AMERICAN WOMEN WRITERS

A Critical Reference Guide
From Colonial Times to the Present

AMERICAN WOMEN WRITERS

A Critical Reference Guide
From Colonial Times to the Present

Second Edition
VOLUME 4 S-Z
Index

Editor
Taryn Benbow-Pfalzgraf

ST. JAMES PRESS

AN IMPRINT OF THE GALE GROUP

DETROIT • SAN FRANCISCO • LONDON
BOSTON • WOODBRIDGE, CT

Taryn Benbow-Pfalzgraf, *Editor*

Glynis Benbow-Niemier, *Associate Editor*

Kristin G. Hart, *Project Coordinator*

Laura Standley Berger, Joann Cerrito, Dave Collins,
Steve Cusack, Nicolet V. Elert, Miranda Ferrara, Jamie FitzGerald,
Laura S. Kryhoski, Margaret Mazurkiewicz, Michael J. Tyrkus
St. James Press Staff

Peter M. Gareffa, *Managing Editor, St. James Press*

Mary Beth Trimper, *Composition Manager*
Dorothy Maki, *Manufacturing Manager*
Wendy Blurton, *Senior Buyer*

Cynthia Baldwin, *Product Design Manager*
Martha Schiebold, *Art Director*

Ronald D. Montgomery, *Data Entry Manager*
Gwendolyn S. Tucker, *Project Administrator*

Library of Congress Cataloging-in-Publication Data

American women writers : from colonial times to the present : a
    critical reference guide / editor: Taryn Benbow-Pfalzgraf. -- 2nd ed.
        p. cm.
    Includes bibliographical references and index.
    ISBN 1-55862-429-5 (set) — ISBN 1-55862-430-9 (vol.1) — ISBN 1-55862-431-7 (vol.2) —
    ISBN 1-55862-432-5 (vol.3) — ISBN 1-55862-433-3 (vol.4)
    1. American literature-Women authors-Bio-bibliography
    Dictionaries. 2. Women authors, American-Biography Dictionaries.
    3. American literature-Women authors Dictionaries. I. Benbow-Pfalzgraf, Taryn
PS147.A42 1999
810.9'9287'03—dc21   99-43293
[B]   CIP

Printed in the United States of America

St. James Press is an imprint of Gale Group
Gale Group and Design is a trademark used herein under license
10 9 8 7 6 5 4 3 2 1

EDITOR'S NOTE

American Women Writers, Second Edition is an important resource for many reasons, the least of which is to disseminate information about hundreds of women writers who have been routinely overlooked. A veritable treasure trove of knowledge, the women profiled in this series have literally changed the world, from Margaret Sanger's quest for reproductive freedom to Jane Addams and Hull House, from Sylvia Earle and Rachel Carson's environmental concerns, to the aching beauty of poems by Olga Broumas, Emily Dickinson, Georgia Douglas Johnson, Marianne Moore, Sylvia Plath, Sara Teasdale, Lorrie Moore, and many others. There are writers who are immensely entertaining (M.F.K. Fisher, Jean Craighead George, Sue Grafton, Helen MacInnes, Terry McMillan, C. L. Moore, Barbara Neely, Danielle Steel), some who wish to instruct on faith (Dorothy Day, Mary Baker Eddy, Catherine Marshall, Anne Morrow Lindbergh), others who revisit the past to educate us (Gwendolyn Brooks, Judith Ortiz Cofer, Paula Allen Gunn, Carolyn Heilbrun, Mary Johnston, Toni Morrison, Alice Walker, Mary White Ovington, Sherley Ann Williams, Mourning Dove), and still more who wish to shock us from complacency of one kind or another (Theresa Hak Kyung Cha, Lillian Hellman, Shirley Jackson, Harriet Jacobs, Shirley Jackson, Carson McCullers, A.G. Mojtabai, Bharati Mukherjee, Carry A. Nation, Flannery O'Connor, Anne Sexton, Phillis Wheatley, and more).

The women filling these pages have nothing and everything in common; they are female, yes, but view their lives and worth in vastly different manners. There is no census of ethnicity, class, age, or sexuality—the prerequisites for inclusion had only to do with a body of work, the written word in all its forms, and the unfortunate limits of time and space. Yes, there are omissions, none by choice: some were overlooked in favor of others (by a voting selection process), others were assigned and the material never received. In the end, it is the ongoing bane of publishing: there will never be enough time nor space to capture all—for there will (hopefully) always be new women writers coming to the fore, and newly discovered manuscripts to test our conceptions of life from a woman's eye.

Yet *American Women Writers* is just what it's title implies, a series of books recounting the life and works of American women from Colonial days to the present. Some writers produced far more than others, yet each woman contributed writing worthy of historical note, to be brought to the forefront of scholarship for new generations to read. Last but never least, thanks to Peter Gareffa for this opportunity; to Kristin Hart for her continual support and great attitude; to my associate editor Glynis Benbow-Niemier; to my editorial and research staff (Jocelyn Prucha, Diane Murphy, and Lori Prucha), and to the beloveds: Jordyn, Wylie, Foley, Hadley, and John.

FOREWORD

In a memorandum to contributors, Lina Mainiero, the founding editor of *American Women Writers* described the project she envisioned in 1978:

> Written wholly by women critics, this reference work is designed as a four-volume survey of American women writers from colonial days to the present. . . Most entries will be on women who have written what is traditionally defined as literature. But *AWW* will also include entries on writers in other fields. . . I see *AWW* as a precious opportunity for women—those who write it and those who read it—to integrate at a more self-conscious level a variety of reading experience.

The result was a document of its time, a period when feminism was associated with building sisterhood and raising consciousness. Even a commercial publishing venture might take on the trappings of a consciousness raising session in which readers and writers met. The idea now seems naive, but the ideal is worth remembering. In 1978 Mainiero was neither young nor revolutionary. She was hesitant about pushing too far; she was content to let traditional definitions stand. But the very inclusion of Rachel Carson and Margaret Mead, Betty Smith and Ursula LeGuin, Rebecca Harding Davis and Phillis Wheatley, Gertrude Stein and Dorothy Parker in a reference work entitled simply and profoundly *American Women Writers* spoke eloquently. Without ever referring explicitly to "canon revision," these four volumes contributed to the process. Having the books on the shelves testified to the existence of hundreds of women who had written across the centuries. Including those whose work was perceived to be "literary" alongside those whose work was not, prefigured debates that continue today both inside and outside of the academy.

Mainiero was especially concerned that contributors not aim their entries at the academic specialist. The "putative reader" was a college senior, who was conversant with literary history and criticism, feminism, and the humanities. This emphasis provoked criticism, because it was expressed during the heyday of academic feminism. *American Women Writers* appeared the same year as Sandra Gilbert and Susan Gubar published *The Madwoman in the Attic*, their influential study of 19th-century English women writers. Nina Baym's *American Women Writers and Women's Fiction: A Guide to Novels by and About Women in America* had appeared the year before. In retrospect, however, the reader Mainiero targeted is precisely the young woman she hoped would join the consciousness session organized by her elders, a woman who would not become an academic, but who would find in women's writing the "necessary bread" to sustain her in living her life.

Ideals and realities clashed in a project that was clearly intended to make money, but declined to pay honoraria to individual contributors. Instead, the publisher promised to contribute a percentage of any profits to "women's causes." The desire to reach the common reader was one reason the volumes were published without a scholarly overview. The decision not to address an academic audience meant the entries contained no critical jargon, but it also meant no authorities checked facts. In fairness, few facts were known about many of the women in the book. Numerous articles profiled women about whom no one had written. One way to gauge the success of feminist scholarship over the past two decades would be to compare the bibliographies of women in this edition with those in the original edition. What we know now about women's writing in the United States is more than we realized there was to know two decades ago. Let me use my contributions as examples. I wrote entries on Gwendolyn Brooks, Frances Watkins Harper, Nella Larsen, and Anne Spencer. These black women lived and worked across almost two centuries. Harper, an abolitionist and women's rights advocate, had been the most popular African American poet of the mid-19th century. Larsen and Spencer published fiction and poetry, respectively, during the Harlem Renaissance. Of Brooks, I concluded, "by any reckoning, hers is one of the major voices of 20th-century American poetry." Yet no biographies existed for any of them. All of the information in print on Harper referred to a single source.

Twenty years later, scholars have explored Harper's life in depth; digging through the archives, Frances Smith Foster discovered three lost novels and a treasure trove of poems. In search of the women of the Harlem Renaissance, scholars have unearthed much more information concerning Larsen and Spencer. Now the subject of a biography by Thadious Davis, Larsen and her novels—*Passing* in particular—have become key texts in the formulation of feminist theory and queer theory. Ironically, though Spencer's oeuvre was the most slender, she was the only one of these writers to have been the subject of a book: J. Lee Greene's *Time's Unfading Garden*, a biographical and critical treatment of the poet along with a selection of her poems. Brooks has begun to receive her due in five biographical and critical studies. As scholars have continued their work, readers have found a valuable reference tool in *American Women Writers*. The fourth and final volume of the original edition appeared in 1982. Soon afterward, Langdon Lynne Faust edited an abridged version, including a two-volume edition in paperback. In part because the original edition concentrated on writers before 1960, a supplement, edited by Carol Hurd Green and Mary G. Mason, was published in 1993. The writers included were more diverse than ever, as a more inclusive understanding of "American" grew.

Fostering that understanding has been a priority of this project since the beginning. That new editions continue to be published confirms the existence of a need that these volumes fill. The explosion of feminist scholarship has enriched each subsequent edition of *American Women Writers*. In this venue at least, the gap between academic specialist and common reader has narrowed. One development that no one would have predicted is the re-emergence of the literary society, a common feature in 19th-century American life. The name has changed; it is now more often called the reading group. But the membership remains mostly female. Such groups have grown up in every segment of American society. Indeed, "Oprah's Book Club" is a macrocosm of a widespread local phenomenon. I hope and suspect members of reading groups, as well as the undergraduates who remain its putative readers, will find this new edition of *American Women Writers* a resource that can be put to everyday use.

CHERYL A. WALL
Professor of English
Rutgers University

BOARD OF ADVISORS

BOARD OF CONTRIBUTORS

Aarons, Victoria
Allegra Goodman
Alice Hoffman
Faye Kellerman
Lesléa Newman
Tillie Olsen
Francine Prose

Adams, Barbara
Aimee Semple McPherson

Adams, Pauline
Marion Marsh Todd

Alldredge, Betty J.
Katherine Mayo
Katharine Pearson Woods

Allen, Carol
Alice Childress

Allen, Suzanne
Martha Moore Avery
Madeleine Vinton Dahlgren
Anna McKenney Dorsey
Ella Loraine Dorsey
Susan Blanchard Elder
Caroline Gordon
Laura Z. Hobson
Lillian Smith

Alonso, Helena
Julia Álvarez
Sandra Cisneros
Achy Obejas

Anderson, Celia Catlett
Beverly Cleary
Marguerite Henry
Florence Crannell Means
Cornelia Meigs

Anderson, Eileen M.
Phyllis Chesler

Anderson, Kathryn Murphy
Beth Henley
Marsha Norman

Anderson, Maggie
Jane Cooper

Anderson, Nancy G.
Dorothy Scarborough
Lella Warren

Antler, Joyce
Lynne Sharon Schwartz

Armeny, Susan
Mary Sewall Gardner
Lillian D. Wald

Armitage, Shelley
Ina Donna Coolbrith
Anne Ellis

Assendelft, Nick
Lisa Alther
Anne Bernays
E. M. Broner
Marilyn Hacker
Joy Harjo
Maureen Howard
Florence Howe
Susanne K. Langer
Meridel Le Sueur

Bach, Peggy
Evelyn Scott

Bakerman, Jane S.
Vera Caspary
Ursula Reilly Curtiss
Dorothea Canfield Fisher
Lois Gould
Elisabeth Sanxay Holding
Emma Lathen
Ruth Doan MacDougall
Margaret Millar
Toni Morrison
May Sarton
Elizabeth Savage
Susan Fromberg Schaeffer
Gene Stratton-Porter
Mary Sture-Vasa
Dorothy Uhnak
Jessamyn West

Bannan, Helen M.
Fabiola Cabeza de Baca
Elizabeth Bacon Custer
Elaine Goodale Eastman
Helen Hunt Jackson
Mary Harris Jones
Kathryn Anderson McLean
Franc Johnson Newcomb
Anna Moore Shaw
Elizabeth G. Stern

Banner, Lois W.
  Harriet Hubbard Ayer

Barbour, Paula L.
  Jane Auer Bowles

Barbuto, Domenica
  Anne Warner French
  Amanda Theodocia Jones

Barnhart, Jacqueline Baker
  Sarah Bayliss Royce
  Elinore Pruitt Stewart

Barr, Marleen S.
  Deborah Norris Logan

Baruch, Elaine Hoffman
  Susan Sontag
  Diana Trilling

Bauer, Denise
  Lucille Clifton
  Alicia Ostriker
  Alix Kates Shulman

Baytop, Adrianne
  Margaret Walker
  Phillis Wheatley

Beasley, Maurine
  Mary E. Clemmer Ames
  Emily Edson Briggs
  Kate Field

Beecher, Maureen Ursenbach
  Susa Young Gates

Bell, Alice
  Paula Fox

Belli, Angela
  Frances Winwar

Ben-Merre, Diana
  Helen McCloy

Benardete, Jane
  Harriot Stanton Blatch
  Abby Morton Diaz
  Mary Abigail Dodge
  Amanda Minnie Douglas
  Malvina Hoffman
  Elizabeth Palmer Peabody
  Lydia Huntley Sigourney
  Sophie Swett

Benbow-Niemier, Glynis
  Jane Kenyon
  Lorine Niedecker
  Jean Valentine

Benet, Sydonie
  Janet Flanner
  Mary McCarthy
  Josephine Miles
  Edna St. Vincent Millay
  Virginia Ramey Mollenkott
  Linda Pastan
  Katherine Paterson
  Marilyn Sachs
  Elizabeth Spencer
  Ruth Stone
  Michele Wallace
  Mae West
  Sherley Anne Williams

Berke, Jacqueline
  Harriet Stratemeyer Adams
  Eleanor Hodgman Porter

Berry, Linda S.
  Georgia Douglas Johnson

Berube, Linda
  Susan Griffin
  Alice Hoffman
  Maxine W. Kumin
  Valerie Miner
  Grace Paley
  May Swenson

Beyer, Janet M.
  Erma Bombeck
  Ellen Goodman
  Lois Gould
  Doris Grumbach
  Nicole Hollander

Biancarosa, Gina
  Erica Jong

Bienstock, Beverly Gray
  Anita Loos
  Shirley MacLaine
  Cornelia Otis Skinner
  Thyra Samter Winslow

Biguenet, John
  Valerie Martin

Bird, Christiane
  Rosamond Neal DuJardin
  Josephine Lawrence
  Harper Lee
  Harriet Stone Lothrop
  Alice Duer Miller

Bittker, Anne S.
  Mary Margaret McBride

Blair, Karen J.
  Jane Cunningham Croly
  Ella Giles Ruddy

Blicksilver, Edith
  Leslie Marmon Silko

Bloom, Lynn Z.
  Natalie Stark Crouter

Bloom, Steven F.
  Wendy Wasserstein

Bloom, Susan P.
  Natalie Babbitt
  Eloise Greenfield

Boisvert, Nancy L.
  Judith Rossner

Bonazoli, Robert
  Kit Reed

Bordin, Ruth
  Elizabeth Margaret Chandler
  Mary Rice Livermore
  Anna H. Shaw

Boyd, Karen Leslie
  Patricia Highsmith
  Nora Roberts

Boyd, Lois A.
  Paula Marie Cooey

Boyd, Zohara
  Sophia Robbins Little
  Josephine Pollard
  Martha Remick
  Mary Jane Windle

Brahm, Laura
  Judy Grahn
  Mary Oliver

Breitsprecher, Nancy
  Zona Gale

Bremer, Sidney H.
  Lucy Monroe
  Elia Wilkinson Peattie
  Eunice Tietjens
  Edith Franklin Wyatt

Brett, Sally
  Inglis Clark Fletcher
  Bernice Kelly Harris
  Edith Summers Kelley
  Ida Tarbell

Broner, E. M.
  Anne Bernays

Brooker-Gross, Susan R.
  Ellen Churchill Semple

Brookes, Kimberly Hayden
  Barbara Deming

Brostoff, Anita
  Gladys Schmitt

Brown, Alanna Kathleen
  Mourning Dove

Brown, Dorothy H.
  Rose Falls Bres
  Elma Godchaux
  Margaret Landon
  Mary Lasswell
  Mary Ashley Townsend
  Jeannette Hadermann Walworth

Brown, Fahamisha Patricia
  Jayne Cortez
  Carolyn M. Rodgers
  Ntozake Shange

Brown, Lois
  Octavia E. Butler
  Terry McMillan

Brown, Lynda W.
  Caroline Whiting Hentz
  Octavia Walton Le Vert
  Anne Newport Royall
  Jennette Reid Tandy

Bryer, Marjorie
  Michele Wallace

Buchanan, Harriette Cuttino
  Corra May Harris
  Helen Kendrick Johnson
  Agnes C. Laut
  Blair Rice Niles
  Marie Conway Oemler
  Josephine Pinckney
  Lizette Woodworth Reese
  Mary Howard Schoolcraft

Bucknall, Barbara J.
  Pearl S. Buck
  Ursula K. Le Guin
  Phyllis McGinley
  Hannah Whittal Smith
  Evangeline Walton

Burger, Mary
  Diane DiPrima

Burns, Lois
  Mary Hunter Austin

Cook, Martha E.
  Virginia Hamilton
  Annie Fellows Johnston
  George Madden Martin
  Katherine Bonner McDowell
  Mary Murfree

Cook, Sylvia
  Olive Tilford Dargan
  Grace Lumpkin

Coultrap-McQuin, Susan
  Eliza Leslie
  Catharine Arnold Williams

Cowell, Pattie
  Bathsheba Bowers
  Martha Wadsworth Brewster
  Elizabeth Sandwith Drinker
  Anna Young Smith
  Annis Boudinot Stockton
  Lydia Fish Willis
  Anna Green Winslow

Cox, Virginia
  Erica Jong

Crabbe, Katharyn F.
  Jane Andrews
  Carolyn Sherwin Bailey
  Katherine Lee Bates
  Margery Williams Bianco
  Claire Huchet Bishop
  Rebecca Sophia Clarke
  Clara F. Guernsey
  Lucy Ellen Guernsey
  Theodora Kroeber
  Elizabeth Foreman Lewis
  Ella Farman Pratt
  Susan Ridley Sedgwick
  Monica Shannon
  Eva March Tappan
  Louisa Huggins Tuthill
  Elizabeth Gray Vining
  Eliza Orne White

Crumpacker, Laurie
  Sarah Prince Gill

Cutler, Evelyn S.
  Rose O'Neill

Dame, Enid
  Edna St. Vincent Millay

Darney, Virginia
  Maude Howe Elliott
  Laura Howe Richards

Dash, Irene
  Carolyn G. Heilbrun

Davidson, Cathy N.
  E. M. Broner
  Laura Jean Libbey
  Tabitha Tenney

Davis, Barbara Kerr
  Ellen Moers

Davis, Thadious M.
  Anna Julia Cooper
  Mollie Moore Davis
  Shirley Graham
  Mary Spring Walker
  Rhoda E. White

Deegan, Mary Jo
  Edith Abbott
  Emily Greene Balch
  Sophonisba Preston Breckinridge
  Helen Merrell Lynd
  Marion Talbott

DeMarr, Mary Jean
  Charlotte Armstrong
  Sarah T. Bolton
  Gwen Bristow
  Doris Miles Disney
  Janet Ayer Fairbank
  Rachel Lyman Field
  Alice Tisdale Hobart
  Agnes Newton Keith
  Alice Hegan Rice
  Mari Sandoz
  Anya Seton
  Ruth Suckow
  Elswyth Thane
  Agnes Sligh Turnbull
  Carolyn Wells

Demetrakopoulos, Stephanie
  Mary Daly
  Mary Esther Harding
  June K. Singer
  Ann Belford Ulanov

Deming, Caren J.
  Gertrude Berg
  Elaine Sterne Carrington
  Agnes E. Nixon
  Irna Phillips

Ferguson, Mary Anne
  Lisa Alther
  Sally Benson
  Doris Betts
  Tess Slesinger

Finger, Mary E.
  Josephine Herbst
  Madeleine L'Engle

Fiore, Jullie Ann
  Annie Dillard

Fish, Virginia K.
  Frances R. Donovan
  Annie Marion MacLean

Fitch, Noel R.
  Sylvia Beach

Fleche, Anne
  Adrienne Kennedy

Fleenor, Juliann E.
  Catharine Esther Beecher
  Caroline Chesebrough
  Susan Hale
  Emily Chubbuck Judson
  Margaret Sanger
  Ann Winterbotham Stephens

Flint, Joyce
  Margaret Craven

Florence, Barbara Moench
  Lella Secor

Fowler, Lois
  Eleanor Flexner
  Frances Dana Gage
  Ida Husted Harper
  Julia McNair Wright

Franklin, Phyllis
  Judith Sargent Murray
  Elsie Clews Parsons
  Jean Stafford

Frazer, Winifred
  Dorothy Day
  Voltairine de Cleyre
  Emma Goldman

Freiberg, Karen
  Kate Wilhelm

Freibert, Lucy
  Georgiana Bruce Kirby
  Jessica N. MacDonald
  Marianne Dwight Orvis

Friedman, Ellen
  Anna Hempstead Branch
  Bettina Liebowitz Knapp
  Dilys Bennett Laing

Fuchs, Miriam
  Beulah Marie Dix
  Maude McVeigh Hutchins

Gabbard, Lucina P.
  Mary Coyle Chase
  Clare Boothe Luce

Galanter, Margit
  Barbara Tuchman

Gallo, Rose Adrienne
  Zelda Sayre Fitzgerald

Garson, Helen S.
  Jacqueline Susann
  Sophie Kerr Underwood

Gartner, Carol B.
  Carman Dee Barnes
  Laura Benét
  Mary Putnam Jacobi
  Kate Jordan
  Myra Kelly

Gaskill, Gayle
  Isabella MacDonald Alden
  Beatrice J. Chute
  Marchette Chute
  Mathilde Eiker
  Sarah Barnwell Elliott
  Jean Kerr

Gensler, Kinereth
  Sandra M. Gilbert

Gentilella, Dacia
  Paula Gunn Allen

Gerson, Risa
  Susanna Anthony
  E. L. Konigsburg
  Eliza Buckminster Lee

Gibbons, Christina Tischler
  Mary Palmer Tyler

Gibbons, Sheila J.
  Mary McGrory

Gilbert, Melissa Kesler
  Gloria Steinem

Giles, Jane
  Elizabeth Elkins Sanders
  Catharine Maria Sedgwick

Kelleghan, Fiona
Marion Zimmer Bradley
Suzy McKee Charnas
Anne McCaffrey
Vonda N. McIntyre
Andre Norton
Kit Reed
Elizabeth Ann Scarborough
Sheri S. Tepper
Connie Willis

Kenschaft, Lori
Martha Ballard
Barbara Ehrenreich
Charlotte Perkins Gilman
Frances Kellor
Carson McCullers
Ann Lane Petry
Ida B. Wells-Barnett

Kern, Donna Casella
Frances Fuller Victor

Kern, Edith
Ann Landers

Kessler, Carol Farley
Elizabeth Stuart Phelps

King, Margaret J.
Clara Jessup Bloomfield-Moore
Peg Bracken
Judith Crist
Maureen Daly
Pauline Kael
Elizabeth Linington
Madalyn Murray O'Hair
Emily Post
Mary Wilson Sherwood
Amy Vanderbilt

Kish, Dorothy
Rebecca Harding Davis

Klein, Kathleen Gregory
Susan Griffin
Ruth McKenney
Anne Nichols
Bella Cohen Spewak
Megan Terry

Klein, Michael
Jean Valentine

Knapp, Bettina L.
Anaïs Nin

Koengeter, L. W.
Ann Eliza Schuyler Bleecker
Maria Gowen Brooks
Hannah Mather Crocker
Margaretta V. Faugeres
Rose Wilder Lane
Adah Isaacs Menken

Kohlstedt, Sally Gregory
Anna Botsford Comstock
Almira Lincoln Phelps

Kolmerten, Carol A.
Frances Wright

Kondelik, Marlene
Mary Shipman Andrews

Koon, Helene
Marian Anderson
Ruth Gordon
Anna Mowatt Ritchie
Elizabeth Robins
Catherine Turney
S. S. B. K. Wood

Koppes, Phyllis Bixlir
Frances Hodgson Burnett

Kouidis, Virginia M.
Mina Loy

Krieg, Joann Peck
Charlotte Mary Sanford Barnes
Susan Fenimore Cooper
Mary Baker Eddy

Kroll, Diane E.
Jean Fritz
Katherine Paterson

Krouse, Agate Nesaule
Rhoda Lerman

Kuenhold, Sandra
Leta Stetter Hollingworth

Kuznets, Lois R.
Esther Forbes
Lois Lenski

Lamping, Marilyn
Hallie Quinn Brown
Pauline Hopkins
Maria W. Stewart
Fannie Barrier Williams

Langhals, Patricia
Florence Wheelock Ayscough
Alice Bacon
Dorothy Borg

Langsam, Miriam Z.
Margaret Bourke-White

Laska, Vera
Marcia Gluck Davenport
Elisabeth Elliot

Lauter, Estella
Diane Wakoski

Levy, Ilise
Alice Hamilton
Jane Jacobs

Lewandowska, M. L.
Marilyn Hacker

Lewis, Janette Seaton
Carrie Jacobs Bond
Joanne Greenberg

Lewis, Sharon A.
Marita Bonner

Lezburg, Amy K.
Ilka Chase

Linden-Ward, Blanche
Andrea Dworkin
Marilyn French
Robin Morgan

Loeb, Helen
Inez Haynes Irwin

Lohman, Judith S.
Crystal Eastman

Londré, Felicia Hardison
Agnes de Mille
Edith Ellis
Anne Crawford Flexner
Harriet Ford
Rose Franken
Ketti Frings
Dorothy Kuhns Heyward
Jeannette Augustus Marks
Frances Aymar Mathews
Adelaide Matthews
Marguerite Merington
Lillian Mortimer
Martha Morton
Josefina Niggli
Charlotte Blair Parker
Lillian Ross
Lillie West
Rida Johnson Young

Lord, Charlotte V.
Sidney Cowell Bateman

Ludwig, Linda
Kathryn Cavarly Hulme
Margaret Mitchell

MacDonald, Maureen
Katherine Bolton Black

MacKay, Kathryn L.
Maurine Whipple

MacPike, Loralee
Emily Kimbrough
Maxine Hong Kingston
Mary Jane Ward

Madsen, Carol Cornwall
Louisa Greene Richards
Emmeline Woodward Wells

Maida, Patricia D.
Lillian O'Donnell

Mainiero, Lina
Willa Sibert Cather

Maio, Kathleen L.
Anna Katharine Green
Mary R. Platt Hatch
Lenore Glen Offord
Metta Fuller Victor

Mallett, Daryl F.
Leigh Brackett
Jane E. Brody
Carolyn Chute
Emma Lathen
Ursula K. Le Guin
Reeve Lindbergh
Bobbie Ann Mason
Rachel Pollack
Anne Rice
Kristine Kathryn Rusch
Joanna Russ
Jessica Amanda Salmonson
Lee Smith
Margaret Truman

Marchino, Lois
Rita Mae Brown

Marcus, Lisa
bell hooks
Sherley Anne Williams

Margolis, Tina
Eva LeGallienne

Marie, Jacquelyn
Chitra Banerjee Divakaruni

Marks, Elaine
  Germaine Brée

Marshall, Kathleen Bonann
  Susan H. Bergman
  Elizabeth Hardwick
  Linda Kaufman Kerber
  Bette Bao Lord
  Lorrie Moore
  Sara Paretsky
  Elaine Showalter
  Mona Van Duyn
  Edith Wharton

Martinez, Elizabeth Coonrod
  Sandra Benítez
  Rosa Guy
  Demetria Martínez
  Cherríe Moraga
  Judith Ortiz Cofer
  Esmeralda Santiago
  Helena María Viramontes

Masel-Walters, Lynne
  Alice Stone Blackwell
  Mary Ware Dennett
  Miriam Follin Leslie
  Inez Haynes Irwin

Mason, Mary Grimley
  Betty Friedan
  Carolyn G. Heilbrun
  Nancy Gardner Prince

Mason, Sarah E.
  Pauline Kael

Masteller, Jean Carwile
  Annie Nathan Meyer
  Elizabeth Seifert

Masters, Joellen
  Gayl Jones

Masters, Jollen
  Susan Fromberg Schaeffer

Matherne, Beverly M.
  Alice Gerstenberg

May, Jill P.
  Ann Nolan Clark
  Ingri Mortenson d'Aulaire
  Maud Fuller Petersham
  Marilyn Sachs

Mayer, Elsie F.
  Anne Morrow Lindbergh

McCarthy, Joanne
  Kay Boyle
  Maeve Brennan
  Mary Maguire Colum
  Hedda Hopper
  Betty MacDonald
  Kathleen Thompson Norris

McCay, Mary A.
  Rosellen Brown
  Louise Erdrich
  Kaye Gibbons
  Ellen Gilchrist
  Patricia Highsmith
  Barbara Kingsolver
  Bobbie Ann Mason
  Brenda Marie Osbey
  Anne Rice
  Helen Yglesias

McClure, Charlotte S.
  Gertrude Atherton

McColgan, Kristin
  Dorothea Lynde Dix

McCrea, Joan M.
  Katharine Coman

McDannell, M. Colleen
  Katherine Eleanor Conway
  Pearl Richards Craigie
  Amanda Smith
  Frances Fisher Tiernan
  Ellen Gould White

McFadden-Gerber, Margaret
  Sally Carrighar
  Annie Dillard
  Wilma Dykeman
  Fannie Hardy Eckstorm
  Josephine Winslow Johnson
  Harriet M. Miller
  Louise Dickinson Rich

McGovern, Edythe M.
  Margaret Wise Brown
  Rachel Crothers
  Susan Glaspell
  Lorraine Hansberry
  Sophie Treadwell
  Charlotte Zolotow

McKay, Mary A.
  Lee Smith

McLennan, Karen
  Harriette Simpson Arnow
  Toni Cade Bambara
  Mary Daly
  Louise Glück
  Virginia Johnson-Masters
  Audre Lorde
  Patricia Meyer Spacks

McQuin, Susan Coultrap
  Sarah Ann Evans

Medeiros, Kimbally A.
  Sandra Harding
  Eleanor Munro
  Anne Truitt
  Anne Waldman

Menger, Lucy
  Ruth Shick Montgomery
  Jane Roberts
  Susy Smith

Mercier, Cathryn M.
  Yoshiko Uchida
  Cynthia Voigt

Miller, James A.
  Margaret Randall

Miller, Marlene M.
  Elizabeth Bishop
  Kelly Cherry
  Elizabeth Cook-Lynn
  M. F. K. Fisher
  June Jordan

Mitchell, Nora
  Olga Broumas
  Louise Glück
  Sharon Olds

Mitchell, Sally
  Francesca Alexander
  Helen Dore Boylston
  Margaret Mayo
  Cora Baggerly Older
  Mary Green Pike
  Rose Porter
  Molly Elliot Seawell
  Mary Ella Waller

Moe, Phyllis
  Abbie Farwell Brown
  Helen Stuart Campbell
  Eliza Cabot Follen
  Emily Huntington Miller
  Sarah Chauncey Woolsey

Mollenkott, Virginia Ramey
  Grace Livingston Hill-Lutz
  Sarah Smith Martyn
  Marjorie Hope Nicolson
  Rosemond Tuve

Montenegro, David
  Linda Ty-Casper

Morris, Linda A.
  Marietta Holley
  Frances Berry Whitcher

Mortimer, Gail
  Katherine Anne Porter

Mossberg, Barbara A. Clarke
  Sylvia Plath
  Genevieve Taggard

Moynihan, Ruth Barnes
  Abigail Scott Duniway

Murphy, Maureen
  Mary E. McGrath Blake
  Helena Lefroy Caperton
  Kathleen Coyle
  Blanche McManus Mansfield
  Mary L. Meaney
  Asenath Hatch Nicholson
  Florence J. O'Connor
  Jessie Fremont O'Donnell
  Katharine A. O'Keeffe
  Clara M. Thompson

Murphy, Miriam B.
  Sarah E. Carmichael
  Martha Spence Heywood

Murphy, Paula C.
  Maya Angelou
  Eleanor Taylor Bland
  Nora Ephron
  Barbara Kingsolver
  Barbara Neely

Mussell, Kay
  Phyllis A. Whitney

Nance, Guin A.
  Gail Godwin
  Nancy Hale
  Virginia M. Satir
  Elizabeth Spencer
  Clara M. Thompson

Neils, Patricia Langhals
  Emily Hahn
  Charlotte Y. Salisbury
  Mary Clabaugh Wright

Neville, Tam Lin
Ruth Stone

Newman, Anne
Julia Mood Peterkin
Elizabeth Sewell
Amélie Rives Troubetzkoy

Nichols, Kathleen L.
Miriam Coles Harris
Ellen Peck
Harriet Waters Preston
Anne Sexton

Nix, E. M.
Gail Godwin

Nochimson, Martha
Carry A. Nation
Martha Harrison Robinson

Norman, Marion
Lucretia Maria Davidson
Margaret Miller Davidson

O'Connor, Christine
Martha Ostenso

O'Loughlin, James
Tillie Olsen

Ockerstrom, Lolly
Mona Van Duyn

Pannill, Linda
Isadora Duncan

Parker, Alice
Ada Jack Carver
Edith Hamilton

Passty, Jeanette Nyda
Isabella Oliver Sharp
Sarah Pogson Smith
Sukey Vickery Watson

Payne, Alma J.
Louisa May Alcott

Pelzer, Linda C.
Patricia Cornwell
Martha Gellhorn
Anita Shreve

Penn, Patricia E.
Del Martin
Annie Smith Peck

Penn, Shana
Lucy S. Dawidowicz

Perez-Guntin, Amiris
Julia de Burgos

Peterson, Margaret
Emily Dickinson
Janet Lewis

Pettis, Joyce
Zora Neale Hurston

Philips, Elizabeth
Sarah Helen Whitman

Phillips, Elizabeth
Elizabeth Ellet
Annie Somers Gilchrist
Estelle Robinson Lewis
Frances Sargent Osgood
Caroline Ticknor
Mabel Loomis Todd

Piercy, Josephine K.
Anne Dudley Bradstreet

Pogel, Nancy
Constance Mayfield Rourke

Poland, Helene Dwyer
Julia Henrietta Gulliver
Susanne K. Langer

Pool, Gail
Cynthia Ozick
Dawn Powell

Pouncey, Lorene
Vassar Miller
Marguerite Young

Preston, Caroline
Annie Trumbull Slosson

Pringle, Mary Beth
Léonie Fuller Adams
Charlotte Perkins Gilman

Puk, Francine Shapiro
Elizabeth Akers Allen
Victoria Lincoln
Dorothy Parker
Frances Gray Patton

Rosenberg, Julia
Emma Manley Embury
Mary E. Moore Hewitt
Rebecca Rush
Caroline Warren Thayer

Rosinsky, Natalie McCaffrey
Anne McCaffrey
Judith Merril
C. L. Moore

Rowe, Anne
Maya Angelou
Elizabeth Madox Roberts
Constance Fenimore Woolson

Rudnick, Lois P.
Mabel Dodge Luhan

Rushin, Kate
Audre Lorde

Ryan, Rosalie Tutela
Jane Starkweather Locke

Salo, Alice Bell
Marjorie Hill Allee
Mabel Leigh Hunt
Elizabeth Yates

Sandberg, Elisabeth
Carolyn Chute
Ruth Seid

Scanzoni, Letha
Anita Bryant
Virginia Ramey Mollenkott

Schiavoni, Andrew
Rochelle Owens
Susan Sontag

Schleuning, Neala Yount
Meridel Le Sueur

Schoen, Carol B.
Hannah Adams
Rebekah Bettelheim Kohut
Emma Lazarus
Penina Moise
Ruth Seid

Schoenbach, Lisi
Germaine Brée

Schofield, Ann
Helen Marot

Schull, Elinor
Adela Rogers St. Johns

Schwartz, Helen J.
Mary Antin
Hortense Calisher
Elizabeth Meriwether Gilmer
Margaret Thompson Janvier
Margaret Woods Lawrence
Tillie Olsen
Grace Paley

Schweik, Joanne L.
Marilyn French
Isabella Gardner
Vivian Gornick
Hettie Jones
Gloria Steinem

Scura, Dorothy M.
Mary Johnston

Seaton, Beverly
Florence Merriam Bailey
Gladys Hasty Carroll
Mary Hartwell Catherwood
Nellie Blanchan Doubleday
Mateel Howe Farnham
Margaret Flint
Helen Morgenthau Fox
Mary Griffith
Susan Huntington
Louisa Yeomans King
Elizabeth L. Lawrence
Alice Lounsberry
Helen Reimensnyder Martin
Sarah Edgarton Mayo
Josephine Clifford McCrackin
Helen Matthews Nitsch
Frances Dana Parsons
Grace Richmond
Gladys Bagg Taber
Anna Bartlett Warner
Susan Bogert Warner
Mary Stanbery Watts
Adeline D. T. Whitney
Kate Douglass Wiggin
Laura Ingalls Wilder
Louise Beebe Wilder
Mabel Osgood Wright

Smith, Susan Sutton
  Elizabeth Cabot Cary Agassiz
  Jane Goodwin Austin
  Delia Salter Bacon
  Sarah G. Bagley
  Mary Edwards Bryan
  Maria Weston Chapman
  Adelaide Crapsey
  Caroline Healey Dall
  Eliza Ann Dupuy
  Harriet Farley
  Eliza Rotch Farrar
  Margaret Fuller
  Caroline Howard Gilman
  Caroline Gilman Jervey
  Elizabeth Dodge Kinney
  Sara Jane Lippincott
  Harriet Hanson Robinson
  Phoebe Atwood Taylor
  Mary Hawes Terhune
  Jean Webster

Sneller, Jo Leslie
  Rosemary Sprague

Snipes, Katherine
  Clara Barton
  Laura Jackson
  Carson McCullers

Snyder, Carrie
  Ana Castillo
  Julia Child
  Jane Cooper
  Mari Evans
  María Irene Fornés
  Shirley Ann Grau
  Bertha Harris
  Erica Jong
  Sandra McPherson
  Valerie Miner
  Alma Routsong
  Anya Seton
  Gail Sheehy
  Leslie Marmon Silko
  Zilpha Keatley Snyder
  Cathy Song
  Danielle Steel
  Mildred Pitts Walter

Sonnenschein, Dana
  Rosalyn Drexler
  Jorie Graham
  Sandra McPherson

Sparks, Leah J.
  Sanora Babb
  Carman Dee Barnes
  Doris Betts
  Germaine Brée
  Olga Broumas
  Octavia E. Butler
  Rachel Carson
  Kim Chernin
  Phyllis Chesler
  Marilyn Chin
  Michelle Cliff
  Judith Crist
  Toi Derricotte
  Diane DiPrima
  Andrea Dworkin
  Suzette Haden Elgin
  Carol Emshwiller
  Marjorie Garber
  Sally Miller Gearhart
  Donna Haraway
  Lillian Hellman
  Susan Isaacs
  Molly Ivins
  Shirley Jackson
  Gerda Lerner
  Del Martin
  Alice Notley
  Martha Craven Nussbaum
  Flannery O'Connor
  Joyce Carol Oates
  Camille Paglia
  Margaret Randall
  Harriet Beecher Stowe
  Lois-Ann Yamanaka

Spencer, Linda
  Jayne Anne Phillips
  Eleanor Roosevelt
  Judith Rossner

Sprague, Rosemary
  Sara Teasdale

Sproat, Elaine
  Lola Ridge

Stackhouse, Amy D.
  Edith Maud Eaton
  Lorine Niedecker

Staley, Ann
  Jane Hirshfield

Stanbrough, Jane
  Elizabeth Manning Hawthorne
  Hildegarde Hawthorne
  Rose Hawthorne Lathrop

Thompson, Ann
  Rosemary Radford Ruether

Thompson, Dorothea Mosley
  Mary Cunningham Logan
  Ruth Bryan Owen
  Irma von Starkloff Rombauer
  Caroline White Soule

Thornton, Emma S.
  Marion Marsh Todd

Tipps, Lisa
  Bertha Harris

Tobin, Jean
  Hilda Morley
  Adrienne Rich
  Ruth Whitman

Townsend, Janis
  Mildred Aldrich
  Gertrude Stein
  Alice B. Toklas

Treckel, Paula A.
  Alice Morse Earle
  Gerda Lerner
  Emily Smith Putnam
  Lucy Maynard Salmon
  Eliza Snow Smith
  Fanny Stenhouse
  Narcissa Prestiss Whitman
  Ann Eliza Young

Turner, Alberta
  Katherine Garrison Chapin
  Ruth Herschberger
  Barbara Howes
  Muriel Rukeyser

Uffen, Ellen Serlen
  Fannie Hurst

Uphaus, Suzanne Henning
  Ann Chidester
  Eleanor Carroll Chilton
  Sarah Norcliffe Cleghorn
  Pamela Frankau
  Maureen Howard
  Marge Piercy

Vasquez, Pamela
  Judith Ortiz Cofer

Vogrin, Valerie
  Alice Adams
  Annie Dillard
  Jamaica Kincaid
  Maxine Hong Kingston
  Carole Maso
  Toni Morrison
  Sharon Olds
  Grace Paley
  Ann Patchett
  Amy Tan

Wahlstrom, Billie J.
  Alice Cary
  Anna Peyre Dinnies
  Betty Friedan
  Zenna Henderson
  Andre Norton
  Joanna Russ

Waldron, Karen E.
  Kim Chernin

Walker, Cynthia L.
  Shirley Barker
  Taylor Caldwell
  Edna Ferber
  Eleanor Gates
  Caroline Pafford Miller
  Myrtle Reed
  Florence Barrett Willoughby

Wall, Cheryl A.
  Gwendolyn Brooks
  Frances Ellen Watkins Harper
  Nella Larsen
  Gloria Naylor
  Anne Spencer

Ward, Jean M.
  Elizabeth Blackwell
  Ella Rhoads Higginson
  Bethenia Owens-Adair

Welch, Barbara A.
  Alice James

Werden, Frieda L.
  Dorothy Dodds Baker
  Kate Millett
  Bernice Love Wiggins

West, Martha Ullman
  Rosellen Brown
  Lynne Sharon Schwartz

ALPHABETICAL LIST OF WRITERS

Abbott, Edith
Abbott, Eleanor Hallowell
Abel, Annie Heloise
Acker, Kathy
Adams, Abigail Smith
Adams, Alice
Adams, Hannah
Adams, Harriet Stratemeyer
Adams, Léonie Fuller
Adams, Louisa Catherine Johnson
Addams, Jane
Adisa, Giamba *See* Lorde, Audre
Agassiz, Elizabeth Cabot Cary
Ai
Akins, Zoë
Alcott, Louisa May
Alden, Isabella MacDonald
Aldon, Adair *See* Meigs, Cornelia
Aldrich, Bess Streeter
Aldrich, Mildred
Alexander, Francesca
Allee, Marjorie Hill
Allen, Elizabeth Akers
Allen, Paula Gunn
Allison, Dorothy
Alther, Lisa
Álvarez, Julia
Ames, Mary E. Clemmer
Anderson, Marian
Andrew, Joseph Maree *See* Bonner, Marita
Andrews, Eliza Frances
Andrews, Jane
Andrews, Mary Shipman
Andrews, V. C.
Angelou, Maya
Angier, Natalie
Anneke, Mathilde Franziska Giesler
Anpetu Waśte *See* Deloria, Ella Cara
Anthony, Susan B.
Anthony, Susanna
Antin, Mary
Anzaldúa, Gloria
Appleton-Weber, Sarah
Appleton, Sarah *See* Appleton-Weber, Sarah
Appleton, Victor, II *See* Adams, Harriet Stratemeyer
Arendt, Hannah
Armstrong, Charlotte
Arnow, Harriette Simpson
Ashley, Ellen *See* Seifert, Elizabeth
Atherton, Gertrude
Atom, Ann *See* Walworth, Jeannette Hadermann

Auerbach, Hilda *See* Morley, Hilda
Austin, Jane Goodwin
Austin, Mary Hunter
Avery, Martha Moore
Ayer, Harriet Hubbard
Ayscough, Florence Wheelock

Babb, Sanora
Babbitt, Natalie
Bacon, Alice
Bacon, Delia Salter
Bagley, Sarah G.
Bailey, Temple
Bailey, Carolyn Sherwin
Bailey, Florence Merriam
Baker, Dorothy Dodds
Balch, Emily Greene
Ballard, Martha
Bambara, Toni Cade
Banning, Margaret Culkin
Barker, Shirley
Barnard, A. M. *See* Alcott, Louisa May
Barnes, Carman Dee
Barncs, Charlotte Mary Sanford
Barnes, Djuna
Barnes, Linda J.
Barnes, Margaret Ayer
Barnes, Mary Sheldon
Barnum, Frances Courtenay Baylor
Barr, Amelia E.
Barr, Nevada
Barton, Clara
Barton, May Hollis *See* Adams, Harriet Stratemeyer
Bateman, Sidney Cowell
Bates, Katherine Lee
Bayard, Elise Justine
Beach, Sylvia
Beard, Mary Ritter
Beattie, Ann
Beebe, Mary Blair *See* Niles, Blair Rice
Beecher, Catharine Esther
Benedict, Ruth
Benét, Laura
Benítez, Sandra
Bennett, Gwendolyn B.
Benson, Sally
Berg, Gertrude
Bergman, Susan H.
Bernays, Anne
Berne, Victoria *See* Fisher, M. F. K.
Bethune, Mary McLeod

Betts, Doris
Bianco, Margery Williams
Bishop, Claire Huchet
Bishop, Elizabeth
Black, Katherine Bolton
Blackwell, Alice Stone
Blackwell, Antoinette Brown
Blackwell, Elizabeth
Blaisdell, Anne *See* Linington, Elizabeth
Blake, Lillie Devereux
Blake, Mary E. McGrath
Bland, Eleanor Taylor
Blatch, Harriot Stanton
Bleecker, Ann Eliza Schuyler
Bloomer, Amelia Jenks
Bloomfield-Moore, Clara Jessup
Blume, Judy
Bly, Nellie *See* Seaman, Elizabeth Cochrane
Bogan, Louise
Bolton, Isabel *See* Miller, Mary Britton
Bolton, Sarah T.
Bolton, Sarah Knowles
Bombeck, Erma
Bond, Carrie Jacobs
Bonner, Marita
Booth, Mary Louise
Borg, Dorothy
Botta, Anne C. Lynch
Bourke-White, Margaret
Bowen, Catherine Drinker
Bowen, Sue Petigru
Bower, B. M. *See* Sinclair, Bertha Muzzy
Bowers, Bathsheba
Bowles, Jane Auer
Boyd, Blanche McCrary
Boyd, Nancy *See* Millay, Edna St. Vincent
Boyle, Kay
Boylston, Helen Dore
Bracken, Peg
Brackett, Leigh
Bradley, Marion Zimmer
Bradstreet, Anne Dudley
Branch, Anna Hempstead
Braun, Lilian Jackson
Breckinridge, Sophonisba Preston
Brée, Germaine
Brennan, Maeve
Brent, Linda *See* Jacobs, Harriet
Bres, Rose Falls
Breuer, Bessie
Brewster, Martha Wadsworth
Briggs, Emily Edson
Brink, Carol Ryrie
Bristow, Gwen
Brody, Jane E.

Broner, E. M.
Brooks, Gwendolyn
Brooks, Maria Gowen
Broumas, Olga
Brown, Abbie Farwell
Brown, Alice
Brown, Hallie Quinn
Brown, Margaret Wise
Brown, Nancy *See* Leslie, Annie Brown
Brown, Rita Mae
Brown, Rosellen
Brown, Sandra
Browne, Martha Griffith
Brownmiller, Susan
Brownson, Sarah N.
Bryan, Mary Edwards
Bryant, Anita
Buchanan, Edna
Buck, Pearl S.
Buckmaster, Henrietta
Burke, Fielding *See* Dargan, Olive Tilford
Burnett, Frances Hodgson
Burnham, Clara L. Root
Burr, Esther Edwards
Burton, Katherine Kurz
Burton, Virginia Lee
Butler, Octavia E.

Cabeza de Baca, Fabiola
Cade, Toni *See* Bambara, Toni Cade
Caldwell, Taylor
Calhoun, Lucy *See* Monroe, Lucy
Calisher, Hortense
Campbell, Helen Stuart
Campbell, Jane C.
Campbell, Juliet Lewis
Caperton, Helena Lefroy
Carlson, Natalie Savage
Carmichael, Sarah E.
Carrighar, Sally
Carrington, Elaine Sterne
Carroll, Gladys Hasty
Carson, Rachel
Carver, Ada Jack
Cary, Alice
Cary, Phoebe
Caspary, Vera
Castillo, Ana
Cather, Willa Sibert
Catherwood, Mary Hartwell
Catt, Carrie Chapman
Caulkins, Frances Manwaring
Cazneau, Jane McManus
Cervantes, Lorna Dee
Cha, Theresa Hak Kyung

Chandler, Elizabeth Margaret
Chapelle, Georgette Meyer
Chapin, Katherine Garrison
Chaplin, Jane Dunbar
Chapman, Lee *See* Bradley, Marion Zimmer
Chapman, Maria Weston
Charnas, Suzy McKee
Chase, Ilka
Chase, Mary Coyle
Chase, Mary Ellen
Chehia *See* Shaw, Anna Moore
Cheney, Ednah Littlehale
Chernin, Kim
Cherry, Kelly
Chesebrough, Caroline
Chesler, Phyllis
Chesnut, Mary Miller
Chidester, Ann
Child, Julia
Child, Lydia Maria
Childress, Alice
Chilton, Eleanor Carroll
Chin, Marilyn
Chopin, Kate
Church, Ella Rodman
Chute, Beatrice J.
Chute, Carolyn
Chute, Marchette
Cisneros, Sandra
Clampitt, Amy
Clapp, Margaret Antoinette
Clappe, Louise Smith
Clark, Ann Nolan
Clark, Eleanor
Clark, Mary Higgins
Clarke, Rebecca Sophia
Cleary, Beverly
Cleghorn, Sarah Norcliffe
Cliff, Michelle
Clifton, Lucille
Coatsworth, Elizabeth Jane
Coit, Margaret L.
Colum, Mary Maguire
Coman, Katharine
Comstock, Anna Botsford
Conant, Hannah Chaplin
Conway, Katherine Eleanor
Cooey, Paula Marie
Cook, Fannie
Cook-Lynn, Elizabeth
Cooke, Rose Terry
Coolbrith, Ina Donna
Coolidge, Susan *See* Woolsey, Sarah Chauncey
Cooper, Anna Julia
Cooper, Jane

Cooper, Susan Fenimore
Corbett, Elizabeth Frances
Cornwell, Patricia
Cortez, Jayne
Cott, Nancy F.
Coyle, Kathleen
Craig, Elisabeth May
Craig, Kit *See* Reed, Kit
Craigie, Pearl Richards
Crapsey, Adelaide
Craven, Margaret
Crist, Judith
Crocker, Hannah Mather
Croly, Jane Cunningham
Crosby, Caresse
Cross, Amanda *See* Heilbrun, Carolyn G.
Cross, Jane Hardin
Crothers, Rachel
Crouter, Natalie Stark
Crowe, F. J. *See* Johnston, Jill
Cruger, Mary
Cumming, Kate
Cummins, Maria Susanna
Curtiss, Mina Kirstein
Curtiss, Ursula Reilly
Custer, Elizabeth Bacon
Cuthrell, Faith Baldwin

Dahlgren, Madeleine Vinton
Dall, Caroline Healey
Daly, Elizabeth
Daly, Mary
Daly, Maureen
Daniels, Dorothy
Dargan, Olive Tilford
d'Aulaire, Ingri Mortenson
Davenport, Marcia Gluck
Davidson, Lucretia Maria
Davidson, Margaret Miller
Davis, Adelle
Davis, Angela Yvonne
Davis, Dorothy Salisbury
Davis, Elizabeth Gould
Davis, Mollie Moore
Davis, Natalie Zemon
Davis, Paulina Wright
Davis, Rebecca Harding
Dawidowicz, Lucy S.
Day, Dorothy
de Angeli, Marguerite Lofft
de Mille, Agnes
de Burgos, Julia
de Mondragon, Margaret Randall *See* Randall, Margaret
de Cleyre, Voltairine
Dégh, Linda

Deland, Margaret Campbell
del Occidente, Maria *See* Brooks, Maria Gowen
Deloria, Ella Cara
Deming, Barbara
Denison, Mary Andrews
Dennett, Mary Ware
Derricotte, Toi
Deutsch, Babette
DeVeaux, Alexis
Dexter, John *See* Bradley, Marion Zimmer
Diaz, Abby Morton
Dickinson, Emily
Didion, Joan
Dillard, Annie
Dinnies, Anna Peyre
DiPrima, Diane
Disney, Doris Miles
Divakaruni, Chitra Banerjee
Dix, Beulah Marie
Dix, Dorothea Lynde
Dix, Dorothy *See* Gilmer, Elizabeth Meriwether
Dixon, Franklin W. *See* Adams, Harriet Stratemeyer
Dodge, Mary Abigail
Dodge, Mary Mapes
Doman, June
Domini, Rey *See* Lorde, Audre
Dominic, R. B. *See* Lathen, Emma
Donovan, Frances R.
Doolittle, Antoinette
D(oolittle), H(ilda)
Dorr, Julia Ripley
Dorr, Rheta Childe
Dorsett, Danielle *See* Daniels, Dorothy
Dorsey, Anna McKenney
Dorsey, Ella Loraine
Dorsey, Sarah Ellis
Doubleday, Nellie Blanchan
Douglas, Amanda Minnie
Douglas, Ann
Dove, Rita
Drew, Elizabeth
Drexler, Rosalyn
Drinker, Elizabeth Sandwith
DuBois, Shirley Graham *See* Graham, Shirley
DuJardin, Rosamond Neal
Dunbar-Nelson, Alice
Duncan, Isadora
Duniway, Abigail Scott
Dunlap, Jane *See* Davis, Adelle
DuPlessis, Rachel Blau
Dupuy, Eliza Ann
Durant, Ariel
Dworkin, Andrea
Dykeman, Wilma

Earle, Alice Morse
Earle, Sylvia A.
Eastman, Crystal
Eastman, Elaine Goodale
Eastman, Mary Henderson
Eaton, Edith Maud
Eberhart, Mignon G.
Eberhart, Sheri S. *See* Tepper, Sheri S.
Eckstorm, Fannie Hardy
Eddy, Mary Baker
Egan, Lesley *See* Linington, Elizabeth
Ehrenreich, Barbara
Eiker, Mathilde
Elder, Susan Blanchard
Elgin, Suzette Haden
Ellet, Elizabeth
Elliot, Elisabeth
Elliott, Maude Howe
Elliott, Sarah Barnwell
Ellis, Anne
Ellis, Edith
Embury, Emma Manley
Emshwiller, Carol
Ephron, Nora
Erdrich, Louise
Estes, Eleanor
Evans, Abbie Huston
Evans, Mari
Evans, Sarah Ann
Evermay, March *See* Eiker, Mathilde

Fahs, Sophia Lyon
Fairbank, Janet Ayer
Fairfield, A. M. *See* Alcott, Louisa May
Farley, Harriet
Farmer, Fannie Merritt
Farnham, Eliza Woodson
Farnham, Mateel Howe
Farquharson, Martha *See* Finley, Martha
Farrar, Eliza Rotch
Faugeres, Margaretta V.
Fauset, Jessie Redmon
Felton, Rebecca Latimer
Fenno, Jenny
Ferber, Edna
Field, Kate
Field, Rachel Lyman
Fields, Annie Adams
Finley, Martha
Fisher, Dorothea Canfield
Fisher, M. F. K.
Fiske, Sarah Symmes
Fitzgerald, Zelda Sayre
FitzGerald, Frances
Flanders, G. M.

Flanner, Hildegarde
Flanner, Janet
Fletcher, Inglis Clark
Flexner, Anne Crawford
Flexner, Eleanor
Flint, Margaret
Flynn, Elizabeth Gurley
Follen, Eliza Cabot
Foote, Mary Hallock
Forbes, Esther
Forché, Carolyn
Ford, Harriet
Ford, Sallie Rochester
Forester, Fanny *See* Judson, Emily Chubbuck
Fornés, María Irene
Forrest, Katherine V.
Forten, Charlotte L.
Foster, Hannah Webster
Fox, Helen Morgenthau
Fox, Paula
Frankau, Pamela
Franken, Rose
Freedman, Nancy
Freeman, Mary E. Wilkins
Fremantle, Anne
French, Alice
French, Anne Warner
French, Lucy Smith
French, Marilyn
Friedan, Betty
Frings, Ketti
Fritz, Jean
Fuller, Margaret

Gage, Frances Dana
Gale, Zona
Gallagher, Tess
Garber, Marjorie
Gardener, Helen Hamilton
Gardner, Isabella
Gardner, Mariam *See* Bradley, Marion Zimmer
Gardner, Mary Sewall
Garrigue, Jean
Gates, Eleanor
Gates, Susa Young
Gearhart, Sally Miller
Gellhorn, Martha
Genêt *See* Flanner, Janet
George, Jean Craighead
Gerould, Katharine Fullerton
Gerstenberg, Alice
Gestefeld, Ursula N.
Gibbons, Kaye
Gilbert, Fabiola Cabeza de Baca *See* Cabeza de
    Baca, Fabiola

Gilbert, Sandra M.
Gilchrist, Annie Somers
Gilchrist, Ellen
Gill, Sarah Prince
Gilman, Caroline Howard
Gilman, Charlotte Perkins
Gilmer, Elizabeth Meriwether
Giovanni, Nikki
Glasgow, Ellen
Glaspell, Susan
Glück, Louise
Godchaux, Elma
Godwin, Gail
Golden, Marita
Goldman, Emma
Goodman, Allegra
Goodman, Ellen
Goodsell, Willystine
Goodwin, Doris Kearns
Goodwin, Maud Wilder
Gordon, Caroline
Gordon, Mary Catherine
Gordon, Ruth
Gornick, Vivian
Gottschalk, Laura Riding *See* Jackson, Laura
Gould, Hannah Flagg
Gould, Lois
Grafton, Sue
Graham, Isabella Marshall
Graham, Jorie
Graham, Katharine
Graham, Shirley
Grahn, Judy
Grant, Margaret *See* Franken, Rose
Grau, Shirley Ann
Graves, Valerie *See* Bradley, Marion Zimmer
Gray, Angela *See* Daniels, Dorothy
Green, Anna Katharine
Green, Anne
Green, Olive *See* Reed, Myrtle
Greenberg, Joanne
Greene, Sarah McLean
Greenfield, Eloise
Greenwood, Grace *See* Lippincott, Sara Jane
Griffin, Susan
Griffith, Mary
Grimes, Martha
Grimké, Angelina
Grimké, Sarah Moore
Gruenberg, Sidonie Matzner
Grumbach, Doris
Guernsey, Clara F.
Guernsey, Lucy Ellen
Guiney, Louise Imogen

Gulliver, Julia Henrietta
Guy, Rosa

H. D. *See* D(oolittle), H(ilda)
Hacker, Marilyn
Hadas, Rachel
Hahn, Emily
Hale, Lucretia Peabody
Hale, Nancy
Hale, Sarah Josepha
Hale, Susan
Hall, Florence Howe
Hall, Hazel
Hall, Louisa Park
Hall, Sarah Ewing
Hamilton, Alice
Hamilton, Edith
Hamilton, Gail *See* Dodge, Mary Abigail
Hamilton, Jane
Hamilton, Kate W.
Hamilton, Virginia
Hanaford, Phebe Coffin
Hansberry, Lorraine
Haraway, Donna
Harding, Mary Esther
Harding, Sandra
Hardwick, Elizabeth
Harjo, Joy
Harper, Frances Ellen Watkins
Harper, Ida Husted
Harris, Bernice Kelly
Harris, Bertha
Harris, Corra May
Harris, Miriam Coles
Harrison, Constance Cary
Hart, Carolyn G.
Hart, Frances Noyes
Hasbrouck, Lydia Sayer
Hastings, Susannah Johnson
Hatch, Mary R. Platt
Haven, Alice Bradley
Hawthorne, Elizabeth Manning
Hawthorne, Hildegarde
Hazlett, Helen
Heilbrun, Carolyn G.
Hejinian, Lyn
Hellman, Lillian
Henderson, Zenna
Henissart, Martha *See* Lathen, Emma
Henley, Beth
Henry, Alice
Henry, Marguerite
Hentz, Caroline Whiting
Herbst, Josephine
Herschberger, Ruth

Hewitt, Mary E. Moore
Heyward, Dorothy Kuhns
Heywood, Martha Spence
Higgins, Marguerite
Higginson, Ella Rhoads
Higham, Mary R.
Highet, Helen MacInnes *See* MacInnes, Helen
Highsmith, Patricia
Hill-Lutz, Grace Livingston
Hirshfield, Jane
Hite, Shere
Hobart, Alice Tisdale
Hobson, Laura Z.
Hoffman, Alice
Hoffman, Malvina
Hogan, Linda
Holding, Elisabeth Sanxay
Hollander, Nicole
Holley, Marietta
Hollingworth, Leta Stetter
Holm, Saxe *See* Jackson, Helen Hunt
Holmes, Mary Jane Hawes
Holmes, Sarah Stone
hooks, bell
Hooper, Lucy Jones
Hooper, Lucy
Hope, Laura Lee *See* Adams, Harriet Stratemeyer
Hopkins, Pauline
Hopper, Hedda
Horlak, E. E. *See* Tepper, Sheri S.
Horney, Karen
Houston, Jean
Howard, Maureen
Howe, Florence
Howe, Julia Ward
Howe, Susan
Howe, Tina
Howes, Barbara
Howland, Marie
Hull, Helen
Hulme, Kathryn Cavarly
Hume, Sophia
Humishuma *See* Mourning Dove
Hunt, Irene
Hunt, Mabel Leigh
Hunter, Rodello
Hunter-Lattany, Kristin
Huntington, Susan
Hurd-Mead, Kate C.
Hurst, Fannie
Hurston, Zora Neale
Hutchins, Maude McVeigh
Huxtable, Ada Louise
Hyde, Shelley *See* Reed, Kit

Ireland, Jane *See* Norris, Kathleen
   Thompson
Irwin, Inez Haynes
Isaacs, Susan
Ives, Morgan *See* Bradley, Marion Zimmer
Ivins, Molly

Jackson, Helen Hunt
Jackson, Laura
Jackson, Rebecca Cox
Jackson, Shirley
Jackson, Ward *See* Braun, Lilian Jackson
Jacobi, Mary Putnam
Jacobs, Harriet
Jacobs, Jane
Jacobs, Sarah Sprague
Jacobsen, Josephine
James, Alice
Jamison, Cecilia Viets
Janeway, Elizabeth
Janvier, Margaret Thompson
Jerauld, Charlotte A.
Jervey, Caroline Gilman
Jewett, Sarah Orne
Johnson, Diane
Johnson, Georgia Douglas
Johnson, Helen Kendrick
Johnson, Josephine Winslow
Johnson-Masters, Virginia
Johnston, Annie Fellows
Johnston, Jill
Johnston, Mary
Jones, Amanda Theodocia
Jones, Edith *See* Wharton, Edith
Jones, Gayl
Jones, Hettie
Jones, Mary Harris
Jong, Erica
Jordan, Barbara C.
Jordan, June
Jordan, Kate
Jordan, Laura *See* Brown, Sandra
Judson, Emily Chubbuck

Kael, Pauline
Kavanaugh, Cynthia *See* Daniels, Dorothy
Keene, Carolyn *See* Adams, Harriet Stratemeyer
Keith, Agnes Newton
Keller, Helen
Kellerman, Faye
Kelley, Edith Summers
Kellogg, Louise
Kellor, Frances
Kelly, Eleanor Mercein
Kelly, Myra
Kemble, Fanny

Kennedy, Adrienne
Kenyon, Jane
Kerber, Linda Kaufman
Kerr, Jean
Keyes, Frances Parkinson
Kilmer, Aline Murray
Kimbrough, Emily
Kincaid, Jamaica
King, Grace Elizabeth
King, Laurie R.
King, Louisa Yeomans
Kingsolver, Barbara
Kingston, Maxine Hong
Kinney, Elizabeth Dodge
Kinzie, Juliette Magill
Kirby, Georgiana Bruce
Kirk, Ellen Warner
Kirkland, Caroline M. Stansbury
Kizer, Carolyn
Knapp, Bettina Liebowitz
Knight, Sarah Kemble
Knox, Adeline Trafton
Koch, Adrienne
Kohut, Rebekah Bettelheim
Konigsburg, E. L.
Kroeber, Theodora
Kübler-Ross, Elisabeth
Kumin, Maxine W.

Laing, Dilys Bennett
Lamb, Martha Nash
Lamott, Anne
Landers, Ann
Landon, Margaret
Lane, Gertrude Battles
Lane, Rose Wilder
Langdon, Mary *See* Pike, Mary Green
Langer, Susanne K.
Larcom, Lucy
Larsen, Nella
Lasswell, Mary
Latham, Jean Lee
Lathen, Emma
Lathrop, Rose Hawthorne
Latimer, Elizabeth W.
Latsis, Mary Jane *See* Lathen, Emma
Laut, Agnes C.
Lauterbach, Ann
Lawrence, Elizabeth L.
Lawrence, Josephine
Lawrence, Margaret Woods
Lazarus, Emma
Le Guin, Ursula K.
Le Sueur, Meridel
Le Vert, Octavia Walton

Lea, Fannie Heaslip
Lee, Eliza Buckminster
Lee, Hannah Sawyer
Lee, Harper
Lee, Marion *See* Comstock, Anna Botsford
Lee, Mary Elizabeth
LeGallienne, Eva
L'Engle, Madeleine
Lenski, Lois
Lerman, Rhoda
Lerner, Gerda
Leslie, Annie Brown
Leslie, Eliza
Leslie, Miriam Follin
Levertov, Denise
Lewis, Elizabeth Foreman
Lewis, Estelle Robinson
Lewis, Janet
Libbey, Laura Jean
Lincoln, Victoria
Lindbergh, Anne Morrow
Lindbergh, Reeve
Linington, Elizabeth
Lippard, Lucy R.
Lippincott, Martha Shepard
Lippincott, Sara Jane
Little, Sophia Robbins
Livermore, Harriet
Livermore, Mary Rice
Livingston, Myra Cohn
Locke, Jane Starkweather
Logan, Deborah Norris
Logan, Mary Cunningham
Logan, Olive
Loos, Anita
Lord, Bette Bao
Lorde, Audre
Lothrop, Amy *See* Warner, Anna Bartlett
Lothrop, Harriet Stone
Loughborough, Mary Ann Webster
Lounsberry, Alice
Lovejoy, Esther Pohl
Lowell, Amy
Lowry, Lois
Loy, Mina
Lucas, Victoria *See* Plath, Sylvia
Luce, Clare Boothe
Luhan, Mabel Dodge
Lumpkin, Grace
Lurie, Alison
Lutz, Alma
Lynd, Helen Merrell

MacDonald, Betty
MacDonald, Jessica N.

Macdonald, Marcia *See* Hill-Lutz, Grace Livingston
MacDougall, Ruth Doan
MacInnes, Helen
MacKinnon, Catharine A.
MacLaine, Shirley
MacLean, Annie Marion
Macumber, Marie S. *See* Sandoz, Mari
Madeleva, Sister Mary
Madison, Dolley
Mairs, Nancy
Malkiel, Theresa S.
Mannes, Marya
Manning, Marie
Mansfield, Blanche McManus
March, Anne *See* Woolson, Constance Fenimore
Marks, Jeannette Augustus
Marot, Helen
Marshall, Catherine
Marshall, Gertrude Helen *See* Fahs, Sophia Lyon
Marshall, Paule
Martin, Del
Martin, George Madden
Martin, Helen Reimensnyder
Martin, Valerie
Martínez, Demetria
Martyn, Sarah Smith
Maso, Carole
Mason, Bobbie Ann
Mathews, Frances Aymar
Matthews, Adelaide
May, Sophie *See* Clarke, Rebecca Sophia
Maynard, Joyce
Mayo, Katherine
Mayo, Margaret
Mayo, Sarah Edgarton
McBride, Mary Margaret
McCaffrey, Anne
McCarthy, Mary
McCloy, Helen
McCord, Louisa Cheves
McCormick, Anne O'Hare
McCrackin, Josephine Clifford
McCrumb, Sharon
McCullers, Carson
McDermott, Alice
McDowell, Katherine Bonner
McGinley, Phyllis
McGrory, Mary
McGuire, Judith Brockenbrough
McIntosh, Maria Jane
McIntyre, Vonda N.
McKenney, Ruth
McLean, Kathryn Anderson
McMillan, Terry
McPherson, Aimee Semple

McPherson, Sandra
Mead, Kate C. *See* Hurd-Mead, Kate C.
Mead, Margaret
Meaney, Mary L.
Means, Florence Crannell
Meigs, Cornelia
Meloney, Franken *See* Franken, Rose
Menken, Adah Isaacs
Merington, Marguerite
Meriwether, Elizabeth Avery
Merriam, Eve
Merril, Judith
Meyer, Annie Nathan
Meyer, June *See* Jordan, June M.
Miles, Josephine
Millar, Margaret
Millay, Edna St. Vincent
Miller, Alice Duer
Miller, Caroline Pafford
Miller, Emily Huntington
Miller, Harriet M.
Miller, Isabel *See* Routsong, Alma
Miller, Mary Britton
Miller, Vassar
Millett, Kate
Milward, Maria G.
Miner, Valerie
Minot, Susan
Mirikitani, Janice
Mitchell, Agnes Woods
Mitchell, Margaret
Mitchell, Maria
Mitford, Jessica
Mixer, Elizabeth
Moers, Ellen
Mohr, Nicholasa
Moise, Penina
Mojtabai, A. G.
Mollenkott, Virginia Ramey
Monroe, Harriet
Monroe, Lucy
Montgomery, Ruth Shick
Moody, Anne
Moore, C. L.
Moore, Lorrie
Moore, Marianne
Moore, Mary Evelyn *See* Davis, Mollie Moore
Moore, Mollie E. *See* Davis, Mollie Moore
Moore, Mrs. H. J.
Moorhead, Sarah Parsons
Moraga, Cherríe
Morgan, Claire *See* Highsmith, Patricia
Morgan, Marabel
Morgan, Robin
Morley, Hilda

Morris, Clara
Morrison, Toni
Morrow, Honoré McCue
Mortimer, Lillian
Morton, Martha
Morton, Sarah Wentworth
Mother Goose *See* Walworth, Jeannette Hadermann
Mott, Lucretia
Moulton, Louise Chandler
Mourning Dove
Mukherjee, Bharati
Muller, Marcia
Munro, Eleanor
Murfree, Mary
Murray, Judith Sargent
Murray, Pauli
Myles, Eileen

Nation, Carry A.
Naylor, Gloria
Neely, Barbara
Neilson, Nellie
Neville, Emily Cheney
Newcomb, Franc Johnson
Newman, Frances
Newman, Lesléa
Newstead, Helaine
Nichols, Anne
Nicholson, Asenath Hatch
Nicholson, Eliza Jane Poitevent
Nicolson, Marjorie Hope
Niedecker, Lorine
Nieriker, Abigail May Alcott
Niggli, Josefina
Niles, Blair Rice
Nin, Anaïs
Nitsch, Helen Matthews
Nixon, Agnes E.
Norman, Marsha
Norris, Kathleen Thompson
Norton, Alice *See* Norton, Andre
Norton, Andre
Norton, Katherine LaForge *See* Reed, Myrtle
Notley, Alice
Nussbaum, Martha Craven
Nye, Andrea
Nye, Naomi Shihab

Oates, Joyce Carol
Obejas, Achy
Oberholtzer, Sara Vickers
O'Connor, Flannery
O'Connor, Florence J.
O'Donnell, Jessie Fremont
O'Donnell, Lillian
Oemler, Marie Conway

Offord, Lenore Glen
O'Hair, Madalyn Murray
O'Hara, Mary *See* Sture-Vasa, Mary
O'Keeffe, Katharine A.
O'Neill, Egan *See* Linington, Elizabeth
Older, Cora Baggerly
Olds, Sharon
Oliphant, B. J. *See* Tepper, Sheri S.
Oliver, Mary
Olsen, Tillie
O'Neill, Rose
Orde, A. J. *See* Tepper, Sheri S.
Ortiz Cofer, Judith
Orvis, Marianne Dwight
Osbey, Brenda Marie
Osborn, Sarah
Osgood, Frances Sargent
Ostenso, Martha
Ostriker, Alicia
Ottenberg, Miriam
Ovington, Mary White
Owen, Catherine *See* Nitsch, Helen Matthews
Owen, Mary Alicia
Owen, Ruth Bryan
Owens, Claire Myers
Owens-Adair, Bethenia
Owens, Rochelle
Ozick, Cynthia

Page, Myra
Paglia, Camille
Paley, Grace
Palmer, Phoebe Worrall
Papashvily, Helen Waite
Paretsky, Sara
Parker, Charlotte Blair
Parker, Dorothy
Parrish, Mary Frances *See* Fisher, M. F. K.
Parsons, Elsie Clews
Parsons, Frances Dana
Parsons, Louella Oettinger
Parton, Sara Willis
Pastan, Linda
Patchett, Ann
Paterson, Katherine
Patton, Frances Gray
Peabody, Elizabeth Palmer
Peabody, Josephine Preston
Peattie, Elia Wilkinson
Peattie, Louise Redfield
Peck, Annie Smith
Peck, Ellen
Pember, Phoebe Yates
Penfeather, Anabel *See* Cooper, Susan Fenimore
Percy, Florence *See* Allen, Elizabeth Akers

Perkins, Frances
Perkins, Lucy Fitch
Pesotta, Rose
Peterkin, Julia Mood
Peters, Sandra *See* Plath, Sylvia
Petersham, Maud Fuller
Petry, Ann Lane
Phelps, Almira Lincoln
Phelps, Elizabeth Stuart
Phillips, Irna
Phillips, Jayne Anne
Piatt, Sarah Bryan
Piercy, Marge
Pike, Mary Green
Pinckney, Josephine
Pine, Cuyler *See* Peck, Ellen
Plain, Belva
Plath, Sylvia
Polacco, Patricia
Pollack, Rachel
Pollard, Josephine
Porter, Eleanor Hodgman
Porter, Katherine Anne
Porter, Rose
Porter, Sarah
Porter, Sylvia F.
Post, Emily
Powell, Dawn
Pratt, Ella Farman
Prentiss, Elizabeth Payson
Preston, Harriet Waters
Preston, Margaret Junkin
Prince, Nancy Gardner
Prose, Francine
Prouty, Olive Higgins
Pryor, Sara Rice
Pugh, Eliza Phillips
Putnam, Emily Smith
Putnam, Mary Lowell
Putnam, Ruth
Putnam, Sallie A. Brock

Raimond, C. E. *See* Robins, Elizabeth
Rampling, Anne *See* Rice, Anne
Ramsay, Martha Laurens
Ramsay, Vienna G. Morrell
Rand, Ayn
Randall, Margaret
Randall, Ruth Painter
Rankin, Fannie W.
Ranous, Dora Knowlton
Rawlings, Marjorie Kinnan
Read, Harriette Fanning
Read, Martha
Reed, Kit

Reed, Myrtle
Reese, Lizette Woodworth
Remick, Martha
Reno, Itti Kinney
Repplier, Agnes
Rice, Alice Hegan
Rice, Anne
Rich, Adrienne
Rich, Barbara *See* Jackson, Laura
Rich, Louise Dickinson
Richards, Laura Howe
Richards, Louisa Greene
Richmond, Grace
Ricker, Marilla M.
Ridge, Lola
Riding, Laura *See* Jackson, Laura
Rinehart, Mary Roberts
Ripley, Eliza M.
Ritchie, Anna Mowatt
Rittenhouse, Jessie B.
Rivers, Alfrida *See* Bradley, Marion Zimmer
Rivers, Pearl *See* Nicholson, Eliza Jane Poitevent
Robb, J. D. *See* Roberts, Nora
Roberts, Elizabeth Madox
Roberts, Jane
Roberts, Maggie
Roberts, Nora
Robins, Elizabeth
Robinson, Harriet Hanson
Robinson, Martha Harrison
Rodgers, Carolyn M.
Rogers, Katherine M.
Roman, Klara Goldzieher
Rombauer, Irma von Starkloff
Roosevelt, Eleanor
Roquelaure, A. N. *See* Rice, Anne
Ross, Helaine *See* Daniels, Dorothy
Ross, Lillian
Rossner, Judith
Rourke, Constance Mayfield
Routsong, Alma
Royall, Anne Newport
Royce, Sarah Bayliss
Ruddy, Ella Giles
Ruether, Rosemary Radford
Rukeyser, Muriel
Rule, Ann
Rusch, Kristine Kathryn
Rush, Caroline E.
Rush, Rebecca
Russ, Joanna
Ryan, Rachel *See* Brown, Sandra

Sachs, Marilyn
St. Johns, Adela Rogers

St. Claire, Erin *See* Brown, Sandra
Salisbury, Charlotte Y.
Salmon, Lucy Maynard
Salmonson, Jessica Amanda
Sanchez, Sonia
Sanders, Elizabeth Elkins
Sandoz, Mari
Sanford, Mollie Dorsey
Sanger, Margaret
Sangster, Margaret E.
Santiago, Esmeralda
Sargent, Pamela
Sarton, May
Satir, Virginia M.
Savage, Elizabeth
Sawyer, Ruth
Scarberry, Alma Sioux
Scarborough, Dorothy
Scarborough, Elizabeth Ann
Schaeffer, Susan Fromberg
Schmitt, Gladys
Schofield, Sandy *See* Rusch, Kristine Kathryn
Schoolcraft, Mary Howard
Schwartz, Lynne Sharon
Scott, Anne Firor
Scott, Evelyn
Scott, Joan Wallach
Scott, Julia *See* Owen, Mary Alicia
Scott-Maxwell, Florida
Scudder, Vida Dutton
Seaman, Elizabeth Cochrane
Seawell, Molly Elliot
Secor, Lella
Sedges, John *See* Buck, Pearl S.
Sedgwick, Anne Douglas
Sedgwick, Catharine Maria
Sedgwick, Susan Ridley
Seeley, Mabel
Seid, Ruth
Seifert, Elizabeth
Semple, Ellen Churchill
Seredy, Kate
Seton, Anya
Settle, Mary Lee
Sewall, Harriet Winslow
Sewell, Elizabeth
Sexton, Anne
Shange, Ntozake
Shannon, Dell *See* Linington, Elizabeth
Shannon, Monica
Sharon, Rose *See* Merril, Judith
Sharp, Isabella Oliver
Shaw, Anna Moore
Shaw, Anna H.
Sheehy, Gail

Sheldon, Ann *See* Adams, Harriet Stratemeyer
Sherwood, Mary Wilson
Shindler, Mary Dana
Showalter, Elaine
Shreve, Anita
Shulman, Alix Kates
Sidlosky, Carolyn *See* Forché, Carolyn
Sigourney, Lydia Huntley
Silko, Leslie Marmon
Simon, Kate
Sinclair, Bertha Muzzy
Sinclair, Jo *See* Seid, Ruth
Singer, June K.
Singleton, Anne *See* Benedict, Ruth
Singmaster, Elsie
Skinner, Constance Lindsay
Skinner, Cornelia Otis
Slade, Caroline
Slesinger, Tess
Slosson, Annie Trumbull
Smedley, Agnes
Smith, Amanda
Smith, Anna Young
Smith, Betty
Smith, Eliza Snow
Smith, Elizabeth Oakes
Smith, Eunice
Smith, Hannah Whittal
Smith, Lee
Smith, Lillian
Smith, Lula Carson *See* McCullers, Carson
Smith, Margaret Bayard
Smith, Rosamond *See* Oates, Joyce Carol
Smith, Sarah Pogson
Smith, Susy
Snedeker, Caroline Dale
Snyder, Zilpha Keatley
Solwoska, Mara *See* French, Marilyn
Somers, Suzanne *See* Daniels, Dorothy
Song, Cathy
Sontag, Susan
Sorel, Julia *See* Drexler, Rosalyn
Soule, Caroline White
Southworth, E. D. E. N.
Souza, E. *See* Scott, Evelyn
Spacks, Patricia Meyer
Speare, Elizabeth George
Spencer, Anne
Spencer, Cornelia Phillips
Spencer, Elizabeth
Spewak, Bella Cohen
Speyer, Leonora von Stosch
Spofford, Harriet Prescott
Sprague, Rosemary
Stabenow, Dana

Stack, Andy *See* Rule, Ann
Stafford, Jean
Stanton, Elizabeth Cady
Steel, Danielle
Stein, Gertrude
Steinem, Gloria
Stenhouse, Fanny
Stephens, Ann Winterbotham
Stephens, Margaret Dean *See* Aldrich, Bess Streeter
Steptoe, Lydia *See* Barnes, Djuna
Stern, Elizabeth G.
Stewart, Elinore Pruitt
Stewart, Maria W.
Stockton, Annis Boudinot
Stoddard, Elizabeth Barstow
Stone, Ruth
Story, Sydney A. *See* Pike, Mary Green
Stowe, Harriet Beecher
Stratton-Porter, Gene
Strong, Anna Louise
Stuart, Ruth McEnery
Sture-Vasa, Mary
Suckow, Ruth
Sui Sin Far *See* Eaton, Edith Maud
Susann, Jacqueline
Swenson, May
Swett, Sophie
Swisshelm, Jane Grey

Taber, Gladys Bagg
Taggard, Genevieve
Talbott, Marion
Tan, Amy
Tandy, Jennette Reid
Tappan, Eva March
Tarbell, Ida
Taylor, Mildred Delois
Taylor, Phoebe Atwood
Taylor, Susie King
Teasdale, Sara
Tenney, Tabitha
Tepper, Sheri S.
Terhune, Mary Hawes
Terry, Megan
Thane, Elswyth
Thanet, Octave *See* French, Alice
Thaxter, Celia Laighton
Thayer, Caroline Warren
Thayer, Geraldine *See* Daniels, Dorothy
Thomas, Dorothy Swain
Thompson, Clara M. (b. c. 1830s)
Thompson, Clara M. (1893-1958)
Thompson, Dorothy
Thorndyke, Helen Louise *See* Adams, Harriet Stratemeyer
Ticknor, Caroline

Tiernan, Frances Fisher
Tietjens, Eunice
Tilton, Alice *See* Taylor, Phoebe Atwood
Tincker, Mary Agnes
Todd, Mabel Loomis
Todd, Marion Marsh
Toklas, Alice B.
Tompkins, Jane P.
Towne, Laura M.
Townsend, Mary Ashley
Treadwell, Sophie
Trilling, Diana
Troubetzkoy, Amélie Rives
Truitt, Anne
Truman, Margaret
Truth, Sojourner
Tuchman, Barbara
Turell, Jane
Turnbull, Agnes Sligh
Turney, Catherine
Tuthill, Louisa Huggins
Tuve, Rosemond
Ty-Casper, Linda
Tyler, Anne
Tyler, Martha W.
Tyler, Mary Palmer

Uchida, Yoshiko
Uhnak, Dorothy
Ulanov, Ann Belford
Underwood, Sophie Kerr
Untermeyer, Jean Starr
Upton, Harriet Taylor

Valentine, Jean
Valentine, Jo *See* Armstrong, Charlotte
Van Alstyne, Frances Crosby
Vandegrift, Margaret *See* Janvier, Margaret Thompson
Vanderbilt, Amy
Van Duyn, Mona
Van Vorst, Bessie McGinnis
Van Vorst, Marie
Vendler, Helen Hennessy
Victor, Frances Fuller
Victor, Metta Fuller
Vining, Elizabeth Gray
Viramontes, Helena María
Voigt, Cynthia
Voigt, Ellen Bryant
Vorse, Mary Heaton

Wakoski, Diane
Wald, Lillian D.
Waldman, Anne
Waldrop, Rosmarie
Walker, Alice

Walker, Margaret
Walker, Mary Spring
Wallace, Michele
Waller, Mary Ella
Walter, Mildred Pitts
Walton, Evangeline
Walworth, Jeannette Hadermann
Ward, Mary Jane
Warfield, Catherine Ware
Warner, Anna Bartlett
Warner, Susan Bogert
Warren, Lella
Warren, Mercy Otis
Wasserstein, Wendy
Watanabe, Sylvia
Watson, Sukey Vickery
Watts, Mary Stanbery
Weber, Sarah Appleton *See* Appleton-Weber, Sarah
Webster, Jean
Weeks, Helen C. *See* Campbell, Helen Stuart
Welby, Amelia Coppuck
Wells, Carolyn
Wells, Emmeline Woodward
Wells, John J. *See* Bradley, Marion Zimmer
Wells-Barnett, Ida B.
Welty, Eudora
West, Dorothy
West, Jessamyn
West, Lillie
West, Mae
Wetherall, Elizabeth *See* Warner, Susan Bogert
Wharton, Edith
Wheatley, Phillis
Wheaton, Campbell *See* Campbell, Helen Stuart
Whipple, Maurine
Whitcher, Frances Berry
White, Anna
White, Anne Terry
White, Eliza Orne
White, Elizabeth
White, Ellen Gould
White, Helen Constance
White, Nelia Gardner
White, Rhoda E.
Whiting, Lillian
Whitman, Narcissa Prentiss
Whitman, Ruth
Whitman, Sarah Helen
Whitney, Adeline D. T.
Whitney, Phyllis A.
Wiggin, Kate Douglass
Wiggins, Bernice Love
Wiggins, Marianne
Wilcox, Ella Wheeler
Wilder, Laura Ingalls

Wilder, Louise Beebe
Wilhelm, Kate
Willard, Emma
Willard, Frances
Willard, Nancy
Williams, Catharine Arnold
Williams, Fannie Barrier
Williams, Sherley Anne
Willis, Connie
Willis, Lydia Fish
Willoughby, Florence Barrett
Wilson, Harriet E. Adams
Windle, Mary Jane
Winnemucca, Sarah
Winslow, Anna Green
Winslow, Helen M.
Winslow, Ola Elizabeth
Winslow, Thyra Samter
Winter, Ella
Winwar, Frances
Wolf, Naomi
Wong, Jade Snow
Wood, Ann *See* Douglas, Ann
Wood, S. S. B. K.
Woodhull, Victoria
Woods, Caroline H.

Woods, Katharine Pearson
Woolsey, Sarah Chauncey
Woolson, Constance Fenimore
Wormeley, Katharine Prescott
Wright, Frances
Wright, Julia McNair
Wright, Mabel Osgood
Wright, Mary Clabaugh
Wyatt, Edith Franklin
Wylie, Elinor Hoyt

Yamada, Mitsuye
Yamamoto, Hisaye
Yamanaka, Lois-Ann
Yates, Elizabeth
Yezierska, Anzia
Yglesias, Helen
Youmans, Eliza Ann
Young, Ann Eliza
Young, Ella
Young, Marguerite
Young, Rida Johnson

Zaturenska, Marya
Zolotow, Charlotte
Zugsmith, Leane

ABBREVIATIONS

A style of all or nothing (initials or complete title) has been employed in this new edition; partial abbreviations have been purged, to limit confusion. In cases where two well-known periodicals have the same initials, only one has the initials and the other is always spelled out in its entirety (i.e. *NR* is New Republic, and National Review is spelled out).

APR	American Poetry Review
CA	Contemporary Authors
CAAS	Contemporary Authors Autobiography Series
CANR	Contemporary Authors New Revision Series
CB	Current Biography
CBY	Current Biography Yearbook
CLAJ	College Literary Association Journal
CLC	Contemporary Literary Criticism
CLHUS	Cambridge Literary History of the United States
CLR	Children's Literature Review
CN	Contemporary Novelists
CP	Contemporary Poets
CPW	Contemporary Popular Writers
CWD	Contemporary Women Dramatists
CWP	Contemporary Women Poets
DAB	Dictionary of American Biography
DLB	Dictionary of Literary Biography
DLBY	Dictionary of Literary Biography Yearbook
DAI	Dissertation Abstracts International
FC	Feminist Companion
FW	Feminist Writers
GLB	Gay & Lesbian Biography
KR	Kirkus Reviews
LATBR	Los Angeles Times Book Review
LJ	Library Journal
MTCW	Major Twentieth–Century Writers
NAW	Notable American Women
NAW:MP	Notable American Women: The Modern Period
NBAW	Notable Black American Women
NR	New Republic
NYRB	New York Review of Books
NYT	New York Times
NYTM	New York Times Magazine
NYTBR	New York Times Book Review
PMLA	Publication of the Modern Language Association
PW	Publishers Weekly
SATA	Something About the Author
SL	School Librarian
TLS	[London] Times Literary Supplement
TCCW	Twentieth–Century Children's Writers
WP	Washington Post
WPBW	Washington Post Book World
VV	Village Voice
WRB	Women's Review of Books
WWAW	Who's Who of American Women

S

SACHS, Marilyn

Born 18 December 1927, New York, New York
Daughter of Samuel and Anna Smith Stickle; **married** Morris
Sachs, 1947; **children:** Anne, Paul

Marilyn Sachs spent her childhood in harsh surroundings, in
a poor neighborhood where the strong victimized the weak. After
graduating from Hunter College (B.A. 1949), she took a job as a
children's librarian at the Brooklyn Public Library. While working, she attended Columbia University (M.S.L.S. 1953). Sachs
and her husband, a sculptor, have two children. She lives in San
Francisco.

With her first books, *Amy Moves In* (1964), *Laura's Luck*
(1965), and *Amy and Laura* (1966), Sachs established herself as a
favorite among preteens. Her characters' conversations ring true,
and the situations are humorous.

In 1968 Sachs began to break from the traditional settings
and themes of children's literature with *Veronica Ganz*. Sachs
once said, ''Veronica was a composite of all the kids who
tormented me while I was growing up in the Bronx,'' yet the
heroine is sympathetically portrayed. The daughter of a broken
marriage, Veronica is one of the main characters in two other
books, *Peter and Veronica* (1969) and *The Truth About Mary
Rose* (1973).

Sachs deftly portrays young girls in their struggles toward
self-identity. Since *Veronica Ganz*, she has continued to probe the
psychological traumas that can create or destroy a personality.
The Bears' House (1971) is a convincing story about an impoverished young girl whose father deserted the family and left them at
the mercy of the welfare authorities. *The Truth About Mary Rose*
describes the effects of Mary Rose's death on her sister Veronica,
her brother, and her young daughter. This story, unlike *The Bears'
House*, has an optimistic ending.

The setting of *A Pocket Full of Seeds* (1973) is France in
World War II. This short novel is a chilling picture of Nazi
terrorism and the ramifications of Jewish refusal to believe
Hitler's power and tyranny could sweep through all the occupied
lands. The story of one French family's extermination is only
slightly softened by the heroine's survival.

Sachs continues to write good, realistic fiction for children.
Her female characters are depicted as spirited young people
squarely facing their emotional problems. Usually the heroine
wins her battle over her environment. In *The Bears' House* and *A
Pocket Full of Seeds*, however, society's impact is devastating.

Critics have complained Sachs's plots are too slick and that
her aloofness from the characters sometimes makes the portrayals

cold and analytical. Although the literary quality of Sachs's work
may be controversial, her contributions in the field of children's
literature are not. Sachs leads young readers into a world of
uncertainty and demands that they themselves consider questions
of society's responsibilities.

Throughout her long career, which has spanned more than 35
years, Sachs has provided young adult readers with enjoyment
and lessons, and though not all critics appreciate her skills she has
won several awards. The aforementioned *The Bears' House*
(1971) won the Australian Children's Book prize in 1977 as well
as the George C. Stone Center's Recognition of Merit award; *The
Truth About Mary Rose* (1973) won the Silver Slate Pencil award
in 1974; *A Pocket Full of Seeds* (1973) won the Jane Addams
Children's Book Honor award in 1974; *Dorrie's Book* (1975) won
both the Silver Slate Pencil and the Garden State Children's Book
award; *Call Me Ruth* (1982) was given an award by the Association of Jewish Libraries in 1983; *Underdog* (1985) won the
Christopher award for 1986; *Fran Ellen's House* (1987) was
given the Bay Area Book Reviewers Association award in 1988
and Sach's second Recognition of Merit award from the George C.
Stone Center for Children's Books; and *The Big Book of Peace*
(edited with A. Durrell, 1990), won both the California Children's
Book award and the Jane Addams Children's Book prize in 1991.
Sachs is a longtime member of the ACLU, PEN, the Sierra Club,
the Author's Guild, and the Society of Children's Bookwriters;
she continues to review books for the *San Francisco Chronicle*.

OTHER WORKS: *Marv* (1970). *Matt's Mitt* (1975). *A December
Tale* (1976). *A Secret Friend* (1978). *A Summer's Lease* (1979).
Bus Ride (1980). *Class Pictures* (1980). *Fleet Footed Florence*
(1981). *Hello. . .Wrong Number* (1981). *Beach Towels* (1982).
Fourteen (1983). *The Fat Girl* (1984). *Thunderbird* (1985). *Baby
Sister* (1986). *Almost Fifteen* (1987). *Just Like a Friend* (1989). *At
the Sound of the Beep* (1990). *Circles* (1990). *What My Sister
Remembered* (1992). *Thirteen Going on Seven* (1993). *Ghosts in
the Family* (1995). *Another Day* (1997). *Surprise Party* (1998). *Jo
Jo and Winnie* (1999).

BIBLIOGRAPHY: Reference works: *CA* (1968, 1999). *SATA* (1972).
WW in America (2000).
    Other references: *PW* (8 Jan. 1973).

—JILL P. MAY,
UPDATED BY SYDONIE BENET

ST. CLAIRE, Erin
See BROWN, Sandra

ST. JOHNS, Adela Rogers

Born 20 May 1894, California; **died** 1988
Daughter of Earl and Harriet Greene Rogers; **married** William
Ivan St. Johns, 1914; second marriage, circa 1930s

The diversity of Adela Rogers St. Johns' reporting may well
have been anticipated by her unusually sophisticated childhood.
She was the daughter of a renowned criminal lawyer and a
displaced Southern Belle—a woman St. Johns has described as
having been extremely unhappy and violently cruel. Her parents'
tumultuous relationship proved a daily trial, and their marriage,
divorce, and remarriage frequently placed her with relatives or at
boarding schools in various parts of California. She charts her
father's career and his tremendous influence on her in *Final
Verdict* (1962). In 1913, when she was eighteen, he introduced her
to William Randolph Hearst, and until 1918 she worked for the
Hearst papers in San Francisco and Los Angeles.

During these early years, St. Johns also began writing for
Hollywood. In order to work at home when her children were
young, she wrote and collaborated on several scripts. She became
''Mother Confessor to the Stars'' for *Photoplay Magazine* and
later wrote biographies of movie stars for a Hearst series called
''Love, Laughter, and Tears'' (a title she would use for her
memoirs of this period).

St. Johns' journalism began setting precedents in the 1920s
when she became the country's first woman sports writer. But it
was in the 1930s, while an International News Service reporter,
that she created her best stories. Among them is her Depression
series on the plight of unemployed women. These articles are
largely based on personal experiences. Despite the artificiality of
the premise—St. Johns set out to look for a job with only a dime in
her pocket—they dramatize the misery of these women and
expose the uncharitableness of several charitable institutions.

In 1934 St. Johns covered the volatile Hauptmann trial
following the Lindbergh kidnapping. At the 1940 Democratic
Convention that nominated Roosevelt for a third term, she scooped
''The Voice from the Sewers'' story, revealing the man largely
responsible for creating a vocal illusion of pro-Roosevelt frenzy in
the convention floor. She subsequently spent several years as a
Washington correspondent.

St. Johns' fiction shares with her journalism a heavily emotive
style (she was known as a ''Sob Sister'') and topical subject
matter and background. She writes about Prohibition and World
War II, and sometimes bases her plot on a publicized crime or
incident. She can write engagingly, but the predominant concerns
of her fiction can be traced to a few fixed themes. One of these
themes, that of the ''modern woman,'' is treated with some depth
in her autobiography, *The Honeycomb* (1969), but in her fiction it
appears as a much less complex phenomenon. It is often merely a
decorative element in stories that are largely examples of wom-
en's escape fiction.

Several of her novels are romances set in Hollywood or in
''high society.'' Women protagonists may, in fact, possess the

characteristics of modern women—they may be important execu-
tives (*Field of Honor*, 1938) or women who freely engage in
affairs (*The Single Standard*, 1928)—but as one critic put it, they
are ultimately unconventional heroines too faithful to the conventions of their type. Characterizations are superficial and limited in
depth and originality by the author's moralizing. Nonetheless, St.
Johns' novels and more than 200 short stories appealed to a large
readership. She published in all the leading fiction and women's
magazines of her time. This commercial success was in all
likelihood the motivation for her 1956 book, *How to Write a Story
and Sell It.*

Unlike some of the characters in her fiction, the people she
describes and the persona she reveals in her autobiographies are
vivid, authentic, and moving. Her memoirs ramble sentimentally,
but they are candid and provide lively insights into political and
cultural history. St. Johns discusses her professional progress as
well as such traumas as the death of a child, divorce and custody
trials, and her alcoholism; her personal philosophy emerges as the
distillation of family values, religious faith, and her self-con-
sciousness as a modern woman. This consciousness, however, has
little to do with any overt alliance with feminist issues. In her
opinion, a ''single standard'' for men and women will remain
unattainable so long as women are mothers. St. Johns approaches
her ideal of modern woman through speculation on the moral
integrity women should maintain in the flux of modern society.
She sees this ideal most inspiringly realized in such admirable
individuals as Eleanor Roosevelt and Anne Morrow Lindbergh.

In recent years, St. Johns's writing explored her deepening
religious faith and her belief in the afterlife. *First Step Up Toward
Heaven* (1959), is the account of the founder of Forest Lawn
Cemetery; *Tell No Man* (1966) is a novel of a religious conversion, and *No Goodbyes: My Search Into Life Beyond Death* (1981,
1982), relates her communications with her deceased son.

St. Johns was one of this century's most famous women
journalists. In 1970, she was awarded the Medal of Freedom by
President Richard Nixon, her former newspaper boy in Whittier,
California.

OTHER WORKS: *A Free Soul* (1924). *The Skyrocket* (1925). *The
Root of All Evil* (1940). *Never Again, and Other Stories* (1949).
Affirmative Prayer in Action (1955). *Love, Laughter, and Tears:
My Hollywood Story* (1978).

BIBLIOGRAPHY: *Adela St. Johns. . .on 60 Minutes with Morley
Safer* (audio recording, 1976). *Adela St. Johns Recounts Her
Career and Dr. Robert Butler Talks About Longevity: On Over
Easy with Hugh Downs* (audio recording, 1979). *Sum & Substance: P. Tillich and A. R. St. Johns* (audiocassette, 1960, 1969,
1980, 1988). *Working with Hearst, A Presentation and Discussion: An Oral History Interview* (1991).

Other references: *Collier's* (24 Jan. 1924). *Foremost Women
in Communications* (1970). *Newsweek* (27 June 1936). *NYTBR* (7

June 1925, 28 Aug. 1927, 3 June 1928, 7 Aug. 1938, 12 June 1949, 10 April 1966).

—ELINOR SCHULL

SALISBURY, Charlotte Y.

Born 12 March 1914, Weston, Massachusetts
Daughter of Benjamin L. and Mary Coolidge Hall Young; **married** Allstom Boyer, 1934; John A. Rand, 1940; Harrison Salisbury, 1964

Charlotte Y. Salisbury grew up in Weston, Massachusetts, and resided in Manhattan and Connecticut. Salisbury's first major publication, *Asian Diary* (1968), is the result of an extensive trip in 1966, on which she accompanied her husband, Harrison Salisbury, a reporter for the *New York Times*, to Hong Kong, Cambodia, Thailand, Burma, India, Sikkim, Mongolia, Siberia, and Japan.

The special quality of *Asian Diary* is its informality and vivid descriptions of everyday scenes. Although Salisbury had the opportunity to mingle with the "notables," she preferred to associate mostly with the "nobodys." She talked with generals, governors, princes and prime ministers, but the people in the cities and villages were the primary focus of her attention. Salisbury describes the magic colors of Cambodia, the melee of life in the Bangkok *klongs*, the grace and beauty of the Southeast Asian people, the charm and fairytale quality of Sikkim, and the surprisingly beautiful landscape of Siberia. Writing during the Vietnam war, Salisbury is acutely aware of the political threats to these Asian cultures. Not surprisingly, the book includes very harsh criticisms of foreign intrusions in general and of American involvement in particular. Salisbury asks, "What are we really doing there except trying to impose our thinking, our way of life, with our army, our bombs, our modern technology, on a small simple peasant country?"

China Diary (1973) is also a descriptive travel book. It is the product of a six-week visit to Peking with her husband. As with her previous writings, *China Diary* is especially valuable for the perceptive observations and impressions of a casual visitor. In this sense it is a refreshing contrast to reports of experts that, though informative, are dull by comparison and lack the warmth which pervades these diaries. Of his wife, Harrison Salisbury noted that she "looks on the world with clear, unclouded eyes and records her response with a warm and frank heart. . . . Her feelings about people are solid and earthy. She senses what is real and what is diplomatic pretense. You can rely on her judgements." In this book, Salisbury takes her readers on a journey through Peking, Shanghai, Hong Kong, Wuhan, Sian, and Changsha. Salisbury also describes the countryside, the farms, the factories, the schools, the hospitals, and the children's facilities. It is a useful guide for the traveler, as well as a description of the life of Chinese peasants and high officials.

A third book resulting from Salisbury's travels with her husband is *Russian Diary* (1974). This time it was Moscow and Leningrad they had the opportunity to visit. Again, Salisbury's dominant concern is for the common people. She is interested in their daily living in an autocratic society. And again, she is not hesitant to be critical—this time of the U.S.S.R.'s oppressive policies. Salisbury writes that the government puts guns ahead of decency, and conformity ahead of creativity.

In one sense, Salisbury's books are travelogues; but they also speak out against all the indignities to the human spirit.

BIBLIOGRAPHY: *Atlantic* (Sept. 1974). *Christian Century* (31 July 1974). *LJ* (1 June 1968, 15 March 1973, 1 June 1974). *Nation* (6 May 1968). *NYTBR* (18 Feb. 1968, 22 April 1973).

—PATRICIA LANGHALS NEILS

SALMON, Lucy Maynard

Born 27 July 1853, Fulton, New York; **died** 14 February 1927, Poughkeepsie, New York
Daughter of George and Maria Maynard Salmon

Lucy Maynard Salmon's father was a staunch Presbyterian and a Republican with abolitionist sentiments. Her mother was head of the Fulton Female Seminary from 1836 until her marriage to George Salmon. With this strong heritage of female education, it is not surprising that Salmon received an excellent education for a woman of her day and age. She attended grammar school in Oswego, New York, and the coeducational Falley Seminar, formerly the Fulton Female Seminary.

Salmon was one of only 50 women at the University of Michigan. Under the tutorship of Charles Kendall Adams, she majored in history and graduated with a B.A. degree in 1876. She received her M.A. degree in 1883, after several years as assistant principal and principal of a high school in MacGregor, Iowa. While teaching at the Indiana State Normal School, Salmon published her first significant historical work, *Education in Michigan during the Territorial Period* (1885). After further graduate study in American history at Bryn Mawr College, Salmon accepted a position as the first professor of history at Vassar College in 1887. Except for a time spent studying in Europe (1898-1900), she remained at Vassar the rest of her professional career.

Salmon became a recognized leader within the Vassar College community. She believed the student should be the principal agent in her own education (Salmon taught her history courses in a seminar format, with emphasis placed on student research) and that the heart of any college is its library. She also anticipated future trends in historical research and methodology when she encouraged the development of a collection of periodical literature at the Vassar college library. Her personal contribution to the periodical collection was the guide *The Justice Collection of Material Relating to the Periodical Press in the Vassar College Library* (1925).

Salmon was a charter member of the American Historical Association. From 1896 to 1899, she served as a member of the association's "Committee of Seven," whose report, *The Study of History in Schools* (1915), formed the guide for teaching history in secondary schools for generations. In addition to her professional activities, Salmon was an active supporter of woman suffrage and an advocate of world peace.

As a scholar, Salmon's work followed no developmental pattern until her later years. Her most important early work is the volume *History of the Appointing Power of the President* (1886), which investigates the creation of the appointing power of the president by the Constitutional Convention, its precedents in English law, and the experience of the states under the Articles of Confederation. While this work is dated, and while Salmon's hopes for a future when presidents would again make appointments based on merit, as they had during the Federalist era, were certainly not borne out by history, it is still a significant historical work for anyone interested in presidential use and abuse of power.

Domestic Service (1897) and *Progress in the Household* (1906) document Salmon's increasing interest in what are considered today to be nontraditional subjects and methods of writing history. *Domestic Service* is based on a survey conducted in 1889 and 1890. It presents an analysis of household employment within a historical perspective, beginning with a discussion of domestic service in colonial America. Salmon suggests there should be specialization in the work of domestic servants—paralleling the division of labor in other fields—and that servants be compensated fairly for their work, through higher wages and profit-sharing plans.

Progress in the Household is, in essence, a supplement to *Domestic Service*, as the essays outline "recent progress in the study of domestic service." These books are dated, and the institutions and problems described by Salmon are for the most part nonexistent today. Still, they present the modern reader with a picture of domestic life and service in the years before the technological revolution of the 20th century and express the issues of concern to American women at the time.

Salmon's departure from the then-current traditional school of history, which emphasized study of the political institutions of America, led to the writing of her most important historical works, *The Newspaper and the Historian* and *The Newspaper and Authority*, both published in 1923. The former discusses the advantages and limitations of newspapers and other periodicals as sources in the writing of history. Salmon points out how the periodical press reveals the personality of its time or environment. The companion volume, *The Newspaper and Authority*, is international in scope and investigates the press with reference to its external government controls.

Just three months prior to her death, Salmon completed *Why Is History Rewritten?* (1929). "History must be continually rewritten because there is always a new history. To the end of time, as far as the human mind can see, history will need to be rewritten and in that very fact the historian finds one of its greatest interests." Salmon was a pioneer in liberating the study of history

from the narrow confines of a political perspective and introducing historians to a new range of sources for historical study.

OTHER WORKS: *History in the German Gymnasia* (1898). *Some Principles in the Teaching of History* (1908). *Patronage in the Public Schools* (1908). *History in the Back Yard* (1913). *The Dutch West India Company on the Hudson* (1915). *"Is This Vassar College?"* (1915). *Main Street* (1915). *What Is Modern History?* (1917). *Historical Material* (1933).

BIBLIOGRAPHY: Brown, L. F., *Apostle of Democracy: The Life of Lucy Maynard Salmon* (1943, reprinted 1967).
Reference works: *DAB. NAW* (1971).

—PAULA A. TRECKEL

SALMONSON, Jessica Amanda

Born Amos Salmonson, 6 January 1950, Seattle, Washington
Daughter of Veronica (Walker) Salerno

Jessica Amanda Salmonson grew up in an itinerant life because her mother, a sword swallower, and stepfather, a fire-eater, worked in carnivals. Abandoned at age seven, Salmonson saw neither for years while growing up in an abusive foster system with an older sister. Running away at the age of twelve, Salmonson lived in "hippy group-houses" until rediscovering her missing father and her stepmother, Lek (also known as Lumchuan), a Thai Buddhist nun who was raised in a temple, with whom she studied Buddhism for several years. Salmonson's short story "Lincoy's Journey" is based on the event that led to Lek's placement in the temple where she was raised, and cites her stepmother as "the only decent adult in my childhood, otherwise I wouldn't have believed decent adults existed."

Salmonson started submitting stories to pulp magazines at the age of ten but didn't get published until age twenty-two in small presses. One of her first works was *Tragedy of the Moisty Morning* (1978), a short story published in chapbook form. *Amazons!* (1979), her first editorial credit in the science fiction and fantasy world, won a World Fantasy award for Best Collection/Anthology of that year. Her first novel, *Tomoe Gozen* (1981), began a fantasy series set in a Japanese milieu and allowed Salmonson to quit a "crappy secretarial job." She hasn't looked back since.

Novels such as *The Golden Naginata* (1982), second in the Tomoe Gozen series, and *The Swordswoman* (1982) followed, along with several more anthologies: *Amazons II* (1982), *Heroic Visions* (1983), and *Tales by Moonlight* (1983). *Hag's Tapestry* (1984), a collection of short stories, was published in chapbook form in England, and two more novels, *Thousand Shrine Warrior* (1984), third in the Tomoe Gozen series, and *Ou Lu Khen and the*

Beautiful Madwoman (1985), would follow in the 1980s. Most of Salmonson's work in that period encompassed anthologies. *The Haunted Wherry, and Other Rare Ghost Stories* (1985) appeared from Miskatonic University Press, named for H. P. Lovecraft's fictional school. Other anthologies included *Heroic Visions II* (1986), *The Supernatural Tales of Fitz-James O'Brien* (1988), *Tales by Moonlight II* (1989), and *What Did Miss Darrington See: An Anthology of Feminist Supernatural Fiction* (1989), which won both the Lambda Literary award and the Readercon Small Press award. During that time, Salmonson also released two short story collections, *A Silver Thread of Madness*(1989) and *John Collier and Fredric Brown Went Quarrelling Through My Head: Stories* (1989).

In the 1990s Salmonson's work focused mostly on short story collections and anthologies, although one novel, *Anthony Shriek, His Doleful Adventures; or, Lovers of Another Realm* (1992), appeared, and *Tomoe Gozen* was republished as *The Disfavored Hero* (1999). Eleven short story collections appeared under Salmonson's pen in a wide variety of topics, ranging from ghosts—*Harmless Ghosts* (1990), *The Mysterious Doom and Other Ghostly Tales of the Pacific Northwest* (1992), and *The Deep Museum: Ghost Stories of a Melancholic* (1999)—to fairy tales,—*Wisewomen and Boggy-Boos: A Dictionary Of Lesbian Fairy Lore* (1992, with Jules Remedios Faye)—from myths and legends—*Mystic Women: Their Ancient Tales and Legends Recounted by a Woman Inmate of the Calcutta Insane Asylum* (1991), *Phantom Waters: Northwest Legends of Rivers, Lakes and Shores* (1995), *Mister Monkey and Other Sumerian Fables* (1995), and *The Eleventh Jaguarundi and Other Mysterious Persons* (1995)—to new creations—*Twenty-One Novels* (1995). She also edited numerous books, including *The Encyclopedia of Amazons: Women Warriors from Antiquity to the Modern Era* (1991), *Master of Fallen Years: The Complete Supernatural Tales of Vincent O'Sullivan* (1995), and *The Phantom Coach: An Antiquary's Ghost Stories* (1999).

One of the reigning experts on feminist and 19th-century fantasy literature, as well as a respected fantasist in her own right, Salmonson's short fiction has appeared in a variety of publications, such as *Deathrealm, Isaac Asimov's Science Fiction Magazine, Pirate Writings, Science Fiction Age, Shadows, Weirdbook*, and *Weird Tales*, as well as in anthologies like Jane Yolen's *Xanadu 2* (1994) and Poppy Z. Brite's *Love in Vein* (1994), among many others.

After getting burned out on paperback originals, Salmonson has been focusing her current and future work on editing mostly limited edition hardcovers and selling antiquarian books through her Violet Books bookstore in her hometown of Seattle, where she lives with artist friend Rhonda Jean Boothe.

BIBLIOGRAPHY: Barr, M. S., *Lost in Space: Probing Feminist Science Fiction and Beyond* (1993). CA. Mallett, D. F., and R. Reginald, *Reginald's Science Fiction and Fantasy Awards: A Comprehensive Guide to the Awards and Their Winners* (1991, 1993). Reginald, R., *Science Fiction & Fantasy Literature,*

1975-1991: A Bibliography of Science Fiction, Fantasy, and Horror Fiction Books and Nonfiction Monographs (1992).

—DARYL F. MALLETT

SANCHEZ, Sonia

Born Wilsonia Benita Driver, 9 September 1934, Birmingham, Alabama
Daughter of Wilson L. and Lena Jones Driver; **married** Etheridge Knight; **children:** Anita, Morani, Mungu

Born in the South, Sonia Sanchez moved north at the age of nine with her family to the Harlem community of New York City. She graduated from Hunter College (B.A., 1955) and did postgraduate work at New York University, where she studied with poet Louise Bogan.

Sanchez worked in the civil rights movement and became further radicalized as a result of hearing Malcolm X. Becoming involved with the burgeoning black arts movement in Harlem during the 1960s and early 1970s as a poet and dramatist, Sanchez became one of the most forceful and best known of the cultural nationalist African American writers of that period. In 1966, she began teaching at San Francisco State College where she was a founder of the nation's first black studies program. Sanchez has since taught at a number of colleges and universities and has been a faculty member at Temple University since 1977.

Following in the tradition of such writers as Langston Hughes, Sterling Brown, and Margaret Walker, Sanchez is widely credited as one of the writers most important in the establishment of "Black English" as legitimate literary diction. In addition to her use of a distinctly African-American syntax and phonetic spelling, she often, particularly in her early work, broke the lines of her poems unusually and used unorthodox spellings that were not phonetic—leaving out certain vowels, for example—forcing the reader to look more carefully at the words themselves and to consider them as a distinctive African-American cultural product. Sanchez also constructs her poetry and her short fiction so as to emphasize the oral performative aspect she sees both as an important part of the African-American tradition and as more accessible to popular audiences. Some of Sanchez's best work engages with African-American music, as in "a / coltrane / poem" from *We a BadddDDD People* (1970), in which Sanchez literally attempts to re-create the structure and sound of John Coltrane's music while connecting it to the oppression of black people and the fight against that oppression.

Sanchez's poems and short stories both celebrate the survival and strengths of the black community in the U.S. and chronicle its losses. Since the beginning of her career, she has gradually adopted a stance rooted in her experiences as an African-American woman that addresses itself beyond a specifically black context to concern with all oppressed peoples. The powerful and moving "MIA's" in *homegirls and handgrenades* (1984), for example, links the disappearance of black children from the streets of Atlanta in the early 1980s to the death squad disappearances in El Salvador and the death of Stephen Biko in South Africa. The volume won the American Book Award for poetry in 1985.

Her concern with social justice has also led Sanchez to write a number of books for children, who she sees as having been particularly poorly served by literature. These include a volume of inspirational poems, *It's a New Day: Poems for Young Brothas and Sistuhs* (1971); *The Adventures of Fat Head, Small Head, and Square Head* (1973); and a collection of stories, *A Sound Investment* (1980), which invites children to draw moral meaning from the tales.

Since the beginning of her career, Sanchez has been a voice for the concerns of women even during the black arts era, when such concerns were generally muted. In this respect, she consciously sets herself in the tradition of female blues, jazz, and rhythm and blues singers who are tough, strong, loving, and often betrayed by love in a harsh world. Several poems in *Wee a BadddDDD People* reflect the suffering in her marriage to poet Etheridge Knight, who had a severe drug problem. *Love Poems* (1973) demonstrates the poet's lyricism, but here too the poems of man—woman relationships reflect their difficulty as well as their passion. Sanchez's work celebrates the power, pride, and solidarity of black women; she also portrays the personal betrayals of love—which often have a larger social implication—as in the poem "Blues" and the short story "After Saturday Night Comes Sunday." *A Blues Book for Blue Black Magical Women* (1974), written while Sanchez was a member of the Nation of Islam (1972-75), praises black women, "Queens of the Universe," and urges them to turn away from false values to "embrace Blackness as a religion / husband." Her concern for women's lives and their freedom reverberates through such later volumes as *I've Been A Woman* (1978) and *Under a Soprano Sky* (1987).

Sanchez has also written a number of significant plays, including *The Bronx is Next* (1968, produced 1970), where she speaks "symbolically" about the need for blacks to destroy urban centers, "to move out of that which is killing them," and the autobiographical *Sister Son/ji* (1969). Sanchez remains one of the most powerful writers, and readers, of poetry, drama, and prose in the U.S. Her voice speaks forcefully, and at times bittersweetly, about racism, sexism, oppression, and the need for revolutionary change. She is also one of the most poignant chroniclers of the social and emotional experience of a woman in the late 20th century in the United States.

In 1995 Sanchez was featured reading her poem "I Have Come into the City" on Sweet Honey in the Rock's CD, *Sacred Ground.* Her poetry has been featured in many other mediums also, such as in the movie *lovejones,* in various black magazines, or on rapper D-Knowledge's CD.

Sanchez's poetry includes a mixture of styles, languages, and dialects, specifically the Black English she has brought to the surface of the literary world. Her 13th book, *Wounded in the House of a Friend*, explores the plights of the African-American people, from the terrain of Africa to the poverty-stricken urban areas of America. It is a journey into racism, anger, and many

issues that have faced blacks throughout history. *Does Your House Have Lions* (1997) mixes the many speech patterns, tones, and styles Sanchez is known for to create and speak of her characters. It recounts her brother's death from AIDS and her family's reaction to the tragedy.

Her 1998 collection, *Like the Singing Coming Off the Drums: Love Poems*, expresses the passions and fire of a new generation. She has dedicated these works to such persons as Ella Fitzgerald and Tupac Shakur. Her recent book, *Shake Loose My Skin: New and Selected Poems* (1999) is a collection from over 30 years of her work. It comes soon after her 1998 nominations for both the NAACP Image and National Book Critics Circle awards. It includes selections from her previous books as well as some unpublished works. Ann K. Van Buren of *Library Journal* said of the collection, "This retrospective of 30 years of work leaves one in awe of the stretches of language Sanchez has helped to legitimize throughout her career."

Donna Seaman of *Booklist* said, "Her ringing voice gives voice to the emotions of many." Yet praise of Sanchez from the literary and black communities is sparse. However, another great black writer, Maya Angelou, has said "The world is a better place because of Sonia Sanchez: more livable, more laughable, more manageable." She goes on to say, "I wish millions of people knew that some of the joy in their lives comes from the fact that Sonia Sanchez is writing poetry. I wish they knew it so they could write her, and thank her, and love her up as I do."

OTHER WORKS: *Home Coming* (1969). *New Plays from the Black Theatre* (edited by E. Bullins, 1969). *Ima Talken bout the Nation of Islam* (1972). *Uh Huh: But How Do It Free Us?* (1975). *Malcolm Man Don't Live Here Anymore* (1979). *I'm Black When I'm Singing, I'm Blue When I Ain't* (1982). *Culture in Crisis: Two Speeches by Sonia Sanchez* (1983). *Generations: Selected Poetry, 1969-1985* (1986).

BIBLIOGRAPHY: Baker, H. A., Jr., "Our Lady: Sonia Sanchez and the Writing of a Black Renaissance," in *Black Feminist Criticism and Critical Theory* (1988). Curb, R., "Pre-Feminism in the Black Revolutionary Drama of Sonia Sanchez," in *The Many Forms of Drama* (1985). Madhubuti, H., "Sonia Sanchez: The Bringer of Memories," in *Black Women Writers (1950-1980): A Critical Evaluation* (1984). Melhem, D. M., *Heroism in the New Black Poetry: Introductions and Interviews* (1990). *Black Women Writers at Work* (1983).*Voices From the Gaps: Women Writers of Color* (1998).

Reference works: *CANR* (1988). *CLC* (1976). *DLB* (1985). *FC* (1990). *MTCW* (1991). *Oxford Companion to Women's Writing in the United States* (1995). *SATA* (1981).

Other references: Beacon Press Online (1999). *MELUS* (Fall 1985, Spring 1988).*Parnassus: Poetry in Review* (Spring-Winter 1985).

—JAMES SMETHURST,
UPDATED BY DEVRA M. SLADICS

SANDERS, Elizabeth Elkins

Born 12 August 1762, Salem, Massachusetts; **died** 19 February 1851, Salem, Massachusetts
Daughter of Thomas and Elizabeth White Elkins; **married** Thomas Sanders, 1782, **children:** four daughters and two sons

Elizabeth Elkins Sanders came from a family of well-to-do colonial merchants, and, at the age of twenty, she married Thomas Sanders, who was to become one of Salem's most successful businessmen. They had four daughters and two sons. Sanders attended the First Unitarian Church of Salem.

Sanders was sixty-six when she wrote her first pamphlet, a plea for compassion for Native Americans entitled *Conversations, Principally on the Aborigines of North America* (1828). This unsigned essay is written in the form of a dialogue between a mother and her young daughter. Its publication coincided with the presidential nomination of Andrew Jackson, who sanctioned the confiscation of Native American lands. Sanders writes of the atrocities committed by federal troops against such tribes as the Creeks of Georgia, and suggests true Christians would not condone these acts. The pamphlet also includes a detailed survey of Native American culture, from Mexico to the Great Lakes. Sanders emphasizes the Native Americans' skill in medicine and agriculture. Her information was drawn from her extensive reading. The following year she wrote a second pamphlet on Native American rights, *The First Settlers of New England* (1829).

During the next 15 years, many of Sanders's articles, book reviews, and letters appeared in New England newspapers. She did not resume writing pamphlets, however, until she was eighty-two, with *Tract on Missions* (1844). This was followed by *Second Part of a Tract on Missions* (1845) and *Remarks on the "Tour Around Hawaii," by the, Missionaries, Messrs. Ellis, Thurston, and Goodrich* (1848). These essays convey her distrust of most foreign missionaries. In the last, Sanders cites Melville's statement that they converted native peoples, not into Christians, but "into beasts of burden." Sanders fears Europeans will destroy the natives' way of life in the Pacific islands, as they had done in the Caribbean during the 16th century. It is her belief that future generations will not feel that too little had been done for foreigners, but instead will regret "the golden opportunity has been lost. . .to perpetuate and improve our institutions, which it is feared are rapidly on the decline."

Sanders's writing style is characterized by its directness. She refers to Andrew Jackson as "a second Robespierre" and plainly states her distaste for what she calls "the gloomy doctrines" and "appalling formulas" of Calvinism. Undaunted by the refusal of her contemporaries to accept her values, this woman of advanced years persisted in voicing her concern for oppressed peoples.

BIBLIOGRAPHY: Reference works: *Critical Dictionary of English Literature* (1872). *Dictionary of American Authors* (1905). *NAW.*

—JANE GILES

SANDOZ, Mari

Born Marie Susette Sandoz in 1896, Sheridan County, Nebraska; **died** 10 March 1966, New York, New York
Also wrote under: Marie S. Macumber
Daughter of Jules A. and Mary Fehr Sandoz

Mari Sandoz grew up in northwest Nebraska, in a frontier area at the edge of Native American country. Despite little formal education and much opposition from her father to a literary career, Sandoz's life was dedicated to writing. In both fiction and nonfiction she depicted the difficulties of frontier life and its violence, the harsh beauty of the country, the changes that have come to the area as Native Americans have been pushed aside and whites have imposed their way of life, the effects of political and social corruption upon the lives of the people, and the relations between ranchers, farmers, and Native Americans.

Sandoz's first published book was *Old Jules* (1935), a biography of her father; three years of research and two years of writing went into it. The book's subject is a vigorous frontiersman, opinionated and cruel as well as creative and foresighted; Sandoz's mixture of fear and admiration for him are ably conveyed. In his story Sandoz epitomized the recent history of her part of the West. Five other works later joined *Old Jules* as parts of the Great Plains series. *Crazy Horse* (1942) is a biography of the Oglala chief, stories of whom Sandoz had heard in her girlhood from old traders, frontiersmen, and Native Americans; *Cheyenne Autumn* (1953) tells of an epic flight of the northern Cheyenne Native Americans. *The Buffalo Hunters* (1954), *The Cattlemen* (1958), and *The Beaver Men* (1964) study aspects of the economic history of the West, evoking people, landscape, and events and showing their interactions through several hundred years. Two projected volumes were never written; one, the introduction to the series, would have dealt with stone-age people, the other with the impact of oil upon the history of the region. Sandoz considered this series the contribution upon which her reputation would rest. As history the books are flawed by lack of documentation and by fuzzy handling of dates and chronology; as evocative recreations of their time and place they are unsurpassed.

Sandoz's fiction uses similar materials. Of her novels, only *Capital City* (1939) is set in the present. One of many antifascist novels of the period, it analyzes a thinly disguised Nebraska and is flawed by its lack of a clear central character and focus.

The four novels set in the past are firmly rooted in historical fact. *Slogum House* (1937), the story of a woman who ruthlessly uses her family to build an empire, vividly depicts frontier violence. Murders, prostitution, and the castration of a man she perceives as an enemy are incidents in the growth of the central character's power. *The Tom-Walker* (1947) follows three generations of war veterans (of the Civil War, World War I, and World War II) from their return home, wounded in body and spirit, through their disillusioning attempts to adjust to a corrupt society. *Miss Morissa* (1955), the story of a young woman doctor who makes a life for herself on the frontier, is dedicated to three actual women doctors of the period. *Son of the Gamblin' Man* (1960) is a

fictionalized biography of painter Robert Henri, son of a frontier gambler and community builder. Through her imaginative recreation of the complicated relationship between father and son, Sandoz mirrored the development of a section of Nebraska.

In her later years, Sandoz received many honors, both as novelist and as historian. Her brutally realistic depictions of frontier violence and lawlessness and her penetrating analyses of Western history give her a secure place among those who have tried to understand that region both as it actually was and as a mythic force in the American consciousness.

OTHER WORKS: *Winter Thunder* (1954). *The Horsecatcher* (1957). *Hostiles and Friendlies: Selected Short Writings* (1959). *Love Song to the Plains* (1961). *These Were the Sioux* (1961). *The Far Looker* (1962). *The Story Catcher* (1963). *Old Jules Country: A Selection from Old Jules and Thirty Years of Writing Since the Book Was Published* (1965). *The Old Jules Home Region* (1965). *The Battle of the Little Bighorn* (1966). *Sandhill Sundays, and Other Recollections* (1966). *The Christmas of the Phonograph Records: A Recollection* (1966, reprinted 1970).

A collection of Sandoz's work is housed at Love Library of the University of Nebraska, in Lincoln.

BIBLIOGRAPHY: Pifer, C .S., *Making of an Author* (1972). Stauffer, H.W., *Story Catcher of the Plains* (1982). Stauffer, H. W. and S. J. Rosowski, eds., *Women and Western American Literature* (1982). Stauffer, H. W., ed., *Letter of Mari Sandoz* (1992). Villager, L. R., *Mari Sandoz: A Study in Post-Colonial Discourse* (1994). Wilkinson, J. L., *Scribe of the Great Plains: Mari Sandoz* (1998).

Reference works: *Oxford Companion to Women's Writing in the United States* (1995). *Benet's Reader's Encyclopedia* (1987).

Other references: *American West* (Spring 1965). *Great Plains Quarterly* (Winter 1992). *PS* (1966, 1967, 1968, 1971).

—MARY JEAN DEMARR

SANFORD, Mollie Dorsey

Born 17 December 1838, Rising Sun, Indiana; died 6 February 1915, Denver, Colorado
Daughter of William Dorsey; married Byron N. Sanford, 1860; children: a son and a daughter

At the age of eighteen, Mollie Dorsey Sanford set out from Indiana with her family on what she considered a journey to the "far west," the Nebraska Territory. After two weeks aboard a waterwheel ship, she arrived in Nebraska City. To earn money for her family, she spent the next three years moving between the family homestead and Nebraska City, working at various odd jobs. In 1860 she married a New York blacksmith; soon after, Sanford was again uprooted. She and Sanford, having caught Pike's Peak fever, spent the next six years moving from mine to

mine in Colorado, but they spent most of the remainder of their lives in Denver, raising a son and a daughter.

Sanford records these experiences in the journal she kept from March 1857 (just before her departure from Indianapolis) to January 1865 (just after the birth of her second child). In 1895 Sanford recopied her journal (unfortunately destroying the original) for her grandson to emulate and to profit by. Selections from the journal were published in *The Echo* in 1925 and in *Colorado Magazine* in 1930. *Mollie: The Journal of Mollie Dorsey Sanford in Nebraska and Colorado Territories, 1857-1866* was published in 1959 (and reprinted in 1975).

The journal's tone is resilient, paralleling the extremes of humor, pathos, and insight which the young and sensitive woman reached during those years. Sanford's themes are both universal and specific: not only morality and religion but male and female relationships in a shifting, mobile society; the importance of home and family to a woman raised on the domestic novel; and the problems a talented woman faces when forced to limit her interests.

Perhaps because of the shock pioneer life delivered to her eastern sensibilities, Sanford's journal combines two literary extremes: the romantic and the realistic. Before her marriage, a single entry might range from a selection of sentimentalized poetry Sanford sometimes wrote to a detailed account of killing a rattlesnake and triumphantly bringing home the trophy. Sanford's marriage and the trip to Denver caused her to lose the security of her home and family and to face the chaos and rigors of mining life: the sentimental becomes religious, her "journey" turns into a "pilgrimage," and the taxing details of existence take over the page.

As a journal writer, Sanford fits into a long tradition of young women who turn to a blank page for the friend life fails to provide, but Sanford also sought a world in which to play the roles of heroine and writer, in which she found release and inspiration.

BIBLIOGRAPHY: *Arizona and the West* 49 (1960). *Nebraska History* 41 (1960). *NYHTB* (6 March 1960). *SR* (7 Dec. 1959).

—LINDA S. COLEMAN

SANGER, Margaret

Born 14 September 1879, Corning, New York; died 6 September 1966, Tucson, Arizona
Daughter of Michael and Anne Purcell Higgins; married William Sanger, 1902; J. N. H. Slee, 1922

Margaret Sanger's mother died, leaving 11 children, when Sanger was seventeen. Profoundly affected by her mother's death, Sanger would later refer to women like her as "breeders," and would dedicate *Women and the New Race* (1920) to her. Although her life was undoubtedly molded in great degree by her iconoclastic and atheistic father, Sanger felt simultaneous fear, anger, and love for him, while expressing love and compassion for her mother. She would later assert her mother was a victim of her father's lust; and her writings suggest that she, like others born in the 19th century, believed women are threatened by men's sinister dual nature that at times can divide itself precipitously into benevolent husband and father and sexual aggressor.

Sanger trained as a nurse, married William Sanger, an architect, had three children, and lived in suburban Hastings-on-Hudson for ten years. After the destruction of their new home (an event which Sanger was later to see as symbolic), the Sangers moved to New York City and became involved in socialist and union activities. This activity and her earlier experiences led to Sanger's feminist writings. The Sangers' 1913 trip to Europe spelled the end of their 11-year marriage. After visiting Glasgow to research an article on the benefits of municipal ownership for women and children, Sanger went to France where she discovered that, in contrast to Scotland and America, contraceptive information was available and poverty was limited. After some time of "inactive, incoherent brooding," Sanger returned to America, with her three children but without her husband.

On her return Sanger took up the cause of woman suffrage, linking it loosely to birth control. In 1914 she founded the journal *The Woman Rebel*, written by women and for women. Contributors included Voltairine De Cleyre and Emma Goldman. The first issue was an unfocused burst of rage, with a rather sharp statement of feminist community and less concern for birth control than for emancipation. Although *The Woman Rebel* never included much birth control information, sending any through the mail was illegal, so Sanger was arrested and forced to flee to Canada and Europe until the charges were dropped.

In 1916 Sanger opened the first birth control clinic in America in the Brownsville section of Brooklyn. She also established the *Birth Control Review*, a publication greatly superior to *The Woman Rebel*. Sanger's feminist rage had become sharply focused on the problem of birth control. *Birth Control Review* continued until 1928.

Sanger's greatest successes came with her association with America's health professionals in achieving the legalization and availability of birth control. With physicians, social workers, and technicians to staff it, she opened the Clinical Research Bureau. When the police raided the clinic in 1929 and seized the confidential physicians' records, the medical profession defended its right to dispense birth control information. In 1936 a U.S. District Court upheld this right, which had been denied previously by the Comstock Law. In 1932 Sanger had rallied individuals across the nation to join the National Committee on Federal Legislation for Birth Control, and in 1937—one year after the court decision—the American Medical Association publicly endorsed birth control, bringing American physicians and their prestige to the side of Sanger's cause. The National Birth Control League and Sanger's clinics were combined in 1942 to form the Planned Parenthood Association of America.

Sanger's many publications consistently express her view that women are victims and need to "free themselves from involuntary motherhood." Concerned mainly for working-class women, Sanger believed they were victimized by their husbands, their doctors, and their priests. They suffered from the sexual appetites and insensitivity of the first, from the passivity of the second, and from the doctrine of the third. Sanger writes in *Woman and the New Race*: "Women are determined to decide for themselves whether they shall become mothers, under what conditions and when. This is the fundamental revolt. . . . It is for woman the key to the temple of liberty."

In *Happiness in Marriage* (1926), Sanger claims men are the sexual aggressors, while women are sexually passive. Female sexuality, she maintains, has not been expressed; if it were, it could become a creative force; and birth control is the means by which it could be released. Influenced by Havelock Ellis, Sanger asserts that only through birth control could the whole female nature be dealt with and the importance of female sexuality be recognized.

Even after her marriage to Slee, a wealthy industrialist, Sanger continued to address the problems of working-class women. *Motherhood in Bondage* (1928) is based on 5,000 of the 250,000 letters she claimed to have received in response to *The New Woman*. The letters are arranged in chapters entitled "Girl Mothers," "The Problem of Poverty," "The Trap of Maternity," "The Struggle of the Unfit," and "The Sins of the Fathers."

To Sanger, the birth control movement meant not only prevention of unwanted babies and abortions but, more importantly, the rational control of the individual woman's body and spirit, synthesized into female sexuality, as well as the subsequent lessening of war and of suffering. Her numerous publications, starting from the premise that women had always been the victims of men and society, are devoted to changing that role.

OTHER WORKS: *What Every Girl Should Know* (1913). *Family Limitation* (1914). *What Every Mother Should Know* (1914). *Dutch Methods of Birth Control* (1915). *Appeals from American Mothers* (1921). *Sayings of Others on Birth Control* (1921). *The Pivot of Civilization* (1922). *Problems of Overpopulation* (1926). *Religious and Ethical Aspects of Birth Control* (1926). *What Every Boy and Girl Should Know* (1927). *My Fight for Birth Control* (1931). *Woman of the Future* (1934). *Margaret Sanger: An Autobiography* (1938). "From Which I Spring" in *Women Without Superstition. . . : The Collected Writings of Women Freethinkers of the Nineteenth and Twentieth Centuries* (1997). "The Goal" in *Motherland: Writings by Irish American Women About Mothers and Daughters* (1999).

BIBLIOGRAPHY: Chesler, E., "Margaret Sanger and the Birth Control Movement" in *Against the Tide: Women Reformers in American Society* (1997). Chesler, E., *New Woman, New World: The Life of Margaret Sanger* (dissertation, 1990). Chesler, E., *Woman of Valor: Margaret Sanger and the Birth Control Movement in America* (1993). Dash, J., *A Life of One's Own: Three Gifted Women and the Men They Married* (1973). Douglas, E. T.,

Margaret Sanger: Pioneer of the Future (1970). Edwards, N. A., "Margaret Sanger: The Transitional Years, 1912-1916" (thesis, 1985). Forster, M., "Birth Control: Margaret Sanger 1876-1966" in *Significant Sisters: The Grassroots of Active Feminism 1839-1939* (1984). Grant, G., *Killer Angel: A Biography of Planned Parenthood's Founder Margaret Sanger* (1995). Gray, M., *Margaret Sanger: A Biography of the Champion of Birth Control* (1978). Johnson, M. S., *Margaret Sanger and the Birth Control Movement in Japan, 1921-1955* (dissertation, 1989). Kennedy, D., *Birth Control in America: The Career of Margaret Sanger* (1970). Mansfield, A. K., *Imperious Women: Margaret Sanger, Blanche Ames and the Birth Control Movement in the United States 1928-1935* (1995). Miller, R. M. and P. A. Cimbala, *American Reform and Reformers: A Biographical Dictionary* (1996). Moore, G., *Margaret Sanger and the Birth Control Movement: A Bibliography, 1911-1984* (1986). Nadler, P. F., "Margaret Sanger's Family Limitation Pamphlet: A Rhetorical and Historical Analysis" (thesis, 1990). Raible, R. E., "Conquering Comstock Law: The Combined Efforts of Mary Ware Dennett and Margaret Sanger" (thesis, 1997). Roldan Ruiz, M., "Margaret Sanger's 'First victory': A Rhetorical Analysis" (thesis, 1981). Topalian, E., *Margaret Sanger* (1984).

Other references: *Margaret Sanger* (microfilm of diaries and correspondence, 1988). *The Margaret Sanger Papers Microfilm Edition: Smith College Collections Series Guide* (1995). *The Margaret Sanger Papers: Documents from the Sophia Smith Collection and College Archives, Smith College (Series 2)* (microfilm, 1994). *The Margaret Sanger Papers: Collected Documents Series* (1997). *The Margaret Sanger Papers: Collected Documents Series* (microfilm, 1996). *Margaret Sanger: A Register of Her Papers in the Library of Congress* (1977). *The Papers of Margaret Sanger* (microfilm, 1976).

—JULIANN E. FLEENOR

SANGSTER, Margaret E(lizabeth Munson)

Born 22 February 1838, New Rochelle, New York; **died** 4 June 1912, Brooklyn, New York

Also wrote under: Margaret Sangster

Daughter of John and Margaret Chisholm Munson; **married** George Sangster, 1858

A precocious little girl, Margaret E. Sangster learned to read at age four, and early showed interest in writing. Her childhood, as she was later to say, was "wholly beautiful and wholly sweet," and in her old age she looked back upon her education with approval: "It was in marked contrast to the education young women are receiving now, but I am inclined to think that, as a practical preparation for life, it may bear comparison with twentieth century methods." She attended schools in Paterson, New Jersey, and Brooklyn, New York.

In 1855, when Sangster was only seventeen, she wrote "Little Janey" and sold it to the Presbyterian Board of Publication, which then commissioned her to write 100 stories for children. After her husband's death in 1871 she began a long, fruitful career of writing and editing. She was, at different times, assistant editor of *Hearth and Home*; assistant editor of *Christian at Work*; family-page editor of the *Christian Intelligencer*; and editor of *Harper's Bazar*. In addition she was connected in various capacities with the *Christian Herald*, *Harper's Young People*, *Ladies' Home Journal*, and the *Woman's Home Companion*.

Sangster's industry was remarkable; over the years she produced an incredible amount of poetry (published in various periodicals), as well as essays, short stories (many for children and young people), and novels. A number of Sangster's books are compilations of her short pieces, and all were popular in her day. Many of Sangster's essays and books were written for girls and young mothers. These combine the elements of "self-help" and inspiration and were well received by contemporary reviewers.

Sociable and friendly, Sangster possessed an unusually sweet and cheerful personality, nourished by an unshakable religious faith. Not one to fret at life's vicissitudes, she remarks serenely of her autobiography (1909) that from her youth she has "had more joy than sorrow, more pleasure than pain, more ease than hardship, and if my little book is optimistic, it is because optimism has been the dominant note of all my years." Such words are noteworthy when one considers Sangster had lived through the Civil War, with people dear to her on both sides of the conflict, and that her husband died when she was just thirty-three, leaving her with a young son.

Sangster's work is dated, but it was popular and respected during a long period of American life. By reading it, one may gain a vivid picture of the middle class in the half-century following the Civil War, what its basic ideals were, and how it felt those ideals to be threatened.

OTHER WORKS: *Manual of Missions of the Reformed Church in America* (1878). *Poems of the Household* (1882). *Some Fairies and Heart Flowers* (1887). *Little Knights and Ladies* (1895). *Easter Bells* (1897). *Home Life Made Beautiful in Story, Song, Sketch, and Picture* (1897). *Cheerful Todays and Trustful Tomorrows* (1899). *Winsome Womanhood* (1900). *Lyrics of Love, of Hearth and Home, and of Field and Garden* (1901). *Janet Ward: A Daughter of the Manse* (1902). *Eleanor Lee* (1903). *Good Manners for All Occasions* (1904). *What Shall a Young Girl Read?* (1905). *Fairest Girlhood* (1906). *Radiant Motherhood* (1906). *Story Bible* (1906). *An Autobiography: From My Youth Up* (1909). *Happy School Days* (1909). *Ideal Home Life* (1910). *Eastover Parish* (1912). *Mother Book* (1912). *My Garden of Hearts* (1913).

BIBLIOGRAPHY: *Christian Herald* (19 June 1912). *NYT* (5 June 1912). *World's Work* (Feb. 1910).

—ABIGAIL ANN HAMBLEN

SANTIAGO, Esmeralda

Born 17 May 1948, San Juan, Puerto Rico
Daughter of Ramona Santiago and Pablo Santiago Díaz; **married**
Frank Cantor, 1978; **children:** Lucas David

Being the oldest of 11 children may have had an impact on Esmeralda Santiago's desire to write. She not only became a surrogate mother to younger children, but also the assistant and translator for her mother in her new English-speaking society. Santiago greeted each experience with eyes wide open, examining everything and putting it to memory. ''Being a writer is like being a collector,'' she told the *Los Angeles Times*. ''Instead of baseball cards, I collect memories, colors. And I carry my collection everywhere I go.''

Memories are important to Santiago in documenting the Puerto Rican and Puerto Rican-American experience. Her first and third books are memoirs, the first, *When I Was Puerto Rican* (1993), of her childhood in Puerto Rico (she came to New York City at the age of thirteen). Her recent book, *Almost a Woman* (1998), is a reminiscence of her teenage years in New York. In between, Santiago published a long novel, *América's Dream* (1996), which is based on the life of a hotel maid in Puerto Rico who flees her abusive spouse to become a nanny and housekeeper for an upstate New York family. In the 1970s, after finishing her bachelor's degree at Harvard University, Santiago volunteered at a center for battered women, and must have learned firsthand the experiences of her character América, who has difficulty leaving the man who beats her. This novel prompted the *Boston Globe* to label Santiago ''one of the most powerful new voices in American fiction.''

Santiago says she wants her readers to know how people live life, and in fact in her extensive novel several issues are examined, both for Latin Americans and for U.S. Americans. In her memoirs Santiago introduces the reader to the scent and feel of guava, the bloody contents of her mother's spicy morcilla sausage, and to the reaction of Puerto Ricans on the island who were taught the four food groups by U.S. health employees in the 1950s. Many of the suggested items in the food groups were not found on the island and therefore seemed as foreign as the English language.

In her second memoir, *Almost a Woman*, Santiago displays the roach-ridden apartments and welfare inspections of Brooklyn, in the second stage of her life, an experience that also included the fists and spit of her classmates. Although she was a bright student, she was placed in a low-intelligence class in New York because she could not ''spik inglis.'' But Santiago excelled in overcoming any obstacle. After high school she attended the Performing Arts school in New York, participated in experimental theater, and found work as a dancer. She appeared on Broadway at age nineteen and had a small role in the 1967 movie *Up the Down Staircase*. Later in life she preferred producing documentary film, her major at Harvard.

Now Santiago is considering writing a third memoir with experiences from her twenties. Her principal language as an adult is English, but it does not keep her from sharing her culture in any and all forms. ''If you don't exist in the arts of a people,'' she told the *Washington Post*, ''you don't exist in a culture.'' On another occasion, in an interview for the *Boston Globe*, she said her ''emotional life is still in Spanish.''

In 1998, shortly after *Almost a Woman* was published, Santiago released another book, coedited with Joie Davidow and titled *Las Christmas*, the word Spanish-speakers give to the Christmas festivities. This book includes 25 essays in English by various U.S. Latino authors about their remembrances as a child and the Cuban, Puerto Rican, Dominican, or Mexican-style Christmas celebrations still held in their homes. In the introduction Santiago notes that for Latinos, the Christmas season is more about getting together with people and eating than it is about shopping and exchanging gifts. She also explains that the Christmas season begins 12 days before December 25 and does not end until January 6, Three Kings' Day. The editors bring several women together to prepare a huge feast with each of their traditional specialties, which is enjoyed at the end of the book. Home and hearth are fond themes for Santiago; she describes a childhood's worth of closets and closetlike spaces in a collection of mini-memoirs by several authors titled *Home*, published in 1995. Half the editors' book proceeds go to homeless assistance groups.

Santiago has also undertaken something few authors do, which is the translation of her own books. She has translated *When I Was Puerto Rican* and *América's Dream* into Spanish, and these books are now distributed throughout Spanish-speaking countries. Santiago lives in a small town in upstate New York.

BIBLIOGRAPHY: Reference works: *Marquis Who's Who Biographies* (1987).

Other references: *Americas* (Sept./Oct. 1996). *Bilingual Review/La Revista Bilingue* (Spring 1998). *Book Report* (Mar./Apr. 1995). *Boston Globe* (20 Sept. 1998). *Hispanic* (May 1994, Dec. 1998). ''Latino Writers Ponder Meaning of Community,'' in *LAT* (14 Dec. 1998). *New Orleans Times-Picayune* (5 Apr. 1998). *People* (22 July 1996). *PW* (25 Mar. 1996). *Sacramento Bee* (17 Jan. 1999). *Seattle Times* (9 June 1997). *WP* (12 Nov. 1998). *WRB* (Jan. 1997).

—ELIZABETH COONROD MARTINEZ

SARGENT, Pamela

Born 20 March 1948, Ithaca, New York

Pamela Sargent has since the late 1970s written science fiction that presents female characters as strong, intelligent, usually empathic individuals, as opposed to earlier, male-dominated science fiction that either ignored or greatly diminished the role of women in fictional societies. Sargent is also known as the editor of *Women of Wonder: Science Fiction Stories by Women about Women* (1975), *More Women of Wonder: Science Fiction Novelettes by Women about Women* (1976), and *The New Women of Wonder: Recent Science Fiction Stories by Women about Women* (1978), all of which portray early classics of pioneering women science fiction writers (such as C. L. Moore) as well as more pointedly feminist fiction of the 1960s and 1970s.

Sargent was born in Ithaca, New York, to parents who both had eclectic careers. Her father was at various times a Marine Corps officer, professional singer, insurance salesman, college admissions director, education professor, and county legislator. Her mother was a pianist and a high school chemistry teacher who worked for the New York State Education Department. Sargent's house was full of books, and she recalls reading children's fantasies such as *Bambi* and *Charlotte's Web*, mythology, and science books like Fred Hoyle's *The Nature of the Universe*. Her mother gave her *The Feminine Mystique* by Betty Friedan, and while in an institution for troubled adolescents at fourteen, Sargent read science fiction such as *The Stars My Destination* by Alfred Bester and claimed it helped her not feel like an outcast. At no time did she feel encouraged to pursue a writing career.

Sargent attended the State University of New York at Binghamton and secured an M.A. in philosophy in 1970. While attending college, she worked as a sales clerk, a runway model, a solderer on an assembly line, a library typist, an office worker, and a teaching assistant in philosophy. She submitted handwritten stories to publishers until a reader at the *New Yorker* advised her to type them before marketing them. At college she was good friends with Jack Dann, who later became a science fiction editor, and George Zebrowski, who later became a science fiction writer. Both of her companions became published while still in college, and they encouraged her to submit one of her own science fiction stories for publication. ''Landed Minority,'' an eerie tale about college students becoming gradually stupider, then dying from an inexplicable epidemic that has turned the college greens into cemeteries, was published by the *Magazine of Fantasy and Science Fiction* in September 1970.

Sargent lived with George Zebrowski after college, though only rarely collaborating with him in her writing. During the early 1970s she wrote several children's stories that were later collected into three anthologies, as well as science fiction stories that were collected in *Starshadows* (1977). Most of her adult science fiction stories deal with children coping with bizarre circumstances and new technology. *Earthseed* (1983), *Eye of the Comet* (1984), and *Homesmind* (1984) were young adult science fiction novels, while *The Sudden Star* (1979), *Watchstar* (1980), and *The Golden Space* (1982) portray children as significant characters. Sargent, it has been claimed by critics, is both acknowledging the power of childhood impressions and decisions that could affect them later as adults and providing role models for the youthful readers of science fiction.

Sargent delved into alternative feminist societies in *The Shore of Women* (1986). Women control the technology while the men are hunter-gatherers in this reverse of stereotypical sex roles. Other topics beckoned, however, as she wrote about ''terraforming''

in *Venus of Dreams* (1986) and *Venus of Shadows* (1988), novels in which, as the planet Venus is made habitable for human life, colonists must create a new world society from scratch. Sargent also wrote a historical novel called *Genghis Khan, Ruler of the Sky* (1991), which emphasizes to some extent the women Mongols as well, and an alternate history novel, *Climb the Wind* (1998), in which Native Americans conquer settlers of the West after the Civil War. Sargent returned to women in science fiction in 1998 with *Firebrands: The Heroines of Science Fiction and Fantasy*, an illustrated guide to fictional women in fantasy and science fiction since the 1600s.

A prolific writer and editor of numerous anthologies, Sargent was awarded the best book for young adults by the American Library Association in 1983 for *Earthseed*, and she was a finalist in 1992 for the Nebula award by the Science Fiction Writers of America for the novelette *Danny Goes to Mars*.

OTHER WORKS: *Bio-Futures: Science Fiction Stories about Biological Metamorphosis* (1976). *Cloned Lives* (1976). *Elvira's Zoo* (1979). *Divide the Night* (1981). *The Alien Upstairs* (1983). *The Mountain Cage* (1983). *Afterlives: Stories About Life after Death* (with Ian Watson, 1986). *The Best of Pamela Sargent* (1987). *Alien Child* (1988). *Fury Scorned* (with George Zebrowski, 1996). *Heart of the Sun* (with George Zebrowski, 1997).

BIBLIOGRAPHY: Reference works: *CANR* 8 (1983). *CANR* 41 (1994). *DLB* 8 (1981). *Encyclopedia of Science Fiction* (1993).

—ROSE SECREST

SARTON, May

Born Eléanore Marie Sarton, 3 May 1912, Wondelgem, Belgium; **died** 16 July 1995
Daughter of George and Mabel Elwes Sarton

May Sarton was an only child. Her father was a noted historian of science; her mother, an artist and designer. Sarton became a naturalized U.S. citizen in 1924. She originally planned a career in the theater and served a valuable apprenticeship in Eva LeGallienne's Civic Repertory Theater. She founded and was director at the Apprentice Theatre (New School for Social Research) and was director of the Associated Actors Theatre in Hartford, Connecticut. From her mid-twenties, however, Sarton devoted herself to the craft of writing.

Sarton's autobiographical writings achieve a clear, candid, conversational tone and are significant explorations of the life of the mind and of the writer at work. It was her belief that genuinely valid autobiography must move beyond reportage of event or even feeling and extend into an examination of motive, impulse, thought, and belief; and her journals are enriched by miniature informal essays which provide these explorations.

I Knew a Phoenix (1959) closely traces Sarton's early life. In *Plant Dreaming Deep* (1968), Sarton uses her renovation of an old house in Nelson, New Hampshire, as an effective metaphor for the establishment of roots and nourishment of the spirit. *Journal of a Solitude* (1973) deals frankly with the pain, frustration, and rage of the human experience. *A World of Light* (1976) is a series of fascinating character sketches of Sarton's friends and relatives. In *The House by the Sea* (1977), Sarton's home in York, Maine, is a symbol of the joys of productive solitude. Her recuperation from a mastectomy becomes the symbol for overcoming emotional deprivation and despondency caused by harsh reviews in *Recovering* (1980), one of her most effective journals.

Sarton's poetry often discusses the balance growing from difficult human choices. Her tenet that "form is freedom" accounts for the frequent employment of traditional poetic forms, although she also works in free verse. She believed the "white heat" of inspiration fuses the poet's critical and emotional selves to trigger artistically productive revision. "Prayer before Work," from *Inner Landscape* (1939), is an evocation of such inspiration. In both poetry and fiction, Sarton treats the social and political questions of the day. "Night Watch," from *A Grain of Mustard Seed* (1971), compares human sickness and social ills. *Faithful Are the Wounds* (1955, reprinted 1985, and again in 1997) fictionalizes the political witch hunts of the 1950s with force, wisdom, and understanding. *Crucial Conversations* (1975, 1994) includes comments about the Watergate scandal.

Mrs. Stevens Hears the Mermaids Singing (1965) is the story of an elderly, successful writer who reviews her life and work during an important interview and in preparation for helping a young friend at odds with himself and his sexuality. Frank, direct, powerful, this novel ranks among Sarton's best work and is an example of why she is often hailed as a spokesperson for women writers.

Death is a topic Sarton treats in all the genres she employs, and the tonal and philosophical span is generous, ranging from the contemplative comments of *The House by the Sea* through the furious protest of Caroline Spencer, the protagonist of *As We Are Now* (1973), who transforms her death into an indictment of society's attitudes toward the aged and the infirm. Brief, spare, blunt, the splendid characterizations of *As We Are Now* elevate it far above most protest fiction.

One of Sarton's constant and most compelling themes is friendship, as in *The Birth of a Grandfather* (1957), in which the terminal illness of a close friend engenders a middle-aged man's reconsideration of himself and his values, and *Kinds of Love* (1970, 1995), a character study of two lifelong women friends.

The Small Room (1961) compares and contrasts Lucy Winter's growth as a teacher with her developing ability to function as an independent person. Her many committed colleagues serve as Lucy's mentors as she seeks to understand not only herself but also a brilliant student who has broken under the demands of personal pride and faculty pressure. Honest, compassionate, discerning, *The Small Room* is a major novel, its treatment of the student-teacher relationship singularly effective.

Steadily productive, unusually successful in her explorations of both isolation and union, Sarton was a serious writer who won great popularity, with significant achievements in three major genres. The last decade of her life, Sarton's work, especially her ever popular journals, dealt with issues of aging and illness and her struggle to remain active as an artist.

OTHER WORKS: *Encounter in April* (1937). *The Single Hound* (1938). *The Bridge of Years* (1946, 1974, 1997). *The Underground River: A Play in Three Acts* (1947). *The Lion and the Rose* (1948). *Leaves of the Tree* (1950). *Shadow of a Man* (1950). *A Shower of Summer Days* (1952, 1979, 1995). *The Land of Silence* (1953). *The Birth of a Grandfather* (1957). *The Fur Person* (1957). *In Memoriam* (1957). *The Writing of a Poem* (1957). *In Time Like Air* (1958). *Cloud, Stone, Sun, Vine* (1961). *The Design of a Novel* (1963). *Joanna and Ulysses* (1963). *Miss Pickthorn and Mr. Hare* (1966). *A Private Mythology: Poems* (1966, 1996). *As Does New Hampshire* (1967). *The Poet and the Donkey* (1969). *Kinds of Love* (1970). *A Durable Fire* (1972). *Collected Poems, 1930-1973* (1974). *Punch's Secret* (1974). *The Leopard Land: Alice and Haniel Long's Santa Fé* (1976). *A Walk Through the Woods* (1976). *A Reckoning* (1978, 1997). *Halfway to Silence* (1980). *Letters from Maine: Poems* (1984, 1997). *May Sarton, Among the Usual Days: A Portrait—Unpublished Poems, Letters, Journals, and Photographs* (1993). *Coming Into Eighty: and Earlier Poems* (1995). *Endgame: A Journal of the Seventy-Ninth Year* (1995). *Beyond the Map: Poems* (1995). *At Eighty-Two: A Journal* (1996). *May Sarton: Selected Letters, 1916- 1954* (1997). *Dear Juliette: Letters of May Sarton to Juliette Huxley* (1999).

Contributor to several anthologies and collections, including: *Through Other Eyes: Animal Stories by Women* (1988), *Family Portraits: Remembrances* (1991), *Images of Women in Literature* (1991), *Writing Women's Lives: An Anthology of Autobiographical Narratives by 20th Century American Women Writers* (1994), *The Beacon Book of Essays by Contemporary American Women* (1996), *Seasons of Women: An Anthology* (1996), and others. She also produced, in creative partnership with several artists, a number of broadsides and limited editions of her poetry.

BIBLIOGRAPHY: Anderson, D. H., in *Images of Women in Fiction* (1972). Blouin, L. P., *May Sarton: A Bibliography* (1978). Evans, E., *May Sarton Revisited* (1989). Hunting, C., ed., *May Sarton: Woman and Poet* (1982). Kallet, M., ed., *A House of Gathering: Poets on May Sarton's Poetry* (1993). Peters, M., *May Sarton: A Biography* (1998). Prenshaw, P. W., ed., *Conversations with May Sarton* (1991). *Sarton Selected: An Anthology of the Journals, Novels, and Poems of May Sarton* (1991). Sibley, A., *May Sarton* (1972). Swartzlander, S. and M. R. Mumford, eds., *That Great Sanity: Critical Essays on May Sarton* (1995).

Reference works: *CA* (1999). *Oxford Companion to Women's Writing in the United States* (1995). *Twayne's Women Authors on CD* (1995).

Other references: *A Service in Celebration of the Life of May Sarton, 1912-1995: Nelson Congregational Church, Nelson, New Hampshire, Saturday, 7 October 1995* (audiocassette, 1995). *World of Light: A Portrait of May Sarton* (video, 1987). *Chrysalis*

(Summer 1975). *Educational Gerontology* (1999). *Essays in Literature* (Fall 1993). *Hollins Critic* (June 1974). *In Their Own Voices: A Century of Recorded Poetry* (CD, 1996). *May Sarton: Woman of Letters* (videocassette, 1995). *May Sarton: Writing in the Upward Years* (video, 1990). *NR* (8 June 1974). *Pilgrimage* (Sept. 1994). *PW* (24 June 1974). *Sojourner* (August 1995).

—JANE S. BAKERMAN

SATIR, Virginia M.

Born 26 June 1916, Neillsville, Wisconsin; **died** 1988
Daughter of Reinhold O. and Minnie Wilke Pagenkopf; **married** Norman Satir, 1951 (divorced 1961)

Virginia Satir was born on a farm in Wisconsin. Her parents moved to Milwaukee when she was twelve. She was married in 1951 and divorced in 1961. In 1936, Satir completed her bachelor's degree in education at Wisconsin State University. For six years, she taught in Wisconsin, Michigan, and Louisiana, with the objective of working with different kinds of children in various settings. During this period, Satir regularly visited the homes of her students and became aware of important psychological and social clues to understanding the behavior of handicapped and of gifted children. Interested in the complex dynamics between the dysfunctional individual and the family, she went back to school "to specialize," earning an M.A. in 1948 in the School of Social Service Administration at the University of Chicago.

Satir has worked as therapist in a broad spectrum of settings—psychiatric clinics, mental hospitals, public welfare programs, and family service agencies. Satir who describes herself as a "teacher-at-large in communications and family therapy," has conducted seminars and workshops for government, industry, hospitals, universities, and other public and private institutions all over the world.

Out of a rich and diversified background of practical experience, Satir evolved a cohesive theory of family systems, which she explains through a step-by-step approach in *Conjoint Family Therapy* (1964). This book challenges the idea that the locus of an individual's illness, or dysfunction, is exclusively within the individual and also the notion that therapists are godlike figures, who should hold themselves aloof from relationships with the patients. Rejecting such a "medical model," Satir offers what she calls the "growth model" of psychotherapy, which is based on the idea that illness is an appropriate communicative response to a dysfunctional system or context.

Peoplemaking (1972) explores the kinds of "factories" (families) and "people-makers" (adults, parents) that make human beings. Intended more for families than therapists, *Peoplemaking* addresses the reader directly, providing exercises intended to allow self-assessment and assessment of the reader's family. Satir again stresses communication systems and family

regulatory systems as indexes to the dynamics of a family, and uses the family context to focus on the experiences and processes which go into the making of a person.

Satir was one of the pioneers in the development of family therapy in the early 1950s. *Conjoint Family Therapy* and *Peoplemaking* are considered "bibles" of family dynamics. In all her books, she is consistent in her affirmation that the human being is capable of continued growth and change. In her writing and her practice, the focus is upon understanding the congruence between the individual and the family context and the processes that go into the making of an effective and happy human being.

OTHER WORKS: *Self Esteem: A Declaration* (1975). *Helping Families to Change* (with others, 1975). *Making Contact* (1976). *Changing with Families* (with others, 1976). *The Satir Model: Family Therapy and Beyond* (1991).

BIBLIOGRAPHY: Andreas, S., *Virginia Satir: The Patterns of Her Magic* (1991). Brothers, B. J., *Virginia Satir: Foundational Ideas* (1991). Caston, C., *Burnout in African American Family Caregivers: Nursing Interventions* (1997). Hardmeier, H., "The System Theory Approach to Family Therapy: Analysis of an Interview by Virginia Satir" (thesis, 1972). Keener, J., *Communication within Families: A Study of the Theories of Virginia Satir and Salvador Minuchin as They Inform the Task of Pastoral Care* (dissertation, 1986). Laping, M., "A Critique of Virginia Satir's Use of System Theory to Build Self-Esteem in Family Members" (thesis, 1979). Loeschen, S., *The Secrets of Satir: Collected Sayings of Virginia Satir* (1991). Loeschen, S., *Systematic Training in the Skills of Virginia Satir* (1998). Schwab, J., ed., *A Resource Handbook for Satir Concepts* (1990).

Other references: *Virginia Satir, M.S.W., Interview with Frederick J. Duhl, M.D* (videocassette, 1976). *Virginia Satir: The Use of Self in Therapy* (videocassette, 1993). Kramer, E., *An Interview with Virginia Satir* (audiocassette, 1960, 1980). *Contemporary Psychology* (March 1977). *Human Behavior Magazine* (Sept. 1976). *LJ* (15 May 1976).

—GUIN A. NANCE

SAVAGE, Elizabeth

Born 15 February 1918, Hingham, Massachusetts; **died** 15 July 1989
Daughter of Robert B. and Mildred Ridlow Fitzgerald; **married** Thomas Savage, 1939; **children:** three

Elizabeth Savage graduated from Colby College in Maine. She married a writer and raised three children. She is primarily known as a novelist but has also published short fiction in such periodicals as the *Paris Review, Cosmopolitan, Redbook,* and the *Saturday Evening Post.*

Savage's earliest novels—*Summer of Pride* (1960), *But Not for Love* (1970), and *A Fall of Angels* (1971)—explore seemingly perfect or privileged families at turning points that reveal the reality and the fallibility beneath the surface. *Summer of Pride* examines the headstrong Olivers and their Western heritage as their unity is threatened by three outsiders. The portraits of the women, especially the matriarch Emily and the matriach-to-be Rea, are rendered vividly and their values are compared with those of the head of the family, who mistakes avoidance of change for dedication to his dependents.

The tone of *But Not for Love* is more ironic. The plot depicts the intricate relationships of the Hollister clan after the disappearance of one member; the climax, a dangerous fire, is rendered in a series of wonderfully funny and frightening scenes. Both books skillfully employ multiple points of view and reveal two of Savage's basic themes: all human beings are both unique and ordinary, both strong and weak, and that genuine love fosters tolerance and compassion.

The point of view of Helena St. John Strider, proud of her marital and professional successes, dominates *A Fall of Angels*. During the Striders' annual Jamaican vacation, the whole fabric of their life and their sense of themselves is twisted when Luke takes a young, bewitching mistress. The relationship between the tourists and Jamaicans serves as a powerful symbol for the unexamined life, and the novel makes effective comments about fidelity and the double standard.

In *Happy Ending* (1972), Savage's conversational tone again reveals her ear for colloquial speech and for dialogue. The struggle of an aging couple to retain independence is compared to the striving of their young employees for some degree of security. These central characters are unsentimentally portrayed as realistic men and women of conscience, trying to live decent lives.

The Last Night at the Ritz (1973) details the long friendship between the unnamed narrator and her college roommate. The protagonist has few illusions about herself or her loved ones, but even in the crises depicted here she displays charity and understanding. Tension and suspense are maintained beautifully during telling glimpses of the publishing world and the 1960s generation gap, and the powerful flashbacks render college life vividly.

South Boston, locale of *A Good Confession* (1975), serves protagonist-narrator Meg O'Shaugnessy Atherton as both background and symbol. Called to her dying grandfather's bedside just as she discovers her husband's infidelity, Meg faces her own shortcomings by evaluating herself against memories of her large Irish-American family. The importance of openness with one's loved ones is a central theme.

The friendship among five high school girls in Missoula, Montana, is the frame for *The Girls from the Five Great Valleys* (1977). Savage again conveys a clear sense of the 1930s Depression by contrasting reports of poverty and suffering with the lives of families who are secure. *The Girls from the Five Great Valleys* reveals that nurturing love teaches strength for survival; selfish possessiveness leads only to tragedy.

Savage's interest in Victorian literature is reflected in *Willowwood* (1978), a story of the Pre-Raphaelite Brotherhood. The novel depicts the complex relationship between Dante Gabriel Rossetti, Elizabeth Siddal, Fanny Cornforth, and Jane Burden Morris. The four central characterizations are brought vividly to life by honest treatment of their motivations—both charitable and selfish—and the supporting figures are beautifully drawn. The setting is enriched by effective details of everyday life and insights into the status of women.

The decisions of several summer residents to "winter over" on Jacataqua Island off the coast of Maine becomes the symbol for crisis and change in *Toward the End* (1980). Effective weather imagery and a well-drawn cast of intriguing characters are the book's greatest strengths.

Savage's novels often feature a central image drawn from the animal kingdom; this device underscores Savage's fine ability to describe the natural world. Always in control of her subject matter and style, Savage is particularly adept at characterization and setting and her fiction is informed by splendid humor and illuminating irony.

BIBLIOGRAPHY: *NYTBR* (5 Feb. 1961, 19 Aug. 1973). *Time* (19 Nov. 1973). *Writer* (Sept. 1972, Dec. 1974).

—JANE S. BAKERMAN

SAWYER, Ruth

Born 5 August 1880, Boston, Massachusetts; **died** 3 June 1970, Hancock, Maine
Daughter of Francis M. and Ethelinda Smith Sawyer; **married** Albert C. Durand, 1911; **children:** one son and one daughter

The only daughter among the five children of an importer, Ruth Sawyer spent her early years on New York City's Upper East Side, summering with the family in Maine; both areas provided subjects and settings for her writings. Sawyer often tagged after her brothers, and undoubtedly the very real and attractive boy protagonists in her stories arose from the warm relationship she had with them. Although Sawyer's father often read aloud from Stevenson and Twain and her mother frequently sang ballads and read from the Bible, it was the folk stories told by her Donegal nurse that made the greatest impression upon Sawyer and awakened in her the love for traditional tales and the wonder of storytelling.

After two years at the Garland Kindergarten Training School in Boston, Sawyer began storytelling and collecting in Cuba, where she went at twenty as a volunteer to help organize kindergartens for orphans of the Spanish-American War. At Columbia University, Sawyer studied folklore and storytelling, at the same time telling stories in schools, libraries, and missions in

New York City and doing features for the *Sun*. She collected tales in Ireland in 1905 while on assignment for the *Sun*, and later in Europe and Mexico.

In 1911 Sawyer married an ophthalmologist and went to live in Ithaca, New York. They had a son and a daughter. Although Sawyer's earlier works have not endured and some of the later works seem contrived and sentimental, the juvenile works that rose out of her personal experiences at home and abroad have justly enjoyed lasting popularity. Sawyer's 1931 Spanish trip, described in the graphic *My Spain* (1941), produced *Toño Antonio* (1934), the humorous story of a boy who travels to Malaga with a herd of playful goats after his family has come upon hard times. Based upon a chance meeting with a shepherd boy at a bakery shop, *Toño Antonio* conveys a strong sense of the Spanish countryside and character. *Picture Tales from Spain* (1936) consists of fresh and vivid traditional stories, including the lively ''The Flea.''

The Least One (1941), a realistic story of the relationship between the son of a burden-carrier and his gray burro, is a warm, genuine account of the life of Mexican peasants and was commissioned by UNESCO for translation into several languages. Among the most highly acclaimed of Sawyer's works are her two autobiographical novels, *Roller Skates* (1936) and its sequel, *The Year of Jubilo* (1940). In *Roller Skates*, as ten-year-old, free-spirited Lucinda Wyman, Sawyer records vividly and sensitively her year in the 1890s with the Misses Peters while her parents are traveling in Europe, a time she spends skating around New York City, involving herself in the lives of the people she meets, most of whom really existed. *The Year of Jubilo* takes Sawyer to Maine after the death of her father.

Sawyer especially enjoyed the Christmas season, and her several collections of holiday folk tales, particularly *The Long Christmas* (1941) and *Joy to the World* (1961), are perennial favorites. The best loved and most widely known of Sawyer's Christmas tales is ''The Voyage of the Wee Red Cap,'' told to her by an itinerant tinker at a crossroads in Ireland. Eleven more traditional stories are included in *The Way of the Storyteller* (1942), in which Sawyer presents her philosophy of storytelling and gives advice about telling tales and putting together a story hour.

Marked by warmth of tone, love of life, and confidence in the goodness of people, Sawyer's writings hold up the old virtues of hard work, perseverance, and faith in God. Always present, regardless of genre, is the sense of the storytelling situation, the effect of Sawyer's sharp eye for ethnic detail, keen ear for the cadence of common speech, and leisurely and loving narrative manner. Sawyer's ability to invest with new life old magic and legend made her the acknowledged great lady of American storytelling.

OTHER WORKS: *The Primrose Ring* (1915). *This Way to Christmas* (1916). *A Child's Year Book* (1917). *Herself, Himself, and Myself* (1917). *Myself* (1917). *Seven Miles to Arden* (1917). *Doctor Danny* (1918). *Leerie* (1920). *The Silver Sixpence* (1921).

Gladiola Murphy (1923). *The Tale of the Enchanted Bunnies* (1923). *Four Ducks on a Pond* (1928). *Folk House* (1932). *The Luck of the Road* (1934). *Gallant* (1936). *The Christmas Anna Angel* (1944). *This Is the Christmas* (1945). *Old Con and Patrick* (1946). *The Little Red Horse* (1950). *Maggie Rose* (1952). *Journey Cake, Ho!* (1953). *A Cottage for Betsy* (1954). *The Enchanted School House* (1956). *The Year of the Christmas Dragon* (1960). *Dietrich of Berne and the Dwarf King Laurin* (with E. Mollès, 1963). *Daddles: The Story of a Plain Hound-Dog* (1964).

BIBLIOGRAPHY: Haviland, V., *Ruth Sawyer* (1965).
    Reference works: *Authors of Books for Young People* (1971). *Junior Book of Authors* (1951). *Newbery Medal Books, 1922-1955* (1955). *TCA* (1942).
    Other references: *Horn Book* (1965).

                                                    —ALETHEA K. HELBIG

SCARBERRY, Alma Sioux

Born 24 June 1899, Carter County, Kentucky; died 10 April 1990
Also wrote under: Beatrice Fairfax, Annie Laurie
Daughter of George W. and Caledonia Lee Patrick Scarberry; married Theodore A. Klein, 1930

Alma Sioux Scarberry is the daughter of a Kentucky fundamentalist minister. Her early home life was difficult; her father, a stern disciplinarian, remarried several times, and Scarberry often had to support herself as a child. She began to write prose and poetry at an early age, and writing always seemed natural to her.

After working her way through a semester at New Bethlehem Business College in Pennsylvania, Scarberry moved in 1917 to New York City, selling varnish to pay her way. Scarberry first found a sales job in a Brooklyn department store, but soon enlisted in the Navy, serving a year as one of the first Yeomanettes. Scarberry took a position with King Features in 1920, first writing daily love columns under the names Beatrice Fairfax and Annie Laurie, but soon writing under her own byline for the New York *American*, *Graphic*, and *Mirror*. She won fame for her feature articles and daring publicity stunts. Scarberry also appeared on Broadway in Irving Berlin's Music Box Revue (1922-23) and in the Shubert revival of *The Mikado* (1924).

In 1926 Scarberry moved to Pittsburgh to write a daily column and features for the Pittsburgh *Sun Telegraph*. On her editor's dare, she wrote her first novel. The tremendous popularity of *Make Up* (1931) won her a contract as columnist and serial writer with Central Press in 1928. After her marriage, Scarberry moved to Chicago, where her first radio drama, *The Girl Reporter*, was purchased and produced by NBC. In 1930 she began to write for the Bell Syndicate and North American Newspaper Alliance. The next 14 years would see all 21 of her romances published serially; only 12 were republished in book form. Scarberry's son was also born in 1930.

In 1940 Scarberry took a publicity job with CBS in Hollywood, soon moving to head the writing department of the Mutual Don Lee Network to write radio dramas and general continuity. From 1944 to 1946, Scarberry directed the Radio Bureau of the National War Fund in New York. The years after 1946 were productive; she wrote features, columns, and songs for films. *The Doofer Family*, a serial fantasy for children which was inspired by songs and jokes she enjoyed with her young son and is Scarberry's own favorite, appeared through General Features (1955-56).

During the Korean War, Scarberry was a soldier-show technician for the U.S. Army, stationed at Fort Chaffee, Arkansas. Scarberry worked as public relations director for Columbus Plastics in Columbus, Ohio, from 1959 until 1965, when she moved to Austin, Texas. Since 1965 she handled public relations for good causes and contributed columns to magazines and newspapers. Scarberry was featured in a local radio talk show and was still writing and starring in television commercials into the early 1980s.

Scarberry's romances are readable, with interesting characters, rapidly developed action, and lively dialogue. The serials reflect the author's experiences and views. Like Janet James of *Make Up* and Rosalie March of *Dimpled Racketeer* (1931), Scarberry's heroines are often attractive and talented country girls who come to the city naive but eager to get ahead. But like singer Elanda Lee of *High Hat* (1930), determined to get a break in radio, or dancer Jan Keats of *Rainbow Over Broadway* (1936), determined to become a Broadway star, Scarberry's heroines are characterized by independence, hard work, and a refusal to compromise values and expectations. After finding independence and success, they can make room in their lives for love, happiness, and a home with a reliable, honest, and sensitive man. All offer readers the vicarious experience of the best of both a brilliant career and a loving family. Each novel climaxes with the happy marriage of hero and heroine, a marriage that resolves all subplots.

For Scarberry, writing always meant the use of a particular kind of talent for profit. Inspiration usually begins with characters; when these are fully developed, a plot forms around them. From the plot outline, the writing comes quickly. As Scarberry puts it: "Writing takes three things. It requires an active creative imagination which leads to a pattern, a formula. And it requires a market. Without a market, a writer really has no purpose." The great popularity of Scarberry's serial fiction indicates her success and understanding in creating for the market of her choice.

OTHER WORKS: *The Flat Tire* (1930). *Flighty: A Romance of Gypsy O'Malley—A Girl Who Lived Down Her Family* (1932). *Puppy Love: A Hollywood Romance* (1933). *Penthouse Love* (1934). *Too Wise to Marry* (1935). *Too Many Beaus* (1936). *Thou Shalt Not Love* (1937). *The Lady Proposes* (1941).

BIBLIOGRAPHY: Web site: www.writepage.com/others/unknown.htm.

—KATHERINE STAPLES

SCARBOROUGH, Dorothy

Born 27 January 1878, Mount Carmel, Texas; died 7 November 1935, New York, New York
Daughter of John B. and Mary Ellison Scarborough

Dorothy Scarborough came from a prosperous Southern background—both grandfathers owned large plantations, and her father was a lawyer and judge. Scarborough received her B.A. (1896) and M.A. (1898) from Baylor University, where she taught from 1905 to 1914. She did advanced graduate work at the University of Chicago, Oxford University, and Columbia University (Ph.D. 1917). She joined the faculty of Columbia, specializing in teaching short story writing.

Scarborough's doctoral dissertation, *The Supernatural in Modern English Fiction* (1917), is an important scholarly work. She establishes the Gothic romance and French, Italian, German, and Russian works as primary influences on the use of the supernatural in modern literature. She discusses the supernatural by categories: modern ghosts, the devil, folktales, and supernatural science. Scarborough concludes that the war was the cause for the contemporary interest in the supernatural and that American writers are essentially responsible for combining humor and the supernatural.

Scarborough contributed book reviews, sometimes covering more than twenty works in a single review, to publications such as the New York *Sun*, *Bookman*, and the *Dial*. She attacks writers who use fiction as a vehicle for propaganda or didacticism. Unfortunately, as many reviewers have noted, this criticism is applicable to her own novels and short stories. Scarborough is praised for her realistic presentation, but condemned for her editorializing.

Many of Scarborough's novels use the Texas farmlands as setting. The plots revolve around romance, but love is frequently hampered by the problems facing the tenant farmer, the economics of the cotton industry, the threat of drought, flood, and the boll weevil. The depiction of natural forces in *The Wind* (1925) has been compared with that of Conrad (*Times Literary Supplement*, 5 Nov. 1925); the 1928 film, starring Lillian Gish, was, however, criticized for excessive use of nature imagery.

Impatient Griselda (1927) is one novel not flawed by propagandizing. Again the setting is a small Texas town with its typical inhabitants: the minister and his wife and children, the doctor, the do-gooder, the busybody, and the Negro cook. Scarborough contrasts two types of women: the seductress (Lilith) and the wife (Irene). The novel opens with the death of one Lilith as she gives birth to a second. Irene marries Lilith's widower (Guinn the minister) and raises the stepdaughter Lilith and her own four children, but feels she never replaces either Lilith in her husband's heart. The book closes with the death of the second Lilith as she gives birth to a third-generation Lilith. Irene sees the cycle continuing as her own daughter must stand in for another Lilith. The types remain unreconciled.

Scarborough did important research in collecting folk songs and ballads; her interest dated back to her early teaching career in Texas. In *On the Trail of Negro Folk-Songs* (1925) and *A Song Catcher in Southern Mountains* (sponsored by ''Project 41'' at Columbia University and published posthumously in 1937), Scarborough discusses origins, influences, instruments, and variations and provides melodies for many songs. (Ola Lee Gulledge collected and transcribed the music in the first book.) *On the Trail of Negro Folk-Songs* includes a chapter on the blues based primarily on a visit with W. C. Handy. Scarborough uses these songs extensively in her novels and the autobiographical *From a Southern Porch* (1919).

Humor pervades Scarborough's writings; she employs informal language, coins words, and puns. A modern reader may be annoyed by Scarborough's facile stereotyping of races (she shows blacks as a happy people singing while they toil in field or kitchen) or amused by her genteel treatment of passion and illegitimate birth, but her novels are entertaining. A scholar may be frustrated by the lack of scholarly apparatus in *The Supernatural in Modern English Fiction*, but Scarborough has made significant contributions to scholarship with her dissertation and folk-song collecting.

OTHER WORKS: *Fugitive Verses* (1912). *Famous Modern Ghost Stories* (edited by Scarborough, 1921). *Humorous Ghost Stories* (edited by Scarborough, 1921). *In the Land of Cotton* (1923). *Can't Get a Red Bird* (1929). *The Stretch-Berry Smile* (1932). *The Story of Cotton* (1933). *Selected Short Stories of Today* (edited by Scarborough, 1935).

BIBLIOGRAPHY: Overton, G. *The Women Who Make Our Novels* (1928).

Reference works: *DAB*. *TCA* (1942).

Other references: *Bookman* (Jan. 1920). *PW* (16 Nov. 1935). *NYT* (8 Nov. 1935). *NYTBR* (11 Nov. 1917, 14 Aug. 1927, 27 Oct. 1929, 14 Feb. 1932, 11 April 1937). *TLS* (15 Nov. 1917, 5 Nov. 1925, 20 Nov. 1937).

—NANCY G. ANDERSON

SCARBOROUGH, Elizabeth Ann

Born 23 March 1947, Kansas City, Missouri

Daughter of Betty Lou and Donald Dean Scarborough; married Richard G. Kacsur, 1975 (divorced 1981).

Elizabeth Ann Scarborough is best known for *The Healer's War* (1988), a novel about a Vietnam nurse, which was inspired by her career after she received an R.N. in 1968 from the Bethany Hospital School of Nursing in Kansas City, Missouri. From 1968 to 1972 she served in the U.S. Army Nurse Corps in Vietnam, earning the rank of captain. She later worked as a surgical nurse at St. David's Hospital in Austin, Texas. In 1987 she earned a B.A. in history from the University of Alaska at Fairbanks, where she lived for 15 years. She has been a freelance writer since 1979 and lives in the state of Washington.

Scarborough is popular for her humorous fantasy, which uses the conventional tropes of witches, dragons, and magic spells in comic, unconventional ways. She has written several series, starting with those about the magical land of Argonia: *Song of Sorcery* (1982), *The Unicorn Creed* (1983), *Bronwyn's Bane* (1983), and *The Christening Quest* (1985). Republished as *Songs from the Seashell Archives*, these stories chronicle the comical, fast-paced misadventures of a young witch named Maggie and her mother, Bronwyn.

The Arabian Nights-influenced novel *The Harem of Aman Akbar* (1984) involves a young bride fighting a genie's curse in the Middle East. Next Scarborough mixed fantasy with western fiction in *The Drastic Dragon of Draco, Texas* (1986) and *The Goldcamp Vampire* (1987), which are set respectively in the Texas plains and the Yukon frontier. Her journalist heroine in these works pursues and confronts the titular monsters.

The Healer's War won the 1989 Nebula award (granted by the Science Fiction Writers of America). Although its subject and incidents are dreadful, the story is warmly narrated with frequent flashes of humor. Nurse Kitty McCulley spends Part I in ''The Hospital'' caring for her American and Vietnamese patients. Kitty describes with sanguine common sense the exhaustion of working long shifts, the grief of losing patients, and the frustrations of finding romance with combat personnel. A dying patient, a Vietnamese ''holy man,'' gives her a magic amulet which allows her to perceive the colorful auras emanating from others' emotions as well as to heal critical injuries. The value of the former ability becomes evident when Kitty is shot down over enemy territory in Part II, ''The Jungle,'' and must evade the Viet Cong and an American soldier prone to homicidal fugues. Kitty learns, or rather confirms, that goodness is found not in political ideology but in ordinary people struggling to survive desperate times. Returning to America, she feels both strengthened by her experiences yet uprooted in a consumer society in which the truths of famine, pain, and death are frivolously disregarded.

Nothing Sacred (1991) is another powerful tale with an intriguing mystery. Viveca Vanachek, a 41-year-old prisoner of war, is kept alive for reasons she cannot fathom in a bizarre POW camp within a secluded valley in Tibet. Her fellow American prisoners are oddly out of date, more concerned with 20th-century baseball than with 21st-century shifting alliances. The guards are downright friendly, ''carelessly'' allowing her to access their computer files and to organize an ancient library while other prisoners rebuild the war-torn building, a palace which the Dalai Lama had previously called home. Viv's haunting dreams of its past glory give clues to the climactic revelation that the prison is as great an ontological mystery as a sociopolitical enigma. The novel ends with nuclear war destroying the world outside, but Viv has found happiness and no longer calls herself a prisoner. In *Last Refuge* (1992), Viv's granddaughter, Chime, ventures out of this magical oasis to seek renewal for a holocaust-burned world.

The humorous Songkiller Saga includes *Phantom Banjo* (1991), *Picking the Ballad's Bones* (1991), and *Strum Again?* (1992). Trouble begins when Torchy, actually the supernatural Faerie Queen, decides to abolish music. Seeking revenge against balladeer Tam Lin, who imprisoned her in the devil's underworld, she especially hates folk songs. As her name foreshadows, Torchy burns the Library of Congress and other musical archives and causes people to forget their fondness for music. Protagonist Willie gathers a fellowship of humans who remember folk music. Aided by a magic banjo, they launch a quest to save their favorite tunes.

Scarborough's friendships with social workers inspired her to write *The Godmother* (1994), in which a magical fairy godmother visits Rose Simpson, a Seattle social worker. In 1995's *The Godmother's Apprentice*, a teenager travels to Ireland to become a fairy godmother herself, and the series was rounded out with *The Godmother's Web* (1998).

Next Scarborough collaborated with fantasy writer Anne McCaffrey on the Petaybee trilogy, consisting of *Powers That Be* (1993), *Power Lines* (1994), and *Power Play* (1995). These novels are set on a faraway planet and concern a rebellion by settlers against the controlling corporation.

Scarborough returned to Earth for her next fantasies. *Carol for Another Christmas* (1996) brings the spirit of Ebenezer Scrooge to visit workaholic Monica Banks, who needs to learn the lessons only Scrooge can teach. In *The Lady in the Loch* (1998), the sheriff of Edinburgh investigates the disappearance of gypsy women at Loch Ness and discovers an ancient evil.

Scarborough's works are accessible and pleasing. The values she promotes in her fiction are trust, caring, and sharing, which her protagonists personify. Her narrative voice is energetic, as are her characters, who ruefully take stock of the evils they confront but who rally enthusiasm to tackle the work of defeating them. These traits promise to keep her popular for years to come.

OTHER WORKS: *An Interview with a Vietnam Nurse* (1989). *The Untold Lives: The First Generation of American Women Psychologists* (1989). *Acorna's People* (with Anne McCaffrey, 1999).

BIBLIOGRAPHY: Everett, G., "The American National Character and the Novelization of Vietnam" (thesis, 1994).
Reference works: *St. James Guide to Fantasy Writers* (1996).
Other references: *Fantasy Magazine* (Fall 1993). *Locus* (June 1990). *New York Review of Science Fiction* (Sept. 1991). *Starlog* (Feb. 1991). SATA (1998). *Science Fiction Chronicle* 11:9 (June 1990).

—FIONA KELLEGHAN

SCHAEFFER, Susan Fromberg

Born 25 March 1941, Brooklyn, New York
Daughter of Irving and Edith Levine Fromberg; **married** Neil J. Schaeffer, 1970; **children:** Benjamin, May

Susan Fromberg Schaeffer is a mother of two. Educated at the University of Chicago (B.A. 1961, M.A. 1963, Ph.D. 1966) and a summer Vermonter, Schaeffer uses these locales in her fiction. She teaches American literature at Brooklyn College.

The Witch and the Weather Report (1972) contains "Ancestors," a series of fine poems about Schaeffer's grandparents, commenting realistically about the tragedy of aging and about death. The tone is peaceful and positive, giving a strong sense of the values of life and of family continuity. "Housewife" captures the tension generated by a woman's desire for freedom and her love for family and home, and the effective imagery of "Wood Fire" celebrates human comfort in an uncertain world.

Granite Lady (1974) reprints selections from the first volume and introduces new poems. The apocalyptic vision of "Reading the Signs" reveals Schaeffer's continuing examination of contemporary social and political problems introduced in the earlier "Sniper" and "Bombing." "Mother and Daughter," "Glimmerings," "The Mother's Curses," and the very powerful "Alphabet" all depict parent-child relationships; imagery based on household objects and fairytales effectively evokes the child's impressions, feelings, and responses. "The Door" offers exciting insights into inspiration and the craft of writing.

Schaeffer's novels all tell family sagas. In *Falling* (1973), the plot details Elizabeth Kamen's struggle for inner peace and mental health. Three generations of the Kamen and Katz-Mazel families are portrayed, and over a dozen members come vividly to life. Flashbacks, often stemming from sessions with her psychiatrist, reveal Elizabeth's background and her steady progress toward self-respect and control. In Elizabeth's growing pride in her capability as a teacher, in her developing acceptance of her looks, and in her newly discovered ability to cope with the conflict between her own needs and her family's demands, Schaeffer documents her protagonist's maturation.

Anya (1974) reveals Schaeffer's remarkable historical imagination through the tale of Anya Savikin, survivor of the Holocaust, who attempts to come to terms with its meaning. The fabric of daily life of Anya's family, Russian Jews living in Poland, is woven with great care so that its destruction is wholly felt, without authorial comment. Details of dress, household chores, food, and drink form one unifying device—a motif that contrasts the comfortable prewar life with ghetto and concentration camp experiences. As existence itself becomes the paramount goal, these details serve to symbolize the characters' enormously altered hopes and dreams.

Time in Its Flight (1978) examines the inner forces operating among the Steeles, a Vermont clan whose story covers most of the 19th and 20th centuries. Flashbacks, letters, diaries, and excellent dialogue all report the ordinary yet important moments in the Steeles' history. John's preoccupation with daguerreotypes provides a good image to point up his wife, Edna's, speculations about the nature of time; both devices serve the central thesis, that little in life changes except the cast of characters, each event renewing the past and invoking the future.

In 1980 Schaeffer published a volume of poetry, *The Bible of the Beasts of the Little Field*; a collection of short fiction, *The Queen of Egypt*; and *Love: A Novel*, the powerful story of Esheal Luria's early life in Russia and his fortunes as an immigrant to the United States. This novel reaffirms Schaeffer's keen interest in family ties, the tensions that threaten these ties, and the impact of historical events as well as of personal choice upon an individual's fate.

In Schaeffer's fiction as in her poetry, mother-daughter relationships are crucial, and both *Anya* and *Time in Its Flight* movingly portray supportive female friendships. Both the damaging and the nurturing factors are honestly presented, making clear that Schaeffer commands a good understanding of the human condition as well as splendid narrative skill enlivened by rich humor.

Although discussion of Schaeffer's fiction has labeled her a Jewish American writer, her recent novels do not deal with Jewish feminism. *The Madness of a Seduced Woman* (1983) involves a young woman in 19th-century Vermont; *Mainland* (1985) and *The Injured Party* (1986) use Brooklyn writers and academics of no discernible ethnic heritage as their heroines. *Buffalo Afternoon* (1989) focuses on a teenage Vietnamese girl and an Italian American soldier.

As in her earlier novels, Schaeffer writes of women who face the power wielded by memory and the often paralyzing trauma inflicted by family. Human inconstancy and vision and blindness are prevalent images complementing themes of enclosure, and Schaeffer's rich development of spatial metaphors stresses depression and isolation as female more than male conditions. Schaeffer's novels are filled with "ghosts"—*The Madness of a Seduced Woman* and *Buffalo Afternoon*, for instance, have narrators who are themselves dead. Voices from the past and dreams haunt her characters. While some have described her fusion of time as "Faulknerian," Schaeffer claims this approach as a feminist one: trapped in the present, her heroines must deal with the unresolved past by rejecting their roles as wives and mothers and often by facing the aggression Schaeffer portrays as a given between mother and daughter. Her peripheral male characters aid the heroines' epiphany because of their constant, albeit marginal, roles. Although *Mainland* and *The Injured Party* depict women who are healed by this recovery and acceptance process, *The Madness of a Seduced Woman* shows the violent consequences when a passionate woman rejects family history in favor of shaping a unique present. *Buffalo Afternoon* departs from these novels in several ways. While it continues Schaeffer's interest in memory, death, and identity, its male protagonist faces the chains of generational influence after the horror he undergoes as a soldier in Vietnam. Thus the hero learns to understand a political as well as a familial past.

Schaeffer tells the story of two seemingly different women in *First Nights* (1993). Her protagonists, a Swedish actress inspired by Greta Garbo and her West Indian housekeeper, reveal similarities in their characters as the reader follows their relationship over 15 years. The elegant Anna interacts with Ivy, and her character moves from melancholy to a more genuine and identifiable woman. Robert Plunket noted in the *New York Times Book Review*, "The problems faced by the most beautiful woman in the world are not the sort that trouble the average reader, and it is not until the conclusion of the book, in an ending both effective and affecting, that Anna becomes a real human being."

Another complex female relationship is explored in *The Golden Rope* (1996). Doris and Florence, identical twins, share the narrative, each with their respective points of view. The sisters' feelings toward the other are contradictory, as one reveals total attachment to her twin while the other denies her sibling's existence. Schaeffer explores the lives of two women whose personality traits clash, as the sisters' reflections alternate throughout the novel. The passive, heartbroken Doris clings to the idea that she and her twin are one spirit in two bodies, while the overemotional Florence sustains the belief that a fierce rivalry is intact. *Publishers Weekly* noted, "Schaeffer's beautifully inflected prose has an affinity with visual art; rich sensory details and vivid imagery give her sentences an almost tactile quality."

Schaeffer is a frequent contributor to the *New York Times Book Review*. She has published new poems in *Prairie Schooner*, the *Southern Review*, and the *Literary Review*, and two novels for young readers: *The Dragons of North Chittendon* (1986) and *The Four Hoods and Great Dog* (1988).

Schaeffer has received many literary awards: the O. Henry award (1978), the Lawrence award (1984), the Friends of Literature award (1984), and the Prairie Schooner's Edward Lewis Wallant Award (1984). She received a Guggenheim Fellowship for 1984-85 and the Centennial Review's Poetry Award in 1985. Schaeffer is Broeklundian Professor of English at Brooklyn College, where she began the M.F.A. program in creative writing. The film rights to Schaeffer's *The Madness of a Seduced Woman* have been purchased.

OTHER WORKS: *Widow* (1973). *Rhymes and Runes of the Toad* (1975). *Alphabet for the Lost Years* (1976). *Times of the King and Queen* (1978). *Autobiography of Foudini M. Cat* (1997).

BIBLIOGRAPHY: Pearlman, M., ed., in *Mother Puzzles* (1989). Pearlman, M., ed., *American Women Writing Fiction: Memory, Identity, Family, Space* (1989).

Reference works: *CA* (1999). *CANR* (1986). *CLC* (1986). *DLB* (1984). *MTCW* (1990). *Oxford Companion to Women's Writing in the United States* (1995). *WW in Writers, Editors and Poets* (1989).

Other references: *APR* (Jan./Feb. 1976). *Best Sellers* (1 Oct. 1974). *Book-of-the-Month Club News* (July 1978). *Centennial Review* (1978). *MELUS* (Winter 1980). *NYTBR* (20 May 1973, 18

May 1975, 30 May 1993). *Poetry* (July 1975). *PW* (6 May 1996). *Southwest Review* (Winter 1984). *Time* (18 June 1973).

—JANE S. BAKERMAN,
UPDATED BY JOLLEN MASTERS AND ALLISON JONES

SCHMITT, Gladys

Born 31 May 1909, Pittsburgh, Pennsylvania; **died** 3 October 1972, Pittsburgh, Pennsylvania
Daughter of Henry H. and Leonore Schmitt; **married** Simon Goldfield, 1937

Gladys Schmitt graduated from the University of Pittsburgh in 1932 and in 1933 became an editor at *Scholastic* magazines. In 1942 Schmitt left *Scholastic* to teach English at Carnegie Institute of Technology, a job she held until her death. Schmitt was married to a musician who gave up his career and devoted his talents to editing Schmitt's writing and taking care of her.

The Gates of Aulis (1942) is an autobiographical novel about a young woman who needs to define herself by being loved. The failure to gain love through sacrificing herself to another person leads to despair and a suicide attempt before she gains more balanced and therefore redemptive insights. The theme is the need to choose and be committed to a societal myth such as religion.

In *David the King* (1946), Schmitt combines introspective detail and a concern over moral issues with material that could sustain serious philosophic themes. Structural and thematic unity exist in David's struggles to reconcile his ambition for power with his commitments to God and his people, and to choose an action when faced with moral ambiguity. David, who can achieve self-fulfillment because everybody loves him, grows in stature as he becomes capable of self-sacrifice and understands the ways of a God who offers no clear moral guidance.

Rembrandt (1961) examines the relationship between the artist, art, and family obligations. Rembrandt's torments arise from conflicts between commitment to art and shame over disloyalty to people he loves, from conflicts between the need to please those who commission his paintings and the need to paint according to his vision and from bitterness over inadequate recognition. Brief popular success ruins Rembrandt; his love of splendor leads to bankruptcy and superficiality.

In *The Godforgotten* (1972), a formerly monastic, medieval community has lapsed into despair, believing that it has been forgotten by God. The church sends a disaffected priest to restore the people to the fold. He succeeds, but by setting inflexible standards disrupts their family relationships and destroys their faith in simple human values.

Sonnets for An Analyst (1973) records the process of Schmitt's recovery after an emotional breakdown. The sonnets give expression to Schmitt's memories and dreams; her emotions; her identifications, loyalties, and insecurities; her need for love. The progression of Schmitt's feelings for the analyst, from anger to love to acknowledgment of his role, parallels the movement of her psyche toward acceptance of her losses—above all, the loss of her commitment to religion—and of herself. Schmitt controls her chaotic emotions through language, wit, and irony, and the structure of the sonnet form.

Schmitt's central concerns are with human relationships and especially the need for compassion in a world where the sustaining myth, and therefore the moral bases, are obscured, decayed, or dead. Her fiction is based in characterization; complexity and irony arise from the technique of multiple point of view—the shifting of points of view between chapters or sections to provide different personal and moral perspectives.

Schmitt is known as a writer of historical fiction, but this categorization does not do her full justice. Schmitt's writing is sometimes too philosophically weighty and too artful, but at its best it contains controlled craftsmanship, past worlds richly recreated on the basis of scanty evidence, and searching psychological and moral depth.

OTHER WORKS: *Alexandra* (1947). *Confessors of the Name* (1952). *The Persistent Image* (1955). *A Small Fire* (1957). *The Heroic Deeds of Beowulf* (1962). *Electra* (1965). *Boris, the Lopsided Bear* (1966).

BIBLIOGRAPHY: Brostoff, A., *Only Human Values* (1973). Brostoff, A., ed., *I Could Be Mute* (1978).
    Reference works: *CA* (1967). *CB* (1943). *TCAS*.
    Other references: *American Scholar* (Summer 1961, Winter, 1973). *WSJ* (16 May 1972).

—ANITA BROSTOFF

SCHOFIELD, Sandy
See RUSCH, Kristine Kathryn

SCHOOLCRAFT, Mary Howard

Born circa 1820 in Beaufort County, South Carolina; **died** date unknown
Wrote under: A Southern Lady
Daughter of Mr. and Mrs. Howard; **married** Henry Rowe Schoolcraft, 1847

There is little biographical information available about Mary Howard Schoolcraft. The only firm facts are her birth place, her marriage in Washington, D.C. to an ethnologist, and her role as his amanuensis. After their marriage, Schoolcraft apparently was instrumental in securing the commission for Henry Rowe Schoolcraft's monumental, six-volume *Historical and Statistical*

Information Respecting the History, Conditions, and Prospects of the Indian Tribes of the United States (1851-57). Because of his paralysis, Schoolcraft helped with the preparation of this classic document.

Schoolcraft's first published work was a pamphlet, *Letters on the Condition of the African Race in the United States* (1852), written to her brother, General John H. Howard. Schoolcraft moves from voicing her concern about the abolitionist sentiment then shaking the capital to a description of the good life of the South Carolina slave, as opposed to the degradation and deprivation of the freed black in the North. She declares that the furor over slavery is not a real issue but merely an expression of "sectional jealousy" used as a rhetorical device for commanding public attention. She details the paternal tenderness with which the South Carolina landowner treats his slaves, explains the philosophical reasons for the Southerners' opposition to abolition, and details the horrors of the freed blacks' life in Philadelphia.

The sentiments in these letters form the core of the novel *The Black Gauntlet* (1860). This book consists of a series of defences of slavery and diatribes against abolition. Schoolcraft has here fleshed out the sentiments of her pamphlet by the addition of numerous lengthy citations from contemporary speeches and magazine and newspaper articles. The clean, comfortable homes and gardens of the plantation blacks and the relaxed lifestyle of these happy, loyal slaves are described glowingly. Schoolcraft bases her defense of slavery on the thesis that it is mandated by God, who directs His people to take slaves among the heathen for the purpose of Christianizing them and saving their eternal souls. The benevolence of such a system is contrasted with the neglect that the abolitionist exhibits once he has tempted the slave to betray his master's loving trust.

This material is loosely attached to a narrative about the Wyndham family of Beaufort District, South Carolina. Schoolcraft uses the story of the Wyndham daughters, of whom Musidora is apparently an autobiographical character, to preach the values of a strict Christian upbringing and the perils of being an orphan raised by a self-centered stepmother.

The Household of Bouverie (1860) repeats some of the themes already treated in *The Black Gauntlet*. The novel opens as the orphaned Lilian de Courcey meets the grandmother who had apparently abandoned her daughter as an infant. With Lilian's questioning of her grandmother's motives and the development of the relationship with her grandmother, the theme of mother love is again explored. Other themes are the visitation of the sins of the fathers on the children and the necessity of expiation of these sins. The plot is skillfully handled, revealing the solutions to the mysteries facing Lilian only at the end of the gothic romance.

Schoolcraft's intentions are clearly didactic. She defends slavery and deplores abolition; she extols Christian duty and motherhood and condemns moral irresponsibility and the lack of altruistic motives in interpersonal relationships. Schoolcraft's style is hyperbolic and ludicrous by 20th-century standards and her ideas exhibit bigotry, but the plot of *The Household of Bouverie* does have merit as an example of the gothic thriller.

OTHER WORKS: *Plantation Life: The Narratives of Mrs. Henry Rowe Schoolcraft* (containing *Letters on the Condition of the African Race* and *The Black Gauntlet*, 1969).

BIBLIOGRAPHY: *Library of Southern Literature* (1970).

—HARRIETTE CUTTINO BUCHANAN

SCHWARTZ, Lynne Sharon

Born 19 March 1939, Brooklyn, New York
Daughter of Jack and Sarah Slatus Sharon; **married** Harry Schwartz, 1957; **children:** Rachel, Miranda

Lynne Sharon Schwartz grew up in Brooklyn, the subject of her most important work to date, *Leaving Brooklyn* (1989), which she describes as a novel about an adolescent girl's transition from youthful self-preoccupation to adult consciousness of the greater world beyond. She graduated from Barnard College (1959), received an M.A. in literature from Bryn Mawr College (1961), and did further graduate study in comparative literature at New York University between 1967 and 1972. Schwartz worked as associate editor for the magazine the *Writer* from 1961 to 1963, and as a writer for Operation Open City, a civil rights-fair housing organization in New York City from 1965 to 1967. She was a lecturer in English at Hunter College of the City University of New York from 1970 to 1975.

Schwartz's other major works include three highly acclaimed novels and two collections of short stories. Her fiction is remarkable for its sharply delineated portraits of the everyday life of the urban middle class; skillfully piercing through the surface of the comfortable, familiar worlds of her characters, she exposes the dreams, anxieties, and absurdities that lie beneath. The rich images with which she paints her characters' foibles and eccentricities have led critics to compare her to the painter Goya or to Flannery O'Connor. Yet while she often deals with idiosyncrasies of personality and behavior, Schwartz strives to portray the universal motivations that channel human desires. She succeeds unusually well in depicting the complex emotional and psychological underpinnings of the "dailiness of life," as one reviewer noted, while at the same time exploring the moral and philosophical dilemmas that confront her characters. Her work is distinguished by its broad intellectual range as well as by its clear style, graceful elegance, and wit.

Much of Schwartz's writing probes the contradictory pull between security and risk, order and change, the "safety of rules and traditions" and the "thrill of defiance." This theme is prominent in *Leaving Brooklyn*, a novel about Audrey, a 15-year-old girl coming of age just after World War II. Narrated by the protagonist, now a mature writer struggling to understand and accept her own history, the story concerns discovery of her physical differences—a ''wandering'' eye that gives her a special ''double vision''—and her seduction by her eye doctor, a seduction in which she is a willing participant. By telling ''the story of an eye, and how it came into its own,'' Schwartz reveals the development of her own ''I,'' as the girl Audrey begins to ''see'' the truths beneath Brooklyn's surface comforts, its rules, and its order, and to distance herself from the conventions of her parents, immigrants once removed, and of Brooklyn. ''Leaving Brooklyn'' becomes a metaphor for reaching beyond custom, convention, and rules, for risk taking, experience, and passion.

In *Disturbances in the Field* (1983), the comfortable, upper-middle class lives of Victor Rowe, a painter, and his talented, well-educated wife, Lydia, a chamber pianist, are suddenly split apart after the deaths of two of their children in a school bus accident. Unable to respond to her husband's emotional needs in the wake of the tragedy, Lydia sets in motion the ''disturbances'' of the title—when ''something gets between the expressed need on the one hand and the response on the other.'' This unsettling, compelling story is told crisply and compassionately: through the accumulation of detail, character, and event, Schwartz compiles a stunningly realistic portrait of an intelligent, but ultimately ordinary woman seeking to find meanings in the terrible loss that wrenched the ''placidity'' from her life.

Rough Strife (1980), Schwartz's first novel, is a chronicle of the emotional dynamics of a marriage over 20 years; Schwartz, in Katha Pollitt's words, ''registers the fluctuations of marital feeling with the fidelity of a Geiger counter.'' The attention paid to detail and to exposing the jumbled, contrapuntal realities beneath the surface of what appears to be a successful conventional relationship predicts the course of much of Schwartz's later fiction.

The theme is realized most vividly in Schwartz's masterful short story collection, *Acquainted with the Night and Other Stories* (1984). In the title story, a successful 47-year-old architect, given to insomnia, confronts terrifying demons of his past, his psyche, and even beyond, something more ''cosmic''—as he seeks sleep in the middle of the night. The characters in the 15 other stories of this anthology also wrestle with the terrors, illusions, and fantasies that compose their reality. For Schwartz, true knowledge is based on an understanding of night—the hidden fears, secrets, and reversals of life—as well as of day.

The characters in the stories collected in *The Melting Pot and Other Subversive Stories* (1987) also confront ''the unending cycles of light and darkness'' that shatter complacency. Nuances of shifting relationships, marriage, and divorce are once again illumined; Schwartz also writes poignantly, and with great good humor, of other subjects—a middle-aged woman undergoing a hysterectomy; another reflecting on the life and death of her opinionated, tempestuous father; a homeless family finding shelter in a Manhattan TV studio. She is particularly concerned with the impact of dream and memory on consciousness: exploring the present, she reaches back to ''subversive'' impulses—among them, tradition, illusion, and fantasy—that guide contemporary

lives. Here, as in *Leaving Brooklyn* and other stories, the daughter of Americanized Jews must confront the meaning of that heritage.

While much of Schwartz's writing defies categorization and she is willing to experiment—*The Fatigue Artist* (1995) includes a series of graphics of an empty swimming pool—she belongs very much to a group of politically oriented Jewish women writers that includes Grace Paley, Rosellen Brown, Cynthia Ozick, and Erica Jong. She is emphatically not an autobiographical writer in her fiction—the long 1996 essay in *Ruined by Reading: A Life in Books* is another matter entirely—but her life inevitably informs her work.

In *The Fatigue Artist*, Schwartz examines and satirizes both traditional and nontraditional medical practice as well as the profound effect a chronic illness (in this case the virus known as Chronic Fatigue Syndrome) can have on the person who has it. The novel was particularly well reviewed by Oregon poet Floyd Skloot, a sufferer of the same disease. A new novel, *In the Family Way*, was published in late 1999 and a book of essays, *Only Connect* is due in 2000.

A widely respected teacher of writing, Schwartz has taught at the graduate level at Washington University in St. Louis, Columbia University, and the University of California at Irvine, as well as in such workshops as Bread Loaf. Schwartz has been widely anthologized in *The Pushcart Prize III; The Best American Short Stories* and many other prize-winning anthologies. Essays, satirical pieces, and translations have appeared in *Harper's, the New York Times, Threepenny Review, Ladies' Home Journal, Dance* magazine, and the *Best American Essays, 1998*, among others.

Schwartz is the recipient of grants from the National Endowment for the Arts, the Guggenheim Foundation, and the New York State Foundation for the Arts. *Leaving Brooklyn* was nominated for the 1989 PEN/Faulkner Award for fiction and was a Literary Guild Selection and the winner of *Hadassah* magazine's Harold U. Ribalow award. Her first novel, *Rough Strife*, was nominated for the PEN/Hemingway First Novel award and a National Book award and received the Great Lakes College Association Honorable Mention.

OTHER WORKS: *Balancing Acts* (1981). *We Are Taking About Homes: A Great University Against Its Neighbors* (1985). *The Four Questions* (text for paintings by O. Sherman, 1989). *Smoke Over Birkenau* (by L. Millu, translated by Schwartz from Italian, 1991). *A Lynne Sharon Schwartz Reader: Selected Poetry and Prose* (1992).

BIBLIOGRAPHY: Reference works: *CA* (1982). *CLC* (1985). *Oxford Companion to Women's Writing in the United States* (1995).
Other references: *American Book Review* (Nov./Dec. 1989). *Hudson Review* (Spring 1984). *NYTBR* (6 Nov. 1983, 26 Aug. 1984, 24 Nov. 1985, 16 Apr. 1989). *Newsweek* (14 Jan. 1985). *Sewanee Review* (Spring 1985). *WRB* (Sept. 1989).

—JOYCE ANTLER,
UPDATED BY MARTHA ULLMAN WEST

SCOTT, Anne Firor

Born 24 April 1921, Montezuma, Georgia
Daughter of John W. and Mary Moss Firor; **married** Andrew M.
   Scott, 1947; **children:** Rebecca, David, Donald

Historian Anne Firor Scott has a unique perspective on remembering when women received suffrage in the United States. Born nine months after the suffrage amendment passed, Scott and women's right to vote came into being nearly at the same time. As the only girl among four siblings, Scott was never taught that girls were inferior. Only when she was in college did a favorite professor warn her that being female might limit her opportunities. Her parents, however, set out to give her every opportunity. Her mother was a full-time homemaker and her father was a college professor. An early influence on Anne was reading. Her father would read aloud to his children. But rather than reading them children's books, he read them his favorites.

This emphasis on the printed word would stand Scott in good stead. She did not set out to be a historian or educator. In her autobiographical essay, ''A Historian's Odyssey,'' Scott read back through her journals, which by 1984 numbered 20 volumes, to examine her choices. She realized that she came to history by chance. ''If my journal is to be believed,'' she wrote, ''I went out into the world in 1940 in search of fame, fortune, and a husband, in no particular order. As to how that search was to be conducted the journal is significantly silent. It was very much a matter of what might turn up.''

Scott attended the University of Georgia and graduated summa cum laude and Phi Beta Kappa in 1941. After graduation, she held a job at IBM and was briefly enrolled in a graduate program for personnel managers. It was a U.S. Congressional internship that marked a pivotal juncture; her internship responsibilities included writing speeches and listening to politicians talking, both of which had a tremendous impact on her. She later wrote, ''[The experiences] made me so painfully aware of my ignorance that I went back to school.'' She chose Northwestern University, where she earned a master's degree in political science. She then took a job with the National League of Women Voters, married, and moved to Cambridge, Massachusetts. She enrolled in the American Civilization program at Harvard because it ''seemed to have few requirements but plenty of scope.'' Before she could finish her dissertation, her husband, who had already finished his degree, secured a job in Washington, D.C. and they moved. Scott mused years later, ''All our planning was for his career; it did not occur to me to think this odd.'' Seven years and three children later, she finished her dissertation and took a job teaching history at Haverford College in Haverford, Pennsylvania.

While Scott's decision to study history may have been indirect, her specialization in the study of women's history was not accidental. Her maternal grandmother had worked for the League of Women Voters. At the age of twenty-three, Scott decided to write a history of women, beginning with Eve. These interests and influences led her to research the history of women of the American South. She soon found ''there was almost no historiographical tradition and no network of established scholars. My temerity rested not on courage but on ignorance; if I had known what was involved I might never have begun.'' Her ''ignorance'' resulted in her first book, *The Southern Lady* (1970), now considered a classic in the field of women's history.

After her temporary appointments at Haverford College and the University of North Carolina at Chapel Hill, she was hired as assistant professor of history at Duke University. In 1980 she earned the distinguished rank of W. K. Boyd Professor of History and in 1991 W. K. Boyd Professor of History Emerita. The recipient of many fellowships, prizes, and honorary degrees, Scott was awarded a university medal from Duke in 1994, a Berkshire Conference Prize in 1980, and honorary degrees from Queens College, Northwestern University, Radcliffe College, and the University of the South.

The author of numerous articles, chapters for books and introductions to the work of other scholars, as well as her own books, Scott is best known as one of the first historians of U.S. women. She is clear in remembering those who went before her. In *Unheard Voices: The First Historians of Southern Women* (1993), she reflected, ''It is impossible to measure the cost to the world of scholarship of their marginality (and that of so many other), or the cost to themselves.'' Scott tried to mitigate this cost for subsequent generations of women historians in service to the profession. She served as president of the Organization of American Historians and president of the Southern Historical Association, and on the advisory boards of the Schlesinger Library, the Princeton University Department of History, and the Woodrow Wilson International Center for Scholars.

OTHER WORKS: *The American Woman: Who Was She?* (1970). *One Half the People* (with A. M. Scott 1975). *Making the Invisible Woman Visible* (1984). *Virginia Women: The First Hundred Years* (with S. Lebsock (1988). *Natural Allies: Women's Associations in American History* (1991).

BIBLIOGRAPHY: Reference works: *American Women Historians, 1700s-1990s: A Biographical Dictionary* (1996). *CA* (1973).

—CELESTE DEROCHE

SCOTT, Evelyn

Born Elise Dunn, 17 January 1893, Clarksville, Tennessee; **died**
   1963, New York, New York
Also wrote under: E. Souza
Daughter of Seely and Thomas Dunn; **married** Frederick C.
   Wellman (Cyril Kay Scott), 1919 (common law); John
   Metcalf, 1928

Although Evelyn Scott's family no longer held the moneyed position it enjoyed before the Civil War, Scott was trained in the values of the Southern aristocratic tradition. At fifteen, she rejected the role of the Southern woman and became an ardent feminist; at eighteen the Dunn family moved to New Orleans. She enrolled in Sophie Newcomb College, but never finished her studies there; instead, she educated herself.

In 1913 Scott ran away to Brazil with the dean of the School of Tropical Medicine of Tulane University, and they changed their names to Evelyn and Cyril Kay Scott. One son was born in Brazil. The Scotts returned in 1920, lived in Greenwich Village and Cape Cod, and separated in Bermuda. In 1928 Scott married British novelist John Metcalf.

Escapade (1923) is an account of Scott's six-year exile with her lover in Brazil. It is written in a subjectively impressionistic style, controlled by a conception: the entanglement of life and death in a conflict between the lush tropical growth soaring above villages of earthy natives and Scott's deathlike isolation. By selecting images that express feelings and actions, Scott balances emotionalism with understanding, and avoids immersion in subjectivity. Scott endured hunger, squalor, severe illness, and a fearful pregnancy. Each episode or carefully composed moment is imbued with Scott's belief that only in the presence of death do we discover life.

Background in Tennessee (1937) is an autobiographical history in which Scott discusses the sociological, economic, religious, and cultural growth of the South, integrating her own experiences and judgements. Scott believed the slow growth of culture in the South was due to the short span of time between the Revolution and the Civil War; most of the important men of the South were orators and politicians, not artists.

Scott wrote several novel trilogies: *The Narrow House* (1921), *Narcissus* (1922), and *The Golden Door* (1925) are about three generations of a family attempting to hold on to their self-made ideals and hollow beliefs. *Migrations* (1927), *The Wave* (1929), and *A Calendar of Sin* (1932) cover American history from 1850 to 1918. In *The Wave*, set during the Civil War, Scott combined over 100 episodes in a deliberately structured mosaic, illustrating the conflict of individuals with society and with themselves. Scott equated the perversion of war with the perversion of love lying in the heart of each individual.

The range of Scott's other publications is broad. *Precipitations* (1920), her first book, is of imagist poetry. *The Winter Alone* (1930) contains poetry more varied in subject and techniques. *Love*, a play, was performed by the Provincetown Players in 1930. Scott wrote a mystery, *Blue Rum* (1930), under the name E. Souza, and three juvenile books: *In the Endless Sands* (1925), *Witch Perkins* (1928), and *Billy, the Maverick* (1934).

Scott possessed the rare combination of emotional intuition and an artistic genius for style and technique. She was a fervent intellectual, sensitive but analytical. She had no strict philosophy, but she consistently strove in her life and work for freedom from every limitation. Scott believed in authorial intrusion and wrote all her fiction from an omniscient point of view, a technique which gave her the freedom she desired. Scott's major works can be read and studied simultaneously on psychological, philosophical, and artistic levels.

OTHER WORKS: *Ideals* (1927). *Eva Gay* (1933). *Breathe Upon These Slain* (1934). *Bread and a Sword* (1937). *Shadow of a Hawk* (1941).

The papers of Evelyn Scott and two unfinished novels are in the possession of Robert L. Welker.

BIBLIOGRAPHY: Scott, C. K., *Life Is Too Short* (1943). Welker, R. L., ''Liebestod with a Southern Accent,'' in *Reality and Myth* (1964).

Reference works: *America Now* (1938). *Living Authors* (1935).

—PEGGY BACH

SCOTT, Joan Wallach

Born 18 December 1941, Brooklyn, New York
Married Donald Scott

With the development of the new social history in the 1960s, history from ''the bottom up'' grew in scope, importance, and diversity. Historian Joan Wallach Scott is a leading figure in the development of women's history, labor history, and gender theory. A renowned teacher and writer, Scott is an influential participant in the ongoing postmodern debate.

The daughter of two high school teachers, Scott knew early in her life that she wanted to be a historian. She attended Brandeis University, graduating with a bachelor's degree magna cum laude in 1962. She received her Ph.D. from the University of Wisconsin in 1969. Her first academic appointment was as assistant professor at the University of Illinois at Chicago Circle. From there she taught at Northwestern University, where she was the first woman faculty member in the history department. Her next appointment was as first assistant and then associate professor at the University of North Carolina at Chapel Hill. In 1980 she was appointed Nancy Duke Lewis Professor at Brown University. She continued to encounter ''firsts'': this time she was the first woman to secure tenure in the history department at Brown. During her time at Brown, she also served as director of the Pembroke Center for Teaching and Research on Women.

Her current position is at Princeton University. She is only the second woman to be invited to join the faculty of the Institute for Advanced Studies at Princeton, an institute founded by Albert Einstein and others in 1930. In an interview with Katherine Hinds, Scott described her appointment to the Institute's faculty as significant to women's studies, a field ''which has been struggling to legitimize itself in the scholarly world for the last ten to fifteen years.''

Scott's first book brought together her interests in French social history and labor history. *The Glassworkers of Carmaux:*

French Craftsmen and Political Action in a Nineteenth-Century City (1974) won the American Historical Association's prize for the best first book written by an American on European history. It made a critical contribution to the developing specialty of the new labor history.

Scott is perhaps best known for her penetrating work in exploring gender dynamics in history and in historiography. She decided to focus more on these issues when students began to demand courses on women. She forthrightly addressed the invisibility of gender (which she herself acknowledged characterized her first book) in her second book, *Women, Work, and Family* (1978). Coauthored with Louise Tilly, this book examines how women figured—actually and symbolically—in working-class history. She told Katherine Hinds in 1985, "Since labor history is my field, it seems appropriate to take these questions about women and gender and work them into labor history."

Most recently, Scott's scholarship has brought her into the center of the sometimes contentious realm of French postmodern theory. Scott has been influential in the consideration of how this theory can apply to the study of history. She borrows from Michel Foucault in arguing that history is the study of politics. Like Foucault, Scott contends that politics cannot be simply defined in governmental terms, but rather as "contests that involve power." Scott and others continue to debate power as not only "a relationship of repression or domination but also a set of relationships or processes that produce positive effects." She maintains all history is decision-making, all history is political.

Scott provides important leadership in opening the historical profession to other women. She gives a great deal of service to the profession, inside and outside her universities. While at Chapel Hill, she chaired the University of North Carolina Committee on the Status of Women. For the American Historical Association, she chaired the Committee on Women Historians. Her expertise includes institution building. She was instrumental in establishing women's studies programs at the University of North Carolina and at Brown.

OTHER WORKS: *Gender and the Politics of History* (1988). *Only Paradoxes to Offer: French Feminists and the Rights of Man* (1996).

BIBLIOGRAPHY: Reference works: *American Women Historians, 1700s-1990s: A Biographical Dictionary* (1996). *CA* (1973, 1978). Other references: *Change* (July/Aug. 1985).

—CELESTE DEROCHE

SCOTT, Julia
See OWEN, Mary Alicia

SCOTT-MAXWELL, Florida

Born Florida Pier MacChesney, 24 September 1883, Orange Park, Florida; **died** 6 March 1979, Exeter, England
Daughter of Robert and Anna Pier MacChesney; **married** Scott J. Scott-Maxwell, 1910 (divorced 1929); **children:** four

In her writing and in her various careers, Florida Scott-Maxwell's life was defined by her curiosity, her allegiance to women's issues, and her devotion to writing. Named for the state of Florida where she was born, Scott-Maxwell grew up in Pittsburgh, Pennsylvania, where she attended public school until the age of fifteen when she moved to New York City.

By age sixteen, she had enrolled in a drama school, which launched her brief career as an actress at the Edwin Mayo Theater Company. In her twenties, she began a second career writing short stories that were published in *Harper's* and *Century* magazines. In due course, she became the first woman hired by the *New York Evening Sun*, where she wrote a weekly column. In 1910 she married Scott Maxwell-Scott; the couple moved to Ballieston, England, near Glasgow, Scotland. Because so few details on her life are available, the names, ages, and gender of their four children are at this time unknown.

Dividing her time between marriage and career, she worked for women's suffrage and wrote a feminist play, *The Flash Point* (1914). After divorcing Scott-Maxwell in 1929, Florida, now forty-six, moved to London, where she supported her family writing columns, short stories, reviews, and the play *Many Women*, which was produced in 1932 at the Arts Theater.

Meanwhile, she became interested in Jungian psychology, trained as an analyst under Carl Jung, and practiced throughout the 1930s in clinics in both Scotland and England. In 1939 she published *Toward Relationships*, which examines the difficulties women face maintaining a sense of individuality while fulfilling their socially assigned roles.

Toward Relationships takes a Jungian approach to feminist themes such as woman as "other," and the importance of feminine, or nurturing, qualities in a world that values achievement and progress—themes current in today's gender debates. After World War II, she began writing plays again. *I Said to Myself* (1946) implemented an experimental narrative approach that used several actors to represent various personality traits of one central character.

Women and Sometimes Men, her second Jungian-feminist tract, elaborated on themes introduced in *Toward Relationships*. While many of Scott-Maxwell's publications and dramas received negative criticism, her most famous and provocative book, *The Measure of My Days* (1968), has been widely anthologized and highly acclaimed. Looking at once back over her life while examining her continued search for self-understanding, this self-critical yet life-affirming journal examines the passions and problems of aging.

Reflecting on old age, adult children and grandchildren, the nature of love and work, and the significance of owning the self comprises a process that makes her "fierce with reality." In a powerful commitment to living in the present, she proclaims: "At my age I care to my roots about the quality of women, and I care because I know how important her quality is."

OTHER WORKS: *The Kinsmen Knew How to Die* (with S. Batcharsky, 1931).

BIBLIOGRAPHY: Allison, K. A. *Florida Scott-Maxwell: Biography of a Woman/Writer* (dissertation, 1990). Cahill, S., *Writing Women's Lives: An Anthology of Autobiographical Narratives by Twentieth Century American Women Writers* (1994). Ireland, N. O., *Index to Women of the World from Ancient to Modern Times: A Supplement* (1988). Moffat, M. J., and C. Painter, *Revelations: Diaries of Women* (1974). Rose, P., *The Norton Book of Women's Lives* (1993).

Reference works: *Biography Index* 8 (1971), 10 (1977). *Encyclopedia of British Women Writers*.

—MIRIAM KALMAN HARRIS, PH.D.

SCUDDER, Vida Dutton

Born 15 December 1861, Madura, India; **died** 9 October 1954, Wellesley, Massachusetts
Daughter of David C. and Harriet Dutton Scudder

Vida Dutton Scudder spent her lifetime attempting to unite literature, socialism, and Christianity. She was a member of the Wellesley College Department of English for 41 years (1887-1928) but achieved her fame as an activist Christian socialist. She helped to found college settlements on the East Coast, working at Denison House in Boston. She was a tireless advocate for higher education for women, took a public role in the debate of the issues of her times (workers' rights, democracy, social community), and was a prolific writer. She was above all an idealist with strong leanings both toward the world and its politics and the church and its organizations.

Born in India where her father served as a Congregationalist missionary, she was related to old New England families through each parent. When her father died suddenly in 1862, the infant Vida and her mother returned to the Dutton home in Auburndale, Massachusetts. Scudder grew up surrounded by doting grandparents, distinguished aunts and uncles, and a devoted mother.

Scudder spent much of her childhood in Europe; she absorbed as much from her mother as from their travels. This exposure set for life her devotion to beauty and tradition. In 1878 she joined the first class of Girls' Latin School in Boston and in 1880 entered Smith College. After graduating from Smith, she spent an academic year at Oxford University, among the first American women to be accepted as special students there, where she heard John Ruskin present the last set of lectures he gave before he retired. Through these lectures she became aware of the "plethora of privilege" in her life. She came away from Ruskin and Oxford filled with a social radicalism, and returned to Smith to obtain her master's degree. Ruskin's ideas gave Scudder a way to link literature to social reality and social purpose.

Scudder accepted a position in the English Department at Wellesley College in 1887. She chose Wellesley over Smith so she could remain with her mother. From the outset, both a great love of letters and a growing social concern animated her teaching. Her two earliest books, *The Life of the Spirit in Modern English Poets* (1895) and *Social Ideals in English Letters* (1898), reflected this combination.

While teaching gave her more self-confidence, Scudder continued to worry about "privilege unshared." This concern led her in 1887 to form a college settlement organization, the college Settlements Association. When the first settlement opened on Rivington Street in New York City in 1889, Scudder, as secretary of the electoral board of the association, promoted its work on college campuses. In 1893 she took a leave of absence from Wellesley to join in the official opening of Denison House in Boston's South End. For the next 20 years she was an integral part of the continued existence of the settlement.

Scudder's deep commitment to social activism informed her teaching career to such a degree that rather than writing the literary criticism that would have given her more prestige among her colleagues, she wrote books designed to convince people that their beliefs should commit them to "social reconstruction." It was perhaps a natural progression for Scudder to decide in 1889 to become a member of William D. P. Bliss' Society of Christian Socialists, a charter member of the Brotherhood of the Carpenter, and an active worker in the Christian Social Union. Her settlement work and her friendships with the women in settlement neighborhoods turned her attention to the practical side of the labor question. Yet these priorities often put Scudder in conflict with the Wellesley College administration over her socialist activities.

In 1911 Scudder was a founding member of the Episcopal Church Socialist League. The goal of the League was to encourage the application of Christian principles to industrial and social relations. In *Socialism and Character* (1912), she tried to reconcile the apparent differences between Christianity and socialism. Through her socialist connections, Scudder was asked to speak in Lawrence, Massachusetts, during the 1912 textile strike, where her speech led to demands for her resignation from Wellesley.

Scudder weathered this storm and remained at Wellesley until her retirement in 1928, when a new phase of her career began. Years of research on the early history of the Franciscans resulted in her major work, *The Franciscan Adventure* (1931), and established her as a leading Franciscan scholar. Her greatest contribution to the growth of Christian social thought in the United States came through her writing. Her autobiography, *On Journey* (1937), provides a perceptive review of 75 years of social history and of her own religious ideals. Only age could curtail her activities, because her interest in the social questions of her time never waned. In 1952 she published *My Quest for Reality*, a sequel to her autobiography. She died suddenly in 1954.

OTHER WORKS: *The Witness of Denial* (1895). *Introduction to the Study of English Literature* (1901). *A Listener in Babel: Being a Series of Imaginary Conversations* (1903). *Saint Catherine of Siena as Seen in Her Letters* (1905). *The Disciple of a Saint* (1907). *Le Morte d'Arthur of Sir Thomas Malory and Its Sources* (1917). *The Church and the Hour: Reflections of a Socialist Churchwoman* (1917). *The Social Teachings of the Christian Year* (1921). *Brother John: A Tale of the First Franciscans* (1927). *The Privilege of Age: Essays Secular and Spiritual* (1939). *Father Huntington* (1940).

BIBLIOGRAPHY: *NAW: The Modern Period* (1980). *DLB: American Literary Critics and Scholars, 1880-1900* (1988).

—CELESTE DEROCHE

SEAMAN, Elizabeth Cochrane

Born 5 May 1865, Cochran's Mills, Pennsylvania; died 27 January 1922, New York, New York
Wrote under: Nellie Bly
Daughter of Michael and Mary Jane Cochran; married Robert L. Seaman, 1895 (died 1910)

Elizabeth Cochrane Seaman, a.k.a. Nellie Bly, spent her youth in a small milltown; her education, except for one year in a local boarding school, was directed by her father, a lawyer and mill owner. After the death of her father, who left only a small legacy, Seaman moved to Pittsburgh with her mother and sought work for their support. Seaman found her first journalism position with the Pittsburgh *Dispatch* at nineteen. At twenty, she moved to New York, attaining a position on Joseph Pulitzer's New York *World* which she kept from 1887 until 1895. She became an international celebrity after her 72-day trip around the world, breaking the record of Jules Verne's fictional hero Phileas Fogg. In the U.S., her exposé stories about urban social conditions and corruption were widely syndicated. Seaman's husband was an industrialist and a New York socialite. After his death in 1910, she controlled his failing business interests through 1919. Returning to journalism, she worked on the New York *Journal* until her death in 1922.

Seaman's writings consisted primarily of articles written for the *Dispatch* and the *World*, some of which appeared as subscription series books. *Ten Days in a Mad-house* (1887) contained three stories written for the *World*, an article about Blackwell's Island Insane Asylum, sketches on servant girls' experiences at employment agencies, and a piece on shop girls working in a paper box factory.

The story of Blackwell's Island, pronounced by the *World* to be "an immense sensation everywhere," established Seaman as a journalist in New York. She pretended insanity in order to "chronicle" the "simple tale of life in an asylum." She illustrated conditions and treatment of patients by describing her personal experiences and the experiences of individual women whom she met. Her narrative, written in unadorned prose, was a dramatic and realistic account. To arouse the reader's emotions Seaman openly expressed sympathy for "her suffering sisters" and her intent to "influence others to make life more bearable for them." While the asylum story and others which Seaman wrote appeared under "sensationalist" headlines—"Behind Asylum Bars" or "Nellie Bly as a White Slave"—her exposé journalism, in both content and style, was an early manifestation of the progressive period's muckraking journalism.

Six Months in Mexico (1888), Seaman's most thoughtful and stylistically pleasing (although often repetitive) book, was an examination of national character and an exposé of corruption and exploitative social conditions. The fact that Seaman went to Mexico as a foreign correspondent in late 1886 made the book a significant document, for this was a period when few other American journalists were providing the public with firsthand information about their neighboring country. Seaman recorded "Mexico in all its splendor," but she also showed that through "civilization's curse or blessing," the country was becoming a "new California." While the book indicated Seaman's sensitivity to unjust social conditions, especially for women and the native Indian population, and provided a record of the responses of an American middle class woman toward a culture both alien and "beautiful" to her, it was occasionally condescending in tone.

The "around the world" story for which Seaman achieved the widest attention was of the "stunt" variety. Chronicling her journey in *Nellie Bly's Book: Around the World in Seventy-two Days* (1890), Seaman presents herself as a "free American girl" encountering diverse cultures, all exciting and exotic, but none measuring up to the American way of life. She provides colorful descriptions of peoples and customs while maintaining the suspense of her race against time. From San Francisco to New York, Seaman was met with extraordinary public adulation; her journey was celebrated in song and dance; toys, clothing, and games carried her name. Seaman's story of "Nellie Bly's stunt" and the public response to it are material for a case study of the rapidly changing relationship between the press and the popular mind in the late 19th century.

BIBLIOGRAPHY: Marzolf, M., *Up From the Footnote: A History of Women Journalists* (1977). Noble, I., *Nellie Bly: First Woman Reporter* (1956). Quillan, J., *Nellie Bly* (produced 1946).

Rittenhouse, M., *The Amazing Nellie Bly* (1956). Ross, I., *Ladies of the Press* (1936).

Reference works: *A Woman of the Century* (1893). *Benet's Reader's Encyclopedia* (1987). *NAW, 1607-1950* (1971). *Oxford Companion to Women's Writing in the United States* (1995).

Other references: *Pittsburgh Press* (8 Jan. 1967, 15 Jan. 1967).

—JENNIFER L. TEBBE

SEAWELL, Molly Elliot

Born 23 October 1860, Gloucester County, Virginia; **died** 15 November 1916, Washington, D.C.
Also wrote under: Foxcroft Davis, Vera Sapoukhyn
Daughter of John T. and Frances Jackson Seawell

Molly Elliot Seawell was born on a Virginia country estate. Educated primarily at home, Seawell learned riding, dancing and household management, and read history, encyclopedias, Shakespeare, and the Romantic poets. After her father's death, Seawell supported her mother and sister by writing stories and as Washington correspondent for a New York daily.

Seawell's earliest books were regional novels. *Throckmorton* (1890) established the basic cast: an elderly old-school southern gentleman, childish but faithful black servants, and young lovers kept apart by family difficulties. Seawell's romantic novels are Ruritanian fantasies tied to some period which allows a historical personage to appear in a minor role—Voltaire in *Francezka* (1902), Robespierre in *The Last Duchess of Belgarde* (1908), Napoleon in *The Fortunes of Fifi* (1903), and so forth. The heroines are active, courageous, stoic, and impeccably pure. The narrative grows from a piquant situation rather than a complex plot.

The books for boys (primarily sea stories) dwell on honor, not action; heroism is demonstrated by dutiful self-sacrifice instead of valiant aggression. *Little Jarvis* (1890) remains at his post and dies when the mast is struck by cannon shot, and the manly officers of *Through Thick and Thin* (1893) risk their lives to bring water to their suffering men.

Despotism and Democracy (1903), published anonymously, and the two books by "Foxcroft Davis," *Mrs. Darrell* (1905) and *The Whirl* (1909), treat Washington society and politics in the silver-fork tradition. The characters are senators, justices, and British diplomats, but the action takes place in drawing rooms and at dinner tables.

Seawell's article "On the Absence of the Creative Faculty in Women," published in the *Critic* in 1891, set off a debate which occupied the letters column for several months. Her thesis was that women had never produced any immortal books or art

because the feminine nature innately lacked the faculty for invention. Seawell then campaigned against suffrage in national magazines and *The Ladies' Battle* (1911). She attacked suffragists as women "born with socialistic and communistic rather than domestic tendencies" who "have an antagonism to men."

Even contemporary reviews of Seawell's work were often lukewarm: her novels were called "wholesome," "slight," and "unpretentious." Plot was never her strong point, and the perfect ladies and gentlemen, the overt racism, and the condescending tone are interesting only because they reflect values once widespread.

OTHER WORKS: *The Berkeleys and their Neighbors* (1888, rev. ed. 1892). *Hale-Weston* (1888). *Maid Marian, and Other Stories* (1891, dramatization, 1893). *Midshipman Paulding* (1891). *Children of Destiny* (1893). *Paul Jones* (1893). *Decatur and Somers* (1894). *Quarterdeck and Fok'sle* (1895). *The Sprightly Romance of Marsac* (1895, dramatization by Seawell, 1900). *A Strange, Sad Comedy* (1896). *A Virginia Cavalier* (1896). *The History of the Lady Betty Stair* (1897). *Twelve Naval Captains* (1897). *The Loves of Lady Arabella* (1898). *The Rock and the Lion* (1898). *The Lively Adventures of Gavin Hamilton* (1899). *The House of Egremont* (1900). *Papa Bouchard* (1901). *Laurie Vane, and Other Stories* (1901). *The Great Scoop* (1903). *The Chateau of Montplaisir* (1906). *The Victory* (1906). *The Secret of Toni* (1907). *The Imprisoned Midshipman* (1908). *The Marriage of Theodora* (1910). *The Jugglers* (1911). *The Son of Columbus* (1912). *Betty's Virginia Christmas* (1914). *Betty at Fort Blizzard* (1916).

BIBLIOGRAPHY: Reference works: *American Women* (1938). *DAB*. *Library of Southern Literature* (1970). *NCAB*. *TCA.* (1942).

Other references: *Bookman* (Jan. 1901). *Critic* (28 Nov. 1891, 19 Mar. 1892). *NYT* (16 Nov. 1916). *North American Review* (Mar. 1914).

—SALLY MITCHELL

SECOR, Lella

Born February 1887, Battle Creek, Michigan; **died** 16 January 1966, Birmingham, England
Wrote under: Lella Secor Florence, Lella Faye Secor
Daughter of William and Loretta Sowle Secor; **married** Philip S. Florence, 1917; **children:** two sons

The youngest of seven children of her mother's two marriages, Lella Secor grew up in a fatherless household. The family was poor. As a child, Secor helped in her mother's boarding house, and after high school, she found work at the Battle Creek *Journal*.

About 1910, Secor followed her brother to Coulee, Washington, homesteading a claim next to his. She later ceded her claim to him when she resumed her newspaper work. In 1915, Secor represented the Seattle *Post-Intelligencer* on Henry Ford's "Peace Ship" to Europe and returned to New York a committed pacifist.

Secor was cofounder of two organizations devoted to keeping the U.S. out of World War I—the American Neutral Conference Committee and the Emergency Peace Federation—for which she wrote impassioned advertisements, articles, and tracts. She describes this period in "The Ford Peace Ship and After," in Julian Bell's *We Did Not Fight: 1914-18 Experiences of War Resisters* (1935), a collection of articles by outstanding British pacificists such as Bertrand Russell, David Garnett, and Roger Angell. Secor's article is also printed in *The History of the Woman's Peace Party*, edited by Marie Louise Degan (1939).

In *Lella Secor: A Diary in Letters, 1915-1922* (1978), edited by her daughter-in-law, Secor's letters to her mother and sisters show a woman indomitable in her quest for independence. Telling of her attempts to enlist all America's antiwar resources under one aegis, Secor's letters blaze with zeal. In 1917 Secor married British economist Philip Sargant Florence; two sons were born. The later letters describe her new life as wife and mother. Resolutely cheerful in tone, they nevertheless reveal weariness and discouragement at her loss of personal freedom.

In 1921 Secor's husband secured a lectureship at Cambridge University, and the family moved to England, where the ready availability of servants freed Secor to take up an activist role. *Birth Control on Trial* (1930) discusses Secor's work at the Cambridge Clinic, of which she was a founder. In 1929 her husband accepted a chair in economics at Birmingham University; there Secor worked to promote world disarmament, Labour politics, women's rights, slum clearance, and family planning.

In 1949, on a trip to Egypt, Secor and her husband were cut off by the outbreak of World War II; they escaped to America, and spent a year in Washington, D.C., before returning to England. Secor describes their adventures in *My Goodness! My Passport!* (1942). Back in England, Secor worked at the American embassy, promoting greater understanding of America by the British. During this period, she also gave radio talks on the BBC and wrote articles for British periodicals and two books. *Only an Ocean Between* (1943) and *Our Private Lives* (1944) are designed for mass consumption, and it is easy to see why Secor's chatty style helped make them popular in England during the war.

After the war, Secor channeled her energies into the Birmingham Family Planning Association, serving for 10 years as its chairperson. *Progress Report on Birth Control* (1956) is based on research into the case histories of the clinic's patients.

Secor's chapter on the Peace Ship in *We Did Not Fight* is perhaps her most outstanding piece of writing, evoking as it does a stirring and little known episode in American history. The account in *My Goodness! My Passport!* of her flight from Egypt, while exceptionally wide-eyed, is still an exciting yarn by a woman possessed of both curiosity and nerve. In contrast to her subjective writing, Secor's two volumes on birth control show considerable restraint. Undertaken in a spirit of scientific inquiry, they nevertheless attest, in the vivid prose of their case histories, to Secor's own belief in the necessity of family planning.

Although Secor was to spend more than half her life in England, she remained a particularly American writer. Her straightforward prose and gift for affecting anecdote reveal her origins as an American journalist and propagandist.

BIBLIOGRAPHY: *Booklist* (15 Sept. 1978). *CSM* (Sept. 1978). *New Directions for Women* (Autumn 1978). *SR* (22 July 1978). *LAT* (17 Oct. 1978).

—BARBARA MOENCH FLORENCE

SEDGES, John
See BUCK, Pearl S.

SEDGWICK, Anne Douglas

Born 28 March 1873, Englewood, New Jersey; **died** 19 July 1935, Hampstead, England
Daughter of George S. and Mary Douglas Sedgwick; **married** Basil de Sélincourt, 1908

Born to gentility and wealth and descended from early settlers of Massachusetts, Anne Douglas Sedgwick developed a strong if idealistic sense of caste and tradition, which later expanded into a Jamesian preoccupation with the social and psychological relationships between people of different cultures. She was intrigued particularly by the confrontation of English and French cultures and by the American's encounter with the mores and values of the old world. Sedgwick's affluent and genteel background also generated a devotion to social manners, costume, and interior design.

As a child, Sedgwick lived in her parents' elegant home in Irvington-on-Hudson, near New York City, and was educated by a governess. Except for two happy years spent with grandparents in Ohio when she was a teenager, childhood provided Sedgwick with her only sustained exposure to her native America. During Sedgwick's tenth year, her father, an attorney, moved his wife and three daughters to London. There Sedgwick lived and studied until she was eighteen. Then she studied painting in Paris for five years.

It is not, however, as a painter but as a novelist that Sedgwick is best known. *The Dull Miss Archinard* (1898), a half-serious venture on Sedgwick's part, became a popular success and gave Sedgwick the impetus to continue writing stories about an existence devoid of emotions and barely touched by the daily vicissitudes of life.

Sedgwick married Basil de Sélincourt, an English essayist, in 1908. Except for the World War I years, when she and her husband worked in France as hospital volunteers, Sedgwick conducted her affairs from her home near the Cotswolds. She cultivated the image of the genteel lady of letters who tended her rosebushes, served tea to the prime minister's wife, and wrote pleasant fiction, and who was equally conversant with fashionable ladies and radical writers. The de Sélincourt ''salon'' admitted aristocrats, prominent politicians, and literary notables. Most of Sedgwick's ''liberal thinking'' and social consciousness was, however, something of a pose, common among the genteel class of her era and more the expression of sentimental idealism than real commitment.

In 1931 Sedgwick was elected to the (American) National Institute of Arts and Letters, having written 17 novels, two collections of short stories, and a rather charming account of the reminiscences of a friend, *A Childhood in Brittany Eighty Years Ago* (1919). She died in 1935 after a lengthy paralytic illness.

Tante (1911) was Sedgwick's most successful novel measured by American sales, but *The Little French Girl* (1924) is artistically better. Though as is characteristic of Sedgwick's fiction, the precocious child of the latter book is a little too precocious, the sensitive man a little too sensitive, and the mysterious lady a little too mysterious. Yet Sedgwick plays out her theme of the tensions created by cultural differences well, and gives the characters some fullness of personality missing in her other books. Also attractive is the juxtaposition of the vitality of the little French girl's promiscuous mother to the insipidness of the child's virginial friend, Toppie. The apparently selfless and saintly Toppie emerges as the character whose selflessness has been an effective cover for a fundamental egocentricity and martyr-complex that threatens to harm not only herself but others. Toppie is an example of Sedgwick's best efforts at irony and perceptive characterization.

Sedgwick's female characters are interesting combinations of conventionality and modernism. Generally the positive heroines are man-and-marriage (but not maternity) oriented. Yet, like Gillian in *The Old Countess* (1927) they reveal an independence of spirit, thought, and emotional reaction that makes the reader wish Sedgwick had devoted more time to character and less to plot.

As novels of manners, Sedgwick's novels are accurate and thorough representations of the social customs and attitudes of the cultures they analyze, but she never quite manages a sustained psychological realism. Invariably, Sedgwick is carried away by romantic plots, idealism, and the social *mise en scene*.

OTHER WORKS: *The Confounding of Camelia* (1899). *The Rescue* (1902). *Paths of Judgment* (1904). *The Shadow of Life* (1906). *A Fountain Sealed* (English title, *Valerie Upton*, 1907). *Annabel Channice* (1908). *Franklin Winslow Kane* (1910). *The Nest* (1912). *Short Stories* (1913). *The Encounter* (1914). *The Third Window* (1920). *Christmas Roses* (English title, *Autumn Crocuses*, 1920). *Christmas Roses, and Other Stories* (1920). *Adrienne Toner* (1921). *The Nest, and Other Stories* (1926). *Dark Hester* (1929). *Phillippa* (1930).

BIBLIOGRAPHY: de Sélincourt, B., ed., *Anne Douglas Sedgwick: A Portrait in Letters* (1936). Overton, G., *The Women Who Make Our Novels* (1928). Overton, G., *An Hour of the American Novel* (1929). Quinn, A. H., *American Fiction* (1936). Swanson, G., ''The Novels of Anne Douglas Sedgwick'' (dissertation, 1956).
    Reference works: *NAW*.

—PATRICIA LEE YONGUE

SEDGWICK, Catharine Maria

Born 28 December 1789, Stockbridge, Massachusetts; **died** 31 July 1867, West Roxbury, Massachusetts
Wrote under: Miss Sedgwick
Daughter of Theodore and Pamela Dwight Sedgwick

Catharine Maria Sedgwick's father was from a family of New England farmers and tavern keepers. He served in both houses of Congress and as Massachusetts Supreme Court chief justice. Her mother belonged to one of the wealthiest colonial families. Because she was sickly, her seven surviving children were raised by a black servant, Elizabeth Freeman, whom they called ''Mumbet.''

Education was an important part of the Sedgwicks' daily life. All the children were required to read Hume, Butler, Shakespeare, and Cervantes. Sedgwick attended the local grammar school at Stockbridge and was sent to Mrs. Bell's School in Albany and Payne's Finishing School in Boston. She later commented that the greatest influence on our characters is our childhood home.

Shortly before her father's death in 1813 he unexpectedly confided his liberal religious beliefs to a close friend, the Unitarian minister William Ellery Channing. At this time, Sedgwick began to express in her journals and letters her own disapproval of Calvinism, the predominant religion of her Berkshire community. Several years later she joined the Unitarian church in New York. Her brothers Theodore and Henry, both noted lawyers and advocates of social reform, also joined the Unitarian church, but other of her relatives objected to Sedgwick's conversion. An aunt told her, ''Come and see me as often as you can, dear, for you know, after this world, we shall never meet again.''

In 1822 Sedgwick began to write a small pamphlet protesting religious intolerance. This work evolved into a full-length novel entitled *A New England Tale*, which was published anonymously that year. The book is set in the New England countryside, and includes characters who speak in the local dialects. It is the story of a virtuous orphan girl, Jane Elton, who is reduced to extreme poverty. The heroine is mistreated by ostensibly pious relatives until she marries a Quaker gentleman and lives happily ever after. The book exposes the hypocrisy of certain church officials, and includes subplots concerning corrupt lawyers, dueling, and gambling. It was an immediate success. At that time, most books read in the U.S. were British imports or American imitations of British works. *A New England Tale* was recognized as one of the first novels to include authentic American settings, situations, and characters and was soon a bestseller on both sides of the Atlantic.

With the publication of her second novel, *Redwood* (1824), Sedgwick became as popular as her contemporaries Cooper and Irving. *Redwood* was translated into German, Swedish, Italian, and French. The novel is about the marriage of a Southern gentleman to the daughter of a Vermont farmer. It also has a subplot involving the Shaker sect and a character study of a strong, outspoken New England spinster.

After her third novel, *Hope Leslie* (1827) was published, Sedgwick became the most famous American woman writer of her day. Sedgwick's own mother had nearly been a victim in a Native American raid, and one of the family ancestors had married a Native American. The book contains lengthy discussions of Mohawk customs and colonial history. It is the story of three American women: Faith Leslie, who is captured by Native Americans, marries into the tribe, and adopts its way of life; her sister Hope, who is pursued by a villainous English admiral until his ship sinks in Boston harbor; and Madawisca, a Native American woman who saves Hope's fiancé when Mohawks attack him, and loses her arm in the process. *Hope Leslie* was hailed by critics as an American masterpiece.

Sedgwick's next novel, *Clarence* (1830), discusses fashionable New York society. *The Linwoods* (1835) is a historical romance set during the Revolutionary War. Sedgwick's last novel, *Married or Single?* (1857) was designed, in her words, "to lessen the stigma placed on the term 'old maid.'"

Sedgwick, who never married, divided her time among the Sedgwick family homes in Stockbridge, Lenox, and New York City. She also toured Europe. Her tea parties were attended by Cooper, Hawthorne, Bryant, Emerson, and Melville. Sedgwick kept a journal for most of her life; it describes her spiritual quest, her travels, and her daily activities. She was an active social reformer: she founded the Society for the Aid and Relief of Poor Women and organized the first free school in New York, primarily for Irish immigrant children.

During the second half of her career, Sedgwick became famous as the author of didactic stories intended for children and working class people. She hoped to convince her readers of the importance of education, democracy, and a close-knit family life. She believed that in America social mobility was largely determined by manners. Her most famous didactic novels were the trilogy consisting of *Home* (1835), *The Poor Rich Man and the Rich Poor Man* (1836), and *Live and Let Live* (1837). These books went through 15, 16, and 12 editions respectively.

Sedgwick lived to the age of seventy-eight and was buried next to her nurse Mumbet in Stockbridge. Her contemporary

Hawthorne called Sedgwick "our most truthful novelist." Her finely crafted writing is more direct than the embellished style of most novels of her time. She was one of the creators of the American literary tradition, and one of the first American novelists to achieve international popularity.

OTHER WORKS: *Letters from Abroad to Kindred at Home* (1841). *The Boy of Mount Rhigi* (1848). *Memoir of Joseph Curtis* (1858).

BIBLIOGRAPHY: Buell, L., *New England Literary Culture: From Revolutionary Through Renaissance* (1986). Dewey, M., ed., *The Life and Letters of Catharine Maria Sedgwick* (1871). Foster, E. H., *Catharine Maria Sedwick* (1971). Kelley, M., *Private Women, Public Stage* (1984). Kolodny, A., *The Land Before Her: Fantasy and Experience of the American Frontiers, 1630-1860* (1984).

Reference works: *NAW* (1971). *Oxford Companion to Women Writing in the United States* (1995).

—JANE GILES

SEDGWICK, Susan (Anne Livingston) Ridley

Born circa 1789; **died** 20 January 1867, Stockbridge, Massachusetts
Daughter of Matthew and Catharine Livingston Ridley; **married** Theodore Sedgwick, 1808

Susan Ridley Sedgwick, whose grandfather was Governor William Livingston of New Jersey, is said to have spent three or four years of her youth "on our frontier, living partly in a fort with General Harrison, afterward President of the United States." Sent back to the East Coast to be educated, she first met Catharine Maria Sedgwick, later her sister-in-law and a successful novelist, at boarding school. After her marriage to Theodore Sedgwick, Catharine's brother, the couple lived for several years in Albany, New York, where Theodore practiced law. Theodore's ill health caused him to retire to the family home in Stockbridge, Massachusetts.

The Morals of Pleasure (1829), written for children, is a collection of didactic stories reflecting the life and values of the genteel and counseling tolerance for the faults of others, "patient diligence and virtuous perseverance," and "courtesy and gentleness of deportment, to which public schools are, in general, so unfriendly." The dialogue is clumsy: in "Twelfth Night," the mother says, "I am really sorry that you should both have forgotten yourselves so far, as to suffer mere general reflections to run into personalities." Sedgwick does, however, attempt effects to show she was not unconscious of style. Almost every story contains an episode in which music plays an important part, and one of Sedgwick's favorite devices is to slip from prose to poetry during those episodes.

Like the short stories of *The Morals of Pleasure* and *The Children's Week* (1830), Sedgwick's novels are written for a young audience. *The Young Emigrants* (1836), the story of a New York family resettling in Ohio in the late 18th century, is, like all of Sedgwick's fiction, sentimental and didactic. It is important, however, as one of the earliest examples of nonreligious fiction for American children.

Theodore Sedgwick is known to have encouraged his sister Catharine's writing. Though contemporaries describe Susan Ridley Sedgwick as a woman of considerable personal charm and intellectual achievement, no record of similar encouragement for her own writing exists.

OTHER WORKS: *Allen Prescott; or, The Fortunes of a New England Boy* (1834). *Alida; or, Miscellaneous Sketches of Incidents During the Late American War* (1841). *Alida; or, Town and Country* (1844). *The Seven Brothers of Wyoming; or, The Brigands of the Revolution* (1850). *Walter Thornley; or, A Peep at the Past* (1859).

BIBLIOGRAPHY: Buell, L. *New England Literary Culture: From Revolution to Renaissance* (1986). Walsh, M. M., *Catharine Maria Sedgwick* (1937).
Reference works: *DAB* (article on Theodore Sedgwick). *Twentieth Century Biographical Dictionary of Notable Americans* (1904).

—KATHARYN F. CRABBE

SEELEY, Mabel

Born 25 March 1903, Herman, Minnesota; **died** 9 June 1991
Daughter of Jacob and Alma Thompson Hodnefield; **married** Kenneth Seeley, 1926; Henry S. Ross, 1956

Mabel Seeley was raised in Minnesota, Illinois, and Wisconsin in a family of storytellers. She worked in Chicago as an advertising copywriter after she obtained her B.A. at the University of Minnesota.

Seeley's nine novels, seven of which fall into the "Had I But Known" subgenre of detective fiction, showcase Midwesterners who are at once regional stereotypes and highly individual characters. In her detective novels, Seeley's slow-talking Norwegian-Americans, mercurial French-Canadians, and ironic heroines all contribute to the sense of the regionally familiar that Seeley consciously works to establish, as she shows Midwesterners at routine jobs in grain elevators (*The Whispering Cup*, 1940) and small-town hospitals (*The Beckoning Door*, 1950), between jobs in seedy rooming houses (*The Listening House*, 1938), and out of their element in Wyoming (*Eleven Came Back*, 1943) and Georgia (*The Whistling Shadow*, 1954). This identification with a specific geographic region and its heritage paves the way for the

special brand of horror and suspense that Seeley develops in her stories of ordinary people caught up in extraordinary circumstances.

The background against which Seeley casts her crimes is solidly middle class, and the predominant work ethic colors the manner in which Seeley's money-oriented crimes are viewed: criminals are those who take economic power from others, while positively viewed characters are those who either work to regain what was theirs or acquire additional property or status. Seeley includes people under proprietary claims, so that murders with economic implications originate in dominating love that turns into jealous and possessive obsession. This money-love nexus can be viewed positively (as when the heroine gets man and money in *The Listening House*) or negatively (as when the villain loses girl and money in *The Beckoning Door*). In the well-ordered, familiar world of Seeley's detective fiction, crime and murder are intrusions which let themselves be felt in the economic and romantic inversions which they effect.

The interlocked themes of love and money run strongly through Seeley's two nondetective novels, the well-received *Woman of Property* (1947) and the thought-provoking *The Stranger Beside Me* (1951). Unlike the seven mysteries, these novels rely on third person narration, and in them Seeley portrays particularly sensitive women who are very different from her wisecracking detective fiction heroines. For Frieda in *Woman of Property* and Christine in *The Stranger Beside Me*, economic success does not go hand in hand with success in marriage. Both novels present sexual incompatibility, men who are not particularly successful at their work, families marred by psychic if not physical abuse, and women who strive for success in what is very obviously a man's world. It is a far cry from the world of Seeley's detective fiction, where the clever woman solves crimes as she falls in love with a man who considerately encourages her in her work.

OTHER WORKS: *The Crying Sisters* (1939). *The Chuckling Fingers* (1941).

BIBLIOGRAPHY: Barzun, J. and W. H. Taylor, eds., *A Catalogue of Crime* (1972). Haycraft, H., ed., *The Art of the Mystery Story* (1946). Haycraft, H., *Murder for Pleasure: The Life and Times of the Detective Story* (1941). Slung, M. B., *Crime on Her Mind* (1975). Symons, J., *Mortal Consequences* (1972).
Reference works: *American Novelists of Today* (1951). *Encyclopedia Mysteriosa* (1994). *TCAS*.

—SUSAN L. CLARK

SEID, Ruth

Born 1 July 1913, Brooklyn, New York; **died** 3 April 1995
Wrote under: Jo Sinclair
Daughter of Nathan and Ida Kravesky Seid

The third daughter and fifth child of Jewish immigrants from Russia, Ruth Seid was born in Brooklyn and the family moved to

Cleveland when she was three. Growing up as a Jewish working-class lesbian in a society that was anti-Semitic, homophobic, and hostile to values not perceived as middle class, Seid devoted her output as a writer to the battle against prejudice and to the reclamation of those whose lives have been crippled by the role of outsider. After graduation from a vocational high school in 1930, she worked in factories and offices, as a ghostwriter and a trade magazine editor, and with the WPA (1936-41) and the American Red Cross (1942-46).

In the mid to late 1930s, she submitted stories to a wide range of political and general interest magazines. *Esquire*, in 1938, was the first to pay for a short story by ''Jo Sinclair.'' Other stories, articles, and poems appeared soon after, and a number have been anthologized. One of her best short works, ''Red Necktie'' (*Common Ground*, Spring 1941), describes the meeting of an elderly, fearful Jewish immigrant with an equally old but cheerful black man, revealing the essential humanity that transcends cultural barriers. Seid also aired a number of radio plays throughout the 1940s; a stage play *The Long Moment* (1951), about a black musician contemplating passing for white to get work, had an eight-week run in Cleveland. Her earlier experiences with the WPA and the American Red Cross were significant influences on her writing. Many of her Red Cross stories are about donating blood, a practical contribution to the war effort that also symbolized for the breaking down of ghetto walls. Donating blood is a central image near the end of the Harper Prize novel *Wasteland* (1946) in which ''John Brown'' learns to accept himself as Jake Braunowitz, an assimilated American Jew, through the help of his strong, caring sister who has learned to accept herself as a lesbian. Seid concentrates on the psychological manifestations of identity, the corroding effects of guilt and shame, and the bitter, twisted family relationships that result. *Wasteland*, which pioneered the use of psychotherapy as a narrative device, is also remarkable both for its focus on a Jewish family at a time when anti-Semitism was peaking in America, and in its presentation, possibly for the first time in 20th century American fiction, of a lesbian as a positive role model.

Sing at My Wake (1951) also details the psychological causes of alienation and loneliness. Catherine Ganly, deeply wounded by her insecure childhood, escapes as a teenager into a romantic infatuation, only to find herself trapped in a shotgun marriage with a man as immature as herself. Divorce frees Cathy to develop a successful career as a journalist, but only when she realizes the threat she poses to the development of her son does she recognize that she remains imprisoned emotionally by her refusal to admit the imperfections of human love.

The Changelings (1955) portrays the destructive effects of racial prejudice on the lives of the immigrant residents of a single street in a large Ohio city. Their fear at the prospect of integration triggers waves of anger and violence that overwhelm the community. The title refers to the children of these immigrants and of the black families, who want to end bigotry and ''leave behind the narrow corner of our frightened elders.'' Of these the best realized is Judith Vincent, the thirteen-year-old gang leader who comes to understand the common humanity of all groups and who takes the first steps toward friendship and justice.

The heroine of *Anna Teller* (1961) is a strong, proud, competent woman who survived the Nazi invasion of Hungary and fought in the uprising against the Russians. At 74, she is relegated to the status of ineffectual dependence in her son's American home. Anna's insistence on her right to prove her usefulness inspires her grandson and two young friends to overcome their own fears, but it creates intolerable friction with her son. Viewed from a number of perspectives that reveal both her strengths and her imperfections, Anna Teller emerges as a compelling and complex personality.

In 1969 Seid completed the still-unpublished *Approach to the Meaning*, dedicated to her sister Fannie, the author's constant emotional and financial supporter. The novel depicts a fragmented woman who must discover herself in order to save her adopted daughter from imitating her own wasted life. Seid herself was saved from the emotional wastelands of her youth when she met Helen Buchman in 1938. Although Buchman was married with two children, Seid lived in her household for almost 30 years, including seven years with Helen's widower. The Feminist Press launched a series of women's autobiographies with a reprinting of Seid's *The Seasons: Death and Transfiguration* (1972, 1993), which describes the author's attempt to keep her own creative death at bay when Helen, her muse and best editor died. In 1973, Joan Soffer, who began their correspondence with a fan letter after *Wasteland*, asked Seid to move in with her in Jenkintown, Pennsylvania. There Seid continued gardening and writing in her lifelong attempt to save walking wastelands with her changeling language. She died in April 1995.

Whether dealing with psychoanalysis or sexual maladjustment, racial tension or the treatment of the elderly, Seid was been far ahead of her contemporaries. Many of her novels deal with Jews, but Seid makes them emblematic of all who feel themselves excluded from the mainstream of American life. Of special value is the attention she gives to women in situations in which the man's problem has usually been emphasized. Seid's narrative skill and rich characterization, her sensitivity, and the objective clarity of her vision more than compensate for the wordiness of her fiction.

BIBLIOGRAPHY: Liptzin, S., *The Jew in American Literature* (1966). Sandberg, E., ''Jo Sinclair: Toward a Critical Biography'' (unpublished dissertation, 1985).

Reference works: *American Novelists of Today* (1951). *CA* (1969). *Contemporary Novelists* (1986). *DLB* (1984). *Oxford Companion to Women's Writing in the United States* (1995). *TCA* (1951).

Other references: *NR* (10 June 1946). *NYT* (25 Sept. 1955). *SR* (20 Aug. 1960).

—CAROL SCHOEN AND ELISABETH SANDBURG

SEIFERT, Elizabeth

Born 19 June 1897, Washington, Missouri; **died** June 1983
Also writes under: Ellen Ashley
Daughter of Richard C. and Anna Sanford Seifert; **married** John Gasparotti, 1920; **children:** four

Elizabeth Seifert was educated in St. Louis; she received a B.A. in 1918 from Washington University and attended the university's medical school for 18 months. She left, she has explained, because the university refused to grant a medical degree to a woman. Seifert did take courses in anatomy, physiology, and dietetics and later used her knowledge of medical subjects in her novels. When her husband, wounded in WWI, became totally disabled in the 1930s, she needed to earn money to support her husband and four children. Again she pursued her interest in medicine. As a clinical secretary in a small hospital, she took case histories and monitored the activities of both the patients and the staff.

A self-described "wife, housewife, and mother who writes," Seifert began a new career at age forty when *Young Doctor Galahad* won the 1938 Dodd, Mead–Redbook Magazine $10,000 prize for a first novel. Since this prominent beginning, Dodd, Mead has published 81 of her novels, some of which have been translated into 17 languages. Until a heart attack in the early 1980s, which prevented her from doing the research necessary for a new book, she had completed an average of two books a year throughout her career.

Almost all Seifert's novels are medical romances. Using her knowledge of medicine, which she continued to update by reading medical journals, she creates an air of authenticity in her medical scenes. She is, however, more interested in personal relationships, and the hospital environment with its life and death crises provides the dramatic stage for personal and professional dilemmas doctors face. Although Seifert's novels tend to follow the formula which she adopted from George M. Cohan ("You have a man, you get him up a tree, you throw rocks at him, you get him down again"), her novels about women doctors are of special interest. These usually emphasize the special conflicts faced by a woman doctor who must not only prove she can succeed in medicine, but who must also juggle her role as woman and as doctor. For such a woman, romance is threatening: she may be asked to surrender her career if she accepts a marriage proposal. Eventually, Seifert's women doctors win both professional status and romantic love.

In *Girl Intern* (1944) Chris (Christine) Metcalfe is repeatedly asked why a pretty girl would try to become a doctor when women are so emotionally and physically unsuited for such a grueling profession. After all, Chris faints when a patient's father pulls a gun on her in the operating room, she weeps and becomes unable to close the incision when a woman dies during a Caesarean section, and she becomes hysterical when rumors accuse her of sexual misconduct. In the end, however, she proves her ability to handle emergencies and to be both a female and a doctor. Even the chief of staff finally relents and admits his love for her. *The Story of Andrea Fields* (1950) and *Miss Doctor* (1951) develop similar themes of the isolation of the professional woman from other women and her fears about accepting a man's love.

Unlike her other novels, which stop when the woman doctor successfully wins the man who had previously fought her career, *When Doctors Marry* (1960) explores the special complications caused by the marriage of two doctors. Even the birth of her child does not deter the heroine from her practice of medicine. Though problems arise, this novel shows one woman combining her roles as wife, mother, and professional.

Seifert has asserted she would not consider writing about failure, and at least in the world of her medical romances, the women doctors eventually solve their dilemmas. They are depicted as emotional and romantic, but Seifert's women doctors remain true to their profession and seek ways to combine marriage and career. Becoming a doctor is not easy for these women: they encounter severe discrimination, but they do not surrender their goals.

Seifert's writing began as a means of self-expression and amusement for a woman in a small town with an invalid husband and four small children. Eventually her writing provided the means of support for her family. When asked how she would like her work to be remembered, she quickly answered, "It saved the life of me and my family."

OTHER WORKS: *A Great Day* (1939). *Hillbilly Doctor* (1940). *Thus Doctor Mallory* (1940). *Bright Scalpel* (1941). *Army Doctor* (1942). *Doctor Bill* (1942). *Surgeon in Charge* (1942). *Bright Banners* (1943). *A Certain Doctor French* (1943). *Girl in Overalls: A Novel of Women in Defense Today* (as Ellen Ashley, 1943). *Doctor Ellison's Decision* (1944). *Doctor Woodward's Ambition* (1945). *Orchard Hill* (1945). *Dusty Spring* (1946). *Old Doc* (1946). *So Young, So Fair* (1947). *Take Three Doctors* (1947). *The Glass and the Trumpet* (1948). *Hospital Zone* (1948). *The Bright Coin* (1949). *Homecoming* (1950). *Doctor of Mercy* (1951). *The Doctor Takes a Wife* (1952). *The Strange Loyalty of Dr. Carlisle* (1952). *The Doctor Disagrees* (1953). *Lucinda Marries the Doctor* (1953). *Doctor at the Crossroads* (1954). *Marriage for Three* (1954). *Challenge for Dr. Mays* (1955). *A Doctor in the Family* (1955). *A Call for Dr. Barton* (1956). *A Doctor for Blue Jay Cove* (1956). *The Doctor's Husband* (1957). *Substitute Doctor* (1957). *Love Calls the Doctor* (1958). *The New Doctor* (1958). *Doctor on Trial* (1959). *Home-town Doctor* (1959). *The Doctor's Bride* (1960). *Doctors on Parade* (including *The Doctor Takes a Wife*, *The Doctor Disagrees*, and *Lucinda Marries the Doctor*, 1960). *Dr. Jeremy's Wife* (1961). *The Doctor Makes a Choice* (1961). *The Doctor's Strange Secret* (1962). *The Honor of Dr. Shelton* (1962). *Dr. Scott, Surgeon on Call* (1963). *Legacy for a Doctor* (1963). *A Doctor Comes to Bayard* (1964). *Katie's Young Doctor* (1964). *Doctor Samaritan* (1965). *Ordeal of Three Doctors* (1965). *Hegerty, M.D.* (1966). *Pay the Doctor* (1966). *Doctor With a Mission* (1967). *The Rival Doctors* (1967). *The Doctor's Confession* (1968). *To Wed a Doctor* (1968). *Bachelor Doctor* (1969). *For Love of a Doctor* (1969). *Doctor's Kingdom* (1970). *The Doctor's Two Lives* (1970). *Doctor in Judgment* (1971). *The Doctor's Second Love* (1971). *Doctor's Destiny* (1972). *The*

Doctor's Private Life (1972). *The Doctor's Reputation* (1972). *The Two Faces of Doctor Collier* (1973). *Doctor in Love* (1974). *The Doctor's Daughter* (1974). *Four Doctors, Four Wives* (1975). *The Doctor's Desperate Hour* (1976). *Two Doctors and a Girl* (1976). *Doctor Tuck* (1977). *The Doctors on Eden Place* (1977). *The Doctors Were Brothers* (1978). *Rebel Doctor* (1978). *The Doctor's Promise* (1979). *The Problems of Dr. A* (1979).

BIBLIOGRAPHY: Seifert, E., in *Writer* (Aug. 1945, Oct. 1961).
Reference works: *American Novelists of Today* (1951). *CA* (1967). *CB* (1951).
Other references: Columbia *Daily Tribune* (16 April 1978).

—JEAN CARWILE MASTELLER

SEMPLE, Ellen Churchill

Born 8 January 1863, Louisville, Kentucky; **died** 11 May 1932, West Palm Beach, Florida
Daughter of Alexander and Emerine Price Semple

Ellen Churchill Semple was the daughter of a prosperous businessman. In 1882 Semple graduated from Vassar College with a B.A. in history. She then taught in a private school in Louisville, and began work on her masters degree in history (Vassar, 1891). During this time, she came into contact with the writings of the renowned geographer Friedrich Ratzel, who coined the word "anthropogeography" to designate the study of the effect of the natural landscape on society. In 1891 Semple went to Leipzig to study with Ratzel. Although women could not matriculate at Leipzig, Semple was permitted to listen to Ratzel's lectures from outside the open classroom door.

In "The Anglo-Saxons of the Kentucky Mountains" (*Geographic Journal*, 1901), Semple adds to a description of life in the isolated mountains of eastern Kentucky explanations of the presumed influence of the natural environment on the development of a way of life. She documents the scarcity of transportation alternatives, and concludes nature is largely responsible. This article displays a preoccupation with the lives of women, and this interest is less pronounced in Semple's other articles and books, most of which are heavily dependent on archival sources and lack the intimate involvement of the researcher with her subjects.

Semple's first book, *American History and Its Geographic Conditions* (1903), explains the pattern of settlement and the political power of the U.S. as influenced by topographic features. The book was widely adopted as a textbook, and Semple became a geographer in demand. In 1906 she became a visiting lecturer at the newly established department of geography at the University of Chicago; she lectured there nearly every other year until 1924.

Influences of Geographic Environment (1911) is a tribute to Ratzel. Initially intended as a translation of Ratzel's *Anthropo-Geographie*, the book was expanded to include documentation of Ratzel's sometimes unsubstantiated claims.

During World War I, Semple lectured on the geography of the Italian front to officers and participated in a special study of the Mediterranean region and Mesopotamia. After the war, she resumed her teaching at the University of Chicago and later at Clark University. Semple was the first geographer solicited for that school. She also gave lectures and taught courses at other universities in both the U.S. and Europe.

Semple's contemporary recognition included election as president of the Association of American Geographers in 1921; medals presented by the American Geographical Society and the Geographic Society of Chicago; and honorary degrees, included one from the University of Kentucky.

Semple's sweeping assertions, in all her works, of the dominant influence of nature, won her the epithet "environmental determinist" and subjected her works to substantial criticism. Semple's eloquence, enthusiasm, and thorough method, however, led to her being highly regarded and influential in the intellectual development of other geographers.

OTHER WORKS: *Geography of the Mediterranean Region* (1931).

BIBLIOGRAPHY: Bronson, J. A. C., *Ellen Semple: Contributions to the History of American Geography* (dissertation, 1974). *Ellen Churchill Semple Papers* (Library of Congress archives, 1900-1932).
Other references: *Annals of the Association of American Geographers* (1933). *Geographical Review* (1932). *Journal of Geography* (1932). *Professional Geographer* (1974). *Science* (1932).

—SUSAN R. BROOKER-GROSS

SEREDY, Kate

Born 10 November 1896, Budapest, Hungary; **died** 7 March 1975, Montgomery, New York
Daughter of Louis P. and Anna Irany Seredy

Kate Seredy was the daughter of a well-known Hungarian teacher and storyteller. She attended the Academy of Art in Budapest for six years, receiving an art teacher's diploma. During World War I, she served for two years as a nurse in frontline hospitals, an experience which left her ill in body and spirit and caused her to become a confirmed pacifist. In 1922 Seredy emigrated to the U.S., where she earned a living by illustrating lampshades, greeting cards, and sheet music, moving on gradually to fashion design and magazine and book illustration. Seredy illustrated books by other writers—including Carol Ryrie Brink's Newbery Medal-winning *Caddie Woodlawn*—as well as her own.

Seredy's most highly acclaimed works rose out of her memories of her Hungarian childhood and the stories her father told her. When Seredy was nine years old, she accompanied her father on a trip to the countryside, where they studied peasant art and life.

The Good Master (1935), Seredy's first and most popular book, is the humorous, episodic story of wild, spoiled, motherless Cousin Kate from Budapest (Seredy herself), who goes to live with her uncle, called "the Good Master" for his wise and gentle ways, his wife, and son, Jancsi, on their horse ranch on the Hungarian plains. Kate gets caught up in the pleasures and responsibilities of farm life, and she calms down and develops a sounder set of values.

A sequel, the more serious *The Singing Tree* (1939), takes Kate through World War I, when Jancsi's father must join the army and the boy is left in charge of the ranch, which becomes a refuge for family, neighbors, and war orphans.

The White Stag (1937) is a stirring retelling of the legendary founding of Hungary. The twins, Magyar and Hunor, Hunor's son Bendeguz, and his son Attila, lead their tribes from their ancient home in Asia steadily westward until they reach their promised land along the Danube. This spirited and rhythmical account of wars and hardships, the drama of the conquest heightened by bold, sweeping drawings, was awarded the John Newbery Medal in 1938.

By contrast with these strongly conceived books, Seredy's novels with American settings seem contrived, shallow, and dated. The most convincing of them, with its sense of history and closeness to nature, is the earliest, *Listening* (1936), the story of the old Dutch colonial house in the Ramapo Mountains of New Jersey in which Seredy lived for a time.

While such values as love of family, respect for authority and the aged, pleasure in hard work, and faith in God reappear throughout Seredy's writings, overriding themes involve confidence in the ultimate goodness of human beings and a deep affection for the soil. The greatest evil is war, a senseless business which hurts most the simple people who are never responsible for bringing it about. Descriptive passages are highly poetic and are particularly rich in visual imagery. Seredy writes with an artist's eye, drawing details from nature and folk life and art. Although didacticism and sentimentality sometimes get in the way of the narrative, the best of Seredy's writing has auditory and visual qualities which draw readers in and carry them along.

OTHER WORKS: *A Tree for Peter* (1941). *The Open Gate* (1943). *The Chestry Oak* (1948). *Gypsy* (1952). *Philomena* (1955). *The Tenement Tree* (1959). *A Brand-New Uncle* (1961). *Lazy Tinka* (1962).

BIBLIOGRAPHY: Reference works: *CB* (1940). *Junior Book of Authors* (1951). *Newbery Medal Books: 1922-1955* (1955). *SAA* (1971).

Other references: *Elementary English* (1968). *Horn Book* (1968).

—ALETHEA K. HELBIG

SETON, Anya

Born 1904, New York, New York; died November 1990, Greenwich, Connecticut
Daughter of Ernest T. and Grace Gallatin Seton; married twice; secondly to Hamilton Chase, circa 1934; children: three

Anya Seton's father was a nature writer and cofounder of the Boy Scouts; her mother was a feminist, explorer, and writer. Seton was educated in England, France, and the U.S. primarily by private tutors, although she also attended Oxford University. She married and had three children, two from her first marriage, and one from her second marriage to Hamilton Chase. She died of heart failure in November 1990 in Greenwich, Connecticut.

She wrote 13 novels, all historical, although her preferred term is "biographical." The variety of periods depicted is remarkable, but the settings are generally either British or American. All tell exciting stories, usually from the point of view of a female protagonist. The heroines of the fictionalized biographies are related in some way to men who made history. *My Theodosia* (1941), Seton's first novel and the story of Aaron Burr's only child, dramatizes an obsessive, almost unnatural relationship between father and daughter. *Katherine* (1954) sympathetically recreates the life of Katherine Swynford, mistress and then wife of John of Gaunt and sister-in-law of Geoffrey Chaucer. *The Winthrop Woman* (1958) centers on Elizabeth Fones Winthrop, niece and daughter-in-law of Jonathan Winthrop, a settler with him of the Massachusetts Bay Colony but a rebel against harsh Puritan rule. *Devil Water* (1962) studies Jenny Radcliffe, daughter of an English Jacobite nobleman who was executed for his participation in the rebellions of 1715 and 1745; her conversion to participation in his cause and her life in England and in Virginia are recreated.

Among the novels not centered on actual events is Seton's best-known work, *Dragonwyck* (1944). Set among Dutch patroons on the Hudson River in the mid-19th century, it contains an effective portrait of a Gothic villain and a heroine who is his innocent accomplice, for her passion and ambition have unconsciously helped cause his crimes. *The Turquoise* (1946), set in late 19th-century New Mexico and New York, shows its destitute heroine's rise to the top of New York society, inadvertently causing a catastrophe. Her repentance and later life of contrition are movingly depicted. *The Hearth and the Eagle* (1948), set in 19th- and 20th-century Marblehead, with a flashback to the 17th century, contains another strong heroine whose passionate and impulsive behavior leads her to a series of disappointments, then to ultimate acceptance of values she had earlier rejected.

In the 1970s Seton's interest in the occult has led her to the theme of reincarnation. In *Green Darkness* (1972), contemporary characters redress evils occurring in 1552 to 1559. *Smouldering Fires* (1975), a mixture of popular psychology and the occult, depicts an ungainly high school girl who must, through hypnosis, relive the anguish of her Acadian ancestress in order to exorcise it and become a normal young woman.

The Mistletoe and the Sword (1955), set in Roman Britain, tells of the relationship between a Celtic girl and a Roman soldier, their initial enmity gradually being transformed to love. *Avalon* (1965), which moves through the British and Norse worlds of the late 10th century, follows the relationship of a Cornish girl and a French-English prince, whose lives are intertwined but who are always at cross-purposes. These two novels are unusual for Seton in that male and female protagonists are balanced against each other, both angles of vision being used about equally.

Foxfire (1950) is the only one of Seton's novels not clearly historical. It is set in Arizona in the 1930s and combines the common western myth of the fabulous lost mine with the motif of a Shangri-la.

Seton's female protagonists are passionate and ambitious. In their youthful romantic idealism, they often rush into relationships doomed to disaster. The novels generally end with the heroines recognizing their responsibility for their fates and either doing penance or making a new beginning. In the process, they become "strong to endure." The historical backgrounds in each novel are based on thorough research. Seton admitted, "I have a passion for facts, for dates and places. I love to recreate the past, and to do so with all the accuracy possible." For *The Winthrop Women*, for example, Seton spent two years reading about the real people on whom she planned to base her story and visiting the places they lived before beginning to write the novel.

Since Seton's death, many of her works have been reissued or republished and remain enormously popular with historical romance fans. Yet because of the age and popularity of her novels, her work is not easy to find. According to her readers, however, it is worth the hunt.

OTHER WORKS: *Washington Irving* (1960).

BIBLIOGRAPHY: Reference works: *CA* (Online, 1999).
    Other references: *NY* (6 Feb. 1946). *NYTBR* (16 March 1941, 16 Feb. 1958, 21 Nov. 1965). *SR* (9 Oct. 1954, 15 Feb. 1958, 3 March 1962).

—MARY JEAN DEMARR,
UPDATED BY CARRIE SNYDER

SETTLE, Mary Lee

Born 29 July 1918, Charleston, West Virginia
Daughter of Joseph E. and Rachel Tompkins Settle; **married** Rodney Weathersbee, 1939; Douglas Newton, 1946; William Littleton Tazewelt, 1978; **children:** Christopher

Although she draws heavily from memories of her Kentucky and West Virginia childhood for her important novel sequence, the Beulah Quintet, Mary Lee Settle defies the regional writer pigeonhole. *Blood Tie* (1977), for which she won the National Book Award in 1978, is set principally in Turkey. *Celebration* (1986) is set all over the world—London, Kurdistan, Africa, Hong

Kong, Virginia—settings reflecting Settle's 17 years of living and working abroad.

The Beulah Quintet, composed of *O Beulah Land* (1956), *Know-Nothing* (1960), *Prisons* (1973), *The Scapegoat* (1980), and *The Killing Ground* (1982), traces four centuries of family networks as they affect the development of what is now West Virginia. Charleston, Settle's birthplace, appears as the fictional town of Canona. The novels reflect Settle's mixed reactions to growing up in the South where, she wrote, children are taught to "ridicule the delicate qualities in ourselves and in others that might interfere with that hard, polite drifting acceptance. The punishment for choosing another path. . .is brutal and unconscious."

Although *The Love Eaters* (1954), *The Kiss of Kin* (1955), *The Clam Shell* (1971), and *Charley Bland* (1989, 1991) are usually considered apart from the quintet, all are set in or near Canona; the latter three include families familiar from the quintet. Settle has called *The Clam Shell* her one autobiographical novel; it is drawn from her years (1936-38) at Sweet Briar College.

Settle's characters, whatever their age, race, sexual preference, or national origin, are psychologically informed by their physical environments. In *Blood Tie*, Ariadne, a middle-aged American divorcee who is diving off the coast of Turkey, discovers a new world, both physical and psychic. "For once, Ariadne realized, I am not searching for someone else's words, only my own will do. Nothing is new in this kneeling in this place. It is the most ancient of homecomings, astonishing familiar water fields of light."

Much of Settle's work is distinctively visual, almost cinematic, although grounded in the psychological. She traces this concentration to her partial blindness, a result of a childhood bout with whooping cough that precipitated a premature eye-straightening operation: "I had consciously to develop a visual sense and that psychic awakening was to me like seeing for the first time." Much of Settle's work similarly echoes her own experiences, both obliquely and, as in *The Killing Ground*, rather slyly.

Settle's casts are often large. Some critics have complained she sometimes tempts the reader with an intriguing portrait, then fails to develop the character satisfactorily. Nevertheless, she has a remarkable eye for texture, for the interweaving of points of view to create transcendent meaning. Plus Deng, the physically imposing African priest who is the hero of *Celebration* appears first as an iconic figure. Later, however, we learn through a shift in the limited omniscient point of view that "he was the youngest of his father's children, a prince in his own tribe, a nigger in Washington, D.C., *ageeb* in Khartoum, nignog in London, and priest everywhere."

In the majority of her novels, Settle uses the omniscient point of view, not to imply a central authority, but to express the irony of discrepancies between various characters' worldviews, and to demonstrate their basic misunderstandings of each other, sometimes despite their best intentions. Her style is conventional only on its surface, profound and innovative in its final effect.

Settle's nonfiction includes *All the Braw Promises: Memoirs of Aircraft Woman Second Class 2146391* (1966), an account of experiences with the Women's Auxiliary of the Royal Air Force during World War II, and *The Scopes Trial: The State of Tennessee vs. John Thomas Scopes* (1972), an intense account of the famous "monkey trial," written for young adults. Over the years, she has supplemented her writing career by teaching, at Bard College in New York, and at the University of Virginia.

OTHER WORKS: *Fight Night on a Sweet Saturday* (1964). *The Story of Flight* (1967, juvenile). *Prisons* (1973); also published as *The Long Road to Paradise*, (1974). *Water World* (1984, juvenile). *The Search for Beulah Land: The Story Behind the Beulah Quintet* (1988). *Turkish Reflections: A Biography of a Place* (1991). *Beulah Quintet* (bound together, 1996). *Choices* (1995).

Contributor to several anthologies and collections, including: *The Best American Essays, 1988* (1988), *Encounters* (1989), *The Sound of Writing* (1991), *Maiden Voyages: Writings of Women Travelers* (1993), *Southern Excursions* (1997), *Bloodroot: Reflections on Place by Appalachian Women Writers* (1998).

Contributor to periodicals, including: *Paris Review, Southern Review, Travel & Leisure, Virginia Quarterly Review, Yale Review* and others.

BIBLIOGRAPHY: Brosi, G., *Contemporary Appalachian Writers* (1988). Flora, J. M., and R. Bain, eds., *Contemporary Fiction Writers of the South: A Bio-Bibliographical Sourcebook* (1993). Garrett, G. P., *Understanding Mary Lee Settle* (1988). Murrey, L. M., *Dream and Reality in Mary Lee Settle's Beulah Quintet* (1993). Pearce, W. M., "Lacunae of Forgetfulness and the Censorship of Memory: Reconstructing History in The Beulah Quintet" (thesis, 1997). Prenshaw, P. W., ed., *Women Writers of the Contemporary South* (1984, 1990). Rosenberg, B., *Mary Lee Settle's Beulah Quintet: The Price of Freedom* (1992).

Reference works: *CAAS* (1992). *CA* (1980). *CLC* (1981, 1990). *DLB* (1980). *Cyclopedia of World Authors, Two* (1989). *FC* (1990).

Other references: *Iron Mountain Review* (special issue, Spring 1991). *NYTBR* (Oct. 1998). *Washington College Magazine* (Winter 1988). *Mary Lee Settle Interview with Kay Bonetti* (audiocassette, 1982). *Tell It On the Mountain: Appalachian Women Writers* (audiocassette, 1997). *The Fiction of Mary Lee Settle* (video, 1990).

—LISA CARL

SEWALL, Harriet Winslow

Born 30 June 1819, Portland, Maine; **died** February 1889, Wellesley, Massachusetts
Daughter of Nathan and Comfort Hussey Winslow; **married** Charles Liszt, 1848 (died); Samuel E. Sewall, 1857

Harriet Winslow Sewall was raised in a traditional Quaker family, and the discussion of personal, social, and political responsibilities in Quaker doctrine deeply concerned her throughout her life.

The serious illness of Sewall's husband's forced him to depend on her for financial support when she was a young wife. By the time Sewall was thirty-seven, her mother, brother, both her sisters, and her husband had died. She remarried her sister's widower. Despite these personal losses, Sewall engaged in philanthropic work and was involved in the abolition and women's rights movements and in the promotion of the interests of labor.

Sewall compiled the *Letters of Lydia Maria Child* (1882). The letters were an inspiration to Sewall, and this collection revealed Child's determination, compassion, and dedication to abolitionism through the frankness of her personal correspondence. Eschewing any recognition for this work, Sewall would not have her name appear in the volume.

It was only after Sewall's death that a book of her poetry was published (*Poems*, 1889). In her more serious poems, Sewall considered the constant fears and doubts of the human condition but reaffirmed faith in human goodness through an appreciation of family, friends, nature, and a moral consciousness. The world-weary were sustained by loved ones in "Pessimist," while the "Optimist" realized that joy would follow sorrow in nature's cycle. In "Why Thus Longing," Sewall teaches that one can find fulfillment and happiness in one's lot through a Romantic reverence for nature. Characterized as a religious verse writer, Sewall extolled the richness of "moral treasures," acceptance of God's will, and perservering effort toward moral progress. In "To S.E.S.," Sewall celebrated the felicitous combination of faith and love in her husband. She wrote to him: "My hopes of what mankind may be / To loftier soarings are encouraged, / Belovéd, when I think of thee."

Sewall was most successful in capturing the "impulse of her own feeling." The poems written out of her own personal relationships were more freshly felt than her versification on other subjects. Her gentle tribute to her husband achieved a subtle meter and imaginative quality.

BIBLIOGRAPHY: Reference works: *Biographical Dictionary and Synopsis of Books Ancient and Modern* (1902). *CAL, A Dictionary of American Authors* (1905). *Famous Women of History* (1895). *NCAB*.

—ELIZABETH ROBERTS

SEWELL, Elizabeth

Born 19 March 1919, Coonoor, India
Daughter of Robert S. and Dorothy Dean Sewell; **married** Anthony Sirignano, 1971

Elizabeth Sewell's parents were English, and they sent her to England as a child to be educated. She received her B.A., M.A., and Ph.D. degrees at Newham College, Cambridge. Sewell became an American citizen in 1972 and has taught at several American colleges, including Fordham University, Hunter College and Notre Dame University. Her scholarship extends to literature, philosophy, religion, language theory, botany, and biology. In her writing, Sewell has concentrated upon theories and methods that attempt to integrate the sciences and the humanities.

The Structure of Poetry (1951), an inquiry into the stasis and dynamics of poetry, shows Sewell's early interest in ideas developed in later works. In *The Field of Nonsense* (1952), Sewell uses works of Lewis Carroll and Edward Lear to define ''nonsense'' as a carefully controlled world directed by reason and subject to its own laws, rather than a merely random reversal of ordinary experience. *The Orphic Voice* (1960) has gained Sewell recognition as an original and important voice in modern theory and criticism. Sewell claims that because of his having been in the worlds of the living and the dead, the figure of Orpheus has been used from ancient times to the present as a symbol of the combined creative forces of mind and body. Sewell supports her theory through detailed and convincing illustrations from the works of many poets, philosophers, and scientists.

In *The Human Metaphor* (1964), Sewell further investigates what she sees as the prevailing empirical method of western thought in the post-Cartesian world. Sewell acknowledges the importance of empiricism, but believes it leads to a split in the human mind and society when it excludes the validity of other modes of thought. Through examples from many major poets, Sewell develops a theory that the metaphoric properties of language can bring apparently divergent methods into meaningful synthesis.

In Sewell's first novel, *The Dividing of Time* (1951), her young heroine lives in two worlds at the same time: the drab world of the civil servant in wartime London and a realm of adventures in lands of fantasy. The two are interwoven, and the ''dividing'' actually leads to integration of the narrator's personality as she gradually loses her fears and comes to know herself.

Sewell's two later novels lack the imagination and intensity of the first. In *The Singular Hope* (1955), set in a school hospital for crippled children in England, the young heroine is also going through a process of increasing self-awareness, but the book remains rather flat and colorless. In *Now Bless Thyself* (1962), characters and action are never fully realized; they serve primarily as vehicles for political, aesthetic, and philosophical discussions.

In her two volumes of poetry, Sewell is especially effective in short lyrics such as ''The Oracle,'' ''Job,'' and ''Archangels in Winter,'' which testify to her fine eye for detail. Several of her longer poems such as ''The Great Darkness'' sustain a dramatic intensity. ''Dialogue,'' the opening poem of *Signs and Cities* (1968) is a fine expression of Sewell's attitude toward art and science; and the final poem of the volume, ''Achievement,'' makes a moving and affirmative statement of Sewell's philosophy of life.

OTHER WORKS: *Paul Valéry: The Mind in the Mirror* (1952). *Poems: 1974-1961* (1962

BIBLIOGRAPHY: Ladner, B., ''Elizabeth Sewell: Poetic Method as an Instrument of Thinking and Knowing'' (dissertation, 1970).
    Other references: *Nation* (4 Feb. 1961). *Soundings* (Summer 1972). *TLS* (17 Oct. 1951, 29 April 1955).

—ANNE R. NEWMAN

SEXTON, Anne

Born 2 November 1928, Newton, Massachusetts; **died** 4 October 1974, Weston, Massachusetts
Daughter of Ralph and Mary Staples Harvey; **married** Alfred M. Sexton II, 1948 (divorced); **children:** two daughters

Although Anne Sexton's childhood included winters with her beloved great-aunt at the spacious family residence in Weston, Massachusetts, as well as happy seaside summers in Maine, Sexton was a demanding, rebellious child who felt rejected by her upper-middle class parents. Her impulsive marriage in 1948 to Alfred Sexton weathered many years of crises before it ended in divorce in 1973. Sexton's sudden bouts of suicidal depression, which for several years necessitated separating her from her two small daughters, continued throughout her life, as did her psychiatric care in and out of mental hospitals. All of these problematic relationships form the basis of much of her poetry.

Discovering her poetic interests at age twenty-eight, this attractive housewife from the suburbs of Boston began studying under mentors such as Robert Lowell. Sexton taught at Boston University from 1970 until she took her life at the age of forty-five.

In *To Bedlam and Part Way Back* (1960), Sexton probed the intensely personal terrain of madness, guilt, and loss. As she undertakes her poetic journey from madness to partial sanity, her most frequent voice is that of the helpless, dependent child searching into the past for the lost parents and the disinherited self. Her two most famous *Bedlam* poems, ''You, Doctor Martin'' and ''Ringing the Bells,'' capture the helpless childishness of mental patients who are ''like bees caught in the wrong hive.'' ''Pushing their bones against the thrust / of cure,'' these ''foxy children'' are dependent on the godlike doctor of the ''oracular / eye,'' who oversees the protective order of their lives. However, the bell-ringing therapy shows that this order is only the regulated passivity of patients directed by the bell-lady's commands. Like the rows of moccasins they make—''waiting on the silent shelf''—the patients are the ''moving dead.'' *Bedlam* also contains numerous elegies to the beloved dead moving through the poet's memories.

In two remarkable mother-daughter poems, "The Double Image" and "Division of Parts," Sexton becomes a female Oedipus investigating the "appalling truths" of identity and guilt. While many readers objected to her subject matter, the raw power of the *Bedlam* poetry quickly established Sexton as a new and significant "confessional" poet.

In the Pulitzer Prize-winning *Live or Die* (1966), religious parallels tend to universalize the dilemma of the "mad" persona; thus in "For the Year of the Insane," Sexton tries to overcome the passivity which keeps her "locked in the wrong house" but fumbling for a fragmented prayer to Mary, the "tender physician" who could heal the spiritual sickness of the "unbeliever." A new voice of awareness and self-irony is also heard. In one of her best poems, "Flee on Your Donkey," Sexton realizes her madness has lost its "innocence." All the years of "dredging" dreams, "like an old woman with arthritic fingers, / carefully straining the water out," have only brought her back to the same "scene of the disordered senses," the "sad hotel" or mental institution from which she urges herself to flee. This book ends on an affirmative note: "I say *Live, Live* because of the sun, / the dream, the excitable gift."

Probably most notable are her poems on womanhood. In "Those Times...," Sexton remembers childhood humiliations and how she "hid in the closet" waiting "among shoes / I was sure to outgrow" while she "planned my growth and my womanhood." The joyous lyric "Little Girl, My Stringbean, My Lovely Woman" is addressed to her daughter who is about to discover that "women are born twice." The frustrations of being female are the focus of poems like "One for My Dame," "Man and Wife," and "Menstruation at Forty," frustrations which, in "Consorting with Angels," culminate in Sexton's weariness with the "gender of things"—her own and that of the "men who sat at my table, / circled around the bowl I offered up."

Sexton's interest in the religious drama of self led to an only moderately successful psychodrama, the one-act play *Mercy Street* (produced at the American Place Theatre, New York City, 1969) as well as several experimental short stories. More successful was Conrad Susa's freeform operatic adaptation of *Transformations* (1971), Sexton's colloquially rendered poetic fairytales, which was produced by the Minneapolis Opera Company in 1973 and televised in 1978. These experiments foreshadow some of the characteristics of Sexton's later poetry: the looser poetic-prose line, the bold image, and the informal interpretations of mythic characters and situations.

Although Sexton's poetry has sometimes been labeled bathetic or hysterical, the startling force of the hyperbolic image is her forte. In her best poetry, Sexton explores the intensely personal but also universal conflict between the creative and self-destructive selves, a schizophrenic drama controlled by formal metrical patterns and casually placed rhymes. The elegiac voice searches for the lost, original self that has been tainted with experience and repressed in shame.

Although the frankness of her approach and the rather limited range of her autobiographical themes will continue to alienate some readers, Sexton attained a significant ranking among contemporary confessional poets.

OTHER WORKS: *All My Pretty Ones* (1962). *Eggs of Things* (with M. Kumin, 1963). *More Eggs of Things* (with M. Kumin, 1964). *Selected Poems* (1967). *Poems* (with D. Livingston and T. Kinsella, 1968). *Love Poems* (1969, 1989). *Joey and the Birthday Present* (with M. Kumin, 1971). *The Book of Folly* (1972). *O Ye Tongues* (1973). *The Death Notebooks* (1974). *The Awful Rowing Toward God* (1975). *The Wizard's Tears* (with M. Kumin, 1975). *45 Mercy Street* (edited by L. G. Sexton, 1976). *Anne Sexton: A Self-Portrait in Letters* (edited by L. G. Sexton, 1977, 1991). *No Evil Star: Selected Essays, Interviews, and Prose* (1985). *Selected Poems of Anne Sexton* (edited by D. W. Middlebrook and D. H. George, 1988, 1991).

Contributor of poetry to: *What Did Miss Darrington See? An Anthology of Feminist Supernatural Fiction* (1989); *No More Masks! An Anthology of Twentieth-Century American Women Poets, Newly Revised and Expanded* (1993); *Eight American Poets: Theodore Roethke, Elizabeth Bishop, Robert Lowell, John Berryman, Anne Sexton, Sylvia Plath, Allen Ginsberg, James Merrill: An Anthology* (1994, 1997); *Nature's Ban: Women's Incest Literature* (1996); *Splash! Great Writing About Swimming* (1996); *An Anthology of Great U.S. Women Poets, 1850-1990: Temples and Palaces* (1997); and others.

BIBLIOGRAPHY: Barnard, C. K., *Anne Sexton* (1989). Bixler, F., et al, eds., *Original Essays on the Poetry of Anne Sexton* (1988). Colburn, S. E., ed., *Anne Sexton: Telling the Tale* (1988). Donovan, J. A., *Her Kind: Personae in Anne Sexton's Poetry* (dissertation, 1993). George, D. H., *Oedipus Anne: The Poetry of Anne Sexton* (1987). George, D. H., ed., *Sexton: Selected Criticism* (1988). Hall, C. K. B. *Anne Sexton* (1989). Hedges, E., and Fishkin, S. F., eds., *Listening to Silences: New Essays in Feminist Criticism* (1994). Heyen, W., ed., *American Poets in 1976* (1976). Hungerford, E., ed., *Poets in Progress: Critical Prefaces to Thirteen Modern American Poets* (1967). Lacey, P. A., *The Inner War: Forms and Themes in Recent American Poetry* (1976). Markey, J., *A New Tradition? The Poetry of Sylvia Plath, Anne Sexton, and Adrienne Rich: A Study of Feminism and Poetry* (1988). McClatchy, J. D., ed., *Anne Sexton: The Artist and Her Critics* (1978). Middlebrook, D. W., *Anne Sexton: A Biography* (1991). Mills, Jr., R. J., *Contemporary American Poetry* (1966). Morton, R. E., *Anne Sexton's Poetry of Redemption: The Chronology of a Pilgrimage* (1988). Northouse, C., and Walsh, R. P., *Sylvia Plath and Anne Sexton: A Reference Guide* (1974). Phillips, R., *The Confessional Poets* (1973). Plimpton, G., ed., *Women Writers at Work: The Paris Review Interviews* (revised edition, 1998). Rosenthal, M. L., *The New Poets: American and British Poetry Since World War II* (1967). *Seduction and Theory: Readings of Gender, Representation, and Rhetoric* (1989). Sexton, L. G., *Searching for Mercy Street: My Journey Back to My Mother, Anne Sexton* (1994). Shaw, R., ed., *American Poetry Since 1960:*

Some Critical Perspectives (1973). Showalter, E., et al, eds., *Modern American Women Writers* (1993). Smith, S. E., *Serious Daring: Sylvia Plath and Anne Sexton* (dissertation, 1998). Wagner-Martin, L., *Critical Essays on Anne Sexton* (1989).

Reference works: *Oxford Companion to Women's Writing in the United States* (1995). *Poetry Criticism* (1991). *Twayne's Women Authors on CD* (CD, 1995).

Other references: *Anne Sexton Reads* (audiocassette, 1999). *Boston Phoenix* (Nov. 1994). *Centennial Review* (Spring 1975). *Contemporary Literature* (Fall 1992). *In Their Own Voices: A Century of Recorded Poetry* (audio cassette & CD, 1996). *Journal of the American Academy of Psychoanalysis* (Winter 1992). *Literature and Psychology* (1993). *Mythlore* (Winter 1994). *NMAL* (Summer 1979). *WRB* (Apr. 1995).

—KATHLEEN L. NICHOLS

SHANGE, Ntozake

Born Paulette Linda Williams, 18 October 1948, Trenton, New Jersey
Daughter of Paul T. and Eloise Owens Willams; **married** David Murray, 1977 (divorced); John Guess; **children:** Savannah

Ntozake Shange was originally named for her father, a surgeon. Her mother was a social worker and educator. In 1971 she renamed herself, taking the Zulu names Ntozake (she who comes with her own things) and Shange (she who walks like a lion). The name reflects some of the cultural and personal concerns of Shange's writings.

Shange's early life was a privileged one. Her home life brought her into contact with many of the giants of black intellectual and cultural life, including W. E. B. Du Bois, Josephine Baker, and musicians Charlie Parker, Dizzy Gillespie, Miles Davis, and Chuck Berry. The impact of black musical traditions remains characteristic of Shange's work today. An avid reader as a child, after the family's move to St. Louis she seems to have immersed herself in the world of her imagination: her novel *Betsey Brown* (1985) is semiautobiographical.

Shange attended Barnard College, graduating in 1970 with honors in American studies. She completed an M.A. in American studies at the University of Southern California (1973) and began her academic career, teaching humanities, women's studies, and Afro-American studies at Sonoma State College, Mills College, and the University of California Extension. During these years, Shange formed and worked with several performing arts groups and began performing her poetry in clubs across the country. Her transition from poet to dramatist began during this period.

In 1975 Shange moved to New York City, a move that brought her work a wider audience. Her Obie award—winning "choreopoem," *for colored girls who have considered suicide/ when the rainbow is enuf* (1977) displayed what would come to be seen as characteristic of Shange's art: mixing dramatic interpretations of her poems with movement, dance, song, music, and

lighting effects to forge a unified woman-centered statement. The poignancy, humor, and rage of the piece delighted some and infuriated others. The work's focus on relationships among women in the face of neglect and mistreatment by men brought attacks from drama, literary, and politico-social critics alike.

Shange herself had attempted suicide in 1966 after separating from her first husband, a law student. In 1976 she described this and subsequent suicide attempts as the result of suppressed rage. Writing and artistic expression, among other things, provided a healthier outlet for this rage.

In subsequent theater pieces, Shange continued the experiments of *for colored girls*, substituting poetry, music, and dance for straight plot narrative and character development. It is only in her adaptations, *Mother Courage and Her Children* (1980, from the Berthold Brecht work) and *Betsey Brown* (1991, from her own novel of the same name), that Shange attempts something approaching conventional drama. And each of these plays makes use of several experimental devices, particularly in their use of music. None of Shange's subsequent work for the theater has received the praise of *for colored girls*.

Shange is primarily a poet who works in the oral tradition. Her strength is in her artistic rendering of the spoken word emanating from her sure ear for the musicality of vernacular speech, its rhythms and intonations. Criticized for "distorting" the language in her written work, she has responded in characteristic language: "i cant count the number of times i have viscerally wanted to attack deform n maim the language that i waz taught to hate myself in / the language that perpetuates the notions that cause pain to every black child as he / she learns to speak of the world & the 'self'. . . / in order to think n communicate the thoughts n feelings i want to think n communicate / i haveta fix my tool to my needs."

Shange's creation of her own black, female image weaves together her prose and poetry, Her novels *Sassafras, Cypress, and Indigo* (1982) and *Betsey Brown* explore various aspects of the black woman's psyche, from Betsey's youthful introspection through the trials of young womanhood of the three plant-named sisters. Fusing her personal and public concerns, Shange also writes cultural criticism and social commentary for a wide variety of publications. In addition, she continues to lecture widely and perform her works as a soloist and in performing arts ensembles.

In addition to her 1977 Obie, Shange also received nominations for the Tony, Grammy, and Emmy awards for the Broadway-recorded and televised versions of *for colored girls*. She has served as artist-in-residence for the New York State Council on the Arts (1977 and 1981). In 1981, additionally, she was awarded a Guggenheim Fellowship and the Columbia University Medal of Excellence as well as an Obie for the off-Broadway production of *Mother Courage and Her Children*.

The Love Space Demands: A Continuing Saga (1991) revisits the blend of poetry, music, dance, and drama that were combined in *for colored girls who have considered suicide*. The pieces in the choreopoem touch on issues ranging from celibacy to crack addiction during pregnancy. Shange hopes, as she told Eileen

Myles in the *Voice Literary Supplement,* "to keep our sensibilities alive. . . . To keep people alive so they know they can feel what is happening as opposed to simply trying to fend it off."

Shange examines race and gender in modern America in her 1994 novel, *Liliane: Resurrection of the Daughter.* The book features monologues delivered by the protagonist, Liliane Lincoln, as she undergoes psychoanalysis. Liliane deals with racial discomfort and her need to assimilate with all cultures, and Shange makes her heroine more identifiable by including appealing qualities, which also add to her complexity. Kelly Cherry noted in the *Los Angeles Times Book Review,* "a daring portrait of a black woman artist recreating herself out of social and psychological chaos. . . . Shange has written a novel that manages to be both risky and stylish."

Combining poetry and Romare Bearden's mixed media art, *I Live in Music* (1994) takes the reader from an metropolitan setting to a bayou. In this all-ages book, Shange again here incorporates more than words in her effort to provide a story that provokes all the senses.

The mid-1990s saw frequent incidents involving racially motivated violence. Tackling the subject in a picture book for children, Shange tells a story of a brother and sister who are victims of a racial attack. *Whitewash*'s (1997) serious tone reflects an honest look at understanding and preventing such incidents.

OTHER WORKS: *Natural Disasters and Other Festive Occasions* (1977). *Nappy Edges* (1978). *Three Pieces: Spell #7; A Photograph; Boogie Woogie Landscapes* (1981). *A Daughter's Geography* (1983). *from okra to greens: poems by ntozake shange* (1984). *see no evil: prefaces, reviews, & essays, 1974-1983* (1984, reissued as *See No Evil: Prefaces, Essays, & Accounts, 1976-1983*). *Melissa and Smith: A Story* (1985). *Ridin' the Moon in Texas: Word Painting* (1987).

Other productions: *A Photograph: A Still Life with Shadow/A Photograph: A Study of Cruelty* (1977, revised as *A Photograph: Lovers in Motion,* 1979). *Where the Mississippi Meets the Amazon* (with T. Nkabinda and J. Hagedorn, 1977). *From Okra to Greens/ A Different Kinda Love Story: A Play/ With Music & Dance* (1985). *Black and White Two-Dimensional Planes* (1979). *Spell #7* (1979). *If I Can Cook, You Know God Can* (1998).

BIBLIOGRAPHY: Betsko, K., and R. Koenig, *Interviews with Contemporary Women Playwrights* (1987). Brater, E., ed., *Feminine Focus* (1989). Foster, K., "Detangling the Web: Mother-Daughter Relationships in the Plays of Marsha Norman, Lillian Hellman, Tina Howe, Ntozake Shange" (thesis, 1994). Keyssar, H., *Feminist Theatre* (1984). Tate, C., ed., *Black Women Writers at Work* (1983).

Reference works: *CA* (1980, 1999). *CANR* (1989). *CLC* (1978, 1983, 1986). *DLB* (1985). *FC* (1990). *MTCW* (1991). *Notable Women in the American Theatre* (1989). *Oxford Companion to Women's Writing in the United States* (1995).

Other references: *LATBR* (18 Dec. 1994). *Ms.* (December 1977). *NYT* (7 May 1989). *PW* (3 May 1985, 10 Oct. 1994, 14 Nov. 1994, 3 Nov. 1997). *Spare Rib: A Women's Liberation Magazine* (May 1987) *Voice Literary Supplement* (Aug./ Sept. 1991).

—FAHAMISHA P. BROWN,
UPDATED BY ALLISON A. JONES

SHANNON, Dell

See LININGTON, Elizabeth

SHANNON, Monica

Born Eastern Canada, 7 March 1893; **died** August 1965
Married Mr. Wing, circa 1927

Monica Shannon and her family moved from Canada to Seattle, Washington, and then to the Bitter Root Valley in the Montana Rockies. There, on a cattle ranch, Shannon lived among the Bulgarian immigrants and the Flatheads, Native Americans who, with her Irish ancestors, provided the inspiration for much of her writing.

After Shannon moved to California with her family, she received a B.L.S. and began work at the Los Angeles Public Library. As a librarian/storyteller and as a doting aunt to two active and inquisitive children, she first told and then wrote the stories that became *California Fairy Tales* (1926). In these tales, elements of several cultures—California Spanish, Irish, Native American—are combined in original fairy tales taking place in a land of bean fields, redwood forests, deserts, and droughts. *Eyes for the Dark* (1928) and *More Tales from California* (1935) are collections similar to *California Fairy Tales* in tone and subject.

Tawnymore (1931), a novel, was a less successful literary venture. Tawnymore, the hero, is a Pericu of the 18th century, and the book begins as the story of his adventures. It is soon taken over by the pirates with whom Tawnymore and his companion sail. The critical consensus was that the book was episodic and marred by the inclusion of distracting incidents.

With *Dobry* (1934), a Newbery Award winner, Shannon showed she could control an extended narrative. Dobry, a young Bulgarian boy, discovers he must be an artist. Against the wishes of his widowed mother, who naturally hopes he will become a productive member of village society, his storytelling grandfather defends Dobry and the primacy of his calling. In addition to celebrating the importance of art, *Dobry* presents a striking portrait of life in rural Bulgaria.

The love for nature, especially for the changing colors and lights of the high mountains, that is so much of the achievement of *Dobry* is also an important feature of Shannon's poetry. Her collection of poems for children, *Goose Grass Rhymes* (1930) is just such an example. Shannon's stories, filled with the sights and sounds of their settings and peopled by whimsical characters, appealed to her young readership.

BIBLIOGRAPHY: Reference works: *Junior Book of Authors* (1951).
Other references: *Horn Book* (Nov. 1928, Aug. 1931, March-April 1935). *LJ* (22 Jan. 1930). *NYT* (24 Dec. 1934). *PW* (29 June 1935).

—KATHARYN F. CRABBE

SHARON, Rose
See MERRIL, Judith

SHARP, Isabella Oliver

Born 1777, Cumberland County, Pennsylvania; **died** 1843
Daughter of Mr. and Mrs. James Oliver, Esq.; **married** (James?) Sharp

Biographical data about Isabella Oliver Sharp can be found in the note "To the Editor," from "R.D." which prefaces *Poems, on Various Subjects* (1805), as well as in several of the poems themselves. Sharp's parents owned a house and farmlands, and her father was highly regarded in the community. He was learned in mathematics and the sciences, and his lessons "improv'd many a youth," as Sharp remembers in her poem "Inscribed to My Brothers." He took pains to instruct his own sons and also the sons of his neighbors, but he virtually neglected the education of his daughters. Sharp's father died around 1791, and her mother was left with a number of small children to raise. Eventually, the house and lands "passed to another hand."

"R.D." states that Sharp never received anything more than a "common english [sic] education." That is, she was taught to read and—just barely!—to write. Still, Sharp became a voracious reader. From her earliest years, hard work was required of her, and while she worked, she composed verses. "Composed on the Banks of the Conodoguinet" actually describes the composition process as it is taking place: while Sharp's hands are laboring to cleanse soiled garments in the river, her mind is busy turning those same clothes into a metaphor for the human soul, and that same river into an analogue for Christ's redemptive sacrifice. The hauntingly beautiful lines of this poem were among the many hundreds Sharp composed and "treasur'd" in her memory over the years until she found someone who could write well enough to transcribe them for her.

As she records in "To the Public," Sharp took an active and empathetic interest in the joys and sorrows of her friends and neighbors. A birth, a death, an illness, a wedding—all were grist for her poetic mill. Deeply read in divinity, Sharp continually sought to explore, as in her speculations "At the Request of B---n," "What strange contact binds / Material things to immaterial minds?" While planted as firmly on the shores of this phenomenal

world as the feet of the washerwoman "on the banks of the Conodoguinet," most of Sharp's poems merge into the noumenal world as well.

Sharp was a popular poet in Cumberland County. She worked with pleasantly musical phrases and ingenious images. It is unfortunate that Sharp's hardworking rural life deprived her of the educational opportunities that might have enabled her to do more.

—JEANETTE NYDA PASSTY

SHAW, Anna H(oward)

Born 2 February 1847, Newcastle-on-Tyne, England; **died** 2 July 1919, Moylan, Pennsylvania
Daughter of Thomas and Nicola Stott Shaw

The daughter of Scotch-English Unitarians, Anna H. Shaw was brought to the U.S. in 1851 and spent her early childhood in New Bedford and Lawrence, Massachusetts. In 1859 Shaw's father established his family in a half-completed log cabin near Big Rapids on the Michigan frontier. An erratic and impractical man, he was seldom at home, and Shaw and her brothers ran the farm with little assistance. Although her formal schooling was fragmentary and frequently interrupted, Shaw was an eager scholar and an avid reader; at fifteen she became the teacher in the local school.

At age twenty, Shaw moved to Big Rapids to live with her sister, and there heard a woman preach for the first time. This encounter reawakened Shaw's childhood desire to make preaching her profession. At about this time Shaw was converted to Methodism; in 1871 she was licensed to preach by the Methodist church. To prepare for a ministerial career, Shaw attended the local high school, Albion College, and the theological school of Boston University, supporting herself by preaching in vacant pulpits. Shaw was the first woman to be ordained by the Methodist Protestant denomination. While serving as pastor of two East Dennis churches, Shaw attended the medical school of Boston University and received her degree in 1886.

Shaw decided, however, that her true vocation lay in furthering the public causes of women. In 1885 she became organizer and lecturer for the Massachusetts Woman's Suffrage Association, and in 1888, she became superintendent of the franchise department of the National Woman's Christian Temperance Union. Although Shaw remained active in the temperance cause, she shifted her major commitment to the suffrage movement in the 1890s. In 1892 Shaw was elected vice-president of the National American Woman's Suffrage Association, and she served as its president from 1904 to 1915. Shaw was a splendid proselytizer but an unsuccessful administrator, and she resigned in the face of rising disaffection and conflict.

In 1917 Shaw was appointed chairman of the Women's Committee of the Council of National Defense. She was highly effective in uniting women's organizations, coordinating their war efforts, and exhorting them to inspirational patriotism; she was later awarded a Distinguished Service Medal. After the war, Shaw joined William Howard Taft and President A. Lawrence Lowell of Harvard on a speaking tour to support the League of Nations.

Shaw was primarily a sermonizer, lecturer, and propagandist. She did not conceive her only book as a literary work, but rather as a personal chronicle of the woman's movement. *The Story of a Pioneer* (1915) is a lively, graphic reminiscence with a strong feminist refrain. Shaw was a witty advocate and told a story well, but she was also a poor concealer of her prejudices; and her memoirs, frank and revealing, bear testimony to her obvious disdain for men and matrimony.

Much of Shaw's literary output consisted of sermons, lectures, and testimony before legislative committees. Several of her sermons have survived. ''The Heavenly Vision,'' delivered before the International Council on Women in 1888, was responsible for convincing Susan B. Anthony that she must convert Shaw to full-time devotion to the suffrage cause. Anthony described Shaw as ''beyond question the leading woman orator of this generation,'' and her sermon, ''The Heavenly Vision,'' as a ''matchless discourse.''

Shaw made frequent use of analogy in her sermons, and she liked rhetorical questions and figurative language. Shaw used humor less in her sermons than in her lectures; her wit was at its best when refuting male arguments against equal suffrage. After she became a highly visible leader of the suffrage movement, Shaw occasionally wrote articles on women and women's rights for popular magazines, but it was as a speaker that Shaw made her major contribution.

BIBLIOGRAPHY: Cott, Nancy F., *The Grounding of Modern Feminism* (1987). Harper, I. H., ed., *The History of Woman Suffrage* (1922). Kraditor, A. S., *The Ideas of the Woman Suffrage Movement, 1890-1920* (1965). Muncy, R., *Creating a Female Dominion in American Reform* (1991). O'Neill, W. L., *Everyone Was Brave: The Rise and Fall of Feminism in America* (1969). Riegel, R. E., *American Feminists* (1963).

Reference works: *HWS*, IV-VI. *Oxford Companion to Women's Writing in the United States* (1995).

Other references: *Journal of Social History* (Winter 1969). *Pacific History* (Oct. 1961).

—RUTH BORDIN

SHAW, Anna Moore

Born Chehia (Pima name), 30 November 1898, Santa Cruz village, Gila River Pima Reservation, Arizona; **died** April 1975
Daughter of Josiah (S-wegi Hapot, Red Arrow) and Rose (Haus Molly) Moore; **married** Ross (Jujul Tonal, Zigzag Light) Shaw, 1920; **children** three

When Anna Moore Shaw's parents, traditional Pimas, converted to Presbyterianism, they chose a new direction for the life of their then-small youngest daughter. Although they trained Shaw in the values and skills central to their Pima heritage, they sent her to American schools and encouraged her to learn a different tradition. After graduating from Phoenix Indian Boarding School in 1918, Shaw completed her high school work and became in 1920 the first full-blooded Native American graduate of Phoenix Union High School. Shortly thereafter, she married her school sweetheart, a Pima-Marcicopa, and settled in Phoenix. During her forty years in the city, Shaw raised three children, cared for her aged parents, led an antiracism project for Church Women United, and was the first woman ordained as an elder in her Presbyterian church.

Shaw and her family always spent weekends and vacations on the reservation, and when Ross Shaw retired in 1960 as a foreman for the Railway Express, they returned to his birthplace, the Salt River Reservation. Shaw's ''retirement'' was active: she edited the tribal newsletter and served with the Pima Mutual Self-Help Housing Program. She also helped start an Aid to the Elderly program, revived basketweaving among Pima women, and founded a tribal museum. Meanwhile, Shaw taught Pima language and culture to young children in the reservation school.

In the 1930s, Shaw began recording Pima legends in order to prevent their loss as the older generation took their memories to their graves. In 1950 she enrolled in a two-year writing course at Phoenix Technical School to gain the skills necessary to actualize her ''plan to help make both Indians and whites aware of the proud heritage of the original Americans.'' Her first major work was a play, *Darkness to Light*, dramatizing the missionary efforts of Dr. Charles H. Cook among the Pimas, which was performed at her Phoenix church.

Shaw's first book, *Pima Indian Legends* (1968), realizes her goal of presenting Pima oral traditions as told by her father in lively, readable English. Although Shaw removes the contextual elements of the telling and uses pseudo-Native American words like ''squaw''—ostensibly to follow white practice —her work has importance as an example of an intermediate stage between oral and written Native American literatures folklore scholars are just beginning to investigate. The tales Shaw includes are those intended traditionally for education and entertainment; only a simplified version of the sacred Pima origin myth appears among many humorous and instructive animal legends and trickster coyote stories. One tale, ''Potsherd Speaks,'' is especially interesting, establishing a living link between the ruins of the ancient Hohokam and ongoing Pima culture.

Conscious of traditional Pima injunctions against being ''boastful and over-talkative about myself'' like Coyote, Shaw begins her autobiography, *A Pima Past* (1974), with her ancestors and ends it with her ''Indian Hall of Fame'' of successful 20th-century Pimas, producing an unusual blend of tribal, family, and personal history. The information Shaw provides about Pima culture in depicting the life of her father, raised by his grandmother, helps readers appreciate the drastic change her own lifestyle represents. Her work lacks the bitterness of many Native American autobiographies, focusing more on the possibilities for intercultural understanding and less on the traumas often experienced by those attempting to reach this goal in a prejudiced society.

While Shaw, a committed Christian, is insistent upon the values of education and cultural adjustment through brotherly love, she is proud of her Pima identity and has helped revitalize her heritage. Her works, as strong statements of dual values, reveal the complexity obscured by the facile dichotomy separating "progressive" from "traditional" Native Americans. Shaw shows us what she calls "a lifetime of treading the bridge between two cultures" can be creative and fulfilling, rather than psychologically debilitating. Her works are important in giving readers a firsthand report on the adaptability of Native American values, and the continued strength of Native American women.

BIBLIOGRAPHY: Reference works: *Indians of Today* (fourth edition, 1971).
Other references: *Arizona and the West* (Summer 1975). *Choice* (May 1969, Oct. 1974). *EJ* (Jan. 1974). *Journal of Arizona History* (Summer 1974). *LJ* (July 1974).

—HELEN M. BANNAN

SHEEHY, Gail

Born 27 November 1937, Mamaroneck, New York
Daughter of Harold M. and Lillian Rainey Henion; **married** Albert F. Sheehy, 1960 (divorced 1967); **children:** one daughter

Gail Sheehy grew up and attended high school in Mamaroneck, New York. After graduating from the University of Vermont in 1958, with a dual major in English and home economics, she worked for the J. C. Penney Company as a consumer representative and then as a filmstrip editor.

In 1960 Sheehy moved with her husband to Rochester, New York, where he entered medical school and she became fashion editor for the *Rochester Democrat & Chronicle*. Her daughter was born a few months after she moved with her husband to New York City. The Sheehys were divorced in 1967.

In New York, Sheehy first wrote for the women's department of the *Herald Tribune*. After a few years she began to write freelance articles and soon became a contributing editor of *New York* magazine. She studied at Columbia University in 1969 and 1970, on a fellowship in interracial reporting, and again later, on an Alice Patterson Foundation fellowship.

Lovesounds (1970) uses alternating points of view—the wife as well as her husband—to relate the breakup of the marriage of a New York City couple of the 1960s. Although not successful as a novel, the book is of interest for its autobiographical elements and analysis of modern marriage.

Speed Is of the Essence (1971) is a collection of articles originally published in *New York*. The book offers case histories

of the prophetic loudmouthed minority Sheehy calls the "speeders," those who first experiment with new life options. The title essay is about amphetamine addicts, but Sheehy's point in the collection is that speed is of the essence in our entire culture.

Panthermania: The Clash of Black Against Black in One American City (1971) is a result of what Sheehy calls an "experiment in interracial journalism." Accompanied by a young black photographer, David Parks, she spent nine months of 1970 in New Haven, Connecticut, investigating the black community's reactions to the trials of the Black Panthers accused of murdering Alex Rackley. Her next book, *Hustling: Prostitution in Our Wide-Open Society* (1973) brings together a series of articles Sheehy wrote about prostitution in New York City—from street hookers to high-society courtesans.

Passages: Predictable Crises of Adult Life (1976) was written in response to Sheehy's personal midlife crisis. She shows there is a pattern of adult development that can be charted and described. She attempts to locate the individual's inner changes, to compare the developmental rhythms of men and women, and to examine the predictable crises for couples. The book is based on case histories of 115 educated middle-class people between the ages of 18 and 55. The enormous success of the book attested to the popular appeal of its theories.

Sheehy followed up her bestselling *Passages* with another popular success. *Pathfinders* (1981), a testament to the American public's need to fit their psyches into a schema, is rife with such generalizations as "What's wrong with me?" is the "archetypal female response." Nonetheless, the book demonstrates Sheehy's genuine concern for "the female psychology."

Pathfinders revives the "Sexual Diamond," of *Passages*, describing the gradual divergence of male and female character traits from 18 to 40 and the slow crossover each sex makes thereafter. Subsequently, Sheehy redirected her analysis of the human personality toward politics aiming at, in her words, an "X-ray of history." *Character: America's Search for Leadership* (1988) concerns the "character" of achievers: the cast includes Al Gore, George Bush, Ronald Reagan, Jesse Jackson, and Gary Hart, examined to substantiate her view on how achievers handle crises and develop. *Character* was followed by a long biography, *The Man Who Changed the World: The Lives of Mikhail S. Gorbachev* (1990). Sheehy describes her journey to Gorbachev's hometown to talk to its residents, her time with the KGB, and her interviews with more than 100 people. *The Man* received almost universally negative reviews across the political spectrum, with several critics noting the inadequacy of her preparation and her popular psychology approach to the massiveness of her subject. To Sheehy's credit, however, she charged into a complicated issue and attempted a comprehensive account; her relatively uncritical fascination is what makes her good at what she does—American journalism.

Sheehy returned to the subject with which she seems most comfortable, female psychology, with *The Silent Passage: Menopause* (1992). The book immediately made the bestseller list although some women were critical in their reviews. Barbara Ehrenreich, in a review titled "All Aboard the Raging Hormone Express," claims Sheehy's description of menopause "drive[s] women to whimper, 'Won't I ever be me anymore?'" Fortunately, as Ehrenreich points out, Sheehy gives plenty of evidence within the book to refute this frightening image.

In 1995 Sheehy published what was originally intended as an update of her 1976 *Passages* but instead became an entirely new look at the progression of adulthood. Life in the past 20 years had changed drastically for many adults, Sheehy found, and in *New Passages: Mapping Your Life Across Time*, she proposed a novel look at the stages of maturity. She suggested the years between 18 and 30 are a time of "provisional adulthood," while ages 30 to 45 are the "first adulthood," and from 45 up is the "second adulthood." Some critics hailed the book as a large improvement from the original, while others found it lacked maturity and depth. Either way, it drew upon Sheehy's strength of collecting stories and data from other sources and weaving it together with her own theories.

Sheehy's next work, *Understanding Men's Passages: Discovering the New Map of Men's Lives* (1998), examines the older, male subgroup of *New Passages*. Again through the use of interviews and other research, Sheehy chronicles the struggles and fears of men over 40 and offers suggestions for overcoming new challenges. Though she often employs what *Kirkus Reviews* calls an "overly and redundantly upbeat tone," the book has been well received as a readable, useful guide striking a good balance between hard psychology and popular psychology.

Despite some mixed reviews, Sheehy has received praise for her journalistic excellence; a March 1991 poll in the *Washington Journalism Review* gave her a high rating and she is widely published in newspapers and magazines. Her self-help books are among the most frequently read within an extremely popular genre, employing a blend of easy reading and easily accepted advice that has proven to be a lucrative combination.

BIBLIOGRAPHY: Reference works: *CA* (1975). *CA* Online (2 June 1999). *CANR* (1981, 1991). *MTCW* (1991).

Other references: Amazon.com (8 June 1999). *Glamour* (Dec. 1977). *KR* (1 May 1998). *NR* (28 Sept. 1987, 27 May 1991). *National Review* (11 Feb. 1991). *Newsweek* (4 Dec. 1972). *NYTBR* (5 Sept. 1971, 30 May 1976, 7 June 1992). *PW* (1 June 1992). *SR* (24 July 1971, 15 May 1976). *Time* (10 May 1976). *Town & Country* (Oct. 1978).

—ANNE HUDSON JONES,
UPDATED BY CARRIE SNYDER

SHELDON, Ann
See ADAMS, Harriet Stratemeyer

SHERWOOD, Mary (Elizabeth) Wilson

Born 27 October 1826, Keene, New Hampshire; **died** 12 September 1903, New York, New York
Daughter of James and Mary Richardson Wilson; **married** John Sherwood, 1851; **children:** four sons

Mary Wilson Sherwood was the oldest of seven children of a distinguished family of Scotch-Irish origin. She attended a fashionable private school for girls in Boston, where the training focused on good manners, not academic studies. Sherwood became part of Washington social life as a hostess during her father's term in Congress (1847-50). Upon her mother's death in 1884 Sherwood also assumed the duties of family management.

After her marriage to a New York lawyer, Sherwood settled in Manhattan. She had four sons; Robert Sherwood, the playwright, was a grandson. Sherwood first began to sponsor literary events in a fundraising effort for the restoration of Mount Vernon. By the 1870s, the Sherwood residence had become an establishment in New York literary and philanthropic circles. Sherwood served as president of the Causeries, a literary gathering of distinguished New York women and was a member of several benevolent societies.

The drain on the family resources induced by entertaining persuaded Sherwood to turn her efforts toward writing professionally. She had already published short stories and occasional verse in New York and Boston magazines. *A Transplanted Rose* (1882), her second novel, about the acceptance of a western girl into New York society, and a later, similar novel, *Sweet-Brier* (1889), were well-received. Sherwood also published a volume of poetry and two autobiographical books, *An Epistle to Posterity: Being Rambling Recollections of Many Years of My Life* (1897) and *Here & There & Everywhere: Reminiscences* (1898). Her style is lively, idiomatic, and touched with humor. Sherwood's most notable works, however, are in the field of etiquette. Sherwood's experience in Washington and Europe, where she traveled extensively, gave her great familiarity with a variety of styles of manners. Her articles on manners appeared in *Atlantic, Scribner's, Harper's, Appleton's Journal*, and *Frank Leslie's Weekly. Manners and Social Usages* (1884) was the most successful of Sherwood's books.

Sherwood wrote popular manuals of style treating such standard topics as table manners and the art of conversation. Like later 20th century philosophers of social convention such as Emily Post, Amy Vanderbilt, and Peg Bracken, Sherwood pointed to kindness and regard for others as the universal law of manners. Sherwood was, however, keenly aware of class differences. She was frank and firm in advocating the leadership of society by a class possessing talent and money. This was largely in reaction to the "upstarts" of the lower orders who were coming into sudden fortunes and social prominence.

Sherwood's several books on etiquette are addressed to a status quo of domestic women in the roles of wives and mothers— ladies of leisure and some means, whose main duties were, in Sherwood's belief, to temper the uncivilized tendencies of men and to serve as exemplars of congenial and decorous interpersonal relations. Like those social arbiters following her, Sherwood sees women as the directors and managers of social setting and action.

Although Sherwood can be criticized for not using her talents for more serious ends, and although her assessment of the role of good manners and the position of women in society was conservative, she should be remembered as the author of the most influential etiquette book of her time.

OTHER WORKS: *The Sarcasm of Destiny; or, Nina's Experience* (1878). *Amenities of Home* (1881). *Etiquette* (1884). *Home Amusements* (1884). *Royal Girls and Royal Courts* (1887). *The Art of Entertaining* (1892). *Poems by M.E.W.S.* (1892).

BIBLIOGRAPHY: Reference works: *AW. NAW* (1971).
    Other references: *NYT* (15 Sept. 1903).

—MARGARET J. KING

SHINDLER, Mary Dana

Born 15 February 1810, Charleston, South Carolina; **died** 1883, Texas
Wrote under: Mary S. B. Dana, Mrs. Mary S. B. Dana Shindler
Daughter of B. M. and Mary S. Palmer; **married** Charles E. Dana, 1830; R. D. Shindler

Mary Dana Shindler's life was beset with tragedies; she lost sister, brother, son, and husband in the span of a few years. Each of these deaths is commemorated by a poem in her collection *The Parted Family, and Other Poems* (1842). These poems reflect how religion enabled Shindler to survive and, not surprisingly, became the dominant theme of her life.

With her first husband, she lived on the Mississippi River in Bloomington, Iowa Territory. After Dana's death, Shindler returned to Charleston; later, she lived in other areas of the South, including Texas, where she composed the *U.S. Labor Greenback Songbook* in 1879. Her writing includes poetry, novels, essays on religion and spiritualism, and, most importantly, *Letters Addressed to Relatives and Friends Chiefly in Reply to Arguments in Support of the Doctrine of the Trinity* (1846), which traces her conversion from Calvinism to Unitarianism. Shindler's later marriage to R. D. Shindler, an Episcopal clergyman, initiated another conversion, to his faith, and produced *A Southerner Among the Spirits: A Record of Investigations into Spiritual Phenomena* (1877).

Shindler's novels, directed mostly toward a young audience, never gained the popularity of her poetry. *Charles Morton; or, The Young Patriot: A Tale of the American Revolution* (1843) is pure romantic history motivated by convenience and circumstance. The seagoing adventures, *The Young Sailor* (1843) and *Forecastle Tom; or, The Landsman Turned Sailor* (1846), are both moral tales; Forecastle Tom becomes a sailor missionary.

The religion permeating Shindler's life also fills her poetry, as does the lavish description of her southern homeland. Her collections *The Southern Harp*, *The Northern Harp*, and *The Western Harp* (published in the 1830s and 1840s) were all well-received, and her poetry found its way into many newspapers and magazines, including particularly the New York *Observor* and the Augusta *Mirror*.

Although Shindler's contributions are minor and often sentimental, they reflect a mind constantly challenging its own earlier assumptions and exploring the limitless possibilities of both the natural and the supernatural worlds.

BIBLIOGRAPHY: Reference works: *Daughters of America; or, Women of the Century* (1883). *Index to Women of the World from Ancient to Modern Times* (1970, incorrect entry).

—THELMA J. SHINN

SHOWALTER, Elaine

Born 21 January 1941, Cambridge, Massachusetts
Daughter of Paul and Violet Rottenberg Cottler; **married** English Showalter Jr., 1963; **children:** Victoria (Vinca), Michael

Elaine Showalter invented gynocriticism, a feminist critical theory and approach that focuses on the woman writer, the meaning of her text, the structure of literature written by women including its history, themes, genres. She introduced this new method of reading specific texts and its application in an essay, "Toward a Feminist Poetics" (1979). Because of the relative success of gynocritics, especially of Showalter herself, whose prolific works demonstrate the method in all its possible combinations (*Daughters of Decadence*—highly praised by the *Times (London) Literary Supplement* when it was published in 1993—applies gynocritics to 19th-century short fiction in Britain), the very foundations of feminism have shifted from practical concerns to intellectual ones. In the *Dictionary of Literary Biography*, Showalter is named "one of the founders of feminist criticism and still one of its most important and influential practitioners." She began by concentrating on British women novelists, studying their work not as part of a tradition dominated by male writers but as a separate tradition altogether, even a subculture with its own "values, conventions, experiences, and behaviors." Her subsequent books, especially *Sexual Anarchy: Gender and Culture at the Fin de Siècle* (1990), include literary histories that contribute to the modern area of "gender studies," since she is concerned with the language, especially the rhetoric, of popular fiction and periodicals as these reflect the changes in themes and tensions at the end of the 19th century and at the beginning of the 20th.

Showalter has had a significant academic career. She earned a B.A. at Bryn Mawr (1962), an M.A. at Brandeis (1964), and a Ph.D. in English at the University of California at Davis (1970). She began teaching at Douglass College, Rutgers University, in 1970 and rose steadily to full professor by 1983. While at Rutgers, she received the Christian and Mary Lindbach Foundation award for distinguished teaching (1976). The following year, she was a Guggenheim fellow (1977-78), and she spent an additional research year as a Rockefeller humanities fellow (1981-82). Since 1984 she has been Avalon Professor of Humanities (and professor of English) at Princeton University, where she remains an active faculty member despite frequent visits to places as diverse as Dartmouth College's Critical Theory School (1986), the Salzburg Seminars (1988), and Oxford University (1989).

Showalter's leap to national prominence came in April 1997 when she appeared with Lynne Cheney on *Crossfire Sunday*, a popular confrontational television show, as a guest during a discussion of the causes of Gulf War Syndrome. Her recent book, *Hystories: Hysterical Epidemics and Modern Culture* (1997), proposes that afflictions like Gulf War Syndrome arise not from exposure to chemicals but from the mind of the individual. Naturally, this was not a popular opinion or one that people suffering from modern maladies like Chronic Fatigue Syndrome were going to admit without loud arguments against it. It must be said that Showalter does not consider these conditions faked or made up; on the contrary, she contests these claims by suggesting that "we're a society that doesn't understand or really take seriously the effects of psychological stress and conflict and anxiety and a certain kind of helplessness on our bodies and on our emotions." After *Crossfire*'s speakers had finished for the evening, one of the hosts (Bob Beckel) remarked that Showalter was driven from a book signing because of a confrontation with "people who have legitimate, legitimate suffering." It cannot be easy for Showalter to keep explaining that psychological suffering can be just as devastating to the body as physical suffering. Nevertheless, she continues to pursue this frequently marginalized line of inquiry and research. One might note that she does not ever connect "hysteria" to "hypochondria" (which is imagined illness), though her critics seem to believe her choice of term means the same thing. In a balanced review of *Hystories*, Jenn Shreve applauds her "slow, well-researched study of the history of hysterical epidemics and their modern day manifestations." The inclusion of alien abduction, satanic ritual abuse, recovered memory, and multiple personality disorder with Gulf War Syndrome has made Showalter the object of intense scrutiny by the very press she says assists in spreading the contagion of these illnesses rooted in the unconscious. There are stories widely circulated on the Internet of people suffering from some of the conditions Showalter lists who appear at events where the author/scholar is present to attack her verbally. These unfortunate people seem to be confirming her diagnosis rather than refuting it. She writes: "The United States has become the hot zone of psychogenic diseases, new and mutating forms of hysteria amplified by modern communications and fin-de-siècle anxiety." It is only fair to point out that David Futrelle, a regular contributor to *Salon* and a self-diagnosed hypochondriac, recognizes a moral vision in Showalter's unmasking of the forces making people sick in modern society. Indeed, the shrill tone of her loudest critics makes it absolutely necessary to read and understand Showalter's position on hysteria and psychosomatic illness. It is characteristic of Showalter that she continues to work as editor of two prestigious

scholarly publications, *Women's Studies* and *Signs: Journal of Women, Culture, and Society*, and to contribute regular essays to respected academic periodicals.

OTHER WORKS: *A Literature of Their Own: British Women Writers from Brontë to Lessing* (1977). *The Female Malady: Women, Madness, and English Culture, 1830-1980* (1985). *Speaking of Gender* (1989). *Sister's Choice: Tradition and Change in American Women's Writing* (1991). *Hysteria Beyond Freud* (coauthor, 1993). *Scribbling Women: Short Stories by Nineteenth Century American Women* (1997).

BIBLIOGRAPHY: Reference works: *CANR* (1997). *DLB* (1988). Feminist Writers (1996).
    Other references: *Crossfire Sunday* (20 Apr. 1997).

—KATHLEEN BONANN MARSHALL

SHREVE, Anita

Born 7 October 1946, Boston, Massachusetts
Daughter of Richard H. and Bibiona Kennedy Shreve; children: Katherine, Christopher

"Love is a very devalued subject to be writing about these days," Anita Shreve has observed. "That strikes me as sad." For Shreve, no subject is "more serious to write about," and her six finely wrought, deftly plotted tales of love, passion, betrayal, and loss give weight to her words. Since the publication of her first novel, *Eden Close*, in 1989, the former English teacher turned journalist turned novelist has been exploring the nature of love—"how it affects people right down to their soul, how it affects their families, how it affects their future"—without exposing its essential mystery. Mystery, in fact, is frequently at the heart of Shreve's novels, serving as the perfect metaphor for her subject.

The eldest of three daughters of an airline pilot and a homemaker, Shreve is a product of the contradictory New England landscape so important to her fiction: she absorbed the appeal of its stark beauty during summers spent roaming the dunes of her native Massachusetts and on the coast of Maine. After graduation with an English degree from Tufts University in 1968, she began teaching high school English and writing the short stories that would find publication in small literary journals. One story, "Past the Island, Drifting," won an O. Henry prize in 1975.

Shreve spent three years working as a journalist in Kenya, where her then-husband attended graduate school. Upon her return to the U.S. in the late 1970s, she was a freelance writer for publications ranging from *Cosmopolitan* to the *New York Times Magazine*. She expanded an award-winning article on working mothers into her 1987 book, *Remaking Motherhood*. Another article, on the consciousness-raising movement, provided the foundation for her second book, *Women Together, Women Alone* (1989). The advance for this second book gave her the freedom to pursue fiction writing, and she published her first novel the same year as well. Subsequent novels have earned her steadily increasing readership and critical acclaim. Her 1997 novel, *The Weight of Water*, won several New England book awards and was shortlisted for the Orange Prize, awarded to a woman author published in Great Britain.

Eden Close, Shreve's first novel, is a gothic tale that strips bare the layers of thwarted love between a husband, wife, and their adopted daughter. Her second novel, *Strange Fits of Passion* (1991), dissects the nature of an abusive relationship, while her third, *Where or When* (1993), explores the legacy of unrequited love that leads a man and a woman to risk all. In *Resistance* (1995), a U.S. bomber crashes in a small Belgian town during World War II, a life-transforming event. Shreve's most critically acclaimed novel, *The Weight of Water*, weaves together parallel plots: the true tale of a 19th-century double murder on the Isles of Shoals, off the New Hampshire coast, and the contemporary story of the disintegration of a marriage. *The Pilot's Wife* (1998), which received rather mixed reviews, exposes the deceptions that lie beneath the surface of a seemingly happy marriage. Clearly, love and marriage lie at the heart of a Shreve plot, but the traditional happy ending frequently eludes her characters. The threat of violence gives her fiction an edge, and when it erupts, as it inevitably does in her human—and therefore flawed—relationships, the consequences are tragic.

Discontinuous plot structures and unconventional points of view give Shreve's fiction an undeniable literariness, but they are not merely tricks of the trade. Instead, they elicit other thematic issues, particularly the nature and burden of truth. The narrator in *Strange Fits of Passion,* for instance, is a journalist who believes she reported the truth about a domestic tragedy, but years later, upon receiving the convicted killer's account of the events, doubts her version of reality. Similarly, in *The Weight of Water*, jealousy blinds the photographer-narrator, a woman with a keen eye for penetrating surface realities. Shreve's literary strategies highlight the subjective nature of truth, the impossibility of ever really knowing another's reality, and the shifting ground on which truth is based.

Shreve hopes to earn a reputation as "a writer who tells a good story and has a beautiful command of the language," and she is well on her way to achieving it. Her plots, which frequently turn on murder, adultery, and incest, are compelling. Her style, which is both luminous and measured, lends its own intensity to these human catastrophes. In only a decade, Shreve has clearly created a body of work that commands both attention and respect for its exploration of the undercurrents of passion, creative and destructive, that lie beneath the surface of our domestic worlds.

BIBLIOGRAPHY: Roche, B. J., "Anita Shreve's Life Stories," in *Boston Globe Magazine* (September 1998).

—LINDA C. PELZER

SHULMAN, Alix Kates

Born 17 August 1932, Cleveland, Ohio
Daughter of Samuel S. and Dorothy Davis Kates; **married** Marcus Klein, 1953 (dissolved); Martin Shulman, 1959 (divorced); **children:** Teddy, Polly.

Praised by the *New York Times* as "the voice that for three decades provided a lyrical narrative of the changing position of women in American society," Alix Kates Shulman is a writer, feminist, and political activist. Through her numerous essays, short stories, novels, and children's books, she has used the landscape of her own life as a white, middle-class Jewish woman to explore the social and political issues shaping many women's lives in late 20th-century American culture.

Born in Cleveland, Ohio, in 1932, Shulman graduated from Bradford Junior College in 1951 and received a B.A. from Case Western Reserve University in Cleveland in 1953. She then moved to New York City, where she briefly studied philosophy at Columbia University (1953-54) and math at New York University (1960-61). She earned her living working as an encyclopedia editor until the late 1960s, when she attended her first meeting of the then burgeoning Women's Liberation Movement, became a member of the radical feminist group Redstockings, and by her own accounts was forever changed.

The publication of Shulman's first novel, *Memoirs of an Ex-Prom Queen* (1972) created a media sensation for its frank depiction of a young Midwestern girl's sexual coming of age. The story recounts the life of a white, middle class girl, Sasha, and the humiliations and degradations that passed as "normal" for girls like her growing up in the 1950s and 1960s. Suffering from unwanted groping by neighborhood boys and valued more for her beauty than her intelligence, by the time she is in her 20s, Sasha ends up married with children and no hope for a life of her own. Critic Lucy Rosenthal called *Memoirs* a "breakthrough book incorporat[ing] all the points of the Women's Liberation Movement and giv[ing] them rare fictional life." The novel sold over a million copies. *Memoirs* was re-released in a special 25th anniversary issue in 1997, when it was widely, and sadly, reviewed as "still relevant."

In both her fiction and nonfiction writing, Shulman often addresses the conflicts inherent in marriage, mothering, and having a creative life. Her first marriage was short lived; her second marriage to Martin Shulman, with whom she had two children, became the basis for one of her most famous essays, "A Marriage Contract." First written in 1969 and subsequently published in such mainstream magazines as *Redbook* and *Life* in 1971 and 1972, this was a contract intended to equally divide housework and childcare duties between spouses. Inspired by the women's movement analysis of the inequities in traditional marriage arrangements, the first principle was the most radical: woman's work is just as valuable as man's work, regardless of pay. Criticized in the popular press at the time, most memorably by Norman Mailer, who said he'd rather have a roommate than be married to her, "A Marriage Contract" has been anthologized in feminist, sociological, and even legal anthologies and textbooks, including one by Harvard Law School Professor Lon Fuller, in *Basic Contract Law.*

Shulman is also the biographer of the feminist anarchist Emma Goldman in *The Anarchist Life of Emma Goldman* (1971). She cites Goldman's work and life as one of her greatest political and literary inspirations. Researching and writing about Goldman's life helped Shulman gain the confidence and personal authority to write from her own life. Shulman also edited *Red Emma Speaks: Selected Writings and Speeches by Emma Goldman* (1972) and most recently, *Red Emma Speaks: An Emma Goldman Reader* (1996).

Other novels by Shulman include *Burning Questions* (1978), about the emergence and ascendance of the women's movement, *On the Stroll* (1981), about a bag lady and a young runaway, and *In Every Woman's Life. . .*(1987), which Shulman describes as a "feminist comedy of ideas."

In recent years Shulman has written two books of her own memoirs. In the first, *Drinking the Rain* (1995), which won the Body Mind Spirit Award of Excellence, Shulman narrates her own continuing journey of personal and spiritual discovery, living alone in a primitive cabin on an island off the coast of Maine. By now a mature woman, divorced, and with grown children, she describes foraging for wild food and relishing her solitude. Shulman's second memoir is a family memoir, *A Good Enough Daughter* (1999).

Shulman has taught literature and writing at New York University, Yale University, and the Universities of Colorado, Arizona, and Hawaii, where she held the Citizen's Chair from 1991-92. She has also been a visiting artist at the American Academy in Rome and the Rockefeller Foundation in Bellagios, Italy. She has been the recipient of awards from DeWitt Wallace-Reader's Digest and the National Endowment for the Arts. In addition to these literary accomplishments, Shulman's most recent feminist activism has included the founding of a Pacific chapter of the pro-choice group No More Nice Girls and work with the Women's Action Coalition (WAC). Today she lives half the year in New York City and the other half in her cabin in coastal Maine.

OTHER WORKS: *Bosley on the Number Line* (1970). *The Traffic in Women and Other Essays* (editor, 1970). *Women's Liberation: A Blueprint for the Future* (contributor, 1970). *Woman in Sexist Society: Studies in Power and Powerlessness* (contributor, V. Gornick and B. K. Moran, eds., 1971). *Awake or Asleep* (1971). *To the Barricades: The Anarchist Life of Emma Goldman* (1971). *Finders Keepers* (1972).

BIBLIOGRAPHY: Ascher, C. et al, eds., *Between Women: Biographers, Novelists, Critics, Teachers, and Artists Write about Their Work on Women* (1984). DuPlessis, R. B., and A. Snitow, eds., *The Feminist Memoir Project: Voices from Women's Liberation* (1998).

Reference works: *CA* 29-32 (1978). *CLC* 2 (1974), 10 (1979). *SATA* 7 (1975).

Other references: *Booklist* (15 June 1971, 15 June 1987). *Children's Literature in Education* 17 (1986). *Commonweal* 94 (21 May 1971). *LJ* (15 June 1971, Aug. 1981). *News & Observer* (12 Sept. 1997). *Newsweek* (1 May 1972). *NYT* (25 April 1972). *NYTBR* (23 Apr. 1972, 26 Mar. 1978, 31 May 1987). *Saturday Review* (20 May 1972).

—DENISE BAUER

SIDLOSKY, Carolyn
See FORCHÉ, Carolyn

SIGOURNEY, Lydia (Howard) Huntley

Born 1 September 1791, Norwich, Connecticut; **died** 10 June 1865, Hartford, Connecticut
Daughter of Ezekiel and Zerviah Wentworth Huntley; **married** Charles Sigourney, 1819; **children:** five, two of whom survived infancy

Lydia Huntley Sigourney was christened "Lydia Howard," in memory of her father's deceased first wife. As a child, she was favored by the widow of Dr. Daniel Lathrop, who employed Sigourney's father as a gardener. Mme. Lathrop made a pet of the clever, bookish girl, read with her and nurtured her sentimental tastes. After Mme. Lathrop's death in 1806, Sigourney became acquainted with Lathrop's relatives, the Wadsworths of Hartford, and with their assistance she and a friend—Nancy Maria Hyde—opened a school in Hartford in 1814. In 1815 Daniel Wadsworth helped her publish her first volume of poetry, *Moral Pieces*. In the following year, Sigourney published her first elegiac volume, a tribute to her former colleague, Nancy Maria Hyde.

In 1819 Sigourney gave up teaching to marry Charles Sigourney, a widower with three young children. Five children were born to her, of whom two survived infancy. When her husband's hardware business began to fail in the 1820s, Sigourney turned to writing as a source of income and quickly became successful. A book of her poems was published by Samuel Goodrich in 1827. By 1830, according to her biographer Gordon Haight, more than 20 periodicals were regularly accepting her occasional verse.

In 1840 Sigourney made a tour of Europe, intending both to meet the literary great and to view the "ruinous castle, where romance lingered, or royal palace, where pomp abode . . .'' Her *Pleasant Memories of Pleasant Lands* (1842) records this trip and gives her probably exaggerated account of "friendships" with Europe's literary elite. Sigourney was, at this time, an attractive woman with a cultivated manner who dressed carefully and was known for her elegant hands, a hallmark of the Victorian lady.

Mrs. Thomas Carlyle's description of this "over-the-water poetess" suggests Sigourney seemed artificial and provincial to her, "beplastered with rouge and pomatum—with long ringlets that never grew where they hung. . .all glistening in black satin. . .staring her eyes out, to give them animation," and even taking "the liberty of poking" Carlyle "now and then to make the lion roar. . . ." Sigourney was nonetheless received by many writers abroad and so enabled to puff her reputation at home in an era when European acceptance virtually guaranteed American success. To the end of her life, Sigourney remained a public figure, well known, even revered, especially in her native Connecticut.

Sigourney was early labeled "the American Hemans," a reference to her English counterpart, Mrs. Felicia Hemans, a popular writer of elegiac verse. Sigourney's work was indeed derivative and, like Heman's, unstintingly sentimental. Best known as a contributor to the "graveyard school" of popular verse, her "tributes," sometimes written at the request of unknown admirers, combine stilted rhetoric, conventional Christian consolation, and commonplace references to the condition or character of the deceased. Collections of her verse catalogue occasions on which the mourning note may be sounded. In one such volume, "The Anniversary of the Death of An Aged Friend" is followed by other verses lamenting deaths—"The Faithful Editor," "The Babe Who Loved Music," "The Good Son," "A Sunday School Scholar," and "The Original Proprietor of Mount Auburn" (a well-known rural cemetery near Boston). Despite the individualized titles, the verses are almost interchangeable evocations of genteel religiosity and the postures of decorous sorrow. Such collections, prettily printed and illustrated, were republished throughout Sigourney's lifetime. Their popularity reflects conventional attitudes toward death, the quality of popular piety, and the widespread admiration for cultured refinement in Victorian America.

Always a popular writer, Sigourney was never respected by contemporary literati. Edgar Allan Poe condemned her imitation of Hemans and her "gemmy," or overcolored, diction. (Sigourney described her home, for example, as a "domain. . .beloved by flowers" where life "in its varied forms, biped and quadrupedal, leaped and luxuriated among us.") Bayard Taylor in *Diversions of the Echo Club* (1876) parodied her verse "to see whether a respectable jingle of words, expressing ordinary and highly proper feelings, can be so imitated as to be recognized." The best known parody of Sigourney's style and its imitators is Mark Twain's "Ode to Stephen Dowling Bots, Dec'd" in *The Adventures of Huckleberry Finn* (1884). However meager its merits, Sigourney's verse is an important index of an era in American taste, and she herself was hailed by Taylor as "good old Mother Sigourney" who had once been "almost our only woman-poet." John Greenleaf Whittier, in a memorial verse of 1887, also noted "She sang alone, ere womanhood had known / The gift of song which fills the air today."

OTHER WORKS: *The Writings of Nancy Maria Hyde* (1816). *The Square Table* (1819). *Traits of the Aborigines of America* (1822). *Sketch of Connecticut Forty Years Since* (1824). *Poems* (1827). *Female Biography* (1829). *Biography of Pious Persons* (1832).

Evening Readings in History (1833). *The Farmer and Soldier* (1833). *How to Be Happy* (1833). *The Intemperate* (1833). *Letters to Young Ladies* (1833). *Memoir of Phebe P. Hammond* (1833). *Report of the Hartford Female Beneficent Society* (1833). *Poems* (1834). *Poetry for Children* (1834). *Sketches* (1834). *Tales and Essays for Children* (1835). *Memoir of Margaret and Henrietta Flower* (1835). *Zinzendorff, and Other Poems* (1835). *History of Marcus Aurelius* (1936). *Olive Buds* (1836). *Poems for Children* (1836). *History of the Condition of Women* (1837). *The Girl's Reading-Book. . .* (1838). *Letters to Mothers* (1838). *The Boy's Reading-Book* (1839). *The Religious Souvenir for 1839* (1839). *Memoir of Mrs. Mary Ann Hooker* (1840). *The Religous Souvenir for 1840* (1840). *Letters to Young Ladies* (1841). *Pocahontas, and Other Poems* (1841). *Poems, Religious and Elegiac* (1841). *The Pictorial Reader. . .* (1844). *The Lovely Sisters* (1845). *Poetry for Seamen* (1845). *Scenes in My Native Land* (1845). *Myrtis, with Other Etchings and Sketchings* (1846). *The Voice of Flowers* (1846). *The Weeping Willow* (1847). *Water-drops* (1848). *The Young Ladies Offering* (with others, 1848). *Illustrated Poems. . .* (1849) *Poems for the Sea* (1850). *Whisper to a Bride* (1850). *Letters to My Pupils* (1851). *Examples of Life and Death* (1852). *Margaret and Henrietta* (1852). *Olive Leaves* (1852). *Voices of Home* (1852). *The Faded Hope* (1853). *Memoir of Mrs. Harriet Newell Cook* (1853). *Past Meridian* (1854). *The Western Home, and Other Poems* (1854). *Sayings of the Little Ones, and Poems for their Mothers* (1855). *Examples from the Eighteenth and Nineteenth Centuries* (1857). *Lucy Howard's Journal* (1858). *The Daily Counsellor* (1859). *Gleanings* (1860). *The Man of Uz, and Other Poems* (1862). *Selections from Various Sources* (1863). *Sayings of Little Ones* (1864). *Letters of Life* (1866). *The Transplanted Daisy: Memoir of Frances Racilla Hackley* (n.d.).

BIBLIOGRAPHY: Haight, G. S., *Mrs. Sigourney: The Sweet Singer of Hartford* (1930). *NAW* (1971).

—JANE BENARDETE

SILKO, Leslie Marmon

Born 5 March 1948, Albuquerque, New Mexico
Daughter of Lee H. and Virginia Marmon; **married** John Silko (divorced); **children:** two sons

Native American novelist, poet, essayist, and short story writer, Leslie Marmon Silko was raised in Old Laguna, New Mexico. The Spaniards had founded a mission there early in the 18th century, but old Laguna had been formed centuries earlier by cattle-keeping Pueblos, successfully repelling raids by the Navajos and the Apaches. Silko's heritage is complicated: her great-grandfather was Caucasian, while her mother was a mixed-breed Plains Indian; she also has Mexican ancestors. Silko uses the heritage as a source of strength: "I suppose at the core of my writing is the attempt to identify what it is to be a half-breed or mixed blooded person; what it is to grow up neither white nor fully traditional Indian." She asserts, however, that "what I know is

Laguna. This place I am from is everything I am as a writer and human being.'' Silko draws from the oral traditions and folklore of her heritage to enrich her work and to relate Native American moral codes, values, and experiences. She insists storytelling is integral to the oral tradition in order to store knowledge, and her themes include pride in transmitting an untouched heritage to scholars, aware that hers is a culture threatened with extinction. She recounts in her short stories and poems what happens when a way of life that as existed for centuries rapidly undergoes cataclysmic and brutal changes with the coming of the Anglos. Community and tribal life break down under the pressure of external conflicts, the advent of reservation life, and the introduction of English-based educational schools. She insightfully interprets her people's plight—disease, wars, broken treaties, relocation, alcoholism, promiscuity—but her characters are seldom embittered or defeated. Instead they cope with adversity, using survival tactics learned from their past to enrich and strengthen their resolution to triumph in spite of a harsh environment or Caucasian society abuse. For Silko, literature is an extension of an oral tradition based on the power of the word to maintain a sense of a Native American tribal and community culture. Although nostalgia and a sense of loss haunt her stories, they frequently end on an optimistic hope for a better future where diverse ethnic groups have learned respect for each other's unique lifestyles.

Silko's first published story, ''The Man to Send Rain Clouds'' (1969) recounts an actual event of an old man found dead and given a traditional Native American burial. Although the local priest sees this as heresy, he nonetheless wisely cooperates by sprinkling holy water on the corpse when Grandpa's relatives tell him the water is necessary so the old man would not be thirsty, and through some form of sympathetic magic ''could send them big thunderclouds.''

''Tony's Story'' (1981), also a fictionalization of an actual event, describes the reasons for an embittered war veteran's killing of a racist state patrolman. *Ceremony* (1977), the first full-length novel published by a Native American woman, also uses a World War II veteran in acute physical and emotional straits, managing to survive by reestablishing contact with his Native American cultural roots. Silko explained that the novel ''is essentially about the powers inherent in the process of storytelling. . . The chanting or telling of ancient stories to effect certain cures or protest from illness and harm have always been a part of the Pueblo's curing ceremonies.''

There is strong moral connection between Silko's artistic delight in crafting a story and the therapeutic functional purpose she hopes it will serve in the Native American community. In both *Ceremony* and the aptly titled *Storyteller* (1981), which also includes poems and photographs as well as short stories, she sketches realistically sympathetic people living in harmony with animals and with the forces of nature. ''Lullaby'' (1974), included in *The Best American Short Stories* (1975) and *Two Hundred Years of Great American Short Stories* (1975), shows the tough, devoted perseverance of an old woman, Ayah, sitting wrapped in a blanket with her husband, Chato, their backs against a rock as a storm beats down. Ayah sings a lullaby as the story ends: ''The

earth is your mother, she holds you. The sky is your father, he protects you. Sleep, sleep. Rainbow is your sister, she loves you. The winds are your brothers, they sing to you. Sleep, sleep. We are together always.'' Thus, Silko draws upon religious and philosophic ideas from her Native American oral and cultural storytelling traditions to create poignant artistic creations.

One of Silko's best critics, Per Seyerstedt, believes her achievement is to have ''raised the life and problems of a minority to the level of general significance.'' *The Delicacy and Strength of Lace: Letters Between Leslie Marmon Silko and James Wright* (1985) chronicles an 18-month exchange of correspondence and friendship-through-the-mail; the letters interpret both writers' concept of brotherly love, sensitivity to nature's beauty, and the clarity of their courageous voices. Silko's sensitivity and humanity are displayed through language always rich, yet controlled and finely tuned, reminding us that the persistent drums of tradition reverberating down the generations powerfully shape lives today.

Silko's second novel, *Almanac of the Dead* (1991), was a 10-year project for the author, evidenced by the wide scope of the story and large cast of characters. Some critics viewed the variety of characters as the novel's weakest feature, but still concluded the story was well worth reading for its strengths.

Yellow Woman and a Beauty of the Spirit: Essays on Native American Life Today (1997) returned to Silko's real strength—short fiction. The collection succeeds in blending Silko's life experiences and ethnicity with ancient Pueblo ideas. Her recent novel, *Gardens in the Dunes* (1999), has been hailed as her best yet. In it she examines differences between white and Native American cultures, and illustrates her preference for the latter. *Kirkus* calls it ''a thoughtful exploration of the incompatibility of dissimilar traditions and an absorbing reading experience.''

Silko's awards and honors include a grant from the National Endowment for the Arts and a poetry award from *Chicago Review*, both in 1974, the Pushcart Prize for poetry in 1977, and a Catherine T. MacArthur Foundation grant in 1983. She has written screenplays for public television and has taught at the University of New Mexico-Albuquerque and the University of Arizona.

OTHER WORKS: *Laguna Woman* (1974). ''Lullaby'' in *The Ethnic American Woman: Problems, Protests, Lifestyle* (edited by E. Blicksilver, 1978). ''Gallup, New Mexico—Indian Capital of the World,'' et al., in *The Third Woman: Minority Women Writers of the United States* (edited by D. Fisher, 1980). *Sacred Water Narratives and Pictures* (1993). *Yellow Woman* (1993). *Love Poem and Slim Man Canyon* (1996).

BIBLIOGRAPHY: Bruchac, J., ed., *Songs From This Earth on Turtle's Back* (1983). Fisher, D., *The Third Women* (1980). Jaskoski, H., *Leslie Marmon Silko: A Study of Short Fiction* (1998). Seyersted, P., *Leslie Marmon Silko* (1980).

Reference works: *CA* (1985, 1988, Online 1999). *CLC* (1983). *CN* (1986). *CP* (1985). *Encyclopedia of Frontier and Western*

Fiction (1983). *FC* (1990). *Oxford Companion to Women's Writing in the United States* (1995).

Other references: *American Indian Quarterly* (Winter 1977-78, 1979). *American Studies in Scandinavia* (1981). *Booklist* (15 February 1996). *Harper's* (June 1977). *KR* (1 January 1996, 1 February 1999). *LATBR* (4 Jan. 1987). *MELUS* (Winter 1978, Summer 1981). *Ms.* (July 1981). *New Leader* (6 June 1977). *Newsweek* (4 July 1977). *NYT* (12 June 1977, 23 April 1978, 25 May 1981). *NYTBR* (12 June 1977). *Prairie Schooner* (Winter 1977-78). *PW* (27 Feb. 1978). *Saturday Review* (May 1981). *Southwest Review* (Spring 1979). *Time* (8 Aug. 1983). *WP* (24 April 1977). *WPBW* (24 April 1977).

Web sites: Engle, S., Review of *Gardens in the Dunes* available online at Amazon.com (4 July 1999). ''Voices From the Gaps: Leslie Marmon Silko,'' available online at voices.cla.umn.edu/authors/LeslieMarmonSilko (4 July 1999).

—EDITH BLICKSILVER,
UPDATED BY CARRIE SNYDER

SIMON, Kate

Born Kaila Grobsmith, 5 December 1912, Warsaw, Poland; **died** 4 February 1990, New York, New York

Daughter of Jacob and Lina Babicz Grobsmith; **married** Dr. Stanley Goldman (common law, died 1942); Robert Simon, 1947 (divorced); **children:** Alexandra

Kate Simon's passionate and daring life provided excellent material for her many popular travel books and the memoirs she produced in old age. Born in the Jewish section of Warsaw, she emigrated to New York with her family at age four and grew up in working-class neighborhoods in the city, where she excelled in the public schools and displayed unusual musical talent. Holding a series of odd jobs, she worked her way through the demanding James Monroe High School and Hunter College (B.A., 1935). A common-law marriage to Dr. Stanley Goldman ended with his death in 1942, leaving Simon to support herself and their daughter, Alexandra, by working at various editorial and reviewing jobs.

After her marriage to Robert Simon, which apparently freed her from financial constraints, Simon began to travel extensively throughout Europe and Mexico. She published her first book, *New York Places and Pleasures: An Uncommon Guidebook*, in 1959. Hailed as a landmark in the travel genre, it went through four revisions and sparked a successful career in travel writing. Simon went on to produce guides to Mexico City, Paris, London, Rome, Italy, and England—all informed by her artistic tastes and graceful prose—as well as the more historically focused *Fifth Avenue: A Very Social History* (1978) and *A Renaissance Tapestry: The Gonzaga of Mantua* (1988).

Acclaimed as these works are, it is Simon's memoirs that distinguish her as more than an elegant and cosmopolitan stylist. *Bronx Primitive: Portraits in a Childhood* (1982, latest reissue 1997) shocked readers with its revelation of intense emotional

conflict and sexual abuse within her family: Simon recounts the strong influence of her mother, who built her own business as a corset maker and encouraged her daughter to acquire an education and the means to be self-supporting. She describes her defiance of her shoemaker father, who insisted she leave high school to become a concert pianist and who, Simon believed, tolerated the sexual abuse by relatives and acquaintances to which she was subjected from early adolescence. Leaving her family in her early teens, Simon eagerly absorbed the influence of leftist politics, antibourgeois sentiment, artistic values, and free love among the 1920s New York City avant-garde. *A Wider World: Portraits in an Adolescence* (1986) reveals, however, that this life was scarcely romantic: Simon was again the victim of sexual predators (sometimes her teachers) and was often desperately poor. She describes shabby lodgings and meager jobs, illegal abortions, and above all, her struggle to nourish her growing aesthetic and intellectual sensibilities.

The posthumously published *Etchings in an Hourglass* (1990) is the most digressive of her books, and also the most bitter and intimate. Here she confronts her grief and anger at the early deaths of Goldman and of her only child, and contemplates a long life filled with as much doubt as comfort: ''At seventeen I was so enamored of life. . .that I promised myself I would experience everything, stipulating no qualities good or bad, and it has pretty much all happened. Little more than I knew at seventeen do I surely know who I am at seventy-five.'' Simon's books document, through the consciousness of a complex and brave woman, the arduous process of living fully.

Also widely published in such magazines as *Harper's, Holiday, National Geographic, Saturday Review*, and *Vogue*, Simon received awards of honor from Hunter College and the English Speaking Union. The National Book Critics Circle listed *Bronx Primitive* as one of the most distinguished books published in 1982.

OTHER WORKS: *New York* (1964). *Mexico: Places and Pleasures* (1965, 1988). *Kate Simon's Paris: Places and Pleasures* (1967). *Kate Simon's London: Places and Pleasures* (1968). *Italy: The Places in Between* (1972, 1987). *England's Green and Pleasant Land* (1974).

BIBLIOGRAPHY: Burstein, J., *Writing Mothers, Writing Daughters: Tracing the Maternal in Stories by American Jewish Women* (1996). Cahill, S. N., ed., *Writing Women's Lives: An Anthology of Autobiographical Narratives by 20th Century American Women Writers* (1994). Norris, G., ed., *The Seasons of Women: An Anthology* (1996). Rose, P., *The Norton Book of Women's Lives* (1993). Yang, M. C., ''From Ethnicity to a Wider World: The Education of Kate Simon and Maxine Hong Kingston'' (thesis, 1992).

Reference works: *CA* (1989, 1990). *MTCW* (1991).

Other references: *Feminist Studies* (Spring 1991). *Los Angeles Times* (4 May 1982). *Ms.* (June 1982, July 1986). *NYT* (5 Feb. 1990). *NYTBR* (19 Aug. 1990). *PW* (14 May 1982). *Time* (14 July 1967, 19 Apr. 1982, 24 Feb. 1986).

—ELIZABETH SHOSTAK

SINCLAIR, Bertha Muzzy

Born 15 November 1871, Cleveland, Minnesota; **died** 23 July 1940, Los Angeles, California
Wrote under: B. M. Bower
Daughter of Washington and Eunice A. Miner Muzzy; **married** Clayton J. Bower, 1890; Bertrand W. Sinclair, 1906; Robert E. Cowan; **children:** four

Bertha Muzzy Sinclair moved to Montana as a youngster, where she gained expertise in ranching and acquaintance with cowboys, which she would later use in her novels. Sinclair lived in the West most of her life; she was married three times and was the mother of four children.

Sinclair wrote nearly 60 Westerns from 1904 to 1940. Her use of initials as a pseudonym led many to assume her works were written by a man. In this guise she was probably the first woman, and certainly the most prolific, to write in the genre of the "formula" Western. *Chip of the Flying U* (1904) furnishes the basic plot for Sinclair's writing and introduces characters for later works. "The Happy Family," the cowboys of the Flying U Ranch, appear in several subsequent novels and furnish prototypes for others. Chip is the first of many young heroes predictably tall, handsome, taciturn, and, by modern standards, remarkably naive about his emotions. Della, the heroine, is petite and dimpled, and has the tiny hands and feet so admired in the 19th century. Their love affair suffers many vicissitudes before it reaches its foregone conclusion, with intimations they will live happily ever after. Later books sometimes offer more violence and villainy, but in most of the novels the happy outcome is predictable.

Sinclair's detailed descriptions of ranch life in the early 20th century make her books attractive. The habits—down to the typical gestures—of the cowboys are well depicted, from the backhand twist the practiced roper uses to catch a calf to the apparently eternal preoccupation of all cowboys with their cigarettes. The men's affection for their horses is an inevitable part of the Western, but, in addition, the actions of horses often affect the stories, with scenes in which the individual characteristics of horses play a major role. Dialogue especially reflects both the Western setting and the period in which Sinclair wrote. When a man declares his love it is apt to be in terms of a card game: "It's my deal. . .do you want to know what's trump?"

Characterization of males is, on the whole, weak, with one hero almost indistinguishable from another and supporting characters flat. Sinclair's women, on the other hand, are often accomplished and independent, indicating Sinclair's interest in unconventional roles for women. She introduces two women doctors in *Chip of the Flying U*, for example, in which the heroine is not only a doctor, she is also a crack shot and brave in the face of danger. Housewifely skills assume little importance in other books as well. In *The Five Furies of Leaning Ladder* (1935), five orphan girls run their ranch in the face of many obstacles; the one sister who is domestic is relegated to a minor role.

The suffering young mother in *Cabin Fever* (1918), whose little boy has been kidnapped, is much more interesting than the male hero in this mining story. The heroine of *The Heritage of the Sioux* (1916) is an Indian. She travels a long distance alone to find the man she loves. Later, when she learns the man she promised to marry has betrayed her friends, she kills herself.

Sinclair's books read like early Western scenarios, and with good reason: the uncluttered scenery and rapid uncomplicated actions of her characters lend themselves easily to film. Several of Sinclair's novels were in fact made into movies. Some books, written in the 1910s, in the early days of the film industry, portray the cowboys forming their own film company and making Westerns in New Mexico.

Sinclair brought a fairytale West to life for her readers. In spite of the realism of her descriptions of Western life and specific details of ranch scenes, Sinclair's description of the larger scene is vague and ephemeral. The background, no matter what state is named, is simply "the West," and her books are typical formula Westerns. There are many weaknesses in Sinclair's writing; nevertheless, her stories are fun—warm and full of humor.

OTHER WORKS: *The Lure of the Dim Trails* (1907). *Her Prairie Knight* (1908). *The Lonesome Trail* (1909). *The Long Shadow* (1909). *The Happy Family* (1910). *The Range Dwellers* (1910). *Good Indian* (1912). *Lonesome Land* (1912). *The Gringos* (1913). *The Uphill Climb* (1913). *Flying U Ranch* (1914). *The Ranch at the Wolverine* (1914). *Flying U's Last Stand* (1915). *Jean of the Lazy A* (1915). *The Phantom Herd* (1916). *The Lookout Man* (1917). *Starr of the Desert* (1917). *Skyrider* (1918). *The Thunder Bird* (1919). *The Quirt* (1920). *Rim o' the World* (1920). *Casey Ryan* (1921). *Cow Country* (1921). *Trail of the White Mule* (1922). *The Parowan Bonanza* (1923). *The Voice at Johnnywater* (1923). *The Bellehelen Mine* (1924). *Desert Brew* (1924). *Black Thunder* (1925). *Meadowlark Basin* (1925). *Van Patten* (1926). *White Wolves* (1926). *The Adam Chasers* (1927). *Points West* (1928). *The Swallowfork Bulls* (1928). *Rodeo* (1929). *Fool's Goal* (1930). *Tiger Eye* (1930). *Dark Horse* (1931). *The Long Loop* (1931). *Laughing Water* (1932). *Rocking Arrow* (1932). *Open Land* (1933). *Trails Meet* (1933). *The Flying U Strikes* (1934). *The Haunted Hills* (1934). *The Dry Ridge Gang* (1935). *Trouble Rides the Wind* (1935). *The North Wind Do Blow* (1936). *Shadow Mountain* (1936). *Pirates of the Range* (1937). *Starry Night* (1938). *The Wind Blows West* (1938). *The Singing Hill* (1939). *The Man on Horseback* (1940). *The Spirit of the Range* (1940). *Sweet Grass* (1940). *The Family Failing* (1941).

BIBLIOGRAPHY: Reference works: *TCA*.
        Other references: *NYHT* (24 July 1940). *NYT* (24 July 1940).

—HELEN STAUFFER

SINCLAIR, Jo
See SEID, Ruth

SINGER, June K.

Born 23 October 1918, Cleveland, Ohio
Daughter of Jonas and Regine Kurlander; **married** Richard E. Singer, 1939; **children:** one daughter

June K. Singer was the first of two daughters; her father was a dentist, her mother a journalist. Singer saw early that a woman could be successful in a "man's world" without losing touch with her feminine roots.

Singer earned a B.S. in English and education from Ohio State University in 1939. She married a rabbi and they had one daughter. In 1959 Singer received an M.A. in counseling and guidance from Northwestern University. She and her husband went to Zurich, where in 1964 they both received their diplomas as analysts from the C. G. Jung Institute. Shortly after their return to the U.S., Singer's husband died. Singer settled in Chicago to practice, where she was one of the founders of two Jungian organizations. She returned to Northwestern University for a Ph.D. in psychology (1968).

The Unholy Bible (1970) is a psychological interpretation of William Blake and an extension of Singer's thesis for her analyst's diploma. It was roundly and often deservedly attacked for the tenuous connections Singer draws between images in the poetry and Blake's unconscious desires and drives. At a time when many literary critics were reviling any use of biographical materials, the reviews of this book often overlooked Singer's many useful insights, such as how Blake's writing, engraving, and drawing gave him the psychic discipline that grounded and controlled the flooding of his unconscious. Singer's style moves unevenly from overlush appreciation to smooth and measured analysis, yet *The Unholy Bible* is an often insightful example of Jungian psychobiography.

Singer's style and thought cohere far better in *Boundaries of the Soul* (1972), and here her view of Jungian thought within its context of contemporary culture reveals a comprehensive, even philosophical, perspective. She departs from some of Jung's ideas, such as his sometimes Victorian concepts of women and his rather limiting and reductionist personality typology. The book is not only an introduction for the general reader but a critique of Jungian thought.

Androgyny (1976) is more difficult to read, but it is also more rich and original. Singer adds a much needed metaphysical and philosophical dimension to the analysis of relationships between the masculine and feminine in both inter- and intrapersonal relationships. She sees the dynamic energy for this development as coming from the alternating union and polarities of masculine and feminine in the archetype of the androgyne. Some feminist reviewers faulted Singer for not presenting a "highly sophisticated, empirical" study or chided her for delving into "esoterica." Singer suggests the universe is winding up, not down, as it develops more complexity and higher consciousness. The book seems to ramble at times because of the great breadth of material included, but Singer's analyses of non-Western systems of thought and their significance are clear and often brilliant. Hers is a hopeful vision, perhaps overly sanguine at times but nevertheless well worth reading.

OTHER WORKS: Has contributed to the following works: *C. G. Jung and the Humanities: Toward a Hermeneutics of Culture* (1990); *To Be a Woman: The Birth of the Conscious Feminine* (1990); *The Allure of Gnosticism: The Gnostic Experience in Jungian Psychology and Contemporary Culture* (1995).

BIBLIOGRAPHY: Rountree, C. *On Women Turning 70: Honoring the Voices of Wisdom* (1999).

Other references: *Contemporary Psychology* (October 1991). *Journal of Analytical Psychology* (1972, 1974, 1977). *Living Your Myths* (video, 1992). *Ms.* (Nov. 1976).

—STEPHANIE DEMETRAKOPOULOS

SINGLETON, Anne
See BENEDICT, Ruth

SINGMASTER, Elsie

Born 29 August 1879, Schuylkill Haven, Pennsylvania; **died** 3 September 1958, Gettysburg, Pennsylvania
Daughter John A. and Caroline Hoopes Singmaster; **married** Harold Lewars, 1912 (died 1915)

Elsie Singmaster's father was of German Lutheran stock; her mother, a descendant of English Quakers. Singmaster seems to have developed along the lines of the former. When she was four the family moved to Macungie, Pennsylvania, and later to Brooklyn, New York, and Allentown, Pennsylvania, where Singmaster graduated from high school. After a year at West Chester Normal School, she attended Cornell for two years. Five years later she entered Radcliffe, graduating in 1907, a member of Delta Gamma and Phi Beta Kappa.

In 1909 she became one of the first women to receive an honorary Litt.D. from Gettysburg College; similar degrees were awarded to her by Pennsylvania College (1916), Muhlenburg College (1929), and Wilson College (1934).

Singmaster married a musician in 1912, but after his death in 1915 she returned to the family home at Gettysburg, where her father was connected with the Lutheran Theological Seminary. Singmaster lived in this historic small town the rest of her life, drawing from it and the surrounding area ample material for her steady writing. From her father and from her surroundings she gained a comprehensive knowledge of the German immigrants who settled so much of Pennsylvania. And with amazing industry she reproduced in fiction (both adult and juvenile) their way of life, their mores, their quaint turns of speech. Creating a typical rural village, Millerstown, she peopled it with appealing characters who appear and reappear throughout her fiction. Occasionally, she builds a story around an historic figure and at times she incorporates actual events into her plot.

From the beginning of Singmaster's career—while she was still in college—magazines were glad to buy her stories; she remarked once that the editors' interest in those first years was probably caught more by the ''local color'' she gave than by any real literary merit. *Kathy Gaumer* (1915) was praised for its picture of the Pennsylvania Germans, but as time went on critics pointed out the technical excellence of her fiction as seen in structure, characterization, and comprehension of life. Hers is perhaps the first fiction to emphasize the importance of the German settlers of Pennsylvania.

History was one of Singmaster's special interests. She wrote several history books for children, as well as a popular life of Martin Luther (published in 1917, on the 400th anniversary of the Reformation). Living most of her life in Gettysburg, Singmaster was able to do a great deal of thorough research on the famous battle, research which she used to good effect in her novels.

Perhaps Singmaster's most widely known work is her controversial *I Speak For Thaddeus Stevens* (1947), a life of the forceful Pennsylvania congressman who advocated the sternest measures of Reconstruction. It is sensitively written; Singmaster tries to show the reasons behind Stevens' passionate advocacy of chastisement for the South, but some reviewers felt Singmaster showed too much partiality for her subject. It remains, however, a vivid picture of a brilliant, iron-willed man who fought for what he considered was right.

I Speak for Thaddeus Stevens is one of Singmaster's outstanding achievements, and it may be ranked with her imaginative recreation of the Gettysburg battle and her beautifully wrought pictures of Pennsylvania German life as her contribution to American literature.

OTHER WORKS: *When Sarah Saved the Day* (1909). *When Sarah Went to School* (1910). *Gettysburg* (1913). *Emmeline* (1916). *The Long Journey* (1917). *Short Life of Martin Luther* (1917). *Basil Everman* (1920). *John Baring's House* (1920). *Ellen Levis* (1921). *Bennet Malin* (1922). *The Hidden Road* (1923). *A Boy at Gettysburg* (1924). *Bred in the Bone* (1925). *Book of the Constitution* (1926). *Book of the United States* (1926). *Book of the Colonies* (1927). *Keller's Anna Ruth* (1926). *''Sewing Susie''* (1927). *Virginia's Bandit* (1928). *What Everybody Wanted* (1928). *You Make Your Own Luck* (1929). *A Little Money Ahead* (1930). *The Young Ravenals* (1932). *Swords of Steel* (1933). *The Magic Mirror* (1934). *Stories of Pennsylvania* (3 vols., 1937-1938). *Rifles for Washington* (1938). *The Loving Heart* (1939). *Stories to Read at Christmas* (1940). *A High Wind Rising* (1942). *The Isle of

Que (1948). *I Hear of a River: The Story of Pennsylvania's Susquehanna* (1950).

BIBLIOGRAPHY: Overton, G., *The Women Who Make Our Novels* (1928).
       Reference works: *American Novelists of Today* (1951). *TCA.* Other references: *Ladies' Home Journal* (March 1925). *NYT* (1 Oct. 1958). New York *Tribune* (1 March 1925).

—ABIGAIL ANN HAMBLEN

SKINNER, Constance Lindsay

Born 7 December 1877, Quesnal, British Columbia, Canada; **died** 27 March 1937, New York, New York
Daughter of Robert J. and Annie Lindsay Skinner

Constance Lindsay Skinner was profoundly influenced by her childhood at a fur trading post in the Peace River area of the Canadian Northwest where her father held a position with the Hudson's Bay Company. Her best works have dealt with this area and the historical interaction of Native Americans and traders.

Skinner began as a journalist writing drama and music criticism for Los Angeles and San Francisco newspapers. She became a freelance writer in New York, writing reviews and poetry. In 1910 her first play, *David*, was produced, and in 1917 her second, in New York, *Good Morning, Rosamund!*

Her first historical works were two volumes in the Yale Chronicles of America, a series addressed to the general reader. The two works, *Pioneers of the Old Southwest* (1919) and *Adventurers of Oregon* (1921), were praised for their ''gusto'' and vitality. They showed her sense of the dramatic and her highly personalized approach to historical work. They were also criticized for their impressionist quality and lack of detailed scholarship.

Skinner placed strong emphasis on the environmentalist approach to history, reflecting the influence of Frederick Jackson Turner. In *Pioneers of the Old Southwest*, she argues that the ''spirit of the frontier was modeling out of old clay a new Adam to answer the needs of a new earth.'' She traces with broad appreciation the development of the various ethnic groups into commonwealth builders. In *Adventurers of Oregon*, she sympathetically portrayed the ''romance of the fur trade'' and the interaction of American, British, and Native American lifestyles.

After the chronicles, Skinner turned to poetry and fiction to reveal her understanding of the origin of the American nation and the importance of the frontier. Her dramatic sense of history found an outlet especially in the 11 adventure stories she wrote for children between 1925 and 1934. In these works she stressed the courage and perseverance of women no less than men.

Beaver, Kings, and Cabins (1933), perhaps Skinner's most ambitious historical work, is an effort to recapture the lost world of the fur trader and his interaction with the natural world and with the Native Americans. Skinner's tone is essentially poetic and romantic; at times she dramatizes her narrative, occasionally inserting dialogue. Tracing the fur traders from their Atlantic coast origins to the Alaskan wilds, she gives primary attention to the era of imperial conflicts when the beaver trade was dominant.

Interspersed in some of Skinner's works are Native American poems. These are her own concepts, not translations; they grew out of her early childhood experiences with Native American culture. In 1930 she published a volume of such poems, *Songs of the Coast Dwellers*; the book won considerable acclaim for Skinner's interpretations of Native American moods and her basic empathy with Native American life.

Skinner's last significant venture in American history was the editing of the Rivers of America series. In an introductory statement, reprinted in most of the early volumes and issued in 1937 as *Rivers and American Folk*, Skinner sets forth her concerns in writing history. What is truly important, she argues, is "folk-centered" history and "history as literature." Her aim is to "kindle imagination and to reveal American Folk to one another." While her historical works lack the closely woven texture and the considered perspectives of trained historians, Skinner succeeded in her own aim. She did indeed "kindle imagination" and portrayed dramatically the frontier experiences of the American folk.

OTHER WORKS: *Adventures in the Wilderness* (with C. Wister, 1925).

BIBLIOGRAPHY: Reference works: *NAW* (1971).
Other references: *American History Review* (Oct. 1920). *NYT* (19 Oct. 1919, 5 Oct. 1930, 25 Sept. 1933). *SR* (31 May 1930, 30 Sept. 1933).

—INZER BYERS

SKINNER, Cornelia Otis

Born 30 May 1901, Chicago, Illinois; **died** 9 July 1979, New York, New York
Daughter of Otis and Maud Durbin Skinner; **married** Alden S. Blodget, 1928; **children:** one son

Cornelia Otis Skinner was the only child born to a theatrical couple. Her mother retired from the stage shortly after Skinner was born, but her father went on to gain national prominence as an actor and matinee idol. Otis Skinner spent much of his time on tour, but the family's desire for a stable and respectable home life led them to settle in Bryn Mawr, Pennsylvania, where Skinner grew up.

Tall and lanky, Skinner thought of herself as an ugly duckling. The autobiographical *Family Circle* (1948) underscores the embarrassing contrast between her mother's effortless charm and Skinner's adolescent gawkiness. Nevertheless, from an early age Skinner gravitated toward the theater. After two years at Bryn

Mawr, where she proved herself hopelessly unmathematical, Skinner departed for Paris. There she attended lectures at the Sorbonne while also receiving classical theater training from Jacques Copeau and Émile Dehelly of the Comédie Francaise. Skinner's father paved her way onto the Broadway stage by providing a small role for her in his own production of the Spanish novel *Blood and Sand*.

While undertaking small roles in a number of productions, Skinner wrote a play for her father. Called *Captain Fury*, it opened in December 1925. Soon Skinner was using her writing talents for her own benefit, creating lively theatrical monologues, which she performed in the U.S. and London. The monologues grew into a series of historical costume dramas, with Skinner herself playing all the roles.

From a sentimental novel of the day, *Edna His Wife*, Skinner developed a monodrama in which she portrayed three generations of women. This ambitious work toured the country in 1938, generating great public enthusiasm, although the New York critics were less kind. She was much better received by them in the title role of Shaw's *Candida* and in other full-fledged productions.

Skinner also contributed light verse and humorous essays to the *New Yorker, Harper's Bazaar, Ladies' Home Journal*, and other magazines. The witty depiction of human social foibles is her particular specialty, and her sketches often turn on comic self-deprecation. Skinner married in 1928 and had one son, and she often wrote of domestic matters. Her satirical treatment of her own ineptness as wife, mother, and social animal is good-natured enough so readers can identify easily with her tales of woe. Her essays have been collected into a number of genuinely funny volumes, among them *Tiny Garments* (1932), *That's Me All Over* (1948), and *Bottoms Up!* (1955).

Skinner's most famous volume is *Our Hearts Were Young and Gay* (1942), an uproarious account of a youthful trip abroad in the company of a schoolmate, Emily Kimbrough. The book details how these two naive young ladies spent the night in a brothel, came down with childhood diseases at inopportune moments, and otherwise found themselves in hot water. It captured the public fancy, and a million copies were sold. Inevitably there was soon a motion picture version (1944), and in 1948 Jean Kerr adapted the book into a popular play. Through all of this, Skinner did not neglect her own stage career. With Samuel Albert Taylor she wrote a successful Broadway comedy, *The Pleasure of His Company* (1959), and played one of the key supporting roles to general acclaim. Her one-woman shows also continued.

Skinner's skills as a biographer were first displayed in *Family Circle*, which is as much about her parents as herself. Her major work on Sarah Bernhardt, *Madame Sarah* (1967), was well received, less for its scholarship than for the vivid and affectionate portrait it draws.

Skinner's reputation in the decades after her death in 1979 rested on the grace with which she moved in several directions at once. Both a master of the comic sketch and a serious researcher into theater history, she brought to her writing projects an effortless quality that tends to obscure her very real talent.

OTHER WORKS: *Excuse It, Please!* (1936). *Dithers and Jitters* (1938). *Soap Behind the Ears* (1941). *Popcorn* (1943). *Nuts in May* (1950). *The Ape in Me* (1959). *Elegant Wits and Grand Horizontals* (1962). *Life with Lindsay & Crouse* (1976).

BIBLIOGRAPHY: Reference works: *Oxford Companion to Women's Writing in the United States* (1995).

Other references: *New Yorker* (21 Nov. 1942). *NYT* (5 Sept. 1948, 10 July 1979). *NYTBR* (8 Jan. 1967). *SR* (19 Nov. 1938, 14 Nov. 1942, 11 Sept. 1948). *TLS* (27 April 1967).

—BEVERLY GRAY BIENSTOCK

SLADE, Caroline

Born 7 October 1886, Minneapolis, Minnesota; **died** 25 June 1975, Saratoga Springs, New York
Daughter of William G. McCormick; **married** John Slade

At the age of seven Caroline Slade moved with her family to Saratoga Springs, New York, where she resided for the rest of her life. She attended Skidmore College and married a lawyer and lecturer at the college. A county social worker for many years, Slade organized and became first director of the Saratoga County Board of Child Welfare. She was also an adviser to the Children's Court. In 1933, she retired and began to write articles, short stories, and novels based on her social work experience.

All Slade's writings portray in realistic detail the lives of the urban poor, and all are strong indictments of the inequities of American society. In *The Triumph of Willie Pond* (1940), *Job's House* (1941), and *Lilly Crackell* (1943), the social welfare system comes under particular attack as Slade reveals the absurdities of the welfare bureaucracy, the insensitive attitudes of many social workers, and the loss of independence and self-esteem suffered by welfare recipients.

The most striking of Slade's works are her three novels about prostitution. These are unusual not only because there are few novels of prostitution by American women but also in the realism and honesty of the treatment. Slade cuts through a variety of stereotypes; her prostitutes are neither "nymphomaniacs" nor innocents who "fall" through one misstep.

Sterile Sun (1936) consists of the life stories of three prostitutes, related in their own words. In *Margaret* (1946), an adolescent girl procures her school friends for a group of men. *Mrs. Party's House* (1948), Slade's best and most complex novel, is told from the point of view of a poverty-stricken widow who becomes a madam and in the process undergoes a complete education on the nature of prostitution. Mrs. Party is surprised to learn it is not "vice rings" which create and maintain the institution of prostitution, but "good men"—the grocer down the street, the judge who tells her she "helps society," the sheriff who compliments her on her clean, disease-free house ("This way,

men are safer"). Mrs. Party gradually loses her initial feelings of guilt and begins to see herself as a "pure" woman, a savior of society; she dreams of "hundreds of clean Houses, a chain of them, little islands free of disease, oases in the midst of killing sand, stepping stones leading the way to a great clean up."

The irony of society's definition of purity runs through all Slade's novels of prostitution. At the same time that Slade portrays the economic basis of prostitution, she exposes the hypocrisy of the ideal of female purity, which she sees as working hand in hand with the economic system. Slade's characters—prostitutes, pimps, and "good men" alike—believe that virginity and ignorance of sex are the center of virtue for women. However, it is this ignorance which leads the young girls in *Sterile Sun* to prostitution and makes Margaret's schoolmates so easily victimized. Margaret, who is more aware, derives comfort from society's glorification of virginity. She does not feel the slightest guilt at procuring her friends, for she knows she is not a "bad girl"—she herself is still a virgin.

Slade's novels were popular and well received, although some reviewers complained about their flat characterization and case history flavor. In general, Slade's work is notable less for its literary merit than for its sensitive and realistic treatment of unusual subject matter. However, the quality of Slade's writing is high enough to lift her novels above the level of sociological tracts, and her effective use of irony saves the novels from sentimentality.

BIBLIOGRAPHY: Farrell, J., "Issues and Writers," in *SRL* (12 April 1941).
Reference works: *American Novelists of Today* (1951). *TCAS*.

—BARBARA A. WHITE

SLESINGER, Tess

Born 16 July 1905, New York, New York; **died** 21 February 1945, Los Angeles, California
Daughter of Anthony and Augusta Singer Slesinger; **married** Herbert Solow, 1928 (divorced); Frank Davis, 1936; **children:** two

Tess Slesinger could be said to have had everything but time: well-to-do parents who sacrificed in order to give her the best education at the Ethical Culture Society School in New York, Swarthmore College, and Columbia University; immediate and continued success when she started to write; a happy marriage and children. But her works show this success was not achieved without pain. Through her first husband she became part of a leftwing circle important in publishing, and she was able to publish her first short story at age twenty-three; but Slesinger found radical theorizing and intellectualizing insufficient to give meaning to life and divorced Herbert Solow. In 1935 Slesinger went to Hollywood to begin a new career as a scriptwriter.

After working on the screenplay for Pearl Buck's *The Good Earth* (produced in 1937), Slesinger began a collaboration with Frank Davis which led to many successful scripts. She was able to combine a happy marriage to Davis and having two children with full professional activity until her untimely death from cancer at thirty-nine. Just a week after her death, *A Tree Grows in Brooklyn*, for which she and her husband had written the script, opened in New York. Slesinger was politically active in helping to make the Screen Writers Guild a viable union and in many other human rights causes.

Received by contemporaries as a realistic portrayal of the "lost generation," *The Unpossessed* (1934, reprinted 1966) reveals Slesinger's profound understanding of her own time. The central character Margaret Flinders attempts to please her egotistical husband, even undergoing an abortion in order to "free" him; Slesinger lets us see her act as a violation of her own being in exchange for his pretentious and selfish ambition. Slesinger reveals his attempts to find meaning through endless discussions with other intellectuals, without any commitment to action, as typical of the futilities of the 1930s. Her skillful use of stream-of-consciousness establishes a light tone while revealing her persona's despair; the reader identifies with her because her problems are questions, her attempts to solve them are processes, not authoritative answers. The final chapter, "Missis Flinders," also published as a short story, is a masterpiece of ironic understatement affirming both the pain and the power to endure of her character.

The tide of Slesinger's 1935 collecton of short stories *Time: The Present* (reprinted 1971 as *On Being Told That Her Second Husband Has Taken His First Lover, and Other Stories*) is ironic in that its very contemporary concerns are timeless. Slesinger touches on the emptiness of middle class life, disillusionment with the American dream, the ruthlessness of the struggle to survive brought on by the Depression, the hypocrisy of whites toward blacks, the ambiguities for women of their relationships to their adulterous husbands and to their mothers, the problems of the artist attempting to reduce the felt hugeness of experience into effective form. Her story on this last theme, "A Day in the Life of a Writer," shows Slesinger's mastery of form and her typical ironic tone. Following the mental ramblings of a male writer trying to overcome a writing block, she shows his "life in the day"—his self-loathing for not being able to repeat the success of his first book, his childish projection of his failure onto his "deaf-mute" typewriter and his wife. The reader understands both his ambivalence toward writing as a prison and the anger of his wife, who supports him.

Slesinger's stories about women show particular acuity. "On Being Told that Her Second Husband has Taken his First Lover" focuses on the continuance of the double-bind for women even with the sexual revolution. A wife who did not originate adultery feels she must accept her husband's announced infidelity as his right to freedom but cannot perceive her right to respond in kind as viable. Her only recourse is to accept his decision, with wit and anguish; rejecting him will only be a repetition of the end of her first marriage. "Mother to Dinner" explores the dilemma of a young wife caught between her husband's demands for her entire devotion and her mother's need for emotional support. The character sees no way out. (Slesinger, in divorcing her first husband, refused such a commitment and devoted herself to her writing.)

Slesinger's works show not truly promise but accomplishment; her short stories and her film scripts will long outlive her. Although her works have been republished, many of her stories remain uncollected. Excerpts from newly discovered notes for another novel, focusing on the real workers of Hollywood, confirm her importance as one who saw through the pretensions and complexities of her own time to basic human issues.

OTHER WORKS: Screenplays: *The Bride Wore Red* (1937). *Dance, Girl, Dance* (with F. Davis, 1940). *Remember the Day* (with F. Davis, 1941). *Are Husbands Necessary?* (with F. Davis, 1942).

BIBLIOGRAPHY: Reference works: *Oxford Companion to Women's Writing in the United States* (1995). *TCA, TCAS.*
Other references: *Antioch Review* (Spring/Summer 1977). *Jewish Social Studies* (Summer 1976). *Michigan Quarterly Review* (Summer 1979). *NYT* (20 May 1934). *Prospects* (1981). *WLB* (Dec. 1934).

—MARY ANNE FERGUSON

SLOSSON, Annie Trumbull

Born 18 May 1838, Stonington, Connecticut; died 4 October 1926
Daughter of Gordon and Sarah A. Trumbull; married Edward Slosson, 1867

A popular and critically admired short-story writer, Annie Trumbull Slosson published over 15 collections of short stories between 1878 and 1912 and was a frequent contributor to the *Atlantic* and *Harper's*. Her first book, *The China Hunter's Club* (1878), a collection of dialect stories situated in her native Stonington and the Fraconia Notch area, was considered, along with Sarah Orne Jewett's *Deephaven* (1877) and Harriet Beecher Stowe's *Pogonuc People* (1878), to be one of the first identifiable examples of the regional or "local color" genre.

In *Seven Dreamers* (1891), her second collection of short stories and her first critical and popular success, Slosson introduces a distinctive style and themes that, as a regional writer, she would develop in her later work. There are seven portraits of "dreamers," people Slosson met in small New England villages who function within the restrictive environment of 19th-century rural communities by discarding social conventions and substituting their own system of rituals and beliefs. Her characters are the natural outcasts of society, frequently mentally or physically defective and without family or friends. She portrays their retreat into a private dreamworld as neither pathetic nor grotesque but rather as a practical means of escaping the hard realities of their lives.

Many of Slosson's characters, such as Lucy Ann Breed who thought she'd written *Pilgrim's Progress* or Miss Prentice who claimed she'd been a pirate, are caricatures of the stereotypical New England eccentric. In her better stories, however, she demonstrated an ability to create more fully realized, realistic characters. In "Deacon Pheby's Selfish Nature," the most powerful story in the collection, she examined the psychological motives behind a young boy's mental disintegration after the death of his sister. Painfully aware of his mother's preference for his deceased sister, he sublimates his own personality and impersonates his sister in the desperate hope of finally winning his mother's love.

In *The Heresy of Mehitabel Clark* she addressed a question that had concerned other regional writers such as Stowe and Mary E. Wilkins Freeman: how the conscience reconciles its more humanitarian instincts with a faith in Calvinist doctrine. Mehitabel Clark, described as tormented and God-fearing, suddenly abandons orthodox Calvinism and substitutes her own religious system, which involves a benevolent "president" and the "president's son." Although her fellow church members feel conscience-bound to dissociate themselves from Mehitabel, even the devout deacon is forced to admit her conversion has made her "a heap happier, that's the melancholy truth." For Slosson, independent thinkers such as Mehitabel Clark performed an invaluable function by questioning and thereby undermining the accepted beliefs and values of the community.

In *Dumb Foxglove, and Other Stories* (1893), Slosson examined the innate religious faith of children and their method for reducing the complexity of Calvinist doctrine to a simple system of beliefs applicable to their own lives. In the title story, a terminally ill child refuses to read the catechism and insists instead on concocting curious tales of what her life will be like "when I get to heaven." Eventually the distressed minister realizes her seemingly heretical fantasies are a way of preparing for her imminent death.

Dumb Foxglove was Slosson's last critical and popular success. Like many other regional writers, she was unable to evolve beyond the limited achievement of her early work. Instead she reworked the characters and themes that had succeeded so well in *Seven Dreamers* and *Dumb Foxglove*, but she no longer displayed the same artistic control over structure and style. Although contemporary critics had compared her early work favorably with that of Freeman and Jewett, *Story-Tell Lib* (1900) and *A Local Colorist* (1912) were faulted for shallow character development and excessive use of dialect.

OTHER WORKS: *Fishin' Jimmy* (1889). *Aunt Leafy* (1892). *Anna Malann* (1894). *White Christopher* (1901). *Aunt Abby's Neighbors* (1902). *Simples From Master's Garden* (1907). *A Dissatisfied Soul* (1908). *A Little Shephard of Bethlehem* (1914). *Puzzled Souls* (1915). *Other People* (1918).

BIBLIOGRAPHY: Reference works: *Oxford Companion to Women's Writing in the United States* (1995).

—CAROLINE PRESTON

SMEDLEY, Agnes

Born 1892, Missouri; **died** 6 May 1950, London, England
Daughter of Charles and Sarah Rails Smedley; **married** Ernest Brundin, 1912 (divorced)

Agnes Smedley's life began in the drab rural poverty of northwestern Missouri. She grew to maturity in the squalor of Colorado mining towns, where her father, an uneducated, hard-drinking, defiant man, had hoped to find his fortune and where her mother took in laundry and died of overwork when Smedley was sixteen.

Determination to avoid her mother's fate led Smedley to leave home, work at odd jobs throughout the Southwest, and supplement her grade school education with a year at Tempe Normal School in Arizona. A brief "egalitarian" marriage ended in divorce.

Around 1917 Smedley began a decade of deep involvement, in New York and Berlin, with the efforts of Indian nationalists to free India from British rule. At the same time she wrote in support of socialist and feminist causes, established birth control clinics, and studied Asian history and Marxism. A relationship during the 1920s with exiled revolutionary leader Virendranath Chattopadhyaya drove Smedley to a nervous breakdown; she wrote her autobiographical novel *Daughter of Earth* (1920, reprinted in 1973, 1986) in an attempt to reorient her life.

Smedley went to China in 1928 and dedicated the rest of her life to the Chinese revolutionary cause. She developed friendships with Communist leaders, traveled with the Red Army as it fought Chiang Kai-Shek's Kuomintang and later the Japanese, and worked unstintingly to secure medical treatment for the wounded. Smedley wrote prolifically, producing three books during the 1930s and a profusion of articles for European, American, and Asian periodicals.

Ill health forced Smedley to return to the U.S. in 1941, and in 1943 she published her widely acclaimed *Battle Hymn of China*. Although she had never joined the Communist Party, the forces of McCarthyism hounded Smedley out of the country in the late 1940s. She died in London en route to the new People's Republic of China; her ashes were buried there.

Daughter of Earth, Smedley's only novel, tells of a working class woman who develops a feminist and a class consciousness as she pits her determination to be a free person against the traps society lays for women and the poor. Marie Rogers, the narrator of this first-person account, attains and preserves her independence—the book's plot is taken from Smedley's own life right up to the moment of its writing—but the emotional cost is high. Marie must cope with the persistent guilt, confusion, and pain of a woman who refuses to fit into expected roles.

Smedley's novel differs from standard proletarian fiction in its outspoken feminism and its emphasis on the psychological. Although it is not reliable autobiography, especially in the concluding sections, the book suffers artistically from its close identification with the still-unfolding events of Smedley's own life. But what this startlingly up-to-date novel lacks in balance and perspective it makes up for in emotional power.

Chinese Destinies: Sketches of Present-Day China (1933), the first of Smedley's five books about China in upheaval, is a collage of articles, stories, and impressions; it communicates a vivid sense of the corruption and utter wretchedness of life in the old China and the revolutionary fervor of those who hoped to build the new. Smedley focuses on individual lives, often women's lives; the tales are well told and the effect is moving. *China's Red Army Marches* (1934) follows a similar but less kaleidoscopic format, its sketches relating loosely to the Red Army's historic progress as it widens and secures its territory in inland China. In *China Fights Back: An American Woman with the Eighth Route Army* (1938), Smedley becomes an active participant in her story, using her journal entries to give the Western world a rare inside account of what life was like in the Red Army as it battled the Japanese invaders. Smedley's zeal and haste sometimes lead to simplistic characterizations and inelegant style, but at their best these books display stirring narrative power.

In *Battle Hymn of China*, history, autobiography, war reporting, and story telling intermingle as Smedley tries to tell wartime America all she had experienced and learned during her 22 years in China. This most comprehensive of Smedley's China books is also Smedley's comprehensive autobiography. Like all her books, this one is strongly partisan, but its very fervor helps promote an understanding of modern Chinese history by capturing and communicating the spirit that made revolution possible.

The Great Road: The Life and Times of Chu Teh, Smedley's enthusiastic biography of the peasant who became commander-in-chief of the Red Army—and Smedley's personal friend—was begun in the 1930s and published posthumously in 1956. Despite stylistic inadequacies, the book is strong in its depiction of rural Chinese society and its detailed look at life and politics within the Red Army.

Smedley saw herself as an interpreter of the Chinese revolution to the West. Her vivid and sensitive observations from the center of one of the century's great dramas constitute her most important professional achievement. But Smedley also saw herself as a woman who, as she once wrote, refused to "live the life of a cabbage."

OTHER WORKS: *Portraits of Chinese Women in Revolution* (edited by J. MacKinnon and S. MacKinnon, 1976).

The papers of Agnes Smedley are housed in several locations, yet the Hayden Library of Arizona State University in Tempe, is the primary repository.

BIBLIOGRAPHY: Howe, F. Afterword to *Portraits of Chinese Women in Revolution* (1976). Huberman, L., and P. M. Sweezy, Publisher's foreword to *The Great Road: The Life and Times of Chu Teh* by A. Smedley (1956). Lauter, P., afterword to *Daughter of Earth* by A. Smedley (1973). Lovett, R. M., preface to *China's Red Army Marches* (1934). MacKinnon, J., and S. MacKinnon,

Agnes Smedley: The Life and Times of an American Radical (1988).

Reference works: *CB* (1944, 1950). *DAB. NAW* (1971). *Oxford Companion to Women's Writing in the United States* (1995). *TCA, TCAS.*

Other references: *Bulletin of Concerned Asian Scholars* (Jan.-March 1975). *Chinese Literature* (Oct. 1980). *Monthly Review* (April 1978). *Nation* (19 Feb. 1949). *NR* (29 May 1950, 14 Dec. 1974). *New Statesman and Nation* (20 May 1950). *NYT* (9 May 1950, 6 April 1978). *Playbooks* (adaptation of *Daughter of Earth*, 1986). *Survey* (Autumn 1974).

—PEGGY STINSON

SMITH, Amanda

Born 23 January 1837, Long Green, Maryland; **died** 24 February 1915, Sebring, Florida
Daughter of Samuel and Mariam Matthews Berry; **married** Calvin Devine, 1854; James Smith, 1863

Born of slave parents, Amanda Smith was the eldest daughter of 13 children. Her father, through persistent hard work, bought his own freedom and that of his wife and family. He moved his family to Pennsylvania where they farmed, worked as domestics, and were a part of the Underground Railroad. Smith worked as a domestic until 1870, when she began her career as an evangelical preacher and missionary. Although she had only a few months of schooling, her natural charismatic character and religious enthusiasm made her a well-known figure in the holiness movement. In 1878 an associate suggested Smith preach in England, and after a year in England she traveled to India where she lived and preached for two years. In 1881, she left for West Africa, returning to the U.S. in 1890. After Smith's missionary works abroad, she settled in Chicago where she focused her attentions on evangelism, temperance, and social work among black orphans.

Smith's contribution to literature is an autobiography published in 1893. Even though her formal education was minimal, her autobiography is rich with sensitive understanding of her life as a black, a woman, and a religious leader. Beginning with her early life, and prior to her full-time commitment to evangelism, the reader senses Smith's struggle with her conversion experience and her understanding of God's direction in her life. Although her faith is strong, Smith candidly writes of her confusion and indecision about her religious convictions. Throughout this first section, she frequently cites examples of the difficulties she encountered as a woman and a black—from burying her small child to not being allowed off the train until all the white people had disembarked.

Smith's descriptions of her travels and adventures in England, India, and Africa give the modern reader a unique view of those countries as seen through the eyes of a 19th-century black evangelical Christian. While in Africa she was particularly sensitive to the plight of women who were sold at an early age to men for wives, and worked like animals in the fields. Her memories of

Africa and Asia would shape her latter involvement with black orphans in Chicago.

The autobiography tells the story of a remarkable woman, and gives a realistic account of 19th-century Protestantism. The holiness doctrine, faith healing, the "Amen Corner," and the missionary movement all figure prominently in the autobiography. Smith extended the role of women in evangelical Christianity, and especially in the Methodist church, by her ability to preach and to personally relate to her Savior.

OTHER WORKS: *An Autobiography* (1893).

BIBLIOGRAPHY: Cadbury, M. H., *The Life of Amanda Smith* (1916). Reference works: *NAW* (1971). *Oxford Companion to Women's Writing in the United States* (1995).

—M. COLLEEN MCDANNELL

SMITH, Anna Young

Born 5 November 1756, Philadelphia, Pennsylvania; **died** 3 April 1780, Philadelphia, Pennsylvania
Wrote under: Sylvia
Daughter of James and Jane Graeme Young; **married** William Smith, 1775; **children:** three

After the death of their mother, Anna Young Smith and her brother were raised at Graeme Park near Philadelphia by their aunt, Elizabeth Fergusson. Fergusson was a prolific poet and correspondent, a circumstance which may have encouraged Smith in her own writing. Smith's early poetry and letters suggest admiration for Fergusson's talent and gratitude for her kindness. Most of Smith's extant poems were written before her marriage, to which her father apparently did not consent. Smith died as a young woman, probably of complications resulting from the birth of her third child (contradictory accounts leave the circumstance and precise date of her death in dispute).

Smith's poems reveal a woman of firm opinions and wide-ranging interests. She treated political and feminist themes as well as the more conventional subjects of love and courtship, gratitude, sensibility, and grief. Her "Elegy to the Memory of the American Volunteers. . . ," for example, places her on the side of the rebels during the Revolutionary War: "Where e'er the Barb'rous story shall be told, / The British cheek shall glow with conscious shame."

Smith was as firm in her demand for fair treatment of women as she was in her politics. She responded to "Reading [Jonathan] Swift's Works" in characteristically strong language: "Ungenerous bard, whom not e'en Stella's charms / Thy vengeful satire of its sting disarms! / Say when thou, dipp'st thy keenest pen in gall, / Why must it still on helpless woman fall? / . . .thy harsh satire, rude, severe, unjust, / Awakes too oft our anger or disgust." Other

more conventional pieces detail Smith's courtship, her gratitude to her aunt, a tribute to her grandfather, and advice to a friend.

Creating in a very short time a body of poetry remarkable for its diversity, Smith leaves one wishing she had more than 24 years to pursue her craft.

OTHER WORKS: Manuscript poems by Anna Young Smith are in Elizabeth Fergusson's commonplace book, Dickinson College Library. Nine poems were published individually in periodicals, one in the *Pennsylvania Magazine* (June 1775) and eight in the *Universal Asylum and Columbian Magazine 5-9* (1790-1792).

BIBLIOGRAPHY: Armstrong, Edward, ed., *Memoirs of the Historical Society of Pennsylvania* (1864). Cowell, P., *Women Poets in Pre-Revolutionary America, 1650-1775* (1981). Reference works: *Oxford Companion to Women's Writing in the United States* (1995).

—PATTIE COWELL

SMITH, Betty (Wehner)

Born 15 December 1896, Brooklyn, New York; **died** 17 January 1972, Shelton, Connecticut
Daughter of John C. and Katherine Hummel Wehner; **married** George Smith, circa 1924 (divorced); Joseph Jones, 1943 (divorced); Robert Finch, 1957 (died); **children:** two daughters

Born and raised in the Williamsburg section of Brooklyn, Betty Smith attended public schools until the age of fourteen when, having completed eighth grade, she began working at a series of factory and clerical jobs. An avid reader as a young girl, she also wrote poems and acted in amateur productions at the Williamsburg YMCA. Moving to the Midwest, she met and married George Smith, a law student at the University of Michigan, and they had two daughters. She audited literature and writing classes at the university and, although not a regular student, had two plays published in a collection of undergraduate work and won an Avery Hopwood prize.

From 1930 to 1934 Smith studied with George Pierce Baker and others at the Yale Drama School. Smith's first two marriages ended in divorce. After the first divorce, Smith accepted a Rockefeller fellowship in playwriting at the University of North Carolina; she remained in Chapel Hill, writing, occasionally lecturing at the university, and playing small roles in local productions. Her third husband, Robert Finch, a writer with whom she had collaborated on several plays, died about a year and a half after their marriage.

A dramatist by inclination, Smith wrote over 70 plays and edited several collections and texts for drama classes. Most of her plays were not published and none received critical acclaim or even major professional performances. Typical of her plays meant for youth groups or schools are *The Boy, Abe* and *First Sorrows*, both about the young Abe Lincoln and the death of his mother. Other one-act plays range in tone from burlesque to sentimentality and in setting from a mid-19th century rural political rally (*Freedom's Bird*, written with Robert Finch) to the sidewalk in front of an illegal abortionist's office on a late depression era Christmas Eve (*So Gracious Is the Time*).

Though she preferred drama, Smith won fame through her fiction. Drawing upon her own memories and those of her mother, she expanded an earlier work, "Francie Nolan," into *A Tree Grows in Brooklyn* (1943), her most successful novel. It sold millions of copies and was made into a movie and a Broadway musical. Whereas the plot and much of the writing can be criticized for excessive sentimentality, the strength of this highly autobiographical novel lies in the richness of detail with which Smith recreates a young girl's childhood and adolescence in the slums of early-20th century Brooklyn, including both the pains of a poverty-stricken childhood and the good times. The characters are vivid and three-dimensional; even the minor characters come alive as recognizable types.

Smith's next novel, *Tomorrow Will Be Better* (1948, in Britain as *Streets of Little Promise*) is set against the same background as her first, but reviewers were not impressed with this effort; they found the dialogue authentic but the book as a whole less spontaneous and more self-conscious than *A Tree Grows in Brooklyn*. In *Maggie-Now* (1958), the character types are similar to those in *A Tree Grows in Brooklyn*—charming, irresponsible men and their long-suffering, hardworking wives and daughters—but this novel too lacks the depth of the earlier one. In her fourth novel, *Joy in the Morning* (1963), Smith shifted the locale from Brooklyn to a Midwestern college campus. In some ways, this book is a sequel to the first novel, as the heroine, a Brooklyn girl with only a grade school education, marries a law student, audits literature and writing classes, and has her work published in a student collection.

Smith obviously drew heavily upon her own experiences for the material for her novels. Her accurate ear for dialogue (a legacy of her dramatic training) is a strength in all of them. But the wealth of detail in *A Tree Grows in Brooklyn* may have exhausted her memories. Each of the succeeding books was less rich in characterization and atmosphere. Her greatest weakness, however, was her inability to shape her novels into realistic and meaningful form; thus they tend to be overly sentimental and to end mechanically or without resolution.

OTHER WORKS: Selected: *Folk Stuff* (1935). *His Last Skirmish* (1937). *Naked Angel* (1937). *Popecastle Inn* (1937). *Saints Get Together* (1937). *Plays for Schools and Little Theaters: A Descriptive List* (edited by Smith, with R. Finch and F. H. Koch, 1937). *Trees of His Father* (1937). *Vine Leaves* (1937). *The Professor Roars* (1938). *Western Night* (1938). *Darkness at the Window* (1938). *Murder in the Snow* (1938). *Silver Rope* (1938). *Youth Takes Over; or, When a Man's Sixteen* (1939). *Lawyer Lincoln* (1939). *Mannequins' Maid* (1939). *They Released Barabbas* (1939). *A Night in the Country* (1939). *Near Closing Time* (1939). *Package for Ponsonby* (1939). *Western Ghost Town* (1939).

Bayou Harlequinade (1940). *Fun After Supper* (1940). *Heroes Just Happen* (1940). *Room for a King* (1940). *Summer Comes to the Diamond O* (1940). *To Jenny with Love* (1941). *25 Non-Royalty One-Act Plays for All-Girl Casts* (edited by Smith, 1942). *20 Prize-Winning Non-Royalty One-Act Plays* (edited by Smith, 1943). *Young Lincoln* (1951). *A Treasury of Non-Royalty One-Act Plays* (edited by Smith et al., 1958). *Durham Station* (1961).

BIBLIOGRAPHY: Reference works: *CA* (1969). *CB* (1943, 1972). *Oxford Companion to Women's Writing in the United States* (1995). *TCAS*.

—ELAINE K. GINSBERG

SMITH, Eliza (Roxey) Snow

Born 21 January 1804, Becket, Massachusetts; **died** 5 December 1886, Salt Lake City, Utah
Daughter of Oliver and Rosetta Pettibone Snow; **married** Joseph Smith, 1842 (died); Brigham Young, 1847

When Eliza Snow Smith, the second of seven children, was very young, her parents migrated to Ohio, where her father successfully took up farming. Smith received the most liberal education allowed a young woman at the time, attending the local schools of Ravenna, Ohio, and a grammar school taught by a Presbyterian minister. In her early teens, Smith began writing poetry. Her first efforts were published in local newspapers and journals under pen names. These verses are typical of her day—sentimental, religious, and didactic.

In the 1820s Smith and her parents joined the Reformed Baptist or "Campbellite" church, and she began a devoted study of the Bible. Smith converted to the Church of Jesus Christ of the Latter Day Saints early in 1835, and left her family's home for the Mormon stronghold of Kirtland, Ohio, where she lodged with the Prophet Joseph Smith and his family. To support herself, Smith founded a select school for young girls in Kirtland. She played an active role in the life of the Mormon community, singing in the Kirtland Temple choir and writing songs and poems for the church.

In 1838 she followed Smith and his flock first to Missouri and then to Illinois, where she began her rise to prominence in the Mormon church. She was the first secretary of the Female (later Women's) Relief Society, a charitable and a spiritual organization associated with the Mormon church. Smith also served as an officer of the Nauvoo, Illinois, Temple and as president of the Nauvoo Endowment House, the building where the important religious ceremonies of the Mormon church took place.

It was in Nauvoo that Joseph Smith quietly introduced the doctrine of plural marriage to his most devoted followers. At first, Smith was repelled by the doctrine, but she came to "esteem it a precious, sacred principle—necessary to the elevation and salvation of the human family—in ridding women from the curse, and the world from corruption." Smith probably became the Prophet's fourth or fifth wife when she secretly wed him in 1842. Their marriage was kept secret until 1852 when Brigham Young, then head of the Mormon church, formally announced polygamy was an integral part of church doctrine.

After the murder of Joseph and the dispersal of the followers, Smith was among the first pioneering companies to reach the valley of the Great Salt Lake. During the course of the journey west, she kept a diary (published in the *Improvement Era*, 1943-44), and wrote patriotic, religious, and eulogistic poetry. Her poetry served as an inspiration to trail-weary Mormons, and encouraged them to continue on their way to the promised land: "Altho' in woods and tents we dwell / Shout, shout O Camp of Israel. / No Christian males on earth can bind / Our thoughts, or steal our peace of mind." On this trip westward, Smith, along with several of Joseph's widows, was married to Brigham Young.

Smith became the most beloved and powerful woman in Utah, as she increased her involvement with charitable, spiritual, and educational projects. In addition to publicly defending polygamy, Smith was an ardent feminist. As head of the Women's Suffrage Society, she worked to dispel the myth that Mormon women lived lives subject to their husband's wills. She worked hard to ensure Utah's women the right to political franchise and won success in 1870.

Smith continued to write poetry, hymns, and religious essays, published in several Utah journals, as well as practical educational texts while living in Utah. Her first volume of poetry, incorporating many of the poems she had written while on the trail from Illinois, was published in 1856, and a second volume was published in 1877. Smith compiled a number of hymnals for the church, containing some of her own hymns, the most popular of which was "O My Father, Thou that Dwellest." She contributed an account of the "assassination" of Smith and his brother and several poems to Lucy Smith's *Biographical Sketches of Joseph Smith* (1853). With her brother Lorenzo Snow, the fifth president of the Mormon church, Smith wrote *The Correspondence of Palestine Tourists* (1875), the record of their missionary trip to the Middle East. Smith was reticent to write of her own experiences, but she did write an autobiographical sketch, which was published in the *Relief Society Magazine* (1944). Smith's best-known work, and an excellent source for historians interested in the foundations of the Mormon religion, is *The Biography and Family Record of Lorenzo Snow* (1884).

Married in turn to the two most important figures in the history of the Mormon church, Smith made a name for herself through her own involvement in church affairs and education, and she pointed with pride to Utah women's right to vote and active participation in church affairs as evidence of Mormon women's freedom and equality. In addition, Smith wrote poems and songs for the church; she provided the young Mormon church with its chief hymns.

OTHER WORKS: *The Story of Jesus* (1845). *Poems, Religious, Historical, and Political* (2 vols., 1856 and 1877). *Bible Questions and Answers for Children* (1883). *Recitations for the Primary Associations* (edited by Smith, 1887). *Hymns and Songs: Selected from Various Authors for the Primary Associations of the Children of Zion* (edited by Smith, 1888). *Recitations for the Primary Associations in Poetry, Dialogues, and Prose* (edited by Smith, 1891).

A copy of Eliza Snow Smith's 1847 diary and her autobiographical sketch are in the Bancroft Library at the University of California.

BIBLIOGRAPHY: Brodie, F. M., *No Man Knows My History: The Life of Joseph Smith, the Mormon Prophet* (1971). Crocherson, A. J., *Representative Women of Deseret* (1884). Gates, S. Y., and L. D. Widstoe, *Women of the Mormon Church* (1926). Hill, D., *Joseph Smith: The First Mormon* (1977). Tullidge, E., *The Women of Mormondom* (1877).

Reference works: *DAB. NAW* (1971).

—PAULA A. TRECKEL

SMITH, Elizabeth Oakes (Prince)

Born 12 August 1806, North Yarmouth, Maine; **died** 15 November 1893, Hollywood, North Carolina

Also wrote under: E., Ernest Helfenstein, Oakes Smith, Mrs. Seba Smith

Daughter of David and Sophia Blanchard Prince; **married** Seba Smith, 1823

As a child, Elizabeth Oakes Smith lived in the country near the south coast of Maine, where she spent much time even after her family moved to Portland when she was eight. At the age of sixteen, Smith married Seba Smith, an editor and publisher and the author of the popular Major Jack Downing stories. Smith's first poems and sketches appeared anonymously in his newspapers. In Portland, Smith had five sons; one died as a young child.

After a series of financial reverses, the Smiths moved to New York in 1837 and took their places in the city's literary circles. Smith contributed to the support of her family through her writing. Her stories, sketches, and poems appeared in the *Ladies' Companion, Godey's Lady's Book, Graham's Magazine*, and other popular monthlies of the day, in addition to her husband's various periodical publications. She contributed to 36 gift books (sentimental annual publications) between 1836 and 1856, editing some of them with her husband and some of them on her own.

From about the midpoint of her life, the "busy devil" with which Smith professed to be afflicted directed her into intense reform activity. She was an active participant in the women's rights conventions of 1848, 1851, 1852, and 1878. In 1851, as an advocate of the working woman, Smith, with Lucretia Mott, sponsored a tailoring cooperative that employed women in Philadelphia. Under the auspices of the YMCA, she was a social worker in New York City. In 1868, she became a charter member of New York's first women's club; she served as its vice-president in 1869. In 1877, after a lifetime of religious searching and questioning, Smith became the minister of an independent congregation in Canastota, New York.

Smith's early writings draw heavily on her immediate environment and include Native American myths and legends, Down East characters, and stories of Maine. These early writings also include sketches of women whose lives were far outside her experience, such as Charlotte Corday and Mme. de Staël, which reappear in later writings and in her lectures on the Lyceum circuit.

Smith won popular and critical acclaim for "The Sinless Child," a long narrative poem which first appeared in the *Southern Literary Messenger*, to which she was a frequent contributor. In the poem, the unworldly heroine is released from a corrupt world through death. Its publication as the title piece in a collection of her poems in 1843 established Smith's reputation.

Smith's first novel, *Riches Without Wings*, was published in 1838. Its themes and values are conventional: the superiority of natural beauty, temperance in all things, modesty, cleanliness. Worldly riches are not to be pursued at the expense of spiritual purity, but wealth and recognition do reward hard work and honesty. Her dialogues and asides to her readers are intended to instruct, and in these, along with the dominant themes, Smith occasionally disparages convention, as when the leading female character asserts the value of passion in women as well as in men, and again when she refuses to wear the prescribed mourning dress on the death of a relative.

In her later work, Smith continued to use the conventional themes of her first novel. A strong strain of mysticism, present in most of her writing, becomes more marked in the later writing. Patriotism and progress are typical themes. The evils of cities, the romantic theme of the superiority of the natural, or country life, is the major theme in *The Newsboy* (1854), a novel credited with influencing social reform in New York.

Smith believed women had the right to develop fully as individuals, and that the current constraints of the marriage relation inhibited their development, were articulated in a series of essays in the New York *Tribune*, published as a monograph in 1851, under the title *Woman and Her Needs* (reprinted in 1974).

As a writer, Smith was spurred always by financial necessity. Her work is remarkable for variety, volume, and inventiveness; it ranges from sonnets to very informal travel sketches and reminiscences, from children's stories to tragic drama. Though in general her characters have the conventional virtues and vices and her intensely romantic themes were chosen to appeal to a wide audience, Smith's fiction, poetry, and essays expose the occasional "burr under the saddle" that placed her among contemporary reformers and made her a significant contributor to the popular literature of the middle third of the 19th century.

OTHER WORKS: *The Western Captive* (1842). *The Sinless Child, and Other Poems* (1843). *The Dandelion, The Rosebud and The Moss Cup* (1845). *The Lover's Gift* (1848). *The Salamander* (1848). *The Roman Tribute* (1850). *The Good Child's Book* (1851). *Hints on Dress and Beauty* (1852). *Shadowland* (1853).

Old New York (1853). *The Sanctity of Marriage* (1853). *Bertha and Lily* (1854). *Black Hollow* (1864). *Bald Eagle* (1867). *The Sagamore of Saco* (1868). *Selections from the Autobiography of Elizabeth Oakes Smith* (edited by M. A. Wyman, 1924).

The New York Public Library has a collection of Elizabeth Oakes Smith's unpublished papers, including the manuscript of her autobiography.

BIBLIOGRAPHY: Wyman, M. A., *Two American Pioneers: Seba Smith and Elizabeth Oakes Smith* (1927).

Reference works: *Appleton's Annual Cyclopedia* (1893). *CAL. DAB. FPA. NAW* (1971). *Oxford Companion to Women's Writing in the United States* (1995).

Other references: *Broadway Journal* (23 Aug. 1845). *Graham's* (June 1843, Sept. 1853, April 1856). *North American Review* (Oct. 1854).

—VIVIAN H. SHORTREED

SMITH, Eunice

Born circa 1770s; **died** death date unknown

Eunice Smith, who wrote during the closing decade of the 18th century, was a resident of Ashfield, Massachusetts. Whatever Smith's personal life may have been like is unknown. From her publishing record it is clear that she experienced a good deal of success as a writer of religious tracts. Smith was a forerunner of the multitude of American women who wrote on religious topics throughout the 19th century.

Smith's success is indicated by the multiple editions and printings of her works, not a common phenomenon in the U.S. of the 1790s. *Practical Language Interpreted in a Dialogue Between a Believer and an Unbeliever in Two Parts* (1793) passed through at least four or five separate editions before 1795, and *Some Arguments Against Worldly Mindedness. . .By Way of a Dialogue or Discourse Between Mary and Martha* (1795) saw seven separate printings before its popularity wore thin.

Smith structured her prose as simple dialogues in which one of the speakers, with the encouragement of the other, changes her state of religious doubt or sin for one of blessed assurance and understanding. The dialogues demonstrate the difference in thought between a sinner and a saint and explore the conception of the role of a Christian vis à vis the Savior. Smith uses these dialogues in an attempt to enliven traditional religious subjects and themes. Whether she was familiar with earlier precedents for such use of dialectic dialogue, she did not reveal.

Smith's tropes, reminiscent of the figurative diction of some of the Puritan Fathers and of the revivalist ministers of the 1740s, also makes her conventional material more vivid. She conjures up explicit images of hell, the "horrible pit." Whereas Smith's tropes and style achieve some complexity, the religious beliefs they illustrate are simple. Smith emphasizes uplifting thoughts rather than the subtle uncertainties and repeated self-doubts of her

Puritan predecessors. Smith was not concerned with fine theological distinctions or knotty religious issues, but with helping the reader to a calm self-scrutiny based on a simple assurance of God's eternal benevolence toward all sinners. She assures the reader that if the individual fights evil diligently, God will intervene with a saving hand.

Smith's religious tracts are not particularly enticing to the modern reader in their simple, antique pious sentiments. But her works are historically interesting as an indication that the better-known moralist women writers of the 19th century, such as Harriet Beecher Stowe, had deep roots in the small towns of 18th-century New England.

—JACQUELINE HORNSTEIN

SMITH, Hannah Whittal

Born 7 February 1832, Philadelphia, Pennsylvania; **died** 1 May 1911, Iffley, England
Wrote under: H.W.S.
Daughter of John M. and Mary Whitall; **married** Robert P. Smith, 1851

After a happy childhood in her Quaker home, Hannah Whittal Smith married in 1851 and had four children. She departed early from strict Quaker ways, which seemed too rigid, to set out on a spiritual pilgrimage. Eventually she began to preach alongside her husband. The Smiths preached the "Higher Life" in America, in England, and on the Continent, being particularly active around 1873. Because Smith's husband was suspected of preaching false doctrine and also of improper conduct with female admirers, they returned to the U.S., but settled permanently in England in 1886.

Smith's preaching was nonsectarian and the influences on her thought were various. After her marriage, Smith came under the influence of the Plymouth Brethren, the Baptists, and the Methodists. But she had inherited from her father an attachment to the works of the 17th-century French quietist Mme. Guyon. Smith also treated as a guide Mme Guyon's friend Fénelon, whose *Spiritual Letters* she quoted with approval.

Because Smith was open to religious enlightenment from any source, she worked out for herself a safeguard against fanaticism, which she offers to her readers in *The Christian's Secret of a Happy Life* (1875, reprinted under several similar titles in 1984, 1985, 1993, and most recently in 1999). Her message is that God's guidance comes to us in four ways: "through the Scriptures, through providential circumstances, through the convictions of our own higher judgement, and through the inward impressions of the Holy Spirit on our minds." In early editions Smith also included a chapter warning against taking emotional states as proof of the baptism of the Holy Spirit.

Both *The Christian's Secret of a Happy Life* and *The God of All Comfort* (1906) are still religious bestsellers today. They owe their appeal to the clarity, simplicity, and directness with which Smith expresses her complete trust in God. Of at least equal interest, but out of print, is Smith's spiritual autobiography, *The Unselfishness of God, and How I Discovered It* (1903, reissued, the latest being in 1987 and 1993).

In the end, Smith found she had returned to a basic Quaker principle: that God has power to save us from sin, not only in a legalistic sense but also in a practical way, by preserving us from it and giving us constant guidance. Because of this interest in the practical applications of Christian teaching, Smith was also active in the temperance and woman suffrage movements.

Smith believed in will power as the chief condition for total trust in God. Her orthodoxy may have been suspect at one time, but her outlook suits the modern Christian, hence her continuing popularity today—not only in scholarly works but in recent reprints of many of her works in the 1980s and into the late 1990s.

OTHER WORKS: *The Devotional Writings of Robert Pearsall Smith and Hannah Whitall Smith* (1870, 1984). *The Record of a Happy Life: Being Memorials of Franklin Whitall Smith* (1873). *John M. Whitall: The Story of his Life* (1879). *Every-Day Religion* (1893). *The Science of Motherhood* (1894). *Religious Fanaticism: Extracts from the Papers of Hannah Whitall Smith* (edited by R. Strachey, 1928, 1976). *Philadelphia Quaker: Letters of Hannah Whitall Smith* (edited by L. P. Smith, 1950). *The Christian's Secret of a Holy Life: The Unpublished Personal Writings of Hannah Whitall Smith* (1990, 1994). *The Hannah Whitall Smith Collection* (1995).

BIBLIOGRAPHY: Pearsall, C. E., et al, *History and Genealogy of the Pearsall Family* (1928). Smith, L. P., *Unforgotten Years* (1939). Smith, R. M., *The Burlington Smiths* (1877). Strachey, R., *A Quaker Grandmother: Hannah Whitall Smith* (1914).
Reference works: *DAB. NAW* (1971).

—BARBARA J. BUCKNALL,
UPDATED BY NELSON RHODES

SMITH, Lee

Born 1 November 1944, Grundy, Virginia
Daughter of Ernest Lee and Virginia Marshall Smith; **married** James E. Seay, 1967; Hal Crowther, 1985; **children:** Josh, Page

As a child, Lee Smith was convinced she was going to be a writer and chose to attend Hollins College in Roanoke, Virginia, because it offered an M.F.A. in Creative Writing. She took writing courses throughout college and found that they taught her elements of a technique that helped her mature as a writer; two teachers, Louis D. Rubin and R. W. Dillard, were especially important to her. She graduated with a B.A. in 1967, and in that year, the novel she wrote in college, *The Last Day the Dogbushes Bloomed* (1968), won a Book-of-the-Month Club Writing Fellowship.

Smith calls herself a storyteller, and her stories range from humorous short stories to novels that seek to understand the artist's search for a self. Some of her characters, like Susan, the narrator of *The Last Day the Dogbushes Bloomed*, watch the world around them and try to transform it into something beautiful. Others, like *Crystal of Black Mountain Breakdown* (1981), cannot accept themselves and escape into a fantasy world.

Something in the Wind (1971), *Fancy Strut* (1973), *Black Mountain Breakdown*, and *Cakewalk* (1981) all received positive reviews, and critics saw in Smith a writer who could combine comic elements with a skilled narrative technique. The books did not sell well, however.

With *Oral History* (1983), Smith's acceptance by reviewers was translated into acceptance by the reading public, and the book, compared by critics to Faulkner's work, was the first to make a profit for her. While Smith deprecates the comparison with Faulkner, the book is a tightly constructed examination of the Old and the New South for the benefit of Jennifer, a young college student who has returned to the Virginia mountains to find her roots. Smith interweaves the history of Appalachia with the legends, songs, and folktales of the region in a way that makes the mountain people live again.

In *Family Linen* (1985), Smith uncovers a family secret, the murder of Jewell Rife by his wife, Elizabeth Bird Hess, the family matriarch who is dying while all her children try to come to terms with her and with their lives. Viewed from the perspective of several family members, the discovery of the secret murder counters the journal that Elizabeth Bird herself leaves to carry on the myth of her devotion to family and duty. Written in the orotund style of the Victorian South, the journal becomes a mockery when contrasted with the lives of Elizabeth's children and when set beside the murder she has hidden for almost half a century.

With *Fair and Tender Ladies* (1988), Smith achieved real popularity as a teller of a wonderful story. The novel, written in the epistolary form, chronicles the lives of Ivy Rowe and again reveals Smith's deep affection for the mountains of Virginia and for the mountain people who have lived, suffered, and endured. Like many of Smith's narrators, Ivy Rowe is chiefly an observer, and her letters vividly depict life in Sugar Fork, where her parents' homestead is, and in the two neighboring towns to which her hard life takes her. Throughout her long life, Ivy Rowe reveals her passions, secrets, hopes, and dreams to a long list of correspondents, but chiefly to her sister, Silvaney, who has lived most of her life in an asylum and whom Ivy keeps alive through her letters. Here Smith again reveals the truth behind the myths of Southern womanhood, and the reality is far more solid and enduring than the fantasy.

In *Me and My Baby View the Eclipse* (1990), a collection of stories, Smith highlights the daydreams of average Southerners and weaves epiphany and loss in the stories of breakdowns, divorces and death. The conflict is often between those like Rose Dee in "Tongues of Fire," who insist on keeping up appearances at all costs, and those like her daughter, who learn to accept the tragedies in their lives and go on living. The stories are full of humor, empathy, and a sense of the irony of being a Southerner in the 20th century. *The Devil's Dream* (1992) is a characteristic blend of Virginia history and wry and loving accounts of family held together by women. Moving back from Nashville to the roots of country music in the lives of the mountain people, the novel again demonstrates Smith's ability as a storyteller. Like generations of Southern writers before her, Smith has a sense of place, an ear for language, and a vision of a South that endures. And *Saving Grace* (1995) touches on a Smith theme that is familiar—rural families.

Smith tells the heartwarming tale of three generations in the same family who write Christmas letters in *The Christmas Letters* (1996). The book is about family tradition, love, and strength as Birdie Pickett, her daughter, Mary, and her granddaughter, Melanie, tuck letters containing stories inside their Christmas cards. The long letters tend to explain their lives as much to themselves as to scattered family and friends. Smith captures vividly the familiar gossipiness of letters that intimates will write each other, women's voices, the clash of generations, and ever-evolving American family life.

In *News of the Spirit* (1997), Smith collects many of her best-loved short stories, following love, longing, despair, imagination, and grace, with family members, brothers, sisters, parents, and friends. Brothers appear in "The Bubba Stories," where character Charlene Christian explains, "I made Bubba up in the spring of 1963 in order to increase my popularity with my girlfriends," but her legendary sibling takes on a life of his own. Another brother appears in "News of the Spirit," as Paula's damaged sibling, Johnny, in the title story, is "writing a new kind of book," constructing another narrative of his tragic life. Parents show up in "Live Bottomless," in which 13-year-old Jenny tells the funny yet hurting tale of her philandering father's fall from grace and the family's subsequent trip to Key West as her parents attempt a "geographical cure" for their troubled marriage. The housekeeper's daughter is the focus as the housekeeper tells prim and proper old maid Sarah about the youngster's "blue wedding." Finally, in "The Southern Cross," Chanel, a girl of easy virtue and dubious reputation, chronicles her cruise around the Caribbean with three Atlanta developers, and Alice Scully talks about her retirement home writers group in "The Happy Memories Club."

BIBLIOGRAPHY: Reference works: *CA* (1985, 1987). *CLC* (1983). *DLBY* (1983). *FC* (1990).

Other references: *NYTBR* (19 July 1992). *New Orleans Times-Picayune* (11 Mar. 1990, 12 July 1992). *Southern Quarterly* (Fall 1983).

—MARY A. MCKAY,
UPDATED BY DARYL F. MALLETT

SMITH, Lillian

Born 12 December 1897, Jasper, Florida; **died** 28 September 1966, Atlanta, Georgia
Daughter of Calvin and Anne Simpson Smith

Lilian Smith was the seventh of nine children. She tasted the "strange fruit" of racial segregation early in her childhood, when her well-to-do, genteel Methodist parents took in an apparently white orphan found living with a black family. The Smiths welcomed the girl until they learned she was part black; then the children were hastily separated, leaving Smith in conflict over the paradox of a culture that teaches hospitality, democracy, and Christian charity at the same time it violently denies the humanity of blacks.

Smith's traditional Southern upbringing led her to value literature, art, and music and to want to be socially useful. Her education (at Piedmont College and Baltimore's Peabody Conservatory of Music) was repeatedly interrupted by declining family fortunes, which had forced the Smiths to move to their summer home in Clayton, Georgia, in 1915. Smith joined the Student Nursing Corps in World War I and, after the Armistice, taught for a year in an isolated mountain school in Georgia. She spent three years teaching music at a Methodist mission school in Huchow, China, and then returned to help run Laurel Falls Camp for Girls, the exclusive summer camp her father founded at their Georgia home, and to act as secretary to her brother Austin, the city manager of Fort Pierce, Florida. In 1928 she attended Columbia University's Teachers College, adding to her already considerable knowledge of child development and Freudian psychology. After her father died in 1930, Smith assumed heavy family responsibilities including the care of her invalid mother. And, in the next five years, she wrote five novels, never published and all lost in a 1944 house fire.

Along with her lifelong companion, Paula Snelling, another young liberal Southern intellectual hired to help run the camp, Smith founded *Pseudopodia*, a little magazine heavily influenced by the editors' Freudian persuasion and their antisegregationist political and social views. At first the magazine concentrated on reviewing works by and about blacks and took a literary stand against, among other things, Margaret Mitchell's *Gone with the Wind* and the Agrarians. It was renamed twice—as the *North American Review* (1937-42) and *South Today* (1942-44)—as the editors broadened their liberal crusade against the consequences of caste in the South and in other countries and as it became a forum also for Smith's fervent views on sexuality and childrearing.

Strange Fruit (1944, reprinted most recently in 1992), Smith's first published novel, sold over 3,000,000 copies and was translated into 16 languages. It was banned from the bookstores and libraries of Boston and from the bookstores of Detroit; Eleanor Roosevelt intervened to remove the Post Office ban. Much of the uproar stemmed from the realistic language and the ironic treatment of miscegenation, sexuality, and abortion. Set in racially segregated Maxwell, Georgia, in the years following World War I, the plot traces from its youthful beginning the secret interracial love affair of Tracy Deen—a war veteran, son of the town's respected white doctor and his aristocratic wife—and Nonnie Anderson—a black college graduate who can only find a job as a maid in Maxwell.

As in Theodore Dreiser's *American Tragedy* and Richard Wright's *Native Son*, Smith's fictional world is deterministic. Characters breaking a taboo in this segregated society must suffer violence. Tracy Deen is murdered by the brother of his pregnant lover. A mob lynches the black servant Deen had paid to marry Nonnie so he could marry as his mother and the town expect him to. Smith handles the stream-of-consciousness technique well, aptly combining it with the sensational plot and subject matter to create a strongly moving, finely detailed picture of the tragedy of racism for both black and white Southerners.

The furor over *Strange Fruit* created the national publishing and speaking outlet Smith needed to wage her campaign against racism. She published a second novel, *One Hour* (1959, 1994), and five nonfiction books that preach racial justice and denounce any person or organization that did not seem as liberal as she. Each book contains eloquent stories about her personal life and the lives of those she encountered on her travels through the South and abroad. Her ability to recreate atmosphere through physical detail allows her to carry out the psychological, social, and political analysis that is her purpose.

Smith also wrote a column for the Chicago *Defender* and articles and book reviews for such widely read magazines as *New Republic, Saturday Review, Redbook*, the *Nation*, and *McCall's*.

Smith's contribution to the cause of racial justice in the U.S. won her the reputation as the most liberal white advocate of civil rights in the South in the 1940s. In the 1950s and 1960s, despite recurrent battles with lung cancer, Smith continued to fight against the evils of segregation by championing the nonviolent movement of Rev. Martin Luther King, Jr.

Her conviction was deep and sincere, but her view of literature and art was limited by the intensity of her belief in the perfectability of mankind. She took daring stands against segregation, but the impact of her writing is diminished by her moralizing. Smith is justifiably recognized as a minor literary figure and a major social reformer.

OTHER WORKS: *Killers of the Dream* (1949, 1994). *The Journey* (1954, 1964). *Now Is the Time* (1955). *Memory of a Large Christmas* (1962, 1996). *Our Faces, Our Words* (1964). *From the Mountain* (writings from *South Today*, edited by H. White and R. S. Suggs, Jr., 1972). *The Winner Names the Age* (edited by M. Cliff, 1978, 1982). *How Am I to Be Heard? Letters of Lillian Smith* (1993). *Lillian E. Smith Papers: 1920-1980* (archives of the Library of Congress, 1980). *Now Is the Time* (1955).

BIBLIOGRAPHY: Blackwell, L., and F. Clay, *Lillian Smith* (1971). Brewer, P. B., *Lillian Smith: Thorn in the Flesh of Crackerdom* (dissertation, 1983). Camacho, R. V., *Woman Born of the South: Race, Region and Gender in the Work of Lillian Smith* (dissertation, 1992). Hill, S. W., "The South Today: A Critical Study of

Lillian Smith's Little Magazine'' (thesis, 1991). Jenkins, M., *The South in Black and White: Race, Sex, and Literature in the 1940s* (1999). Loveland, A. C., *Lillian Smith, a Southerner Confronting the South: A Biography* (1986). Miller, K. A. *Out of the Chrysalis: Lillian Smith and the Transformation of the South* (dissertation, 1986). Morehouse, L. ''Bio-Bibliography of Miss Lillian Smith'' (thesis, 1956). O'Dell, M. D., ''Sites of Southern Memory: The Autobiographies of Katharine DuPre Lumpkin, Lillian Smith, and Pauli Murray'' (dissertation, 1997). Sosna, M., *In Search of the Silent South: Southern Liberals and the Race Issue* (1977). Sullivan, M., *A Bibliography of Lillian Smith & Paula Snelling* (1971).

Reference works: *CB* (1944). *Oxford Companion to Women's Writing in the United States* (1995).

Other references: *Great Women Writers Read Their Work* (audiocassette, 1974, 1986).

—SUZANNE ALLEN

SMITH, Lula Carson
See McCULLERS, Carson

SMITH, Margaret Bayard

Born 20 February 1778, near Philadelphia, Pennsylvania; **died** 7 June 1844, Washington, D.C.
Daughter of John B. and Margaret Hodge Bayard; **married** Samuel H. Smith, 1800

Margaret Bayard Smith married the editor of the Jeffersonian newspaper the *National Intelligencer* and brought with her to Washington in 1800 a lively curiosity, a warm understanding of human relationships, and an openness to experience.

During her early life in Washington, Smith wrote privately, chiefly letters and notebooks. Her public career as a writer began in the 1820s. She published two novels based on Washington life, *A Winter in Washington* (1824) and *What is Gentility?* (1828). She also wrote short stories, essays, and verse for such publications as *Godey's Lady's Book*, the *National Intelligencer*, and the *Southern Literary Messenger*. In addition, Smith wrote several biographical accounts for James Herring and John B. Longacre's *National Portrait Gallery of Distinguished Americans*.

Smith's reputation as a writer rests primarily on the collection of her letters and notebook entries edited by Gaillard Hunt in 1906 and published under the title *The First Forty Years of Washington Society*. This miscellany revealed Smith as a person of wit, insight, and affection and as a discerning observer of the society of her time.

Smith's Jeffersonian sympathies are evident in her work, but her circle of friends far transcended party lines. She found the transition from Jeffersonian republicanism to Jacksonian democracy a difficult one. Though flexible by nature, Smith belonged to an earlier age of gentility and ordered society. Her writing about the pre-Jacksonian period combined the personal world and public political concern; in the latter period, her focus was more on the private side of Washington life.

Smith was a novelist whose primary concern was the changing ways and values of society. *A Winter in Washington* had its elements of suspense and mystery, including an abducted child and a murder. But the central theme of this book and of *What is Gentility?* is the clash of moral values and cultural ways. Smith saw the Jeffersonian era as a kind of republican golden age, and she sought to convey the values of that period to a later generation.

Smith portrayed the political scene as women saw it—as outsiders. For her novels, she drew on some of the sketches of real-life events she had recorded previously in her notebooks as historical memoirs. On the whole, Smith held traditional views about women and their role in society. In *A Winter in Washington* she did voice, through Mrs. Mortimer, perhaps the most original and nonconformist of her female characters, some of the discontent experienced by women of the day. An incipient feminist, Mrs. Mortimer thinks it folly for women to talk of government when they are ''slaves to all'' or ''mill horses'' or ''captive birds.'' But Smith herself affirmed the theory of separate spheres and home as the ''place of highest duties. . .and most enduring pleasures.''

As a novelist Smith is on soundest ground in depicting the social and political world of which she had been a part. Her private papers have proved a storehouse of information about this society. As a letter writer, Smith has charm and liveliness. She clearly enjoyed people, and her portraits of the personalities of her age are drawn with an affectionate yet keen-eyed view. It is both the quality of the person Smith is and the perceptive insight she brings to bear on her society that give her work its vitality and durability.

BIBLIOGRAPHY: Green, C. M. *Washington: Village and Capital, 1800-1878* (1962). van der Linden, F., *The Turning Point: Jefferson's Battle for the Presidency* (1962).
Reference works: *NAW* (1971).

—INZER BYERS

SMITH, Rosamond
See OATES, Joyce Carol

SMITH, Sarah Pogson

Born circa 1790, Woodside House, Essex, England; **died** death unknown, in Charleston, South Carolina
Wrote under: ''A Lady''
Daughter of John and Ann Wood Pogson; **married** Judge Peter Smith

Very little is known about Sarah Pogson Smith's life. The date of her arrival in Charleston, South Carolina was recorded there on her tombstone, but the date on the original stone was nearly indecipherable and may have been 10 May 1788 or 1793. She was the daughter of a planter of St. Kitts, West Indies, and his second wife, from Sussex, England. At some point, Smith was married to Judge Peter Smith of Peterboro, New York, by whom, if we are to regard the introduction to her *Essays* (1818) as autobiographical, she had one son and more than one daughter. Colonel Alston Deas, a relative who restored the tombstone and who has corresponded with this contributor, states Smith was "noted for her witty and sometimes caustic conversation," and that she "lived with her sister, Mrs. William Blamyer. . .in later life." William S. Kable has firmly established Smith's claim to the *Essays*, previously attributed in error to Maria Henrietta Pinckney; he has also published evidence supporting the attribution to Smith of *The Female Enthusiast* (1807).

The Female Enthusiast, a five-act drama, offers a sympathetic portrayal of Charlotte Corday, who killed the demagogue Marat during the French Revolution. The play explores the moral reasons that might impel a "good" girl from a respectable, upper-middle class home to commit a political assassination. While Smith has relied quite heavily on Shakespeare for various stylistic devices, *The Female Enthusiast* is a remarkably capable apprentice piece.

Essays, Religious, Moral, Dramatic, and Poetical is a random and extensive collection of Smith's writings. The first section consists of seven essays that champion Christian virtue and criticize a variety of moral and religious failings. By far the most interesting is Essay Seven, in which Smith very effectively castigates the fanaticism and vanity of "Camp-Meeting" (revivalist) preachers and laments the fatuousness of their followers.

The second section consists of three five-act plays. In "The Young Carolinians; or, Americans in Algiers," various young Americans en route to Europe are captured by pirates and sold in Algiers. While much is made of the sufferings of these "Christian slaves" at the hands of their cruel and cunning Mohammedan captors, Smith does briefly acknowledge that the captives themselves come from a slave-based economy. The play concludes happily, with the repatriation of all the principal captives. Far less happy is "A Tyrant's Victims," a tragedy about Agathocles, the self-made king of Syracuse, whose "soaring ambition" and overweening selfishness play havoc with multitudes; but ironically, Agathocles himself escapes unscathed. Three young English girls, heroines of "The Orphans," are defrauded by their guardian and cast out unprotected into the world. Fortunately, they are rescued by their hearty, sea-going brother, who arrives back in England just in time.

The third section consists of several poems on such subjects as friendship, virtuous conduct, love, and bereavement. A recurrent theme is the mutability of the "shadow" things of earth and the permanence of the heavenly reward promised to the believing Christian.

The 13 long poems of *Daughters of Eve* (1826) tell colorful tales set in several lands at different stages of human history; most are loosely bound by the theme of human, and especially female, suffering. As Smith reminds the reader in the 13th poem, it was "Woman," the "first *Transgressor*" who bore Christ, and "Woman" who first saw Him after the Resurrection. The afflicted Christian "Daughters of Eve," represented by the needy deaf-mutes in the book's first poem, and the non-Christian "Daughters of Eve," symbolized by the innocent pagan girls so cruelly "degraded" and slaughtered in the second poem, pass through various permutations and emerge as America's regenerate "virtuous Daughters" in the final lines of the concluding poem.

In the heroic couplets of Smith's 1133-line poem *The Arabians*, her poetic gifts reach their full fruition. In splendidly fluid lines, rich in ingenious imagery, exotic scenery, and powerful emotional appeal, Smith recounts the conversion to Christianity of Abdallah and Sabat, two young Arabs of virtuous character and noble family, and the martyrdom of one.

Not only were many of Smith's works intended to inspire right conduct, but the proceeds from these works were frequently applied to good causes, although Smith herself was probably much in need of income. Thus, *Daughters of Eve* helped to educate and care for "the indigent deaf and dumb"; *Zerah* (1837) laid the cornerstone for a church; the first edition of *The Arabians* provided essential aid for two "important Institutions" in Charleston, while a later edition helped to fund a "Seamen's floating Church." If the record of Smith's life remains incomplete, the record of her benevolence endures. But it is her considerable achievement as a writer that is Smith's chief claim to modern scholarly consideration.

BIBLIOGRAPHY: Deas, A., *Information on Sarah Pogson Recorded in the Files of the Charleston Library Society* (n.d.). Kable, W. S., "South Carolina District Copyrights: 1794-1820," in *Proof: The Yearbook of American Bibliographical and Textual Studies 1* (1971).

Other references: *South Carolina Historical [and Genealogical] Magazine* (1903-1934).

—JEANETTE NYDA PASSTY

SMITH, Susy

Born 2 June 1911, Washington, D.C.
Daughter of Merton M. and Elizabeth Hardegen Smith; married M. L. Smith, 1934 (divorced)

Suzy Smith's childhood was rootless because of frequent moves. After her father's death in 1933, Smith married but later divorced and lived with her mother until her mother's death in 1949. Subsequently, she has generally lived alone.

Her loneliness led Smith to the paranormal. In 1955, success in contacting her deceased mother with a Ouija board initiated Smith's interest in the field. Desiring to learn, Smith worked briefly with Dr. J. B. Rhine's Parapsychology Laboratory at Duke University in Durham, North Carolina. This association, together with many years in newspaper work, have had a lasting influence on Smith's writing. From Durham, Smith moved to Florida and thence to New York, where she resided until 1965. During this period, Smith received grants from the Parapsychology Foundation, which enabled her to prepare her first published books. Since 1965 when writing began to provide a modest living, Smith has traveled and lectured widely.

Smith's works fall roughly into two categories: those reporting psychic occurrences and those about herself. Smith's books on the psychic constitute an extensive data resource. Because Smith was deeply impressed by the methods of Dr. Rhine's laboratory, she has striven to bring similar objectivity and precision to her books. She rarely expresses her own opinions, but instead presents, simply and lucidly, the matters she is reporting and leaves the readers to form their own conclusions.

In sharp contrast, Smith's autobiographical works, *Confessions of a Psychic* (1971) and *Conversion of a Psychic* (1978), are deeply personal. Smith writes openly, even ingenuously, of herself and her psychic experiences. Her honesty provides the very evidence needed by skeptics to explain away her psychic life as the fabrication of her unconscious mind. She reveals herself as physically crippled, unwillingly single, and lonely. Yet the seemingly clear pattern of need fulfillment proves not to be clear. The spirit mother is bossy but not all—knowing. The spirit admirer is, as he was at death, ignorant, selfish, and dull. Nor does Smith's handling of her painful psychic misadventures draw attention; she does not discuss her difficulties until she has them under reasonable control. Smith's conversion to a born-again Christian, described in her second autobiography, provides skeptics with similar ammunition—but ammunition still not sufficient to prove her insincerity.

Smith has made a unique literary contribution. Her many works documenting psychic events and processes have brought an unprecedented amount of information on this subject to the public view, in simple, easily understandable language. Her books on herself provide a different, more moving insight. Smith shares with her readers the difficult, sometimes painful, process of becoming a psychic and, finally, of finding a living Jesus and the close comfort of a loving God.

OTHER WORKS: *ESP* (1962). *The Mediumship of Mrs. Leonard* (1963). *The World of the Strange* (1963). *The Enigma of Out-of-Body Travel* (1965). *ESP for the Millions* (1965). *A Supernatural Primer for the Millions* (1966). *Haunted Houses for the Millions* (1967). *More ESP for the Millions* (1967). *Prominent American Ghosts* (1967). *Reincarnation for the Millions* (1967). *Adventures in the Supernormal* (1968). *Out-of-Body Experiences for the Millions* (1968). *Understanding ESP* (1968). *ESP: Widespread Psychic Wonders* (1970). *Ghosts Around the House* (1970). *Psychic Animals* (1970). *Today's Witches* (1970). *Susy Smith's Supernatural World* (1971). *ESP and You* (1972). *How to Develop Your ESP* (1972). *She Spoke to the Dead* (1972). *ESP and Hypnosis* (1973). *The Book of James* (1974). *Do We Live After Death?* (1974). *Exorcism: #5, Widespread Psychic Wonders* (1974). *Life is Forever: Evidence for Survival After Death* (1974). *Power of the Mind* (1975). *Strangers from Space* (ca. 1976).

Voices of the Dead? (1977). *Ghost Writers in the Sky: More Communication from James* (1990).

BIBLIOGRAPHY: Reference works: *WW of American Women* (1978).

—LUCY MENGER

SNEDEKER, Caroline Dale

Born 23 March 1871, New Harmony, Indiana; **died** 22 January 1956, Bay St. Louis, Mississippi
Wrote under: Caroline Dale, Caroline Dale Owen
Daughter of Charles A. and Nina Dale Owen Parke; **married** Charles H. Snedeker, 1903

Caroline Snedeker was the great-granddaughter of Robert Owen, the Welsh reformer who brought together scientists and educators in an attempt to found a model "village of cooperation" in New Harmony, Indiana, in 1825. Snedeker grew up in nearby Mt. Vernon. Nourished on her grandmother's stories of New Harmony and its ideals and her mother's singing and love for music, Snedeker early developed a keen interest in history, literature, and classical music. The family moved to Cincinnati for the children's schooling, and there Snedeker later entered the College of Music to study piano and composition. After the death of their father, Snedeker and her three sisters gave instrumental concerts to support the family, with Snedeker serving as pianist as they toured the Midwest. She was also an instructor of music before her marriage to the Dean of the Cathedral of Cincinnati. The couple moved to Hempstead, New York, where Snedeker was encouraged and advised in her writing by her husband.

Snedeker's writings comprise 13 juvenile novels, all but one of them historical fiction for older children and young adults, two novels for adults, and articles, stories, and poems. *The Coward of Termopylae* (1911), Snedeker's first novel, grew out of her great love for ancient Greece. Intended for adults, but gaining success when reissued in 1912 as *The Spartan*, for young people, it is based on two passages from Herodotus about a Spartan soldier during the Persian Wars who was branded a coward and who later acquitted himself by a noble death. In *Theras and His Town* (1924), written in response to a request for a child's version of *The Spartan*, an eleven-year-old Athenian boy goes to live with his uncle in Sparta, where he observes the tremendous differences in life and values between the two states. The strength of both books is their revelation of ancient life and thought.

The strength of other Snedeker novels about ancient Greece and Rome is this depiction of everyday life; their weaknesses are events that strain credulity, plots based on too little material, and explanatory and moralistic digressions that impede the plot. *The*

Perilous Seat (1923), about the daughter of a priest at Delphi; *The White Isle* (1940), which takes Lavinia and her patrician family from Rome to frontier Britain; and *The Forgotten Daughter* (1933) are romances. The last, the best crafted, tells of the romance of a Greek slave girl and a Roman aristocrat during the period when Tiberius Gracchus tried to break up the big estates of the nobles and parcel out the land to Roman peasants.

Snedeker also wrote a series of books based on American history. *Downright Dencey* (1927) deals with friendship that develops between a little Quaker girl and a waif after she has injured him by thoughtlessly throwing a stone at him. Carefully delineated details of Quaker life on Nantucket at the beginning of the 19th century, Dencey's forthright personality, and the mystery of the waif's parentage have a certain charm, making this probably the most read of Snedeker's books today. *The Beckoning Road* (1929) takes Dencey's family west to New Harmony.

Snedeker first wrote about New Harmony in *Seth Way: A Romance of the New Harmony Community* (1917), a fictionalization for adults of the life of the zoologist Thomas Say. Although too slow-moving, this book does give a good sense of the community's potential and its problems. *The Town of the Fearless* (1931) is the fictionalized history of Snedeker's own family and its connection with New Harmony. Snedeker contributed further to the knowledge of Robert Owen's experiment by editing the diaries of another resident, Donald Macdonald, which she discovered in Ireland after a lengthy search.

Snedeker's books are distinguished by conscientious research and careful attention to details of setting, but, particularly in her books for children, Snedeker frequently intrudes upon her story with explanatory and moralistic comments, imposing the value judgements of her time upon the mores of the past. Although generally well received by critics and popular when they came out, Snedeker's books have not stood the test of time. Too labored in movement, romanticized, and stiff in dialogue to appeal to modern audiences, they are seldom read except by those who have a deep interest in their period or a scholarly concern with the history of literature for young people.

OTHER WORKS: *The Black Arrowhead* (1929). *Uncharted Ways* (1935). *The Diaries of Donald Macdonald* (edited by Snedeker, 1942). *Luke's Quest* (1947). *A Triumph for Flavius* (1955). *Lysis Goes to the Play* (1962).

BIBLIOGRAPHY: Miller, B. M., "Caroline Dale Snedeker," in *Horn Book* (April 1956). Snedeker, C. D., "Trilobite Door: Chapters from my Life," in *Horn Book* (1947-1948).
Reference works: *Authors of Books for Young People* (1967). *Indiana Authors and Their Books* (1949). *Junior Book of Authors* (1951). *Yesterday's Authors of Books for Children* (1978).

—ALETHEA K. HELBIG

SNYDER, Zilpha Keatley

Born 11 May 1927, Lemoore, California
Daughter of William S. and Dessa Jepson Keatley; **married** Larry A. Snyder, 1950; **children:** Melissa, Douglas, Ben

The daughter of a rancher and driller, Zilpha Keatley Snyder grew up in rural Southern California; she recalls that her world was quiet and revolved around animals and books. She attended Whittier College, where she met her husband, a music student. While her husband completed his graduate studies at the University of California at Berkeley, Snyder became a master teacher and demonstrator for education classes there. After she began to write, Snyder retired from teaching. The Snyders have three children, one a foster child from Hong Kong.

Snyder has written one book of poetry, *Today Is Saturday* (1969), but most of her books are novels. The most convincing of these are the earliest, each of which is grounded firmly in reality before moving into the world of fantasy. *Season of Ponies* (1969), based on a dream, combines Snyder's two childhood interests, horses and magic. A lonely girl on an isolated farm uses her grandmother's amulet, which she thinks is magical, in imaginary games with the free-spirited Ponyboy and his herd of pastel-colored ponies, very like the glass ponies on her bedroom shelf. Expressive writing succeeds in mingling magic with the reality of the heroine's life.

Black and Blue Magic (1966), written for Snyder's son, who wanted a funny story about a boy, also uses a magic device—an ointment that causes a twelve-year-old boy to grow wings. Although contrived, the book moves along with much realistic dialogue and deftly portrays an adolescent who gradually gains a greater sense of self-worth.

In *Eyes in the Fishbowl* (1968), a suspense story for older readers, Dion, a shoeshine boy, spends his spare time in the basement of a department store. He becomes aware that Madame Stregovitch in the cosmetics department has summoned the "Others," the spirits of needy children, who terrify the clerks with their antics and cause so much confusion the store eventually goes out of business. The plot is spun out and slightly didactic, but Dion's strained relationship with his casual, easygoing musician father is true to life, and the department-store setting is vivid with realistic details.

Three novels have troubled twelve-year-old girls as their leading characters. *The Velvet Room* (1965) develops around dreamy, intelligent Robin Williams, the daughter of migrant workers, and a migrant worker herself, who finds a special haven in the library of a deserted mansion where the owners of a large fruit ranch used to live. *The Truth About Stone Hollow* (1974) is deft and rich in its characterization of both adults and children and in its portrayal of smalltown relationships and prejudices. Both these novels are set in rural California during the Depression. *The Witches of Worm* (1972) takes place in a modern urban apartment complex. Jessica thinks either she herself is a witch or that her cat is a witch's cat. Whatever causes her to do the spiteful things she does, it is clear that she is hostile and angry and feels misunderstood by her mother and playmates. Although, like many of Snyder's conclusions, this one is abrupt and unsatisfying, the story is fast paced and presents an intriguing picture of a girl's attempts to come to grips with the painful realities of her life.

One of Snyder's most highly regarded books, both by critics and children, is *The Egypt Game* (1967), with characters based on children Snyder taught at the Washington School in Berkeley. The story arose out of her desire for a book to encourage close and proud identification with minority characters. A group of children play in the yard of the strange and aloof Professor—who runs a secondhand store—and imagine themselves to be rulers and gods in ancient Egypt, until a child is murdered in the neighborhood and the old Professor is suspected of being responsible. Although the story moves with suspense and humor, the interracial cast seems too deliberately assembled and the plot too carefully concocted to thrill young readers.

Snyder produced seven books for children and two young adult novels in the 1980s. One of these novels, *The Birds of Summer* (1983), received the Parent's Choice award and the PEN Literary award. Numerous others were given the Dell Yearling Edition distinction. The year 1990 brought *Libby on Wednesday*, which was named by the ALA as a Best Book for Young Adults. More recently, Snyder's work *Cat Running* (1994) highlights her characterization skills and concern with social interaction. The book is set in the dust bowl during the Depression and shows how a young, slightly self-absorbed girl overcomes problems within her family and reaches beyond prejudice. Snyder drew on her descriptive powers for the next novel, *The Trespassers* (1995), which tells the tale of children exploring a deserted mansion.

Thirty years following publication of *The Egypt Game*, Snyder picks up the story of the young characters of this novel to play in *The Gypsy Game* (1997). The sequel was not nearly as well received as *Egypt*, in part because reading the first novel is almost essential to understanding the second and because the children never actually pretend to be gypsies, which is a large part of the charm of the original.

Snyder continued with a 1998 publication of *Gib Rides Home*, a work based on the life of her father, which features an eleven-year-old orphan boy who is eventually sent to work for a family. Reviewer Susan Lempke credits the story with "deft pacing and characterization, along with a background rich in sensory detail. . .[which] makes this a touching, satisfying tribute to Snyder's father and to all children who face difficult lives with courage." In 1999, Synder's book, *The Runaways* was released, receiving starred reviews from both *Publishers Weekly* and *School Library Journal*.

Snyder draws her ideas chiefly from memories of her own childhood, from her teaching, and from her life with her family. Recurring themes involve friendship, curiosity, coming to terms with oneself and life, and the power of the imagination. Snyder's work is distinguished by her ability to build suspense, by her literate use of sprightly and vigorous language to capture the cadence and content of children's speech, and by her skill in creating sympathetic protagonists who are imaginative, highly intelligent, lonely preteens with psychological problems arising from their domestic circumstances.

OTHER WORKS: *The Changeling* (1970). *The Headless Cupid* (1971). *The Princess and the Giants* (1973). *Below the Root* (1975). *And All Between* (1976). *Until the Celebration* (1977). *Heirs of Darkness* (1978). *The Famous Stanley Kidnapping Case* (1979). *A Fabulous Creature* (1981). *Come On, Patsy* (1982). *Blair's Nightmare* (1984). *The Changing Maze* (1985). *The Three Men* (1986). *And Condors Danced* (1987). *Squeak Saves the Day and Other Tooley Tales* (1988). *Janie's Private Eyes* (1989). *Song of the Gargoyle* (1991). *Fool's Gold* (1993).

BIBLIOGRAPHY: Hopkins, L. E., *More Books by More People* (1974). Reference works: *CA* (1974, Online 1999). *SATA. Third Book of Junior Authors* (1972).
    Other references: *Booklist* (1 Sept. 1994, June 1995, 1 Feb. 1997, 1 Jan. 1998). *Claremont Reading Conference Yearbook* (1973). *Elementary English* (1974).
    Web sites: www.microweb.com/1snyder/.

—ALETHEA K. HELBIG,
UPDATED BY CARRIE SNYDER

SOLWOSKA, Mara
See FRENCH, Marilyn

SOMERS, Suzanne
See DANIELS, Dorothy

SONG, Cathy

Born 1955, Honolulu, Hawaii
Married Douglas Davenport; children: two

The selection in 1982 of Cathy Song's *Picture Bride* (1983) as the winning manuscript in the Yale Series of Younger Poets competition marked the young poet's rather sudden literary emergence. In a review of *Picture Bride*, Shirley Geok-lin Lim hails Song as "a major figure on the Asian American literary scene." Song received her B.A. from Wellesley College (1977) and an M.F.A. from Boston University's creative writing program. After her graduation from the program in 1981, Song returned to Honolulu. She now teaches creative writing at several universities in addition to working on her own literary projects.

In many of the poems in *Picture Bride*, Song writes about her family's history and interrelationships. In the title poem she imagines her grandmother, joined to a stranger through a prearranged marriage, leaving home to meet her husband for the first time. Insightful and sensitive in capturing her evolving relationship with her mother, Song intimates in several poems that she must escape her mother's presence, but eventually realizes what she draws from her mother is vital to her own identity. "When I stretch a canvas / to paint the clouds, it is your spine that declares itself."

The poems of *Picture Bride*, though driven by the specific details of Song's past, also help to illuminate the Asian-American experience in general. In "Lost Sister," about a Chinese-American who finds herself alienated from both East and West, and in her unflinching portrayal of Chinatowns, Song addresses the difficult realities faced by Asian-American immigrants. Song has expressed concern that critics encountering her acute cultural awareness may marginalize her work. Her strengths as a poet—startlingly clear description, lines quietly unfolding a story in short breaths, images running threadlike throughout a poem, weaving a unified work—stand independent of her Asian themes.

Song further explores her past in *Frameless Windows, Squares of Light* (1988), her second volume of verse. These poems, writes Song, focus on "the mind. . .tunneling into memory, released by imagination. Out of that depth, squares of light form, like windows you pass at night." In these new poems, Song returns to many of the themes and scenarios introduced in *Picture Bride*. Also familiar are her characteristic straightforward diction and her strong sense of closure. "A Small Light" captures with rhythmic repetition the feel of a distant memory. In "A Child's Painting" Song reaffirms her ability to transform commonplace events into beautiful portraits.

Song's third collection, *School Figures* (1995), continues to explore her familial relationships. Her position as both daughter and mother is captured in verse; both the loss of her father and the challenges of raising children are addressed. "Neither woundedly angry at nor sentimentally accepting of her family and its heritage, Song explores the nuances of intimacy with admirable clarity and passion," writes Pat Monaghan of *Booklist*.

In addition to her poetry, Song has edited (with Juliet Kono) *Sister Stew* (1991), an anthology of writings by Asian-American women. Her poems have also appeared in several anthologies and in such periodicals as *Asian-Pacific Literature*, *Hawaii Review*, *Poetry*, and *Seneca Review*.

BIBLIOGRAPHY: Cheung, K.-K., *Asian-American Literature* (1988). Chock, E., *Talk Story: An Anthology of Hawaii's Local Writer* (1978). Fisher, D., *The Third Woman: Minority Women Writers of the United States* (1980). Lim, S. G. and A. Ling, eds., *Reading Literatures of Asian America* (1992).

Reference works: *CA* (Online, 1999). *Oxford Companion to Women's Writing in the United States* (1995).

Other references: *Booklist* (1 Oct. 1994). *International Examiner* (2 May 1984). *MELUS* (Fall 1983, Spring 1988). *WRB* (Oct. 1988).

—JEROME CHOU,
UPDATED BY CARRIE SNYDER

SONTAG, Susan

Born 16 January 1933, New York, New York
Married Philip Rieff, 1950 (divorced); **children:** one son

Susan Sontag, the elder of two daughters of a traveling salesman and a teacher, was raised in Arizona and California. She studied at the University of California at Berkeley and the University of Chicago, from which she received her B.A. when she was only eighteen, a year after marrying sociologist Philip Rieff. Her M.A. degree in philosophy is from Harvard University. In the late 1950s, she divorced her husband and settled with her son (born in 1952) in New York City, although she has spent a good portion of each year in Europe. Through the mid-1960s she taught English and philosophy at several American colleges and universities. She began writing fiction and critical essays and reviews when she was twenty-eight. She is also a writer and director as well as a critic of films: the provocative *Duet for Cannibals* (1969) and *Brother Carl* (1971) were both made in Sweden; *Promised Lands* (1974) is a documentary about Israel. As PEN's American Center president (1987-89), she joined a protest at an international conference in Seoul, South Korea, against this government's treatment of writers and publishers. Among her other achievements and awards, including being named in 1984 by the French government an Officier de Arts et des Lettres, she is a member of the American Academy and Institute of Arts and Letters. In 1990 she was also granted a five-year fellowship from the MacArthur Foundation.

Sontag has become a cultural icon of our age. Her intellectual precociousness and her unique critical perspective that takes the influence of American and European thought equally into account has carved her a niche in "the modern critical canon." One critic lauded her by saying Sontag's career as a writer "has been marked by seriousness of pursuit and a relentless intelligence that analyzes modern culture on almost every possible level: artistic, philosophical, literary, political, and moral. . .Sontag has produced a stimulating and varied body of work which entertains the issues of art while satisfying the rigors of her own intellect." Another critic sees Sontag's critical writing as primarily concerned with discovering "what is the central tradition of Western thought in the 20th century and which writers have contributed most to its creation." While her importance can be interpreted in many ways, she is nonetheless a central figure in both the discovery and the codification of our contemporary intellectual culture. Sontag has disappointed some of the feminist community because of her lack of interest in feminist scholarship. However, averse to labels and stereotypes, Sontag says her writing is "based on freedom and self-revelation."

While Sontag has always insisted she is a fiction writer, she is one of our most influential cultural critics. Her subjects have been European writers, thinkers and filmmakers, and photography, pornography, and the problems with assigning metaphorical meaning to epidemic illness. Throughout, Sontag has insisted her work and the work of her models be allowed to stand on their own as art, to maintain their aesthetic, not decimated by interpretation: "Criticism in all the arts. . .treats the work of art as a statement being made in the form of a work of art."

Against Interpretation, and Other Essays (1966, reissue 1986) is a brilliant expression of the modernist sensibility. Despite the title, she does interpret, making accessible the most striking experiments in avant-garde film and criticism. From her treatment of new-wave critics to her famous "Notes on Camp," she is always provocative and original, so much so that one critic observed: "Perhaps what makes *Against Interpretation* valuable and exciting is not so much its erudition, which is considerable. . .as its passionate irresponsibility, its determined outrageousness." In *Under the Sign of Saturn* (1980, 1989), which Sontag has described as "seven portraits of consciousness," she explores how modernism has become "the dominant tradition of high literary culture instead of its subversion" through essays on artists who are also her models, particularly Walter Benjamin, Paul Goodman, Antonin Artaud, Roland Barthes, and Elias Canetti. She thus makes European intellectuals not only available, but also relevant in the United States.

In *Styles of Radical Will* (1969, 1989), Sontag again investigates the difficulties of confronting new artistic modes. Part of her appeal lies in her ability to move from the world of high culture to low—from Karl Marx to Harpo Marx, for instance. She flirts with the demonic, the underside of human experience. Her "dark and complex vision of sexuality" is not to feminists' taste, but it is worth paying some attention to what she has to say about our impulses towards violence and destruction. Elsewhere, as in "The Third World of Women" (*Partisan Review*, 1973), she shows she can be, at times, a brilliant spokeswoman for feminism.

Politically, Sontag takes the part of adversary, as in the autobiographical *Trip to Hanoi* (1968). She sees art as something that expands consciousness; thus, in *Styles of Radical Will*, her views on politics and art are related, "for it is sensibility that nourishes our capacity for moral choice."

As a novelist, Sontag has never been autobiographical. The heroes of her full-length works are male. *The Benefactor: A Novel* (1963, reissue 1994) is about a European man who looks back on his 60-plus years and on such surrealistic adventures as selling his mistress to an Arab merchant. Despite the brilliance of isolated perceptions, the work as a whole lacks the passionate conviction of those writers (Djuna Barnes, Dostoevsky, Nietzsche) who influenced it. For many readers, the work requires an interpreter to give it meaning.

In *Death Kit* (1967, reissue 1986), Sontag wittily combines mythical, religious, and philosophical elements within the structure of a whodunit making use of the journey-to-hell theme. Despite the high praise of some critics, such as Granville Hicks, most readers are more excited by Sontag's criticism than her fiction.

The reader of the short story collection *I, etcetera* (1978, 1996) has a greater sense of the intimate self with all its pain and longing than is usual in her fiction. Travel imagery is pervasive. "Unguided Tour" counterpoints a broken love affair and the return to a past pervaded by the cliché-ridden language of tourism. "When I travel, it's always to say goodbye," the narrator laments. "I don't consider devotion to the past a form of snobbery. Just one of the more disastrous forms of unrequited love."

In *Illness as Metaphor* (1977, 1988), Sontag describes "not what it is really like to emigrate to the kingdom of the ill and live there [a theme that would have had autobiographical relevence], but the punitive or sentimental fantasies concocted about that situation: not real geography, but stereotypes of national character." She applies a moralist's scorn to the use of tuberculosis and cancer as metaphor. *AIDS and Its Metaphors* (1988) examines the language and interpretation surrounding the disease and argues against the degradation and guilt AIDS patients suffer due to ill-chosen metaphors.

Yet Sontag's own metaphoric power is freely employed in equally dubious contexts, as when, in *On Photography* (1979, 1989), she labels those who take or view photographs as junkies, rapists, and murderers. In some ways, the aesthetic position here is the antithesis of *Against Interpretation* and *Styles of Radical Will*: art, at least the art of the photographer, is now an amoral force rather than one which enlivens sensibilities and consciousness. "By getting us used to what, formerly, we could not bear to see or hear, because it was too shocking, painful, or embarrassing, art changes morals. . . ."—for the worse, it is implied.

After years of important political and cultural work, including speaking out against martial law in Poland at Town Hall in New York City (1982), Sontag became drawn to the particular plight of besieged Sarajevo. In summer of 1993, Sontag braved the Sarajevo siege and directed a production of *Waiting for Godot*. Her devotion to the arts brought her to the war-torn city to help inspire and bring unity to people oppresses by racial hatred. Deftly, she assembled actors and crew members from all ethnic groups to symbolize the possibility for peace through creativity. Her efforts are extraordinary not just because she orchestrated performances in the midst of bombings and explosions, but because she succeeded in bringing hope to the besieged people. Recognized and respected by the citizens of Sarajevo, she became one of only two foreigners to be named an honorary citizen.

In other projects, Sontag has continued to look toward Europe for her subjects. Her fourth film, *Unguided Tour* (1983), from the short story of the same title, tells of a relationship that is fragmenting as the couple tours the decaying ruins of Italy. In *Sarah* (1988), a documentary film about Sarah Bernhardt, Sontag narrates the voice of the actress. She has directed two other plays: *As You Desire Me* by Luigi Pirandello, whom she calls "the most influential playwright of the 20th century," ran in Italy (1979-81). *Jacques and His Master* by Milan Kundera played at the American Repertory Theater in Cambridge, Massachusetts (1985). In addition to essays on dance, Dutch painting, and Robert Mappelthorpe, Sontag collaborated with Cesare Colombo on *One Hundred Years of Photography* (1988), and included 10 of her poems, collectively entitled "In Memory of Their Feeling," in a catalog for a London exhibition entitled *Cage, Cunningham, and Johns: Dancers on a Plane* (1989).

Some 25 years after the publication of her previous novel *Death Kit* (1967), Sontag's *The Volcano Lover* (1992, reissue 1993) found a new kind of success. Accepted publicly with greater enthusiasm than her previous fiction met, the historical romance is based on the love triangle between Sir William Hamilton, the famous British ambassador to the court of Naples, his much younger wife Emma, and her lover, Lord Nelson. The novel is said to have a "coolly modern narrative voice that recounts action while commenting on love and grief, cracking jokes, digressing to discuss artistic philosophies, referring to developments. . .that her 18th-century characters should know nothing about." It's style is difficult for some because of the historical license taken, but most found this temporal aberration "a satisfying saga of high literary quality, a brainy page-turner."

With intellectual passion and great human compassion, unconfined by genre, Sontag has been a renaissance woman with both critical and artistic offering. Like the camera, to which she is addicted at the same time she bewails it, Sontag always brings to the reader a new awareness of the world.

OTHER WORKS: *Cage-Cunningham-Johns: Dancers on a Plane—In Memory of Their Feelings* (1990). *Illness as Metaphor; and AIDS and Its Metaphors* (1991). *The Way We Live Now* (1991). *Who Was the Much Admired Sir William Hamilton* (1992). *Alice in Bed: A Play in Eight Scenes* (1993, reissue 1994). *Conversations with Susan Sontag* (1995). *In America* (1999).

Contributor of short stories, reviews, essays, and articles to periodicals including *New Yorker, Atlantic Monthly,* and *Harper's.*

BIBLIOGRAPHY: Bruss, E., *Beautiful Theories* (1982). *Hiding in Plain Sight: Essays in Criticism and Autobiography* (1993). Kennedy, L., *Susan Sontag: Mind as Passion* (1995). Markgraf, S. T., "Novelty of/as Metaphor: Susan Sontag, Adrienne Rich, and Yvonne Rainer" (thesis, 1994). Misrach, R., *Violent Legacies: Three Cantos* (1992). Plimpton, G., ed., *Women Writers at Work: The* Paris Review *Interviews* (1998). Poague, L. A., *Susan Sontag: An Annotated Bibliography, 1948-1992* (2000). Sayres, S., *Susan Sontag: The Elegiac Modernist* (1990). Stead, A. A., "Mapping Spiritual Dangers: The Novels of Susan Sontag" (thesis, 1993). *The Other Within Us: Feminist Explorations of Women and Aging* (1997). Tydeman, W. E., "Photography, Meaning and Methodology: American Writings on Photography Since 1945" (thesis, 1985). Willis, L. A., "Womanist Intellectuals Developing Tradition" (thesis, 1996).

Reference works: *Benet's* (1991). *CA* (Online, 1999). *CANR* (1988). *CN* (1986). *DLB* (1985). *FC* (1990). *Oxford Companion to Women's Writing in the Untied States* (1995).

Other references: *American Literary History* (Fall, 1989). *Book Review Digest* (1992, 1994). *Feminist Review* (Summer, 1991). *Journal of American Studies* (April 1990). *LATBR* (1993). *Midwest Quarterly* (Winter, 1988). *Nation* (1992). *National Review* (31 Aug. 1992). *NR* (7, 14 Sept. 1992). *NYTBR* (24 Oct. 1982, 9 Aug. 1992, 24 Oct. 1992). *NYTM* (2 Aug. 1992). *October* (Summer, 1989). *Performing Arts Journal* (interview, 1985). *SR* (Oct. 1972). *Sewanee Rev.* (Fall, 1984). *Theater* (1993). *Time* (24 Oct. 1988). *VVLS* (Nov. 1990). *WP* (1992).

—ELAINE HOFFMAN BARUCH AND ANDREW J. SCHIAVONI, UPDATED BY JULIET BYINGTON

SOREL, Julia

See DREXLER, Rosalyn

SOULE, Caroline White

Born 3 September 1824, Albany, New York; **died** 6 December 1903, Glasgow, Scotland
Also wrote under: Aunt Carra
Daughter of Nathaniel and Elizabeth Merselis White; **married** Henry B. Soule, 1843 (died 1852); **children:** five

Despite her family's limited means, Caroline White Soule was educated at the Albany Female Academy, from which she graduated with high honors at seventeen. Soule, like others in her family a member of the Universalist church, took a job as principal of the female department of the Clinton Liberal Institute, a secondary school operated by that church in Clinton, New York. She taught for only two terms before marrying a Universalist minister, with whom she made frequent moves from one parish to another. Henry Soule died of small pox in 1852, leaving Caroline with five small children. She immediately wrote *The Memoir of Rev. H. B. Soule*, published the following summer. The anguish and grief of Soule's loss come through the simply told narration of his life.

Soule supported her family as a part-time teacher and, increasingly, as a contributor of stories and articles to various story-papers and magazines. In 1853 Soule migrated to Boone County, Iowa. In Iowa, she became western editor of the *Ladies Repository*, and her stories and novellas appeared at regular intervals.

A serious eye ailment forced Soule to return to the East for treatment in 1864. She did not resume editorial work until 1868, when she founded and edited the *Guiding Star*, a Sunday school paper. She was also children's editor for the *Christian Leader* and contributed to other Universalist papers under several pseudonyms, one of which was "Aunt Carra." Soule helped to found what became the Woman's Centenary Association, the first national organization of churchwomen in the U.S.; she was its president from 1869 to 1880. From an office in New York City, she ran fund raising activities netting the organization over $100,000 in five years, a substantial sum for that time.

Her activities for the association undermined her health, and Soule went for a visit to England and Scotland to recuperate. She interrupted her rest many times, however, to lecture on temperance and the higher education of women. She helped organize a Scottish Universalist Convention and finally became minister of

St. Paul's Universalist in Glasgow; she was officially ordained in 1880. Soule remained in Scotland for the rest of her life except for a period between 1882 and 1886 when she again worked for the Centenary Association in the U.S.

Soule's stories appeared in the 1850s, the era of the sentimental novel, when many women writing for the numerous weeklies and monthlies were also pleading the various causes of women's rights, abolition, and temperance. *Home Life; or, A Peep across the Threshold* (1855) is a collection of Soule's ''little moral tales'' published by a Universalist publisher. Soule intended *Wine or Water* (1862) as a novel, but it is really three separate tales loosely bound by the moral thread of its temperance theme.

Soule's moral tales are notable for their emphasis on the virtues of happy home life as a bulwark against vice and degradation. She wrote in the preface to *Home Life*, ''we wrote of home-life. . .because we have thought much on the secret influences which gladden or madden human homes. . .that if a peep across the threshold showed a happy home—. . .we might cross the sacred steppingstone and look thence upon a world of beauty, peace, and joy.''

Soule's concern for nurture and education was lifelong, and her stories and novellas illustrate her sensitive and sensible ideas on the raising of children. In ''The Only Daughter,'' for example, she criticizes parents who raise children with no useful skills, no healthful sports in their daily activity, and no appropriate discipline. In *Wine or Water*, she describes the type of family life she hoped to inspire in her readers: ''both parents were yet firm in their requirements, and as they never were forgot, as too many do, that their children were not yet men and women, but simple-hearted little ones, their commands were suited to their varied ages and dispositions, and their home was thus a fair type of the Christian's thought of heaven, care with comfort for an accompaniment, labor made light by love.''

Much of Soule's writing exhibits the flowery sentimentality and effusive moralizing of the late 19th century. A thread of common sense and down-to-earth intelligence, however, pervades her sermonizing and exemplifies her lifelong concern for home and family. She summed up her own life by writing: ''I have written everything from a sermon to a song, and done everything from making sorghum molasses in a log cabin on a prairie to preaching three times a Sunday in the city of London.''

OTHER WORKS: *The Pet of the Settlement* (1860).
Some letters and papers of Caroline W. Soule are at the New York Public Library.

BIBLIOGRAPHY: Reference works: *Appleton's Cyclopaedia of American Biography* (1900). *Daughters of America* (1883). *NAW* (1971). *Our Woman Workers* (1882).

—DOROTHEA MOSLEY THOMPSON

SOUTHWORTH, E(mma) D(orothy) E(liza) N(evitte)

Born 26 December 1819, Washington, D.C.; **died** 30 June 1899, Washington, D.C.
Wrote under: Mrs. E.D.E.N. Southworth
Daughter of Charles L. and Susanna Wailes Nevitte; **married** Frederick H. Southworth, 1840

E. D. E. N. Southworth and her sister were educated in Washington, D.C., at the school run by her stepfather, Joshua Henshaw, whom her mother had married after the death of Captain Nevitte. Southworth taught school in Washington after her graduation. Deserted by her husband within a few years of their marriage, Southworth was left with two young children to support. Despite ill health, which plagued her for many years, she returned to teaching in Washington and began to write.

Southworth's first publication was a short story, ''The Irish Refugee,'' which appeared in the Baltimore *Saturday Visitor*. This was followed by other short stories. Her first novel, *Retribution* (1849), was serialized in 1847 in the columns of the Washington *National Era*, which published most of her early stories. It is reported Southworth never knew how long her serials would be; she would continue on week after week, with characters presumed dead sometimes reappearing. When the serial had reached a certain length, the book publisher would bring out as one volume the work written so far and later publish the rest as a sequel. Many of her works were reprinted in other countries and translated into several languages.

Southworth produced about three novels per year throughout most of the rest of her life and even at that rate could hardly satisfy the demands of her readers, so popular were her works. *The Hidden Hand* (1888), first published serially in the New York *Ledger*, is said to have been the most popular work that paper ever printed. In book form it sold almost two million copies; it was also transformed into several dramatic versions, one of which starred John Wilkes Booth. *Ishmael* (1876) and *Self-Raised* (1876) sold over two million copies each. Others tried to capitalize on Southworth's popularity by writing under names such as S. A. Southworth, Ella Southworth, or Emma S. Southworth; her publishers insisted however that the only genuine novels were those signed with the famous initials E.D.E.N.

A typical theme in Southworth's novels is the ''rags and riches'' romance, exemplified in *The Curse of Clifton* (1853). Clifton, heir to an ancestral fortune, loves a humble mountain girl. Clifton's ''curse'' is his stepmother—one of Southworth's more malignant villains, who in her most furious soliloquies echoes the most evil moments of Lady Macbeth. Some critics consider *The Hidden Hand* Southworth's best work. The heroine, Capitola, is a multifaceted character, though she is portrayed as thoroughly good. The plot has a great deal of variety, with pranks, outlaws, and much mystery. The villain, Colonel LeNoir, is a model of the type; he grinds his teeth in impotent rage and vows revenge for affronts both real and imagined. Southworth considered *Self-Made* her best work. It was originally published in 1876 in two parts, the first called *Ishmael; or, In the Depths* and the second *Self-Raised; or, Out of the Depths*. This novel has an interesting rags-to-riches theme, a degenerate villain, and a highborn young woman who refuses to marry the hero, Ishmael, because of his low birth but who is justly punished for her pride. It also has a fine touch of humor and well-handled descriptions of setting and costume.

Villains in Southworth's novels are thoroughly evil, heroes and heroines thoroughly pure. The situations in which they are brought together are the familiar fare of most novels written originally in serialized form: sudden catastrophic illnesses, bankruptcies, murders or other calamitous deaths, ancestral secrets revealed, hidden passions unleashed. A voracious reader herself, Southworth perhaps unconsciously echoes in her work such 19th-century authors as Scott, Dickens, and Cooper. Some of her favorite settings—wild mountain roads and fearful chasms—are reminiscent of the novels of the Brontës. Finally, however, the enormous popularity of Southworth's novels seems to be attributable to the simple black and white morality of her tales, her fine melodramatic touch, and her innate storytelling ability.

OTHER WORKS: *The Deserted Wife* (1850). *The Mother-in-Law* (1851). *Shannondale* (1851). *The Discarded Daughter* (1852). *Old Neighborhoods and New Settlements* (1853). *The Lost Heiress* (1854). *India: The Pearl of Pearl River* (1855). *The Missing Bride* (1855). *Vivia; or, The Secret of Power* (1857). *Virginia and Magdalene* (1858). *The Lady of the Isle* (1859). *The Haunted Homestead* (1860). *The Gipsy's Prophecy* (1861). *Hickory Hall* (1861). *The Broken Engagement* (1862). *Love's Labor Won* (1862). *The Fatal Marriage* (1863). *The Bridal Eve* (1864). *Allworth Abbey* (1865). *The Bride of Llewellyn* (1866). *The Fortune Seeker* (1866). *The Coral Lady* (1867). *The Widow's Son* (1867). *Fair Play* (1868). *The Bride's Fate* (1869). *The Changed Brides* (1869). *The Family Doom* (1869). *How He Won Her* (1869). *The Prince of Darkness* (1869). *The Christmas Guest: A Collection of Stories* (1870). *The Maiden Widow* (1870). *Cruel as the Grave* (1871). *Tried for Her Life* (1871). *The Artist's Love* (1872). *The Lost Heir of Linlithgow* (1872). *A Noble Lord* (1872). *A Beautiful Fiend* (1873). *Victor's Triumph* (1874). *The Mystery of Dark Hollow* (1875). *The Spectre Lover* (1875). *The Fatal Secret* (1877). *The Red Hill Tragedy* (1877). *The Phantom Wedding* (1878). *Sybil Brotherton: A Novel* (1879). *A Leap in the Dark* (1889). *Nearest and Dearest* (1889). *Unknown* (1889). *For Woman's Love* (1890). *The Lost Lady of Lone* (1890). *Broken Pledges* (1891). *David Lindsay* (1891). *Gloria: A Novel* (1891). *Lillith* (1891). *The Unloved Wife* (1891). *''Em'': A Novel* (1892). *Em's Husband: A Novel* (1892). *Brandon Coyle's Wife* (1893). *Only a Girl's Heart* (1893). *A Skeleton in the Closet* (1893). *Gertrude Haddon* (1894). *The Rejected Bride* (1894).

The papers of E.D.E.N. Southworth are in the Perkins Library of Duke University, and at the Library of Congress in Washington, D.C.

BIBLIOGRAPHY: Baym, N., *Women's Fiction* (1978). Boyle, R. L., *Mrs. E.D.E.N. Southworth, Novelist* (1939). Coultrap-McQuin, S., *Doing Literary Business* (1990). Hart, J. D., *The Popular Book* (1950). Kelly, M., *Private Women, Public Stage* (1984). Mott, F. L., *Golden Multitudes* (1947). Pattee, F. L., *The Feminine Fifties* (1940).

Reference works: *DAB. Oxford Companion to Women's Writing in the United States* (1995).

—ELAINE K. GINSBERG

SOUZA, E.
See SCOTT, Evelyn

SPACKS, Patricia (Ann) Meyer

Born 17 November 1929, San Francisco, California
Daughter of Norman B. and Lillian Talcott Meyer; **married** Barry B. Spacks, 1955; **children:** Elizabeth

As an academic writer and professor of English, Patricia Meyer Spacks writes literary criticism on 18th-century authors, the structure of the novel, and women writers; nonfiction that elucidates aspects of mind (or age) such as the imagination, gossip, boredom, and adolescence; and essays on pedagogy and the literary profession. Presently the Edgar F. Shannon Professor of English at the University of Virginia, Spacks also held the positions of chair of the English Department and president of the Modern Language Association (1994). She received her education at Rollins College in Winter Park, Florida (B.A., 1949), Yale University (M.A.), and the University of California (Ph.D., 1955). Her academic appointments include instructor at Indiana University at Bloomington (1954-56) and the University of Florida at Gainesville (1958-59). At Wellesley College she began as an instructor and was promoted to professor. Her awards include the Shirley Farr Fellowship of the American Association of University Women (1962-63), Guggenheim Fellowship (1969-70), National Endowment for the Humanities Senior Fellowship (1974), National Humanities Institute Fellowship (1976-77), Honorary Doctor of Letters from Rollins College (1976), and American Council of Learned Societies Fellowship (1978-79).

In six books about 18th-century literature, Spacks writes with a vision that considers the writer and the genre in the social and cultural context of the period as well as the history of literary evolution and significance. *Imagining a Self: Autobiography and Novel in Eighteenth-Century England* (1976) is a comparative study between the two genres. The pairing of each autobiography with a work of fiction, e.g., Edward Gibbon's *Autobiographies* (1776) and Laurence Sterne's *Tristram Shandy* (1760), reveals that the clear distinctions between the two genres invented in the 18th century are more apparent than true. As in her other studies, Spacks looks to the common ground: "the meaning of technique, the insistence of theme, and the implications of genre." "Autobiographies affirm identity" and novels in the development of character and plot assert identity. In the 20th century, the aim of either genre, "imagining a self," requires borrowings and blurring of the differences as self becomes the central subject.

Similarly, in *Desire and Truth: Functions of Plot in Eighteenth-Century English Novels* (1990), Spacks explores the question: What truth does fiction tell? She shows, although "desire" is a critical term of the 20th century, its priority is for building plots and assigning meaning: "Truth, dressed—like Falsehood—by Desire, becomes Fiction." Several studies associate fictional structures and reality, the making of novels, and social, ultimately, ethical, truth.

In all of her literary analyses, Spacks includes women writers and their writings, many of whom were unknown and excluded from traditional criticism. *Imagining a Self* (1976) presents several 18th-century writers: Fanny Burney, Charlotte Lennox, Jane Barker, Susannah Rowson, Lady Mary Wortley Montagu, Laetitia Pilkington, Charlotte Charke, Hester Lynch Thrale, Mary Wollstonecraft, Mary Davys, Penelope Aubin, and Sarah Fielding. Spacks edited *Series: Women Writers in English, 1350-1850* (1999). *The Female Imagination: A Literary and Psychological Investigation of Women's Writings* (1975), Spacks' first full-length text about women writers, introduces the integral relationship between the imagination and freedom. The text examines the "special female awareness [that] emerges through literature in every period."

Three themes predominate that reveal the social limitations of women's lives and the power of writing in obviating those restraints: the problems of women writing about women; the threat and the appeal of dependency, usually represented by marriage; and children or care-taking as a central justification of women lives. The imagination becomes the way to reproduce the reality that makes awareness and thus change possible and to represent other possibilities that bode for freedom.

The Adolescent Idea: Myths of Youth and the Adult Imagination (1981), *Gossip* (1985), and *Boredom: The Literary History of a State of Mind* (1995) share ideas, concepts, and states of mind that concern the 20th century, yet, through literary example, Spacks demonstrates the historical continuity. Adolescence as a social and psychological phenomena is a 20th century construct but earlier times represented this stage of life.

Gossip, like relationships, forms the subject, structure, and subtext of literature, as explored in *Gossip*. It functions as a plot device, as the source of malice or intimacy, as a mirror from the private to the public life. It is "the language of shared experience" transformed into story. Where gossip is social, boredom is lonely. *Boredom* examines how writing protects the writer against its vacuum, and reading admits the reader into the created antithesis to boredom: an active state of mind. "All writing—at least since 1800 or so—is about boredom. . . . The ideal dynamic between writing and reading depends in part on boredom as displaced, unmentioned, unmentionable possibility. The need to refute boredom's deadening poser impels the writer's productivity and the reader's engagement."

Spacks' recent articles discuss pedagogy. The title of her presidential address to the MLA (1994) links the structural and ethical concerns of her criticism with those of teaching: "Reality—Our Subject and Discipline" (1995). She asks, "So what. . .Why does it matter that we struggle to understand others'

words and to shape our own language to convey meaning and feeling?" Her present work-in-progress is a study of self-love in the 17th and 18th centuries.

OTHER WORKS: *The Varied God: A Critical Study of Thomson's "The Seasons"* (1959). *The Insistence of Horror: Aspects of the Supernatural in Eighteenth-Century Poetry* (1962). *John Gay* (1965). *The Poetry of Vision: Five Eighteenth-Century Poets* (1967). *An Argument of Images: The Poetry of Alexander Pope* (1971).

BIBLIOGRAPHY: *CA* Online (1999). *Oxford Companion to Women's Writing in the Untied States* (1995).

—KAREN J. MCLENNAN

SPEARE, Elizabeth George

Born 21 November 1908, Melrose, Massachusetts; **died** 14 November 1994
Daughter of Harry A. and Demetria Simmons George; **married** Alden Speare, 1936; **children:** son and a daughter

After graduation from college during the Depression, Elizabeth George Speare taught English in Massachusetts high schools for several years. She married an industrial engineer and then settled in Wethersfield, Connecticut. Speare did little writing until her son and daughter were in their teens, when she began to do articles for women's magazines and an occasional story and play. Two of Speare's books, *The Witch of Blackbird Pond* (1958) and *The Bronze Bow* (1961) received the Newbery Award.

While reading about the history of the Connecticut River valley, Speare came upon *A Narrative of the Captivity of Mrs. Johnson*, the personal account of the actual experiences of Susanna Johnson during the French and Indian War. This pioneer woman and her family were taken by Indians to Montreal, where they were sold to the French, who held them for ransom. Among the captives was Mrs. Johnson's younger sister, Miriam Willard. *Calico Captive* presents events from Miriam's point of view, adding details and characters and elaborating upon the romantic aspects to produce an engrossing story and an interesting view of the period. Although Speare often seems overly conscious of her audience and many of the characters are types, Miriam emerges as a strong and likable young woman.

The Witch of Blackbird Pond also had its origin in a chance reading encounter. Speare happened to learn how children used to be sent from Barbados to Boston to be educated and wondered what life would have been like for a girl from those sunny surroundings in colonial Wethersfield with its grim, hard Puritan way of life. The result was the story of sixteen-year-old orphaned Kit Tyler—free-spirited, Anglican, and reared in luxury in the tropics—who travels to Connecticut to live with her aunt in 1687. Her recklessness brings her into conflict with the duty-ridden Puritans and culminates with her trial for witchcraft. Although the book's three romances seem contrived to please a teenaged audience, Kit's rigidly principled Uncle Matthew; the gentle, old but despised Quaker woman, Hannah; and the lonely, frightened child, Prudence, whose testimony saves Kit from conviction, are well-drawn characters, while the sense of Puritan ways and values is particularly strong.

An equally strong protagonist is Daniel bar Jamin in *The Bronze Bow*, an imaginary story set in Jesus' time, which rose out of Speare's wish to give her teenaged Sunday School class the feeling of what it must have been like to live in Palestine during the Roman occupation. It excels in making credible the intense hostility the ancient Jews felt for their conquerors and their deep frustration at being unable to stand up to the military might of the Romans.

In *The Prospering* (1967), Speare fictionalizes the actual experiences of the settlers who participated in the experiment of the Stockbridge mission in western Massachusetts. This was the plan of the visionary and zealous young John Sergeant to prepare the Native Americans to live and work in English ways upon land he hoped would remain theirs forever. The story is related by Elizabeth, youngest daughter of the Williams family, which was among the earliest settlers there. She sees the village grow over a 50-year period into a beautiful town, observing how the experiment fails because the Native Americans are unable to change their ways and the colonists increasingly use the Native Americans and the land for their own purposes. This novel is less successful as fiction than Speare's award-winning novels because its heroine is too objective and impassive and too much on the fringes of events to involve the reader deeply.

Speare knows how to tell a story well and create sympathetic central characters and memorable minor ones. Her best books move fast through well-researched, judiciously selected detail and are enlivened with much realistic dialogue. Speare is most outstanding for her ability to recreate past times believably and to give them life and immediacy by integrating the personal problems of her protagonists with those of the era. Although her output has not been large, Speare is ranked among the best of contemporary writers of historical fiction for young people.

OTHER WORKS: *Life in Colonial America* (1963).

BIBLIOGRAPHY: Reference works: *CB* (1959). *More Books by More People* (1974). *More Junior Authors* (1963). *Newbery and Caldecott Medal Books: 1956-65* (1965). *SAA* (1973).

—ALETHEA K. HELBIG

SPENCER, Anne

Born 6 February 1882, Henry County, Virginia; died 27 July 1975, Lynchburg, Virginia
Daughter of Joel C. and Sarah Cephus Scales; married Edward Spencer, 1901

Anne Spencer was the only child of divorced parents; she had no formal education before the age of eleven, when she entered Lynchburg Seminary. Spencer lived with her husband in Lynchburg, where for the next 20 years her local fame derived chiefly from the beautiful garden she cultivated. Throughout this period, Spencer also wrote poems for her private pleasure, and at the urging of James Weldon Johnson, in 1920 she began to publish her work. Over the next three decades, her poems appeared in almost every major anthology of black American poetry.

In many of her poems, Spencer rejects this world of ugliness, impurity, and hate and replaces it with a visionary world of beauty and love. The sonnet "Substitution" is the clearest statement of this theme. A love for natural scenery in general and for her garden in particular provided a metaphorical setting for several works. The central conceit of "Life-Long Poor Browning" mourns the fact the poet never enjoyed the beauties of Virginia. Here and elsewhere, Spencer reveals an affinity for the technical devices and philosophical concerns of the metaphysical poets.

Spencer used the traditions of English poetry, but she was not a conventional poet. Her best poems remain fresh and strikingly original. "At the Carnival" offers a finely hued, evocative description of a tawdry street fair. Onlookers like "the limousine lady" and "the bull-necked man," "the unholy incense" of the sausage and garlic booth, the dancing tent where "a quivering female-thing gestured assignations," and the crooked games of chance combine to produce an atmosphere of unrelieved ugliness and depravity. Yet the possibility of beauty exists even here, in the person of a young female diver, the "Naiad of the Carnival Tank." Her presence transforms the scene.

Usually Spencer's references to the world of reality were more oblique. That she was aware of life's travails, particularly as they affect women, is nonetheless evident. Her poem "Letter to My Sister" begins: "It is dangerous for a woman to defy the gods." Despite her participation in the civil rights struggle and her work as a librarian in the local black high school, Spencer rarely employed racial themes in her poetry. An autobiographical statement she wrote for Countee Cullen's anthology, *Caroling Dusk* (1927), suggests the reason: "I write about the things I love. But have no civilized articulation for the things I hate." Spencer's posture was typical of the black female poets of her generation.

Several of her critics have drawn comparisons between Spencer and Emily Dickinson. They share a penchant for cryptic imagery and perhaps a similar method of composition, but Spencer is not the major poet Dickinson is. As her biographer, J. Lee Greene, attests, the wonder is that Spencer became a poet at all. A Southern black woman with little education, who belonged to no literary coterie and lived her entire life in small, provincial towns, Spencer proved by writing poetry of the quality she did, when she did, though dangerous, it is not impossible to defy society's gods.

OTHER WORKS: Anne Spencer's poems may be found in the following volumes: Brown, S., A. P. Davis, and U. Lee, *The Negro Caravan* (1941); Greene, J. L., *Time's Unfading Garden: Anne Spencer's Life and Poetry* (1977); Johnson, J. W., *The Book of American Negro Poetry* (1931).

BIBLIOGRAPHY: Brown, S., *Negro Poetry and Drama* (1937). Gilbert, S. and S. Gubar, eds., *Shakespeare's Sister* (1979). Greene, J. L., *Time's Unfading Garden: Anne Spencer's Life and Poetry* (1977). Honey, M., ed., *Shadowed Dreams: Women's Poetry of the Harlem Renaissance* (1989). Stetson, E., ed., *Black Sister: Poetry by Black American Women, 1746-1980* (1981).

Reference works: *Notable Black American Women* (1992). *Oxford Companion to Women's Writing in the United States* (1995).

Other references: *A Journal* (March 1978). *Echoes from the Garden: The Anne Spencer Story* (documentary film, 1980).

—CHERYL A. WALL

SPENCER, Cornelia (Ann) Phillips

Born 20 March 1825, Harlem, New York; died 11 March 1908, Cambridge, Massachusetts
Daughter of James and Judith Vermeule Phillips; married James Spencer, 1855 (died 1861); children: one daughter

The year after Cornelia Spencer's birth, her family moved to Chapel Hill, North Carolina, where her father became professor of mathematics at the University of North Carolina. Spencer was educated at home and always felt her education had been inferior to that received by her brothers. For this reason, she was a tireless crusader for women's education later in life. After her husband, an Alabama lawyer, died in 1861, she and her daughter returned to the Phillips home in Chapel Hill.

After the Civil War, Spencer began teaching Latin and Greek to children in the community. To make ends meet, she also tutored, ran a boarding house, painted china, worked for the university, and contributed occasional articles to the newspapers. An offer from the *North Carolina Presbyterian* to write a column on subjects of her choice at $400 per year provided some measure of financial security.

Spencer used her column to promote her two favorite projects—the restoration of the University of North Carolina and education for women. The university had been closed during the Civil War, and when it reopened it was under the control of a president and professor appointed by the "Carpetbag" Republican government. Spencer not only criticized the politics of the faculty, but their lack of educational qualifications. When the university was reorganized again in 1875, and the Republicans dismissed, Spencer climbed the belfry to ring out the good news. In 1895 the university awarded her an honorary degree for her

lifelong devotion, the first ever given to a woman by that institution. Her crusade for better education for women also bore fruit in 1877 when the university opened a summer normal school for girls. Spencer was instrumental in founding the Normal and Industrial School for Women in 1891, which later became the Women's College of the University of North Carolina at Greensboro.

In 1894 Spencer moved to Cambridge, Massachusetts, to live with her daughter and son-in-law. She wrote her first book, *The Last Ninety Days of the War in North Carolina* (1866), at the urging of her good friend David L. Swain, president of the University of North Carolina. Swain and former Confederate Governor Zebulon B. Vance offered her access to their private wartime papers to give the work authenticity and accuracy. Called a "Whig review of the War" by the press, *The Last Ninety Days* is a bitter condemnation of secession and the Confederate leadership. "That North Carolina accepted a destiny which she was unable to control, when she ranged herself in the war for Southern independence, is a fact which cannot be disputed." As a result, the state was left ravaged and penniless by Sherman's invasion, and its people broken in spirit. Spencer firmly believed, as most North Carolinians did, that her state had sent more men to the Confederate army than any other but was the least honored in civil and military appointments. She has only high praise for Governor Vance's attempts to feed and clothe his people, even when his actions violated Confederate law. "Looking back at our delusions, errors, and miscalculations for the four years of the war," she concludes, "the wonder is that the Confederacy lasted as long as it did."

Spencer's second book, *Pen and Ink Sketches of the University of North Carolina* (1869), first appeared as a series of articles in the Raleigh *Standard*. Her last book, published in 1888, is a children's history of the state.

OTHER WORKS: *First Steps in North Carolina History* (1888). *Selected Papers of Cornelia Phillips Spencer* (edited by L. R. Wilson, 1953).

Cornelia Phillips Spencer's diaries, journals, and letters are in the Southern Historical Collection of the University of North Carolina Library in Chapel Hill, North Carolina.

BIBLIOGRAPHY: Chamberlain, H. S., *Old Days in Chapel Hill* (1926). Russell, P., *The Woman Who Rang the Bell* (1949).

—JANET KAUFMAN

SPENCER, Elizabeth

Born 19 July 1921, Carrollton, Mississippi
Daughter of James L. and Mary McCain Spencer; married John Rusher, 1956 (died 1998)

A native of Mississippi and the progeny of a family whose ancestors had lived in Carroll County, Mississippi, since the

1830s, Elizabeth Spencer spent her childhood in the kind of rural South she depicts with topographic precision in several of her novels. Spencer studied English at Belhaven College in Jackson, Mississippi, (B.A. 1942) and Vanderbilt University (M.A. 1943); and went on to teach for two years, first in Mississippi and then in Tennessee, resigning from teaching to work as a reporter for the Nashville *Tennessean*. In 1946 Spencer abandoned the craft of the journalist for that of the novelist, and her first novel, *Fire in the Morning*, was published two years later. Recipient of a Guggenheim Fellowship in 1953, Spencer traveled to Italy, the scene of two later novels, *The Light in the Piazza* (1960) and *Knights & Dragons* (1965). She has served as writer-in-residence at several colleges and universities in the U.S. and Canada, including Bryn Mawr (1962), the University of North Carolina (1969), Hollins College (1972), and Concordia University (1977-78).

Her first novel, *Fire in the Morning* (1948, reprinted 1998, 1999), published with the encouragement of the Fugitive poet Donald Davidson, reveals Spencer's firsthand knowledge of the intricate workings of a small Southern town—its layers of intrigue and the complexities of relationships that span several generations. With the Southerner's sense of local story as possessing the power of myth, Spencer delineates the history and works out the fate of two antagonistic families in Tarsus, Mississippi, in a fashion recalling the conflicts in various "houses" of Greek drama. The movement of the novel is predicated on a young man's gradual discovery of the interwoven affairs of love, fraud, and violence which underlie one family's dominance of the town. In the process of uncovering the private histories which link together the inhabitants of Tarsus, he comes to terms with the town, his own family, and himself in relationship to what had seemed an inexplicable past.

In *Fire in the Morning*, Spencer suggests there are sociological differences between the regions of Delta and hill country in Mississippi. In *This Crooked Way* (1952, reprinted 1999), these regions provide symbolic points of reference for charting Amos Dudley's odyssey from poverty to riches and from damnation to salvation. Convinced as a consequence of a religious experience that God will support him in his opportunistic endeavors, Dudley leaves the Yocona hills, striding into the Delta in Colonel Sutpen fashion to wrest a plantation out of the overgrown land. His success, however, leaves destruction in its wake; and it is not until he brings the remnants of his hill country family to the Delta to share his affluence that he finds a measure of peace and is able to reconcile himself with his past.

Spencer's third novel, *The Voice at the Back Door* (1956, reprinted 1994), which treats politics and the cost of equal justice for blacks and whites in a Southern town, is the last to deal with the Mississippi South. She returns in *The Snare* (1972) to a Southern locale; but in this novel it is to the New Orleans atmosphere of the French Quarter, where her heroine becomes involved in the city's underworld of jazz musicians.

In 1960, with the publication of *The Light in the Piazza*, Spencer shifts locales, delineating in this novella the crisis of conscience of an American woman who decides to allow her beautiful but mentally retarded daughter to marry her young Italian suitor. Spencer treats such a dilemma, which might otherwise be too ponderous, with grace and charm; and her evocation of the Florentine atmosphere and its impact upon the Americans makes the city a powerful force in the story. *The Light in the Piazza* was made into a Metro-Goldwyn-Mayer film in 1962, starring Olivia de Havilland, Yvette Mimieux and George Hamilton.

Critics distressed by the power of the manipulative American mother in *The Light in the Piazza*, saw Spencer following the international theme of Henry James. Few acknowledged the ironic force of the idea that many men might prefer a pretty obedient woman with the mind of a ten-year-old. *Knights & Dragons* (1965), also set in Italy, reflects a recurrent theme in Spencer's work: the tension between a woman's need for independence and her social conditioning and psychological need to live for others. Perhaps because critics considered this work too allegorical, Spencer's next two novels, *No Place for an Angel* (1967) and *The Snare* (1972), are rich in realistic detail. Both attempt to record the demoralized affluent life of post—World War II America and each features a strong heroine who refuses to connect meaning in life with men.

Spencer continued to expand her vision of life both in terms of setting and ideas. Early identified as a Southern writer influenced by William Faulkner and Eudora Welty (a close friend) because of the regional themes and precise local details in her first three novels, she has kept challenging her original identity both geographically and spiritually. Like many women writers trained by men she remains intensely aware of the importance of craft, and she has created as many heroes as heroines. She has also learned over the years, however, to identify and articulate the human problems that women's lives often exemplify more clearly than men's.

The Stories of Elizabeth Spencer (1981, 1983), 33 stories written over more than 30 years, appeared with Welty's foreword paying tribute to Spencer's seriousness. Asked in a 1980 interview about recurrent themes in her writing, Spencer remarked that many stories were "about liberation and the regret you have when you liberate yourself." Such ambivalence might well isolate Spencer from more ideological feminists but links her with the divided self that remains a valued part of American literary tradition. *Jack of Diamonds and Other Stories* (1988), a shorter collection of stories including two O. Henry Award winners, reveals Spencer to be one of our most skillful literary artisans.

In *The Salt Line* (1983, reprinted 1995) Spencer returned to the novel to create a more complex social reality. Here the academic upheavals of the 1960s and the natural disaster of a hurricane help shape her characters' needs. Once again using the South as a convincing background she explores the problematic nature of marriage. *The Night Travellers* (1991, reprinted 1999), her most political work to date, uses the war in Vietnam as a focus for generational conflict. Beginning in the traditional South, perhaps reflecting her personal growth toward a cosmopolitan conscience, Spencer carries her characters to Canada and the mid-Atlantic states and finally even to Vietnam. Again, a mother-daughter relationship becomes the most unforgettable aspect of this record of social upheaval.

Spencer returned to the South from Canada in 1986 to teach at the University of North Carolina in Chapel Hill, and retired in 1992. She is a writer who has continued to grow, struggling to give her readers more than just a slice of life or a neat ideology. Although her effort to create mythology and enhance themes may make her work seem old-fashioned, the precision of her observations, the subtlety of her style, and the diversity of backgrounds she evokes marks her place as an important writer of the 20th century and beyond. Her novels, moving as they do from the fixed geography and traditions of the South to an international scene, demonstrate the scope of a writer who may have begun under the shadow of the mythic South but whose vision is not regionally limited. She has explored in several contexts and with considerable artistry the individual as an outsider to the environment, whether that environment be the Mississippi Delta, Vietnam, Canada, or an Italian city.

By the end of the 1990s, Spencer had written nine novels, three short story collections (not including three reprints), a dramatic play (*For Lease or Sale*, produced in 1989), a compilation of interviews from varied sources, entitled *Conversations with Elizabeth Spencer* (1998), and her memoirs, *Landscapes of the Heart* (1998). Her works have been translated into a myriad of foreign languages, including French, Finnish, German, Norwegian, Japanese, Polish, and Bengali. She is also the recipient of many fellowships (McGraw-Hill, NEA, Bryn Mawr, Guggenheim Foundation, and the *Kenyon Review*), awards (Award of Merit from the American Academy, 1983; John Dos Passos Award for Literature, 1992; Salem Award for Distinction, 1992; North Carolina Governor's Award, 1994; J. William Corrington Award for Fiction, 1997; Richard Wright Literary Excellence Award for Fiction, 1997; Fortner Award for Literature, 1998) and holds honorary degrees from Rhodes University (Memphis, 1968), Concordia University (Montreal, 1988), University of the South (Sewanee, Tennessee, 1992), the University of North Carolina at Chapel Hill (1998), and Belhaven College (Jackson, Mississippi, 1999).

OTHER WORKS: *Ship Island, and Other Stories* (1968). *Marilee: Three Stories* (1987). *On the Gulf* (1991). *The Light in the Piazza and Other Italian Tales* (1996).

Contributor to *Opera News, Sewanee Review, Southern Review*, the *Writer*, and others.

BIBLIOGRAPHY: Bradbury, J. M., *Renaissance in the South: A Critical History of Literature, 1920-1960* (1963). Clayton, M. E., "Rejecting Tradition: A Contemporary View of Place and Identity in the Short Stories of Elizabeth Spencer" (thesis, 1997). Entzminger, B., "Frustrated Passions: Emotional Distance as Narrative Strategy in Elizabeth Spencer's Fiction" (thesis, 1993). French, W. C., ed., *The Fifties: Fiction, Poetry, Drama* (1970). Jones, J., *Mississippi Writers Talking* (1982). Prenshaw, P. W., *Elizabeth Spencer* (1985). Roberts, T., *Self and the Community in the Fiction of Elizabeth Spencer* (1993). Rubin, L. D., and R. D.

Jacobs, *South: Modern Southern Literature in its Cultural Setting* (1961).

Reference works: *CANR* (1990). *CLC* (1982). *DLB* (1980). *Oxford Companion to Women's Writing in the United States* (1995).

Other references: *Mississippi Quarterly* (Fall 1976, Spring 1994, Fall 1994, 1996). *NYTBR* (January 1998). *South Atlantic Quarterly* (Summer 1964). *Southern Quarterly* (special issue, 1997). *Style* (Fall 1993). *Elizabeth Spencer Interview with Kay Bonetti* (audiocassette, 1993).

—GUIN A. NANCE,
UPDATED BY EUGENIA KALEDIN AND SYDONIE BENET

SPEWAK, Bella Cohen

Born 15 March 1899, Bucharest, Rumania; **died** December 1987
Daughter of Adolph and Fanny Lang Cohen; **married** Samuel Spewak, 1922

Born in Hungary (now Rumania), Bella Cohen Spewak moved to New York in her youth. She graduated from Washington Irving High School (1917) and began her career reporting for various New York newspapers, writing features. She later assisted her husband as a foreign correspondent in Europe and Russia from 1922 to 1926. They returned to New York to collaborate on Broadway dramas and musicals and Hollywood film and television scripts. After World War II, Spewak returned to Europe for material to broadcast an ABC series on the work of United Nations Refugee Relief Association and conditions abroad. She once served as national publicity director of the Camp Fire Girls; she was a member of the Dramatists Guild and the Screen Writers Guild.

Although they experimented with different styles, the Spewaks wrote primarily comedy and satire. The commercial failure of *Spring Song* (produced 1934, published 1936) with its affectionate portrayal of New York's ethnic East Side neighborhood and its tragedy apparently convinced them to challenge social ills through humor. The effects of fortune and fame upon the individual became subjects for satiric attack. Characters are manipulated to satirize institutions—generally connected with the mass media—they represent. The Spewaks expose romantic love, movie stardom, and wartime heroism to unsentimental analysis. While sometimes too extravagant to be truly satiric, their works invariably center on the exploitation of reality and universal emotion which characterizes the mass media.

The Spewaks' best play, *Boy Meets Girl* (1935, film version, 1938), winner of the Roi Cooper Megrue Prize (1936), is a hilarious comedy in which theme, content, structure, subplots, satire, and even the movie scripts being discussed duplicate each other by presenting variations on the boy-meets-girl cliché. The traditional love story is complicated by the presence of baby Happy, around whom all the developments center. His not so innocent mother, widowed by a bigamist, is only the most visible "girl" whose love life is rearranged when the baby becomes a movie star. Hollywood and its film audiences are unmercifully satirized as the Spewaks expose formulaic composition, deliberate inaccuracy, and shameless pandering to the lowest public taste. A spirit of fun pervades the criticism as the play inevitably concludes with the boy getting the girl—and the baby.

The Spewaks' most popular work is *Kiss Me Kate* (produced 1948, published 1953, television version 1959), with music by Cole Porter. The plot meshes a theatre company's on-stage production of Shakespeare's *The Taming of the Shrew* with the similar backstage marital battles of the actors playing Kate and Petruchio, who carry their dramatic roles into their private lives. Genuinely humorous, the musical avoids mechanical complications and purely slapstick gags.

Spewak employed her extensive working experience in newspapers, television, Broadway, and Hollywood to provide an unquestionably authentic atmosphere; her characters, dialogue, and action are believable. Even though her satire is based on the extremes of behavior, the total circumstances seem realistic and the resultant humor is good natured and unthreatening. The success of Spewak's dramas results from a judicious blend of mockery and acceptance of the vagaries of human nature.

OTHER WORKS: All written with Samuel Spewak: *Poppa* (1929; produced, 1935). *Clear All Wires* (1932; produced, 1932; film version, 1933). *Solitaire Man* (1934; produced, 1926). *Trousers to Match* (1941; produced, 1941; produced as *Miss Swan Expects*, 1939). *Woman Bites Dog* (1947; produced, 1946). *My Three Angels* (1953; produced, 1953; television version, 1960). *Festival* (1955; produced, 1955). *Boy Meets Girl and Spring Song: Two Plays* (1973, 1987). *Streets: A Memoir of the Lower East Side* (1995).

BIBLIOGRAPHY: *From Russia to* Kiss Me, Kate: *The Careers of Sam and Bella Spewack: An Exhibition at the Alan and Margaret Kempner Exhibition Room Rare Book and Manuscript Library, 8 March 1993 to 9 July 1993* (1993). *Professional Luncheon Meeting Guest Speaker, Miss Bella Spewack* (audiocassette, 1966).

—KATHLEEN GREGORY KLEIN

SPEYER, Leonora von Stosch

Born 7 November 1872, Washington, D.C.; **died** 10 February 1956, New York, New York
Wrote under: Leonora Speyer
Daughter of Count Ferdinand von Stosch; **married** 1893 (divorced); Sir Edgar Speyer, 1902; **children:** four daughters

Daughter of a Prussian father who fought for the Union in the Civil War and a New England mother, Leonora von Stosch

Speyer's first career was as a violinist. Having attended public schools, then the Brussels Conservatory, she made her debut at eighteen with the Boston Symphony and later played with the New York Philharmonic. Speyer had four daughters during her first marriage, which ended in divorce. In 1902, she married Sir Edgar Speyer, a banker, who gave up his British title to become an American citizen. In 1915 the couple moved to the U.S. and Speyer, already in her forties, began writing poetry.

When acute neuritis forced Speyer to give up the violin, she turned seriously to writing. Her career was highlighted by receipt of several prizes, among them the Pulitzer Prize in 1927 for her second book of poems, *Fiddler's Farewell* (1926). Speyer was president of the Poetry Society of America from 1934 to 1936; beginning in 1937, she taught a writing workshop at Columbia University for a number of years.

Speyer was obviously influenced by her friend Amy Lowell and other Imagist poets, and she is noticeably derivative of Edna St. Vincent Millay. Even so, her own voice is distinctive; it is direct, personal, and immediate, even when the subject is a remote place or distant time. Speyer writes in "House of Calvin" (*Slow Wall*, 1939), that she is one "who loved the lovely things of God," an attitude clearly reflected in her many nature poems. Music often provides subject or image, and she was praised for the "melodious and rhythmical sound effects" in her work. Speyer employs such diverse forms as free verse, prose poetry, ballads, and sonnets.

Speyer often uses fresh or startling images, as in "Bird in a Tree" (*Slow Wall*), when she writes of "The beak like tiny scissors / Snipping the sound to shape." Occasionally her images are strained or precious, but many succeed dramatically, as when "thunder crumbles the sky" in "Squall" (*A Canopic Jar*, 1921). The linking of antithetical terms is another of her favorite devices: in "Of Mountains" (*Fiddler's Farewell*) the hills are "stone wings" in "granite flight."

Least successful of Speyer's poems are those in which she invents female characters in the tradition of folklore. These tend to be melodramatic, sentimental, or even silly. "Monk and Lady" and "Ballad of Old Doc Higgins" (both from *Naked Heel*, 1931) are prime examples. More successful are poems whose heroines, such as Sappho, Medusa, Salome, Mary Magdalene, are drawn from myth or history. Also successful are poems that explore the relationships of modern women and men. The speaker of "The Ladder" (*A Canopic Jar*), for example, reveals herself a martyr to a faithless man, saying she "kissed the foot that bruised [her] as it passed." The sequence "Sonnets of a Not Unusual Situation" (*Naked Heel*) describes a woman with casual lovers in her past who now finds herself unable to establish intimacy with the man she loves.

From the study and practice of the violin, Speyer learned, she said, "the patience, the concentration, the knowledge of how to work" that helped her with her writing. But it was the writing, she also said, that gave her "a sense of. . .high noon in the soul."

OTHER WORKS: *American Poets: An Anthology of Contemporary Verse* (edited by Speyer, 1923). *Nor Without Music* (published with *Slow Wall*, 1946).

BIBLIOGRAPHY: Reference works: *TCA*.
Other references: *Bellman* (4 Jan. 1919). *NYT* (3 May 1927, 11 Feb. 1956). *Poetry* (July 1940). *SR* (23 May 1946).

—JEANNINE DOBBS

SPOFFORD, Harriet (Elizabeth) Prescott

Born 3 April 1835, Calais, Maine; **died** 14 August 1921, Deer Island, Massachusetts
Also wrote under: Harriet Prescott
Daughter of Joseph N. and Sarah Bridges Prescott; **married** Richard S. Spofford, 1865; **children:** one child, who died as an infant

Harriet Prescott Spofford was born into a distinguished New England family that had suffered economic reversals since the War of 1812. Spofford spent most of her early years in a household of women, including her mother and four Prescott aunts, while her father sought his fortune in the West. In 1849 she settled with her mother in Newburyport, Massachusetts, where she attended Putnam Free School, finishing her education later at the Pinkerton Academy in Derry, New Hampshire. In 1856, when her father returned an invalid and her mother soon was stricken, Harriet became the support of the family. She turned to writing, one of the few lucrative careers open to women in her day. This early work, published anonymously in Boston family story-papers in the 1850s, remains uncollected and unacknowledged. Quantity was demanded rather than quality, as these pieces earned Spofford between $2.50 and $5 each. Only with the publication of her short story "In a Cellar," in the young *Atlantic Monthly* (February 1859) did her career really begin.

Spofford's marriage to Richard S. Spofford, a Newburyport lawyer, was long and successful, although their only child died as an infant in 1867. They lived briefly in Washington (*Old Washington*, 1906, is based on Spofford's memories); traveled abroad twice; and finally settled on Deer Island, a five-acre island in the Merrimac River near Newburyport. The scenery, legends, and people of her New England home supplied much of the material for Spofford's writing, especially her poetry. In "June on the Merrimac," John Greenleaf Whittier called attention to the setting in which "Deer Island's mistress sings." Spofford lived on Deer Island for the rest of her life, visiting and often visited by a circle of women writers in Boston including Sarah Orne Jewett, Elizabeth Stuart Phelps Ward, and Julia Ward Howe.

From the 1860s until her death, Spofford was one of the most widely published of American authors. Many stories, essays, and poems appeared in *Harper's Bazar*, *Atlantic Monthly*, the *Knickerbocker*, the *Cosmopolitan*, and in juvenile magazines such as *Youth's Companion*.

Two strengths save Spofford from being dismissed as merely a popular magazine contributor producing only "romantically frothy tales." The first, for which she is alternately highly praised and condemned, is her vivid and often graphic description. In *Sir Rohan's Ghost: A Romance* (1860), for instance, her description of a wine cellar was so convincing and memorable connoisseurs sent her tributes of wine for years afterward. In a century when a woman's sphere was domestic, Spofford utilized her special knowledge to make textures, jewelry, even furniture definitive of character. In *Art Decoration Applied to Furniture* (1878), Spofford observed that furniture is "emblazoned, as one might say, with the customs of a people and the manners of a time." Her ability to capture character through setting and inanimate objects is nowhere more stunning than in the title story of *The Amber Gods* (1863), where the two women, Yone and Lu, are defined by the jewels they wear ("This amber's just the thing for me, such a great noon creature!") and the materials that suit them ("I never let Lu wear the point at all; she'd be ridiculous in it,—so flimsy and open and unreserved; that's for me.").

Spofford's second strength is that although she too divides her women into opposites reminiscent of the fragile blondes and passionate brunettes who represent saint and sinner for most romantics—and only too accurately represent the roles in which contemporary women were cast—Spofford reveals the woman within the role. If she takes sides, her vibrant heart urges her to admire the passionate Yones over the dutiful Lus; but Lu, too, is always loved. In "Desert Sands," for instance, the submissive wife Eos has artistic talent that is recognized immediately and appreciated by the seductive Vespasia, and her cousin Alain berates her husband for suppressing it: "This aptitude, this power, this whatever you choose to call it, genius or inspiration, for which you refuse her utterance, this has produced a spiritual asphyxia."

Beginning her career in the 1850s, Spofford found herself caught between the dying school of romanticism and the newly-vociferous advocates of realism. Her discerning eye and ability to capture the character of her New England neighbors in dialect and description earned the praise of W. D. Howells and the young Henry James, but they were both bothered by her romantic lushness and discouraged her from "fine writing." Although her realistic talent would culminate in her last collection, *The Elder's People* (1920), it could at best earn her recognition as a strong minor writer scarcely comparable to Mary Wilkins Freeman. It is in her romantic tendencies that the uniqueness of Spofford's writing can be found, even though in response to the fickle changes in popular taste and literary approach, she often either abandoned (always reluctantly) or failed to develop and control the poetic promise of her early romantic work.

OTHER WORKS: *Azarian: An Episode* (1864). *New England Legends* (1871). *The Thief in the Night* (1872). *The Servant Girl Question* (1881). *Hester Stanley at St. Marks* (1882). *The Marquis of Carabas* (1882). *Poems* (1882). *Ballads About Authors* (1887).

House and Hearth (1891). *A Lost Jewel* (1891). *A Scarlet Poppy, and Other Stories* (1894). *A Master Spirit* (1896). *In Titian's Garden, and Other Poems* (1897). *An Inheritance* (1897). *Stepping-Stones to Happiness* (1897). *Hester Stanley's Friends* (1898). *Priscilla's Love-Story* (1898). *The Maid He Married* (1899). *Old Madame, and Other Tragedies* (1900). *The Children of the Valley* (1901). *The Great Procession, and other Verses for and about Children* (1902). *That Betty* (1903). *Four Days of God* (1905). *The Fairy Changeling: A Flower and Fairy Play* (1911). *The Making of a Fortune: A Romance* (1911). *The King's Easter* (1912). *A Little Book of Friends* (1916).

BIBLIOGRAPHY: Bendixen, A., ed., *"The Amber Gods" and Other Stories* (1989). Cooke, R. T., *Our Famous Women* (1883). Halbeisen, E. K., *Harriet Prescott Spofford* (1935). Hopkins, A. A., *Waifs, and Their Authors* (1879). *The Development of the American Short Story* (1923). Pattee, F. L., *A History of American Literature Since 1870* (1915). Ward, E. S. P., , "Stories That Stay," in *The Century Magazine* (Nov. 1910). Richardson, C. F., *American Literature (1607-1885)* (1902).

Reference works: *NCAB*, IV. *Oxford Companion to Women's Writing in the United States* (1995).

Other references: *Bookman* (Nov. 1925).

—THELMA J. SHINN

SPRAGUE, Rosemary

Born 29 June 1920, New York, New York; **died** 25 September 1991
Daughter of Percy C. and Nell Andersen Sprague

Rosemary Sprague was the only child of a comfortable Episcopalian family that stressed both manners and the arts. Her early years in Cleveland, Ohio, were filled with the best that city had to offer from the Hathaway Brown School for Girls in Shaker Heights to concerts, museums, and instruction in piano, dance, and fine embroidery. Sprague received her B.A. from Bryn Mawr and her M.A. and Ph.D. degrees from Western Reserve University, where she specialized in Chaucer, Shakespeare, and Victorian literature. Further study was done at the Shakespeare Institute, Stratford-on-Avon; Oxford University; and the University of London. Sprague lectured at colleges and universities in England and the U.S.; she was the Board of Visitors Distinguished Professor in English at Longwood College, Virginia, where she taught beginning in 1962.

Well-researched historical novels for young adults comprise the bulk of Sprague's literary production. Her characters range from a ballerina in the court of Louis XV to the great grandson of Aeneas, who in legend escaped Greece to found a kingdom in Britain. Sprague's characters have pluck and energy whether they are historical people or fictitious participants of actual historical events.

All of Sprague's books are action-filled, but the characters are given believable motivation and emotions and Sprague always provides authentic history along with high entertainment. An example is *Fife and Fandango* (1962), in which a young convent-reared Spanish aristocrat suddenly loses her family and fortune, due to the invasion of Napoleon and the English. Because of her courage and resourcefulness, Juanita reveals the traits necessary for survival in chaos. And in *Red Lion and Gold Dragon* (1967) young Alfred, who has been carefully taught to avoid violence, is suddenly forced to make decisions about supporting the last king of the Saxons at the time of William's 1066 invasion of England. The conflicts between relatives, beliefs, and, of course, the two armies are backdrops for the interior suffering and growth of Alfred.

Sprague has written excellent biographical studies for young adults, of Robert Browning and George Eliot. In *Imaginary Gardens* (1970), she writes about five American poets: Emily Dickinson, Amy Lowell, Sara Teasdale, Edna St. Vincent Millay, and Marianne Moore. As in all her work, Sprague avoids sentimentality and substitutes concrete accuracy. Her writing reveals the human in her subjects and she avoids letting any one aspect of a subject's life (such as Browning's romance) distort her presentation.

Sprague's work emphasizes the importance of honor, courage, and fidelity in human lives. She connects the exterior system of manners to the interior morality of her characters, as she creates believable characters in historical situations. She had a good ear for language and successfully shifted from one culture or period to another. Her universe has order, meaning, and hope. Her young villains see the errors of their pasts, and adult villains, once caught, are disposed of quickly. Sprague's books give young adults a positive introduction to history while providing role models who handle realistic human problems with dignity.

OTHER WORKS: *Northward to Albion* (1947) *A Kingdom to Win* (1953). *Heroes of the White Shield* (1955). *Heir of Kiloran* (1956). *Conquerors of Time* (1957). *Dance for a Diamond Star* (1959). *The Jade Pagoda* (1964). *The Poems of Robert Browning* (Crowell Poets Series; edited by Sprague, 1964). *Forever in Joy: The Life of Robert Browning* (1965). *George Eliot: A Biography* (1968). *Imaginary Gardens* (1970). *Longwood College: A History* (1989).

BIBLIOGRAPHY: Reference works: *CA* (1968). *Ohio Authors and Their Books* (1962).

Other references: *Best Seller* (15 May 1968). *Book Week* (7 May 1967). Chicago *Sunday Tribune* (27 April 1958). *Horn Book* (May 1947). *KR* (1 March 1956). *LJ* (15 Sept. 1965). *NYHTB* (31 July 1955). *NYT* (12 July 1953).

—JO LESLIE SNELLER

STABENOW, Dana

Born 27 March 1952, Anchorage, Alaska

Dana Stabenow has followed a growing trend in crime fiction in recent years of putting emphasis on regional settings. The particularities and peculiarities of an author's home can add interesting flavor to an otherwise blasé story line. Following in the footsteps of other regional writers, like Tony Hillerman who writes about his home in the Southwest, Stabenow has made her home in the Pacific Northwest an intricate part of her contemporary mysteries.

One of Stabenow's most popular of her three writing series features Alaskan Kate Shugak, a feisty, courageous, and yet very independent freelance investigator. Throughout the series, Stabenow makes effective use of the Alaskan settings, Aleutian culture, and Kate's personal heritage passed down from her grandmother to add depth and meaning to her tales of mystery and intrigue. Kate is an ex-investigator for the Anchorage district attorney and has turned part-time private detective while trying to maintain a low profile after retiring to her native home in a fictional national park somewhere near the town of Cordova.

Stabenow herself was born in Anchorage and raised on a 75-foot fish tender in the Gulf of Alaska. She worked many odd jobs, including being a gofer for Cook Inlet Aviation and an egg grader, bookkeeper, and expediter for Whitney-Fidalgo Seafoods. Along the way, she learned the traditions of her homeland and the industries located there. After saving her earnings during the bustling days of the oil pipeline, Stabenow was able to pay her way through the University of Alaska's M.F.A. program. She began her writing career penning science fiction—the subject of another of her series starring Star Svensdotter. Her science fiction work has been described as "almost cinematic vividness" by Roland Green of *Booklist*. However, the Kate Shugak series remains her most well known.

Stabenow won an Edgar award for the first book in the Kate Shugak series, *A Cold Day for Murder* (1992). This first whodunit features a popular formula for the contemporary crime story: a female investigator, a remote setting, and a conflict between the traditional culture (in this case Aleutian) and the modern American way of doing things. The story line explores how the Aleutian culture is pressured into fitting into the mostly white society. Stabenow seamlessly weaves Aleut traditions and customs into the plot, as she does in all the books in the series. She has the ability to relate to the reader the majesty of Alaska, as well as the rugged terrain and the toll it takes on its inhabitants.

Stabenow's Kate Shugak series offers readers a welcome change to the ever present urban crime drama. Moving the mystery out of the city and into the beauty of Alaska makes for a pleasant change for crime fiction followers. She now competes head on with Alaskan mystery writer John Straley, the creator of Sitka private detective Cecil Younger, with one difference—Stabenow's character being a woman adds a whole new twist to the mystery novel and attracts a whole new crop of readers.

Both Staley and Stabenow, however, have the ability to describe in great detail the eccentric and interesting characters that inhabit the towns they write about. This is one of the most intriguing elements to the regional novel—the reader feels like they get to know the small-town folks depicted in the story. Take, for instance, Kate's crafty grandmother, Ekaterina, a leader of the Niniltna Native Association, and Olga (*Dead in the Water*, 1993),

a skilled Native basket weaver. Learning the Native stories is intriguing to the reader and teaches a little bit of the local color.

In 1998 Stabenow introduced a new character and, in doing so, a new series. Again the backdrop for her mysteries is Alaska, but this time the hero is Alaskan State Trooper Liam Campbell. Campbell's character debuted in *Fire and Ice*, the story of another Anchorage native who has left behind the city to retreat to smalltown life in Newenham. This story is filled with turmoil and twisted plots, but is led to a smooth ending by the sure writing of Stabenow.

With both the Kate Shugak series and the newest Liam Campbell series, Stabenow ably weaves tales of the region where she was born. She writes splendid, intriguing mysteries, successfully interplaying the beauty and harshness of the Alaskan wilderness, the eccentric but unique inhabitants, and the Native Aleut customs and traditions. Stabenow ably blends thrills and chills, fact and fiction, and danger and peace to tell compelling tales of mystery and crime.

OTHER WORKS: *Second Star* (1991). *A Handful of Stars* (1991). *A Fatal Thaw* (1993). *A Cold-Blooded Business* (1994). *Play with Fire* (1995). *Red Planet Run* (1995). *Blood Will Tell* (1996). *Breakup* (1997). *Killing Grounds* (1998). *So Sure of Death* (1999).

BIBLIOGRAPHY: Reference works: *CA* Online (1999).
Other references: *PW* (1991, 1993, 1998). *Seattle Times* (online, 1998). Dana Stabenow website (1999).

—DEVRA M. SLADICS

STACK, Andy
See RULE, Ann

STAFFORD, Jean

Born 1 July 1915, Covina, California; **died** 26 March 1979, White Plains, New York
Daughter of John and Mary McKillop Stafford; **married** Robert Lowell, 1940; Oliver Jensen, 1950; A. J. Liebling, 1959 (died 1963)

Jean Stafford spent her childhood in California and Colorado. She received a B.A. and an M.A. from the University of Colorado and did postgraduate work at the University of Heidelberg (1936-37). Stafford was married three times: to the poet Robert Lowell; to Oliver Jensen, staff photographer for *Life*; and to A. J. Liebling, a writer associated with the *New Yorker*. Liebling died in 1963. Stafford's literary achievement was recognized early and rewarded by several grants and prizes.

Boston Adventure (1944), Stafford's first published novel, is an ironic story of a lonely child. After years of daydreams of escaping the hostility of her own chaotic home by living with the impeccable, wealthy Miss Pride of Boston, Sonie Marburg, daughter of poor immigrants, has her dream come true. Sonie learns Miss Pride's world is not as simple or as superior as she had imagined. Despite some ambivalence and a sense that the price of order and peace may be high (paid for, perhaps, by a loss of spontaneity and ''normal'' love), Sonie commits herself to Miss Pride and her well-ordered world. Freudian overtones suggest Sonie's choice is unfortunate, but at the same time, Stafford conveys well the dearth of options women have to shape their lives. Although some critics consider the prose uneven, *Boston Adventure* was well-received and remains in print.

Stafford's most successful novel, *The Mountain Lion* (1947), set partly in a middle class home in Covina and partly in the rougher, simpler atmosphere of a Colorado cattle ranch, is primarily the story of Ralph Fawcett's coming of age. Traditional in its insistence that entering the male adult world requires courage, skill, and loss of innocence, *The Mountain Lion* is also the story of Ralph's sister Molly's failure to achieve initiation, of her refusal to accept realities of the flesh or tolerate adult compromise with banality. Thus the book ultimately resists the traditional simplicities of initiation, revealing certain mindless aspects of the male adult world and the fact that in such a world females must be ruthlessly excluded and may even be sacrificed.

The Catherine Wheel (1952) tells of the strength, order, and beauty—as well as of the isolation, jealousy, guilt, and fear—engendered by unrequited love. Stafford explores two kinds of disappointed love: between men and women, and between friends. This is also a story of delayed maturity, painfully achieved only after the protagonists realize those they love are unworthy. Although the novel has been criticized because it is stylized and overly populated with grotesques, it retains the power to charm and to raise uncomfortable questions about the value of requited and unrequited love.

Stafford contributed short stories to a wide range of magazines, particularly to the *New Yorker*, and published several collections. *Collected Stories* (1969) contains most of the short fiction she published from 1945 through 1968. In 1970 it received the Pulitzer Prize for fiction. The stories are arranged in four geographic groupings, dealing generally with Americans abroad, the New England area, the West, and Manhattan. Stafford considers most frequently the lonely—those few with strength to carve narrow places for themselves and those who fail even at this, strangers in strange lands, physically or spiritually isolated or trapped in hollow social rituals with people who are sometimes thoughtless and cruel.

Most effective are the stories set in Adams, Colorado: to these Stafford brings not only impressive narrative skill but also a warmth, range of tone, and richness of observation not so apparent elsewhere in her work. Such a story is ''The Tea Time of Stouthearted Ladies,'' which gives us middle class women down on their luck and making the best of it; another is ''In the Zoo,'' which gives us a longer perspective on the lives of the sensitive children and adolescents Stafford so successfully draws.

In evaluating Stafford's achievement in *Collected Stories*, one may also evaluate her general achievement, which is considerable. Although she was criticized for some preciousness and for including selections that seem closer to sketches than stories, she was rightly praised by the Pulitzer Committee for ''her range in subject, scene and mood'' and for her ''mastery of the short story form.'' She achieves here, as in much of her work, what she argued writers should try for: the vivid presentation of truth without moral judgement.

OTHER WORKS: *Children Are Bored on Sunday* (1953). *The Interior Castle* (1953). *The Lion and the Carpenter* (1962). *Elphi, the Cat with the High I.Q.* (1962). *Bad Characters* (1964). *A Mother in History* (1966).

BIBLIOGRAPHY: Avila, W., *Jean Stafford: A Comprehensive Bibliography* (1983). Goodman, C. M., *Jean Stafford: The Savage Heart* (1990). Hulbert, A., *The Interior Castle: The Art and Life of Jean Stafford* (1992). Roberts, D., *Jean Stafford: A Biography* (1988). Ryan, M., *Innocence and Estrangement in the Fiction of Jean Stafford* (1987). Walsh, M. E. W. *Jean Stafford* (1985).

Reference works: *Oxford Companion to Women's Writing in the United States* (1995).

Other references: *Criticism* (1962, 1967, 1975). *SAQ* 61 (Autumn 1962). *Southern Review* 9 (Summer 1973). *SR* (Summer 1969). *Studies in the Novel* (Fall 1976). *TriQ* (Winter 1973). *WAL* (1973). *Writer* (Spring 1955).

—PHYLLIS FRANKLIN

STANTON, Elizabeth Cady

Born 12 November 1815, Johnstown, New York; died 26 October 1902, New York, New York

Daughter of Daniel and Margaret Livingston Cady; married Henry Brewster Stanton, 1840; children: seven

Elizabeth Cady Stanton was the fourth of six children. Her father was a lawyer, politician, and judge. Listening to his clients and reading his law books, she learned at an early age of the injustices women suffer. When the family's only son died in 1826, she resolved to take his place. She was tutored in Greek by her Presbyterian minister and later studied Latin and mathematics at the Johnstown Academy. She graduated from Emma Willard's Troy Female Seminary in 1832.

A strong advocate of the reforms of the day—temperance, abolition, and women's rights—she had the word ''obey'' omitted from the ceremony at her marriage to Henry Brewster Stanton, an antislavery lecturer. On their honeymoon, the couple attended a world antislavery convention in London, where Stanton met Lucretia Mott, a delegate the convention refused to seat because she was a woman. After the European tour, they settled in

Johnstown, where the first of their seven children was born in 1842. They moved to Boston shortly thereafter and, in 1847, to Seneca Falls, New York. Stanton and Lucretia Mott organized the first convention for women's rights there in 1848. Stanton was commissioned to draft the Declaration of Principles (later *Declaration of Sentiments*), in which she included a most controversial resolution demanding suffrage.

Stanton met Susan B. Anthony in 1851, and the two formed a very fruitful collaborative friendship which spanned the next half century. Stanton was the writer and speaker whenever possible; Anthony the strategist, organizer, and intrepid traveler. In the years after the Civil War there were increasing divisions in the women's movement, due partly to differing assessments of priorities. Stanton campaigned against the 14th and 15th Amendments because they did not extend rights to women. This alienated many reformers who argued "this is the Negro's hour." In 1868 Stanton and Anthony published a magazine, *Revolution*, financed by erratic entrepeneur George Francis Train, in which they included his controversial views on economics and labor unions as well as their own radical views on marriage and divorce. In 1869 Stanton and Anthony formed the National Woman Suffrage Association, which Stanton led as president for 21 years. Other reformers, generally more conservative, formed the American Woman Suffrage Association. When the two suffrage associations merged and became the National American Woman Suffrage Association (NAWSA) in 1890, Stanton served as president for two years.

In order to finance her children's education, Stanton spent many years delivering lectures, on subjects such as the education of women and divorce, for the New York Lyceum Bureau. Throughout a 50-year career, she wrote many letters and articles, not only on suffrage but on a wide range of social and political questions affecting women, for feminist and general newspapers. In addition to numerous tracts and pamphlets reprinting her speeches and articles, she published three major works.

With Anthony, Stanton edited the first three volumes of the monumental *History of Woman's Suffrage* (1881-86), covering the years from 1848 to 1885. Admittedly one-sided, their history contains a rich store of speeches, summarized debates, letters, and evaluations of the early women's rights conventions, both national and state. Stanton's most controversial work is *The Woman's Bible* (2 vols., 1895-1898, reprinted 1999). Her unorthodox views had been known for years, through essays like "The Effect of Woman Suffrage on Questions of Morals and Religion," included in pamphlets such as *The Christian Church and Women* (1881) and *Bible and Church Degrade Women* (1885). Stanton believed "whatever the Bible may be made to do in Hebrew or Greek, in plain English it does not exalt and dignify woman." Although she invited a panel of women scholars to assist her, most declined. The bulk of the brief notes on each book are Stanton's, and the results are eclectic and sketchy. Despite an appeal from Anthony for tolerance of differing opinions, the 1896 national convention of the NAWSA passed a resolution dissociating the organization from the work.

Stanton's autobiography, *Eighty Years and More* (1898), contains the candid and delightful reminiscences of a woman who, at eighty-three, was still trying to expand the frontiers for her sisters.

OTHER WORKS: *Elizabeth Cady Stanton as Revealed in Her Letters, Diary, and Reminiscences* (edited by T. Stanton and H. S. Blatch, 2 volumes, 1922, reprinted 1969). *The Elizabeth Cady Stanton-Susan B. Anthony Reader: Correspondence, Writings, Speeches* (1992). *Selected Papers of Elizabeth Cady Stanton and Susan B. Anthony* (1997).

BIBLIOGRAPHY: Banner, L. W., *Elizabeth Cady Stanton: A Radical for Women's Rights* (1987). Blatch, H. S., and A. Lutz, *Challenging Years: The Memoirs of Harriot Stanton Blatch* (1940). Cimbala, P. A., and R. M. Miller, eds., *Against the Tide: Women Reformers in American Society* (1997). Cimbala, P. A., and R. M. Miller, eds., *American Reform and Reformers: A Biographical Dictionary* (1996). DuBois, E. C., *Feminism and Suffrage: The Emergence of the Independent Women's Movement in America, 1848-1869* (1978). DuBois, E. C., ed., *Elizabeth Cady Stanton and Susan B. Anthony: Correspondence, Writings, Speeches* (1981). Gaylor, A. L., ed., *Women Without Superstition: "No Gods—No Masters": The Collected Writings of Women Free-thinkers of the 19th and 20th Centuries* (1997). Griffith, E., *In Her Own Right: The Life of Elizabeth Cady Stanton* (1984). Lutz, A., *Created Equal* (1940), Lutz, A., *Susan B. Anthony: Rebel, Crusader, Humanitarian* (1959). McFadden. M., *Golden Cables of Sympathy: The Transatlantic Sources of 19th-Century Feminism* (1999). Oakley, M. A. B., *Elizabeth Cady Stanton* (1972). Strange, L. S., *Pragmatism and Radicalism in Elizabeth Cady Stanton's Feminist Advocacy: A Rhetorical Biography* (dissertation, 1999). Wagner, S. R., *Elizabeth Cady Stanton Through Her Stories* (1994). Ward, G. C., *Not for Ourselves Alone: The Story of Elizabeth Cady Stanton and Susan B. Anthony: An Illustrated History* (1999). Watson, M., *Lives of Their Own: Rhetorical Dimensions in Autobiographies of Women Activists* (1999).

Reference works: *Norton Book of American Autobiography* (1999). *Oxford Companion to Women's Writing in the United States* (1995).

—NANCY A. HARDESTY

STEEL, Danielle

Born 14 August 1947, New York, New York.
Daughter of John and Norma Stone Schuelein-Steel; **married** Claude-Eric Lazard, 1967 (divorced 1975); Danny Zugelder, 1975 (divorced 1978); William Toth, 1978 (divorced); John Traina, 1981 (divorced 1997); Thomas Perkins, 1998 (separated 1999); **children:** five daughters, four sons (one deceased).

The life of Danielle Steel, an enormously popular author throughout the 1980s and 1990s, has developed like the plot of one of her novels. As the only child of wealthy parents, Steel was born in 1947 in New York, New York. She lived with her father after her parents divorced when she was seven but had what she describes as a lonely childhood, with most nurturing coming from relatives and servants. She spent her childhood and teenage years in Paris and New York and graduated from the Lycée Français at fourteen. She entered New York's Parsons School of Design but left soon after because of a stomach ulcer. Instead, she studied at New York University from 1963 to 1967.

Steel's first marriage began at age eighteen with a wealthy French banker, Claude-Eric Lazard. Money wasn't a problem, but Steel grew bored after several years and insisted on finding a job. A public relations firm in Manhattan hired her as vice president of public relations, where she stayed from 1968 to 1971. In 1973 she began working as a copywriter for Grey Advertising but not before writing her first novel, *Going Home*. Dell published it as a paperback in 1973 with moderate sales. During these years, Steel's marriage to Lazard was ending, and she more seriously turned to writing. It took five rejected novels, however, before *Passion's Promise* (1977) changed her fortune. Ironically, this novel's plot, featuring a socialite who falls for an ex-convict, mirrors her own experience in 1975: while visiting another inmate at a prison in Vacaville, California, Steel met and fell in love with Danny Zugelder. They were married that year inside the prison while he served a sentence for robbery and sexual assault

Another four of Steel's novels were published in the late 1970s: *The Promise* (1978), *Now and Forever* (1978), *Seasons of Passion* (1979), and *Summer's End* (1979). *The Promise* was her first big hit, with sales of over 2,000,000 copies. During these years in her personal life, Steel divorced her second husband and married William Toth, a recovering heroine addict. They were divorced shortly after. Not surprisingly, Steel's 1981 novel, *Remembrance*, is about a beautiful woman who marries a heroine addict.

Private life for Steel settled down somewhat in 1981 with her marriage to John Traina, but her writing career was just taking off. Both Steel and Traina brought two children to their marriage, and in the coming years they had an additional five. Steel spent time with her family by day but would write for hours every night while they slept. This schedule produced novels at a breakneck speed: 17 works were published between 1981 and 1989.

All told, Steel has amassed nearly four dozen bestselling novels during her career thus far, and almost two dozen of those have been adapted to made-for-TV movies. But despite her popularity among readers, critics are still not fond of Steel's somewhat cookie-cutter approach to plots, which are often not realistic, and her shallow handling of character development. Most of her books center around a glamorous, wealthy woman facing great trials and challenges. While her books do not typically conclude with a storybook ending, they often focus on the growth and personal triumph of the main character. She is credited, however, with artfully weaving romance and often history into the journey of the protagonist.

More recently, Steel has strayed from her traditional story lines. She addresses love between siblings in *Kaleidoscope* (1987)

and *No Greater Love* (1991), and chooses a male lead in *Fine Things* (1987) and *Daddy* (1989). She focuses on more realistic situations in some novels: *Mixed Blessings* (1992) deals with issues of infertility, *Accident* (1994) shows how one family copes with their teenage daughter's serious car accident, and *The Gift* (1994) tells of a 1950s family that must deal with the loss of their daughter but welcomes an unwed mother into their home. Steel's other writing ventures include two series of books for children, which actually began as a project for her own children, a collection of her poetry written during the 1970s, and coauthorship of the nonfiction work, *Having a Baby* (1984).

Steel's personal life again took a rocky turn in 1994 with the publication of an unauthorized biography, the release of which she fought unsuccessfully in court. Her marriage to Traina ended within two years, in part because of the embarrassing revelations in the biography (many of which Steel denies are true). Further heartbreak struck with the suicide of Steel's 19-year-old son Nicholas, who struggled with manic depression throughout his childhood and teenage years. It was during this difficult time that she was charged with plagiarism by another popular writer, and the matter was ended with an out-of-court settlement. To assuage her pain over Nicholas, Steel wrote a book about his life and death called *His Bright Light* (1998). But just like the women who overcame trials in her novels, Steel's work has not been diminished by these hurdles and in fact may prove to have been enhanced by them. She has developed a winning formula that draws millions of faithful readers, and by all indications she will continue producing popular novels for years to come.

OTHER WORKS: *The Ring* (1980). *Loving* (1980). *Palomino* (1981). *To Love Again* (1981). *Love Poems: Danielle Steel* (1981, abridged edition 1984). *Crossings* (1982). *Once in a Lifetime* (1982). *A Perfect Stranger* (1982). *Changes* (1983). *Thurston House* (1983). *Full Circle* (1984). *Secrets* (1985). *Family Album* (1985). *Amando* (1985). *Wanderlust* (1986). *Zoya* (1988). *Star* (1989). *Martha's Best Friend* (1989). *Martha's New Daddy* (1989). *Martha's New School* (1989). *Max and the Baby-Sitter* (1989). *Max's Daddy Goes to the Hospital* (1989). *Max's New Baby* (1989). *Martha's New Puppy* (1990). *Max Runs Away* (1990). *Message from Nam* (1990). *Max and Grandma and Grandpa Winky* (1991). *Martha and Hilary and the Stranger* (1991). *Heartbeat* (1991). *Freddie's Trip* (1992). *Freddie's First Night Away* (1992). *Freddie's Accident* (1992). *Freddie and the Doctor* (1992). *Jewels* (1992). *Vanished* (1993). *Wings* (1994). *Five Days in Paris* (1995). *Lightning* (1995). *Malice* (1996). *Silent Honor* (1996). *The Ranch* (1997). *Special Delivery* (1997). *The Ghost* (1997). *The Long Road Home* (1998). *The Klone and I* (1998). *Mirror Image* (1998). *Bittersweet* (1999).

BIBLIOGRAPHY: *CA* Online (6 Apr. 1999). *DISCovering Authors* Online (7 Apr. 1999). *Entertainment Weekly* (20 Dec. 1996). *SATA* 66 (1991). *Twentieth-Century Romance and Historical Writers* (1994).

—CARRIE SNYDER

STEIN, Gertrude

Born 13 February 1874, Allegheny, Pennsylvania; **died** 27 July
  1946, Neuilly-sur-Seine, France
Daughter of Daniel and Amelia Keyser Stein; **life partner**
  Alice B. Toklas

Gertrude Stein was the last of seven children. Her father was
an intense, restless, argumentative man who moved his family
about Europe during her early years, before settling in Oakland,
California. The death in 1888 of her mother, who came from a
well-to-do German-Jewish family of artistic and mercantile accomplishment, plunged Stein into a painful, lonely adolescence.
Her father's death three years later left her with a sense of release
from firm restraint. Her principal companion as a child and until
she was well into her thirties was her brother, Leo, a brilliant but
erratic lifelong student of the arts.

In 1893 Stein enrolled in the Harvard Annex (renamed
Radcliffe College the following year). She studied under Hugo
Münsterberg in the Harvard Psychological Laboratory and with
William James. Her college compositions, collected by Rosalind
Miller, exhibit her passionate temperament and also her insecuri-
ty. She published a number of technical papers while at Harvard,
including one with fellow student Leon Solomons, reporting their
joint study of automatic responses. The behaviorist psychologist
B. F. Skinner believes her writing style is in essence automatic
writing and rooted in her undergraduate research experience.

At James's prompting, Stein went on to Johns Hopkins
Medical School in 1897. There she completed two satisfactory
years, but then became less disciplined in her work and did not
receive her medical degree. She did research in neurology, lived in
London and New York, and then joined Leo in Paris at 27, rue de
Fleurus, the site of her now legendary salon.

Under Leo's guidance, she began to collect modern art. Her
friendship with Picasso began in 1905; the following year, she sat
for her portrait. In 1907 Alice B. Toklas arrived in Paris, and the
two women soon established the love relationship that would
endure for the remainder of their lives. In 1909 Toklas joined
Stein at the rue de Fleurus and became a counter to Leo's
vociferous disparagement of Stein's writing. Gertrude and Leo
formally separated in 1913, with the women staying on at the rue
de Fleurus.

Except for a visit to America in 1934 and 1935, Stein spent
the rest of her life in Europe, mostly in France. Between 1916 and
1919, Stein and Toklas did war-relief work for the American Fund
for French Wounded, and Stein was awarded the Médaille de la
Reconnaissance in 1922 for this work. Following the war, Stein's
studio became a haven for expatriate American writers and
continued to be a showcase for abstract painters. In the 1930s, her
reputation grew, especially with the extensive promotion of *The
Autobiography of Alice B. Toklas* (1933, reissued several times,
most recently in 1993). She and Toklas spent much of World War
II in the French countryside, where their fellow villagers protected
them as Jews during the Nazi Occupation. Late in 1944, the two

women returned to Paris and opened their apartment to American
soldiers. Stein died in 1946, after an operation for cancer.

The range of her work is great, and her innovations in style
make strict classifications difficult and misleading. She wrote
poems, plays, novels, autobiography, theory, and criticism; and,
in addition, she created new kinds of works, such as the "portraits."

Her first full-length work charts the dynamics of a lesbian
love triangle. *Q. E. D.* was written in 1903 and published posthumously in 1950 as *Things as They Are*. Adele, the principal
character, is modeled in Stein's own image, and the plot is
patterned after her thwarted love affair at medical school. The
novel is largely realistic, with an established set of characters and
a sequential plot line. Stein is most concerned with the revelation
of character through plot and believes character determines events.
In this respect, she differs from contemporary naturalistic and
realistic writers and their concern with the effects of deterministic
forces external to the individual. She introduces a notion essential
to her theory of character, the notion of "personal time," by
which she means the integral patterning of response and event
transcending any single response of the individual to experience,
and which is unique to that individual.

Written between 1903 and 1911 but not published until 1925
(reprinted 1995), *The Making of Americans; or, the History of a
Family's Progress* is Stein's most voluminous and possibly most
accomplished prose work. Her original intention was to write a
history of every American "who ever can or is or was or will be
living," but her goal changed in the course of writing the novel. It
begins in the realistic mode, with attention to delineation of time,
place, and character, but swiftly becomes an autobiographical
record in which she meditates on partially transformed aspects of
her past and the movement of her consciousness at the moment of
composition. Stein seeks to express the "bottom nature"—that
rhythmic movement of consciousness that is what one essentially
is, that makes up one's identity. As a consequence, the work
becomes increasingly abstract, for narrative is abandoned and
associative patterning determines the ordering of word and phrase
and sentence.

Three Lives (1909, 1990) contains three stories of lower-
class women. The heroines of "The Good Anna" and "The
Gentle Lena" are lightly sketched, flat characters. "Melanctha,"
the most accomplished work of *Three Lives*, represents a great
change and advance in Stein's style. Ostensibly, "Melanctha"
concerns the relationship between a young mulatto woman and a
black doctor; the fairly sympathetic portrayal of black characters
is remarkable for the time. The work also concerns the same love
triangle Stein had written of earlier. Now the focus is on Jeff
Campbell who shares the cerebral, bourgeois quality of Stein's
alter ego Adele in *Q. E. D.*; Melanctha, a vibrant, sensual woman
corresponds to Adele's beloved. Stein later contended the detailed
and complex characterization was the result of writing in the spirit
of a Cézanne portrait, for she accords substantial attention to each
aspect of her characters' composition. She was praised for using
sentence forms that reflect her characters' mode of dealing with
reality. For example, compound declarative sentences, replete

with participial modifiers, represent Campbell's habitual recoiling from experience into endless rumination.

During the years from 1908 to 1913, Stein wrote one- to three-page prose "portraits" of her friends and acquaintances. The portraits were published in a variety of places: Alfred Stieglitz published "Picasso" and "Matisse" in *Camera Work* (1912); many were included in *Portraits and Prayers* (1934). In far shorter works than "Melanctha," Stein continues her study of how sentence forms can express character. The portraits have two prominent stylistic features: they contain repeated phrases and clauses and are lyrical. Repetition illustrates a character's essential rhythm and thus portrays the essential self.

The portraits are helpful in charting the increasing abstraction of Stein's style, the change from the minimal narrative and direct characterization of *Three Lives* to the hermetic style of *Tender Buttons: Objects, Food, Rooms* (1914, 1991). Instead of portraying the character of others, in the latter she meditates on her own individual mode of perceiving and reacting to experience. Virtually without referents and narrative, *Tender Buttons* is unified by a single consciousness. In each of three parts ("Objects," "Food," and "Rooms"), Stein meditates on some element—a thing, a foodstuff, her role in society. It is, as Weinstein puts it, "a master score of phenomenology and psychology, naiveté and wisdom, nonsense and sense."

Stein's early plays, some of which are included in *Geography and Plays* (1922), use conventional dramatic elements in an idiosyncratic way to call attention to their mere conventionality. "Counting Her Dresses," for example, contains numerous "parts" and "acts" randomly assigned; most have one line, only one has three. Yet the subject is fairly accessible: the eccentricities, frailties, and vanities of women who identify with their outward appearance.

Composition as Explanation (1926) builds on the substance of talks Stein addressed to the literary societies of Oxford and Cambridge about her own work and that of other avant-garde writers and artists. The central concepts are the nature of composition, the necessary ugliness of masterpieces, and the continuous present.

By "composition," she means both the world as a set of phenomena perceived in any moment of time and the expression of this perception in a work of art. The artist creates an impression of what is seen in her time, but because her realization is far more sensitive and acute than that of others, her work is termed ugly by contemporaries. The greater the masterpiece, the more surely it will be judged ugly. Only in the future will the validity and beauty of such a work be established. The artist is, then, very much in and of her time, while her public lags behind. Such a theory served Stein's own minimal reputation in 1926.

Operas and Plays (1932) contains works spanning the years 1913 to 1931, including Stein's best-known opera, *Four Saints in Three Acts* (1927), for which Virgil Thomson composed the music. It deals with the condition of being a saint—of being constant in faith, of sustaining internal balance, of knowing one's identity clearly and truly. Like Stein's other dramatic pieces, it treats dramatic conventions in an unconventional manner. There are not four saints, but many; there are not three acts, but many; there is no identifiable setting, no external plot development. The setting is a state of mind, the plot a meditation on being. The religious significance of many lines has been explicated by critics, but the religiosity is not doctrinal.

The Autobiography of Alice B. Toklas is Stein's most popular work and also her most stylistically accessible. By writing as if she were Toklas, she distances herself from her material and creates her own legend, and she takes advantage of a certain latitude with the truth allowed by the semifictional mode that results from her innovative use of narrative voice. It remains unclear to what degree Toklas herself contributed to the work's composition and editing. Stein recounts with sympathy and wit Toklas's life in San Francisco and arrival in Paris in 1907, relates her own early years (not necessarily accurately), and then treats the women's lives in Paris. The years before World War II are recalled with delight; the war and its aftermath as if in shadow. Her treatment of fellow artists is frequently severe and vituperative. It prompted the "Testimony Against Gertrude Stein" published by Eugene and Marie Jolas (in *Transition* in 1935) and signed by Braque, Matisse, and others who contend Stein understood very little of what was going on around her.

Lectures in America (1935) is Stein's theoretical explanation and justification of her work. It is fairly straightforward, highly egocentric, and thoroughly charming. Her assessment of her place in the history of literature must be looked at in the light of her intense sense of self-importance, but the lectures are significant because in them she sets up the critical framework (relating her writing to the goals of cubist painters) that is the most frequent means of explaining her style.

The Geographical History of America; or, The Relation of Human Nature to the Human Mind (1936) is Stein's formal treatise on the nature and operation of consciousness. She distinguishes between the two major aspects of consciousness: human nature and human mind. Human nature is the agent of individual perception; it is bound to the sensible world and considers the concepts it creates to be reality. From human nature arise notions of past and future time that limit one's self-awareness. "What is the use of being a little boy if you are growing up to be a man," she writes, and by this she means that notions of time and identity limit the individual by diverting attention from the experience of the present. Human mind, for Stein, takes as its province abstract thought and has knowledge of the rhythm that underlies and organizes all experience, independent of individual perception. The artist who is aware of human nature—and there are few such besides herself, Stein believes—creates the finest work.

Everybody's Autobiography (1937, 1993) was intended to capitalize on the interest in Stein's work that *The Autobiography of Alice B. Toklas* and her 1934-35 visit to America had generated. It recounts her experiences as a visitor to America after an absence of 30 years. The general subjects are the American character, the American landscape, people she met there, and the production of *Four Saints in Three Acts*. Throughout, her overriding concern is with who she is. She seems to have suffered a substantial identity crisis when she finally achieved an audience and is here moving back inside herself to separate out the essential Stein from the public Stein

In *The World Is Round* (1939), Stein puts the traditional fairytale motif of individuation to her own use in a story for children. She recounts the experiences of two children, Rose and Willie, who seem to be projections of dual aspects of one self. The final union of Rose and Willie in marriage seems to represent knowledgeable self-acceptance gained through experience. The story may also be Stein's treatment of partners—sister and brother, woman and lover—which were essential to her own developing sense of identity. The tone of the work is quite different from her other work: it is wistful, even sad, although there are humorous moments.

Wars I Have Seen (1945), begun in 1942, is a journal of living in an occupied land and owes much to her friend Mildred Aldrich's work *On the Edge of the War Zone* (1917), written in similar circumstances during World War I. The subject matter is highly accessible, despite the lengthy sentences and absence of section headings. Of particular interest is Stein's almost exclusive focus on domestic affairs and her acceptance of the Vichy regime. Her placid attitude may be the result of her age—she was then seventy—her consistently conservative political views, and her lifelong need to bring events within the spectrum of her personal philosophy, often at the expense of the truth.

Brewsie and Willie (1946), Stein's last novel, demonstrates her sure ear for dialect and slang. Brewsie and Willie are polar characters. Brewsie is a thoughtful, restrained young man absorbed in the meaning of events. Stein identifies with his views in an addendum to the book. Willie is unconcerned with issues, loud, boisterous, and critical of others' seriousness. Their portraits are intended to represent American types and Stein's contention that Americans had become too rich and too self-satisfied. Although Stein rarely concerned herself with politics, she was reactionary for her time: a 19th-century rugged individualist at sea in the technological 20th century.

Stein's 43-year career was as prolific as it was long. It is however, her lot to be remembered primarily for her support and encouragement of other artists, and neglected for her own accomplishments as a writer. Undoubtedly, Stein's patronage of abstract painters encouraged and supported Picasso, Matisse, and others in their work. Her friendship with and close reading of such writers as Ernest Hemingway and Sherwood Anderson clearly affected the direction of their writing. Her own work was read by American and European writers, and the simplicity and purity of her language was well appreciated by a number of them. Stein's salon was a site of intellectual ferment at a time when Americans and Europeans were forging an artistic community in Paris. Still, Stein was accomplished as a writer herself, and it is time that increased critical attention is paid her and the measure of her innovative work made.

OTHER WORKS: *Useful Knowledge* (1928). *Lucy Church Amiably* (1930). *How to Write* (1931, 1995). *Matisse, Picasso, and Gertrude Stein, with Two Shorter Stories* (1933). *Narration* (1935).

Picasso (1938). *Paris, France* (1940, 1996). *Ida: A Novel* (1941). *Four in America* (1947). *Blood on the Dining Room Floor* (1948). *The Gertrude Stein Reader and Three Plays* (1948). *Last Operas and Plays* (1949). *The Unpublished Works of Gertrude Stein* (8 vols., 1951-58). *A Novel of Thank You* (1958, 1994). *Gertrude Stein: Writings and Lectures, 1909-1945* (1967). *Gertrude Stein on Picasso* (edited by E. Burns, 1970). *Fernhurst, Q. E. D., and Other Early Writings* (1971). *Sherwood Anderson/Gertrude Stein: Correspondence and Personal Essays* (1972). *A Book Concluding with As a Wife Has a Cow: A Love Story* (1973). *Reflections on the Atomic Bomb* (1973). *How Writing Is Done* (1974). *In Savoy; or, "Yes" Is for Yes for a Very Young Man* (1977; produced, 1949). *Really Reading Gertrude Stein: A Selected Anthology with Essays by Judy Grahn* (1989). *A Stein Reader* (1993). *Stanzas in Meditation* (1994). *The Letters of Gertrude Stein and Thornton Wilder* (1996). *History, or Messages from History* (1997). *Writings, 1903-1932* (1998). *Writings, 1932-1946* (1998). *Baby Precious Always Shines: Selected Love Notes Between Gertrude Stein and Alice B. Toklas* (1999).

The papers of Gertrude Stein are housed in several locations, including the the Bancroft Library at the University of California, Berkeley; Beinecke Library of Yale University; and the Humanities Research Library of the University of Texas at Austin.

BIBLIOGRAPHY: Alfrey, S., *The Sublime of Intense Sociability: Emily Dickinson, H. D., and Gertrude Stein* (1999). Berry, E. E., *Curved Thought and Textual Wandering: Gertrude Stein's Postmodernism* (1992). Bloom, H., *American Women Fiction Writers, Volume Three, 1900-1960* (1998). Bowers, J. P., *Gertrude Stein* (1993). Bridgman, R., *Gertrude Stein in Pieces* (1970). Brinnin, J. M., *The Third Rose: Gertrude Stein and Her World* (1959). Gallup, D., ed., *The Flowers of Friendship: Letters Written to Gertrude Stein* (1953). Galvin, M. E., *Queer Poetics: Five Modernist Women Writers* (1999). Gygax, F., *Gender and Genre in Gertrude Stein* (1998). Hobhouse, J., *Everybody Who Was Anybody: A Biography of Gertrude Stein* (1975). Hoffman, F., *Gertrude Stein* (University of Minnesota Pamphlets on American Writers, 1961). Hoffman, M., *The Development of Abstractionism in the Writings of Gertrude Stein* (1965). Hoffman, M., *Gertrude Stein* (1976). Klaich, D., *Woman + Woman: Attitudes Towards Lesbianism* (1974). Knapp, B. L., *Gertrude Stein* (1990). Kostelanetz, R., *Gertrude Stein Advanced: An Anthology of Criticism* (1991). Marren, S. M., "Passing for American: Establishing American Identity in the Work of James Weldon Johnson, F. Scott Fitzgerald, Nella Larsen and Gertrude Stein" (thesis, 1995). Mellow, J. R., *Charmed Circle: Gertrude Stein & Company* (1974). Miller, R., *Gertrude Stein: Form and Intelligibility* (1949). Parini, J., ed., *The Norton Book of American Autobiography* (1999). Quartermain, P., *Disjunctive Poetics: From Gertrude Stein and Louis Zukofsky to Susan Howe* (1992). Riddel, J. N., *The Turning Word: American Literary Modernism and Continental Theory* (1996). Ruddick, L. C., *Reading Gertrude Stein: Body, Text, Gnosis* (1990). Simon, L., *Gertrude Stein Remembered* (1995). Souhami, D., *Gertrude and Alice* (1999). Sprigge, E., *Gertrude Stein: Her Life and Work* (1957). Stewart, A., *Gertrude Stein and the Present* (1950). Sutherland, D., *Gertrude Stein: A Biography of Her Work* (1951). Toklas, A. B.,

Staying on Alone: Letters of Alice B. Toklas (1973). Toklas, A. B., *What Is Remembered* (1963). Watson, S., *Prepare for Saints: Gertrude Stein, Virgil Thomson, and the Mainstreaming of American Modernism* (1998). Wilson, R. A., *Gertrude Stein: A Bibliography* (1994). Wineapple, B., *Sister Brother: Gertrude and Leo Stein* (1997 1996).

Reference works: *Oxford Companion to Women's Writing in the United States* (1995). *Poetry Criticism* (1997).

Other references: *American Literature* (1973, 1996). *American Scholar* (1998). *Ascent* (Autumn 1958). *Biography* (Spring 1999). *College Literature* (June 1996). *Forum for Modern Language Studies* (1996). *Massachusetts Review* (Fall 1997). *Midstream: A Monthly Jewish Review* (June 1996). *Modern Fiction Studies* (1996). *NYRB* (8 April 1971). *South Dakota Review* (Fall 1997).

—JANIS TOWNSEND,
UPDATED BY NELSON RHODES

STEINEM, Gloria

Born 25 March 1934, Toledo, Ohio
Daughter of Leo and Ruth Nuneviller Steinem

As a child, Gloria Steinem moved around from city to city in a house trailer while her father Leo, who "never wore a hat and never had a job," looked for work. Her parents divorced when she was ten, and Steinem became the sole caretaker of her mentally ill mother. As a teenager, Steinem was an avid reader who dreamed of "dancing [her] way out of Toledo," not of following in the footsteps of her pioneer feminist grandmother, Pauline Steinem, who was president of the Ohio Women's Suffrage Association and one of two U.S. representatives to the 1908 International Council of Women.

In her teens Steinem worked part-time dancing for $10 a night at conventions. She left Toledo during her senior year in high school and moved to Washington, D.C., to live with her older sister. Winning an academic scholarship to Smith College, she graduated with a B.A. in government, Phi Beta Kappa and magna cum laude (1956). Travel in southern India after graduation as a Chester Bowles Asian Fellow helped her develop a lifelong understanding and empathy for oppressed peoples and started her writing career freelancing for Indian newspapers. In India she joined a group called the Radical Humanists and worked as part of a peacemaking team during the caste riots. Her first monograph, *The Thousand Indias*, a guidebook for the government in New Delhi, appeared in 1957. When Steinem returned to the U.S. in 1958, filled with an "enormous sense of urgency about the contrast between wealth and poverty," she became the codirector of the controversial Independent Research Service, an offshoot of the National Student Association.

Steinem moved to New York in 1960 to establish herself as a journalist. Her first job was as a writer of photo captions and celebrity liaison for *Help!*, a political satire magazine. In 1962 her first bylined article, a study of the contraceptive revolution called "The Moral Disarmament of Betty Co-ed," appeared in *Esquire.* Her second monograph, *The Beach Book* (1963), a coffee-table semibook filled with excerpts from literature about beaches, featured suggestions of things to do while sunbathing, beach fantasies, and a foil jacket that could double as a sun reflector.

"I Was a Playboy Bunny," written in 1963 for *Show* magazine, helped launch Steinem's freelance writing career and celebrity status by bringing her assignments on fashion, culture, celebrities, and books from such mass circulation magazines as *Glamour, McCall's,* and *Look* and from the *New York Times*. The essay, in the form of a diary, recounts Steinem's undercover experiences working in the New York Playboy Club, waiting on tables with a Kleenex-stuffed bosom. It is full of the beginnings of her feminist consciousness, the recognition of power differences, and illustrations of indignities suffered by the body. Looking back, Steinem refers to this work as "schizophrenic."

In 1968 she began taking on more serious writing assignments, becoming a cofounder, contributing editor, and political columnist for *New York* magazine. After attending a 1969 hearing on illegal abortions, organized by the radical feminist group Redstockings, Steinem wrote "After Black Power, Women's Liberation," her first openly feminist essay, which won her the Penney-Missouri Journalism award. Having come to believe that only a magazine controlled by women would advance women's issues, in 1972 Steinem was a cofounder, with Pat Carbine and others, of *Ms.*, the first feminist mass circulation magazine.

Steinem's first major collection of articles, essays, and diary entries, *Outrageous Acts and Everyday Rebellions* (1983), chronicles her 20-year writing journey from prefeminist pretty "girl reporter," who never thought her work was good enough, to feminist editor of *Ms.* and spokeswoman-icon of American women's liberation. The collection begins with "I Was a Playboy Bunny," which was adapted for an ABC television movie, *A Bunny's Tale,* in 1985 starring Kirstie Alley.

Outrageous Acts also includes pieces on politicking with McGovern, McCarthy, Kennedy, King, and Chavez, the contradictory messages of the right-wing, the institution of marriage, the media, and the comical "If Men Could Menstruate." Steinem shows us where feminism has been and encourages women to network, find their sisters, and perform outrageous acts in order to advance the liberation of women and other powerless groups. Her personal journey to feminism is accompanied by empathic sketches of a diverse group of notable women that includes Marilyn Monroe, Jackie Onassis, Alice Walker, Pat Nixon, and Linda (Lovelace) Marchiano, and a moving tribute to Steinem's mother in "Ruth's Song." Like herself, the women Steinem profiles are both victims and survivors, sexual objects and, in most cases, feminist protagonists.

Steinem's biography of Marilyn Monroe, *Marilyn: Norma Jean* (1986), expands on her profiles of emblematic women. In a series of essays, Steinem provides a feminist and psychological portrait of a multidimensional sex goddess who is a prisoner of her neglected childhood and of an age characterized by sexual exploitation. Steinem explores her own identification with the actress, remembering that as a teenager in 1953 she walked out of *Gentlemen Prefer Blondes* in embarrassment at the "whispering, simpering, big-breasted child-woman" who dared to be just as "vulnerable and unconfident" as she was. Focusing on the private, inner life of Norma Jean, not the mythical, public Marilyn Monroe, Steinem's sensitive portrayal weaves together the story of a neglected, abused, unparented child with a vulnerable woman, an "interchangeable pretty girl," living behind a mask of sexuality, struggling for independence, wanting only to please others but longing to be taken seriously.

Revolution from Within: A Book of Self-Esteem (1992) is also a modern parable of a woman whose image of herself is very distant from the image others had of her. Steinem employs her autobiographical account of the search for identity and self-worth to help explore internal barriers to women's equality. She takes the reader from a rat-infested Toledo home where she is her mentally ill mother's caretaker to a television studio where her "imposter" self has become the mother of a movement. While supporting her argument that inner strength and self-esteem are the bases of liberation with extensive summaries of psychological research and exegeses of *Jane Eyre* and *Wuthering Heights*, she also makes central the voices of diverse people: a lesbian, a man-junkie, a Cherokee Indian, and others whose comparable journeys of personal growth are linked to social activism. She associates women's loss of self-esteem with such factors as stereotypical gender roles, a preoccupation with romantic love, and male-imposed standards of female beauty. Steinem encourages both men and women to find their inner child, unlearn, reparent themselves, and imagine a future self in order to begin their own positive personal and social change.

Moving Beyond Words (1994) is another of Steinem's essay collections, this time containing three original essays, the wicked satire "What If Freud Were Phyllis? or, The Watergate of the Western World"; "Revaluing Economics"; and "Doing Sixty"; and three that were recastings of articles that had originally appeared in *Ms.*, "The Strongest Woman in the World" (on body-builder Bev Francis); "The Masculinization of Wealth" (an analysis of the position of wealthy women); and the much-reprinted and frequently taught indictment, "Sex, Lies, and Advertising."

While her earlier books were and are still bestsellers, *Moving Beyond Words* has not enjoyed this success, though the book continues to demonstrate Steinem's intellectual acumen, her writing ability, and her admirable candor. "Doing Sixty," written as its author enters her seventh decade, identifies herself as "a nothing-to-lose, take-no-shit older woman," and exults, "I'm looking forward to trading moderation for excess, defiance for openness, and planning for the unknown. . . . More and more, there is only the full, glorious, alive-in-the-moment, don't-give-a-damn yet caring-for-everything sense of the right now."

Steinem was chosen by the *World Almanac* as one of the Twenty-five Most Influential Women in America for nine consecutive years and has received the Front Page, Clarion, and ACLU Bill of Rights awards, the United Nations' Ceres Medal, and the first Doctorate of Human Justice awarded by Simmons

College (1973). In 1978 she studied the impact of feminism on the premises of political theory as a Woodrow Wilson Scholar at the Smithsonian Institution. Arguing that "we teach what we need to learn and write what we need to know," she has been credited with inventing the phrase "reproductive freedom" and popularizing the usage of "Ms." to address women. Her nearly constant travel as a lecturer and feminist organizer (nearly two decades of plane travel every week is documented) and her constant presence in connection with *Ms.* magazine since its founding have earned her the distinction of being, probably, the leading American feminist of her time, although throughout she has also been one of the most controversial—and, assuredly, much misunderstood—of famous Americans.

She has served as a board member or adviser to the Ms. Foundation for Women, the National Women's Political Caucus, Voters for Choice, Women's Action Alliance, and the Coalition of Labor Union Women. At her sixtieth birthday party, organized by friends and other famous feminist leaders, a "Gloria fund" was established at the Ms. Foundation, which raised more than $2,000,000 in two months. The object was, according to Marlo Thomas, to enable Steinem "to continue doing what she always did—giving away every cent of every dollar she had."

Bella Abzug, the former U.S. congresswoman, said about Steinem, "She's served as our most vivid expression of our hopes and demands. She's our pen and our tongue and our heart. She's Elizabeth Cady Stanton and Susan B. Anthony and Emma Goldman all rolled up into one." There have been several biographies of Steinem, one for children, and, most notable, *The Education of a Woman: The Life of Gloria Steinem* (1995) by Carolyn G. Heilbrun (which Steinem authorized), and *Gloria Steinem: Her Passions, Politics, and Mystique* (1997) by Sydney Ladensohn Stern.

Assessing Steinem's impact, Stern concluded her book by saying, "Bella [Abzug] and Stan Pottinger and Marie Wilson and so many others inside and outside the movement understand [Steinem's] place in history. Feminism's second wave had better theorists. There were more graceful writers. There were more eloquent speakers. There was no better leader."

OTHER WORKS: The Steinem papers are in the Sophia Smith Collection and College Archives at Smith College

BIBLIOGRAPHY: Cohen, M., *The Sisterhood: The Inside Story of the Women's Movement and the Leaders Who Made It Happen* (1988). Daffron, C., *Gloria Steinem* (1988). Davis, F., *Moving the Mountain: The Women's Movement in America since 1960* (1991). Diamonstein, B., *Open Secrets: Ninety-Four Women in Touch with Our Time* (1970). Echols, A., *Daring to Be Bad: Radical Feminism in America, 1967-1975* (1989). Gilbert, L., and G. Moore, *Particular Passions: Talks with Women Who Have Shaped Our Times* (1981). Heilbrun, C. G., *The Education of a Woman: The Life of Gloria Steinem* (1995). Henry, S., and E. Taitz, *One Woman's Power: A Biography of Gloria Steinem* (juvenile, includes afterword by Steinem, 1987). Lazo, C., *Gloria Steinem:*

Feminist Extraordinaire (1998). Stern, S. L., *Gloria Steinem: Her Passions, Politics, and Mystique* (1997).

Reference works: *CANR* 28 (1990). *CBY* (1988). *CLC* 63 (1991). *Encyclopedia of Twentieth Century Journalists* (1986). *FC* (1990). *MTCW* (1991).

Other references: *Booklist* (15 Sept. 1995). *Boston Globe* (17 Jan. 1973, 15 Jan. 1992, 22 Jan. 1992). *Chicago Tribune* (20, 22 Jan. 1992). *Christianity and Crisis* (14 Dec. 1992). *Commentary* (May 1992). *Humanist* (May/June 1987). *LAT* (3 Feb. 1992). *LJ* (1 Oct. 1995). *Nation* (6 Nov. 1995). *Newsweek* (16 Aug. 1971, 2 Oct. 1995). *TLS* (8 June 1984). *NYT* (11 Dec. 1984; 9 Feb. 1995; 9 Oct. 1997; 2 Nov. 1997; 14, 19 Dec. 1997; 25 Jan. 1998; 3 May 1998; 22, 24, 25, 27, 28 Mar. 1998; 11 Oct. 1998). *NYTBR* (21 Dec. 1986, 2 Feb. 1992, 10 Sept. 1995). *Sewanee Review* (Fall 1984). *WSJ* (6 Mar. 1992). *WP* (9 Oct. 1983, 12 Jan. 1992). *WRB* (Dec. 1983, June 1992, Dec. 1995). *Yale Review* (Winter 1988).

—MELISSA KESLER GILBERT,
UPDATED BY JOANNE L. SCHWEIK

STENHOUSE, Fanny

Born 12 April 1828, St. Heliers, Jersey, England; **died** date unknown
Married T. B. H. Stenhouse, 1850; **children:** six

Little is known of Fanny Stenhouse's biography except what she recorded in her two books. Stenhouse was one of the younger children of a large English farming family. At the age of fifteen she took a job teaching English at a convent school in France and shortly afterwards became governess to a wealthy French family. At eighteen, Stenhouse was formally engaged to the cousin of her employer, but she gave up all thought of the marriage when, in 1849, she visited England and discovered her family had converted to the Mormon religion. Two weeks later, Stenhouse herself became a convert, and in 1850 she married the Scottish Mormon missionary responsible for her conversion. She had six children. The Stenhouses did missionary work in Switzerland before they migrated in 1855 to New York and in 1859 to Utah. In Salt Lake City, Stenhouse founded and edited the *Daily Telegraph*, the city's first daily paper.

Tolerant of the Mormon doctrine of plural marriage, Stenhouse became its opponent when it invaded her own home. For 15 years, Stenhouse and her husband had maintained a monogamous marriage. Yet as Stenhouse became more prominent in the community, he succumbed to pressure to meet his religious obligation to take another wife (who bore him two more children). At about the same time her husband was considering taking a third wife, Stenhouse's eldest daughter became the fourth wife of Brigham Young's eldest son. Stenhouse began to doubt the divinity of Joseph Smith's revelation about polygamy; she believed the doctrine was created by Smith to justify his own amorous activities. Stenhouse's doubts concerning the revelation placed her faith

in the Mormon religion in jeopardy, and her husband came to share her doubts. In 1870 Stenhouse and her husband withdrew from the church, and his second wife soon divorced him.

While visiting gentile (non-Mormon) friends in New York, Stenhouse was encouraged to write the story of her life in the Mormon church and discuss the institution of polygamy. Stenhouse's first effort, *Exposé of Polygamy in Utah: A Lady's Life Among the Mormons* (1872), was written in a few short days. A small volume, illustrated with woodcuts, the book briefly outlined Stenhouse's life and presented her arguments against the doctrine of polygamy. *Exposé of Polygamy in Utah* was a popular book widely read by a population hungry for sensational news of the Mormons' bizarre practice of polygamy. One of Brigham Young's wives, Ann Eliza Webb Young, claimed the influence of this book as one reason why she left and later divorced her husband. Stenhouse's *Exposé* is an accurate book, less melodramatic than most written in that day and age, and as a result of its popularity, she embarked on a lucrative lecture tour. In 1874 Stenhouse published a second book covering the same issues but in greater detail.

The value of Stenhouse's work rests in her attempt at objectivity on a very controversial subject. The books are significant for the student of Mormon history because of what they reveal about the Mormon missionary system and the role played by English and European converts in the settlement of Utah.

—PAULA A. TRECKEL

STEPHENS, Ann (Sophia) Winterbotham

Born 30 March 1810, Humphreysville (now Seymour), Connecticut; **died** 20 August 1886, Newport, Rhode Island
Wrote under: Jonathan Slick, Mrs. Ann S. Stephens
Daughter of John and Ann Wrigley Winterbotham; **married** Edward Stephens, 1831; **children:** two

Ann Winterbotham Stephens was the third of 10 children, raised by her stepmother after the death of her own mother. Stephens was educated in local schools in Connecticut. After her marriage, she moved with her husband to Maine, where she edited and contributed to his publication, the *Portland Magazine*. In 1837 Stephens and her husband moved to New York, where she became active in literary circles and continued to edit and contribute to magazines. Her longest association was with *Peterson's Magazine*; she served as an editor, from 1842 to 1853, and contributed numerous serials later published as books. Stephens had two children and contributed significantly to the support of her family.

Stephens wrote humorous sketches (*High Life in New York*, published under the name Jonathan Slick, 1843), thrillers (such as

Henry Langford; or, The Forged Will, 1847), novels with Indian themes (such as *Malaeska: The Indian Wife of the White Hunter,* 1860), and, especially, historical romances. Stephens' romances feature little action and focus instead on long descriptions of female clothing, which appealed to the women who were the primary readers of *Peterson's.* Stephens' stories fit in well with the other contents of the magazine, whose pages were filled with patterns for slippers and children's clothes and richly colored illustrations of house dresses, walking dresses, carriage dresses, etc. In fact, some passages of Stephens' stories read like modern advertising copy.

The romances also illustrate Stephens' conception of women. Women are always described externally, as if they appear on a stage. Many of her romances are merely a series of historical tableaux, silent scenes selected from well-known novels or legends set within a frame for an audience to view. The women posture in these serials, posing in the view of others. They are acted upon by others; or they wait for some lover to arrive. The women's clothes and jewelry conceal their emotions from others. In "The Pillow of Roses," Mary, Queen of Scots, constantly aware of the prying eyes of others, uses her jewels to conceal her mood.

As the magazines which Stephens edited and contributed to were aimed at the upper-class woman, so was her fiction. Although it contained many pictures of poverty, it was a sentimentalized poverty which only served to make her heroines attractive, innocent, and humble. As *Peterson's* declared, "*This is emphatically the Magazine for ladies.*"

During her lifetime Stephens was an important writer and editor. Recognized and respected, she had a writing career of over 40 years and was read by the daughters of her original readers. Her work was being gathered into a 23-volume edition at her death in 1886. Today, however, her work can no longer find acceptance.

OTHER WORKS: *The Portland Sketchbook* (edited by Stephens, 1836). *Alice Copley: A Tale of Queen Mary's Time* (1844). *David Hunt and Malina Gray* (1845). *The Diamond Necklace, and Other Tales* (1846). *The Tradesman's Boast* (1846). *The Red Coats; or, The Sack of Unquowa: A Tale of the Revolution* (1848). *Fashion and Famine* (1854). *The Ladies' Complete Guide to Crochet, Fancy Knitting, and Needlework* (1854). *Zana; or, The Heiress of Clair Hall* (1854). *Frank Leslie's Portfolio of Fancy Needlework* (edited by Stephens, 1855). *The Old Homestead* (1855). *Myra, the Child of Adoption* (1856). *The Heiress of Greenhurst: An Autobiography* (1857). *Mary Derwent* (1858). *The Works of Mrs. Ann S. Stephens* (23 vols., 1859-1886). *Ahmo's Plot; or, The Governor's Indian Child* (1860). *Victor Hugo's Letter on John Brown, with Mrs. Ann S. Stephen's Reply* (1860). *Sybil Chase; or, The Valley Ranche: A Tale of California* (1861). *Esther: A Story of the Oregon Trail* (1862). *Mahaska: The Indian Princess* (1863). *The Rejected Wife; or, The Ruling Passion* (1863). *The Indian Queen* (1864). *A Pictorial History of the War for the Union* (2 vols., 1863-1865). *The Wife's Secret* (1864). *Silent Struggles* (1865).

The Gold Brick (1866). *Double False* (1868). *Mabel's Mistake* (1868). *The Curse of Gold* (1869). *Ruby Gray's Strategy* (1869). *Wives and Widows; or, The Broken Life* (1869). *Married in Haste* (1870). *A Noble Woman* (1871). *Palaces and Prisons* (1871). *The Reigning Belle* (1872). *Lord Hope's Choice* (1873). *The Old Countess; or, The Two Proposals* (A sequel to *Lord Hope's Choice*, 1873). *Bellehood and Bondage* (1874). *Bertha's Engagement* (1875). *Norston's Rest* (1877). *The Lady Mary* (1887).

BIBLIOGRAPHY: Brown, H. R., *The Sentimental Novel in America, 1789-1860* (1940). Douglas, A., *The Feminization of American Culture* (1977). Papashvily, H. W., *All the Happy Endings* (1956). Stern, M. B., *We the Women* (1963).

Reference works: *NAW* (1971). *Oxford Companion to Women's Writing in the United States* (1995).

—JULIANN E. FLEENOR

STEPHENS, Margaret Dean

See ALDRICH, Bess Streeter

STEPTOE, Lydia

See BARNES, Djuna

STERN, Elizabeth G(ertrude Levin)

Born 14 February 1889, Skedel, Poland; **died** 9 January 1954, Philadelphia, Pennsylvania
Wrote under: Eleanor Morton, Leah Morton, E. G. Stern, Elizabeth Stern, Elizabeth Gertrude Stern
Daughter of Aaron and Sarah Rubenstein Levin; **married** Leon T. Stern, circa 1911

The infant Elizabeth Stern emigrated with her parents in 1890 from Poland to Pittsburgh, where she was raised and educated, graduating from the University of Pittsburgh in 1910. After a year at the New York School of Philanthropy, she married penologist Leon Stern, and began a career that successfully combined marriage and motherhood with social work and writing. Stern was a night school principal in New York and Galveston, supervised welfare work for Wanamaker's in Philadelphia, and directed two New York settlement houses. A journalist from 1914 to 1937, Stern included features in the *New York Times* and a regular column in the *Philadelphia Inquirer* among her accomplishments. In the 1940s she wrote, lectured, and was active in many Quaker and philanthropic organizations. She died at sixty-four after a long illness.

Stern's best works are fictionalized autobiographies that focus on her movement from Polish-Jewish ghetto to American mainstream. Theodore Roosevelt introduced Stern's first book, *My Mother and I* (1917), which poignantly describes how education loosens bonds between an immigrant mother and her daughter. While the young protagonist is proud of her achieved status as middle-class housewife, she regrets her mother's alienation from the world maternal self-sacrifice helped her reach. In *I Am a Woman—and a Jew* (1926), Stern explores the confrontation between a rebellious daughter and her rabbi father, with the mother as mediator. The first person narrator's rejection of both orthodox Judaism and feminine domesticity is complicated by a lingering sense of responsibility to both traditions, and inability to escape anti-Semitism and sexism.

Stern also used her work experience as raw material for fiction. With her husband, she wrote *A Friend at Court* (1923), the "casebook" of an idealized female probation officer. The work is marred by a predictable romantic subplot and panegyrics on probation as a social panacea. The middle-aged social worker in *When Love Comes to Woman* (1929) provides no such pat answers to women involved in unconventional living arrangements; Stern's ideal is a dual-career marriage promising lifelong friendship. Her telling comparisons between the sexual experimentation of the "new women" of the 1920s and the seriousness of the suffragists of her youth offer insights into important and still-contemporary issues.

Family relationships are central to Stern's other novels. In *A Marriage Was Made* (1928), a mother's domination of her daughter thwarts the girl's promising career by making her too passive to express emotion in her music or life. The mother-daughter theme is also important in *Gambler's Wife* (1931), which traces a strong but self-sacrificing woman from her youth in the Arkansas hills, through her elopement with a drifter who repeatedly abandons her, to her last years with her grown, but immature children.

Later in life, Stern moved from fiction to essay and biography. A collection of her newspaper columns, *Not All Laughter* (1937), reveals her consuming interest in relationships, and her version of woman's true role: the thinking wife, the comrade. Stern wrote biographies of a businesswoman (*Memories: The Life of Margaret McAvoy Smith*, 1943) and a Quaker inventor (*Josiah White: Prince of Pioneers*, 1946). In her last book, *The Women Behind Gandhi* (1953), Stern concentrates on Gandhi's wife and his Indian and European female disciples, highlighting the women's rights phase of his movement for India's full liberation.

In her works, Stern accurately accounts the costs and benefits of both the Americanization process and the application of feminist principles to life. Her books may appear dated by their romanticism and frequent concentration upon battles considered long won (particularly on the right of married women to work), but Stern's emphasis upon the sacrifices involved in family relationships complicated by cultural change is of continuing interest, and her perspective as a daughter of immigrants makes her insights especially important.

OTHER WORKS: *This Ecstasy* (1927).

BIBLIOGRAPHY: Baum, C., P. Hyman, and S. Michel, *The Jewish Woman in America* (1976).

Reference works: *NCAB. Oxford Companion to Women's Writing in the United States* (1995).

Other references: *Bookman* (Aug. 1917). *NYT* (8 July 1917, 24 April 1929, 19 Feb. 1928, 12 April 1931, 10 Jan. 1954). *SR* (18 Dec. 1926, 7 Sept. 1929, 8 Aug. 1953). *Survey* (15 Oct. 1923, Feb. 1947).

—HELEN M. BANNAN

STEWART, Elinore Pruitt

Born 1878; **died** 1933
Wrote under: Elinore P. Stewart, Elinore Rupert
Married n.d., widowed; Clyde Stewart, 1909; **children:** one daughter and three sons (one died young)

Almost nothing is known of Elinor Pruitt Stewart's early life. She was one of six children who were raised by their grandparents after their parents died "within a year of each other." She grew up in Indian Territory (Oklahoma), married, but lost her first husband in a railroad accident. As a widow with a two-year-old daughter, Jerrine, she went to work in Denver as "washlady." In 1909 intending to homestead a place for herself and her daughter, Stewart accepted a position as housekeeper for a Wyoming cattle rancher, Clyde Stewart. Stewart filed on the 160 acres adjoining Clyde Stewart's property but after six weeks as housekeeper she accepted Stewart's proposal of marriage. They had three sons, the first dying of erysipelas. Stewart never regretted her hasty marriage nor did she give up her determination to "prove-up" her own land without the help of her husband.

Stewart's literary contribution is in the form of letters to Juliet Coney, her former employer in Denver. The letters were first published in the *Atlantic Monthly* in 1913, and in book form in 1914 as *Letters of a Woman Homesteader*. A second volume, *Letters on an Elk Hunt*, was published in 1915 (both were reprinted in 1993). In the foreword of the 1961 edition, Jessamyn West writes that Stewart "was a born storyteller with a novelist's eye for those persons and events which have in them the seeds of development. . .which make good narrative possible." The "stories" paint a vivid picture of life on the Wyoming frontier. Stewart's enjoyment of life and her interest in everything around her are revealed in her writing. She was an energetic, adventurous woman who was not afraid of new experiences. She wrote to her friend that "homesteading is the solution of all poverty's problems," especially for women. She would like to urge all the "troops of tired, worried women, . . .scared to death of losing their places to work, who could have plenty to eat, who could have. . .comfortable homes of their own, if they but had the courage and determination to get them" homesteading.

Stewart's letters are not only interesting stories; they are the essence of social history.

OTHER WORKS: *The Adventures of the Woman Homesteader: The Life and Letters of Elinore Pruitt Stewart* (1992).

BIBLIOGRAPHY: Dykstra, N. A., "Eve in the New World Garden: The Autobiographies of Marjorie Kinnan Rawlings and Elinore Pruitt Stewart" (thesis, 1992). George, S. K., "Elinore Pruitt Stewart" in *By Grit & Grace: Eleven Women Who Shaped the American West* (1997). Lindau, S. K., *My Blue and Gold Wyoming: The Life and Letters of Elinore Pruitt Stewart* (dissertation, 1990). West, J., foreword to *Letters of a Woman Homesteader* (1961).

Other references: *Booklist* (Spring 1914). *Dial* (1 July 1914). *Nation* (16 July 1914). *NYT* (7 June 1914). *Outlook* (1 Aug. 1914). *Review of Reviews* (Aug. 1914). *Wisconsin Library Bulletin* (July 1914).

—JACQUELINE B. BARNHART

STEWART, Maria W. (Miller)

Born 1803, Hartford, Connecticut; **died** 17 December 1879, Washington, D.C.
Married James W. Stewart, 1826 (died 1829)

Maria W. Stewart was the daughter of black parents whose name was Miller. According to biographical information in the introduction to *Meditations from the Pen of Mrs. Maria W. Stewart* (1879), Stewart was orphaned at "five years of age; was bound out in a clergyman's family." She left this family when she was fifteen and attended "Sabbath schools" until she was twenty. This appears to be the only formal education she acquired though her "soul thirsted for knowledge." Her marriage in Boston to a navy veteran of the War of 1812 lasted until 1829 when she was widowed. Experiencing a religious conversion in 1830 and making a "public profession of. . .faith in Jesus Christ" in 1831 evidently led to her writing an essay, "Religion and the Pure Principles of Morality: The Sure Foundation on Which We Must Build," which was printed in tract form in Boston by the young

abolitionist editor of the *Liberator*, William Lloyd Garrison. Another essay, "Meditations from the Pen of Mrs. Maria W. Stewart," was printed by him in 1832. In 1832 and 1833, Stewart gave three public addresses which were subsequently printed in the *Liberator* (28 April 1832, 17 Nov. 1832, 27 April 1833). Discouraged by the lack of support and disheartened by the criticism of her friends, she gave a farewell speech in September 1833, and moved to New York City where she became involved with a Female Literary Society for black women. She taught school in Manhattan and in Brooklyn until 1852 when she moved to Baltimore, again teaching school there. In 1861 she moved to Washington, D.C., where she organized a school during the Civil War period. Later while working as a matron at the Freedmen's Hospital in Washington, she claimed a pension under a law passed granting funds to widows of veterans of the War of 1812. Not long before her death, using these funds and again with Garrison's help, Stewart published *Meditations from the Pen of Mrs. Maria W. Stewart*, a collection of all her speeches and writings.

It appears that Stewart was the first American-born woman to speak in public halls in America. Hers are the only extant speeches, although British-born women had spoken in public and American-born women had spoken in churches, particularly Quaker meetings, before her. All of Stewart's speeches and essays exhibit certain general characteristics. Most obvious and pervasive is her strongly emotional appeal to Christian virtue. A second characteristic is her appeal to blacks to help themselves; she speaks of the "great necessity of turning your attention to knowledge and improvement." Her special concern with black women's importance is evidenced frequently as she cries, "O ye daughters of Africa, awake, awake."

Stung by criticism of her public speaking, in her farewell speech in 1833 Stewart justifies her personal virtue and morals and her public speaking with many historical and Biblical references. These allusions attest to the scope of what must have been largely her "self-education." In all her speeches, Stewart laments the injustices inflicted on black people, both free and slave, and takes to task white women, addressing them as "ye fairer sisters." She chides white Americans further, lamenting, "But how few are there among them that bestow one thought upon the benighted sons and daughters of Africa who have enriched the soil of America with their blood and tears."

A dedicated feminist, Stewart was an equally dedicated pacifist. In early speeches she advocates moderation saying, "Far be it from me to recommend to you, either to kill, burn, or destroy." Later she admonishes her listeners to "sheath your swords and calm your angry passions." Her strongest appeal for action is that black men "sign a petition to Congress to abolish slavery in the District of Columbia."

Stewart's early essay, "Meditations from the Pen of Mrs. Maria W. Stewart," is the most literary in form of her writings. A series of fourteen meditations written in a variety of rhyme schemes, most commonly couplets and quatrains, it is somewhat reminiscent of the style of Edward Taylor's meditations written more than a century earlier. Interspersed among the meditations are seven prayers written from the intimately personal and unique viewpoint of a black woman.

To characterize Stewart as an abolitionist is to put the case too strongly; to name her as an early feminist is to describe her accurately. Her writings and speeches indicate her total awareness of her femininity first, her blackness second.

OTHER WORKS: *Productions of Mrs. Maria W. Stewart* (1835).

BIBLIOGRAPHY: Bormann, E.G., "Female Antislavery Speakers," in *Forerunners of Black Power: The Rhetoric of Abolition* (1971). Flexner, E., *Century of Struggle* (1959). Golden, J. L., and R. D. Rieke, "Separation," in *The Rhetoric of Black Americans* (1971). Lerner, G., *Black Women in White America: A Documentary History* (1972). Loewenberg, B. J., and R. Bogin, eds., in *Black Women in Nineteenth-Century American Life* (1976). O'Connor, L., *Pioneer Women Orators* (1954). Porter, D., *Early Negro Writing 1760-1837* (1971).
Reference works: *NAW* (1971). *Oxford Companion to Women's Writing in the United States* (1995).
Other references: *Journal of Negro Education* (5 October 1936).

—MARILYN LAMPING

STOCKTON, Annis Boudinot

Born 1 July 1736, Darby, Pennsylvania; **died** 6 February 1801, Burlington County, New Jersey
Wrote under: "Emelia" (sometimes spelled "Amelia")
Daughter of Elias and Catherine Williams Boudinot; **married** Richard Stockton, circa 1755 (died 1781); **children:** six

Although few records of Annis Boudinot Stockton's childhood remain, her extant manuscripts and Stockton family histories leave a considerable body of material for reconstructing her adult life. Born to a tradesman of French Huguenot descent, Stockton apparently received a more substantial education than was common for girls of her time. Her first poems were written before her marriage to Richard Stockton, a well-known New Jersey lawyer, landowner, and future signer of the Declaration of Independence. Some of these poems celebrate their courtship: ". . .I find on earth no charms for me / But what's connected with the thought of thee!" After her marriage, Stockton moved to the Stockton estate near Princeton, naming her home "Morven," after the imaginary land of Ossian's (James Macpherson's) Fingal. The romance of that title and the elaborately stylish gardens Stockton cultivated at Morven reflect the impulses of much of her verse: pastoral, sentimental, and imitative of popular British modes.

The quiet life at Morven was interrupted by the Revolutionary War. Because both Stockton and her husband were committed patriots, Morven was occupied by the British under Cornwallis during the Battle of Princeton in December 1776. The estate was sacked; plate and papers (including some of Stockton's early poems) were stolen. And although the family had been evacuated, Richard Stockton was taken prisoner soon after their escape. Washington's quick recapture of Princeton allowed Stockton and her children to return to their ruined home. Richard Stockton was released later in 1777, but ill treatment in prison probably hastened his death in 1781.

Stockton's watch by her husband's deathbed occasioned two of her most moving elegies: "But vain is prophesy when death's approach, / Thro' years of pain, has sap'd a dearer life, / And makes me, coward like, myself reproach, / That e're I knew the tender name of wife." Stockton continued to live at Morven until the marriage of her eldest son, at which time she left the estate to him and moved to the home of her youngest daughter, Abigail Field of Burlington County, where she died in 1801.

Much of Stockton's life had been occupied with the raising of her six children and the managing of a sizeable household. But however demanding those responsibilities became, she continued to make time for her verse. Her husband encouraged her work, and Stockton's audience gradually expanded beyond the family circle. She exchanged verses, for example, with Philadelphia poet Elizabeth Graeme Fergusson. Noting the support she found in her "sister" poet, Stockton addressed Fergusson directly in "To Laura" (Fergusson's pseudonym): "Permit a sister muse to soar / To heights she never try'd before, / And then look up to thee. . . ." Additionally, Stockton became a close friend of Esther Burr, who preserved two of Stockton's poems in her journal. She wrote a number of odes to George Washington, many of them warmly acknowledged in his letters to her. Such encouragement from family and friends may have suggested to Stockton the possibility of an even wider audience: her first known publication, "To the Honorable Colonel Peter Schuyler," appeared in the *New-York Mercury* on 9 January 1758, and in the *New American Magazine* in January of 1758. Although other Philadelphia, New York, and New Jersey periodicals printed Stockton's verse from time to time, most of her work remained in manuscript.

Throughout her life, Stockton continued to work in the couplets and alternately rhymed quatrains of Pope, Young, Thomson, and Gray. Using these models, she developed themes of courtship, marriage, nature, friendship, patriotism, old age, and grief. But even as she imitated conventional forms, Stockton worried about the propriety of her activities: she confided to her brother Elias in a letter dated 1 May 1789, about one of her odes to Washington, that "if you think it will only add one sprig to the wreath the country twines to bind the brows of my hero, I will run the risk of being sneered at by those who criticize female productions of all kinds." Fearful for her reputation, yet wishing recognition for her work, Stockton faced a dilemma common to colonial women poets. The number of her publications and the size of her extant manuscript collection may indicate that the desire to write finally outweighed her fear of impropriety.

OTHER WORKS: Poems by Stockton were published in the *New-York Mercury, New American Magazine, Pennsylvania Magazine, Columbian Magazine,* and *New Jersey Gazette.* Some poems are appended to the Reverend Samuel Stanhope Smith's *Funeral Sermon on the Death of the Hon. Richard Stockton. . .* (1781).

Manuscripts (poetry notebooks) are in the Princeton University Library, Historical Society of Pennsylvania, Library of Congress, and the New Jersey Historical Society.

BIBLIOGRAPHY: Bill, A., *A House Called Morven* (1954, revised 1978). Cowell, P., *Women Poets in Pre-Revolutionary America,* 1650-1775 (1981). Ellet, E., *Women of the American Revolution* (1850). Glenn T., *Some Colonial Houses and Those Who Lived in Them* (1899). Green, H. C., and M. W. Green, *Pioneer Mothers in America* (1912). Mulford, C. J., *The Poetry of Annis Boudinot Stockton* (1994). Stockton, J., *A History of the Stockton Family* (1881). Stockton, T. C., *The Stocktons of New Jersey, and Other Stocktons* (1911).

Reference works: *Oxford Companion to Women's Writing in the United States* (1995).

—PATTIE COWELL

STODDARD, Elizabeth (Drew) Barstow

Born 6 May, 1823, Mattapoisett, Massachusetts; **died** 1 August 1902, New York, New York
Wrote under: Elizabeth Stoddard
Daughter of Wilson and Betsey Drew Barstow; **married** Richard H. Stoddard, 1851; **children:** three, all of whom died young

Elizabeth Barstow Stoddard grew up in prosperous circumstances. She did not like school, but briefly attended Wheaton Female Seminary in Norton, Massachusetts. At home, her eager and intelligent personality attracted the attention of the town minister, Thomas Robbins, who gave her access to his excellent library. Taking full advantage of the opportunity to read widely, she became acquainted with the work of the best 18th-century authors. Stoddard moved to New York City after her marriage to Stoddard, a young writer. In spite of poverty and the early deaths of all three of the couple's children, the marriage was happy. Importantly, it resulted in Stoddard's acquaintance with many prominent contemporary literary figures, who made the Stoddard home a meeting place. She began writing, and produced numerous stories and poems, which appeared in the *Atlantic Monthly, Harper's, Knicker-bocker,* and *Appleton's Journal.* Stoddard's *Lolly Dinks' Doings* (1874) is a book for children. None of her works are noteworthy today; however, her three novels are worth consideration in that they presage the trend toward realism in American literature.

The Morgesons (1862) is concerned with the development of Cassandra Morgeson, who seems remarkably like Stoddard herself. Daughter of an old family, Cassandra is intensely individualistic, not very well liked by those about her, but respected nevertheless. Sent to a distant town to attend an academy, she falls desperately in love with her cousin, Charles, in whose home she stays. After his death, she falls in love with wild, handsome Desmond Somers, an hereditary alcoholic. He goes abroad to reform, returns cured, and marries her. His brother, Ben, marries her elfish sister, Veronica, but six months after the birth of their child dies of drink. The story ends with the discovery that the baby is mentally defective.

Two Men (1865) is the story of two strangers who come into the Parke family and after many years find their happiness in each other's love, despite disparity of age. Jason Auster is the first ''interloper.'' He marries proud Sarah Parke, who is secretly in love with her half-cousin, Osmond, long gone from home. When Jason and Sarah's son, Parke, is nine years old, Osmond returns to leave his ten-year-old daughter, Philippa, the second stranger, to grow up in the family. The years pass and Jason is more and more remote; Sarah and Philippa dislike each other intensely. The girl, however, loves the charming Parke and is sure she, and only she, can make him happy. Parke, unconscious of her devotion, has a love affair with a beautiful mulatto who dies bearing his child. His mother, Sarah, dies also, and he goes off to adventure in South America. Jason and Philippa, left alone, are after many months drawn together.

Temple House (1867) describes the strange doings and passions of the inhabitants of a great, decayed, barely furnished house. They are the owner, the retired sea captain Argus Gates; his worthless brother, George; George's wife; and their daughter, Temple. A shipwreck off the coast brings another member to the family—the mysterious and half-Spanish Sebastian Ford.

Both Van Wyck Brooks and Arthur Hobson Quinn praise Stoddard for attempting stark realism, and both see evidence of a spirit much like that of Emily Brontë. Her style is rough and occasionally difficult; at times her characters speak in riddles. Descriptions of nature are arresting, full of strange conceits and jolting figures. The reader is aware that Stoddard is determined never to glamorize life, though every so often she does lapse into Victorian sentimentality.

OTHER WORKS: *Poems* (1895).

Papers of Elizabeth Barstow Stoddard are located in many institutions, including the American Antiquarian Society, the Boston Public Library, Columbia University, Duke University, Harvard University, the New York Public Library, and others.

BIBLIOGRAPHY: Buell, L. and S. Zagarell, *''The Morgesons'' and Other Writings, Published and Unpublished by Elizabeth Stoddard* (1984). Harris, S., *19th-Century American Women's Novels: Interpretive Strategies* (1990). Matlack, J. A., ''The Literary

Career of Elizabeth Barstow Stoddard'' (unpublished dissertation, 1967). Stoddard, R. H., *Recollections, Personal and Literary* (1903).

Reference works: *AA. DAB. Oxford Companion to American Literature* (1965). *Oxford Companion to Women's Writing in the United States* (1995).

Other references: *Academy* (24 Oct. 1896). *Bookman* (Nov. 1902). *Legacy* (1991). *San Jose Studies* (Fall 1984). *Studies in American Fiction* (1985).

—ABIGAIL ANN HAMBLEN

STONE, Ruth

Born 6 August 1915, Roanoke, Virginia
Daughter of Roger and Ruth Ferguson Perkins; **married** twice; second to Walter B. Stone; **children:** Marcia, Phoebe, Abigail

Ruth Stone is a poet, born in Virginia and raised in Indianapolis. She attended the University of Illinois and received her B.A. from Harvard University. The author of five books of poetry, she has also taught at universities across the country. Stone's poems are fresh and original, quirky and funny. Gaiety and loneliness are all mixed up together and self-pity does not stand a chance. The poems are marked throughout by a strong sense of rhythm that never loses touch with the first primitive body rhythms, ''the natural singing mind'' she absorbed from her parents as a child. Her mother taught her poems by heart, and by the time she was two, both the cadence of the language and the music of poetry and forms had become part of her body. Her father was a musician; hearing him play drums at home was another way she took in rhythms by ear at an early age. By the time she was six, Stone was writing poems and ballads with a strong, uninhibited attachment to form. This is particularly evident in her first book, *In an Iridescent Time* (1959). In her later books, though the feeling for rhythm remains, the poems become more elastic and are less often strictly rhymed.

Stone's life and work are closely bound together. Her second book, *Topography* (1971), begins with a strong rhymed love poem, ''Dream of Light and Shade,'' a poem of young marriage, enchantment, and stability. ''I watch him sleep, dreaming of how to defend/ his inert form.'' But soon death, with a horrible abruptness, makes a mockery of normality and order. After the suicide of her husband the book becomes heavier, tilted, and ''chaotic with necessary pain'' (''The Plan'').

In *Topography* Stone begins the long letter to her deceased husband that in a sense becomes the body of the rest of her work. Sometimes, as in ''Tenacity,'' he is addressed directly: ''I sit for hours at the window / preparing a letter; you are coming toward me.'' At other times, as in the poem ''Salt'' (''I saw the long hair

roots, / The long arms and the boots / of despair''), it is guilt and the impossibility of reconciliation that keep the wound open and drive the poet.

In an interview with Robert Bradley, Stone said, ''What is this living in the present? It seems your past drags behind you like a great huge snake or worm. . . . You can't help but live in your past.'' But Stone's particular past makes her present very vivid, intense with the work of seeing for two. Her vision, never subdued and dutiful, is shot through with a respect for the crazy perverse fertility of life.

The poses and props of ''the literary life'' hold no attraction for her and her poems work hard to demystify poetry. In her third book, *Cheap: New Poems and Ballads* (1975), the reader often glimpses the underbelly of life. In ''Codicil,'' an ornithologist's widow recounts trips with her husband: ''Yes, / he would send her up a tree / And when she faltered he would shout, / 'Put it [the egg] in your mouth. Put it in your mouth.' / It was nasty, she said.'' These glimpses are seldom ''pretty'' or decorative but they speak with their own bold vitality. The events of her life have made Stone impatient with convention. She shrugs off distinctions between morbidity and fertility and chooses instead to walk, grieving fiercely, along the messy borders where decay and regeneration overlap (''Overlapping Edges'').

Stone's development, with its wild quirky ups, downs, and turns, is exhilarating to follow. The pure girlish delight of her first book's title poem, ''In an Iridescent Time,'' surfaces again in an odd, funny, matronly form in the title poem of *Second Hand Coat: Poems New and Selected* (1987, reprinted 1991). In this book, and particularly in her 1991 book, the exuberant, irreverent *Who Is the Widow's Muse?* Stone's strong survivor's instinct has brought her through. Confronting late middle age with buoyancy, she speaks in a rich, original voice of courage that makes you want to be near her. She has been many things—a young bride, an exasperated mother, a wild granny who has sat wailing with an apron over her head. Stone gives us a fresh, unconventional eye with which to look at women's lives.

OTHER WORKS: *Unknown Messages* (chapbook, 1974). *American Milk* (chapbook, 1986). *The Solution* (chapbook, 1989). *Nursery Rhymes from Mother Stone* (chapbook, 1992). *Simplicity* (1995). *Ordinary Words* (1999).

BIBLIOGRAPHY: Ferguson, M. A., ed., *Images of Women in Literature* (1991). Gilbert, S., and W. Barber, *The House Is Made of Poetry: The Art of Ruth Stone* (1996, 1999). Hamlin, S., ''We Are Alive! A Cycle of Women'' (thesis, 1999). Howe, F., ed., *No More Masks! An Anthology of Twentieth-Century American Women Poets, Newly Revised and Expanded* (1993). Myers, J. E. and R. E. Weingarten, eds., *New American Poets of the '90s* (1991). Stankard, L. J., ''The 'We' of 'Me': Relational Feminism in the Poetry of Ruth Stone'' (thesis, 1992).

Reference works: *CANR* (1981). *FC* (1990). *Oxford Companion to Women's Writing in the United States* (1995). *The 1997 Pushcart Prize XXI: Best of the Small Presses* (1996). *Sextet One:*

Six Powerful American Voices: A Pennywhistle Poetry Anthology (1996).

Other references: *Associated Writing Programs Chronicle* (Oct./Nov. 1990). *Hudson Review* (Summer 1988). *English Studies* (Oct. 1988). *Iowa Review* (1981).

—TAM LIN NEVILLE,
UPDATED BY SYDONIE BENET

STORY, Sydney A.

See PIKE, Mary Green

STOWE, Harriet (Elizabeth) Beecher

Born 14 June 1811, Litchfield, Connecticut; **died** 1 July 1896, Hartford, Connecticut
Wrote under Christopher Crowfield
Daughter of Lyman and Roxana Foote Beecher; **married** Calvin E. Stowe, 1836; **children:** Eliza, Isabella, Henry, Frederick, Georgiana, Samuel, Charles

Harriet Beecher Stowe was born on 14 June 1811, in Litchfield, Connecticut, the daughter of Congregational minister Lyman Beecher and his first wife, Roxana, who died when Stowe was four. Lyman Beecher was a devout Puritan and a believer in orthodox Calvinism, so Stowe and her siblings received a primarily theological education from their father, although they also attended the local academy. Her intellectual promise appeared early, and when she was seven years old her father wrote to a friend, "Hattie is a genius. I would give a $100 if she was a boy."

She left Litchfield in 1824 to attend the Hartford Female Seminary, which had been founded by her elder sister Catharine. While at Hartford, Stowe began her first major literary endeavor, which was a tragedy in blank verse depicting a young Roman's conversion to Christianity at the court of the emperor Nero. It was also during this time Stowe began to suffer from periodic episodes of paralyzing depression that would follow her throughout her life. At the age of fourteen, a year after moving to Hartford, Harriet had a highly emotional "conversion" to the Christian faith in which she believed she had truly experienced God's saving grace. This event would remain with her and be dramatized in several of her works.

In 1832 Stowe and Catharine moved with their father to Cincinnati, Ohio. Within a year of their arrival, Catharine started a new school, the Western Female Institute, and Stowe worked there as a teacher from 1833 to 1836. During this time she published a geography textbook, *An Elementary Geography* (1835), under her sister's name and assisted her brother, Henry Ward Beecher, with the publication of his daily newspaper, the *Cincinnati Journal*. She also contributed to the magazine *Western Monthly*, which awarded her a short story prize in 1834.

In 1836 Stowe married Professor Calvin E. Stowe of the Lane Theological Seminary and quit teaching to care for twin daughters born later the same year. She wrote only intermittently during these years, but it was her writing that allowed the family to hire domestic help for their growing brood. Stowe had her first true encounter with slavery when one of her servants was accused of being a runaway slave, and Henry Ward Beecher and Stowe's husband helped her to escape. An intellectual and author of religious books, her husband was a widower who suffered from visions and depression. The early years of their marriage were not happy ones because of her difficulty in adjusting to married life and her unhappiness with the frontier life in Ohio.

Cincinnati was a conflict-torn border town between the slave-holding South and the free North. Lane Theological Seminary became a seat of abolitionist fervor, and Stowe developed a growing awareness of the evils of slavery and the plight of runaway slaves during the early years of her marriage. She was not an ardent abolitionist at this point, however, and wrote virtually nothing on slavery during the 1840s. Her concerns were primarily for her family's well-being, because her husband was poorly paid and they suffered increasing poverty and hardship during their first 14 years of marriage. Harriet still found time to write occasionally, however, and her first book, a collection of short stories called *The Mayflower: or, Sketches of Scenes and Characters of the Descendants of the Pilgrims* (1843), was published to good reception both in the U.S. and in England, where its title was changed to *Let Every Man Mind His Own Business*.

Stowe's family situation improved in 1850 when her husband became the Collins Chair of the Natural and Revealed Religion at Bowdoin College in Brunswick, Maine. Two years later he received a professorship at Andover Theological Seminary and the family moved to Massachusetts. Happier in her native New England and with much of her flagging health restored, Stowe began to write in earnest.

Uncle Tom's Cabin: or, Life Among the Lowly (1852) would become Stowe's most famous work and indeed one of the most well-known books in American literature. This novel was inspired by Stowe's increasing distress over slavery and her outrage over the Fugitive Slave Act of 1850. The idea for the book came to her when she had a vision of the triumphant death of Tom while at a Communion church service. Harriet's brothers, Henry Ward and Edward, both ministers, urged their sister, in the words of Edward's wife, "to make this whole nation feel what an accursed thing slavery is."

Uncle Tom's Cabin contains the stories of dozens of slaves but focuses on two who live on the Shelby plantation in Kentucky. Eliza Harris runs from the plantation because her child is to be sold and eludes the hired slave catchers by crossing the broken ice of the Ohio River into the free state of Ohio. Aided by the underground railroad, Eliza and her son are eventually reunited in Canada with her husband, George. As Eliza and her son head north toward freedom, "Uncle Tom," the other protagonist in the novel, is sent "down the river" for sale. Too noble to run away from the plantation and too Christian to resent his master for selling him, Tom befriends a sickly white child named Evangeline St. Clare and is purchased by her father, Augustine. Eva eventually dies, but not before convincing her father to free his slaves. St. Clare does not fulfill his pledge, however, because he dies suddenly, thus representing those who want to help slaves but take no action on their behalf.

Tom is sold farther downriver to Simon Legree, the epitome of a cruel slaveholder, whose abuse of Tom ends in the latter's death by whipping. Eliza and Tom thus both triumph over slavery, although Tom's triumph is in his martyr's death while Eliza's is in her successful escape. Stowe's story ends with her narrator demanding that readers consider whether slavery, which separates families, leads to pain and suffering, and violates Christian principles, can be tolerated.

As some of Stowe's early and modern critics pointed out, however, *Uncle Tom's Cabin* does not provide a ringing endorsement for integration and coexistence. Escaped slave Eliza and her family settle in the African state of Liberia rather than live in North America, which many readers see as an indirect endorsement of colonization. Critics, including those who praised the novel, assert that it perpetuates racial stereotypes and 19th-century prejudicial views on the innate differences between blacks and whites. Many critics have now begun to reinterpret the novel and praise little-mentioned aspects of it, such as Stowe's portrayal of women as strong figures.

Uncle Tom's Cabin was published first as a serial novel in the Washington antislavery newspaper *National Era* in 1852 and later that year as a novel by John P. Jowett of Boston. The book sold 300,000 copies within a year and would sell over 1,000,000 more in England. Stowe herself allowed the *National Era* to publish the work but thought it too mild for abolitionists and was surprised when it became a mobilizing force for the entire antislavery movement. The poet Longfellow echoed the feelings of many when he wrote the following of Stowe in his journal: "How she is shaking the world with her Uncle Tom's Cabin!. . . At one step she has reached the top of the stair-case up which the rest of us climb on our knees year after year." Author Henry James noted that the novel was "less a book than a state of vision, of feeling, and of consciousness."

Although *Uncle Tom's Cabin* was not aimed at Southern slaveholders, this group became its chief opponents, just as abolitionists became its staunchest supporters. The book aroused so much fervor on both sides of the slavery issue that many, including a future president of the U.S., credited it with contributing to the outbreak of the Civil War. When President Abraham Lincoln met Harriet Beecher Stowe in 1862, he is reported to have said to her, "So you are the little woman who wrote the book that created this great war!"

Uncle Tom's Cabin led to over 30 anti-Tom novels within three years claiming to show slavery's positive effects on slaves. Stowe published *A Key to Uncle Tom's Cabin* in 1853 to document some of the anecdotes she used in the novel. Critics were far from finished with attacking the book, however, and an overly dramatic although hugely popular stage version was largely

responsible for the "Uncle Tom" stereotype of a servile black trying to please whites that persists today.

Stowe's second and last real antislavery novel, *Dred: A Tale of the Great Dismal Swamp* (1856), sold well but was less successful because it had no heroic central figure like Tom. The case of Dred, a runaway slave living in the Dismal Swamp and preaching of a Holy War to end slavery, reveals the ill effects of slavery on slaveholders. Like *Uncle Tom's Cabin*, however, this novel does not call for widespread emancipation and an end to slavery.

A year after the publication of *Dred,* Stowe's eldest son, Henry, a freshman at Dartmouth College, drowned in a swimming accident, and Stowe's religious faith was called into question. She eventually regained her faith in God but converted from staunch Calvinism to the Episcopalian Church. Although she never again achieved the fame which *Uncle Tom's Cabin* brought to her, she continued to write, and her collected works eventually filled 16 volumes.

Stowe did have another brush with notoriety in 1869, however, when she published an article in the *Atlantic Monthly* about her friend Lady Byron. Stowe had met the poet's wife when she and her husband visited England and Scotland after the publication of *Uncle Tom*, which was enormously successful in the United Kingdom. The two women had become good friends, and Stowe, defending Lady Byron against detractors, used her *Atlantic Monthly* article to reveal Lord Byron's incestuous relationship with his sister. The furious English and American publics accused Stowe of lying, and Stowe responded in turn by elaborating on her article in the book *Lady Byron Vindicated* (1870), which was a departure from the works that made her famous.

Other well-known novels by Stowe include *The Minister's Wooing* (1859) and *Pearl of Orr's Island* (1862). The latter is about angelic Mara Lincoln, a "pearl of great price," and her life in a Maine fishing village. Mara, like many of Stowe's heroines, is somewhere between saint and angel. Her religious convictions and sudden death, like that of the virginal Eva in *Uncle Tom*, brings salvation to her loved ones. Stowe does a marvelous job in rendering the dialect and daily life of the inhabitants of Orr's Island, and critics agree the local-color movement in New England began with *Pearl of Orr's Island*.

The Minister's Wooing is set in late-18th-century Newport, Rhode Island, and is one of a group of novels set in the New England Stowe remembered from girlhood. The principal character in the novel is Mary Scudder, who loves her cousin James but refuses to marry him because he is not a Christian. Mary agrees to wed Minister Samuel Hopkins after James is reportedly lost at sea, but Hopkins releases her from her obligation when James, having made his fortune and become a Christian, returns to Newport.

Like many of her novels, *The Minister's Wooing* is romantic and sentimental, with a rather formulaic plot culminating in marriage and the salvation of a soul. Although Stowe's characters—the young, pure heroine who often suffers an untimely fate; the noble mother figure; the hypocritical minister; and the young man in need of Christian salvation—are stereotypical, readers can identify with their problems and beliefs because they mirror those of the day. Stowe was not a complex or sophisticated writer, but she gave readers characters they could understand and problems they could relate to.

In the aftermath of the Civil War, Stowe adopted a pseudonym, Christopher Crowfield, and began to write essays on domestic life for the *Atlantic Monthly*. Crowfield's personality was that of a congenial old busybody. The essays themselves were on such diverse topics as women's suffrage, parlor furniture, problems with servants, reading suggestions for young girls, and the employment of former slaves in the new South. These writings were collected into three volumes, *House and Home Papers* (1865), *Little Foxes* (1866), and *The Chimney-Corner* (1868).

Revenue from the sales of Stowe's works brought prosperity to her family and allowed them to purchase a winter home in Mandarin, Florida, in 1868, where Stowe hoped to employ former slaves. She also wanted to provide a permanent home for her alcoholic son, Frederick, who had never quite recovered from wounds received in the Battle of Gettysburg. Although she was not as successful in either venture as she would have liked, she and her husband did spend much of each winter in Florida until shortly before his death in 1886, when ill health prevented them from returning.

Stowe's own health began to fail in 1890 and her mind began to wander. She lived out the remaining six years of her life in Hartford, Connecticut, with her minister son, Charles, and his family. Mark Twain, a longtime neighbor, would often find her, "vague and cheerful," picking flowers in his garden. Not long before her mind began to fail, Stowe wrote the following in a letter to Oliver Wendell Holmes: "And now I rest me, like a moored boat, rising and falling on the water, with loosened cordage and flapping sail." Though she may not have been aware of it at the end, Stowe's contributions to literature and to humanity would ensure her immortality.

OTHER WORKS: *The Two Altars* (1852). *Uncle Tom's Emancipation* (1853). *Sunny Memories of Foreign Lands* (1854). *My Expectations* (1858). *My Strength* (1858). *Our Charlie and What To Do with Him* (1858). *Strong Consolation* (1858). *Things That Cannot Be Shaken* (1858). *A Word to the Sorrowful* (1858). *Agnes of Sorrento* (1862). *Stories about Our Boys* (1865). *Religious Poems* (1867). *Daisy's First Winter and Other Stories* (1867). *Queer Little People* (1867). *Men of Our Times* (1868). *The American Woman's Home* (with C. E. Beecher, 1869). *Oldtown Folks* (1869). *Little Pussy Willow* (1870). *My Wife and I* (1871). *Pink and White Tyranny* (1871). *Sam Lawson's Old Town Fireside Stories* (1872). *Palmetto Leaves* (1873). *Women in Sacred History* (1873, reissued as *Bible Heroines*, 1878). *Deacon Pitkin's Farm* (English version, 1875, similar American collection, *Betty's Bright Idea, and Other Tales*, 1876). *We and Our Neighbors* (1875). *Footsteps of the Master* (1876). *Poganuc People* (1878).

A Dog's Mission; or, The Story of Old Avery House, and Other Stories (1881). *Nellie's Heroics* (1888). *Our Famous Women* (1884). *The Collected Works of Harriet Beecher Stowe* (16 vols., 1896).

BIBLIOGRAPHY: Adams, J. R., *Harriet Beecher Stowe* (1963). Crozier, A., *The Novels of Harriet Beecher Stowe* (1969). Ellsworth, M. E. T., "Two New England Writers: Harriet Beecher Stowe and Mary Wilkins Freeman" (thesis, 1981). Elrod, E. R., "Reforming Fictions: Gender and Religion in the Works of Harriet Beecher Stowe, Rose Terry Cooke, and Mary Wilkins Freeman" (thesis, 1991). Hedrick, J., *Harriet Beecher Stowe: A Life* (1994). Jakoubek, R. E., *Harriet Beecher Stowe: Author and Abolitionist* (1989). Kirkham, E. B., *The Building of Uncle Tom's Cabin* (1977).

Reference works: *American Authors, 1600-1900* (1966). *Benet's Reader's Encyclopedia of American Literature* (1991). *DAB* (1957). *NAW* (1971). *The Reader's Companion to American History* (1991).

—LEAH J. SPARKS

STRATTON-PORTER, Gene

Born Geneva Stratton, 17 August 1863, Wabash City, Indiana; **died** 6 December 1924, Los Angeles, California
Daughter of Mark and Mary Shellabarger Stratton; **married** Charles Dorwin Porter, 1886; **children:** one daughter

Gene Stratton-Porter was the youngest of 12 children. She married in 1886; there was one daughter. From early childhood, Stratton-Porter spent most of her time outdoors with her father and brothers and was fascinated by plants and birds. From her father, she learned her first lessons as a naturalist.

Few authors claim to write so directly from life. Stratton-Porter stressed that she based fictional characters on her beloved family and admired friends, insisting that true-to-life portraits need not focus on undesirable human traits. Similarly, the three areas in which she lived—the Wabash River Basin, the Limberlost Swamp in northeastern Indiana, and Southern California—figure importantly in her work.

Although Stratton-Porter was enormously popular and successful at several types of imaginative writing (magazine articles, short stories, poetry, and novels), she considered herself primarily a naturalist. In natural history as in fiction, Stratton-Porter relied wholly on her own observations, devoting enormous energy and facing considerable danger to achieve veracity. Largely self-educated, Stratton-Porter also trained herself as an expert photographer and polished her drawing skills to illustrate the nature books. Although critics have questioned the accuracy of some of her observations, Stratton-Porter had total confidence in her field work as in her personal experience.

Stratton-Porter's aim was to teach love of nature, God, and one's fellow man, and these themes regulate all her fiction. An equally important motif is familial heritage and relationships. Often a mystery about the family's background lends tension. Another powerful pattern is the consistent strength and capability of the females. Although these characters believe that their first obligation is to run a perfect home and to nurture husband and children, they are also frequently committed to a life work of their own. They are able, productive citizens, usually equal partners in their marriages, who value the money earned for the independence it represents.

Stratton-Porter's enduring popular reputation is based largely on her novels. *Freckles* (1904), the story of a maimed orphan who works his way to fame, position, and wealth through honesty, bravery, and tremendous effort, is a prime example of the pluck-makes luck school of American fiction. The sequel, *A Girl of the Limberlost* (1909), portrays Elnora Comstock, born in the Limberlost and dedicated to studying and earning her way out of it and to resolving a severely damaged relationship with her mother. Some of the values the Limberlost youngsters share—the desires for urban life, fine clothing, wealth, and social position—have been sharply criticized, but for Stratton-Porter, these were the logical rewards of ability and extremely hard work. These two novels celebrate the swamp's danger as well as its beauty and are surprisingly little concerned with conservation; Stratton-Porter depicts the area as a natural prey to progress.

Other novels clearly reflect Stratton-Porter's lifelong commitment to conservationism, and their protagonists value money in part as a means of serving humanity. David Langston in *The Harvester* (1911) and Linda Strong in *Her Father's Daughter* (1921) earn their livings from the flora, but they also make deliberate efforts to harvest wisely and to save threatened species.

Though accused of preoccupation with happy endings and the sunny side of life, Stratton-Porter intended thoughtful examination of serious human problems. *At the Foot of the Rainbow* (1907) and the long narrative poem, "Euphorbia" (*Good Housekeeping*, Jan.—Mar. 1923) treat serious marital discord, and *The Magic Garden* (1927) explores problems faced by children of divorced parents. In *Michael O'Halloran* (1915), Stratton-Porter examines the work ethic as spiritual salvation for both Mickey, a slum child, and Nellie Minturn, a woman whose inherited wealth has barred her from genuine love. Mahala, of *The White Flag* (1923), struggles for self-definition as well as purity. Always, the Stratton-Porter formula prevails: central love stories embellished by nature lore, a pattern devised deliberately to make nature study and moral guidance palatable and salable.

More than 20 films were based on the novels, and Stratton-Porter organized her own company, Gene Stratton-Porter Productions, to protect the moralistic tone of her work. The movies she produced were popular but not landmark productions.

Perhaps the most widely read female American author of her day, Stratton-Porter is generally considered somewhat limited in her world view, but she is an author of power, invention, and strong narrative ability.

OTHER WORKS: *The Song of the Cardinal* (1903). *What I Have Done with Birds* (1907). *Birds of the Bible* (1909). *Music of the Wild* (1910). *After the Flood* (1911). *Moths of the Limberlost* (1912). *Laddie* (1913). *Birds of the Limberlost* (1914). *Morning Face* (1916). *Friends in Feathers* (1917). *A Daughter of the Land* (1918). *Homing with the Birds* (1919). *The Firebird* (1922). *Jesus of the Emerald* (1923). *Wings* (1923). *The Keeper of the Bees* (1925). *Tales You Won't Believe* (1925). *Let Us Highly Resolve* (1927).

BIBLIOGRAPHY: Hart, J. D., *The Popular Book: A History of America's Literary Taste* (1950). Long, J. R., *Gene Stratton-Porter: Novelist and Naturalist* (1990). MacLean, D. G., *Gene Stratton-Porter: A Bibliography and Collector's Guide* (1976). Overton, G., *American Night's Entertainment* (1923). Porter-Meehan, J., *Life and Letters of Gene Stratton-Porter* (1927, 1972). Richards, B., *Gene Stratton-Porter* (1980). S. F. E. [E. F. Saxton], *Gene Stratton-Porter: A Little Story of the Life and Works and Ideals of "The Bird Woman"* (1915).

Reference works: *Oxford Companion to Women's Writing in the United States* (1995).

Other references: *Harper's* (Oct. 1947). *The Old Northwest* (June 1977). *Smithsonian* (April 1976).

—JANE S. BAKERMAN

STRONG, Anna Louise

Born 14 November 1885, Friend, Nebraska; died 29 March 1970, Peking, China
Also wrote under: "Anise"
Daughter of Sydney and Ruth Tracy Strong; married Joel Shubin, 1932

Anna Louise Strong descended from Puritan families who arrived in New England in 1630. Her father was a Congregational minister; her mother an important figure in the church's missionary organizations. Strong completed secondary schooling by the age of fourteen, studied languages in Germany and Switzerland, and obtained her bachelor's degree at Oberlin. Her first writing, poetry and stories, was published in *Youth's Companion* during her teens.

After college, Strong took her first journalism position as an associate editor and writer for a fundamentalist weekly, the

Advance, where she was overworked and fired by the publisher as soon as she had increased circulation. "As for their exploitation of myself, I was only eager to do more work for the salary than anyone else could do; this seemed the road to advancement." Partially to save face, she enrolled in a philosophy program at the University of Chicago. At the age of twenty-three, Strong defended her doctoral thesis on the psychology of prayer before the combined theology and philosophy faculties and became the youngest student ever awarded such a degree at the university.

For several years, Strong worked in urban social reform projects, including organizing child welfare exhibits in cities across America. She began to combine political activism and journalism after rejoining her father in Seattle, Washington, in 1915. Strong was elected to the Seattle School Board, but was recalled in 1918 because of her activism in antiwar groups and her reportage (under the pseudonym "Anise") for the Seattle *Daily Call* and the Seattle *Union Record*, both socialist newspapers. Her first major article was a rather detached, "impartial" account of the Everett Massacre (*New York Evening Post*, 4 February 1919). As events led to the Seattle General Strike of 1919, Strong became their major chronicler. After the strike, she analyzed what happened and the lessons to be learned in a pamphlet, *The Seattle General Strike* (1918). Roger Sale, a historian of Seattle history, considers the chapter on the strike in Strong's autobiography, *I Change Worlds: The Remaking of an American* (1935), as the "best single work on Seattle in one of its most critical periods."

In 1921 Strong did publicity work on the famine in Poland and Russia for the American Friends Service Committee, and she reported on the famine in both countries for the International News Service. From Moscow she wrote in defense of the Bolsheviks' new government and made several trips to the U.S. to lecture and raise money for projects aimed at promoting friendship between the two nations. In 1930 Strong founded the *Moscow News*, an English-language newspaper for foreigners in Russia. Despite working as hard as she once did for the *Advance*, Strong's ultimate inability to reconcile her American view of the proper style and philosophy of reporting with the perspectives of the Russian staff, caused her to leave the newspaper. Eventually concluding she would always remain an "outsider," Strong ceased to dream of "becoming a creator in chaos" declining to "organize" further and determining to continue writing. For the next 45 years, Strong reluctantly embraced a life of "roving to revolutions and writing about them for the American press."

In addition to her coverage of Russia from the 1920s through the 1940s, Strong reported on the course of revolutionary change in Mexico, the civil war in Spain, the advance of the Red Army against the Germans in Poland—her only novel, *Wild River* (1943), is a celebration of the courage shown by Russians during the German invasion—and, most regularly, on the revolution in China. Strong's most famous single piece of reportage is "The Thought of Mao Tse-Tung" (*Amerasia*, June 1947), an article she based on an interview with the leader at the Chinese Revolutionary Army's headquarters in Yenan in 1946. Mao's first use of the

phrase "paper tiger" is found here. Perhaps the most widely read of Strong's writing among intellectuals, academics, and government officials is *Letter from China*, a monthly newsletter which she published from 1962 until January 1969. During this period, it represented one of the few reliable sources of information about life in China and the position of the Chinese leadership on their rift with the Soviet Union.

In addition to her China reportage, Strong's best works are her only book on the U.S., *My Native Land* (1940), and her autobiography, *I Change Worlds*. The first belongs to the genre of documentary reportage in which American intellectuals sought to "discover America." Her account is moving, filled with human interest stories, and governed by a simple—although not reductive—vision of the world. Strong condemns the failures of the American capitalist system; yet she does not entirely deny the past, but rather affirms a kind of populist democracy.

Strong wrote the first volume of her autobiography, *I Change Worlds*, partially as a result of urging from Lincoln Steffens. She identified herself as "motor-minded," one who thinks "in terms of actions." Critical of American civilization and resigned to a "haunting feeling of not being wanted," Strong documents the history of her times in the context of her largely unsuccessful attempts to be an "insider" in social movements for change. Despite a tone of innocent wonder, which is at the same time the tone appropriate to a manifesto, Strong's autobiography is a "rare tale" of "chosen" change in the consciousness of a remarkable woman. The second volume of her autobiography, which it is reported she was finishing at the time of her death, remains in China, unpublished.

Most of Strong's journalism is flawed by a consistent naiveté, a disinterest in explaining theory, and an overabsorption in portraying personality and action. The best of her work, however, is informative and meaningful "for the great Middlewestern masses," because of Strong's well-constructed images, dialogue, and use of the human-interest story.

OTHER WORKS: *The Psychology of Prayer* (1909). *Child Welfare Exhibits: Types and Preparation* (1915). *The First Time in History: Two Years of Russia's New Life* (1924). *Children of Revolution* (1925). *China's Millions* (1928). *Red Star in Samarkand* (1929). *The Soviets Conquer Wheat* (1931). *The Road to the Grey Pamir* (1931). *The Soviet World* (1936). *The Soviets Expected It* (1941). *The Chinese Conquer China* (1949). *Cash and Violence in Laos and Vietnam* (1962). *Letters from China, Nos. 1-10* (1963). *Letters from China, Nos.21-30* (1966).

The papers of Anna Louise Strong are housed at the University of Washington in Seattle.

BIBLIOGRAPHY: Chen, P., *China Called Me* (1979). Friedham, R. L., *The Seattle General Strike* (1967). Milton, D., and N. Dall, *The Wind Will Not Survive* (1976). Nies, J., *Seven Women: Portraits from the American Radical Tradition* (1977). Ogle, S. F., "Anna Louise Strong: Seattle Years" (thesis, 1973). Pringle, R. W.,

Anna Louise Strong: Propagandist of Communism (dissertation, 1972). Sale, R., *Seattle: Past to Present* (1976).

Reference works: *NAW: MP* (1980). *Oxford Companion to Women's Writing in the United States* (1995).

Other references: *Eastern Horizon* (1970). *NR* (25 April 1970). *Newsweek* (13 April 1970). *NYT* (30 March 1970). *Survey* (Oct. 1964).

—JENNIFER L. TEBBE

STUART, Ruth McEnery

Born 21 May circa 1849, Marksville, Louisiana; **died** 6 May 1917, New York, New York

Daughter of James and Mary Routh Stirling McEnery; **married** Alfred Oden Stuart, 1879 (died 1883); **children:** Stirling (died 1905)

During the 1890s Ruth McEnery Stuart was one of the South's most popular women writers, rivaling Kate Chopin in her fame. Praised as the "laureate of the lowly," she became best known for her African-American dialect fiction, and at her death the *New York Times* observed that she "left no successor" in the genre. Although racial stereotypes, sentimentality, and Old South nostalgia now date much of her work, Joel Chandler Harris, creator of the Uncle Remus stories, said Stuart "got nearer the heart of the negro" than any other white author of that era.

Stuart was born on a plantation, but she grew up in New Orleans, the nation's most exotic setting for regionalist writing. After the Civil War, her father failed to regain his earlier prosperity, and Stuart contributed to the family's support by teaching. She moved to Washington, Arkansas, after marrying an affluent widower, but he died four years later, apparently leaving most of the estate to his grown children.

Stuart returned with her young son to New Orleans, where she met Dorothy Dix, Mollie Moore Davis, Eliza Jane Poitevent Nicholson, and other women writers. She probably resumed her teaching career, but an encounter with the editor of *Harper's Monthly*, Charles Dudley Warner, led her to submit stories to Northern magazines and by 1892 she made a permanent move to New York. She occasionally substituted for editors of various journals, turning down offers of regular staff positions in order to focus on her writing, which she published everywhere from the *Youth's Companion* to the *Century Magazine*.

A favorite of the "Harper set," Stuart mixed well in artistic and literary circles, both in New York and at her summer home in the Catskills. Her friends were diverse, from William Dean Howells, George Washington Cable, and Mark Twain to *St. Nicholas* editor Mary Mapes Dodge, General George Armstrong Custer's widow, Elizabeth, the Tiffany Company designer Candace Wheeler, and the Boston twin physicians Augusta and Emily Pope.

Thanks to her sister Sarah Stirling McEnery's support as household manager, Stuart was able to travel throughout the country reading to enthusiastic audiences from her own works, as Twain and Cable—but few women—did. Progressive on such issues as African-American education and women's suffrage, she opposed America's entry into World War I and recited one of her poems at a large peace demonstration in New Orleans.

Most of the stories in Stuart's first collection, *A Golden Wedding and Other Tales* (1893), are black dialect fiction. Her characters include an elderly ex-slave couple, who are poignantly reunited in New Orleans after decades apart, and a mischievous country boy whose mother dresses him in his sisters' hand-me-downs. Reviewers liked Stuart's blend of "humor and pathos" in such accounts of African-American life and also in her early portrayals of urban immigrants and genteel Arkansas spinsters.

Soon matching the black dialect stories in popularity were Stuart's Deuteronomy Jones monologues, narrated in folksy style by a middle-aged farmer from the fictitious Simpkinsville, Arkansas, who dotes on his precocious child. Stuart collected these comic pieces in the bestselling collection *Sonny: A Christmas Guest* (1896) and the sequel *Sonny's Father* (1910). Stories about the Jones' fellow townspeople appeared in *In Simpkinsville: Character Tales* (1897), which includes "The Unlived Life of Little Mary Ellen," a widely read portrayal of a young woman who is jilted at the altar, loses her mind, and goes to an early grave believing that her niece's talking doll is her own baby.

Most of Stuart's women characters, both black and white, cope better with adversity than the fragile Mary Ellen does. Stories in *Solomon Crow's Christmas Pockets and Other Tales* (1897) depict a cheerful widow with several children who earns "a scant living" at newspaper work but hosts a holiday dinner for all her boarding-house neighbors; an ancient African-American candy woman in New Orleans, who always claims Easter Sunday as her birthday; and a teenage girl who collaborates with her old mammy to start a new life in the city after the family plantation is sold for debts.

Until her son died from an accidental fall in 1905, Stuart published a story collection or novella almost every year. An interviewer reported that her intense program of writing and platform reading would exhaust even a strong man. But Stuart cut back drastically on her work and her social life for about four years after Stirling's death. Even though the market for local color fiction was shrinking, all but one of Stuart's later volumes reprise the Southern settings, dialects, and character types that made her famous. The exception is her last book of fiction, *The Cocoon: A Rest-Cure Comedy* (1915). Drawing on her experiences at the Jackson Health Resort in Dansville, New York, Stuart uses the genre of romantic burlesque to comment on such issues as infertility, eugenics, and women's nervous diseases. Critics have noted resemblances to Charlotte Perkins Gilman's feminist classic "The Yellow Wallpaper" (1892), and Stuart had met Gilman's bane, Dr. Weir Mitchell—a likely model for the presiding physician of the Virginia sanitarium in *The Cocoon*. Stuart's protagonist, Blessy Heminway, is a witty New Yorker who spends much of her stay undermining the rest cure regimen.

In the 1920s, plays about African-American life were attracting attention, and Sarah McEnery tried unsuccessfully to find a dramatist who would adapt her sister's black dialect fiction for the New York stage. Racially insensitive as some of these stories now look, one obituary described the author as a "friend of the negro," and Kate Chopin—whose literary reputation has fared much better than Stuart's—emphasized that her body of work was unmarred by "prejudices" of any sort.

OTHER WORKS: *Carlotta's Intended and Other Tales* (1894). *The Story of Babette: A Little Creole Girl* (1894). *Gobolinks or Shadow-Pictures for Young and Old* (with Albert Bigelow Paine, 1896). *The Snow-Cap Sisters: A Farce* (1897). *Moriah's Mourning and Other Half-Hour Sketches* (1898). *Holly and Pizen and Other Stories* (1899). *Napoleon Jackson: The Gentleman of the Plush Rocker* (1902). *George Washington Jones: A Christmas Gift That Went A-Begging* (1903). *The River's Childen: An Idyl of the Mississippi* (1904). *The Second Wooing of Salina Sue and Other Stories* (1905). *Aunt Amity's Silver Wedding and Other Stories* (1909). *The Haunted Photograph, Whence and Whither, A Case in Diplomacy, The Afterglow* (1911). *Daddy Do-Funny's Wisdom Jingles* (1913). *Plantation Songs and Other Verse* (1916).

The main collection of Stuart's papers is in the Manuscripts Department of Howard-Tilton Memorial Library, Tulane University, New Orleans.

BIBLIOGRAPHY: Fletcher, M. F., "Ruth McEnery Stuart: A Biographical and Critical Study" (dissertation, 1955). Frisby, J. R., Jr., "New Orleans Writers and the Negro: George Washington Cable, Grace King, Ruth McEnery Stuart, Kate Chopin, and Lafcadio Hearn, 1870-1900" (dissertation, 1972). Halsey, F. W., ed., *Women Authors of Our Day in Their Homes: Personal Descriptions and Interviews* (1903). Harkins, E. F., and C. H. L. Johnston, *Little Pilgrimages Among the Women Who Have Written Famous Books* (1902). Knight, D. D., ed., *Nineteenth-Century American Women Writers* (1997). McKee, K. B., "Writing in a Different Direction: Women Authors and the Tradition of Southwestern Humor, 1875-1910" (dissertation, 1996). Simpson, E. C., Introduction to *Simpkinsville and Vicinity: Arkansas Stories of Ruth McEnery Stuart* (1983). Sneller, J. E., "Bad Boys/Black Misfits: Ruth McEnery Stuart's Humor and 'The Negro Question,'" in *Images of the Child* (1994). Sneller, J. E., "Man-Figs and Magnolias, Ladies and Lariats: Humor and Irony in the Writings of Three New Orleans Women, 1865-1916" (dissertation, 1992). Sneller, J. E., "'Old Maids' and Wily 'Widders': The Humor of Ruth McEnery Stuart," in *New Directions in American Humor* (1998). Sneller, J. E., "'Sambo' and 'The Southern Lady': Humor and the (Re)Construction of Identity in the Local Color Fiction of Ruth McEnery Stuart," in *Gender, Race, and Identity* (1993). Taylor, H., *Gender, Race, and Region in the Writings of Grace King, Ruth McEnery Stuart, and Kate Chopin* (1989).
Reference works: ANB (1999). DAB. DLB 202. *Library of Southern Literature* (1909). *Nineteenth-Century American Fiction Writers* (1998). NAW, 1607-1950 (1971). *Southern Writers: A Biographical Dictionary* (1979).
Other references: *Bookman* (1904). *Harper's Bazaar* (1899). *Legacy* (1993). *Louisiana Literature: A Review of Literature and Humanities* (1987). NYT (8 May 1917). *Studies in American Fiction* (1998). *Xavier Review* (1987).

—JOAN WYLIE HALL

STURE-VASA, Mary (Alsop)

Born Mary O'Hara Alsop, 10 July 1885, Cape May Point, New Jersey; **died** 15 October 1980, Chevy Chase, Maryland
Wrote under: Mary O'Hara
Daughter of Reese Fell and Mary Lee Spring Alsop; **married** Kent K. Parrott, 1905; Helge Sture-Vasa, 1922

Mary Sture-Vasa was privately educated, with the emphasis on languages and music. She traveled widely during her youth in the eastern U.S., and she also lived in California and Wyoming, locales important to her career as popular novelist, screen writer, and composer. For example, *The Catch Colt* (1964), a musical drama, blends all these influences. Sture-Vasa was married twice and had two children.

In *Wyoming Summer* (1963), a fictionalized autobiography, Sture-Vasa defines a story as "a reflection of life plus beginning and end (life seems not to have either) and a meaning." She applied her definition to ranch life as recorded in her journals to create this book and her best-known works, the Flicka series. Like the straight autobiographical works, *Novel-in-the-Making* (1954) and *A Musical in the Making* (1966), *Wyoming Summer* conveys a clear sense of the artist, writer, and composer at work. Episodic but smooth, highly personal but detached, it includes poignant comments about women and their careers and is embedded with tiny, insightful essays about adversity, loneliness, religion, creativity, happiness, and love.

Now regarded as young people's classics, the very popular series *My Friend Flicka* (1941), *Thunderhead* (1943, film version, 1945), and *Green Grass of Wyoming* (1946) shares these themes and reflects Sture-Vasa's knowledge and love of animals. These novels trace the maturation of Ken McLaughlin and his development of a line of horses destined to realize his family's dreams. In the first novel, Ken's struggle to master the filly is clearly the symbol for his efforts to discipline himself. The parallelism continues in the next two books, where Ken's development is symbolized by the difficulty of training Flicka's colt, Thunderhead, a promising but wild stallion. Ken learns to differentiate between absolute freedom and freely exercised responsibility, between dream and reality, and is thus prepared for his role as young man and young lover. The characterization is well wrought, persuasive, and sound.

Thunderhead and *Green Grass of Wyoming* are more intricately plotted than *My Friend Flicka* and more appealing to adults, for in each an important subplot explores the sometimes strained marriage (complicated by possessiveness, financial worries, and parenthood) of Rob and Nell McLaughlin. Nell's portrait is particularly strong in its presentation of the tensions engendered by traditional women's roles. Defining herself only as Rob's wife, the mother of Ken and Howard, Nell learns to subordinate herself to her husband in *Thunderhead*. In *Green Grass of Wyoming*, she finds herself at a stage of life she has always desired—she has at last borne a daughter, has taught her sons to be self-reliant young men, and has helped her husband achieve some financial security. But Nell is unprepared for this new era, and it precipitates a physical and emotional breakdown. Her resolution of these difficulties remains traditional and is honestly depicted; she does not alter her self-definition, but she does learn to invest herself in herself as well as in others. Beautifully rendered natural settings and details of ranch life underscore the realism of all three works.

Christian faith is a major theme in Sture-Vasa's work. *Let Us Say Grace* (1930) explains the Trinity in a fable framing a parable. The parable compares the function of the monetary system to the relationships within the Trinity. In the Flicka series, Nell's musings and her talks with her sons often concern religion. *The Son of Adam Wyngate* (1952), a less well-received novel, portrays a clergyman whose faith is tested when he confronts his wife's adultery. The hero, Bartholomew Wyngate, is a mystic, and the novel attempts to make his mysticism readily understandable to the average reader. More successfully, it probes the relationships of several generations of a large family, and the insights into sibling rivalry in both young and older characters are vivid. Set in New York, this book continues the religious theme which is rooted in Sture-Vasa's serious study of Christianity and Eastern philosophy and theology.

Sture-Vasa is considered a talented, careful writer who reveals a genuine understanding of human nature and a fine ability to project into animal "mentality" without anthropomorphizing.

BIBLIOGRAPHY: Witham, W. T., *The Adolescent in the American Novel, 1921-1960* (1964).

Other references: *NYTBR* (24 Aug. 1941, 27 Oct. 1946). *SR* (1 Nov. 1941, 17 May 1952).

—JANE S. BAKERMAN

SUCKOW, Ruth

Born 6 August 1892, Hawarden, Iowa; **died** 23 January 1960, Claremont, California
Daughter of William J. and Anna Kluckhohn Suckow; **married** Ferner Nuhn, 1929

The second daughter of a Congregational minister, Ruth Suckow grew up in Iowa. A moving and useful account of her childhood, which examines many of the materials used in novels and stories, is "A Memoir," published in *Some Others and Myself* (1952). She was educated in Iowa schools, Grinnell College, the Curry School of Expression in Boston, and the University of Denver (B.A. 1917, M.A. 1918—her thesis dealt with woman

novelists). Learning the apiary business, she later supplemented her earnings by bee-keeping. In 1929 she married Ferner Nuhn, another Iowa writer. Arthritis eventually necessitating a dry climate, she spent her last years in Southern California.

A regional realist, Suckow created fiction that is remarkably even in quality and consistent in theme and tone, although her stories treat a wider variety of character types than are fully portrayed in the novels; they also tend to end less hopefully. Her almost invariable setting is rural Iowa. Early reviewers praised her knowledge of her characters and her skill in description; often they also accused her of stressing the unpleasant side of Iowa life and of the indiscriminate piling up of detail. In mid-career, she was praised for her realism and for the warmth now seen in her work. Critics found the late novels nostalgic and less pessimistic than the early works. But today they seem very much of a piece: all show disappointed lives but end on a positive note. What changed was not Suckow's view of her world but the critical expectations of her.

Country People (1924) tells the story of August Kaettcrhenry, dour son of German immigrants. Years of toil, leading finally to prosperity, leave him unable to enjoy the results of his labor. After his death, however, his wife discovers an unsuspected independence in herself and lives more happily than ever before. This novel seems static, for it is presented almost entirely through narration; dialogue and dramatized action are lacking.

The next four novels, *The Odyssey of a Nice Girl* (1925), *The Bonney Family* (1928), *Cora* (1929), and *The Kramer Girls* (1930), make effective use of dramatized scenes and of accurately rendered and functional dialogue. All are concerned with family relationships, but most particularly with women. Their fully and sympathetically drawn characters are ordinary people about whom Suckow makes us care.

The Odyssey of a Nice Girl and *Cora* follow the lives of two Iowa girls from childhood into adulthood. In the first, Marjorie is a middle-class girl; while "nice," she is also shallow. Her marriage strikes many readers as an unsatisfactory, conventional ending to a pointless "odyssey." Cora is from working-class backgrounds; her success in a career and her failed marriage leave her facing the future with courage; although not happy, she is strong and would not change her life. The experiences of both women are so presented as to be typical for their time and place.

The Bonney Family and *The Kramer Girls* deal with families. The Bonney family consists of parents, two sons, and two daughters; in the novel, the initially happy family is followed to its eventual breakup. The final focus is on Sarah, the oldest daughter, as she sets out on a new career. In *The Kramer Girls*, the central family group is three sisters, the two eldest sacrificing themselves to give the youngest a chance. All three lead narrow lives, but the youngest, after years of struggle, eventually reaches a balance, content in her marriage and in her job. The depictions of the mannish Georgie and feminine Annie, the two older sisters, breathe new life into the stereotype of the "old maid."

The Folks (1934), Suckow's most ambitious novel, shows a natural progression from earlier themes and techniques. Fred Ferguson, his wife Annie, and their children are all developed fully and believably. Each of the children is given a section of the novel, while the opening and closing sections focus on their parents. All four children ultimately disappoint the parents: Carl, the most apparently successful, is trapped in an unhappy marriage, and Bunny marries a young woman whom his parents can neither approve nor understand. Dorothy, conventionally pretty and popular, makes an apparently ideal marriage; her section, set near the center of the novel, describes her wedding as a perfect moment against which everything else is measured. Margaret's section, the longest, follows her from college, through a Bohemian period in New York City, into an obsessive affair with a married man. The novel's structure is thematic rather than chronological, presenting some key events from several viewpoints. Margaret is the most complex of the characters; the depiction of her rebellion against middle class Midwestern standards is well handled.

Only two more novels followed. They continue Suckow's earlier themes but are more heavily symbolic, abstract, and moralistic. *New Hope* (1942) is a parable of the American experience. The town of New Hope is presented in the first optimism of its early years. But the settlers bring their old sins with them, and Suckow makes it clear New Hope will never become more than a village. The novel centers around two families, those of a businessman and a minister. The minister's arrival and departure several years later give the novel its form; events are seen through the perspective of the little son of the businessman. A central theme is the loss of innocence. Like *The Folks*, *New Hope* is organized thematically, though without any complication of chronology or point of view.

The John Wood Case (1959) studies the effects on family, church, and community of the revelation that a trusted smalltown business and church leader is an embezzler. The town's hypocrisy is revealed, but some characters behave well under the pressure. The novel ends hopefully, as the culprit's son is shown courageously facing the future.

While never considered a major writer, Suckow has always been deservedly respected for her contributions to regional realism, her sensitive characterizations of Iowa women and men, and her honest, unflinching studies of decent people meeting the disappointments of their lives with dignity. Her fiction is always carefully crafted; to read her work is to be carried to rural Iowa as it was not long ago.

OTHER WORKS: *Iowa Interiors* (1926). *Children and Older People* (1931). *Carry-Over* (1936).

BIBLIOGRAPHY: Kissane, L. M., *Ruth Suckow* (1969). McAlpin, S., "Enlightening the Commonplace: The Work of Sarah Orne Jewett, Willa Cather, and Ruth Suckow" (dissertation, 1971). Omreanin, M. S., *Ruth Suckow: A Critical Study of Her Fiction* (1972). Stewart, M. O., "A Critical Study of Ruth Suckow's Fiction" (dissertation, 1960).

Reference works: *Oxford Companion to Women's Writing in the United States* (1995).

Other references: *BI* (Nov. 1970). *Palimpsest* 35 (Feb. 1954).

—MARY JEAN DEMARR

SUI SIN FAR
See EATON, Edith Maud

SUSANN, Jacqueline

Born 20 August 1921, Philadelphia, Pennsylvania; **died** 21 September 1974, New York, New York
Daughter of Robert and Rose Jans Susann; **married** Irving Mansfield, 1939; **children:** one son

Jacqueline Susann was an only child. After graduation from high school, she went to New York City, where she married television and film producer Irving Mansfield in 1939 (date and place vary in interviews). They had one son. Susann worked as a model, an actress, and television performer. In 1946, she wrote the play *Lovely Me*, collaborating with Beatrice Cole. Seventeen years later she began to publish.

Every Night, Josephine! (1963, reprints in 1970 and 1974), Susann's only book of nonfiction, tells about her French poodle. In depicting the hedonism of her dog's life, Susann also describes her own lifestyle in New York and Hollywood, her friendships, and her television and theater work. Some critics think the book is Susann's best; it is unique in showing the author's sense of humor and is funny except for occasional slips into coyness. Animal lovers often find the story irresistible.

Susann considered but never wrote a sequel about Josephine. Instead, she turned to fiction. Although critics scorned her work, Susann was a popular success and a literary phenomenon, the first author to have two number-one bestsellers back to back.

In *Valley of the Dolls* (1966), using character types and settings that would become part of a familiar format, Susann traces the lives and loves of three women in the entertainment business. Each gains money and prominence in the neon-lighted world, but a heavy penalty is exacted. The actress commits suicide; the singer becomes a drunken drug addict; the television star finds marriage brings sorrow and a need for drugs, the "dolls" of the title. Susann manages to keep several plots going simultaneously in the novel, but the content is that of a soap opera, the characters are wooden, and the dialogue clichéd.

Robin Stone of *The Love Machine* (1969, 1981) leads a fast-paced, self-centered existence in the wheeling-dealing world of show business and television. Although women flock to him, he cannot love until he gains understanding through psychoanalysis.

The novel, a "fast-read," is almost as quickly forgotten. Its attraction lies in the author's ability to interweave numerous subplots with the major plot and to keep the storyline going. Susann is less skillful in her depiction of characters, who are lifeless and whose speech makes no distinction for education, position, regionalism, or personality traits.

Once Is Not Enough (1973, 1976) has more violence and more varieties of sexual types and behavior than Susann's other novels. This time the multiple plots concern characters from the movie and publishing world. The major female character has incestuous feelings for her father, which lead her into disastrous relationships; when her father dies, she commits suicide. Many of the characters are vaguely familiar; they seem to have come from gossip columns and movie magazines. Nevertheless, Susann has some success in creating sympathy for her unhappy, driven women.

Susann's shortest and last work, *Dolores* (1976), is an obvious portrait of Jacqueline Kennedy. The novel is Susann's weakest, lacking any of the vitality of her previous works. Thinly disguised characters become caricatures of actual persons in public life. Had the novel been written by a lesser-known author, it probably would not have been published. Readers must be impressed, however, by the courage of Susann, who wrote the novel during her final bout with cancer.

Susann wrote with warmth and knowledge about developmentally disabled children and about cancer; they were the tragedies that touched her own life. She looked with less sympathy at many other aspects of existence. Although she detailed with gusto the sins of a select group of people, behind the glitter of the prose stood a moralist who granted as little happiness to transgressors as any writer of earlier periods.

OTHER WORKS: *Yargo* (1979).

BIBLIOGRAPHY: Hanna, D., *The World of Jacqueline Susann* (1975). Mansfield, I., *Life with Jackie* (1984). Seaman, B., *Lovely Me: The Life of Jacqueline Susann* (1987, 1996). Ventura, J., *The Jacqueline Susann Story* (1975).

Other references: *Harper's* (Oct. 1969). *Life* (19 Aug. 1966, 30 May 1966). *Nation* (1 Sept. 1969). *NYT* (23 Sept. 1974). *NYTM* (12 April 1973).

—HELEN S. GARSON

SWENSON, May

Born 28 May 1919, Logan, Utah; **died** 4 December 1989, Ocean View, Delaware
Daughter of Dan Arthur and Anna Margaret Hellberg Swenson

One of a large family, May Swenson grew up and was educated near the State University in Logan, where her father was professor of mechanical engineering. After graduation, Swenson worked as a reporter on the Salt Lake City *Deseret News* and then moved to New York where she held various jobs, becoming an editor for New Directions in 1959. In 1966 she resigned to devote full time to her writing, with interludes as poet-in-residence at several American and Canadian universities. Swenson received numerous honors for her poetry, including Guggenheim and Rockefeller Fellowships, the Shelley Memorial Award, and an Award in Literature from the National Institute of Arts and Letters. In 1970 she was elected to membership in the institute.

Though Swenson did translations from the work of the Swedish poet Tomas Tranströmer and wrote a play and some prose, she was best known as a poet. Her first book, *Another Animal* (1954), indicated the directions and methods much of her later work would follow; it demonstrates the qualities of freshness, vitality, and keen and often unusual observations of natural phenomena and a magical balancing of surface and interior meanings. Often the balancing takes the form of metaphor as in the equation between landscape and the human body in "Sketch for a Landscape." In this book she begins, too, the riddling pattern often followed later of refusing to name lest naming interfere with the observer's truly identifying the object.

Swenson's second book, *A Cage of Spires* (1958), a solid volume both in length and quality, continues the pressure upon the things of this world, turning them into emblems of other, deeper structures. For example, in "Promontory Moment," the poem evolves from the image of a yellow pencil tilted in sand like the mast of a ship, to the whole relationship of the works of man, nature, the sea, and sun where "little and vast are the same to that big eye / that sees no shadow." But Swenson's cosmic images are rarely solemn, so interspersed are they with vivid accounting of the immediate world. Depth and wit come together in this book described by Richard Wilbur as "happy throughout in both senses of the word."

To Mix with Time: New and Selected Poems (1963) reproduces most of the poems of her first two volumes, along with an entire new collection. Some of the poems came as a response to France, Italy, and Spain, which Swenson visited in 1960 and 1961 with an Amy Lowell Traveling Scholarship. Of particular interest is "Death Invited," in which Swenson combines an awareness of the ongoingness of death with the ritual of the bullfight.

Half Sun Half Sleep (1967) continues the search for "the clarities of Being" through the landscapes of city, country, and the sea. She continues also her experiments with unusual typography suited to the material of the poem which has marked her work from the beginning.

All the poems in *Iconographs* (1970) are in such shapes. It is important to notice, however, that Swenson has never sacrificed the sense of the poem to its iconography; the shapes are imposed upon the poems after composition. *Iconographs* marks too a further expression of passion in such poems as "Feel Me," "A Trellis for R.," "Wednesday at the Waldorf," and "The Year of the Double Spring." Here Swenson releases some of the intense feeling that remained as a strong undercurrent in many of the earlier poems.

Besides her original verse, Swenson has published several books for young readers. Most of the poems in the first two, *Poems to Solve* (1966) and *More Poems to Solve* (1971), have been chosen from her already published work.

Swenson has carried the perception of visual detail farther than any other contemporary poet, and probably none so successfully joins freshness of vision with serious undercurrents of ideas. Moreover, she is aware of the textural connotations of sound, consistently using them to enhance meaning. Wit, too, enlivens poem after poem in the metaphysical sense, being a play between intellect and object in a serious sleight of hand. As Richard Howard has said, "her attention is to the quality of being itself in order to encounter, to espouse form as it *becomes* what it is." Swenson's poetry is unique in such encounter and well deserves the high praise it enjoyed in a career spanning 35 years. Swenson published some 450 poems, and amid the many that speak of nature, science, and technology, there are also a number of love poems. Those originally published in earlier works, along with 13 not previously published, have been collected in *The Love Poems of May Swenson* (1991). Included in this volume are visual and nature poems that treat love and sexuality while also interpreting the world through human hearts. Swenson's metaphorical use of flowers to communicate a frank sexuality and sensuality has much in common with the more erotic interpretation of the Song of Songs. Love is not always pleasure, and Swenson is quick to point out the isolation occurring in a life without love as an anchor. "In love we are set free" certainly, and Swenson implies that without love we are truly imprisoned in ourselves.

OTHER WORKS: *The Contemporary Poet as Artist and Critic* (1964). *Windows and Stones: Selected Poems* by Tomas Tranströmer (translated by Swenson, 1972). *The Guess & Spell Coloring Book* (1976). *New and Selected Things Taking Place* (1978). *In Other Words: New Poems* (1987, reprinted 1992). *American Sports Poems* (with R. R. Knudson, 1989). *The Complete to Solve* (juvenile, 1993). *Nature* (1993). *The Centaur* (1994). *Nature: Poems Old and New* (1994). *May Out West: Poems of May Swenson* (1996). *Made with Words* (1998).

Contributor to many journals, including: *American Poetry Review, Nation, Paris Review, Parnassus, Poetry,* and *Yale Review.*

Contributed to anthologies, most recently: *No More Masks! An Anthology of Twentieth-Century American Women Poets, Newly Revised and Expanded* (1993); *The Best American Poetry 1994* (1994); *An Anthology of Great U.S. Women Poets, 1850-1990: Temples and Palaces* (1997).

May Swenson's papers are housed at Washington University in St. Louis, Missouri.

BIBLIOGRAPHY: Gilbert S. M., and S. Gubar, eds., *Shakespeare's Sisters: Feminist Essays on Women Poets* (1979). Hotelling, K. R., "After Autonomy: The Feminist Poetics of Marianne Moore, Elizabeth Bishop, and May Swenson" (dissertation, 1998). Knudson, R. R., *May Swenson: A Poet's Life in Photos* (1996).

Mullaney, J. P., ed., *Truthtellers of the Times: Interviews with Contemporary Women Poets* (1998).

Reference works: *AWP* (1986). *CA* (1969, 1990). *CANR* (1992). *CLC* (1975, 1980, 1990). *CP* (1985). *DLB* (1980). *FC* (1990). *MTCW* (1991). *Oxford Companion to Women's Writing in the United States* (1995). *SATA* (1979).

Other references: *American Poetry Review* (March-April 1978, Sept. 1994). *Bulletin of Bibliography* (March 1987). *CSM* (12 Feb. 1979). *Explicator* (Fall 1979). *Hudson Review* (Summer 1988). *Nation* (10 Aug. 1963, 28 Feb. 1972). *NR* (7 March 1988). *NYT* (obituary, 5 Dec. 1989). *NYTBR* (7 May 1971, 11 Feb. 1979, 19 Jan. 1992). *Parnassus* (Fall 1978, 1985, 1990). *Paris Review* (Summer 1993). *Poetry* (Nov. 1971, Feb. 1979, Feb. 1980, July 1989). *Poetry Criticism* (1996). *Southern Review* (Winter 1969). *Twentieth Century Literature* (1998). *TriQuarterly* (7 Fall 1966). *Wilson Quarterly* (1997). *WRB* (Jan. 1995).

—ANN STANFORD,
UPDATED BY LINDA BERUBE

SWETT, Sophie (Mariam)

Born Brewer, Maine, 1858; **died** 12 November 1912
Daughter of Nathaniel and Susan Braston Swett

Sophie Swett was educated in public and private schools in Boston, Massachusetts. She served for a time as an associate editor of *Wide Awake*, the juvenile periodical established by Daniel Lothrop, a Boston-based publisher of children's books. In later life, Swett made her home in Arlington Heights, Massachusetts.

Swett's stories for young people characteristically combine a "Horatio Alger" plot and a Down-East setting. *A Cape Cod Boy* (1901), for example, tells of a "little Portugee," swept ashore in a storm, who masters the Yankee virtues of the Cape Codders who adopt him and, in time, prospers and repays his benefactors. In *Mary Augusta's Price* (1903), a homebody who yearns to be "like those brilliant girls who taught school and gave music lessons and could learn to paint portraits," turns her domestic skills to profit and demonstrates both good character and ability as a "business girl" by selling preserves to repay a moral debt. Swett's *Stories of Maine* (1890) is a local history intended as a school reader.

Swett should be regarded as both a juvenile author and a practitioner of the New England "local color" style best known through the works of Sarah Orne Jewett. Swett's sister, Susan Hartley Swett (1860-1907) was a poetess and author of local color fiction who also published in the juvenile periodicals.

OTHER WORKS: *Captain Polly* (1889). *Flying Hill Farm* (1892). *The Mate of the Mary Ann* (1894). *Cap'n Thistletop* (1895). *The*

Lollipops' Vacation (1896). *Pennyroyal and Mint* (1896). *The Ponkaty Branch Road, and Other Stories for Young People* (1896). *Tom Pickering of "Scutney"* (1897). *Bilberry Boys and Girls* (1898). *The Boy from Beaver Hollow* (1900). *The Littlest One of the Brown* (1900). *Sarah the Less* (1902). *The Wonder-Ship* (1902). *The Young Ship-Builder* (1902). *The Lion Tamer's Little Girl* (1903). *Long Tom and How They Got Him* (1903). *Peaseblossom's Lion* (1903). *The Yellow-Capped Monkey* (1903). *Sonny Boy* (1904). *Polly and the Other Girl* (1906). *Princess Wisla* (1908). *The Six Little Pennypackers* (1911). *How the Pennypackers Kept the Light* (1912).

BIBLIOGRAPHY: *Herringshaw's Encyclopedia of American Biography of the Nineteenth Century* (1911). *Who Was Who in America, 1899-1942* (1966).

—JANE BENARDETE

SWISSHELM, Jane Grey

Born 6 December 1815, Pittsburgh, Pennsylvania; **died** 22 July 1884, Sewickley, Pennsylvania
Also wrote under: Jennie Deans, J. G. S.
Daughter of Thomas and Mary Scott Cannon; **married** James Swisshelm, 1836 (separated); **children:** one daughter

When Jane Grey Swisshelm was seven, her father died of tuberculosis. Her mother, who had previously lost four children to the disease, disregarded the doctor's prescription when Swisshelm showed symptoms, treating her with fresh air, fresh food, and exercise. Swisshelm recovered, and at the age of fourteen was teaching in the public school in Wilkinsburg, Pennsylvania. Swisshelm joined the church of her Scotch Covenanter parents at the age of fifteen, after a period of torment. The church provided her with a sense of purpose and a source of conflict throughout her life. In 1836 she married James Swisshelm, entering upon a marriage that was stormy and intermittent.

A short stay in Louisville, Kentucky, where her husband went into business, provided Swisshelm with material for her later writing against slavery. She started a school for blacks, but gave it up when threats were made to burn down her house. From 1840 on, Swisshelm's articles attacking capital punishment, advocating woman suffrage and the right of women to hold property, and urging the abolition of slavery appeared, at first anonymously, in newspapers in and around Pittsburgh. She contributed stories and poems as well. When Pittsburgh was left without an abolitionist paper in 1847, Swisshelm resolved to edit one herself. She delighted in the criticism she drew as a woman editor with pronounced political views. She continued to write for the Pittsburgh *Saturday Visiter* after it merged with Robert Riddle's

Journal in 1852. Her zeal for reform included advocacy of the "watercure treatment," advice on woman's health, dress, reading, and education.

An opponent of the Mexican War, Swisshelm went to Washington, D.C., in 1850 to observe the debate over disposition of Mexican territory acquired through the War. Horace Greeley engaged her as a Washington correspondent to the New York *Tribune*, and as the first woman to have such a regular assignment, she sought and secured a seat in the Congressional reporters' gallery.

In 1857 Swisshelm severed her connection with the *Family Journal and Visiter*, left her husband, and took her small daughter to northern Minnesota. There she agreed to revive and edit a defunct Democratic newspaper, which had as a major purpose attracting immigration to Minnesota. Her agreement with its proprietor included, however, the right to express her own views. The St. Cloud *Visiter* readily offended one of the leading political powers in the territory, and in March 1858, three men broke into her office and destroyed her press. Swisshelm first discovered she had an aptitude for public speaking at a meeting to raise funds to procure a new press, and for some years afterward made a lecture tour each year. As she traveled, she sent vivid letters to the St. Cloud *Democrat*, the weekly which had emerged under her editorship in July 1858 when, in order to avoid a libel suit, she had promised never again to use the *Visiter* as a political organ.

In 1863, following a revolt by the Sioux, Swisshelm went on a lecture tour through the East to arouse opinion in favor of sterner treatment of Native Americans. At this time, she characterized the Washington scene as "treason, treason, treason all around about—paid treason—official treason." She served as a nurse in military hospitals around Washington, while waiting to begin her duties as a clerk in the War Department. Her letters continued, castigating all whose conduct she disapproved: public officials, the Sanitary Commission, women who knit in the office.

Her last journalistic venture, the *Reconstructionist* (1865), was a radical newspaper, outspoken in its criticism of Andrew Johnson. Johnson responded by dismissing her from her post in the War Department, and without this source of income, she could not continue publication of the *Reconstructionist*.

Swisshelm's autobiography, *Half a Century* (1880), is unquestionably flawed by her biases. In addition, it was reconstructed from memory, as she had systematically destroyed letters and diaries during her unhappy marriage. It is, nevertheless, an important first-hand account of events of her time, as well as of her struggle as a woman. The last third of the book contains her picture of her experiences nursing the sick and wounded during the Civil War, putting to use her powers of keen observation, willingness to sacrifice herself, her sense of humor, her strong will, and her personal warmth.

A journalist who espoused many reform causes, Swisshelm was best known as an abolitionist. Her unrestrained style often provoked violent response, physical as well as verbal. Her writing is simple and direct, distinguished by dramatic narrative, graphic description, and vivid characterization. Although Swisshelm is noted and remembered for her ruthlessness, invective, and sarcasm, her brilliant style is equally effective in describing men and women she admired, and in conveying her warmth and her sense of pride in places and events which, to her, meant progress.

OTHER WORKS: *Letters to Country Girls* (1853). *True Stories About Pets* (1879). *Crusader and Feminist: The Letters of Jane Grey Swisshelm, 1858-1865* (edited by A. J. Larsen, 1934).

Files of the St. Cloud *Visiter* and the St. Cloud *Democrat* and a partial file of the Pittsburgh *Saturday Visiter* are in the Minnesota Historical Society. A file of the Pittsburgh *Saturday Visiter* and a few issues of the *Reconstructionist* are in the Carnegie Library in Pittsburgh.

BIBLIOGRAPHY: Stuhler, B. and G. Kreuter, eds., *Women of Minnesota* (1977). Thorp, M. F. *Female Persuasion* (1949).

Reference works: *DAB. NAW* (1971). *Oxford Companion to Women's Writing in the United States* (1995).

Other references: *Abraham Lincoln Quarterly* (Dec. 1950). *American Historical Review* (July 1932). *Minnesota History* (March 1951). *Mississippi Valley Historical Review* (Dec. 1920). *NYT* (23 July 1884). *Western Pennsylvania Historical Magazine* (July 1921).

—VIVIAN H. SHORTREED

T

TABER, Gladys Bagg

Born 2 April 1899, Colorado Springs, Colorado; **died** 11 March 1980, Hyannis, Massachusetts
Daughter of Rufus M. and Grace Raybold Bagg; **married** Frank A. Taber, 1922 (died 1964); **children:** one daughter

Gladys Bagg Tabor was born in the West, grew up in the Midwest, and lived her adult life in Virginia, New York, and New England. She graduated from Wellesley in 1920; took an M.A. at Lawrence College, Appleton, Wisconsin, in 1921; and did graduate work at Columbia University. In 1922 she married a professor of music at Randolph-Macon College in Virginia, who lost his hearing and had to leave his profession. Tabor had one daughter.

Tabor's early work includes a play and a book of poems, but most of it is popular romance, sometimes serialized in magazines such as the *Ladies' Home Journal.* Her fiction is light and uplifting; her heroines usually find true love despite an unsympathetic father or class differences. In later novels, her heroines are long-suffering middle-aged housewives. Tabor's fiction shows a remarkable concentration on her own life, with the same themes and characters appearing again and again, and, as often happens with popular writers about whom the public is very curious, she became increasingly open about her own life when she turned completely to nonfiction after publishing her last novel, a barely disguised autobiography, in 1957.

Tabor's father is a perennial character in her books, fiction or autobiography. She wrote one book about him, *Especially Father* (1949), and portrays him in detail again in *Harvest of Yesterdays* (1976). He is harshly dealt with in her fiction, where he is the tyrant who keeps his daughter from marrying the man she loves, but in Tabor's nonfiction she tries to sympathize with him. Nevertheless, Tabor always portrays him as a hyperactive domestic tyrant with the social responsibility of a sand flea. Tabor's literary treatment of her father is an interesting case history in the making of capital from one of life's burdens.

Tabor's fiction is not the work which gained her the loyal fans she has attracted over the years; rather, her magazine columns and the books she made from them are the cornerstone of her success. From November 1937 to December 1957, her column "Diary of Domesticity" ran in the country's leading women's magazine, the *Ladies' Home Journal,* where she was also assistant editor (1946-58). Then for 10 or more years the column continued, in *Everywoman's Family Circle,* the supermarket magazine, as "Butternut Wisdom." These columns, and the books she made from them, chronicle the life of Tabor and her family at Stillmeadow, a farmhouse built in 1690, near Southbury, Connecticut. The first Stillmeadow book, *Harvest at Stillmeadow,* was published in 1940. There is a lot of repetition in the Stillmeadow books, which are organized seasonally, but these are the most popular mid-20th century examples by a woman of the subgenre of semiautobiographical books about country life.

Sharing Stillmeadow with Tabor and her daughter is Jill (Eleanor Mayer), Tabor's beloved "lifelong friend," and her two children. Jill was widowed in 1943. Tabor's husband, who is seldom mentioned, died in 1964. Throughout the series, the reader follows the changes coming to the lives of Tabor and Jill as their children grow up and they struggle with the usual problems of country life. Jill is portrayed by Tabor as the stereotyped demon gardener; her death in 1960 was acknowledged in Tabor's columns and became the subject of a book on coping with grief, *Another Path* (1963). Tabor characterizes herself, like the usual middle-aged heroines in her later novels, as timid and incompetent in mechanical things, unable to use the telephone or the vacuum cleaner.

Like other women who write for the popular audience, Tabor portrays herself as much more of an average housewife than she could have been. In *Mrs. Daffodil* (1957), an autobiographical novel in which the heroine is a columnist who lives in an old house in New England, an interviewer asks Mrs. Daffodil why she is so successful as a writer. "I think it's because I am not a special person at all. . . . I am just any woman with a house and a family and dogs and a garden. So if I put down what I feel, others feel the same way. I've often wished I were a literary writer, like Virginia Woolf, but I'm just the common garden variety." Such is indeed the nature of popular appeal; the readers want to read what they already think.

OTHER WORKS: *Lady of the Moon* (1928). *Lyonesse* (1929). *Late Climbs the Sun* (1934). *Tomorrow May Be Fair* (1935). *The Evergreen Tree* (1937). *Long Tails and Short* (1938). *A Star to Steer By* (1938). *This is For Always* (1938). *Nurse in Blue* (1943). *The Heart Has April Too* (1944). *Give Us This Day* (1944). *Give Me the Stars* (1945). *Especially Spaniels* (1945). *The Family on Maple Street* (1946). *Stillmeadow Kitchen* (1947). *The Book of Stillmeadow* (1948). *Stillmeadow Seasons* (1950). *When Dogs Meet People* (1952). *Stillmeadow and Sugarbridge* (with B. Webster, 1953). *Stillmeadow Daybook* (1955). *What Cooks at Stillmeadow* (1958). *Spring Harvest* (1959). *Stillmeadow Sampler* (1959). *Stillmeadow Road* (1962). *Another Path* (1963). *Stillmeadow Cookbook* (1965). *Stillmeadow Calendar* (1967). *Especially Dogs* (1968). *Stillmeadow Album* (1969). *Amber: A Very Personal Cat* (1970). *My Own Cape Cod* (1971). *My Own Cook Book* (1972). *Country Chronicle* (1974). *Conversations with Amber* (1978). *Still Cove Journal* (1981).

BIBLIOGRAPHY: *Ladies' Home Journal* (Oct. 1946). *NYT* (9 Oct. 1955). *WLB* (April 1952).

—BEVERLY SEATON

TAGGARD, Genevieve

Born 28 November 1894, Waitsburg, Washington; **died** 8 November 1948, New York, New York
Daughter of James N. and Alta Arnold Taggard; **married** Robert Wolf, 1921; Kenneth Durant, 1935; **children:** one daughter

Genevieve Taggard was the eldest child of schoolteacher-missionaries, whose Scots-Irish pioneer ancestors had migrated to Washington from Vermont. Feeling alienated from the spiritual and cultural sterility of eastern Washington, Taggard's devout parents moved the family to Hawaii when she was two. Except for two traumatic returns to Washington necessary for her father's health, Taggard lived 18 years in what she later idealized as innocent, exotic poverty.

The contrast between Hawaii, where caste, race, and wealth seemed irrelevant, and Waitsburg's smalltown prejudice and rude materialism, focused Taggard's moral vision. Her social conscience was a logical extension of her parents' preachings, but their faith as fundamentalist Disciples of Christ allowed only biblical reading; Keats and Ruskin were illicit pleasures. Defiantly, Taggard embarked upon her writing career at age twelve.

By the time she graduated from the University of California at Berkeley (1920), Taggard was both poet and socialist. Nationally published, Taggard was offered work in New York by Max Eastman at the *Liberator*. She took a leading role in the literary and social developments of the 1920s and 1930s, working first for B. W. Huebsch's avant-garde *Freeman* and helping found and edit the *Measure*, a lyric poetry journal. Taggard taught at several colleges, traveled in Europe and Russia, raised a daughter, and was active in humanitarian and proletarian causes. Her two husbands were also radical writers. Taggard retired in 1946 in Vermont; she died in 1948 of the effects of hypertension.

Known primarily to scholars for her biography of Emily Dickinson (1930), a passionate, bold interpretation of the father-daughter relationship and Dickinson's psychology, Taggard received wide recognition throughout her career as a literary activist and poet, who was published and reviewed in journals ranging from the *New Yorker* to *New Masses*.

Her first book of poetry, *For Eager Lovers* (1922), established her unique idiom as a metaphysical Marxist, a lyric intellectual who incorporates Hawaiian exotica into poems about revolution and a woman's experience in love. Even such Marxist visions of doomed decadence as "Twentieth Century Slave-Gang" eschew rhetoric and combine modern directness ("the ants are hurried") with extraordinary images: oaks bend knotted knees in labor, a pond is wrinkled with velvet oil, wasps carry spider-spoil to where crude honey hangs in mud.

While this volume commemorates a first year of marriage, and Taggard occasionally speaks as an "eager lover," she insists on the necessary independence—even defiance—of soul, voice,

whole being, especially in the potentially compromising love relationship. Her resolute quest for freedom (personal, artistic, social, and political) is the dominant theme of Taggard's poetry; here the tone is "caged arrogance" as the voice celebrates its emancipation.

In *Collected Poems, 1918-1938*, Taggard juxtaposes early and late poems to show their essential continuity, that love of beauty and hatred of oppression are not contradictory. She brings her modernist and ideological rebellion against romanticism to the lives of "mothers, housewives, old women" to capture with compassion, "the kitchens they knew, sinks, suds, stew-pots, and pennies. . . / Dull hurry and worry, clatter, wet hands and backache." While Taggard's Marxism and moral upbringing lead her to respect "those timid slaves of breakfast" who "get out in the line, drop for once dish rag and broom," her tolerance turns to scorn for artists who care only for aesthetics. That she feels the odds are against a "middle-class middle-aged woman" succeeding either socially or aesthetically at "useful" lyrics is told in "Words Property of the People," where Taggard cites the cost of her convictions. She finds herself "stammering/Anxious to show that a poet's mind / Is as useful as a carpenter's hammer."

In *Slow Music* (1946), Taggard is still working to support her lifelong conviction that the desire to be socially relevant and the belief that art obeys its own laws must coexist. Charges that her poetry lacks a "unified sensibility" point to what makes Taggard's poetry unusual: the lifelong synthesis of her experience and vision as sister, daughter, mother, wife, lover, professor, activist, and poet, whose words were heard on records and on the radio, sung at Carnegie Hall to music of Copland and Schuman, and read in Moscow and in bean fields. She lived paradox as naturally as she wrote metaphysical verse. The synthesis of mangoes, metaphor, and Marx makes Taggard's poetry complex. But her passion for precision makes abstract idea and mood arresting and accessible: Taggard renders psychological and social states through metaphors of the physical world.

OTHER WORKS: *Hawaiian Hilltop* (1923). *Continent's End* (edited by Taggard, with G. Sterling and J. Rorty, 1925). *May Days* (edited by Taggard, 1925). *Words for the Chisel* (1926). *The Unspoken, and Other Poems* by Anne Brenner (edited by Taggard, 1927). *Travelling Standing Still* (1928). *Circumference: Varieties of Metaphysical Verse, 1459-* (1929). *The Life and Mind of Emily Dickinson* (1930). *Remembering Vaughan in New England* (1933). *Ten Introductions* (with D. Fitts, 1934). *Not Mine to Finish* (1934). *Calling Western Union* (1936). *Long View* (1942). *Falcon* (1942). *A Part of Vermont* (1945). *Origin Hawaii* (1947).

BIBLIOGRAPHY: Aaron, D., *Writers on the Left* (1961). Lins, K. L., "An Interpretive Study of Selected Poetry by Genevieve Taggard" (thesis, 1956). Mossberg, B.A., and C. L. Mossberg, *Genevieve Taggard* (Western Writers Series). Peck, D. R., "Development of an American Marxist Literary Criticism: The Monthly New

Masses'' (dissertation, 1968). Wilson, E., ''A Poet of the Pacific,'' in *The Shores of Light* (1952).

Reference works: *DAB. NAW* (1971). *Oxford Companion to American Literature* (1965). *Oxford Companion to Women's Writing in the United States* (1995). *TCA.*

Other references: *Masses and Mainstream* (Jan. 1949). *Ms.* (1979). *Nation* (19 Jan. 1927). *New Masses* (Jan. 1927). *Poetry* (Dec. 1934, May 1936, Feb. 1947). *SR* (7 Nov. 1936; 14 Dec. 1946). *Scholastic* (17 May 1938). *Time* (22 Nov. 1948). *WLB* (Jan. 1930).

—BARBARA CLARKE MOSSBERG

TALBOTT, Marion

Born 31 July 1858, Thun, Switzerland; **died** 20 October 1948, Chicago, Illinois
Daughter of Israel T. and Emily Fairbanks Talbott

Marion Talbott's was an intellectual, well-established New England family; her father was the first dean of the medical school of Boston University, and her mother was active in establishing the Girls' Latin School in Boston. Talbott was encouraged by her parents in her advocacy of women's rights in academic institutions. She received a B.A. from Boston University in 1884 and a B.S. degree from the Massachusetts Institute of Technology in 1888.

In 1892 Talbott joined the University of Chicago faculty as an assistant professor in the Department of Sociology and Anthropology, where she taught sanitary science and was appointed the first women's dean in a coeducational institution. In 1906 she established the Department of Household Administration. After her retirement in 1925, Talbott served as acting president of Constantinople Women's College in Turkey (1927-28, 1931-32).

Talbott's pioneering work in women's education was complemented by her scholarly study of the application of science to the home. This latter interest was probably sparked by her association with Ellen H. Richards, a leader in the home economics field, a family friend, teacher, and colleague. With Richards, Talbott edited *Home Sanitation: A Manual for Housekeepers* (1887) and wrote ''Food as a Factor in Student Life'' (1884). The latter is a more scholarly study of food services in dormitory settings and how to set nutritious standards at a low cost. Both books are simplistic and outdated but were important beginning steps in the study of nutrition and home economics.

The Modern Household (1912) is an introductory text intended for housewives and college students to help them adapt to modern social changes affecting the home. The book covers a variety of topics ranging from the mundane care of the house to ethics in consumerism and the community.

The Education of Women (1910) describes the educational opportunities available to girls and women in the U.S. Talbott'

defense of social hygiene, exercise, and training for rational thinking dates the book, but she was advocating ''daring'' ideas at the time. Talbott's emphasis on women in the home pervades her writing, and in this way she makes her more ''radical'' ideas acceptable to a skeptical readership.

The History of the American Association of University Women, 1881-1931 (1931), written with Lois Mathews Rosenberry, is a detailed account of the committees, work, and goals of the association Talbott helped to found.

Anyone interested in the turbulent, innovative founding days of the University of Chicago will find Talbott's *More Than Lore* (1936) a delight to read. She is forthright in her statements about discrimination against women professionals at the university. Talbott believed women should be ''ladies,'' polite and well-bred, and that a higher education prepared women to be better wives and mothers. In this way, she supported the traditional roles of women. Her writings are also interspersed, though, with a sharp appreciation of women's contributions to society and the difficulty of managing a home, and these analyses sound similar to modern writings on the sociology of housewives and housework. Most clearly, her critiques of discrimination against women in academia are relevant and accurate today.

BIBLIOGRAPHY: *NAW* (1971). *Oxford Companion to Women's Writing in the United States* (1995). *Publications of the Members of the University of Chicago: 1902-1916* (1917).

—MARY JO DEEGAN

TAN, Amy

Born 19 February 1952, Oakland, California
Daughter of Daisy (Tu Ching) and John Tan; **married** Lou de Mattei, 1974

Amy Tan's fiction, infused with the spirit of the fairytales she read avidly as a child, earned the author a fairytale success in real life. While still in her thirties, Tan published two novels to spectacular critical acclaim and commercial gain. She grew up in San Francisco, the child of Chinese immigrant parents who made it out of China just before Mao came to power. Drawing on the tensions and dislocations of this background, her novels depict a new aspect of an honored American literary experience, the immigrant adventure.

In the first, *The Joy Luck Club* (1989), and even more so in the second, *The Kitchen God's Wife* (1991), Tan exhibits an extraordinarily satisfying storytelling gift: pacing, imagery, descriptive vividness, laced with suspense, humor, emotion, and psychological reality. Clearly a writer with a modern sensibility, she also includes acute social observations in the manner of the 19th-century novel, and the mix results in a masterful tapestry of individual and social anguish. Both novels describe mother-daughter relationships in which exotic elements of Chinese background clash against a contemporary feminist point of view. The mothers are oppressed, but not victims; the daughters strive to place themselves beyond the control of these strong mothers, claiming their own space and time, without losing the richness of their beginnings and their loyalties. The resolutions of the conflicts are emotionally satisfying, without a trace of romanticizing lies or sentimentality.

In ''Two Kinds,'' a short story published in the February 1989 *Atlantic Monthly*, Tan describes the narrator's mother's background: ''She had come to San Francisco in 1949 after losing everything in China: her mother and father, her family home, her first husband, and two daughters, twin baby girls.'' Tan's fiction tells and retells variations of this story, while engaging a modern audience with the further labyrinthine irony and pain of oth-er-daughter love, complicated by dual, conflicting cultures and needs. Further, in *The Kitchen God's Wife*, the reader is swept into the detailed horrors of the havoc and devastation suffered by the Chinese people throughout the social upheavals of this century.

Tan's father was an engineer and Baptist minister. She knew her mother had been married before, but she learned only at twenty-six that she had half sisters from that marriage still living in China. Tan herself was a middle child and only daughter of her mother's second marriage. Both her father and her older brother died of brain tumors in the 1960s. Her remarkably resourceful mother took Tan and her younger brother from the ''diseased'' house to Montreux, Switzerland, where Tan finished her high school years. When the family returned to the Bay Area, Tan enrolled in Linfield College, a Baptist school in Oregon, but soon followed her boyfriend to San Jose State University (B.A., 1963), changing her major from premed to English. Her mother had harbored unrealistic hopes for her daughter. ''Of course you will become a famous neurosurgeon. . .and, yes, a concert pianist on the side.''

What Tan had always wanted to be was a writer, ever since she won a writing contest at age eight. Disappointing her mother, she married her boyfriend, Lou de Mattei, earned a master's degree in linguistics (San Jose State, 1974), worked at a variety of freelance technical writing jobs, and wrote her stories on the side. She and her mother became more and more estranged until a trip to China resolved Tan's ambiguities about her past heritage and her present sense of herself. For the first time, she felt Chinese as well as American. ''When I began to write *The Joy Luck Club*, it was so much for my mother and myself,'' to explain the turbulent disagreements of their lives together. She has reported that the writing of her first novel was like ''taking dictation from an invisible storyteller.'' One is reminded of Harriet Beecher Stowe's statement that God had dictated *Uncle Tom's Cabin*.

Tan's third published book is for children. *The Moon Lady* (1992) is ''set in the China of long ago. . .a story of a little girl who discovered that the best wishes are those she can make come true herself.''

Superficially, Amy Tan's next book, her third novel, *The Hundred Secret Senses* (1995), has much in common with its predecessors. The mother-daughter paradigm in those books is only slightly altered; Tan presents Olivia, a California-born, modern, practical, skeptical career woman and her much older half-sister Kwan, who is nurturing, Chinese-born, unassimilated, accented; Kwan also communicates with the ''world of yin,'' a ghost world. Again, the two women are set in opposition; in Olivia's eyes Kwan is odd, intruding, unsophisticated—a nearly lifelong source of embarrassment and guilt.

The book's plot sends Olivia, her husband, Simon, and Kwan on a pilgrimage back to China. Nineteenth-century China is again explored, this time through Kwan's account of the lives of hers and Olivia's reincarnated selves. However, the heart of the story rests in the resolution of the two sisters' world views, which occurs in Olivia's acceptance of mystery and opening herself to a spiritual life—rather than the acceptance of anything specifically generational or Chinese.

Tan is undoubtedly the best known (and bestselling) Chinese-American author. The film adaption of *The Joy Luck Club*, for which she cowrote the script, was a box office hit. While her success may have opened doors for other young Asian-American writers, it is also true that every Asian-American writer published in the 1990s has had his or her work compared to Tan's. Though Tan enjoys her fame, she does not relish being pigeonholed as an ethnic writer; she'd like her work (and that of other hyphenated American writers) to be found not on multicultural reading lists but on ones simply for American literature. Regarding her own work, she points out that ''the obsessions I write about are very American—marriage, love, the idea that you can create your own life.''

Tan doesn't take herself too seriously as a literary star. She's appeared on *Sesame Street*, and her second children's book, *The Chinese Siamese Cat* (1994), is the tale of a mischievous, independent-thinking kitten who changes history. Tan has also appeared as the leather-clad, whip-yielding lead singer of a band called the Rock Bottom Remainders with fellow band members (and fellow authors) Dave Barry and Stephen King.

BIBLIOGRAPHY: Cosslett, T., ''Feminism, Matrilinealism, and the 'House of Women' in Contemporary Women's Fiction,'' in *Journal of Gender Studies* (Mar. 1996).

Reference works: *Bestsellers* (1989). *CA* (1992). *CLC* (1990).

Other references: *Asian Week* (21 Oct. 1994). *Far Eastern Economic Review* (27 July 1989, 14 Nov. 1991). *Independent* (10 Feb. 1996). *KR* (15 July 1994). *LATBR* (12 Mar. 1989). *Newsday* (11 Nov. 1995). *New Statesman and Society* (30 June 1989, 12 July 1991, 16 Feb. 1996). *Newsweek* (17 Apr. 1989). *NYT* (4 July 1989, 31 May 1991, 11 June 1991, 20 June 1991, 17 Nov. 1995). *NYTBR* (19 Mar. 1989, 16 June 1991, 8 Nov. 1992, 29 Oct. 1995). *St. Louis Post-Dispatch* (11 Nov. 1995). *Time* (27 Mar. 1989, 3 June 1991). *WP* (8 Oct. 1989). *WPBW* (5 Mar. 1989, 16 June 1991). *WRB* (Sept. 1991).

—HELEN YGLESIAS,
UPDATED BY VALERIE VOGRIN

TANDY, Jennette Reid

Born 27 September 1889, Vevay, Indiana; **died** 24 August 1968, Dillsboro, Indiana
Daughter of Carroll S. and Jennette Carpenter Tandy

Descended on her father's side from Swiss immigrants, Jennette Reid Tandy was the oldest of six daughters in a locally prominent and well-educated family. Both parents encouraged the girls in reading, needlework, music, and art. The family valued academic achievement, and all of the daughters attended universities or art school. Tandy and her sister Elizabeth earned doctorates. After studying at Wellesley College for two years, Tandy went to the University of Chicago for her Ph.B. (1911), then studied library science at Western Reserve University. During the 1910s she worked as librarian and teacher in Ohio and Indiana. In the 1920s, Tandy studied and taught at Columbia University where she received her M.A. (1920) and her Ph.D. (1925).

At Columbia, Professors William P. Trent and Carl Van Doren guided Tandy and other graduate students to undertake some of the necessary groundwork for establishing American literature, then a just barely respectable subject for academic inquiry, as a legitimate discipline. Always independent and iconoclastic, Tandy more than met the challenge for a pioneering study. Her dissertation, published as *Crackerbox Philosophers in American Humor and Satire* (1925), goes beyond mainstream American literature to include what she calls the "underbrush of literature," that is, the popular writing of newspapers and almanacs. Her book, one of the landmarks in the study of American humor, has been overshadowed by Constance Rourke's *American Humor* (1931) but is notable on several counts.

Although *Crackerbox Philosophers* is a study in American letters, Tandy is mindful of the cultural context out of which literature comes. In assuming a broad definition of literature that includes folk and popular material and in treating literature as an artifact of culture, Tandy, her mentors, and colleagues helped to establish a perspective that eventually gave rise to the American studies and popular culture movements. Tandy's work anticipates Rourke's later recognition that a study of American humor is a study of American character. In her book, Tandy describes and analyzes the provincial character type she calls "crackerbox philosopher." Her study is the earliest full treatment of this unlettered American social critic. The crackerbox philosopher in literature and in life is a variant of the "wise fool" a person deficient in book learning but strong in common sense. In her chapter, "The Development of Southern Humor," Tandy gives the first serious attention to a group of journalistic writers later to be identified as "frontier" or "Old Southwestern" humorists. Since frontier humor is often described as "masculine," it is noteworthy that a woman became one of its earliest scholars.

Serious illness and a long recuperation ended Tandy's career as a scholar. She returned to her native Ohio River Valley and as a therapeutic continuation of her interest in textiles and needlework started weaving tapestries on a small hand loom. Always a willing traveler and always questing after knowledge and new experiences, Tandy studied art and weaving in this country and Europe, most intensely with the Navajos in Arizona. A collector of Native American jewelry and crafts, she incorporated Navajo motifs into some of her tapestries.

When Tandy returned to Vevay, she chose for her studio an early 19th-century building, formerly used as a saloon and tavern, where Daniel Boone is reputed to have stayed overnight. In her weaving, she continued some of the same interests that had occupied her as a literary scholar: local culture and ordinary folk. Many of Tandy's tapestries depict scenes along the Kentucky and Ohio Rivers: shanty boats, tobacco market, and provincial architecture. Her interest in popular culture shows in woven representations of a hamburger stand and pool hall. Some of her portrait tapestries are caricatures. In her depiction of "Mrs. Uppercrust," for instance, Tandy pokes fun at the pretensions of social class in the spirit of a crackerbox philosopher.

Never content with mediocrity, Tandy experimented with technique, floss, and color and became an accomplished artisan. In the 1940s and 1950s, she produced hundreds of tapestries and exhibited them in one-woman shows in art museums in the U.S. and Canada. Life as a New York City intellectual and life as a village weaver seem unconnected, but a common thread runs through Tandy's diverse activities and achievements: in her art and in her scholarship, she focused on Native American culture.

BIBLIOGRAPHY: Louisville *Courier-Journal Magazine* (1 Oct. 1950). Indianapolis *Star Magazine* (5 Dec. 1954).

—LYNDA W. BROWN

TAPPAN, Eva March

Born 26 December 1854, Blackstone, Massachusetts; **died** 29 January 1930, Worcester, Massachusetts
Daughter of Edmund M. and Lucretia Logee Tappan

Eva March Tappan, whose father died when she was six years old, spent most of her childhood at various ladies' seminaries where her mother supported them both by teaching. Indeed, the first half century of Tappan's life belonged, one way or another, to educational institutions. After receiving a B.A. from Vassar in 1875, Tappan taught in secondary schools, first at the Wheaton Seminary in Norton, Massachusetts (1875-80), and later at the Raymond Academy in Camden, New Jersey, where she was also an associate principal (1884-94). In 1894 Tappan entered the University of Pennsylvania full time. There she earned an M.A. (1895) and a Ph.D. (1896), writing her dissertation on the 17th-century English poet, Nicholas Breton. In the same year she published her first book, *Charles Lamb, the Man and the Author*.

The following year, 1897, Tappan returned to teaching, this time as head of the English department of English High School, Worcester, Massachusetts. During the next seven years, she balanced the demands of teaching and authorship, writing several successful textbooks in history and literature, including *In the Days of Alfred the Great* (1900), *England's Story* (1901), and *Our Country's Story* (1902). In 1904, determined to devote all her energies to writing, Tappan resigned her post at English High School.

Tappan's books are characterized by a simple, direct style, extensive use of picturesque detail, and a pervasive sense of drama. Although the use of details and dramatization may not seem unusual now, it was at the time, for Tappan was among the first writers to present history in terms of the customs, culture, and manner of living of a people, rather than in terms of battles and political settlements. In addition, although Tappan's style is dramatic, she does not make the mistake of dramatizing at the expense of accuracy. Among her contemporaries and ours, the consensus is that her research was thorough and her interpretations sensitive. For example, her *Little Book of the War* (1918) is a careful attempt to explain the causes of World War I without recourse to the frenzied propaganda of the time.

In all of her more than 40 books, Tappan manages to be scholarly without being pedantic, informative without being didactic, and entertaining without being trivial. Her conviction that history was more than a record of wars helped to change the nature of historical writing for children.

OTHER WORKS: *In the Days of William the Conqueror* (1901). *Old Ballads in Prose* (1901). *In the Days of Queen Elizabeth* (1902). *The Christ Story* (1903). *In the Days of Queen Victoria* (1903). *Robin Hood, His Book* (1903). *A Short History of England's Literature* (1905). *The Golden Goose, and Other Fairy Tales* (1905). *A Short History of America's Literature* (1906). *American Hero Stories* (1906). *A Short History of England's and America's Literature* (1906). *America's Literature, with Selections from Colonial and Revolutionary Writers* (1907). *The Chaucer Story Book* (1908). *Letters from Colonial Children* (1908). *The Story of the Greek People* (1908). *Dixie Kitten* (1910). *A Friend in the Library* (12 vols., 1910). *An Old, Old Storybook* (1910). *The Story of the Roman People* (1910). *Old World Hero Stories* (1911). *When Knights Were Bold* (1912). *The House with the Silver Door* (1913). *Diggers in the Earth* (1916). *The Farmer and His Friends* (1916). *Makers of Many Things* (1916). *Travelers and Traveling* (1916). *The Little Book of the Flag* (1918). *Our European Ancestors* (1918). *Food Saving and Sharing* (1918). *The Little Book of Our Country* (1919). *Hero Stories of France* (1920). *Heroes of Progress* (1921). *Story of Our Constitution* (1922). *Ella, a Little Schoolgirl of the Sixties* (1923). *American History Stories for Very Young Readers* (1924). *Barry, the Dog Hero of the St. Bernard Pass* (1924). *Stories of America for Very Young Readers* (1926). *The Prince from Nowhere* (1928).

BIBLIOGRAPHY: Smith, D. V., *Fifty Years of Children's Books* (1963).

Reference works: *DAB*. *NAW* (1971).

Other references: Boston *Evening Transcript* (30 Jan. 1930).

—KATHARYN F. CRABBE

TARBELL, Ida (Minerva)

Born 5 November 1857, Erie County, Pennsylvania; **died** 6 January 1944, Bridgeport, Connecticut
Daughter of Franklin S. and Esther McCullough Tarbell

Ida Tarbell grew up in what was then the heartland of America's oil region. As a child, she evinced considerable intellectual curiosity and independence, which her parents (both former teachers) encouraged. The Tarbell family was closely knit and espoused the typical virtues of the early American Dream: hard work, honesty, thrift, and moral good. To the end of her life, she tended to judge all character (of person or corporation) on the basis of its adherence to what she called "the fair and open path." It was this high moral sense that animated her best writing.

An adolescent struggle to reconcile the Holy Writ with scientific fact (she found a solution in theories of evolution) led Tarbell to study biology at Allegheny College, as the sole female in a freshman class of 40. After graduating in 1880, Tarbell took an onerous and poorly paid teaching position with a Poland, Ohio, seminary (like her college, not far from her family home). In 1882 she returned home and soon became a staff member of the *Chautauquan*, a monthly magazine connected with the Chautauqua movement and its home studies program. Beginning as an editorial secretary, Tarbell advanced during her eight-year employment on the magazine to writer and annotator.

At the age of thirty, Tarbell decided she was "dying of respectability" and gave vent to her need for adventure by quitting her job and going to Paris to write a biography of a French revolutionary, *Madame Roland: A Biographical Study* (1896).

Despite her own (and others') assessment of her ability as "not a writer but a dead scholar," Tarbell supported herself in France by writing for American magazines. In this manner she was noticed by S. S. McClure, publisher of the fledgling *McClure's* magazine. Her contribution on Napoleon, in 1894, boosted the magazine's popularity and Tarbell's reputation as a journalist of note. From 1894 until 1906 Tarbell was a writer for *McClure's*; from 1906 to 1915, for *American Magazine*. In this 21-year period as a staff writer, Tarbell produced the works which support her journalistic reputation. Almost all resulted from assignments for articles, which later were published separately as books; they are either biographies (not critical or analytical but thoroughly researched) or studies of complex issues (such as the oil corporations or tariffs), which Tarbell could explain in concepts and language understandable to the average person. These studies, however, are not purely objective analyses but reflect the attitudes and values of her background. Tarbell was one of the investigative journalists popular in the early 20th-century who were given the name "muckrakers" by Theodore Roosevelt.

Like many others, Tarbell was profoundly affected by World War I and its alteration of traditional beliefs; this is reflected in her focus, from 1911 until the 1920s, on war and peace and resultant social problems. Her writings after WWI are fewer; in these years, Tarbell was more active as lecturer or delegate to various national and international conferences. She herself considered her postwar writings "musty"-it seems probable she no longer was able to write from the fierce certainties of youth and that the concerns of the reading public had been altered substantially by the war.

Perhaps Tarbell's best writing from the later years of her life is her autobiography, *All in the Day's Work* (1939), written when she was eighty-two. She relates that at fourteen, she had prayed never to be married; as a college student, she avoided "entangling alliances." The phrase (hers) is telling; throughout her autobiography, Tarbell repeatedly notes her need for independence and freedom—freedom from marriage and from groups, especially the suffragists or other women's groups.

Tarbell was not a feminist; she opposed the woman suffrage movement because she felt suffragists belittled women's contributions to society. As her autobiography, her study of Mme. Roland, and her two treatises on "womanhood"— *The Business of Being a Woman* (1912) and *Ways of Woman* (1915)—reveal, she answered "the woman question" with the cliché that the hand that rocks the cradle rules the world. The home, which Tarbell felt to be a sufficient and necessary sphere in which women could operate, was the most vital unit in a healthy society. Thus she approved patriarchal practices by big business (such as Henry Ford's workers communities) and she herself flourished under the direction of patriarchal males. In fact, the staff at *McClure's* operated as a family, with Tarbell the laudable "big sister," training younger men to become editors. Her aversion to equally independent and talented women, especially feminists, can be traced to early rebuffs by female suffragists and scientists; recalling these incidents in her autobiography, Tarbell concludes, "men have always been nicer to me than women."

Tarbell deserves recognition, however, for her pioneering role in journalism and especially for her classic study of the oil industry, *The History of the Standard Oil Company*, a two-volume work first published in 1904 (reissued in one volume, 1963; abridged, by D. Chalmers, 1966). H. H. Rogers, a Standard Oil executive, guided Tarbell through selected corporate documents during her two-year research effort, but she consulted other sources, as the massive documentation reveals. The *History* does not by any means whitewash Standard Oil; Tarbell frankly regards the corporation as guilty of "commercial sin." But she is equally honest in recognizing the genius of John D. Rockefeller: he early understood control of the oil industry depended on control of the transportation of that oil. While he embodied the industry and verve she had been taught to admire, he created the corporate entity she recognized as death to the individual businessman—a clear negation of the American dream. *The History of the Standard Oil Company* is a landmark in both business and journalism because it represents Standard Oil's first serious attempt at public relations and because it was in the vanguard of serious investigative reporting by American periodicals.

OTHER WORKS: *A Short Life of Napoleon Bonaparte* (1895). *Early Life of Abraham Lincoln* (1896). *The Life of Abraham Lincoln* (2 vols., 1900). *Napoleon's Addresses* (1902). *He Knew Lincoln* (1907). *Father Abraham* (1909). *Selections from the Letters, Speeches, and State Papers of Abraham Lincoln* (1911).

The Tariff in Our Times (1911). *New Ideals in Business: An Account of Their Practice and Their Effects upon Men and Profits* (1916). *The Rising of the Tide: The Story of Sabinsport* (1919). *In Lincoln's Chair* (1920). *Boy Scout's Life of Lincoln* (1922). *He Knew Lincoln, and Other Billy Brown Stories* (1922). *Peacemakers, Blessed and Otherwise: Observations, Reflections, and Irritations at an International Conference* (1922). *In the Footsteps of the Lincolns* (1922). *Life of Elbert H. Gary: The Story of Steel* (1925). *A Life of Napoleon Bonaparte* (1927). *A Reporter for Lincoln: Story of Henry E. Wing, Soldier and Newspaper Man* (1927). *Owen D. Young: A New Type of Industrial Leader* (1932). *The Nationalizing of Business, 1878-1898* (Volume 9, A History of American Life series, 1936). *Women at Work: A Tour Among Careers* (1939).

Ida Tarbell's papers are in the collections of the Reis Library of Allegheny College and the Sophia Smith Collection at Smith College.

BIBLIOGRAPHY: Chalmers, D., *The Social and Political Ideas of the Muckrakers* (1964). Filer, L., *Crusaders for American Liberalism* (1939). Fleming, A., *Ida Tarbell: First of the Muckrakers* (1971). Marzolf, M., *Up from the Footnote* (1977). Tomkins, M., *Ida M. Tarbell* (1974).

Reference works: *Oxford Companion to Women's Writing* (1995).

Other references: *American Heritage* 21 (April 1970).

—SALLY BRETT

TAYLOR, Mildred Delois

Born 1943, Jackson, Mississippi
Daughter of Wilbert L. and Deletha Davis Taylor

In writing realistic stories about the African American experience in the South, Mildred Delois Taylor juxtaposes the warmth and safety of family love and community solidarity against the burning injustices of racism. Emotionally powerful and often graphic in its horrifying verisimilitude, Taylor's relatively small but critical body of work celebrates the physical and spiritual survival of her heroic black characters and the indomitability of the human spirit.

Taylor graduated from the University of Toledo and pursued graduate study in journalism at the University of Colorado, but her most valuable education took place at home and through life experiences. Storytelling was an integral part of Taylor's family life. From her father, a master storyteller, she learned the black history absent from the textbooks she studied at school—a history that emphasized the pride, dignity, and values of African American life despite the sorrows and defeats experienced in an unjust society. During two years (1965-67) spent in Ethiopia with the Peace Corps, Taylor was frequently reminded of her father's stories, and her determination to write the truth about the black experience further solidified.

Taylor's first book, a novella called *The Song of the Trees* (1975, most recent reissue 1997), won first prize in the African American category of a competition sponsored by the Council on Interracial Books for Children. Told from the perspective of eight-year-old Cassie Logan, the book begins the saga of the proud Logan family, and in particular the children, which continues in much of Taylor's subsequent work. The Logan books chronicle the family's hardships and joys in Depression-era Mississippi, exploring what it means to grow from childhood to adulthood as an African American in the United States. Themes of strength, dignity, determination, integrity, love of the land, and the importance of family are woven through works alive with drama and vivid with sure characterization, quick dialogue, and a skilled narrative style.

Taylor incorporates into her stories much of what she learned in her own childhood, and incidents about which she read or heard. The result are stories that bristle with life, read like autobiography, and have an aural, poetic quality. *Roll of Thunder, Hear My Cry* (1976, reissued 1997), the first full-length novel about Cassie and her family, won the 1977 Newbery Medal, was chosen as a National Book award finalist, and was named a *Boston Globe-Horn Book* honor book for 1977. *Let the Circle Be Unbroken* (1981, reissued 1991) was nominated for the American Book award and won the Coretta Scott King award for 1981. *The Friendship and Other Stories* (1987, 1993), like *The Song of the Trees*, focuses on a single incident in the life of the Logans, and is also intended for a younger audience. It received the 1989 *Boston Globe—Horn Book* award. *The Road to Memphis* (1990, 1995) brings the Logan children into explosive young adulthood, and was chosen as the 1990 Coretta Scott King award winner.

In *The Gold Cadillac* (1987, 1998), a Christopher award winner, Taylor introduces the reader to new characters, 'lois and her sister, Wilma, who discover for the first time what it is like to be scared because of the color of their skin. *Mississippi Bridge* (1990) is written from the point of view of a white boy, Jeremy Simms, who witnesses a tragic bus accident that results in ironic justice for the blacks who have been ordered off the bus. Both books resonate with honesty and emotionally wrenching incidents.

In all of her work, Taylor draws upon the well of history and the "cauldron of story." As a writer, she considers herself only a link in the storytelling chain, drawing from a long tradition that has enabled her to write of herself, but ultimately to write of others. Taylor's work rises above the personal to the universal, standing as a historical monument to how things used to be, and a contemporary reminder of how much work remains to be done in the eradication of racial discrimination.

In 1988 Taylor was honored by the Children's Book Council "for a body of work that has examined significant social issues and presented them in outstanding books for young readers." She is widely acknowledged as a talented voice whose groundbreaking contributions have greatly enriched the field of children's literature. Many critics consider *Roll of Thunder, Hear My Cry* already a classic work in the tradition of realistic fiction. Nearly all of her

books were reprinted in the late 1990s; an enduring testament to her consummate skill and popularity.

OTHER WORKS: *The Well: David's Story* (1995, 1999).

BIBLIOGRAPHY: *African-American Voices and Visions: Biographies of Some of our Most Prestigious Author and Illustrators* (1997). Crowe, C., *Presenting Mildred D. Taylor* (1999). Hohn, H., *Nevada Women Military Pilots of World War II* (1998). Ketter, J., *Responding to Roll of Thunder, Hear My Cry: A Reading/Writing Connection* (1991). McDougal L., ed., *Roll of Thunder, Hear My Cry and Related Readings* (1997). Pilgrim, I., *Roll of Thunder, Hear My Cry, Mildred D. Taylor: Notes* (1997). Rediger, P., *Great African Americans in Literature* (1996). *The Marble in the Water: Essays on Contemporary Writers of Fiction for Children and Young Adults* (1980). Vick, D., *Favorite Authors of Young Adult Fiction* (1995). Wood, M., *Twelve Multicultural Novels: Reading and Teaching Strategies* (1997).

Reference works: *Black Authors and Illustrators of Children's Books* (1988). *CA* (1980, 1989). *CANR* (1989). *CLC* (1982). *CLR* (1985). *DLB* (1986). *Oxford Companion to Women's Writing in the United States* (1995). *SATA* (1979, 1988). *TCCW* (1989).

Other references: *Booklist* (1 Dec. 1990). *Children's Literature Association Quarterly* (Summer 1988). *Horn Book* (Aug. 1977, Mar./Apr. 1989).

—CAROLYN SHUTE

TAYLOR, Phoebe Atwood

Born 18 May 1909, Boston, Massachusetts; died 8 January 1976, Boston, Massachusetts
Also wrote under: Alice Tilton
Daughter of John D. and Josephine Atwood Taylor; married Grantley W. Taylor

Phoebe Atwood Taylor's parents were both natives of Cape Cod; her father was a physician. Taylor graduated from Barnard College in 1930, published her first detective novel in 1931 and published up to three detective novels a year, every year afterwards for almost 20 years. She wrote between midnight and 3:00 a.m., "after housekeeping all day," usually "beginning three weeks before the deadline for the novel to be delivered to her New York publishers." (Her Leonidas Witherall novels include heartfelt depictions of the harried popular author, besieged by telegrams from his publisher, struggling to meet his deadlines.) Taylor married a prominent Boston surgeon of the same surname and lived in Newton Highlands and then in Weston, suburbs of Boston, always keeping a summer home at Wellfleet on Cape Cod. She died of a heart attack.

Taylor's first book, *The Cape Cod Mystery* (1931), features her most famous detective, Asa Alden (Asey) Mayo. A "man of all work" to the wealthy Porter family, he is a "fine and bleak"

Cape Cod native who chews tobacco and must be sixty but could be anything from thirty-five to seventy. Using what he calls "common sense," he extricates a Porter scion suspected by incompetent local officials of murdering a popular novelist and identifies the actual killer—the 300-lb. widow of a Boston minister who bashed the writer with an advance copy of his latest book, a sensational account of her husband's life.

By the last of the Cape Cod mysteries, *Diplomatic Corpse* (1951), the hero's character has evolved and, like many of his fellow series detectives, he has become a superman. "Tall, lean, salty Asey Mayo" has changed from chewing tobacco, as in the first two books, to smoking a pipe, and from being the Porters' handyman to being Chairman of the Board of Porter Motors. In intervening novels he has been revealed as a more and more expert marksman, knife-thrower, hand-to-hand fighter, driver, sailor, and cook.

The charm of the Cape Cod novels lies not only in Asey's role as the wryly humorous Yankee, but also in their settings. Taylor's eye for detail and lively sense of place combine with many glimpses of the daily life of the times, and now increase the historical interest and fun of her novels.

Leonidas Xenophon Witherall, hero of the mysteries Taylor wrote under the pen name of Alice Tilton, solves crimes taking place in a recognizable prewar and wartime Boston and its suburbs. He is a master, then headmaster and owner of Meredith's Academy, a private boys' school. His escapades are even crazier and more convoluted, if possible, than Asey Mayo's. *The Hollow Chest* (1941) concerns a samurai sword as murder weapon, an antique horse car, a Lady Baltimore cake, a papier-maché lion's head, and the manuscript of a treatise on the "11th-century vowel shift," and requires a massive suspension of disbelief.

Many of Taylor's works are notable for their brisk, even breathless, pace. Both detectives encounter problems and solve them within a day or two, and their chases—by car, on foot, by plane, by motorboat, or via antique horsecar—often make their adventures tests of physical stamina and agility as well as mental ability. This pace and Taylor's zany plots rife with eccentric characters and odd props often make her mysteries seem the literary equivalents of the classic screwball film comedies of the 1930s.

Taylor's mystery comedies also incorporate many elements of the classic detective story. Asey has a trio of Dr. Watsons and a Lestrade. Taylor includes one case of young love per story: the ingénue is never guilty, nor is the young man who falls in love with her. Like many British detective stories of the same era, Taylor's works are touched with xenophobia, racism, and anti-Semitism. Some of this narrowness is of the "Napoleon was a great man and a great general, but he was an off-Islander" variety and goes with Taylor's regional-comedy territory.

Taylor's mystery-farces will never appeal to those who want realism in their criminal fiction, but they have withstood the passage of time at least as well as those of her Golden Age sisters, Agatha Christie and Ngaio Marsh. Taylor's characters, settings, and historical interest still provide excellent entertainment, and explain why the novels have been reissued in the 1960s, in the 1980s, and again in the 1990s.

OTHER WORKS: *Death Lights a Candle* (1932). *The Mystery of the Cape Cod Players* (1933). *The Mystery of the Cape Cod Tavern* (1934). *Sandbar Sinister* (1934). *Deathblow Hill* (1935). *The Tinkling Symbol* (1935). *The Crimson Patch* (1936). *Out of Order* (1936). *Beginning with a Bash* (1937, reprinted 1972). *Figure Away* (1937). *Octagon House* (1937). *The Annulet of Gilt* (1938). *Banbury Bog* (1938). *The Cut Direct* (1938). *Cold Steal* (1939). *Spring Harrowing* (1939). *The Criminal C.O.D.* (1940). *The Deadly Sunshade* (1940). *The Left Leg* (1940). *The Perennial Boarder* (1941). *The Six Iron Spiders* (1942). *Three Plots for Asey Mayo* (1942). *File for Record* (1943). *Going, Going, Gone* (1943). *Dead Ernest* (1944). *Proof of the Pudding* (1945). *The Asey Mayo Trio* (1946). *Punch with Care* (1946). *The Iron Clew* (1947, in Britain as *The Iron Hand*).

Phoebe Atwood Taylor's manuscripts are collected in the Mugar Memorial Library of Boston University.

BIBLIOGRAPHY: Haycraft, H., *Murder for Pleasure* (1941). Klein, K. G., ed., *Great Women Mystery Writers: Classic to Contemporary* (1994). Waugh, C. R., ed., *Murder and Mystery in Boston* (1987).

Reference works: *A Catalogue of Crime* (1971). *Detecting Women* (1994). *Encyclopedia Mysteriosa* (1994). *Encyclopedia of Mystery and Detection* (1976). *St. James Guide to Crime & Mystery Writers* (1996). *TCA, TCAS. Twentieth-Century Crime and Mystery Writers* (1980).

Other references: *Barnard Alumnae Monthly* (Oct. 1932, March 1936). *NYT* (12 Jan. 1976). *WP* (17 Jan. 1976).

—SUSAN SUTTON SMITH

TAYLOR, Susie King

Born 6 August 1848, Isle of Wight, Georgia; **died** after 1902
Daughter of Hagar and Raymond Baker; **married** Edward King, 1862 (died 1866); Russell Taylor, 1879

Susie King Taylor was the first of nine children born to slaves on the Grest family plantation. When she was seven years old, her grandmother took her to Savannah. There Taylor learned to read and write at the home of a free black woman. She used her knowledge to make life more bearable for her grandmother and other urban slaves by forging passes for them to be out after the nine o'clock curfew.

While on a trip to St. Catherine's Island in 1862, Taylor and her family came within Union lines and asked for protection. She was then asked by the commander to take charge of a school for freedmen on St. Simon's Island. In August 1862 Captain C. T. Trowbridge came to St. Simon's to recruit freed slaves for a new regiment, the first U.S. Colored Troops, later the 33rd U.S. Colored Infantry. Taylor and her new husband enlisted. Technically, Taylor was enrolled as a laundress, but according to her reminiscences, her duties were far greater: she taught the soldiers to read and write, helped them clean their muskets and prepare ammunition, cooked the food, and nursed the wounded. She and King served with the occupation forces in Charleston, Augusta, and Savannah before being mustered out in February 1866.

Taylor's life after the war was a succession of hardships. King died in September 1866, leaving her broke and pregnant. She tried teaching, first in a school she and King had opened in Savannah; later she taught in a school in Liberty County and then in a night school for adult freedmen in Savannah. But Taylor's teaching career was less than successful and in the 1870s, she worked as a laundress, first in Georgia and later in Boston. In 1879 she married Russell Taylor, a free black man of Boston.

For the rest of her life, Taylor's major interest was the lot of veterans of the Union army, especially of its colored regiments. In 1886 she helped found the Boston Corps of the Women's Relief Corps, an auxiliary of the Grand Army of the Republic. She became its president in 1893 and compiled a survey of the Massachusetts veterans of the war.

Taylor's autobiography, *Reminiscences of My Life in Camp*, was published in 1902 with an introduction by her old friend and commander, Thomas Wentworth Higginson. It is a brief but fascinating look at the Civil War and Reconstruction from the perspective of a former slave. Taylor skips quickly over her life under slavery, a subject of much interest to and speculation by historians. Nevertheless, a sense of excitement—a feeling she and others were participants in a great experiment—comes through vividly. The reader can sense her fear of capture by Confederate soldiers and her joy at the reading of the Emancipation Proclamation. Taylor's pride in the loyalty and bravery of the colored troops, despite lack of pay and hazardous front-line duty to which blacks were routinely assigned, is also evident.

Reminiscences of My Life in Camp ends on a somber note. On a trip to Louisiana to visit her dying son, she was subjected to the indignities of segregation on trains, in hotels, and on the street. (Although segregation was still widely practiced in both North and South for many years after the war, Taylor found her adopted home of Massachusetts a paradise in comparison to the South.) Saddened and angered, she asked: "I wonder if our white fellow men realize the true sense or meaning of brotherhood? For 200 years we had toiled for them; the war of 1861 came and was ended, and we thought our race was forever free from bondage, and that the two races could live in unity with each other, but when we read almost every day of what is being done to my race by some whites in the South, I sometimes ask, 'Was the war in vain? Has it brought freedom, in the full sense of the word, or has it not made our condition more hopeless?'" The question is still pertinent today.

BIBLIOGRAPHY: Cornish, D. T., *The Sable Arm* (1956). Higginson, T. W., *Army Life in a Black Regiment* (1870). McPherson, J. M., ed., *The Negro's Civil War* (1965). Pierce, E., "The Freedmen at Port Royal," in *Atlantic Monthly* (Sept. 1863). Rose, W. L., *Rehearsal for Reconstruction: The Port Royal Experiment* (1964).

—JANET E. KAUFMAN

TEASDALE, Sara

Born 8 August 1884, St. Louis, Missouri; **died** 29 January 1933, New York, New York
Daughter of John W. and Mary Willard Teasdale; **married** Ernst B. Filsinger, 1914

The youngest of four children, Sara Teasdale was born into comfortable circumstances provided by her father, a prominent businessman, and her independently wealthy mother. Because of her nervous temperament, she was educated at home until she was nine. After attending Mary Institute (founded by T. S. Eliot's grandfather) for a year, she completed her education at Hosmer Hall, a school designed to prepare young women for college. She was already writing poetry, and she received much encouragement from her teachers; she also read Heine and Sappho, who, along with Christina Rossetti, were the greatest influences on her own work.

Following graduation in 1902, Teasdale, together with several of her friends, published a manuscript magazine, the *Potter's Wheel*, in which many of her early poems appeared. Her first professional publication came in May, 1907, when her dramatic monologue "Guenevere" appeared in *Reedy's Mirror*. The poem attracted much attention, as did *Sonnets to Duse, and Other Poems* published that same autumn, though the book was not a financial success.

Teasdale literally sacrificed herself to poetry, and therein lay her tragedy. Frail and high-strung, she lived perforce a disciplined life which brought both unhappiness and loneliness, for she was innately an outgoing person, capable of great emotional depth. Her line, "O, beauty, are you not enough? Why am I crying after love?" reveals her constant ambivalence. She experienced two major romantic involvements, one with the poet Vachel Lindsay, and the other with Ernst Filsinger, a St. Louis businessman whom she married in December 1914. But the demands of poetry brought about a gradual estrangement, and the marriage was dissolved in 1929 by Teasdale's decision. After courageously enduring four years of rapidly deteriorating health and acute depression, exacerbated by the fear that she might become a helpless invalid, she took an overdose of barbiturates and died in 1933.

At first glance, Teasdale's poetry appears to be simple, but its simplicity is deceptive. Although it does not lend itself to involved critical exegesis, its highly connotative language can imply deeply felt emotion which evokes an equal response. Teasdale treads a fine line between revelation and reticence. *Sonnets to Duse* and

Helen of Troy, and Other Poems (1911) reveal her experimentation to find her own poetic voice, and successive volumes demonstrate her constant striving to speak from her own experience, honestly and without sentimentality. Her constant theme is love, its joys, and, as her own life grew more difficult, its tragedies. The source of her imagery is invariably nature, which serves equally well for moments of exaltation—"I am the pool of gold/ Where sunset burns and dies/ You are my deepening skies,/Give me your stars to hold,"—or, as in her posthumous volume *Strange Victory* (1933), for moments of deepest pain: "Nothing but darkness enters this room,/ Nothing but darkness and the winter night,/ Yet on this bed once years ago a light/Silvered the sheets with an unearthly bloom;/ It was the planet Venus in the west/ Casting a square of brightness on this bed,/ And in that light your dark and lovely head/ Lay for a while and seemed to be at rest." Here the controlled objectivity of the language deepens the sense of anguish and desolation; the words must be read for implication and nuance, as well as for obvious meaning. In Teasdale's poetry, every word is important.

Though deprecated by critics of the post-*Wasteland* generation, Teasdale continues to be read and admired. One reason for her popularity doubtless derives from her ability to write about bitter experience without bitterness, and to laugh wisely, especially at herself. But even more important is a sense of that inner courage and integrity, which compelled her to write in her own way, uninfluenced by the work of her contemporaries: "Let the dead know, but not the living see—/ The dead who loved me will not suffer, knowing/ It is all one, the coming or the going—/ If I have kept the last essential me./ If that is safe, then I am safe indeed. . . ." She recognized her way inevitably incurred suffering. Even at her moments of deepest despair, however, Teasdale exercises a control born of a conscious choice, and the ultimate effect of her poetry is one of confident affirmation: "If this be the last time/ The melody flies upward/ With its rush of sparks in flight,/ Let me go up with it in fire and laughter. . . ."

OTHER WORKS: *Rivers to the Sea* (1915). *The Answering Voice: Love Lyrics by Women* (edited by Teasdale, 1917). *Love Songs* (1917). *Flame and Shadow* (1920). *Rainbow Gold* (edited by Teasdale, 1922). *Dark of the Moon* (1926). *Stars To-Night* (1930). *Collected Poems of Sara Teasdale* (1937, 1996). *Mirror of the Heart: Poems of Sara Teasdale* (1984).

BIBLIOGRAPHY: Brenner, R., *Poets of Our Time* (1946). Carpenter, M. H., *Sara Teasdale: A Biography* (1960). Drake, W., *Sara Teasdale: Women and Poet* (1979). Dubois, J., *The Same Sweet Yellow* (1994). Howe, F., *No More Masks! An Anthology of Twentieth-Century American Women Poets, Newly Revised and Expanded* (1993). Lester, D., ed., *I Lay Me Down: Suicide in the Elderly* (1994). Lupack, A., *Modern Arthurian Literature: An Anthology of English and American Arthuriana from the Renaissance to the Present* (1992). Maser, F. E., *Sara Teasdale: A Returning Comet: An Essay* (1993). Moore, M., *Nevertheless* (1983). Ruihley, G. R., ed., *An Anthology of Great U.S. Women Poets, 1850-1990: Temples and Palaces* (1997). Schoen, C. B., *Sara Teasdale* (1986). Sprague, R., *Imaginary Gardens: A Study of Five American Poets* (1969). Untermeyer, L., *The New Era in American Poetry* (1919). Walker, C., *Masks Outrageous and Austere: Culture, Psyche, and Persona in Modern Women Poets* (1991). Woodard, D., *This More Fragile Boundary: The Female Subject and the Romance Plot in the Texts of Millay, Wylie, Teasdale, Bogan* (dissertation, 1993).

Reference works: *Oxford Companion to Women's Writing in the United States* (1995).

Other references: *Turn-of-the-Century Women* (Summer/ Winter 1990).

—ROSEMARY SPRAGUE

TENNEY, Tabitha (Gilman)

Born 7 April 1762, Exeter, New Hampshire; **died** 2 May 1837, Exeter, New Hampshire
Daughter of Samuel and Lydia G. Gilman; **married** Samuel Tenney, 1788 (died 1816)

Tabitha Tenney was descended from early pioneers in New Hampshire who had raised themselves to prominent social positions in the town of Exeter. She was the oldest of the seven children, and probably remained at home with her mother to help raise her younger siblings after the death of her father. Tenney was somewhat older than was typical for her time and social class when she married; the couple had no children. Her husband, who served as a physician in the Revolutionary army, later directed his attention chiefly to politics and scientific inquiry.

Although Tenney was described as an "accomplished lady," it is unlikely her formal schooling differed greatly from that of other respectable 18th-century American women, or from that form of "female education" which she satirizes in her novel, *Female Quixotism: Exhibited in the Romantic Opinions and Extravagant Adventures of Dorcasina Sheldon* (1801). Her education, like Dorcasina's, would have provided her with a command of the fine points of fashion and household management, some acquaintance with the classics, and a fuller knowledge of contemporary novels. While married, Tenney produced two books which largely derived from her reading. After her husband's death in 1816, she spent the remainder of her life concentrating on her needlework, which was renowned for its intricacy.

Tenney's first publication was *The Pleasing Instructor* (1799), an anthology of classical literature addressed to young women. It was intended to "inform the mind, correct the manners, or to regulate the conduct" while at the same time blending, in best classical fashion, "instruction with rational amusement." Tenney dedicated *Female Quixotism* ''to all Columbian Young Ladies, who Read Novels and Romances.'' But unlike most novels so dedicated, Tenney's book satirizes both sentimentality and sentimental fiction in general. *Female Quixotism* is roughly modeled on Charlotte Ramsay Lennox's *The Female Quixote; or, The Adventures of Arabella* (1752), but Tenney alters the pattern of her model to emphasize a different message. In the earlier book, the main character is basically innocent but is corrupted by the ideals of the sentimental fiction she reads. Tenney, however, portrays a character who rationalizes her foolishness by blaming it on the novels she has read.

This change gives *Female Quixotism* an effective focus. Dorcasina, who is an adolescent when we first see her, remains frozen in the kind of prolonged adolescence that sentimental fiction requires. She is intelligent, occasionally witty, but entirely blind to the increasing disparity between her own life and the sentimental life she envisions for herself. Dorcasina early rejects a sensible suitor, Lysander, because his letter proposing marriage fails to use words like ''angel'' or ''goddess.'' Ironically, Lysander is as close as Dorcasina ever comes to making the sentimental match she aspires to.

Over the years, Dorcasina is duped by and deceives herself about men who seek to humiliate her or gain her fortune. Finally, the malicious ridicule of Seymour, a most despicable character who intends to marry the toothless, white-haired Dorcasina and then have her committed to a mental institution so he can enjoy her fortune unhindered by her company, leads Dorcasina to recognize the folly of her life and warn her young readers ''to avoid the rock on which I have been wrecked.''

The novel is a satire, but it is written with a sensitivity to its main character seldom encountered in satire. As silly as Dorcasina's version of reality is, it is in many ways preferable to the world she faces. Most of the men she meets are singularly cruel, spiteful, misogynistic creatures, and, on this level, Tenney's novel covertly warns women that they must be particularly cautious in a world where they have little place and little power. Tenney's satire is also effectively double-edged in another sense. While she criticizes the women who get their education from fiction, she equally criticizes a social system that denies women any real education.

F. L. Pattee once described *Female Quixotism* as the most popular novel written in America before *Uncle Tom's Cabin*. This is not the case, but Tenney's novel did run through at least six separate editions between the time of its publication and 1841. No current edition, however, of the novel is available. Ironically, *Female Quixotism* fell into obscurity by the middle of the last century, while novels it satirized, such as Susanna Rowson's *Charlotte Temple* (1791), continued to be popular into our own century, and even now are available in modern editions.

BIBLIOGRAPHY: Bell, C. H., *History of the Town of Exeter* (1888). Brown H. R., *The Sentimental Novel in America, 1789-1860* (1940). Davidson, C. N., *Revolution and the Word: The Rise of the Novel in America* (1986). Gilman, A., *The Gilman Family* (1869). Hoople, S. C. *Tabitha Tenney:* Female Quixotism (dissertation, 1985). Loshe, L. D., *The Early American Novel, 1789-1830* (1907). Petter, H., *The Early American Novel* (1971). Tenney, M. J., *The Tenney Family; or, The Descendants of Thomas Tenney of Rowley, Massachusetts, 1638-1890* (1891).

Reference works: *CAL* (1965). *NAW* (1971). *Oxford Companion to Women's Writing in the United States* (1995).

—CATHY N. DAVIDSON

TEPPER, Sheri S(tewart)

Born Shirley Stewart Douglas, 16 July 1929 in Colorado
Wrote under A. J. Orde, B. J. Oliphant, E. E. Horlak, Sheri S. Eberhart
Married Gene Tepper; **children:** one son, one daughter

Sheri Tepper was born in Colorado. She sold poetry and children's stories as Sheri S. Eberhart while working for the relief agency CARE, then in 1962 launched a 24-year career in the Rocky Mountain Planned Parenthood, becoming executive director and writing pamphlets on topics such as sex instruction for children and self-assertiveness for young women. She married Gene Tepper in the late 1960s.

Her first fictional works were *King's Blood Four* (1983), *Necromancer Nine* (1983), and *Wizard's Eleven* (1984), later collected as *The True Game* (1996). These are narrated by Peter, who grows up on another planet ruled by Game-players, who wield supernatural powers such as shape-shifting and teleportation. The Gamelords carelessly throw away their Gamesmen and ''pawns''— unTalented farmers, traders and craftsmen—in bloody feuds.

Peter, who seems to have no Talents, learns otherwise when he discovers special figurines, representing the Eleven forebears of the Gamesmen, which lend him their powers. Peter is forced to join the Game, and his adventure-filled quest to defeat tyranny leads him to discover the historic colonization of the planet and the reasons behind the terrible Game. The tripartite bildungsroman concludes with a revelation of Peter's identity and his own, unforeseen Talent. This trilogy is continued in the Mavin Manyshaped series and the Jinian series, collected as *The End of the Game*(1986).

The True Game books exemplify the plot format Tepper uses in most of her works: young protagonists dwelling on an old planet become aware of the mysteries of their world and discover their strengths as they fight those who delight in destruction and enslavement. Through their journeys they learn of the foolish ambitions that led to the planet's colonization, realize the deceptions and self-deceptions upon which their government is based, ally themselves with the natives, and create a balance in which human and alien can live harmoniously. In each case, revelation opens up to greater and greater revelations, considered delightful by some reviewers and implausible by others; novels like *Grass* (1989) and *The Family Tree* (1997) are particularly famous for their wondrous plot surprises.

Tepper is a didactic writer. These early books attack the evils of despoliation and coercion, arguing that humans must learn self-restraint in politics and religion, the thoughtless destruction of dimly understood ecologies and population control. Her villains are two-dimensional, as though Tepper considers tyrants merely stupid rather than criminal masterminds. Though preachy, she provides nonstop thrills and stunningly imagined landscapes that make her books compulsively readable.

Tepper's feminist polemical streak turned bitingly satiric in *The Gate to Women's Country* (1988), an important novel that sparked a continuing controversy between male and female readers. Feminists loved the book; men found it disturbing. Stavia grows up in a postapocalyptic society in which women govern all aspects of culture except, seemingly, the military, which men maintain in closed garrisons. Adolescent males must choose to join the garrisons or enter the walled Women's Country, where they are educated and become "servitors." Most choose the former, though over the centuries more men seek the gentler way of life. Foolishly running away, Stavia learns the "true nature" of men in the wilderness. She is raped, then confined and tortured in a settlement made up of the worst aspects of Mormonism and Islam. Returning to Women's Country, she learns the ruling clique of women has been selectively breeding men for feminine traits such as cooperation and caring.

Many readers consider Tepper's finest novel to be *Grass* (1989), a *New York Times* Notable Book and Hugo awards nominee. Marjorie Westriding Yrarier is sent as ambassador to Grass, the one planet immune to a plague devastating other worlds. There she learns of the bizarre relationship between the local human nobility and the native creatures and discovers the truth that will lead to a cure for the pandemic. "*Grass* is about man's relationship to God" and "what religion does to man: environmentalists don't worship the same god as those who are out to destroy the world. Western religions are all about getting even," Tepper said in a 1989 interview. Marjorie also appears in *Raising the Stones* (1990), which considers "what would we do if we had a god that actually gave us peace?," and *Sideshow* (1992), a blistering attack upon the complacent relativism that condones atrocities perpetrated in the name of freedom of religion.

Tepper became increasingly didactic on the issues of ecology and women's rights. *Beauty* (1991) interweaves and revises the tales of Sleeping Beauty, Cinderella, and Snow White. *A Plague of Angels* (1993) shows that female dictators can be evil too, as a witch prepares an army of androids to kill or subjugate everyone in a far-future America. The protagonists ally with talking animals and mythological monsters to overthrow her and reforest the wastelands. In *Plague* and *Shadow's End* (1994), alien superbeings

sit in judgement upon humanity and take extreme measures to end oppression and order men not to ruin and discard one planet after another. *Gibbon's Decline and Fall* (1996), a near-future tale set in the U.S., rages against antiabortionists.

The Family Tree (1997) and *Six Moon Dance* (1998) continue these polemics, but in a more lighthearted vein. *Six Moon Dance* again considers allowing women to control breeding. Both novels argue that humans are not superior beings, but part of a beautiful biosphere. Tepper feels we must learn to treasure our planet in its majestic variety.

Tepper has also written mysteries under the pseudonyms A. J. Orde and B. J. Oliphant, and a few horror novels under her own name and as E. E. Horlak. Her canon is widely praised for its overall high quality and boldness in tackling controversial themes, chiefly her celebration of biodiversity and transformations of all types; her demand for equality and symbiosis not only among humans but between humans and their environment; and her promise that the antagonistic relationships between men and women can evolve into something precious and life-affirming.

OTHER WORKS: *The People Know* (1968). *The Perils of Puberty* (1974). *The Problem with Puberty* (1976). *This Is You* (1977). *So Your Happily Ever After Isn't* (1977). *So You Don't Want To Be a Sex Object* (1978). *The Revenants* (1984). *The True Game* (1985). *Marianne, the Magus, and the Manticore* (1985). *The Song of Mavin Manyshaped* (1985). *The Flight of Mavin Manyshaped* (1985). *The Search of Mavin Manyshaped* (1985). *Jinian Footseer* (1985). *Blood Heritage* (1986). *Dervish Daughter* (1986). *The Bones* (1987). *Northshore* (1987). *Southshore* (1987). *The Awakeners* (1987). *After Long Silence* (1987, as *The Enigma Score*,1989). *Marianne, the Madame, and the Momentary Gods* (1988). *Marianne, the Matchbox, and the Malachite Mouse* (1989). *Still Life* (1989). *The Marianne Trilogy* (1990). *Singer From the Sea* (1999).

As A. J. Orde: *A Little Neighborhood Murder* (1989). *Death and the Dogwalker* (1990). *Death for Old Times' Sake* (1992). *Looking for the Aardvark* (1993, retitled *Dead on Sunday*, 1993). *A Long Time Dead* (1995). *A Death of Innocents* (1997).

As B. J. Oliphant: *A Ceremonial Death* (1985). *Dead in the Scrub* (1990). *The Unexpected Corpse* (1990). *Death and the Delinquent* (1992). *Deservedly Dead* (1992). *Death Served Up Cold* (1994). *Here's to the Newly Dead* (1997).

As E. E. Horlak: *Still Life* (1989).

BIBLIOGRAPHY: Bogstad, J., "Gender, Power and Reversal in Contemporary Anglo-American and French Feminist Science Fiction" (thesis, 1992). Canty, J. F., "Does Eugenics = (E)Utopia? Reproductive Control and Ethical Issues in Contemporary North American Feminist Fabulation" (thesis, 1995). Carroll, L., "Mythological Backgrounds in Sheri S. Tepper's Fiction" (thesis, 1996). Harris, D. L., "Acts of Genesis: A Feminist Look at the Changing Face of the Mother in Selected Works of Science

Fiction by Women'' (thesis, 1997). Jesser, N. S., ''Troubling Worlds: The Transformation and Persistence of Violence in Contemporary Feminist Utopian Narratives'' (thesis, 1998). Zaman, Sobia, ''The Feminist Appropriation of Dystopia: A Study of Atwood, Elgin, Fairbairns, and Tepper'' (thesis, 1995).

Reference works: *Encyclopedia of Fantasy* (1997). *Magill's Guide to Science Fiction and Fantasy Literature* (1996). *St. James Guide to Fantasy Writers* (1995).

Other references: *Denver Post* (15 Oct. 1989, 30 July 1990, 3 Dec. 1995) *Journal of the Fantastic in the Arts* 7 (1996). *Locus* 41 (Sept. 1998). *New York Review of Science Fiction* 8 (July 1996). *Science-Fiction Studies* 19 (1992).

—FIONA KELLEGHAN

TERHUNE, Mary (Virginia) Hawes

Born 21 December 1830, Dennisville, Virginia; **died** 3 June 1922, New York, New York
Wrote under: Marion Harland
Daughter of Samuel P. and Judith Smith Hawes; **married** Edward P. Terhune, 1856; **children:** six, three of whom died in childhood

Mary Hawes Terhune was tutored at home and began contributing regularly to Richmond papers at fourteen. She wrote a version of her first published novel at sixteen and had published two very successful novels when she married a Presbyterian minister at twenty-six. She continued to write while she successively moved with her husband to Newark, New Jersey; Springfield, Massachusetts; and Brooklyn, New York. He assisted her in her work, providing ''the first reading and only revision of her manuscripts, before they are given into the hands of the printer.'' She bore six children, three of whom survived childhood. Daughters Christine Terhune Herrick and Virginia Terhune Van de Water followed their mother as writers on domestic matters, and son Albert Payson Terhune became ''the collie's Balzac,'' an enormously popular author of dog stories.

Alone (1854), the first of Terhune's many novels and her most popular, follows the trials of Ida Ross, who must live ''alone'' at fifteen after the death of her widowed mother, ''a being more than human—scarcely less than divine.'' The first scene of the book depicts Ida throwing herself upon her mother's coffin as it is lowered into the grave. She must leave her plantation home and live in Richmond with a cynical, worldly guardian who has raised his daughter to be as coldhearted as himself. For a time, under their influence, Ida becomes almost misanthropic, but she blossoms again when she meets the loving and merry Dana family. She finds and loses and finds again her true love, the Reverend Morton Lacy, and they are happily married at the novel's end. *Alone* depicts life in Richmond and a prewar plantation—slaves are all happy, devoted family ''servants.'' In a closing scene Ida strikes the book's keynote: ''A woman is so lonely without a home and friends! They are to us—I do not say to you [men]—necessaries of life.''

Many of Terhune's 25 novels and three collections of short stories have the same antebellum Southern background and sentimental message: women can and should be educated and able to support themselves, but their truest position is dependence and their proper sphere the home. Her most famous book on household affairs, *Common Sense in the Household: A Manual of Practical Housewifery* (1871), became a bestseller and was translated into French, German, and Arabic. She advocates learning by doing, attention to the presentation of food and a varied menu, and she deprecates the ''vulgar prejudice against labor-saving machines.'' Here, the housewife can consult a 13-page essay on how to handle her servants; she can find out how to clean and cook a catfish or restore luster and crispness to black alpaca and bombazine. The style is informal, the advice practical.

Terhune's books of advice are by no means confined to the culinary and domestic. *Eve's Daughters; or, Common Sense for Maid, Wife, and Mother* (1892) covers all facets of the growing girl's physical, mental, and moral health, including the way in which a mother should educate her daughter about sex: ''Get some good familiar treatise upon Botany,—I know of none better than Gray's 'How Plants Grow,'—and read with her of the beautiful laws of fructification and reproduction.''

Eve's Daughters also counsels women through marriage and motherhood to menopause—the ''climacteric''—and a postmenopausal ''Indian Summer.'' In the chapter ''Shall Baby Be?'' Terhune voices her convictions on the sin of childlessness; she believed American mothers had a duty to bear ''troops'' of boys and girls to withstand the invasion of ''massed filth''—''Irish cottiers and German boors, and loose and criminal fugitives from everywhere.''

Terhune's ideas on women's roles seem as dated today as her methods for healing cuts, but her cookbooks and domestic advice profoundly influenced Americans for half a century.

OTHER WORKS: *The Hidden Path* (1855). *Nemesis* (1860). *Miriam* (1862). *Husks* (1863). *Moss-Side: Husbands and Homes* (1865). *Colonel Floyd's Wards* (1866). *Sunnybank* (1866). *The Christmas Holly* (1867). *Phemie's Temptation* (1869). *Ruby's Husband* (1869). *At Last* (1870). *The Empty Heart: ''For Better, for Worse''* (1871). *True as Steel* (1872). *Jessamine* (1873). *From My Youth Up* (1874). *Breakfast, Luncheon, and Tea* (1875). *My Little Love* (1876). *The Dinner Year-Book* (1878). *Loiterings in Pleasant Paths* (1880). *Our Daughters: What Shall We Do with Them?* (1880). *Handicapped* (1881). *The Cottage Kitchen* (1883). *Judith: A Chronicle of Old Virginia* (1883). *Cookery for Beginners* (1884). *Common Sense in the Nursery* (1885). *Country Living for City People* (1887). *Not Pretty, but Precious* (1887). *Our Baby's First and Second Years* (1887). *A Gallant Fight* (1888). *House and Home* (1889). *Stepping-Stones* (with V. F. Townsend and L. C. Moulton, 1890). *With the Best Intentions* (1890). *His Great Self* (1892). *The Story of Mary Washington* (1892). *Mr. Wayt's Wife's Sister* (1894). *The Premium Cook Book* (1894). *The Royal Road* (1894). *Home of the Bible* (1895). *Talks Upon Practical Subjects* (1895). *Under the Flag of the Orient* (1895). *The Art of Cooking by Gas* (1896). *The National Cook*

Book (with C. T. Herrick, 1896). *The Secret of a Happy Home* (1896). *An Old-Field School-Girl* (1897). *Ruth Bergen's Limitations* (1897). *Some Colonial Homesteads and Their Stories* (1897). *The Comfort of Cooking and Heating by Gas* (1898). *Where Ghosts Walk* (1898). *Charlotte Brontë at Home* (1899). *Cooking Hints* (1899). *Home Topics* (1899). *More Colonial Homesteads and Their Stories* (1899). *William Cowper* (1899). *Dr. Dale* (with A. P. Terhune, 1900). *Hannah More* (1900). *John Knox* (1900). *In Our County: Stories of Old Virginia Life* (1901). *Marion Harland's Complete Cook Book* (1903). *Everyday Etiquette* (with V. Van de Water, 1905). *When Grandmamma Was Fourteen* (1905). *The Distractions of Martha* (1906). *Marion Harland's Cook Book of Tried and Tested Recipes* (1907). *The Housekeeper's Week* (1908). *Ideal Home Life* (with M. E. Sangster et al., 1910). *Marion Harland's Autobiography* (1910). *The Story of Canning and Recipes* (1910). *Home Making* (1911). *The Helping Hand Cook Book* (1912). *Should Protestant Ministers Marry?* (1913). *Looking Westward* (1914). *A Long Lane* (1915). *The Carringtons of High Hill* (1919). *Two Ways of Keeping a Wife* (n.d.).

BIBLIOGRAPHY: Baym, N., *Woman's Fiction: A Guide to Novels by and about Women in America, 1820-1870* (1978). Griswold, W. M., *A Descriptive List of Novels and Tales, Dealing with the History of North America* (1895). Halsey, F. W., *Women Authors of Our Day in Their Homes* (1903). Pattee, F. L., *The Feminine Fifties* (1940).

Reference works: AA. *The Living Female Writers of the South* (1872). *The Living Writers of the South* (1869). NAW (1971). *Oxford Companion to Women's Writing in the United States* (1995). *Southland Writers* (1870). *Women of the South Distinguished in Literature* (1861).

Other references: *Harper's* (Nov. 1882). *NYT* (4 June 1922).

—SUSAN SUTTON SMITH

TERRY, Megan

Born 22 July 1932, Seattle, Washington
Daughter of Harold Joseph Duffy, Jr., and Marguerite Cecelia Henry Duffy

Formerly adjunct professor of theater at the University of Nebraska, Omaha, and later playwright-in-residence at the Omaha Magic Theater (OMT), Megan Terry is also a founding member of the New York Theatre Strategy and the Women's Theatre Council; she was one of the playwrights-in-residence of the Open Theatre (1963-68) with Joseph Chaiken, Jean-Claude van Itallie, and others. In 1973 Terry won the *Village Voice* Obie award for best off-Broadway play for *Approaching Simone*.

Two concerns of the Open Theatre have characterized much of Terry's work and her approach: ensemble creation and performance and the presentation of abstraction and illusion to clarify complex human attitudes. The "transformation" which marks so much of her work involves, first, characters, place, time, and action changing unpredictably and, second, different actors replacing each other as characters. These are present also in the "musicals" which Terry has composed for OMT (a regional company which presents only new "musicals"), her new works, and the workshops she conducts.

Terry's best-known play, *Viet Rock: A Folk War Movie* (1967), was developed in the playwright's workshop for the Open Theatre. Parodying and satirizing attitudes toward war, *Viet Rock* is less an anti-American political statement than a universal condemnation of the wastefulness, hypocrisy, and senselessness of war. The transformations of scenes, characters, and actors guarantee that each production will be individuated by its cast and circumstances. In Brechtean fashion the slogans and clichés, songs and battles can be revised or updated, but the theme of war's destructiveness remains. The mythic conclusion, when the Viet Cong kill and devour a G.I. and a native woman, intensifies the audience's repugnance and reveals the universal character of the military as one soldier ingests another—transforming another's flesh into his own. Terry's earlier theatrical transformations had made soldiers into senators or witnesses, sweethearts into soldiers, or actors into babies and mamas.

Approaching Simone (1970) has received the best reviews of all Terry's plays. It presents a totally self-aware hero, Simone Weil, in her struggle to gain complete truth. In the two most strikingly dramatic scenes ("Simone at Fourteen—When and Why She Wants to Kill Herself" and "The Visitation") the physical pain of migraine headaches and battle wounds is symbolic of the lacerating agonies she endures. At fourteen, Simone is challenged by the chorus with her inadequacies: gender, ignorance, awkwardness, arrogance. Urged to kill herself, she slowly is drawn back to the will to live, to "know truth." During the "visitation," Simone focuses on the metaphysical poet George Herbert's "Love" as her pain is assumed by the physically and emotionally supportive ensemble. Believing love is the disintegration of the self, and truth is to be found in love, Simone is Terry's heroic woman, an individual not described or circumscribed by sexual conflicts. Terry writes of Simone as a model for other women to "know that a woman can make it and think clearly in a womanly way."

Terry is a somewhat iconoclastic combination, an experimental dramatist who advocates entrepreneurial management and espouses the "pioneer values" of hard work and self-sufficiency. A designer early in her career, she still thinks of her work as "a kind of architectural process in which she 'builds' plays," and not only as a metaphor. She believes theater is a hands-on-business, and that one must be willing to build sets, create audiences, and manage finances, as well as conceive of "theater."

Called "The Mother of American Feminist Drama" by Helene Keyssar, Terry writes plays characterized by rapid transformation of character and situation, by a great deal of physical action, and by a deep political commitment. The body of her work has continued to grow, as has the range of her styles. Critic David Savran has said her plays constitute "a virtual compendium of the styles of modern drama, ranging from collaborative ensemble work to performance art to naturalism."

Terry is a feminist whose critique of society is less "ideological" than it is grounded in humanist values and in a deep commitment to community. In her work she explores such issues as "production and reproduction, the language of patriarchy, gender roles. . .the victimization and heroism. . .and the pain and power of women," according to Keyssar and Jan Breslauer. Directing her critiques less at systems than "as protests against individual circumstances, institutional corruption, or verbal and conceptual distortions," her feminism, Keyssar says, is "a precise criticism of gender roles, an affirmation of women's strength, and a challenge for women to use their own power." Terry puts these principles into practice in her own professional life, encouraging other women playwrights, collecting and distributing bibliographies, and building networks as she crosses the country.

One of her own best expositors, she says of the legacy of the Open Theatre in New York, "I feel we democratized the theater." She also feels she contributed to the form of American musicals by proving "that rock music worked on the stage" and by "speed[ing] up exposition." Of her work now, she says the playwright's responsibility is "to critique [her] society," and she wishes to convey through her plays "that life is possible."

OTHER WORKS: *Calm Down Mother* (1966). *Ex-Miss Copper Queen on a Set of Pills* (1966). *Keep Tightly Closed in a Cool Dry Place* (1966). *Comings and Goings* (1967). *The Gloaming, Oh My Darling* (1967). *Home* (1968). *The Magic Realists* (1969). *Fireworks* (1970). *The People vs. Ranchman* (1970). *One More Little Drinkie* (1971). *The Tommy Allen Show* (1971). *Massachusetts Trust* (1972). *Megan Terry's Home; or, Future Soap* (1972). *Sanibel and Captive* (1972). *American Wedding Ritual* (1973). *Couplings and Grouplings* (1973). *Hothouse* (1975). *Nightwalk* (with S. Sheppard and J. C. van Itallie, 1975). *The Pioneer* (1975). *Pro Game* (1975). *Women and the Law* (1976). *Willa-Willie Bill's Dope Garden* (1977). *American King's English for Queens* (1978). *Babe in the Bighouse* (1978). *100,001 Horror Stories of the Plains* (1978). *Attempted Rescue on Avenue B* (1979). *Brazil Fado* (1979). *Goona-Goona* (1980). *Scenes from Maps* (1980). *Comings and Goings* (1980). *Fireworks* (1980). *The Gloaming, Oh My Darling* (1980). *The Trees Blew Down* (1980). *Flat in Afghanistan* (1981). *Katmandu* (1981). *Molly Bailey's Traveling Circus Featuring Scenes from the Life of Mother Jones* (1983). *Fifteen Million Fifteen-Year-Olds* (1983). *The Pioneer* (1984). *Pro Game* (1984). *Retro* (1985). *Kegger* (1985). *Objective Love* (1985). *Sea of Forms* (with J. A. Schmidman, 1986). *Sleazing Towards Athens* (1986). *Amtrak* (1988). *Dinner's in the Blender* (1988). *Headlights* (1989). *Snow Queen* (for children, 1990). *Walking Through Walls* (1991). *Sound Fields* (with J. A. Schmidman and S. Kimberlaine, 1991). *India Plays* (1992). *Right Brain Vacation Photos: New Plays and Production Photographs, 1972-1992* (edited with others, 1992). *Belches on Couches* (with J. A Schmidman and S. Kimberlaine, 1993). *Remote Control* (1994). *Body Leaks* (1994). *Star Path Moon Stop* (1996). *Fireworks* (1996).

BIBLIOGRAPHY: Barron, E. A., *A Structural Analysis of Representative Plays of Megan Terry* (dissertation, 1984). Benzel, K. N. and L. P. de la Vars, eds., *Images of the Self as Female: The Achievement of Women Artists in Re-envisioning Feminine Identity* (1992). Betsko, K. and R. Koenig, eds., *Interviews with Contemporary Women Playwrights* (1987). Chinoy, H. K. and L W. Jenkins, *Women in American Theatre* (1981). Cohn, S. B., ed., *Comic Relief: Humor in Contemporary American Literature* (1977). Hart, L., ed., *Making a Spectacle: Feminist Essays on Contemporary Women's Theatre* (1989). Keyssar, H. *Feminist Theatre* (1985). Kolin, P. C., ed., *American Playwrights Since 1945* (1989). Kolin, P. C. and C. Kullman, eds., *Speaking on Stage: Interviews with Contemporary American Playwrights* (1996). Larson, J. *Public Dreams: A Critical Investigation of the Plays of Megan Terry, 1955-1986* (dissertation, 1989). Marranca, B. and G. Dasgupta, eds., *American Playwrights: A Critical Survey* (1981). Savran, D., *In Their Own Words* (1988). Schlueter, J., ed., *Modern American Drama: The Female Canon* (1990). Senelac, L., ed., *Gender in Performance* (1992). Wagner, P. J., *Megan Terry: Political Playwright* (dissertation, 1980). Winner, C. A., *A Study of American Dramatic Productions Dealing with the War in Vietnam* (dissertation, 1977).

Reference works: *CA* (1979). *CD* (1973, 1977, 1982, 1988). *CLC* (1981). *Contemporary Theater, Film, and Television* (1988). *DLB* (1981). *FC* (1990). *Notable Women in American Theater* (1976). *Oxford Companion to Women's Writing in the United States* (1995). *Prize-Winning Drama: A Bibliographic and Descriptive Guide* (1973). *TCAD* (1981).

Other references: *Art and Cinema* (1987). *Centennial Review* (Summer 1988). *Interview with Megan Terry* (audiocassette, 1981). *Megan Terry* (audiocassette, 1984). *Mississippi Folklore Register* (Spring-Fall 1988). *Modern Drama* (Dec. 1984). *Notes on Contemporary Literature* (March 1990). *Performing Arts Journal* (1983). *Studies in American Drama* (1987, 1989). *University of Mississippi Studies in English* (1992).

—KATHLEEN GREGORY KLEIN,
UPDATED BY MARCIA HEPPS AND NELSON RHODES

THANE, Elswyth

Born 16 May 1900, Burlington, Iowa; died July 1984
Married William Beebe, 1927

The wife of naturalist and writer William Beebe, Elswyth Thane made her permanent home on a farm in Vermont. As an author, however, she is most closely associated with Virginia and with England, where from 1928 to 1939 she worked each summer in the British Museum. A prolific writer, she produced works of fiction, historical and biographical studies, autobiographical books, plays, and several books for children.

Thane identified herself as a historian and scholar. Although her historical and biographical works lack the elaborate apparatus of academic studies and employ novelistic devices, and although they sometimes have been criticized for blending fact and fiction, they rely heavily on primary source material. *The Tudor Wench* (1932; on Elizabeth I) and *Young Mr. Disraeli* (1936), written near the beginning of Thane's career, study the early lives of their subjects. Thane also dramatized episodes from each, under the same titles. Later she concentrated on Virginia history, particularly the Revolutionary period, examining Martha Washington in *Washington's Lady* (1960) and George Washington in *Potomac Square* (1963), and the children they reared in *Mount Vernon Family* (1968), a book for children. In addition, *Mount Vernon Is Ours* (1966) and *Mount Vernon, the Legacy* (1967) relate the history of their home's preservation as a national shrine.

Thane's best fiction grew from her historical interests. Most ambitious is the series of Williamsburg novels, which epitomize American history from the Revolutionary War until World War II through the experiences of two Williamsburg families and their English relatives. The seven novels are *Dawn's Early Light* (1943; the Revolution), *Yankee Stranger* (1944; the Civil War), *Ever After* (1945; the Spanish-American War), *The Light Heart* (1947; World War I), *Kissing Kin* (1948; the end of World War I to Hitler's coming to power), *This Was Tomorrow* (1951; the Nazis and the prelude to World War II), and *Homing* (1957; the beginnings of World War II).

The early novels, which are set in times when Williamsburg played a significant historical role, are most successful. In the later novels, the Williamsburg connection becomes strained as most action necessarily takes place elsewhere, and the symbolic use of the town (now a forgotten backwater) as a refuge from war and suffering doesn't really work. All are romances, the lovers frequently being a very young woman and a mature, masterful man; some are star-crossed, but more often love conquers all. In the ideal relationship, the man cherishes and protects the woman, while she adores him.

Similar romantic relationships and themes occur in the nonhistorical fiction, and an additional motif used in several novels is the occult. *Tryst* (1939) tells of the love of a young girl for a man she has never met in life; their souls are united in death, when she is killed in an automobile accident. *Remember Today* (1941) is narrated by the heroine's guardian angel; this device is not very successful, and the guardian angels seem oddly helpless to affect the lives of their charges.

Thane's autobiographical writings are informal and somewhat diffuse. *England Was an Island Once* (1940), centering on Thane's last two summers in England before World War II, includes digressions on her previous summers there, on English history, and on people she has known. It effectively conveys both a sense of change in England's relations with the world and the feeling of impending war. *Reluctant Farmer* (1950, reprinted as *The Strength of the Hills*, 1976) is a very personal account of how Thane turned a rundown Vermont farm with a ramshackle house into a working farm and her real home. Full of local color, it avoids both preciousness and sentimentality.

Thane managed both to please the popular taste with her light fiction and to write serious biography. Melodramatic and sentimental elements mar her fiction, and some plots are excessively

contrived. Her most significant accomplishments are in her historical works, which are based on careful research, are imaginatively recounted, and always readable.

OTHER WORKS: *Riders of the Wind: A Romance* (1926). *Echo Answers* (1927). *His Elizabeth: A Novel* (1928). *Cloth of Gold: A Novel* (1929). *Bound to Happen* (1930). *Queen's Folly: A Romance* (1937). *From This Day Forward* (1941). *The Bird Who Made Good* (1947). *Melody: A Romance* (1950). *The Lost General* (1953). *Letter to a Stranger* (1954). *The Family Quarrel: A Journey Through the Years of the Revolution* (1959). *The Virginia Colony* (1969). *Dolly Madison: Her Life and Times* (1970). *The Fighting Quaker: Nathanael Greene* (1972).

BIBLIOGRAPHY: *Atlantic* (Jan. 1946). *NYHTB* (29 Jan. 1950). *NYTBR* (11 Sept. 1932, 22 March 1936, 23 May 1943). *SR* (14 March 1936, 10 Aug. 1963).

—MARY JEAN DEMARR

THANET, Octave
See FRENCH, Alice

THAXTER, Celia Laighton

Born 29 June 1835, Portsmouth, New Hampshire; died 26 August 1894, Appledore Island, Isles of Shoals, Maine
Daughter of Thomas B. and Eliza Rymes Laighton; married Levi L. Thaxter, 1851 (separated); children: three sons

Raised on a lighthouse island in the Isles of Shoals 10 miles off the New Hampshire coast, Celia Laighton Thaxter grew up within the sound and sight of the sea and early learned to appreciate its beauty and its cruelty. This dual awareness became a major theme in her poetry, which established her literary reputation at a relatively young age.

Thaxter's father became the lighthouse keeper when she was four years old. She, her father, mother, and two brothers were the sole human inhabitants of the island for many years. In 1841 the family moved to another of the islands, Smutty-Nose, where they began receiving paying summer guests. As this proved a successful venture, Thomas Laighton in 1847 began building a resort hotel on Appledore Island, the largest of the Shoals island group. This he completed in 1848 with the help of Levi L. Thaxter, a young Harvard graduate.

The Appledore House opened the following year and became a major summer resort attracting artists and writers including

Hawthorne, Thoreau, Emerson, Whittier, Lowell, Mark Twain, Charlotte Cushman, Ole Bull, Lucy Larcom, Sarah Orne Jewett, Annie Adams Fields, and Childe Hassam. Hassam completed a series of remarkable paintings of the islands, including some of Thaxter in her garden (1892), which are now in the Smithsonian. Many of these artists were attracted by Thaxter as well as by the scenery, and she established a kind of literary salon on the islands beginning in the 1860s.

Levi Thaxter had become Celia's tutor in her early teens, and in 1851 they married and later had three sons. The marriage was not successful, as Thaxter pined for her island home when, off and on in the 1850s, they lived on the mainland in several Massachusetts towns. Levi, on the other hand, began to resent her literary success. By the end of the 1860s, Thaxter and her husband lived essentially separate lives, although they never divorced. She remained on Appledore with her mother and her oldest son Karl, who was developmentally disadvantaged.

The death of her mother in 1877 was a severe shock to Thaxter, precipitating a religious crisis wherein she attempted to communicate through seances with her mother. This endeavor may have inspired a similar experience described fictionally by Sarah Orne Jewett in her spiritualistic story, ''The Foreigner'' (1900). Although a religious skeptic in her early years, Thaxter did turn to spiritualism, theosophy, and Eastern religions in her later years.

Thaxter was an extraordinarily accomplished watercolorist; this is an overlooked aspect of her considerable talent. Her prose publications, *Among the Isles of Shoals* (1873) and *An Island Garden* (1894), also remain as gems of descriptive prose.

Thaxter's first poem, significantly entitled ''Land-Locked,'' appeared in the *Atlantic Monthly* in March 1861. She continued to publish poems in the major literary journals of her day, namely *Scribner's, Harper's*, the *Independent*, the *Century*, and the *Atlantic*. She also published juvenile material in *Our Young Folks* and *St. Nicholas Magazine*. The first collection of Thaxter's poetry, *Poems*, appeared in 1871. Many subsequent revised editions were printed.

Most of Thaxter's poetry deals with nature, not the benign nature of the Romantics, but a harsh, indifferent ocean. Several poems deal with actual shipwrecks that occurred on the Isles of Shoals while she was there. In ''The Wreck of the Pocohantas,'' Thaxter asks: ''Do purposeless thy children meet / Such bitter death? How was it best / These hearts should cease to beat?'' She returns often in her poetry to this basic theological question. Thaxter's tones is sometimes bitter and despairing, and occasionally somewhat cynical about traditional religious explanations. At times her austere, harsh imagery anticipates that of 20th-century poets such as Anne Sexton and Sylvia Plath. Probably some of Thaxter's bitterness, like theirs, stemmed from the frustrations she encountered trying to play the many and conflicting roles of wife, mother, and artist. These conflicts are apparent in her letters, published in 1895.

OTHER WORKS: *Drift-Weed* (1878). *Poems for Children* (1884). *The Cruise of the Mystery* (1886). *Idyls and Pastorals* (1886). *My Lighthouse, and Other Poems* (1890). *Stories and Poems for Children* (1895). *The Letters of Celia Thaxter* (edited by A. A. Fields and R. Lamb, 1895). *The Heavenly Guest, and Other Unpublished Writings* (edited by O. Laighton, 1935).

BIBLIOGRAPHY: Faxon, S., et al., *A Stern and Lovely Scene: A Visual History of the Isles of Shoals* (1978). Hawthorne, N., *The American Notebooks* (1881). Laighton, O., *Ninety Years at the Isles of Shoals* (1930). Spofford, H. P., *A Little Book of Friends* (1916). Thaxter, R., *Sandpiper: The Life and Letters of Celia Thaxter* (1962). Westbrook, P. D., *Acres of Flint, Writers of Rural New England 1870-1900* (1951).
Reference works: *Oxford Companion to Women's Writing in the United States* (1995).

—JOSEPHINE DONOVAN

THAYER, Caroline (Mathilda) Warren

Born 1787 (?); **died** 1844
Wrote under: Caroline Mathilda Warren, Caroline Mathilda Thayer
Married Mr. Thayer (died); **children:** three

Caroline Warren Thayer was reared in New England in what seems to have been an intellectually stimulating and affectionate environment. She married a Mr. Thayer and had three children, but husband and children died within a few years. She made her living as a writer and schoolteacher, heading the ''Female Department'' at various schools. Many of Thayer's books went through several editions. The prefaces are the best source of biographical information. Nothing, however, is known of her later years.

The Gamesters; or, Ruins of Innocence (1805), a warning against the ''vices of gaming,'' is Thayer's only novel. Its hero, Leander Anderson, is physically appealing and morally upright, but the potential weakness in his character is that his sensibility overwhelms his judgement; he is purposefully corrupted by his close friend, Somerton, a libertine. Several other stories, meant to provide moral guidance, are intertwined with Leander's, but all the digressions do not save or even enliven *The Gamesters*. The pace of the novel is very slow, and the characterization weak. Leander is the greatest disappointment; in response to Thayer's own question, ''Why did he fall?'' she answers, ''Inquiry is vain.''

Thayer's other works are nonfiction, and all were published under the name of Thayer. *Religion Recommended to Youth* (1817) is a plea for Methodism, to which she converted in her early twenties, in the form of letters addressed to a former pupil. *Letter to the Members of the Methodist Episcopal Church* (1821) is a pamphlet about her conversion to Swedenborgianism and subsequent dismissal from Wesleyan Seminary. In a clear and lively style, she outlines the points at which Methodism and

Swedenborgianism differ and her reasons for accepting the latter. In Thayer's account of her dismissal, one also learns a good deal about the way the seminary was run.

Poems Moral and Sentimental by Mrs. Harriet Muzzy, which Thayer edited in 1821, contains some verses of Thayer's own. Her literary merit, such as can be found, surfaces when she speaks in her own voice, that of an intelligent and religious teacher, and not when, as in her novel, she follows various popular formulas for success.

OTHER WORKS: *First Lesson in the History of the U.S.* (1825).

BIBLIOGRAPHY: Cowie, A., *The Rise of the American Novel* (1948). Peter, H., *The Early American Novel* (1971).

—JULIA ROSENBERG

THAYER, Geraldine
See DANIELS, Dorothy

THOMAS, Dorothy Swain

Born 13 August 1898, Barnes, Kansas; **died** 22 September 1990
Daughter of Willard I. and Augusta Dodge Thomas; **married** John W. Buickerood, 1939

Dorothy Swain Thomas was a member of a large and talented family of a minister. The Reverend Thomas' family moved often: to several towns in Kansas and then, when Thomas was seven, to a homestead in Alberta, Canada; 40 miles from a railroad. Six years later, the family moved back to the Midwest, eventually to Lincoln, Nebraska, where Thomas attended high school and college. She interrupted her college education from time to time to teach in country schools, in small towns, and eventually in Lincoln. She moved to New Mexico in 1934, but the locale of her stories remains primarily the Midwest.

Thomas published numerous stories, several poems, and books for children. She also wrote one-act plays; one is included in *Best One-Act Plays of 1950*. Her novels, *Ma Jeeter's Girls* (1932, reissued 1986) and *The Home Place* (1936, 1966) are actually collections of short stories. All episodes use the same cast of characters, however, and the continuity of theme makes a unified novel.

Ma Jeeter's Girls is told from the point of view of the young school teacher who "boards" with Ma Jeeter and teaches at the school across the road. Living at home with Ma are her apparently virginal son Pete, her unmarried daughter Laura, and Laura's little daughter. But Ma has five other daughters, and every chapter delineates the courtship of one of the daughters, each of whom, with only one exception, has become pregnant without the sanction of marriage.

Ma Jeeter is particularly well-drawn. Although her physical appearance is rather horrible, she is a wonderfully sympathetic character as she relates the downfall of her daughters, the emotions of the family concerning "the family weakness," and the various ways in which the problems of paternity and marriage are resolved. The novel seems at first glance to be a lighthearted treatment of an age-old problem, but Thomas' understanding of the moments of sorrow and defeat in the particular situation of each daughter is notable.

The first chapter of *The Home Place* won second prize for the O. Henry Memorial Awards in 1935; the editors considered it one of the best in depicting the effects of the Depression on family life. Subsequent chapters, all published earlier as short stories, have merit but do not achieve the harmony found in *Ma Jeeter's Girls*. Events cover a year during the Depression on the Nebraska farm to which the three sons and their families return when they lose their jobs and homes. The small, crowded house becomes the scene of conflict and resolution between the varied members— particularly the women—of four generations of the family. It is through the eyes of Phyllis, the young, pregnant wife of the second son, that the other characters and their problems are sympathetically developed. Thomas' book is rich in details of Midwestern farm life during the Depression and shows both humor and warmth in development of character.

H. L. Mencken's *American Mercury* named Thomas one of the ablest of American short story writers. Several of her stories have been anthologized or marked for special honors. As did Ruth Suckow in Iowa and Bess Streeter Aldrich in Nebraska, Thomas explores the everyday lives of ordinary people. Her stories are, she has said, pretty sure to be about love and happiness sought for. In contrast to Mari Sandoz, writing in Lincoln, Nebraska, at the same time, Thomas believed life to be more kind than cruel; her work, while realistic, often reflects an optimistic point of view. The author's skill lies in her fidelity to physical detail and her ability to develop her characters and present their story from a clean, clear, and unmannered viewpoint.

OTHER WORKS: *Hi-Po the Hippo* (1942). *Eliphant Dilemma* (1946). *The Child in America: Behavior Problems and Programs* (with W. I. Thomas, 1928, reissued 1970).

BIBLIOGRAPHY: Daniels, S., *Dorothy Thomas: The Woman and the Work* (videocassette, 1989). *Getting Away* (film based on Thomas' short story, 1980).
Other references: *American Mercury* (Dec. 1946). *CSM* (4 Jan. 1941). *Quill Minutes*, Nebraska State Historical Society,

Lincoln, Nebraska (1931-32). San Angelo *Standard-Times* (6 Mar. 1977). *Saturday Evening Post* (10 April 1937).

—HELEN STAUFFER

THOMPSON, Clara M.

Born circa 1830s; **died** death date unknown
Also wrote under: Logan

While Clara M. Thompson was one of the more important Victorian popular novelists, she is barely mentioned in contemporary literary encyclopedias. Her sentimental, moralistic novels are informed by complicated plots: young women seduced and ruined, families separated and reunited, insanity, miscegenation, kidnapping, ransom, and religious bigotry.

The Chapel of St. Mary (1861) is characteristic. Agatha Douglass comes to live with her uncle Rodney Douglass at Maple Cliff; she is befriended by Papsy, Douglass' black-Native American maid and neighbors Honora and Gregory Clarendon. Honora's friend Charlotte Morgan comes to Maple Cliff to teach Agatha and Anne Walbridge, whose dissolute brother Dick seduces Papsy. When Douglass goes to Scotland, Agatha's brother Chauncey arrives to run Maple Cliff and falls in love with Charlotte, who rejects him after being warned by Mrs. Douglass never to marry a Douglass.

Three other families are introduced: the pious, self-righteous Ridgeways, the scheming Winchesters, and the Fergusson sisters who provide further romantic complications. In the end Gregory and Agatha reject Isabelle and Duncan Winchester and marry each other. The Fergusson sisters are reunited with their brother Robert Walton; Charlotte marries Chauncey Douglass. Papsy and her brother Chet are discovered to be Rodney Douglass' children.

While plot construction is Thompson's strength, characterization is not. Most of the characters are conventional Victorian types; however, those Thompson says she based on real life—Papsy, Chet, and the Judge—are more fully developed, and the generous Aunt Polly, another black-Native American character, is a foil to the smug hypocrisy of the Ridgeways and their Ladies' Sewing Circle. Although the theme of this didactic novel is hypocrisy, the contrast between the Christian charity of the black-Native Americans of the Gorge and the narrow sectarianism of the other characters, *The Chapel of St. Mary* actually reflects the anti-Catholic nativism of the period in its allusion to Maria Monk and its mention of Ursuline nuns fostering vocations, perhaps a veiled reference to the burning of their convent by a Charleston mob in 1834.

Thompson is undistinguished as a stylist, but, as a writer of sensational novels, her work is of some interest to those concerned with the popular literature of the Victorian period.

—MAUREEN MURPHY

THOMPSON, Clara M(abel)

Born 3 October 1893, Providence, Rhode Island; **died** 20 December 1958, New York, New York
Daughter of T. Franklin and Clara Medberry Thompson

Clara M. Thompson graduated from the Women's College of Brown University and began her medical training at Johns Hopkins University in 1916. It had at one time been her ambition to become a medical missionary, but at Johns Hopkins her interest in psychoanalysis intensified. After her internship at the New York Infirmary for Women and Children, Thompson completed her residency in psychiatry at the Phipps Clinic at Johns Hopkins in 1925.

Thompson's career was varied and its course inextricably linked to changes occurring in the field of psychoanalysis as the culturally oriented analysts challenged many of the Freudian theories to which the classical psychotherapists ascribed. After establishing a private practice, teaching at Vassar and the New York Psychoanalytic Institute, and studying at Budapest with Sandor Ferenczi, Freud's pupil and colleague, Thompson, along with other proponents of the cultural approach to psychoanalysis, formed the American Association for the Advancement of Psychoanalysis. Thompson was elected vice president. With others, she established the William Alanson White Institute in New York in 1943. As its executive director for many years, she provided the leadership that allowed the institute to preserve its ideal of open scientific investigation.

Although Thompson published over 50 papers, articles, reviews, and interviews, the works which make her most accessible to the lay reader are three books, only one of which was published during her lifetime. *Psychoanalysis: Evolution and Development* (1950) is a study of the major trends and developments in psychoanalysis. Thompson builds her discussion of the most significant theories of Freud, Adler, Jung, Ferenczi, Sullivan, Fromm, and others on the thesis that a thread of continuity runs through the evolution of psychoanalysis, even as it develops in divergent directions. No polemicist, Thompson approaches this study as a reconciler whose perspective is based on the belief that it is premature to assume any one school of psychoanalysis has discovered final truth.

Interpersonal Psychoanalysis: The Selected Papers of Clara M. Thompson (1964) is addressed primarily to a professional audience. The selections in the first two-thirds of the book deal with changing concepts in psychoanalysis, the contributions of Ferenczi, Sullivan, and Fromm, and various clinical problems in psychotherapy. The last portion of the work contains professional articles and an uncompleted manuscript on the psychology of women. This material has been edited a second time and presented for a more popular audience under the title *On Women* (1971).

In her exploration in these two books of what might be called "female distinctiveness," Thompson is interested in the extent to which the basic experiences that set women apart from men affect their essential makeup. She is sufficiently Freudian to acknowledge the impact of woman's biological distinctiveness on her role in life, but she differs with Freud over the degree of biologic determinism. Many of the characteristics which Freud saw as being innate in the female Thompson attributes to cultural factors, and she imputes the preponderance of distorted ideas about the female psychosexual life to the unavoidable bias of male theorists.

Thompson credits Freud with having developed the most comprehensive and detailed theories about women, but she opposes his view that a woman is essentially a castrated male. Thompson insists that a woman's psychology is "something in its own right and not merely a negation of maleness;" she was one of the very early psychoanalytic theorists to insist many of the "truths" about the innate nature of women have to be examined in light of the culture that has defined the woman, and she was one of the pioneers in asserting that the female experience has an inherent validity of its own.

In her contributions to the literature of psychoanalysis, Thompson was both evaluator and originator. She assessed the work of others in the field from the perspective of one capable of realizing continuity in divergence. In her own divergence from the classical psychoanalytic concepts, Thompson provided new ways of looking at human problems. Her theories concerning the impact of culture on the psychosexual development of women foreshadowed many of the perspectives on women which only emerged in popular literature after her death in 1958.

BIBLIOGRAPHY: Green, M. R., *Interpersonal Psychoanalysis: The Selected Papers of Clara M. Thompson*, Part VI (1964).
Other references: Chicago *Sun* (13 June 1950). *NYTBR* (28 Feb. 1965).

—GUIN A. NANCE

THOMPSON, Dorothy

Born 9 July 1894, Lancaster, New York; **died** 30 January 1961, Lisbon, Portugal
Daughter of Peter and Margaret Grierson Thompson; **married** Josef Bard, 1923; Sinclair Lewis, 1928 (divorced); Maxim Kopf, 1943 (died)

Dorothy Thompson was the daughter of an English clergyman who married an American woman and settled in upper New York State. Left motherless when she was still a child, she turned early to history, literature, and languages for pleasure as well as study. She attended the Lewis Institute in Chicago, and received the B.A. degree from Syracuse University in 1914.

Thompson began her writing career as a publicist for woman suffrage groups and the Red Cross. This work took her abroad, where she secured freelance writing assignments and made influential friends among the overseas press corps. Within a few years she had become a regular correspondent for the Philadelphia *Public Ledger* and the New York *Evening Post*. Later she became a bureau chief in Berlin.

Thompson was fluent in German and thoroughly at ease with German culture and politics—which was perhaps why she was among the first, and among the most perceptive and persistent, critics of Nazism. Her enduring reputation rests chiefly on the worldwide recognition and respect she won as the plain-speaking reporter who, through her widely syndicated New York *Herald Tribune* column "On the Record," alerted the English-speaking world to the brutality and menace of the Hitler regime.

Although she broke with the *Herald Tribune* over her support for President Franklin Roosevelt in 1940 (she had originally favored the paper's candidate, Wendell Willkie), Thompson continued writing until virtually the end of her life. In addition to her newspaper column, she contributed a monthly article to the *Ladies' Home Journal* and did regular radio broadcasts. A series of wartime talks sent by short wave to Germany was published under the title *Listen, Hans* (1942). *Let the Record Speak* (1939) was culled from her political columns. *The Courage to be Happy* (1957), drawn from Thompson's *Journal* pieces and dealing mainly with personal and social topics, reflects the rigorous, work-centered ethic of her Methodist childhood.

By the 1940s, Thompson was one of the most widely read columnists in the country, and the press of travel and speaking engagements made her writing of necessity a collaborative effort with researchers and editorial aides. Critics should look to her early work for the full flavor of her journalistic style. In *The New Russia* (1928), for example, she combines cogent political analysis with vivid personal detail to give a memorable picture of the Soviet Union after ten years of Communist rule. Thompson compares the pioneering work of the Soviet experiment to the development of the American frontier. She is, however, astute and clearsighted in her recognition of the ways in which classical communist ideals have been jettisoned for practical political purposes.

Perhaps Thompson's greatest gift as a journalist was her ability to maintain an enthusiastic receptivity to her subject while tempering enthusiasm with objective judgement. She was considered a highly opinionated writer, but in general, her opinions represent moral convictions which the reader can easily detect and allow for. In *I Saw Hitler* (1932) Thompson's scorn for the subject of her interview is everywhere apparent, yet personal antipathy does not lead her to underestimate the leadership potential of the Nazi dictator.

One of Thompson's biographers suggests she felt keenly her failure to produce a body of writing that would transcend the topical. In particular, she seems to have wanted to write her own autobiography, and she made several efforts, which she abandoned as unsatisfactory. Thompson seems to have been a writer with greater powers than her subjects called forth.

OTHER WORKS: *Depths of Prosperity* (with P. Bottome, 1925). *Refugees* (1938). *Political Guide* (1938).

BIBLIOGRAPHY: Kurth, P., *American Cassandra: The Life of Dorothy Thompson* (1990). Sheean, V., *Dorothy and Red* (1963).

Sanders, M., *Dorothy Thompson: A Legend in Her Time* (1973). Schorer, *Sinclair Lewis: Am American Life* (1961).

Reference works: *Benet's Reader's Encyclopedia* (1987). *Oxford Companion to Women's Writing in the United States* (1995).

Other references: *Atlantic* July (1945). *CB* (1940). *Colliers* (June 1945). *Newsweek* (20 Oct. 1944). *NY* (20 April 1940, 27 April 1940).

—ANN PRINGLE ELIASBERG

THORNDYKE, Helen Louise
See ADAMS, Harriet Stratemeyer

TICKNOR, Caroline

Born 1866, Boston, Massachusetts; **died** 11 May 1937, Boston, Massachusetts
Daughter of Benjamin H. and Caroline Cushman Ticknor

As a member of a family prominent in the publishing business, from childhood Caroline Ticknor knew many men and women in the literary establishment and was devoted to their work. She was the granddaughter of William D. Ticknor, who founded Ticknor and Fields. The firm published the most successful authors of the period; directed the old Corner Bookstore, rendezvous for the intellectuals of Boston, Cambridge, and Concord at the time of their dominance in the country's cultural life; and also published the *Atlantic Monthly*, whose contributors included leading writers of America and England. Her father continued in the business, and Ticknor became an author and editor.

Having been educated privately, except for a year in public school and a special course at Radcliffe College, Ticknor began writing at the age of eighteen "for the fun of it." She wrote both short fiction and articles for *Harper's, Century*, the *Independent, Cosmopolitan*, the *New England Magazine*, and *Atlantic*. Although a collection of minor stories and a light satire appeared in 1896, her work as a biographer is more important.

Hawthorne and His Publisher (1913) is an account of the mutually rewarding relationship between the major American author and William Ticknor from 1851 to 1864, when they both died. The work relies on family recollections of the two men and their acquaintances, as well as 150 letters from Hawthorne to Ticknor's grandfather. Consonant with the spirit of a memorable friendship, Ticknor neither intrudes nor shows partiality in the depiction of the two men. Sympathetic in her characterization of Hawthorne, she thereby reflects the integrity of the self-effacing and loyal publisher on whom the man of letters counted not only for good advice but magnanimous favors.

The second biographical study by Ticknor is *Poe's Helen* (1916), a tribute to Sarah Helen Whitman, preeminent among the literary women closely associated with the controversial writer. The substance of the book is derived from Whitman's manuscripts

and correspondence, including Poe's previously published letters to her. Poe figures in the biography as a romantic poet, a fascinating and morbid genius; "Helen" is the woman "of poetry and moonlight," but one with whom he had intellectual and spiritual ties. Whitman is praised for being free from bias, generous in her attitudes toward Poe's "eccentricities," and keen in her critical judgements. The praise is weakened, however, by Ticknor's failure to consider even briefly Whitman's bold defense of him in *Edgar Poe and His Critics* (1860).

In *Glimpses of Authors* (1922), Ticknor takes advantage of experiences she enjoyed as a member of a family hospitable to "the great and near great" writers associated with the publishing house. The book is, in fact, semiautobiographical, but its author is modest, discreet, and gently amusing in her reminiscences. Because she is dependent upon a variety of sources—the testimony of relatives and friends, letters, proof sheets, and other memorabilia—some of which are inconsequential, *Glimpses of Authors* is composed of fragments. Those about Lew Wallace, Joel Chandler Harris, and Thomas de Quincey, for example, prove more interesting than those about Henry James and Mary N. Murfree. Her sketches evoke the manners, tastes, diversions, and anxieties of American and English literary circles before the rise of modernism.

Ticknor was aware of the vicissitudes of those who write for a livelihood; she observed that originality is always theoretically in great demand but finds itself scantily appreciated when it appears. Nonetheless, at the time when a radical change in perspectives necessitated a reappraisal of the history of American literature, Ticknor ratified the accepted 19th-century view of its achievement. There is a suggestion of nostalgia in Ticknor's adherence to the aims of conserving records of an earlier period.

OTHER WORKS: *A Hypocritical Romance, and Other Stories* (1896). *Miss Belladonna: A Child of Today* (1896). *Miss Belladonna: A Social Satire* (1897). *The "Old North" Signal Lights, 1723-1923; or, Christmas Comes to Boston* (1923). *May Alcott: A Memoir* (1928). *Washington's Surprising Ancestor* (n.d.).

BIBLIOGRAPHY: Flagg, M. B., *Boston Authors Now and Then* (1966).
Reference works: *Oxford Companion to Women's Writing in the Untied States* (1995).
Other references: Boston *Globe* (12 May 1937).

—ELIZABETH PHILLIPS

TIERNAN, Frances (Christine) Fisher

Born 5 July 1846, Salisbury, North Carolina; **died** 24 March 1920, Salisbury, North Carolina
Wrote under: Christian Reid
Daughter of Charles F. and Elizabeth Caldwell Fisher; **married** James M. Tiernan, 1887 (died 1898)

Frances Fisher Tiernan was born into an aristocratic Southern family. Her father, president of the Western North Carolina

Railroad, was a Confederate officer killed at the Battle of Bull Run. Tiernan was educated primarily at home. At twenty-two, she converted to Roman Catholicism.

Tiernan was able to support herself and several family members by her writing. Her career began in 1870, with the publication of *Valerie Aylmer*, the first of a series of five "plantation novels" romanticizing the domestic life of the antebellum South. As with most of Tiernan's romances, the plantation novels are melodramatic accounts of women turning men's heads and men breaking women's hearts. Many of Tiernan's romances were serialized in Catholic magazines before publication in book form.

Although she wrote primarily fiction, her travel sketch, *The Land and the Sky* (1876), won much acclaim for its vivid portrayal of the back country of western North Carolina. Tiernan's fondness for the wilderness also is expressed in her novels. *After Many Days* (1877) is set in the preindustrial South and emphasizes the pride of land ownership, natural refinement, and simple rural existence. In 1879 Tiernan decided she needed to "broaden the narrow little world in which my life, so far, has been spent" so she traveled for a year on the Continent. Upon returning to America her writing assumed a "European" flavor. *Hearts of Steel* (1883), *Armine* (1884), and *Weighed in the Balance* (1900) are located in European cities but still focused on the love troubles and triumphs of the ruling class.

The geographical flavor of Tiernan's novels changed again in 1887, when she moved with her husband, a widowed land speculator, to Mexico. Several books are attempts to capture what she understood as the life of Mexico and its people. Trips to the West Indies and the Dominican Republic produced two adventure novels: *The Man of the Family* (1897) and *The Chase of an Heiress* (1898).

After James Tiernan's death in 1898, Tiernan returned to North Carolina where she became active with the Daughters of the Confederacy. Proceeds from the play *Under the Southern Cross* (1900) were used to construct a monument to Jefferson Davis. Tiernan firmly believed that reading was a means of moral enlightenment, and to this end she established two Catholic women's reading circles. Her literary, civic, and religious achievements were commemorated in 1909 when she was awarded the Laetare Medal by Notre Dame University.

In 1911 Tiernan wrote what was considered her most successful work, *The Light of Vision*. The theme is central to many of her other novels: the Christian way of life, especially for women, is one of personal sacrifice. A Catholic convert remarries her divorced, good-for-nothing husband after he becomes a helpless invalid. Through her patient care she is able to save her husband from self-destruction and lead him to a holy death.

The Light of Vision echoes the common Victorian theme of the suffering, saintly wife (or innocent child) leading the sinful man back to a life of piety and goodness. In her more than forty novels, Tiernan sought to portray life not as it was, but as it should be—restrained and refined. Her Southern, aristocratic characters abhorred excess wealth, strove for purity, and attempted to

preserve an idyllic preindustrial society. Although Tiernan traveled in areas seldom frequented by other Southern women, her novels show only the geographical change; characters, plots, and morals remain unchanged. Her portrayal of the "proper" life had contemporary popularity, but the novels are too steeped in turn-of-the-century mentality to say much to the modern reader.

OTHER WORKS: *Morton House* (1871). *Ebb-Tide, and Other Stories* (1872). *Mabel Lee* (1872). *Carmen's Inheritance* (1873). *Nina's Atonement, and Other Stories* (1873). *A Daughter of Bohemia* (1874). *Hearts and Hands* (1875). *A Question of Honor* (1875). *Bessie's Six Lovers* (1877). *Bonny Kate* (1878). *A Summer Idyl* (1878). *A Gentle Bell* (1879). *A Child of Mary* (1885). *Roslyn's Fortune* (1885). *His Victory* (1887). *Miss Churchill* (1887). *Philip's Restitution* (1888). *A Cast for Fortune* (1890). *Carmela* (1891). *The Lost Lode* (1892). *A Little Maid of Arcady* (1893). *A Comedy of Elopement* (1893). *The Land of the Sun* (1894). *The Lady of Las Cruces* (1896). *The Picture of Las Cruces* (1896). *A Woman of Fortune* (1896). *Fairy Gold* (1897). *A Daughter of Sierra* (1903). *Vera's Charge* (1907). *Princess Nadine* (1908). *The Coin of Sacrifice* (1909). *The Wargrave Trust* (1911). *The Daughter of a Star* (1913). *A Far Away Princess* (1914). *A Secret Bequest* (1915).

BIBLIOGRAPHY: Becker, K. B., *Biography of Christian Reid* (1941). Reference works: *The Book of Catholic Authors* (1942). *NAW* (1971). *NCAB*.

—M. COLLEN MCDANNELL

TIETJENS, Eunice (Hammond)

Born 29 July 1884, Chicago, Illinois; died 6 September 1944, Chicago, Illinois
Also wrote under: E. H., Eloise Briton, Guy Trevor MacKenzie, Frances Trevor
Daughter of William A. and Idea Strong Hammond; married Paul Tietjens, 1904; Cloyd Head, 1920; children: two daughters and one son

"Born under a wandering star," Eunice Tietjens lived on Chicago's suburban North Shore until her banker father drowned in 1897. She and three younger siblings were schooled in Geneva, Dresden, and Paris, where her mother was an exhibiting painter. Tietjens married a composer and bore two daughters, burying one before she returned alone to Chicago in 1909.

Tietjens established her financial independence by writing pseudonymous serials. In 1912 she experienced an aesthetic "birth," and, encouraged by friends in the Chicago literary movement, she turned to poetry and began her 25-year association with Harriet Monroe's *Poetry*. Tietjens became assistant editor of the literary journal in 1915.

In 1917 Tietjens published the first of her four volumes of poetry. She spent 1917 and 1918 in Paris, as the Chicago *Daily*

News' first woman war correspondent. After the war, she remarried, bore a son, and became active in Chicago's major literary clubs. Travels in China and Japan, three winters in Tunisia, and a year in the South Seas confirmed Tietjens' fascination with non-Western cultures. She wrote an unsuccessful play, *Arabesque*, with her husband in 1925 and edited a successful Oriental anthology. After 1929 she wrote mostly children's travel books. When her husband Cloyd Head joined the Miami Players in 1934, Tietjens taught college there, wrote her autobiography, became involved in Pan-American affairs, and worked on an epic poem about the Caribbean.

During her lifetime, Tietjens was best known for her earliest poems, collected in *Body and Raiment* (1919). "Proem: A Plaint of Complexity," a finely wrought catalogue of her "too many selves," implicitly acknowledges the biographical basis for her successes, reflected in several notoriously sensuous lyrics and occasional poems to famous contemporaries.

Among this youthful collection's best poems, "The Great Man" is the first example of Tietjens' mastery of free verse, while "The Drug Clerk" and "The Steam Shovel" introduce contemporary, sociological subject matter. Most of the poems, however, rely on regular rhymes and conventional forms and emotions, which often undermine Tietjens's psychological insights and sensory perceptions. Thus in her frequently anthologized poem "A Bacchante to her Babe," trivial rhymes reduce mythic eroticism and powerful images of birth to a harmlessly playful song of maternal joy.

Such weaknesses do not mar Tietjens' most consistent volume of poetry, *Profiles from China* (1917). Written after most poems in *Body and Raiment*, these free verse sketches are rooted in a complex cross-cultural perspective with perceptual and emotional power. In "The Cormorants," for instance, her painterly skill focuses unblinkingly on an Oriental scene her Western mind finds revolting: the semistarved slavery of fishing birds whose string collars prevent them from swallowing the catches their "lousy lords" require.

Characteristic of Tietjens' work are the uncensored sensory details of fermenting toilet pots in "Spring," the troublesome shadow of brutality underlying exotic mystery in "The Hand," and her condemnation in "My Servant" of the inhumanity of praising as "golden lilies" thumping, bound feet. But only "The City Wall" and "The Most-Sacred Mountain" were often anthologized. Pressing squalor is muted by references to the European middle ages and countered by distant beauty in the former, while memorable lines with clear, open tones fully realize the pure "white windy presence of eternity" in the latter, her most admired poem.

Profiles from Home (1925), which Tietjens wrote at a distance from her subjects and on the self-derivative model of her free verse Chinese "profiles," lacks both sensory immediacy and personal response. These qualities appear frequently, however, in *Leaves in Windy Weather* (1929)—for instance, in the burnished, tactile images of "Old Friendship" and the sibilant, sizzling burst of primitive passion in "Fire."

This final, miscellaneous volume of Tietjens' poetry also includes her best poetic narratives. "From the Mountains," a sonnet sequence that her family had suppressed in 1915, plots a brief, parabolic love affair. "The Man Who Loved Mary" is the best of several dramatic narratives. For her personal prose, as well as her poetry, however, the vignette—with its sharply etched description and compressed emotional force—was Tietjens' best form. Her novel *Jake* (1921) relies more on lyric description than narrative development, and her 1938 autobiography is loosely episodic.

Tietjens' contemporaries accurately identified painterly perception, not formal technique, as the most dependable quality of her literary oeuvre. Clichéd closing lines often mar promising poems, although her best poems exhibit an emotionally direct poetic voice that responds honestly to even the most complex experiences.

OTHER WORKS: *Japan, Korea, and Formosa* (edited by B. Holmes, 1924). *Boy of the Desert* (1928). *Poetry of the Orient* (edited by Tietjens, 1928). *The Romance of Antar* (translated by Tietjens, 1929). *China* (with L. S. Hammond; edited by B. Holmes, 1930). *The Jaw-Breaker's Alphabet* (with J. Tietjens, 1930). *Boy of the South Seas* (1931). *Manga Reva, the Forgotten Island* (with R. L. Eskridge, 1931). *The Gingerbread Boy* (1932). *The World at My Shoulder* (1938). *An Adventure in Friendship* (edited by Tietjens, 1941).

The Eunice Tietjens Papers are housed in the Newberry Library in Chicago, Illinois.

BIBLIOGRAPHY: Love, W. N. S., "Eunice Tietjens: A Biographical and Critical Study" (dissertation, 1960).

Reference works: *Oxford Companion to Women's Writing in the United States* (1995).

Other references: *Bookman* (Aug. 1925, April 1929). *Masses* (Aug. 1917). *NYHTB* (6 Oct. 1929). *NYT* (19 Oct. 1919). *Poetry* (Sept. 1917, Oct. 1917, Feb. 1920, July 1925, Sept. 1938). *SR* (7 Oct. 1944).

—SIDNEY H. BREMER

TILTON, Alice
See TAYLOR, Phoebe Atwood

TINCKER, Mary Agnes

Born 18 July 1831, Ellsworth, Maine; died 27 November 1907, Dorchester, Massachusetts
Daughter of Richard and Mehitabel Jellison Tincker

Mary Agnes Tincker was a precocious child who had progressed from the role of student to that of full-time teacher in the public schools of Ellsworth by age thirteen. Within two years she had begun her lifelong involvement with the literary world by contributing anonymous sketches to local newspapers and journals.

Tincker became a Catholic in 1851, an event which shaped much of the content, characterization, and setting of her works. Her most frequent contributions were made to the *Catholic World* which serialized her first novel, *The House of York* (April 1871-June 1872). The setting for this novel is Ellsworth, during the Know-Nothing period (1854-55). The story follows the developing vocation of Dick Rowan, an impetuous young man whose maturation takes place through suffering and persecution not unlike that which the author herself endured after her acceptance of Catholicism.

In 1863 Tincker volunteered as a Civil War nurse serving in Judiciary Square Hospital, Washington, D.C., until ill health prevented her from continuing. Some of the destruction and conflict of this period is reflected in her writing, particularly in the poem ''A Soldier's Daughter,'' from the collection, *Autumn Leaves* (1889). In this work the war is seen from a child's point of view. There is a poignant description of a New England home—of the children, the land, and the death of the father.

Tincker struggled with the theme of death throughout her life and work. Perhaps her most mature expression is in a short sketch ''Palingenesis,'' in which she concludes the arch enemy humanity must conquer is the fear of death. In addition, one must conquer death not by despising life but by enjoying life to its fullest, so there will be no final fear in that change in the form of individual life called death.

Tincker's father served as a sheriff of Hancock County and as warden of the Maine state prison. A persistent interest in the criminal, from both a legal and religious point of view, permeates her work. For example, in *Grapes and Thorns* (1874) the plot includes unravelling the mysterious death of the mother of a devout parish priest. This work also provides a look into late-19th-century prison life and the inadequacies of rural penal systems, as well as observations on the motivations and weaknesses in the human person.

Although Tincker holds Catholicism in great esteem, this does not preclude a tolerance which enables her to recognize the depth of goodness in all creation, as well as the proclivity to evil. In *Grapes and Thorns*, the conversion of Mr. Schöninger from Judaism to Christianity is treated as a gradual transition in which Judaism is never renounced but, in his own eyes, fulfilled. Tincker spent 14 years in Italy (1873-87) during which time she also traveled in Spain and France. This sojourn formed the setting for her remaining novels. Tincker became known in England with the publication there of *Six Sunny Months* (1878) and *Signor Monaldini's Niece* (1879). On the continent, *Grapes and Thorns* was translated into French; *By the Tiber* (1881) and *Two Coronets* (1889) were translated into German.

The critics of her time singled out Tincker's power of description and her astuteness in developing the most minute details of personality in characters as her greatest gifts. Yet all of the works suffer from the clichés and coincidence characteristic of many novels of this period. Tincker's own struggle as a single

woman in the turn-of-the-century world became a focus in much of her work. She protests the restrictions placed on women's freedom; the stereotype of woman as a being of inferior intelligence is consistently reversed in her novels. Tincker, however, did achieve recognition for her work and was accepted as a member of the Ancient Academy of the Aracadia in Rome.

OTHER WORKS: *The Winged Word* (1873). *The Jewel in the Lotus* (1884). *Aurora* (1886). *San Salvador* (1892).

BIBLIOGRAPHY: Reference works: *Catholic Encyclopedia* (1913). *DAB. NCAB. Novels and Tales by Catholic Writers* (1946). *Supplement to Allibone's Critical Dictionary of English Literature* (1891).

Other references: *Catholic World* (June 1872). *Literary World* (27 Sept. 1878, 12 Dec. 1885). *Nation* (March 1879, 9 June 1881).

—VIRGINIA KAIB RATIGAN

TODD, Mabel Loomis

Born 10 November 1856, Cambridge, Massachusetts; **died** 14 October 1932, Hog Island, Muscongus, Maine
Daughter of Eben J. and Mary Wilder Loomis; **married** David Todd, 1879; **children:** one

Mabel Loomis Todd, an only child, was a descendant of Priscilla and John Alden of Plymouth Colony. Todd's father, astronomer at the U.S. Naval Observatory, poet, and naturalist, was a friend of Asa Gray, Henry David Thoreau, and Walt Whitman. Educated at private schools in Cambridge and Georgetown, D.C., Todd later studied at the New England Conservatory of Music. She married an astronomer, and their one child was born in 1880. They moved to Amherst College in 1881, when her husband became director of the observatory and a member of the faculty. Upon his retirement in 1917, they made their winter home in Coconut Grove, Florida, where Todd fostered the movement to establish the Everglades National Park; her Maine island, where they had a summer house, became a National Audubon Society wildlife sanctuary.

Todd, who was responsible for the publication of the first volumes of Emily Dickinson's poetry, undertook the editorial work at a time when no one else would. The Todds had been initially well-received, when they moved to Amherst, by Susan Gilbert Dickinson and her husband Austin, treasurer of the College and the poet's brother. A liaison developed between Todd and Austin in the fall of 1882 and continued until his death in 1895. Although the men remained friends, animosity between the wives extended to family imbroglios over Todd's legitimate claims as the editor, at the request of the poet's family, of Dickinson's verse and selected letters.

The editing was a formidable job. Dickinson's handwriting was idiosyncratic; her grammar and punctuation were not always conventional. There were tentative words, alternate lines, or different versions of the same poem between which to choose. The labor required a sure grasp of the poet's intentions, but also anticipation of readers' resistance to an original and imaginatively daring language. Todd enlisted the help of her husband, of Austin, and of the reluctant T. W. Higginson, editor of the *Atlantic*, with whom Dickinson had begun correspondence as early as 1862. A modest selection, *Poems by Emily Dickinson*, appeared in 1890 with a preface by Higginson (known as the First Series, followed by the Second Series, 1891), who assisted in securing a publisher and launching the book. "You," he told Todd, "did the hardest part of the work."

Todd is less well known for the books she wrote. She first published *Footprints* (1883), which in retrospect seems fictionalized autobiography. The story of a quiet, lonely man—a forty-year-old physician for whom life's mysteries are cold and bleak—ends as he comes to know a spirited young woman who shares his sense of the autumnal beauty of the New England seacoast and they glimpse a promise of joy together. Lyrical descriptions of an austere landscape with its granite cliffs, wild flowers, and expanse of sky and ocean suggest emotions that are not overtly described in the narrative.

Todd wrote *Total Eclipses of the Sun* (1894), the first volume in the Columbian Knowledge series, edited by her husband. She traces the separation of modern scientific astronomy from the inaccurate poetic views characterized by mysticism, superstition, and terror of the past. Authoritative without being pedantic, Todd writes a muted poetry describing an eclipse she witnessed with her husband in Japan during 1887. "A startling nearness to the gigantic forces of nature," she concludes, "seems to have been established," and personalities, hates, jealousies, even mundane hopes "grow very small and very far away."

Todd also collaborated with her husband in other scientific writing. She published informal essays, reviews of new books, three serialized novels, and a sonnet sequence. She also wrote two travel books: *Corona and Coronet* (1898) is a leisurely account of a yacht trip to Japan to view the total eclipse of the sun in 1896, and *Tripoli the Mysterious* (1912) describes Libya's ancient desert city, its changeless etiquette, sandblown ruins, architecture, crafts, trades, and the people Todd met on two "eclipse trips" in 1900 and 1905. In the tour de force, *A Cycle of Sunsets* (1910), she observes changes of light, hues, tones, and atmosphere at the end of every day throughout a year as attentively as an artist like J. M. W. Turner Studies sky and land. Sixty of her paintings are in the Hunt Institute for Botanical Documents, Carnegie-Mellon University.

Todd's judgements are apt to be aesthetic rather than conventionally moral; her condescension toward "village" insularity is tempered if not tolerant. Her tensions are disciplined, her feelings cultivated. Graceful in manner, she values decorum appropriate to occasions and is sensitive to the nuances of the moment. Human presences rarely dominate the scenes or subjects to which Todd responds with subtlety, composure, and intelligent interest.

OTHER WORKS: *Letters of Emily Dickinson* (edited by Todd, 1894; enlarged edition, 1931). *A Cycle of Sonnets* (1896). *Poems by Emily Dickinson* (edited by Todd; Third Series, 1896). *Steele's Popular Astronomy* (edited by Todd, with D. P. Todd, 1899). *Bolts of Melody: New Poems of Emily Dickinson* (edited by Todd, with M. T. Bingham, 1945). *The Thoreau Family Two Generations Ago* (Thoreau Society Booklet No. 13, 1958).

BIBLIOGRAPHY: Bingham, M. T., *Ancestor's Brocades* (1945). Blake, C. R., and C. F. Wells, eds., *The Recognition of Emily Dickinson* (1967). Sewall, R. B., *The Life of Emily Dickinson* (1974).

Reference works: *NAW* (1971).

—ELIZABETH PHILLIPS

TODD, Marion Marsh

Born March 1841, Plymouth, New York; died after 1914
Daughter of Abner K. and Dolly Wales Marsh; married Benjamin Todd, 1868 (died 1880); children: one daughter

Marion Marsh Todd was one of seven children. Her family moved to Eaton Rapids, Michigan, in 1851. Her father, a Universalist preacher, died in 1852. She attended Ypsilanti State Normal School, then taught until she married a lawyer, who, like her father, encouraged Todd to pursue a career. She had one daughter.

In the late 1870s, the Todds moved to San Francisco, where Todd enrolled in Hastings Law College. In 1880 her husband died and the following year she withdrew from school without a degree but was admitted to the bar. Todd, like many women lawyers, became politically active although women had no vote. She ran for state attorney general on the Greenback-Labor ticket in 1882; although she lost, she led her party in votes. By 1886, having returned to Michigan, she continued in reform politics: as delegate to the Knights of Labor General Assembly in Richmond, Virginia; as cofounder in 1887 (with Sarah Emery and others) of the Union Labor Party. In 1890 she moved to Chicago to edit the *Express*, a nationally circulated reform weekly. She later returned to Michigan, first to Eaton Rapids, then to Springport.

Between 1886 and 1902, Todd published five books on critical political issues and three novels. The political books are well documented and cogently argued; they reflect her legal training, yet are seasoned with wit. In *Protective Tariff Delusions* (1886), Todd, addressing a general audience, takes on the political issue of the day. She asserts, with supporting statistics, that protective tariffs help neither the farmer nor the laborer and hence should be abolished.

Senator John Sherman (formerly secretary of the Treasury) was a primary target of the Populists in the 1880s and 1890s.

Accused of selling his vote and political influence to big bankers, he was held partly responsible for the nation's problems, which the Populists saw as resulting from deflation. In two works, *Honest (?) John Sherman; or, a Foul Record* (1890) and (an elaboration) *Pizarro and John Sherman* (1891), Todd reenforces the Populist attack.

Her chief effort on behalf of the woman suffrage movement is a delightful book, *Prof. Goldwin Smith and His Satellites in Congress* (1890). This is a response to Smith's article, "Woman's Place in the State" (*Forum*, January 1890). Smith, a respected historian at Cornell, attacked the feminist movement. In her counterattack, Todd uses quotes from Smith as her text and pursues them to their ludicrous but logical ends. She leavens her caustic analysis with anecdotes from diverse sources: literature, periodicals, hearsay. The book remains clear, persuasive, and amusing.

One of Todd's best known work is *Railways of Europe and America* (1893). She presents tables comparing aspects of the 1890 American and European railway industries: equipment, stock, trackage, workers, accident records, and passenger and freight rates. These are the groundwork for her major recommendation: nationalize the American railroad industry since, "They know no people, no party, no God—but the God of Greed, based upon unrighteous dividends and watered stock." Like her previous works, though weighted with facts, this book is readable.

It is difficult to believe the woman who wrote these interesting books also wrote novels so meretricious as Todd's three romances. The stories are unexciting, the characters undeveloped, the stabs at "social issues" superficial. *Claudia* (1902), for example, revolves around a well-born woman's search for a husband among three suitors. There is little action and much talk—about evolution, growth, reincarnation, the burdens of the rich. All this talk is shallow and unrealistic. Inexplicably, Todd's social concerns in her nonfiction are mocked by the middle class trivia in her fiction.

Scholars of Populism are aware of Todd's work on railroads; scholars of feminism have yet to discover her work on suffrage. Readers of novels are unaware of her romances; perhaps it's better so. It is difficult to accept sentimental novels written by women who have demonstrated their insightful understanding of the political and economic world in which they live.

OTHER WORKS: *Rachel's Pitiful History* (1895). *Phillip: A Romance* (1900).

BIBLIOGRAPHY: Davis, W. J., *History of Political Conventions in California* (1893).

Reference works: *AW. NAW* (1971).

Other references: *Arena* (July 1892). *Green Bag* (Jan. 1890, April 1890). *Michigan Pioneer and Historical Collections* (1892).

—PAULINE ADAMS,
UPDATED BY EMMA S. THORNTON

TOKLAS, Alice B.

Born Alice Babette Toklas, 30 April 1877, San Francisco, California; **died** 7 March 1967, Paris, France

Daughter of Ferdinand and Emma Levinsky Toklas; **life partner** Gertrude Stein (died 1946)

Alice B. Toklas was born into San Francisco's upper-middle class Jewish society. When she was thirteen, Ferdinand Toklas moved his family to Seattle, where Toklas enrolled in the music conservatory of the University of Washington to study piano, but her mother's failing health forced the family to return to San Francisco. After her mother's death in 1897, Toklas became the "responsible granddaughter" to a house full of male relatives. She made brief contact with the bohemian life in San Francisco, but largely concentrated on domestic duties. Henry James' novels filled her with longing for Europe and fueled her desire to escape her situation.

In 1907 Toklas left America. Soon after her arrival in Paris, she met Gertrude Stein and the two became intimate friends. Toklas recalled her first impression of Stein, of a "golden brown presence, burned by the Tuscan sun." The two women agreed to a marital relationship in 1908. Toklas soon joined Stein and her brother Leo in their apartment—Leo Stein left in 1913—and the two women lived together until Stein's death in 1946.

Toklas devoted herself to the care, ease, and fulfillment of Gertrude Stein. As Stein's secretary, Toklas typed, edited, and organized the writer's manuscripts. As her companion, she made travel arrangements, scheduled meetings, entertained visitors, and maintained their home. In the years following Stein's death, Toklas was instrumental in publishing Stein's unpublished works, worked with biographers and critics of Stein whose approaches pleased her, and annotated abstruse and allusive aspects of Stein's writing. In 1957 Toklas formally entered the Catholic Church to insure an afterlife with Stein.

Toklas collaborated with Stein on at least two books. She helped, in Stein's words, "to reduce tenses grammar spelling and genders into some kind of order" in Stein's *Picasso* (1938), then translated this work into English. It is problematic how much Toklas contributed to Stein's *The Autobiography of Alice B. Toklas*, but clearly she contributed anecdotes, observations, and judgements. There is some evidence Toklas and Stein jointly wrote Stein's "Ada" (1908 to 1912, exact date uncertain) and *A Novel of Thank You* (1925, 1994).

After Stein's death, Toklas published a number of books and articles. The most substantial of these is her volume of memoirs, *What Is Remembered* (1963). The material here is much the same as that in *The Autobiography of Alice B. Toklas*, but the tone is frequently more caustic and the scenes more carefully composed. The anecdotes are finely polished; they have the ring of having been told many times before and so brought to this final form.

Toklas' skill in rendering an event and portraying an acquaintance displays her finely honed intelligence. Though she devotes herself largely to fleshing out Stein's legend in her memoirs, Toklas' accomplished style shows her to be a prose writer in her own right.

The same anecdotal style pervades Toklas' *The Alice B. Toklas Cookbook* (1954, reprinted several times, most recently in 1994 and 1995). This work consists of both her own recipes and those of friends. More importantly, it includes reminiscences of friends, servants, and journeys. Toklas' writing is witty, laconic, and precise; her anecdotal style taut and ironic. The book reads as a memoir, with foods the emblems of memory. *Aromas and Flavors of Past and Present* (1958), edited by Poppy Cannon, is simply a collection of Toklas' recipes.

Toklas also wrote several articles in which she reminisces about literary life in Paris. In 1956, she published a translation of a book of fables, *The Blue Dog and Other Fables for the French*, written by the adolescent daughter of some friends. After her death, a volume of her letters appeared. *Staying on Alone: Letters of Alice B. Toklas* (1973) includes only letters written after Stein's death. They are gossipy, irreverent, and full of devotion to Stein's memory. They deal with Toklas' adjustment to life as a widow and her difficulties with Stein's heirs. When Toklas writes of herself as a woman, it is in the reflected glow of Stein's genius.

Toklas' writing is largely autobiographical. She presents an impression of herself as a loving woman devoted to the comfort of her spouse. She writes a carefully controlled prose, precise of phrase, concise and strong in its evocation of person and place. Toklas' role as secretary to Stein and her involvement with several generations of writers and artists earn her special interest as a participant in the expatriate American world of letters.

OTHER WORKS: *Baby Precious Always Shines: Selected Love Notes Between Gertrude Stein and Alice B. Toklas* (with G. Stein, 1999).

BIBLIOGRAPHY: Bridgman, R., *Gertrude Stein in Pieces* (1970). Levy, H., *920 O'Farrell Street* (1947). Friedrich, O., *The Grave of Alice B. Toklas and Other Reports from the Past* (1991, 1989). Lord, J., *Six Exceptional Women: Further Memoirs* (1994). Mellow, J. R., *Charmed Circle: Gertrude Stein & Company* (1974). Rogers, W. G., *When This You See Remember Me* (1948). Simon, L., *The Biography of Alice B. Toklas* (1977, 1991). Souhami, D., *Gertrude and Alice* (1999). Stein, G., *The Autobiography of Alice B. Toklas* (1993). Steward, S. M., *A Pair of Roses* (1993). Thomson, V., *Virgil Thomson* (1966). Windham, D., *The Roman Spring of Alice Toklas: 44 Letters by Alice Toklas in a Reminiscence* (1987).
Reference works: *Norton Book of Women's Lives* (1993). *Oxford Companion to Women's Writing in the United States* (1995).
Other references: *Biography* (Spring 1999). *Modern Fiction Studies* (1996). *People Weekly* (February 1996). *Prose* (Fall, 1973). *Twentieth Century Literature* (1999). *Women's Studies International Forum* (May 1993).

—JANIS TOWNSEND

TOMPKINS, Jane P.

Born 18 January 1940, New York, New York
Daughter of Henry and Lucille Reilly Parry; married Daniel P. Tompkins, 1963 (divorced); E. Daniel Larkin, 1975 (divorced); Stanley Fish, 1982

Nominated for a Pulitzer Prize in 1992 for nonfiction, Professor of English Jane P. Tompkins lets her unabashed affection for the work of Louis L'Amour, Zane Grey, and John Ford provide the backdrop for her examination of male Westerns and cultural polarities in gender and power in *West Of Everything: The Inner Life of Westerns* (1992). Tompkins combines a loving tribute with an unflinching condemnation and she shares her own inner great divide over male Westerns. Tompkins' work on Westerns followed her study of 19th-century sentimental novels; she sees the Westerns as a "cannon-burst" against sentimental women's fiction in the 19th century, against the dominance of women's culture and the women's invasion of the public sphere between 1880 and 1920. "It's about men's fear of losing their mastery, and hence their identity, both of which the Western tirelessly reinvents."

Tompkins had previously argued that serious study of the sentimental novels America produced in the 19th century offered substantial rewards. Her primary question is: What makes a literary classic? She argued it is not the intrinsic merit of a text, but rather the circumstances of its writing. She contends that writers like Brockden Brown, Cooper, Stowe, and Warner wrote in order to alter the face of the social world, not to elicit aesthetic appreciation. Thus the value and significance of the novels, for readers of their time, depended on precisely those characteristics that formalist criticism has taught us to deplore: stereotyped characters, sensational plots, and clichéd language. *Sensational Designs: The Cultural Work of America Fiction* (1985) angered some critics who saw her attempts to open up the literary canon to "classics" that the current critical tradition has ignored as "suffocatingly nationalistic."

Tompkins graduated from Bryn Mawr College with a B.A. magna cum laude in 1961 and did her graduate work at Yale University; she received an M.A. in 1962 followed by a Ph.D. in 1966. She began her teaching career at Connecticut College and Greater Hartford Community College. She taught at Temple University, Columbia University, and the Graduate School and University Center of the City University of New York. Since 1985 she has been professor of English at Duke University.

Tompkins' commitment to bringing heretofore unheralded "classics" to the reading public is reflected in her introduction to the Penguin Twentieth-Century Classic edition of Zane Grey's *Riders of the Purple Sage*. Her efforts have also recovered a novel first published in 1852. *The Wide Wide World* by Susan Warner is often acclaimed as America's first bestseller. Tompkins finds the value in these two texts, works often discounted and ignored.

In her most recent work, Tompkins turns the lens on herself. *A Life in School: What the Teacher Learned* (1997) is a painful and exhilarating story of Tompkins' spiritual awakening. She looks back on her own life in the classroom and discovers how much of what she learned there needs to be unlearned—she offers a critique of our educational system while also paying tribute to it. Tompkins identifies the key problem as an obsessive quest to educate as opposed to a shared exploration by student and teacher. "The university has come to resemble an assembly line, a mode of production that it professes to disdain. Each professor gets to turn one little screw—his specialty—and the student comes to him to get that screw turned. Then on to the next. The integrating function is left entirely to the student." Her prescription is for teachers to adopt a style of instruction that uses open discussions, intensive interaction, and more fluid syllabi.

In her literary criticism, Tompkins frequently unsettled the more traditional literary canon by examining texts often relegated to the margins. *A Life in School* takes as its starting point what is often most marginalized: the emotional dimensions of teaching. She describes the fear of shame and the desire for admiration and love that motivate the behavior of both teachers and students in higher education. Tompkins relates her four years of experimental teaching as an effort to unsettle and reform the authoritarian patterns that molded her as a teacher.

BIBLIOGRAPHY: *CANR* (1986, 1992).

—CELESTE DEROCHE

TOWNE, Laura M(athilda)

Born 3 May 1825, Pittsburgh, Pennsylvania; **died** 22 February 1901, St. Helena Island, South Carolina
Daughter of John and Sarah Robinson Towne

Laura M. Towne's father was from Massachusetts, her mother from Coventry, England. After the early death of her mother, the family moved to Boston, where the children were educated, and later to Philadelphia.

The Towne family became interested in abolition in Boston and had its abolitionist convictions reinforced by the sermons of Dr. William Henry Furness at the First Unitarian Church in Philadelphia. Towne became active in the movement while studying at Woman's Medical College and with Dr. Constantine Hering, the famous homeopath. When the Civil War began, she immediately sought to do what she could in the Union cause.

What came to be called the Port Royal Experiment provided Towne with the opportunity to engage in the teaching and medical and missionary work that was to occupy her for the last 40 years of her life. When Union forces occupied the Sea Islands of South Carolina seven months after the fall of Fort Sumter, resulting in the total abandonment of the islands by the white planters, the islands became an experiment in freedom for 10,000 slaves far behind Confederate lines.

Northern abolitionists, philanthropists, and antislavery government forces quickly organized contingents of volunteer teachers and labor superintendents to travel to the Sea Islands. In April 1862, Towne sailed from New York to Port Royal with one such group, sponsored by the Freedmen's Aid Society of Pennsylvania.

The freed slaves of the Sea Islands had been kept by the cotton aristocracy in abject poverty, superstition, and ignorance. Facing not only the difficulties of providing education, health care, and food and clothing for the people but also the unhealthy, smallpox-ridden climate and the constant threat of the return of Confederate soldiers, the Northern "Gideonites," as many were called, had to be a hardy, dedicated lot to remain and to succeed.

Not all remained, and not all succeeded with the tasks of the experiment in freedom, but Towne did, and she recorded her experiences in letters and a diary. She established the Penn School on St. Helena Island—a school which had continuous independent existence until 1948, when it became part of the South Carolina state school system—and soon impressed the community, Northern visitors, and the Freedmen's Bureau with the progress of pupils who received warm personal encouragement and no corporal punishment. Her medical training also made her the closest thing to a doctor the island had, and she spent long hours doctoring and nursing blacks and whites alike.

Towne eventually bought one of the abandoned St. Helena Island estates, Frogmore, and lived and worked out her life there with her friend Ellen Murray, returning to the North infrequently for holidays and family visits.

The manuscripts of Towne's diary and letters are more complete and somewhat more pungent in rebuking the rebels than is the version edited by Rupert S. Holland in 1912. But the edited version of Towne's writing, *The Letters and Diary of Laura M. Towne*, nevertheless gives a lively, personal account of an important sideline in Civil War history. Towne's letters and notes not only cover her comments on the major military and political figures and events of the Port Royal Experiment but are also sensitive descriptions of ex-slaves, of day-to-day existence, of the halting progress she sees in education, health care, and self-sufficiency. The primary historical account of the Port Royal Experiment, *Rehearsal for Reconstruction*, by Willie Lee Rose, relies heavily on the firsthand accounts of Towne and other similar Northern workers.

The impact of Northern white women school teachers on Southern black education after the Civil War is often forgotten. Towne was a forerunner, and her book is a forgotten link in our history.

OTHER WORKS: Laura M. Towne's diary is at the University of North Carolina; many letters from Towne are in the James Miller McKim Collection at Cornell University.

BIBLIOGRAPHY: Abbott, M., *The Freedmen's Bureau in South Carolina, 1865-1872* (1967). Evans, M., *Martha Schofield: Pioneer Negro Educator* (1916). Rose, W., *Rehearsal for Reconstruction* (1964). Simkins, F., and R. Woody, *South Carolina during Reconstruction* (1932). Tindall, G. B., *South Carolina Negroes: 1877-1900* (1966). Williamson, J., *After Slavery: The Negro in South Carolina during Reconstruction, 1861-1877* (1965). Other references: *Journal of Negro History* (1923).

—CAROLYN WEDIN SYLVANDER

TOWNSEND, Mary Ashley (Van Voorhis)

Born 24 September 1832, Lyons, New York; **died** 7 June 1901, Galveston, Texas
Also wrote under: Mary Ashley, Crab Crossbones, Michael O'Quillo, Henry Rip, Xariffa
Daughter of James G. and Catherine Van Voorhis; **married** Gideon Townsend, 1852

Mary Ashley Townsend was the only child of her mother's second marriage. Her father died when she was one year old, and her mother subsequently married a third time. The family, with five children, lived in pleasant circumstances in the country, and Townsend attended the district school and the academy. She married a first cousin and after living in Fishkill, New York, and Iowa City, they moved in 1860 to New Orleans, where they lived for the remainder of their lives. Townsend became known as the "poet laureate of New Orleans." Her husband, Gideon, was a successful businessman and they led an active social life. Three daughters were born to them.

The first in a long series of contributions by Townsend to newspapers was published in the *Daily Delta* (19 Sept. 1850), while she was in New Orleans visiting a married sister. In her many years as a writer, Townsend adopted different pseudonyms for her work in various genres. "Xariffa" was the signature used for a great many of her poems, especially in her early period. For essays on topics ranging from bonnets to warfare and in tones from light to serious, she used the name "Michael O'Quillo." She signed her name as "Crab Crossbones" to "Crossbones Papers," which were often didactic or satiric comments on society's foibles. "Henry Rip" was the signature to "My Penny Dip," a popular moral tale. Her own name, Mary Ashley, was signed to both prose and poetry late in her career. Her work was published in newspapers, magazines, and anthologies.

Townsend published a number of short stories, but her only novel was *The Brother Clerks: A Tale of New Orleans* (1857). The novel is concerned with the coming of age of two very different brothers, who move to New Orleans from New York, and with their experiences in a strange city. It has interesting sketches of what life was like in New Orleans in the early 19th century, but the characters do not really come alive. In common with the better-known fiction writers of the 19th century, Townsend has an intrusive manner in addressing comments directly to the reader.

Townsend was best known and widely praised for her poetry. It reflects her wide diversity of interests; much of it is of a moral or religious nature. Her love of the region is also evident. She was asked to write poems for many special occasions, which she did (but asked others to read for her, feeling her gift was for writing and not public reading). Her most popular poem was "Creed," first published in 1868, and reprinted many times. It is included in *Xariffa's Poems* (1870).

James Wood Davidson wrote in 1869, "Her blank verse is remarkable for its ease, vigour, and spirit." He compared her poetry favorably with all other women writers of the time. Four of her poems were printed in the *Louisiana Book* by Thomas McCaleb in 1894, and he quoted Henry Austin on her essentially Southern style, saying further: "This poet, I think, has written finer passages than any other American woman, except perhaps, Emma Lazarus and Sarah Helen Whitman." Grace King eulogized Townsend in 1901 as a poet and a woman who would be greatly missed by readers throughout the South.

OTHER WORKS: *The World's Cotton Centennial Exposition* (1885). *Easter Sunrise* (1889). *Distaff and Spindle* (1895). *Down the Bayou: The Captain's Story, and Other Poems* (1902).

BIBLIOGRAPHY: McCaleb, T., *The Louisiana Book* (1894). Manly, L., ed., *Southern Literature from 1579-1895* (1900). Meyer, A. M., "Mary Ashley Townsend: A Biographical and Critical Study" (thesis, 1938). Thompson, T. P., *Louisiana Writers, Native and Resident* (1904).
Reference works: *AA. DAB. Living Female Writers of the South* (1872). *Living Writers of the South* (1869). *LSL. Poets of America* (1886). *The South in History and Literature: A Handbook of Southern Authors* (1907).

—DOROTHY H. BROWN

TREADWELL, Sophie

Born 5 October 1885, Stockton, California; **died** 20 February, Tuscon, Arizona
Daughter of Alfred B. and Nellie Fairchild Treadwell

Sophie Treadwell was the only child of a pioneer California family. From her father, a judge whose maternal grandmother had raised him in Mexico, Treadwell inherited a passion for all things Spanish and Mexican.

During her years at the University of California at Berkeley, from which she graduated in 1906, Treadwell wrote some one-act plays and acted both on campus and in little theaters in nearby Oakland. Then after one year as a teacher in a one-room school at Yankee Jims, in the Mother Lode Country—where she impressed the natives with her insistence on feminist ideas—Treadwell returned to San Francisco, to work as a reporter on the San Francisco *Bulletin*, soon becoming a feature writer with her own byline. She attained verisimilitude for her "sob stories" by masquerading, for example, as a prostitute in order to prove the established churches gave "only a stone" to the poor unfortunate women who "asked for bread."

In 1910 Treadwell married a sports writer for the San Francisco *Chronicle*; in 1915, she went with him to New York, where he took a position with the New York *Herald Tribune*. The connection served Treadwell well; she persuaded the *Herald Tribune* newspaper to send her to Europe as a war correspondent during World War I.

Treadwell continued to write plays; by 1920 she had written nearly three dozen. In 1921 she used her Mexican connection to secure the only American interview with Pancho Villa at his ranch near Durango, Mexico. This visit resulted in her first professionally produced Broadway play, *Gringo* (1922). Throughout the rest of the decade, Treadwell concentrated on work for the theater. *Plumes in the Dust*, the story of Edgar Allan Poe, was originally written for John Barrymore but ultimately produced in 1936 with Henry Hull in the lead.

Treadwell's most successful effort, *Machinal* (1928), also was the result of her newspaper work—as a reporter covering the infamous Snyder-Gray murder case in 1927. *Machinal* provided the first starring role for the then-unknown Clark Gable. The play was staged in England and in many European cities, including two productions in Moscow. Treadwell was the first American playwright to be paid royalties in the U.S.S.R.

In 1938, insisting on the potential for achieving the "good life" through a return to traditional American values, Treadwell wrote *Hope for a Harvest*. When the play was produced in 1941, with Frederic March in the lead, it was rejected by a public that, on the eve of Pearl Harbor, no longer agreed that a simple return to farm life and hard work could be the solution to all problems.

Throughout most of the 1950s Treadwell lived in Spain, continuing to write and rewrite her plays. A novel was published in 1959. A careful craftsman, Treadwell never relinquished hope for another box office success to equal that of *Machinal*, and she left many versions of a great number of efforts in this direction. The only play produced in her final years was *Now He Doesn 't Want to Play*, set in Mexico. Even at eighty, Treadwell was actively engaged in the production at the University of Arizona, working with the director and rewriting throughout rehearsals, in

the vain hope the play would go to Broadway. As it turned out, Treadwell was destined to be remembered only for *Machinal*, which in itself is no small accomplishment.

In "real life" both lovers, Snyder and Gray, were found guilty of the murder of Snyder's husband and executed. But, with consumate skill, Treadwell concentrates in *Machinal* on the woman, making her female protagonist a genuinely universal character, a simple person, frustrated in every relationship through no fault of her own. Ultimately, the killing of her husband becomes an almost symbolic act—committed to free herself from a mechanistic world with which she cannot cope. She is very nearly acquitted, but the prosecutor reads aloud a deposition from her absent lover, now living in Mexico, in which he "tells all." This final, callous disregard for their relationship elicits a tortured admission of guilt, and the young woman goes to her death without understanding how the sin of murder made her "free and not afraid for one minute." *Machinal* was done on BBC-TV in England and on several American television programs in the 1950s. When it was revived at the off-Broadway Gate Theatre in 1960, it won the Vernon Rice Award.

Machinal, an eloquent statement about the stultifying effects of the mechanization and meaninglessness of the modern world and the lack of human concern for others, is a fitting obituary for Treadwell, a woman who strove passionately throughout her long life for the right to be an individual dedicated to old-fashioned humanistic principles.

OTHER WORKS: *Oh, Nightingale* (1925). *Lone Valley* (1933). *One Fierce Hour and Sweet* (1959).

There is a collection of Sophie Treadwell's unpublished plays at the University of Arizona, Tuscon.

BIBLIOGRAPHY: Gassner, J., *Best American Plays* (Early Series, 1900). Himelstein, M. Y., *Drama was a Weapon* (1976). Mantle, B., *Best Plays, 1928* (1929). Ross, I., *Ladies of the Press* (1936).

Reference works: *Oxford Companion to Women's Writing in the United States* (1995).

Other references: *Theatre Magazine* (Jan. 1929).

—EDYTHE M. MCGOVERN

TRILLING, Diana

Born 21 July 1905, New York, New York
Daughter of Joseph and Sadie Forbert Rubin; married Lionel Trilling, 1929 (died 1975); children: one son

Diana Trilling has spent most of her life in New York City, except for brief sojourns abroad, mainly at Oxford and London. In

1925 she received her B.A. from Radcliffe College, where she majored in fine arts. In 1929 she married literary critic and professor Lionel Trilling, who died in 1975. They had one son, who is an art historian.

From 1955 to 1957, Trilling was chairman of the board of the American Committee for Cultural Freedom. She has also served on the board of the *American Scholar* and is a member of the American Academy of Arts and Sciences. She awarded a Guggenheim fellowship in 1950, and in 1977 received a joint grant from the National Endowment for the Humanities and the Rockefeller Foundation for an oral history of the advanced literary-intellectual culture of New York from 1925 to 1975.

Trilling was fiction critic for the *Nation* from 1942 to 1949. A collection of the *Nation* reviews appears in *Reviewing the Forties* (1978). During the 1950s, Trilling frequently contributed penetrating essays on McCarthyism and civil liberties to the *New Leader*. Trilling has published widely, in periodicals ranging from the popular *Redbook* to the intellectual *Encounter* and *American Scholar*.

The *Claremont Essays* (1964) is a brilliant collection that demonstrates Trilling's salient qualities as a cultural critic—her fusion of literary, social, and political commentary in which the personal and the public, the thinking and feeling selves are combined. The critical analysis of *"The House of Mirth Revisited"* is no mere *explication de texte* but an explication of life as well. Granville Hicks has called "The Death of Marilyn Monroe" a masterpiece of analysis. "The Oppenheimer Case: A Reading of the Testimony" is political analysis informed by the examination of one thousand pages of court records.

In the more recent *We Must March, My Darlings* (1977), it is primarily the 1960s that are under scrutiny, and again the pen is far-ranging. This collection includes "The Assassination of President Kennedy," "Celebrating with Dr. Leary"—which Irving Howe praised as a "major demolition of everything in the late 1960s and beyond, that yielded to the soft swoon of unthinking"—and "On the Steps of Low Library," about the university revolts. One can never count on Trilling for the expected or comfortable ending. She defends anticommunists in "Two Symposiums," arguing one can be opposed to both communism *and* McCarthyism. Trilling sees the critic's function as a "moralizing function, whatever additional critical purpose he may also be pursuing," but she is never a propagandist. The title essay deals with the author's return in 1971 to Radcliffe, where she lived for almost nine weeks in a coed dorm. Trilling's detractors have accused her of siding with the older generation and of accommodating herself to institutional authority; but, in fact, she resists categories, and in many instances the young end up agreeing with her.

Trilling is not popular with radicals, partly because of her desire to point out ambiguities in the arguments of advocates of social theories. Unlike many feminists, she refuses to discount biology. Though she urges women to "direct their sensibility

outward, to the world of social and human fact," she is keenly aware of the significance of sexuality and its effect on personal freedom. In her provocative piece "The Liberated Heroine" (*Partisan Review*, 1978), Trilling contrasts contemporary "heroines" with earlier "heroines of spirit"—classical literary figures—and shows that women are still capitulating to men and accommodating to their fantasies.

Trilling is a critic in the liberal tradition. Her humanism recognizes the realities of lust and rage, whose boundaries Freud had mapped out, at the same time that it upholds the virtues of manners and form. One might say of her what she said of President Kennedy, that she has had the "ability to bring past and present together, with the hope that this [offers] of a continuing life in civilization—which is to say, a future."

OTHER WORKS: *The Portable D. H. Lawrence* (edited by Trilling, 1947, 1981). *The Selected Letters of D. H. Lawrence* (edited by Trilling, 1958). *Of This Time, of That Place, and Other Stories* (1980). *Uniform Edition of the Works of Lionel Trilling, 1978-80* (edited by Trilling, 1981). *Mrs. Harris: The Death of the Scarsdale Diet Doctor* (1981, 1982). *The Last Decade: Essays and Reviews, 1965-1975* (1982). *The Beginning of the Journey: The Marriage of Diana and Lionel Trilling* (1993).

BIBLIOGRAPHY: *From the Library of Lionel and Diana Trilling* (1998). Ozick, C. and Atwan, R., *The Best American Essays 1998* (1998). Podhoretz, N., *Ex-Friends: Falling Out with Allen Ginsberg, Lionel & Diana Trilling, Lillian Hellman, Hannah Arendt, and Norman Mailer* (1999). Thomson, V., *A Virgil Thomson Reader* (1981).

Reference works: *Oxford Companion to Women's Writing in the United States* (1995).

Other references: *Change* (March 1979). *Commentary* (July 1977). *New Leader* (23 May 1977). *NR* (20 Aug. 1977). *NYTBR* (15 March 1964). *Partisan Review* (1978). *SR* (14 March 1964).

—ELAINE HOFFMAN BARUCH

TROUBETZKOY, Amélie Rives

Born 23 August 1863, Richmond, Virginia; died 16 June 1945, Charlottesville, Virginia
Wrote under: Amélie Rives
Daughter of Alfred and Sarah Macmurdo Rives; married John Chanler, 1888 (divorced 1895); Pierre Troubetzkoy, 1896

Both of Amélie Rives Troubetzkoy's parents were of prominent Virginia families. Her father was a colonel of engineers on Robert E. Lee's staff. Soon after her birth, Troubetzkoy and her mother were moved to Castle Hill, the home of her father's parents, a gracious colonial estate in the foothills of the Blue Ridge Mountains not far from Charlottesville. Her grandparents took a great interest in Troubetzkoy's education, and she developed sophisticated tastes in the rich cultural milieu of Castle Hill. It became a center of security for her throughout her active life and provided the setting for a number of her novels.

By all accounts, Troubetzkoy was a beautiful and dynamic woman; and many of her heroines are reflections of herself in their vivacity, intelligence, sensitivity—and their luxuriant blond hair. She traveled widely and maintained contacts with many outstanding English and American authors of her time. Her first marriage proved incompatible and ended, amicably, in divorce in 1895. Her second marriage, to Prince Pierre Troubetzkoy, a young portrait painter who had given up his wealth and position in Russia, was long and happy.

Troubetzkoy's writing career spanned several American literary movements and several trends in American reading tastes. Frequently, the fiction that appealed most strongly to the public was not her strongest work. Troubetzkoy's first published story, "A Brother to Dragons" (*Atlantic*, March 1886), is a romantic, sentimental tale written in Elizabethan diction. Weak novels appealing to the public primarily for their exotic settings or melodramatic situations are interspersed throughout her career; still, the strength and development of Troubetzkoy's talents can be seen.

In *Virginia of Virginia* (1888), we can see the beginning of the strong Troubetzkoy heroine. Most critics praised its realism and dialogue while pointing out that it is an uneven work. The novel *The Quick or the Dead?* (1888) caused a public furor. The heroine is a young widow, and her debate on whether to remarry shocked propriety; yet more shocking were the scenes of sensuality, especially implications they were instigated by the heroine herself. But the novel is more than a deliberately sensational one; it is a sincere portrayal of the painful self-questioning Barbara undergoes as she considers the conflict between what she sees as her duty and feels as her need for fulfillment. Tinged with sentimentality and flowery diction, it is not consistently realistic; but in many ways *The Quick or the Dead?* is a more open, honest statement of the sexuality of women than the major realists of the period allowed.

As a result of its notoriety, *The Quick or the Dead?* became a bestseller. In its sequel, *Barbara Dering* (1893), Barbara continues to show a conflict between her true nature and her expected role. In both novels, Troubetzkoy uses nature imagery to reveal this conflict.

Another strong heroine is Phoebe, the protagonist of *World's End* (1914), a novel winning high critical praise and had large sales. Phoebe, like earlier heroines, is a young woman of feeling and intellect; but she is less perfect and more realistic and develops more as a character than her predecessors. In this novel, for the first time, the heroine is matched by a fully developed,

strong male character. Troubetzkoy's later works move more and more to sympathetic, less stereotyped male characters, possibly because of her years of happy marriage with Pierre. In *World's End*, the conflict is resolved in the sense that the heroine comes to some self-knowledge; but, as is usual in Troubetzkoy's novels, there is no totally happy ending.

Troubetzkoy's *Shadows of Flames* (1915)—reflecting her own experience with drug addiction—*The Queerness of Celia* (1926), and her last novel, *Firedamp* (1930), are all among her best works, but do not quite equal the achievement of *World's End*.

In addition to her novels, Troubetzkoy wrote drama and poetry throughout her career. She published several plays written in blank verse and a long narrative poem, *Seléné* (1905), which shows a skillful handling of sustained verse, with many fine sensuous passages.

During and after World War I, Troubetzkoy wrote a series of plays which had successful Broadway runs, including *Allegiance, The Fear Market* (of which a movie version was made), and an adaptation of Mark Twain's *The Prince and the Pauper*. *Love-in-a-Mist* (1927) was an effective comedy of manners, and her only commercially successful play to be published after its Broadway run. Her last play, *The Young Elizabeth* (1938), shows her admiration for the young queen who is torn between love and duty; Elizabeth becomes a true Troubetzkoy heroine.

Troubetzkoy has been called a realist, a fine local colorist, and an important social historian; she has also been called a semierotic, a sensationalist, a romantic who revels in morbid scenes and hysterical passions. Both strengths and weaknesses can be found in her work. Troubetzkoy did not always use her many talents to their best artistic effect; her active life and spontaneity may have led her away from careful revision. But the vitality and sincerity of much of her work remain fresh and significant for modern readers.

OTHER WORKS: *A Brother to Dragons, and Other Old-Time Tales* (1888). *Herod and Mariamne* (1888). *The Witness of the Sun* (1889). *According to Saint John* (1891). *Athelwold* (1893). *Tanis, the Sang-Digger* (1893). *A Damsel Errant* (1898). *Augustine, the Man* (1906). *The Golden Rose: The Romance of a Strange Soul* (1908). *Trix and Over-the-Moon* (1909). *Pan's Mountain* (1910). *Hidden House* (1912). *The Ghost Garden* (1918). *As the Wind Blew* (1920). *The Sea-Woman's Cloak and November Eve* (1923).

BIBLIOGRAPHY: Clark, E., *Innocence Abroad* (1931). Longest, G., *Three Virginia Writers: Mary Johnston, Thomas Nelson Page, and Amélie Rives Troubetzkoy: A Reference Guide* (1978). Manly, L., *Southern Literature from 1579-1895* (1895). Meade, J., *I Live in Virginia* (1935). Painter, F., *Poets of Virginia* (1907). Taylor, W., *Amélie Rives (Princess Troubetzkoy)* (1973).

Reference works: *LSL*, 10.

Other references: *Lippincott's* (Sept. 1888). *Mississippi Quarterly* (Spring 1968). *Virginia Cavalcade* (Spring 1963).

—ANNE NEWMAN

TRUITT, Anne

Born 16 March 1921, Baltimore, Maryland
Married James Truitt (divorced 1971); **children:** Alexandra, Mary, Sam

''I will be going along, doing one thing on the surface—while underneath something else is brooding and preparing itself—the thing I'm going to do next,'' Anne Truitt said in an interview with Eleanor Munro. On the surface, Truitt is an astonishing artist of sculptures, paintings, and drawings. Since her first exhibit, a one-artist show with dealer Andre Emmerich in New York City in 1963, Truitt has proven herself to be one of the most profound artists of this century. She has won several awards, like the Guggenheim Fellowship in 1971 and the National Endowment of Arts Fellowship in 1972 and 1977.

Truitt earned her B.A. in psychology at Bryn Mawr College in 1943. Afterward, she decided to turn down a scholarship from Yale and took a night class in sculpture in Cambridge. She went on to formally educate herself in art at the Institute of Contemporary Art in Washington, D.C. (1949-50). During the time of her education and private work, Truitt destroyed the art she created from 1950 to 1961, saying, ''My eye was off then.'' As she realized herself as an artist, Truitt became a writer. Merely accounting her own life, she wrote three insightful journals: *Daybook: The Journal of An Artist* (1982, reprinted 1987, and with an excerpt published in *The Norton Book of Women's Lives*, 1993), *Turn: The Journal of An Artist* (1986, 1987), and *Prospect: The Journal of An Artist* (1996).

Committing herself to introspection through writing, Truitt began *Daybook* on 6 June 1974, the day she visited a friend in Arizona. The visit was an attempt for rest after she had just accomplished two retrospective exhibits: one at the Whitney Museum of American Art in December 1973 and the other at the Corcoran Gallery of Art in Washington in April 1974. The journal was inspired after the exhibits were displayed and she experienced a disturbing realization that her life had gone by without attention to her feelings. She concealed them with her art. Her writing articulates her thoughts of growing old and how it had been artistically recorded. She is aware that she had not given much thought to the time in between young and old when she wrote of her modeling of human bodies: ''Classical beauty held no interest to me. I pursued the marks of experience. . .'' She then added, ''When I modeled one marked, used female body after another, I was recording adumbrations of what I have now, at the age of fifty-three, become.''

While writing *Daybook*, Truitt continued her daily routine: gardening, taking care of her three children and home, and working in the studio. She wrote this diary for seven years and, at the end of those years, brought ''the artist of the present together with the artist of the past.'' The private writing of the journal was not unlike Truitt. Seeing her sculptures with clear vision, she always worked on them in seclusion, insomuch as to put her work in storage for no public eye. That was until Ken Noland, the owner of the studio she rented, asked to see the sculptures. After a progression of talks by Noland to friends in the art circle, Emmerich took her work, displayed them appropriately, and her identity as an artist became public.

In *Turn*, Truitt's consideration of her age and death is pursued further for two-and-one-half years of writing. She begins in July 1982, after her ex-husband, James Truitt, killed himself in November 1981. She struggles with the pain of the loss, noting they had been divorced 10 years prior to his death, while contemplating her own death.

Her writing is moving and bounces the reader through all emotions with grace and ease. *Turn* brings both laughter and tears as Truitt shares her happiness in the publication of *Daybook* and her sadness of James' death. Despite her melancholy feeling toward his suicide throughout the diary, Truitt's writing in *Turn* is lighter, even happier, than that of *Daybook* because she is no longer concerned with finding herself as an artist. She has already done so in *Daybook*. Truitt has a change in attitude, a ''turn,'' in her second disclosure. She revels in her joys of being a grandmother, takes in daily life as a teacher and gardener, and enjoys the company of family and friends. *Turn* is the emergence of a defined artist and woman of wisdom.

Spring 1991 through spring 1992 Truitt finds herself ''as a person who is preparing to reach the end of a long life.'' She considers this closeness to death in *Prospect*, a journal she begins to write as a last attempt to bring her life together as a whole. Burdened by the fears of death, illness, decreased finances, and worry for her children and grandchildren, Truitt's writing forces her to face harsh reality. The diary becomes a remembrance of her life as she prepares for a retrospective exhibition, an attempt to increase her financial worth once more, with Emmerich's gallery—this time showing 30 years of her art. As she goes through piece by piece of her sculptures, paintings, and drawings from 1961 to 1991, she recollects her life with literary eloquence. ''The work demanded to be answered to,'' she wrote, giving her art the honor it deserves. She successfully brings a sense of completeness as she fully understands the meaning of her past and courageously accepts her fated future.

Aside from her work as an artist and writer, Truitt spent much of her time as a professor at the University of Maryland beginning in 1975. She also served one year as acting Director of Yaddo, a retreat for artists.

OTHER WORKS: *Anne Truitt: Sculpture and Drawings, 1961-1973* (exhibition catalogue, 1974). *Anne Truitt: Sculpture and Painting: 17 October-19 November 1976, University of Virginia Art Museum* (exhibition catalogue with E. Carmean, 1976). *Originals: American Women Artists* (1979).

BIBLIOGRAPHY: Berger, M., *Beyond Formalism: Three Sculptors of the 1960s: Tony Smith, George Sugarman, Anne Truitt : 18*

September-24 October 1986, Hunter College Art Gallery, New York City (exhibition catalogue, 1986). Harrop, J. F., "Anne Truitt and the Minimalist Movement" (thesis, 1983).

Reference works: *Newsmakers* (1993).

Other references: *Anne Truitt: The Influence of Willa Cather on Her Art* (videocassette, 1985). *NYTBR* (April 1996). *Studies in Art Education* (Winter 1991). *The Future of the Object in Art* (audiocassette, 1979).

—KIMBALLY A. MEDEIROS

TRUMAN, Margaret

Born Mary Margaret Truman, 17 February 1924, Independence, Missouri

Writes under: Margaret Truman Daniel

Daughter of Harry S. and Elizabeth Virginia "Bess" Wallace Truman; **married** Clifton Elbert Daniel, 1956; **children:** Clifton, William, Harrison, Thomas

Like Reeve Lindbergh, Margaret Truman is another famous daughter-turned-writer. The child of President Harry S. Truman and First Lady Bess Wallace Truman, Margaret grew up around Washington, D.C., politics and politicians; her friends include Drucie Snyder Horton, daughter of John W. Snyder, Secretary of the Treasury for the Truman Administration. So it is no wonder that her writings, both fiction and nonfiction, center around her famous family, those involved in politics and history, and the nation's capital.

Truman attended public school in Independence, Missouri, until 1934, when her father was elected to the U.S. Senate. A talented singer, Truman began taking voice lessons at the age of sixteen and made her concert debut singing over a nationwide radio hookup with the Detroit Symphony Orchestra. She graduated from George Washington University in 1946, receiving a B.A. in history. Her father, then the president, gave the commencement address and presented her with her diploma. In 1949 she made a concert appearance with the National Symphony Orchestra at Constitution Hall in Washington. In 1956 Truman married Clifton Daniel, who would later become the chief of the *New York Times* Washington Bureau.

Beginning her career as a writer of nonfiction, Truman's *Souvenir: Margaret Truman's Own Story* came out in 1956, the story of growing up in the White House and in politics. *White House Pets* (1969), a chronicle of the "First Pets" (animals in the Oval Office), followed. In 1972 she released a book about her father titled *Harry S. Truman*, a thorough biography of one of the most important political figures of the 20th century, containing unequaled insight and understanding of the man's extraordinary life and offering rare glimpses of the personalities and politics behind the world events of his time.

More books about the Truman family followed, with *Letters from Father: The Truman Family's Personal Correspondence* (1981) with and about her father, and then *Where the Buck Stops: The Private and Personal Writings of Harry S. Truman* (1989), by her father, and edited by Margaret, containing the 33rd president's interesting theories and opinions on leadership and leaders, plus his Letterman List of picks for the best and worst presidents, all penned in President Truman's bluntly honest "give 'em hell" style. Truman's son Clifton Truman Daniel also wrote *Growing Up with My Grandfather: Memories of Harry S. Truman* (1994), and Truman wrote a book about her mother, *Bess W. Truman*, published in 1986.

Women of Courage came out in 1976, called by some the female version of John F. Kennedy's *Profiles in Courage*. The book contains brief biographies emphasizing the courage of 12 women both famous (such as Susan B. Anthony and Dolly Madison) and little known in U.S. history, including Susan Livingston, Sarah Winnemucca, Ida Wells-Barnett, Elizabeth Blackwell, Marian Anderson, and others.

First Ladies (1995) examines the lives of the women who occupied the White House with their husbands. As a First Daughter, Truman has known and met First Ladies from Frances Cleveland to Hillary Clinton. The book also contains interviews with Lady Bird Johnson, Betty Ford, Nancy Reagan, Rosalynn Carter, Barbara Bush, and Mrs. Clinton; and recollections of Pat Nixon, Jacqueline Kennedy Onassis, Edith Wilson, and Eleanor Roosevelt. In addition, Truman wrote about Dolly Madison, Mary Todd Lincoln, Grace Coolidge, Julia Tyler, Julia Grant, and Mamie Eisenhower. The result is a remarkable group portrait of the women who have more than merely resided in the house on Pennsylvania Avenue.

Truman has won numerous accolades as both writer and political figure. In 1984 she was the recipient of the Harry S. Truman Public Service award presented annually by the City of Independence (Missouri) to an outstanding American citizen, an ironic honor considering her lineage and city of birth are both represented therein.

In 1980 her first novel, *Murder in the White House*, was published, beginning a long career as a mystery writer. She subsequently released a novel a year until 1987. *Murder at Kennedy Center* came out in 1989, followed by *Murder at the National Cathedral* (1990), *Murder at the Pentagon* (1992), *Murder on the Potomac* (1994), *Murder at the National Gallery* (1996), *Murder in the House* (1997), and *Murder at the Watergate: A Novel* (1998). Three of her books were collected in *Margaret Truman: Three Complete Mysteries* (1994). Many mystery writers seem to try and capitalize on a theme—Sue Grafton with her alphabet mysteries, guaranteeing her at least 26 novels, Lillian Jackson Brown and her cat series, Dick Francis favoring horses. All of Truman's mystery novels center around the nation's capital and its monuments. Called the Capital Crimes Mysteries, starting in the White House in 1980 (a good place for a former First Daughter to begin), Truman takes us to Capitol Hill, the Supreme Court, the Smithsonian, Embassy Row, the FBI, to Georgetown, and the CIA before 1989, often featuring the elegant couple Mackensie "Mac" Smith and Annabel Reed as they become enmeshed in political imbroglios and murder.

Though not known for stellar dialogue, well-developed characters, or gripping cliffhangers, Truman's thoughtful meditations and sarcastic snickers about politics and politicians are a delight. We've yet to see the monuments (Washington, Jefferson, or Lincoln), the Treasury building, and others. What happens, though, when she runs out of famous places in Washington, D.C., about which to write?

OTHER WORKS: *Murder on Capitol Hill* (1981). *Murder in the Supreme Court* (1982). *Murder in the Smithsonian* (1983). *Murder on Embassy Row* (1984). *Murder in the FBI* (1985). *Murder in Georgetown* (1986). *Murder in the CIA* (1987).

BIBLIOGRAPHY: Ferrell, R. H., ed., *The Autobiography of Harry S. Truman* (1980). McCollough, D., *Truman* (1992). Daniel, C. T., *Growing up with My Grandfather: Memories of Harry S. Truman* (1994). Klein, K. G., *Great Women Mystery Writers: Classic to Contemporary* (1994).

—DARYL F. MALLETT

TRUTH, Sojourner

Born circa 1797, Ulster County, New York; **died** 26 November 1883, Battle Creek, Michigan
Daughter of Elizabeth and James; **married** Thomas; **children:** five

Sojourner Truth, born a slave approximately 30 years before New York State abolished the institution, was originally given the name Isabella. From 1810 to 1827, she belonged to John Dumont, but left him when he broke his promise to manumit her one year before he was legally required to do so. She took the surname Van Wagenen from a family with whom she subsequently resided. In 1843 she adopted the name "Sojourner Truth" after hearing a call to become an itinerant preacher.

Much of Truth's early life is undocumented. Her first language was Dutch, and she spoke with a Dutch accent throughout her life. As a slave, she gave birth to a minimum of five children, one of whom likely died in infancy and two of whom were sold as children. Truth's eventual public commitment to justice was foreshadowed when her son Peter was sold, contrary to New York law, to an Alabama plantation owner. Despite her inexperience with the judicial process, Truth sued successfully for his return.

After attaining her freedom, Truth moved to New York City and worked as a domestic. She participated in several churches, eventually aligning herself with Robert Matthews, who, calling himself Matthias, founded the Kingdom of Mathias. In 1833 he organized a short-lived and scandal-ridden communal society of which Truth was a member. After this organization foundered, Truth lived more quietly and conventionally until she became Sojourner Truth in 1843.

Despite her lifelong illiteracy, Truth spent the summer of 1843 walking across Long Island and through Connecticut, singing at revivals and speaking at various church meetings, and acquiring the beginnings of her reputation as an orator. She spent the subsequent winter in Northampton, Massachusetts, within another communal society, this one organized by George W. Benson, the brother-in-law of William Lloyd Garrison. Through this association she became a resolute abolitionist. After several years in Massachusetts, she began to travel throughout the Midwest, sharing public speaking responsibilities with such other abolitionists as Frederick Douglass.

Her autobiography, *Narrative of Sojourner Truth* (1850), an as-told-to narrative transcribed and edited by Olive Gilbert, was published in 1850. This narrative is comparatively brief; it is at its liveliest when Truth describes her determination to take her freedom from Dumont despite his attempt to renege on his promise and when she anxiously pleads for the return of her son Peter. Later she describes her distress after Peter goes to sea; he rarely wrote and didn't return home when expected. At the time the *Narrative* was composed, Truth hadn't heard from Peter in nearly 10 years; he never reappeared in her life. During her speaking tour after its publication, Truth lived primarily off the profits from the book's sale.

She became a women's rights advocate at this point, a decision that permitted her to continue her career as an orator during the years following the Civil War. Although Truth lived as a free woman for over 50 years, including nearly 20 following the Civil War, she would die two generations before passage of the woman suffrage amendment.

Truth is perhaps most well known for her "Aren't I a Woman" speech, which she also delivered in 1850. The exact text of this speech is unknown, for although it was transcribed by a newspaper reporter, he portrayed Truth's accent and diction as stereotypically Southern rather than the Dutch-accented English she spoke. This speech was prompted by a rumor that Truth was in fact a man, an accusation made in part because of her physical appearance, particularly her height, and her voice. When someone asked her to prove she was a woman, she did by lifting her blouse and baring her breast. The speech interrogates stereotypes regarding gender—she is strong, hard-working, and muscular, but she has also borne and raised children and suffered the anxiety and grief mothers suffer. Although men have not treated her as a "lady," she refuses to conflate the definition of "lady" with "woman" and continues to insist on her own femininity. She concludes with the assertion that if the first woman was strong enough to disrupt all of human history, then a crowd of contemporary women should be able to accomplish at least as much in the way of good.

After her *Narrative* was published, Truth moved to Battle Creek, Michigan, where she would eventually settle permanently. She worked during the Civil War to see that African-American regiments were adequately supplied, and worked with newly freed slaves for a year in Virginia. In 1864 she was received by President Lincoln in the White House, an unusual honor for African-Americans even during the Lincoln presidency. Back in Battle Creek, she received flocks of visitors until she died in 1883. She is buried in Oak Hill Cemetery in Battle Creek.

BIBLIOGRAPHY: Painter, N. I., *Sojourner Truth: A Life, A Symbol* (1996).

Reference works: *NAW* (1973).

—LYNN DOMINA

TUCHMAN, Barbara

Born 30 January 1912, New York, New York; **died** 6 February 1989, Greenwich, Connecticut

Daughter of Maurice and Alma Morgenthau Wertheim; **married** Lester R. Tuchman, 1940

Barbara Tuchman was a distinguished American historian who created narratives that brought to life people, places, and events of the past. Although academics at times criticized her approach, she earned the respect of many historians and had a loyal following among lay readers. She strongly believed history should be readable, and her grounded attitude carried through in her fascinatingly plotted history books.

Tuchman's first book, *The Lost British Policy: Britain and Spain since 1700*, appeared in 1938. During the following 50 years, she received critical and popular acclaim for her studies in history, with subjects ranging from 14th-century England to late 20th-century America. Two won Pulitzer prizes and several became bestsellers. Her commentaries on American and world policies also appeared in distinguished journals.

Tuchman's grandfather was Henry Morgenthau Sr., the businessman and diplomat; her uncle was Henry Morgenthau Jr., Roosevelt's Secretary of the Treasury; and her father was an international banker and owner of the *Nation*. Tuchman was educated at Radcliffe College. Her first job, with the Institute of Pacific Relations, took her to Tokyo in 1935. One of her earliest works is an essay on the Japanese character published in the prestigious *Foreign Affairs* when she was only twenty-three.

Tuchman's work as a journalist during the next seven years, reporting from the war in Spain and writing in London for the magazine *The War in Spain*, led to the publication in England of her first book, *The Lost British Policy*.

Tuchman's *Bible and Sword: England and Palestine from the Bronze Age to Balfour* (1956) argues that support for the Jewish homeland in Palestine had a double root: imperial strategy in defense of Suez, India, and Middle Eastern oil fields, and the attitude toward what Thomas Huxley called the "national epic of Britain," the Bible. In 1958 came *The Zimmerman Telegram*, a historical work that aroused both professional respect and popular notice. It tells the story, only partly known until then, of efforts by German Foreign Minister Arthur Zimmerman, before America's entrance into World War I, to bring about an alliance with Mexico in return for territorial concessions in the United States.

The Guns of August (1962), which brought Tuchman a Pulitzer, applied a similar technique to a broader and more significant moment in World War I. Beginning with the description of the funeral of Edward VII, Tuchman sketches the familial and political ties of Germany, England, and France and makes clear the interrelatedness of their world on the eve of its dissolution. It is typical of Tuchman's style in its mix of detail and long view, character, and event. She aims at an account of the way things happened, rather than seeking the underlying causes or attempting to convert events into arguments for historical theory.

Nevertheless, in her next book, *The Proud Tower: A Portrait of the World Before the War, 1890-1914* (1966), Tuchman describes her interest in writing about the decade before World War I as coming in part from a desire to understand the war. Although the individual chapters—for example, on the Dreyfus case—are beautifully done, it is not easy to see how these particular parts of a social history support a coherent conception of the origins of the war.

In *Stilwell and the American Experience in China, 1911-45* (1970), for which Tuchman received her second Pulitzer prize, the career of General Joseph W. Stilwell becomes the central focus of an examination of the relationship of America and China. Tuchman sees Stilwell as quintessentially American and his career in China as a "prism of the times," representing America's greatest effort in Asia as well as the "tragic limits" of America's experience there. Tuchman believes the efficiency and aggressiveness Stilwell brought were like the Christianity and democracy he also represented—all foreign to Chinese society and not assimilable.

While the response of professional historians to *Stilwell and the American Experience in China* was very positive, *A Distant Mirror: The Calamitous 14th Century* (1978) has been the most criticized of any of Tuchman's books. It has, however, received an enthusiastic greeting from the layperson eager to read well-shaped narrative about an unfamiliar period. Tuchman regards the 14th century as a period like our own, "a distraught age whose rules were breaking down under the pressure of adverse and violent events." Her original plan to follow the effects of the bubonic plaque was changed to allow her to explore the marriage alliances and treaties that made up medieval diplomacy and to examine the code of chivalry. Whatever professional questions have been raised about the book's overarching concept, its sense of time and place are as brilliant as in any of Tuchman's works.

Practicing History (1981) is a collection of essays in which Tuchman discusses the techniques and role of the historian. She also comments on some crucial events of her own day: the Six Day War, Watergate, and Vietnam. Tuchman's *The March of Folly: From Troy to Vietnam* (1984) examines four episodes of evident governmental blunder across a broad sweep of time, attempting to discern their commonalities. Her subjects include the Trojans' decision to bring a mythical Greek horse within their city walls, the refusal of six Renaissance popes to arrest the church's growing corruption, British misrule under King George III, and the mishandling of Vietnam by the U.S. She notes three vital connections between these highly varied events: that those responsible were all forewarned of outcomes of "folly"; that feasible alternatives existed; and that a group rather than an individual perpetrated foolishness. Although the book was criticized for its lack of a true common thread, Tuchman was praised for her thoroughness, imagination, and valuable insight into the political process.

In her final book, *The First Salute: A View of the American Revolution* (1988), Tuchman turns to the subject of the American Revolution and the reasons for Britain's defeat. Focusing on the failure of famed British naval officer Sir George Brydges Rodney to pursue the French fleet from his Dutch West Indian island base, Tuchman places the Revolution in international context. She draws parallels between the Dutch struggle for independence and that of the American colonies and, with great admiration for the leadership of George Washington, examines the forces on both the British and American sides that resulted in the American victory.

In addition to books and articles, Tuchman produced a significant paper on disarmament in the early 1980s entitled "The Alternative to Arms Control" for the Center for International Strategic Affairs at the University of California. Tuchman's many honors include honorary degrees from Yale, Columbia, Harvard, and New York University; the Regent Medal of Excellence from the State University of New York; and the Order of Leopold from the Kingdom of Belgium.

OTHER WORKS: *The Other One* (alternate title *Possessed*, 1955). *Notes from China* (1972). *The Book* (1980).

BIBLIOGRAPHY: *Atlantic* (Dec. 1988). *Nation* (26 Apr. 1971, 6 Mar. 1989). *NYRB* (22 Dec. 1988). *NYT* (19 Oct. 1958; 7 Mar. 1984; 7, 8, 13 Feb. 1989). *NYTRB* (28 June 1962, 3 Feb. 1968, 28 Sept. 1978, 11 Mar. 1984, 2, 16 Oct. 1988, 12 Nov. 1989). *Time* (3 Oct. 1988, 7 Nov. 1988, 20 Feb. 1989). *Times* [London] (8 Feb. 1989).

—LOIS HUGHSON AND MARGIT GALANTER,
UPDATED BY JANETTE GOFF DIXON

TURELL, Jane

Born 25 February 1708, Boston, Massachusetts; **died** 26 March 1735, Medford, Massachusetts
Daughter of Benjamin and Jane Colman; **married** Ebenezer Turell, 1726; **children:** four, all died young

Jane Turell's father was minister of the innovative Brattle Street Church and an influential figure in Boston's cultural and religious life. Like the fathers of other notable 18th-century New England women, Colman carefully attended to his daughter's education, so that by the time Turell was four she had amassed amounts of knowledge remarked upon by her father's peers. She began writing poetry under her father's guidance when she was about eleven years old. Throughout her life, Colman remained her mentor in spiritual and literary matters, partly through a lively, intimate exchange of letters and poems.

Turell's husband, a Congregationalist minister, had a pastorate in Medford, Massachusetts, where the couple settled. Of their four children, three died in infancy; one survived to age six. Turell suffered from bouts of illness and depression for many years and died at age twenty-seven.

Turell wrote poetry and prose throughout her adolescent years, and her poetic ambitions were not diminished by domestic duties and pregnancies. Her reading ranged from divinity to history, medicine, public debates, and poetry. After her death, her husband wrote a short biography, interspersed with selections from her works, to illustrate her talent and piety. He wished her life and work to serve as examples for young New England women. First published in Medford in 1735 as *Reliquiae Turellae et Lachrymae Paternal*, the slim volume contains correspondence, diary extracts, short religious essays, and verse—the only extant samples of Turell's writing. Unfortunately, because he published her work to illustrate her piety, her husband excluded material, such as her humorous verse, that he judged unsuitable.

It is probable that, even before her death, Turell's works circulated in manuscript form among her friends and acquaintances, as was customary in 18th-century New England. She achieved enough contemporary fame as a writer to warrant a second edition of the biography, published in 1741 as *Memoirs of the Life and Death of the Pious and Ingenious Mrs. Jane Turell*.

Like many of her female contemporaries, Turell had no wish to compete with male writers or to be published; she wrote privately, discussing personal events and religious ideas. She read widely in the neoclassic English poets and copied their style, adapting it to her religious subjects. Even her eulogies of other writers find their meaning in religious themes. She praises the English moralist poet Elizabeth Singer because Singer attacked evil: "A Woman's Pen Strikes the curs'd Serpents Head, / And lays the Monster gasping, if not dead."

Turell's neoclassicism is evident in a poetic enticement to her father to pass the hot summer months in Medford. "An Invitation into the Country in Imitation of *Horace*'' is exactly what the title indicates. She compares harsh city life to the joys of innocent country living, transforming her small New England village and rural domicile into a model Arcadia. She lures her father with pastoral descriptions of ''soft Shades'' and ''balmy Sweets / of Medford's flow'ring Vales, and green Retreats'' and an occasional New England touch: ''Yet what is neat and wholsom. . .Curds and Cream just turn'd.''

She again mixed the neoclassic, religious, and personal in what is perhaps her most moving work, a lament for her dead children, written during her last pregnancy. She recollects the pains of childbirth in vivid tropes, but ends the poem with a reaffirmation of faith in Christ, as she pledges her next child to God's service.

The major portion of Turell's verse consists of skillful paraphrases of psalms and canticles, which reveal her understanding of Puritan ideas and historiography. For example, she transforms Psalm 137 to dramatize the Puritan's experiences in the New World, changing a Babylonian landscape into American wilderness.

Most of Turell's prose pieces are simple meditations on religious subjects, often expressing doubts and fears over the state of her soul. In letters to her father, she repeatedly sought comfort from anxiety. Often, in more serene moments, she wrote short, essaylike letters to her younger sister, guiding her towards a life of virtue and pietry and advising her to abandon the frivolities of youth. Her prose works are thoughfully serious, although undistinguished in style and content.

Since only fragments of Turell's work are available, a thorough assessment remains impossible. Clearly, she imitated her father's style and ideas, and she followed the prescriptions of early-18th-century poetics. Religious themes are ever present, and abstractions and personifications are common in her poetry. Much of her later verse indicates a potential never realized.

BIBLIOGRAPHY: Brooks, C., *History of the Town of Medford* (1855). Evans, C., *American Bibliography* (1912).
Reference works: *NAW* (1971).

—JACQUELINE HORNSTEIN

TURNBULL, Agnes Sligh

Born 14 October 1888, New Alexandria, Pennsylvania; **died** January 1982
Daughter of Alexander H. and Lucinda McConnell Sligh; **married** James Turnbull, 1918; **children:** one daughter

Of Scots Presbyterian background, Agnes Sligh Turnbull grew up in western Pennsylvania and graduated from Indiana (Pennsylvania) State College in 1910. She then attended the University of Chicago for one year. She was married in 1918 and had one daughter.

Turnbull's fiction is varied and uneven. She began with a number of sentimental and undistinguished narratives about actual and imagined Biblical women. Scattered throughout her career are a few children's books: *Elijah the Fishbite* (1940), *Jed, the Shepherd's Dog* (1957), *George* (1965), and *The White Lark* (1968).

Her best fiction deals with Scottish settlers in the coal country of western Pennsylvania. Major concerns are the difficult lives of pioneer women and the effect upon them of their strict Presbyterianism. Her attitude toward this faith is ambivalent. While she dramatizes the psychological damage done by adherence to the Calvinistic doctrine of predestination and portrays Episcopalianism as gentler (see especially *The Rolling Years*, 1936, and *The Bishop's Mantle*, 1947), she also shows the comfort and sense of community given by the faith. In some books (notably *The Gown of Glory*, 1952, and *The Nightingale*, 1960) set in the early years of this century, she writes nostalgically of smalltown life centered around the local Presbyterian church. Her women are strong and self-reliant, but they also are traditionally home and family centered.

Two of Turnbull's finest novels are set on the Pennsylvania frontier during the Revolutionary War. Vividly depicting the joys and hardships of the frontier, *The Day Must Dawn* (1942) tells of a gently bred pioneer woman who schemes to have her daughter go east to an easier life. The novel climaxes with an Native American raid, based on an actual incident, and ends with her dying acceptance of the fact her daughter will marry a frontiersman and go West to still wilder country, postponing the dream for another generation.

The King's Orchard (1963), set in the same period and using some of the same historical material, is a fictionalized biography of James O'Hara, who came to this country shortly before the Revolution, traveled west to Indiana, became Washington's quartermaster during the war, and was prominent in the early history of Pittsburgh. Many other historical personages, of minor as well as major importance, figure in its pages. It effectively contrasts settled Philadelphia, rough young Pittsburgh, and the wilderness that would become Indiana and Illinois.

For other novels Turnbull turned to the late 19th and early 20th centuries. The most ambitious of these, *The Rolling Years*, studies three generations of Scots Presbyterian women in western Pennsylvania. Sarah McDowell bears 12 children (of whom five survive) to her dour Calvinistic husband; her bitterness about her repeated, difficult confinements is effectively shown. Her last child, Jeannie, has an easier and yet more restricted life. A gay and loving girl, she marries a minister and moves to town. As a young widow, she rears her daughter, Constance, with the help of her spinster sisters, who are also strikingly portrayed. Engaged to a Presbyterian divinity student, Constance faces her crisis when he denies some of the tenets of their faith. Thus the novel dramatizes the gradual weakening of the strict Calvinism of the Scottish immigrants as their life grows increasingly easy.

Remember the End (1938) tells of Alex MacTay, a poetic young Scotsman who comes to Pennsylvania in 1890. Suppressing his aesthetic interests, he rises to great wealth and power, but at the cost of deeply wounding his wife and alienating his only son. Sympathetically portrayed, he typifies the strengths and weaknesses of the great tycoons of the period, such as his own model, Andrew Carnegie.

Much of Turnbull's fiction tends toward the sentimental and some of her novels seem written to inculcate an easy and conventional morality. In addition, her novels tend to use trite plot devices. But at her best, in the novels studying her Scottish background in western Pennsylvania, she has created moving and believable pictures of women's joys and sufferings.

OTHER WORKS: *Far Above Rubies* (1926). *The Wife of Pontius Pilate: A Story of the Heart of Procla* (1928). *In the Garden: A Story of the First Easter* (1929). *The Four Marys* (1932). *The Colt that Carried a King* (1933). *Old Home Town* (1933). *This Spring of Love* (1934). *Dear Me: Leaves from the Diary of Agnes Sligh Turnbull* (1941). *Once to Shout* (1943). *The Golden Journey* (1955). *Out of My Heart* (1958). *Little Christmas* (1964). *The Wedding Bargain* (1966). *Many a Green Isle* (1968). *Whistle and I'll Come to You: An Idyll* (1970). *The Flowering* (1972). *The Richlands* (1974). *The Winds of Love* (1977).

BIBLIOGRAPHY: *NYHTB* (26 Oct. 1947). *NYTBR* (9 Feb. 1936, 27 Nov. 1938, 25 Oct. 1942, 26 Oct. 1947, 16 March 1952). *SR* (17 Oct. 1942, 19 Nov. 1955).

—MARY JEAN DEMARR

TURNEY, Catherine

Born 16 December 1906, Chicago, Illinois
Daughter of George W. and Elizabeth Blamer Turney; **married** Cyril Armbrister, 1930; George Reynolds, 1940

When Catherine Turney was six months old, her family moved to Rome, New York, where she grew up. In 1921 they moved to Pasadena, California. She studied play and short story writing at Columbia School of Journalism. In the summer of 1926, she began to work at the Pasadena Playhouse, where she assisted Gilmore Brown on the world premiere of Eugene O'Neill's *Lazarus Laughed*. She became director of the Playhouse Workshop and received a scholarship when the School of Theatre was officially established; she graduated in the first class in 1931.

Turney organized the Bandbox, a small touring company that later became the Leo Carillo Theater on Olvera Street in Los Angeles. As the difficulties of maintaining such theaters multiplied, she turned more and more to writing. She first wrote scripts for radio, a medium to which she returned from time to time. In 1936 Turney's first stage play, *Bitter Harvest*, opened in London, concerning the ill-fated love of Byron for his half sister. *My Dear Children*, produced on Broadway in 1938, was an excellent starring vehicle for John Barrymore. It capitalized on his reputation as a romantic figure and reveals the strong sense of theater characterizing much of Turney's work.

She wrote for Metro Goldwyn Mayer for a year during the 1930s, and for Warner Brothers from 1942 to 1948. Among her screen credits are *Mildred Pierce* (first draft, 1945), *A Stolen Life* (1946), *Winter Meeting* (1948), *My Reputation* (1946), and *Cry Wolf* (1947). In 1949 she moved to New York to write television scripts for Studio One and Starlight Theater, later returning to California where she continued to write for television shows such as Ford Theater, Lux Video, One Step Beyond, and Walt Disney.

Turney wrote one novel, *The Other One* (1955, later called *Possessed*), a supernatural story. Its dramatic quality led to its being made into a film, *Bring Back the Dead* (1956). *Byron's Daughter* (1972) is a biography of Medora Leigh, daughter of Byron and his half sister. It is a readable and well-documented study of an element in the poet's life that had previously been ignored.

Turney's films, particularly those written for Warner Brothers, are often characterized as "women's pictures," in part because the starring roles went to actresses like Bette Davis, Barbara Stanwyck, and Eve Arden; in part because the subject matter supposedly appeals to a female audience. Like her stage plays, however, they are theatrically effective vehicles with strongly characterized roles for all the players.

OTHER WORKS: *Surrender the Seasons* (1981).

BIBLIOGRAPHY: *Chicago Tribune* (9 May 1939, 21 Jan. 1973). *LAT* (19 Nov. 1972). New York *Daily News* (1 Feb. 1941). *NYRB* (22 Feb. 1973). *TLS* (14 June 1973).

—HELENE KOON

TUTHILL, Louisa (Caroline) Huggins

Born 6 July 1799, New Haven, Connecticut; **died** 1 June 1879, Princeton, New Jersey
Wrote under: Mrs. Louisa C(aroline) Tuthill, Louisa Tuthill
Daughter of Ebenezer and Mary Dickerman Huggins; **married** Cornelius Tuthill, 1817 (died 1825); **children:** four

Educated in seminaries for young ladies in New Haven and Litchfield, Connecticut, Louisa Caroline Huggins Tuthill apparently expected to settle down into an unexceptional life as a lawyer's wife, but a religious experience caused her husband to give up the law for the ministry and an attack of typhoid fever forced him to give up the ministry for a brief attempt at publishing a literary magazine. Tuthill encouraged his wife to write. After his death in 1825, she began to write steadily and seriously in order to support herself and her four children.

Tuthill's guidebook for young girls leaving school, *The Young Lady's Home* (1839) is a combination of vignette, sermon, and sentiment typical of her work. It is dedicated "to my young friends, who, in completing school education, have arrived at an important era in life, hoping it may aid you in estimating the value of knowledge already acquired, in the momentous task of self-education, and the performance of the duties at home." Throughout, the emphasis is on the qualities and accomplishments that make one "a good, useful American woman!" In the modest fictional frame of the book, three girls leave school together. Clara, who feels "every inch of the United States is home to me," returns to her mother to learn domestic economy and later marries a kind and distinguished U.S. senator. Isabel, who longs for the lights of New York, is gradually brought to an understanding of the dangers of pride and, with the guidance of Clara and her husband, exercises her Christian usefulness by rescuing from poverty the third friend, Geraldine, who, searching for the excitement of Europe, has married "a dissipated gambler."

Tuthill counsels young women to be silent in company and to respect their elders, but she also insists on good nutrition, plentiful exercise, and fresh air. She advocates a much broader curriculum than was generally recommended for female education at the time: systematic and continuous study of history, literature, natural science, composition, classical and modern languages, and the fine arts—especially architecture. Tuthill wrote the first history of architecture published in the U.S. (1848).

Among the most successful of her guidebooks for behavior were *I Will Be a Lady: A Book for Girls* (1845) and *I Will Be a Gentleman: A Book for Boys* (1846). A popular author, whose works often ran to many editions and were reprinted in England, Tuthill wrote with a clear intention to instruct, to edify, and to raise the moral tone of the women and children who read her books.

OTHER WORKS: *James Somers: The Pilgrim's Son* (1827). *Love of Admiration* (1828). *Mary's Visit to Boston* (1829). *Ancient Architecture* (1830). *Calisthenics* (1831). *The Young Lady's Reader* (edited by Tuthill, 1839). *The Belle, The Blue, and the Bigot* (1844). *Onward! Right Onward!* (1844). *Any Thing for Sport* (1846). *When Are We Happiest* (1846). *My Wife* (1846). *Hurrah for New England* (1847). *The Mirror of Life* (edited by Tuthill, 1847). *My Little Geography* (edited by Tuthill, 1847). *The Boarding-School Girl* (1848). *The Boy of Spirit* (1848). *History of Architecture from the Earliest Times* (1848). *Goals and Guerdons* (1848). *The Nursery Book* (1849). *The Merchant* (1850). *A Strike for Freedom* (1850). *Braggdocio: A Book for Boys and Girls* (1851). *Queer Bonnets* (1852). *Tip-top* (1853). *Joy and Care* (1855). *Beautiful Bertha* (1855). *Reality* (1856). *Edith, the Backwoods Girl* (1859). *Caroline Perthes, the Christian Wife* (edited by Tuthill, 1860). *I Will Be a Soldier* (1862). *Romantic Belinda*

(1864). *Larry Lockwell; or, I Will Be a Sailor* (1864). *True Manliness* (1867). *The Young Lady at Home and in Society* (1869). *Get Money* (1871).

BIBLIOGRAPHY: Reference works: *Appleton's Cyclopedia of American Biography* (1889). *NAW* (1971).

—KATHARYN F. CRABBE

TUVE, Rosemond

Born 27 March 1903, Canton, South Dakota; **died** 21 December 1964, Bryn Mawr, Pennsylvania
Daughter of Anthony G. and Ida Larsen Tuve

With a father who was president of Augustana College and a mother who taught music at the same institution, Rosemond Tuve lived her entire life in the climate of higher education. She earned her B.A. from the University of Minnesota in 1924 and her M.A. from Bryn Mawr in 1925, studied at Johns Hopkins (1926-28) and Oxford the next year, and completed her Ph.D. at Bryn Mawr in 1931. Tuve taught at a number of American colleges and universities; she was a professor of English at Connecticut College for Women for 28 years.

A Democrat, Tuve spent three summers teaching at the Bryn Mawr School for Women Workers in Industry and was a member of the National Association for the Advancement of Colored People (NAACP). She was a member also of many professional and literary organizations and the recipient of honorary degrees and awards. She contributed incisive articles on Spenser, Chaucer, Ramus, and other medieval and Renaissance authors to scholarly journals and wrote several books. Characteristic of her perspective is the stress on the importance of historical scholarship as opposed to "criticism without footnotes."

Elizabethan and Metaphysical Imagery: Renaissance Poetics and 20th Century Critics (1947) distinguishes between imagery as defined by Romantic criticism and Symbolist poetics, and the theories and practices of Renaissance poetry. Citing "modern man" as "surely the timidest host any century has produced," Tuve emphasizes that Renaissance poets, who saw their art as concerned with truth and directed to the reasoning mind of humankind, produced "imagery such as no period since has matched. . .images of such profound reach that our own more self-conscious attempt to 'be suggestive' cannot rival them in penetration." Her style is clear, forceful, and quietly witty, as when she comments that "no one who leaps to his feet to announce a critical error ever sits down without adding some new one."

In the words of medievalist Dorothy Bethurum, Tuve's next book, *A Reading of George Herbert* (1925), "rescued Herbert from the Freudian critics and returned the study of his poems to their traditional background of liturgical symbolism." "What kind of readers do we make," Tuve asks, "whom circumstances have intervened to make ignorant of what every literate man once knew?''

Tuve's *Images and Themes in Five Poems by Milton* (1957) focuses on earlier poems rather than on the great epics or *Samson Agonistes*. In 1958 Tuve gave a BBC talk (''Rosemund Tuve on John Milton,'' *Listener*, 1958) in which she explains that works of art are ''irrevocably born one of a kind,'' and that ''the way *peculiar to him* in which a great poet uses a common archetypal image or a familiar symbol is part of that uniqueness.''

Essays by Rosemond Tuve (1970) gathers previously published essays into one convenient volume: three on education, seven on Edmund Spenser, two on George Herbert, and two on John Milton. There is also a bibliography of all of Tuve's articles and reviews and all books, except for the unaccountable omission of *Allegorical Imagery: Some Medieval Books and Their Posterity* (1966) a posthumously published book based on an almost complete manuscript.

The value of Tuve's work lies in her constant faith in the importance of literature, her particularized onslaughts on modern arrogance and ignorance, and her patience in teaching students how to rise above the problems surrounding the art of reading well. Her disciplined studies made her not only the foremost authority on the subject of Renaissance imagery but also a leading exponent of the relationship between pictorial and verbal imagery and of the significance of *which* books an author had read and *how* the author had read them.

OTHER WORKS: *Seasons and Months: Studies in a Tradition of Middle English Poetry* (1933). *Palingenius' ''Zodiake of Life''* (Introduction by Tuve, 1947).

BIBLIOGRAPHY: Roche, T. P., Jr., Introduction to *Essays by Rosemond Tuve* (1970).
Other references: *CA* (1964). *NYT* (22 Dec. 1964). *PMLA* (June 1960). *TLS* (5 Sept. 1958, 9 Sept. 1958, 26 Sept. 1958).

—VIRGINIA R. MOLLENKOTT

TY-CASPER, Linda

Born 17 September 1931, Manila, Philippines
Daughter of Francisco Figueroa Ty and Catalina Velasques-Ty; married Leonard Casper, 1956; children: Gretchen, Kristina

Although Linda Ty-Casper has lived for over 35 years in the U.S. with her husband, writer and critic Leonard Casper, and their two daughters, she has maintained her Philippine citizenship and makes frequent visits there. She has published nine novels and two collections of short stories, all of which focus on life in the Philippines, with a strong concern for historical and political crosscurrents and developments, particularly the long history of

colonialism and revolution and the imposition of martial law. One of her recent novels, *Awaiting Trespass* (1985), could not be published there for political reasons during the last years of the dictatorship of Ferdinand Marcos, which came to an end in 1986 with the Peoples Revolution. Published in Britain and the U.S., it recounts the mysterious death by torture of a prominent citizen.

Trained as a lawyer, with law degrees from both the University of the Philippines (1955) and Harvard University (1957), Ty-Casper began writing fiction almost immediately upon graduation from law school. She started her first novel in 1957, she says, ''because I'd read some historical accounts which were derogatory to the Philippines and I wanted to answer them.'' The result was *The Peninsulars* (1964), in which Ty-Casper brings to life the impact of Spanish colonialism on the Philippines in the 18th century, heightened by the English invasion of Manila and early, unsuccessful attempts by various local factions at gaining independence.

With a precision of detail and observation, Ty-Casper documents in short stories and novels the personal and political lives of her characters with great subtlety. Moral choices are often at the center of the conflicts faced by her characters, but these choices evolve naturally out of the lives of the characters themselves; they are not imposed on them by the author. Ty-Casper's writing often joins the precision of a legal brief with a poetry of brilliantly ambiguous imagery. With careful and understated language, she explores the difficult decisions encountered by ordinary people confronted with violence and political treachery.

Ty-Casper's approach to writing and to her characters is that of the storyteller. Her writing takes on a cumulative trancelike quality that weaves the reader into the events that it recounts by maintaining a cool and distanced objectivity that is at the same time passionate and deeply felt. Her later work, such as *Wings of Stone* (1986), becomes almost surrealistic as her characters encounter the frenetic tensions of modern-day life in the Philippines and the United States. Her storyteller's voice, she says, was inherited from her grandmother, who told her stories during World War II.

The post-Marcos Philippines is the backdrop for Ty-Casper's novel *DreamEden* (1997). Although a number of books have been written using this venue in the years since the 1989 coup, Ty-Casper is uniquely qualified to handle the issues and weaves a story which, in her own words, ''focuses on the experiences of the people.'' The story involves the conflicts and dreams of a jaded attorney, the politician he works for, and others who adjust daily to the changes brought about by revolution. As always, her characters are three-dimensional and pull the reader into their lives. Filipinos rejoiced at their new freedom after the overthrow of Marcos but were then faced with adjusting to a life with less structure and order. This same type of conflict is evident in the lives of the characters in *DreamEden*. Ty-Casper's research into newspaper archives and interviews with those who have lived the revolution make this a believable piece of fiction.

Ty-Casper is working on a yet to be released novel on the Philippine-American War of 1899, provisionally titled *The Stranded Whale*. She is an officer of the Boston Authors, the oldest continuing writers group in the U.S., originally founded in 1900. She has had fellowships at Harvard, Radcliffe College, and the Massachusetts Artists Foundation. In 1993 Ty-Casper won a UNESCO/PEN short story prize and the Southeast Asia WRITE award.

OTHER WORKS: *The Transparent Sun and Other Stories* (1963). *The Secret Runner and Other Stories* (1974). *The Three-Cornered Sun* (1979). *Dread Empire* (1980). *The Hazards of Distance* (1981). *Fortress in the Plaza* (1985). *Ten Thousand Seeds* (1987). *A Small Party in a Garden* (1988). *Common Continent: Selected Stories* (1991).

BIBLIOGRAPHY: Bresnahan, R., *Conversations with Filipino Writers* (1990). Casper, L., *New Writing from the Philippines* (1966). Lumbera, B., *Revaluation: Essays on Philippine Literature, Cinema, and Popular Culture* (1984). Montenegro, D., *Points of Departure: International Writers on Writing and Politics* (1991). Valeros, F., and E. Greunberg, *Filipino Writers in English* (1987).

Reference works: *CA* (1983). *CANR* (1988). *Encyclopedia of World Literature* (1992). *Oxford Companion to Women's Writing in the United States* (1995).

Other references: *Belles Lettres* (May-June 1987). *Philipinas* (Fall 1987). *PW* (26 May 1997). *World Literature Today* (Winter 1998). Geocities web site: http://www.geocities.com/Paris/4485/linda.html.

—DAVID MONTENEGRO,
UPDATED BY REBECCA C. CONDIT

TYLER, Anne

Born 25 October 1941, Minneapolis, Minnesota
Daughter of Lloyd P. and Phyllis Mahon Tyler; married Taghi Mohammad Modaressi, 1963; children: two daughters

Anne Tyler was raised in North Carolina. She graduated from Duke University with a major in Russian (1961) and pursued graduate work at Columbia University (1962). She served as Russian bibliographer at the Duke University Library and as assistant to the librarian at McGill University Law Library in Montreal. In 1963 Tyler married a child psychiatrist, and they had two daughters.

Tyler has been prolific: she has written several phenomenally bestselling novels and numerous short stories, which appear in many diverse magazines, from *McCall's* to the *New Yorker*. Tyler introduces most of the major characteristics of her novels in her first, *If Morning Ever Comes* (1964). Plots involve the complexities of family life and are geographically bound to small towns in North Carolina or to withering row houses or more fashionable Roland Park in Baltimore. The title of each novel appears in the text and focuses on a major theme. Humor, often bittersweet, is important. Characterization is Tyler's greatest strength, especially

of old people who are presented with compassion and of invincible and usually eccentric women. Tyler uses diction and grammar to establish her characters' backgrounds and imagery reflecting their problems and traits: "Pieces of Emerson were lodged with Elizabeth like shrapnel." She has established herself as a writer of unquestioned talent.

Jeremy Pauling, of *Celestial Navigation* (1974), is a sensitive and shy artist who lives in his own mind and who finds forays into the real world puzzling and, finally, destructive. The chapters centering on him employ a narrative voice, but the six chapters devoted to four women in Jeremy's life all use first person voices. Ironically, Jeremy experiences his greatest happiness and creativity after his mother's death (an event his sisters thought would devastate his life) and after Mary and their children depart, leaving only a note on the refrigerator door. Both Jeremy—"Wasn't that what life was all about: steadfast endurance?"—and Mary—"I don't know which takes more courage: surviving a lifelong endurance test because you once made a promise or breaking free, disrupting your whole world"—embody the trait Tyler insists on for most of her characters: endurance.

Searching for Caleb (1975) juxtaposes the comic and the serious, chronicling three generations of a Baltimore family of Roland Park. Family strife climaxes when the first cousins, Justine and Duncan, marry each other. These two set out on adventures best symbolized by the Mayflower truck that moves their rosewood chests and crystal from Roland Park and by the orange U-Haul van that, much later, moves only their books and clothes to a circus' winter trailer park. Like *Celestial Navigation*, this novel brings characters into Chekhovian scenes where people talk to unlistening ears. Daniel and Caleb Peck, Tyler's most endearing old people; Justine, Daniel's fortune-telling, nomad-like granddaughter; other Pecks; and eccentric strangers make up this comic novel, which details man's foibles, charms, mores, weaknesses, and flaws.

In *Earthly Possessions* (1977), Charlotte Emory gives a minute account of being kidnapped in a Maryland bank and abducted to Florida. In alternate chapters she tells the history of her own life (a struggle to dispossess herself of encumbering possessions) and the histories of the peculiar and unhappy families of her mother and husband. Richly humorous, this novel epitomizes in Charlotte a woman Tyler frequently portrays—a woman denied the autonomous existence she craves. No shrill feminist cries rise from Tyler's fiction, but an existential longing for freedom does.

Eccentric characters are prominent in Tyler's work; they settle into a private world, unconcerned with the day-to-day activities that dominate the lives of others. *Morgan's Passing* (1980) presents a highly eccentric character, Morgan Gower, in fascinating detail. The reader, however, is left somewhat at a loss, never completely sure of the character or of his personae.

A skillful writer, Tyler treats serious and often tragic themes without sacrificing the comic. Her prose, as some critics charge, is not stylistically daring, and her concerns are not with depressed minorities or with mythic ghosts. Instead, she writes truly about the lives of middle class Americans, and her characters dwell, as

John Updike has said, ''where poetry and adventure form as easily as dew.''

Tyler's critical and popular success has increased steadily. Since *Morgan's Passing* she has published more critically acclaimed and prize-winning novels and many short stories. In 1988, *The Accidental Tourist* (1985, a National Book Critics award-winner) became a major motion picture starring William Hurt; in the same year, Tyler received the Pulitzer Prize for fiction for *Breathing Lessons* (1988).

All of Tyler's novels take place in Baltimore, where she has lived for many years. They are portraits of families who, behind the appearance of normality, shelter idiosyncrasies, pain, and secrets. *Dinner at the Homesick Restaurant* (1982) begins with 85-year-old Pearl Tull looking back on her life and the three children she raised alone after being abandoned by her husband. Gradually, the reader sees the profound effect this desertion has had on each character, and the inability of these children to escape their past, even as adults. In the end, however, the bonds of family overcome the pain of years of misunderstandings and lack of communication.

The Accidental Tourist is about the Learys, another abandoned family. Most of the story centers around Macon Leary, a man controlled by structure and routine. His apparent refusal to grieve after the brutal murder of his son drives away his wife, causing Macon to draw even more inward. Not until he meets Muriel Pritchett, whom he hires to train his unruly and sometimes vicious dog, does Macon finally begin to live. The Learys are an excellent example of Tyler's ability to portray a seemingly ordinary family with all their quirks and hangups in a subtle, ironic, and humorous way.

Breathing Lessons (1988) takes place in one day, with periodic flashbacks. During the journey to and from a friend's funeral, Ira and Maggie Moran come to certain realizations about their children and themselves, particularly how different from their expectations their life has become. Recognizing their regrets, they also come to know the importance of the bond they share.

The Bedloe family in *Saint Maybe* (1991) has also failed to live up to its own expectations. It is the ''ideal'' family, but through a series of tragic events, the course of all their lives changes drastically and permanently. The novel focuses on Ian, the youngest son, who sacrifices his own goals and dreams in an effort to make amends for what has happened. With more sadness and less humor than Tyler's previous work, the novel delves beautifully into the lives of ordinary people and the necessity for endurance.

Winner of the 1996 O. Henry award, *Ladder of Years* (1996) tells the adventures of Mrs. Delia Grinstead, who, following a chance encounter at a grocery store while on vacation with her family, runs away to begin a new life as Miss Grinstead. Life's little complications happen to Miss Grinstead just as they did to Mrs. Grinstead. *Ladder of Years* is a novel about marriages of all sorts, family relationships, and the interaction of people in general. The theme of *Ladder of Years* alludes to *King Lear*: when all

three of his boss's daughters are lined up in front of him, Sam Grinstead chooses the youngest, Cordelia (''Delia'') to become his bride. A fairy tale of sorts ensues, but for Delia all is not the ''happily ever after'' of fairytales. *Publisher's Weekly* said Tyler ''engages our sympathy and growing respect for a character who finally realizes that the ladder of years is a time trip to the future.''

A *Patchwork Planet* (1998) again is a study of family life and interpersonal relationships. Tyler once again makes the ordinary magical as she weaves the story of Barnaby, a wealthy ne'er-do-well, as he tries to make something of his life. The reader comes to care about Barnaby, struggling along with him as he tries to turn his life around. Tyler's first foray as a writer of children's literature came in 1993 with the publication of *Tumble Tower*. Written for children ages four to eight, *Kirkus* called it ''a gently subversive fable celebrating the rewards of disorder.'' It is the story of Molly, whose discomfortingly messy room ultimately offers comfort to the rest of her family.

Tyler continues to write novels of family life peopled with characters who are true-to-life in middle-class oddball families, dealing with loneliness, isolation, human interaction. A psychologist analyzing her characters might call them dysfunctional, but they continue to be endearing to the reader. All of Tyler's main characters face crossroads, and while deciding what to do, waver, just like ''real'' people. The rest of her novels deal with the results of the decision ultimately made. Her work retains its clarity of style, and her ability to combine the tragic with the comic gives her characters a genuine humanity. She consistently addresses the individual struggle for identity, happiness, and fulfillment, and demonstrates that the simple, even the apparently trivial, is sometimes the source of what is most rich and complex in life, and well worth examination.

OTHER WORKS: *The Tin Can Tree* (1965). *A Slipping-Down Life* (1970). *The Clock Winder* (1972). *The Best American Short Stories of 1983* (edited with S. Ravanel, 1983).

BIBLIOGRAPHY: Petry, A. H., *Understanding Anne Tyler* (1990). Rainwater, C. and W. J. Scheick, eds., *Contemporary American Women Writers: Narrative Strategies* (1985). Stephens, C. R., ed., *The Fiction of Anne Tyler* (1990). Sternburg, J. ed., *The Writer on Her Work: Contemporary Women Reflect on Their Art and Situation* (1980). Voelker, J., *Art and the Accidental in Anne Tyler* (1989).

Reference works: *CA* (1974). *CANR* (1984, 1991). *CLC* 7 (1977, 1979, 1981, 1984, 1987, 1990). *CBY* (1981). *DLB* (1980). *DLBY* (1982). *MTCW* (1991). *Oxford Companion to Women's Writing in the United States* (1995). *SATA* (1975).

Other references: *Atlantic* (Mar. 1976). *Atlantis: A Women's Studies Journal* (Fall 1987). *Classical and Modern Literature* (Fall 1989). *English Journal* (Fall 1987). *Hollins Critic* (Apr. 1986). *Iowa Journal of Literary Studies* (1981). *KR* (1997). *Mississippi Quarterly* (Winter 1988). *New England Review and Bread Loaf Quarterly* (Spring 1985). *NY* (29 Mar. 1976, 6 June 1977). *People* (26 Dec. 1988). *Southern Literary Journal* (Fall

1983). *Southern Quarterly* (Summer 1983). *SR* (Jan. 1978, Fall 1984).

Web sites: Amazon.com, and various reviews and articles available online at: http://auxiliaries.ba.kent.edu/pages/Book/ Bizs/fiction.html; http://books.realcities.com/reviews/0420/patch- workworkplanet1/.htm; http://www.canoe/ca/JamBooksReviews/jul5_ patchwork.html; and http://www.kirjasto.sci.fi/atyler.htm; http:// www.randomhouse.com/.

—ELIZABETH EVANS,
UPDATED BY SHAUNA SUMMERS AND HEIDI HARTWIG
DENLER

TYLER, Martha W.

Born circa 1830s; **died** death date unknown

The only surviving biographical information about Martha W. Tyler is what can be surmised from her only known novel, the autobiographical *A Book Without a Title; or, Thrilling Events in the Life of Mira Dana* (1855).

Mira Dana, Tyler's heroine, challenges any definition of womanhood forcing her to submit to tyrannical authority. Her early battles with the Lowell mill owners who employ her as a factory operative become the model for her subsequent encounters with all representatives of male power, be they husbands, doctors, lawyers, bankers, or publishers. In this, the first American novel to depict a strike, Mira convinces her coworkers to oppose an arbitrarily imposed pay cut. The decision to become a striker entails a new definition for womanhood, a definition predicated on woman's right to justice and self-expression. Mira explains, "ought we not [to strike], when they are striving to crush our very souls for cursed gold? They'll find that there is *one* girl in Lowell who *dares* to speak of liberty and act like a true woman."

In her preface Tyler explains that her novel should be read not as a work of art but as a direct attack on the misuses of mate authority. She describes a world in which the supposedly reciprocal relationship between the sexes has broken down. She asks how women can be expected to behave properly within their own sphere when men neither respect women's sphere nor fulfill their obligations within the male sphere.

Although difficult to read because of its erratic plot and often tortured prose, the novel merits resurrection because of the intriguing information it provides for both the historian and the literary critic. Tyler pays attention to the early women factory workers, the mid-19th-century phenomena of bank failures and financial crises, and the consequences of structuring a society according to the doctrine of separate sexual spheres.

Like her contemporaries Harriet Beecher Stowe and Fanny Fern, Tyler wrote fiction in explicitly political terms, while writing within the popular tradition of domestic fiction written for women. Like many of the female novelists who wrote during the mid-19th century, Tyler, in drawing attention to various aspects of women's position in society, was in part responsible for the popularization of those issues which would eventually develop the struggle for women's rights into a mass movement.

BIBLIOGRAPHY: Blake, F., *The Strike in the American Novel* (1972). Hill, V. L., "Strategy and Breadth: The Socialist-Feminist in American Fiction" (dissertation, 1979).

—VICKI LYNN HILL

TYLER, Mary (Hunt) Palmer

Born 1 March 1775; **died** 7 July 1866
Also wrote under: An American Matron
Daughter of Joseph P. and Elizabeth Hunt Palmer; **married** Royall Tyler, 1794 (died 1826); **children:** 11

Mary Palmer Tyler was born of a respected family in Boston on the eve of the American Revolution. At the age of nineteen she married her father's close friend and contemporary, Royall Tyler, a lawyer who was already celebrated for writing the first native comedy to be produced in America. The couple moved to Brattleboro, Vermont, where Tyler bore and raised her 11 children (all surviving childhood and most prospering as adults), nursed her husband through his final illness (1821-6), and then survived him by 40 years. In her later years, she was supported by her children and revered in her community where she was known affectionately as "Madam Tyler." Tyler's obituary describes her as "imparting a tone of elevation and refinement, and an ambition for literary pursuits, to the new and unformed society around her."

In 1810 Tyler, already the mother of eight children, wrote a child-care manual, *The Maternal Physician*. This book was reprinted in 1972 as part of a series on medicine and society in America because it is the first book of its genre to have been written in the new world. In correspondence with his publisher, Royall Tyler notes that his wife insisted on remaining anonymous, even though she was offered more money for the book if she would sign it.

Tyler's intent in *The Maternal Physician* was to give medical advice to families based on her own successful experience. In an age when infant death was a common and accepted occurrence, she criticizes the tendency to be passive in the face of illness. She asserts that the mother is the child's best guardian and must be ever vigilant, vigorous in the treatment of the slightest ailment, and willing to call a doctor if the complaint is serious.

The book includes advice on bathing, sleeping, teething, weaning, obedience, exercise, diet, and disease. If Tyler didn't have firsthand experience with an illness, she quoted from British medical authorities of the day. Her remedies, including a wide variety of herbal treatments, sound totally unfamiliar now, but her basic philosophy of childrearing remains remarkably fresh and sound: she advocates gentle, firm, consistent guidance.

Grandmother Tyler's Book was undertaken by Tyler in her eighty-third year at the request of her children and grandchildren.

It is a series of vivid reminiscences of her girlhood and marriage. Through the efforts of her descendants, it was finally published in 1925. The earliest stories, dealing with the events of the Revolution in and around Boston, are interspersed with quotations from her mother's memoirs. Although too young to remember it, Tyler had been told of her father's participation in the Boston Tea Party. Her mother actually describes her fright when he came home in his Native American costume.

From the age of nine, Tyler had admired her father's friend, Royall Tyler. She discloses the story of his disastrous love affair with Abby Adams (daughter of John Adams), which ended as a consequence of his having "lived too gay a life." When they did marry, the marriage was kept a secret for a while, owing apparently to the opposition of Tyler's mother.

During the time Tyler was secretly married, pregnant, and waiting at home for her husband to establish a law practice in the wilds of Vermont, she suffered a great sense of sinfulness and a crisis of faith. This was resolved after many months by a dream in which she was chased by wolves to the edge of a precipice only to be rescued at the last minute by the figure of Christ. He encircled her waist with his arm and said, "Lean on me and I will save you." From this time on, Tyler's profound faith sustained her through many trials, including the lingering and painful cancer which killed her husband, and the consequent poverty and reliance on friends and neighbors to sustain the family. She accepted good and bad fortune alike with the comment that all was God's will.

Tyler's observations of family life are as unsentimental and spirited as her advice on childrearing. Her faith and her maternal orientation gave meaning to her life and to the books she wrote as an expression of gratitude for and pleasure in that life.

OTHER WORKS: Mary Palmer Tyler's letters and a journal (1821-40) are preserved by the Vermont Historical Society at Montpelier, Vermont, in the Royall Tyler Collection.

BIBLIOGRAPHY: Tanselle, G. T., *Royall Tyler* (1867).

Other references: Boston *Transcript* (16 Dec. 1925). New York *Tribune* (10 May 1925). *SR* (28 March 1925). *Vermont Quarterly* 20 (1952). *Vermonter* (1924).

—CHRISTINA TISCHLER GIBBONS

U

UCHIDA, Yoshiko

Born 24 November 1921, Alameda, California; **died** 21 June 1992
Daughter of Dwight Takashi and Iku Umegaki Uchida

A tenacious belief in the power of literature and education directed Yoshiko Uchida's work as an author. A cum laude graduate of the University of California at Berkeley (1942), Uchida received an M.Ed. from Smith College (1944). Her publications included articles on folk arts and crafts for the *Tokyo Nippon News* and columns for *Craft Horizons*; her diverse contributions to children's literature span the genres of picture book, chapbooks for young readers, adolescent novels, collections of folklore, and historical novels. In addition, an adult novel, a number of nonfiction titles, and countless short stories illustrate Uchida's versatility.

Of her work, Uchida stated: "I try to write of meaningful relationships between human beings, to celebrate our common humanity." The realistic stories set in the United States often depict immigrant Japanese families and first-generation Japanese Americans struggling to make a good life in a new land. *The Promised Year* (1959), *The Birthday Visitor* (1975), *A Jar of Dreams* (1981, 1996), *The Best Bad Thing* (1983, 1993), and *The Happiest Ending* (1985) especially portray the promises of America and the hopes of a better future.

Journey to Topaz (1971) and *Journey Home* (1978, 1996) never abandon such hope even as they chronicle a dark chapter of America's history. As a college student, Uchida was evacuated with her family from California to the Tanforan Racetrack with 8,000 other Japanese Americans, and four months later moved to the Topaz concentration camp in Utah. In writing of the Japanese internment during World War II from an eleven-year-old child's perspective, Uchida not only describes the physical treatment of prisoners, but also captures the individual and collective bafflement at America's imprisonment of its own citizens. She also speaks openly about her experience in a Japanese relocation center, where she worked as a teacher. In her two novels, Uchida recreates the family's sparse and crowded living quarters, and contrasts their physical humiliation and poverty with a triumphant spirit and tenacious belief in goodness.

Well-developed, complex characters, provocative situations, and gifted storytelling account for Uchida's success with critics and readers alike. She garnered many awards and honors, including citations from the National Council of Teachers of English, the American Library Association, the California Association of Teachers of English, chapters of the Japanese American Citizens League, the International Reading Association, the National Council for Social Studies, and the Children's Book Council. A Ford Foundation Fellowship in 1952 enabled Uchida to travel to Japan. This and later trips brought authority and authentic settings to her writing. Books set in Japan include the series about the endearing young Sumi, *Rokubei and the Thousand Rice Bowls* (1962), and *In-Between Miya* (1967). An early work, *The Full Circle* (1957), is a compelling story of postwar peace in Japan and of the dubious privilege of being Umeko Kagawa, the adolescent daughter of a prominent religious leader. Based on conversations between Uchida and Kagawa, the novel is essentially a biography.

Ceremony, tradition, and revered customs influenced Uchida's creations. Both old and young are respected; joyous friendships between young and old promote genuine intergenerational understanding. The centrality of family, and its unquestioning support of individual contributions and invaluable uniqueness, fosters the growth of all of Uchida's characters. A strong sense of morality inhabits the center of her work, but it never overpowers nor seems artificial. Uchida's early commitment to education flows through her books that teach in the best possible ways: answers are never simple, growth never easy but always possible. Her memoir, *The Invisible Thread* (1991), chronicles the relationship between her adopted country, her Japanese legacy, and her growth as a writer. Sharing her own cultural heritage, Uchida defeated stereotypes and presented to "Japanese-American young people an understanding of their own history and pride in their identity."

OTHER WORKS: *The Dancing Kettle and Other Japanese Folk Tales* (1949). *New Friends for Susan* (1951). *We Do Not Work Alone: The Thoughts of Kanjiro Kawai* (1953). *The Magic Listening Cap: More Folk Tales from Japan* (1955). *Takao and Grandfather's Sword* (1958). *Mik and the Prowler* (1960). *The Forever Christmas Tree* (1963). *Sumi's Prize* (1964). *The Sea of Gold and Other Tales from Japan* (1965, reprinted with M. Yamaguchi 1991). *Sumi's Special Happening* (1966). *Sumi and the Goat and the Tokyo Express* (1969). *Kisako's Mysteries* (1969). *Makoto, the Smallest Boy* (1970). *Samurai of Gold Hill* (1972). *The History of Sycamore Church* (1974). *The Rooster Who Understood Japanese* (1976). *Tabi: Journey Through Time: Stories of the Japanese in America* (1981). *Desert Exile: The Uprooting of a Japanese American Family* (1982, reprinted 1989). *The Foolish Cats* (1987). *Picture Bride* (1987, expanded, 1997). *Bird Song* (1992). *The Bracelet* (1993, reprinted 1996). *The Magic Purse* (1993). *The Wise Old Woman* (1994).

Contributor to numerous anthologies and collections, including: *Animal Tales* (1990); *The Graywolf Annual Seven: Stories from the American Mosaic* (1990); *Tales of Justice* (1990); *Humorous Tales* (1990); *Six Short Stories by Japanese American Writers* (1991); *Growing Up Female: Stories by Women Writers from the American Mosaic* (1993); *Berkeley! A Literary Tribute* (1997); and others.

Yoshiko Uchida's manuscripts and papers are in several collections across the country: in the Kerlan Collection at the University of Minnesota; manuscripts prior to 1981 at the University of Oregon Library; and manuscripts, papers, and all published materials since 1981 are in the Bancroft Library at the University of California, Berkeley.

BIBLIOGRAPHY: Allman, B., et al, eds., *Children's Authors and Illustrators* (1991). Chang, C. E. S., *Language Arts* (1984). Dreyer, S. S., *The Bookfinder: A Guide to Children's Literature about the Needs and Problems of Youth Ages Two through Fifteen* (1981). Flora, S. B., *Famous Asians & Their Culture* (video, 1992). Marvis, B. J., *Contemporary American Success Stories: Famous People of Asian Ancestry Vol. II* (1994, 1997).

Reference works: *Asian American Literature: Reviews and Criticism of Works by American Writers of Asian Descent* (1999). *CA* (1975). *CANR* (1982, 1988). *Children's Book World* (1967). *MTCW* (1991). *SATA* (1971, 1989). *TCCW* (1989).

Other references: *NYHTBR* (8 Mar. 1949, 15 May 1955). *NYT* (4 Nov. 1942, 9 Mar. 1958, 24 June 1992). *TLS* (3 Oct. 1968).

—CATHRYN M. MERCIER

UHNAK, Dorothy

Born 1931, Bronx, New York
Married; **children:** one daughter

For fourteen years, Dorothy Uhnak served as a member of the New York City Transit Police, achieving the rank of detective first class. She is married and the mother of one daughter.

Her first book, *Policewoman* (1964), is a partially fictionalized account of the transformation of the narrator (who shares Uhnak's name and background) from applicant to full-fledged working member of the New York City Police Department. No attempt is made to gloss over the frustrations engendered by tedious procedures, the reluctance of citizens to testify against offenders, the use of influence to free criminals justly apprehended, or the hardening process through which a beginning officer must pass. In contrast, however, the excitement of the work and the sense of service rendered and assignments well done is also dramatized, making *Policewoman* a strong, compelling first book.

Uhnak then introduced a cast of continuing characters who appear in a series of three novels. The protagonist, Detective Christie Choriopoulos Opara, works for the district attorney's Special Investigations Squad. The problems common to working mothers—Opara is a young widow whose husband, also a policeman, was killed while on duty—and the presence of Opara's family, which serves as a support group, both contribute to the realism of the series. The developing personal and professional relationships between Opara and her boss, Casey Reardon, one of fiction's best realized "tough cops," provide subplots throughout the trilogy. Other members of the squad lend depth, color, comic relief, and effective detail.

The plot of *The Bait* (1968) springs from an arrest Opara unwillingly makes while on her way to the culmination of a seemingly more important undercover assignment. Uhnak's development of the background and motivation of the murderer enhances the suspense and offsets the book's dependence on coincidence. The organization and the machinations of the Secret Nation, a black religio-political gang, form the subplot of *The Witness* (1969); seen through the eyes of initiate Eddie Campion, the scenes involving the Nation are especially powerful. Elena Vargas of *The Ledger* (1970) is one of Uhnak's most vibrant and complex characters, and her attitudes and history are fully explored. Vargas and Opara engage in a long, absorbing battle of wills which contributes enormously to the book's success.

Law and Order (1973) is not a crime novel but rather the panoramic saga of a family of New York policemen, their connections, their work, their sense of self and place. The central character, Brian O'Malley, is a study of an essentially decent man struggling to master himself, his work, and the necessarily shady world into which that work takes him. Next came Sergeant Joe Peters, the officer investigating the murder of two little boys, who is the protagonist and narrator of *The Investigation* (1977). Both the police and public opinion point to Kitty Keeler, the children's mother, as the killer, and Peter solves a double mystery to achieve the book's climax. Much of the tension springs from the contradictory and intense appraisals other characters make of the accused. She is believed by some to be nearly saintly in her generosity, warmth, and kindness and believed by others to be a sensual, self-indulgent, fiendish woman. Kitty Keeler's real motivations and personality are the plot's true mystery.

False Witness (1981) portrays two women who have achieved success in professions dominated by men. Sanderalee Dawson, model, television personality, and political activist, is the victim of rape and attempted murder; Lynne Jacobi, a bureau chief in the New York City District Attorney's Office, investigates the crime, forcing the two women into an uneasy alliance. The extreme violence of the attack on Sanderalee underscores the brutality of the struggles for power and control the protagonists experience professionally. *False Witness* is a superior novel whose characterizations are especially strong.

The Ryer Avenue Story (1994) is a departure for Uhnak from her tried and true police/crime novels. In this story, six childhood friends bound by a secret, shared act of violence are followed throughout several generations. As kids, the six friends—boys and girls—beat a man to death in the Bronx borough where they live. One of their fathers is eventually tried and put to death for the crime, which the six friends continue to hide. The book follows them to success and in some cases fame, through their tragedies and joys, until their secret is finally revealed.

In *Codes of Betrayal* (1997), Uhnak returns to crime drama in this tale of NYPD cop, Nick O'Hara. Although Nick was raised by an "Irish cop uncle," his estranged mother is a product of the Ventura crime family. Nick's son is killed while spending time with a cousin—from the Ventura side of the family. At the same time, Nick finds that his father was also killed by the Venturas years ago. Nick's life falls apart, but his anger eventually saves him when he is offered a deal by the FBI to help bring down the Venturas.

Ulnak has her own method of writing and says she has never found anyone else who works the way she does. Hers is not a nine-to-five routine, and often she will construct entire chapters mentally "until the pictures, words, and actions must absolutely be on paper." Characters are the unifying force in her novels. As she states, "What I must know, absolutely, before I start a novel is who each character is at the beginning and who he will be at the end. I'm never sure how the characters will get from the first place to the last, but I am positive where they will end up." Remarkably able to convey tellingly the ambiences of home, squad room, and mean streets, Uhnak is a good writer noted for her mastery of realistic detail in plot, setting, and characterization.

OTHER WORKS: *Victims* (1987). *Secrets and Mysteries* (1993).

A manuscript collection of Dorothy Uhnak is housed at the Muger Memorial Library at Boston University.

BIBLIOGRAPHY: Reference works: *Best Sellers* (1 Feb. 1964). *Detecting Women* (1994). *Encyclopedia Mysteriosa* (1994). *Mystery Fancier* (Jan. 1978). *Newsweek* (13 Apr. 1973). *Oxford Companion to Women's Writing in the United States* (1995). *St. James Guide to Crime & Mystery Writers* (1996).

Other references: *Booklist* (15 Sept. 1997). *LJ* (15 Sept. 1997). *PW* (15 Feb. 1993).

—JANE S. BAKERMAN,
UPDATED BY REBECCA C. CONDIT

ULANOV, Ann Belford

Born 1 January 1938, Princeton, New Jersey
Daughter of Ralph J. and Ruth Belford; married Barry Ulanov, 1968; children: one son.

Ann Belford Ulanov was the youngest of three children. Her father was a surgeon and her mother a nurse. She earned her B.A. cum laude from Radcliffe in 1959. She received a Master of Divinity magna cum laude (1962) and a Ph.D. in psychiatry and religion (1967) from the Union Theological Seminary. Ulanov received her analytical training from the C. G. Jung Training Center in New York City (1963-67). She has been in private practice in New York since 1965 and a professor of psychiatry and religion at the Union Theological Seminary since 1974. Her husband is an English professor (and former chairman of the Department of Religion at Barnard College). They have one son.

In *The Feminine in Jungian Psychology and in Christian Theology* (1971), Ulanov investigates the implications for Christian theology of Jung's special insights into the feminine. Ulanov emphasizes Jung's idea that the psyche is structured in polarities; she believes that the masculine-feminine polarity encompasses in its symbolism all the other psychic polarities. She goes on to demonstrate that of these two poles, the feminine has been most neglected in psychoanalytic literature. It is usually treated as auxiliary to the masculine and confined to its literal sexuality. Ulanov analyzes and then rejects what she calls the "biological

approach" of Freud and the "cultural approach" of more current socioanthropological studies. Using the theories of Kant and Cassire, as well as of Jung, she maintains that all perceptions of reality are symbolic and partially subjective. She describes aspects of the feminine—both as the predominant approach to reality in a woman and as it appears in a man's psyche as the contra-sexual element, the anima—and the negative effects of its repression in western religion. This book delineates the religious significance for our culture of accepting the experience and consciousness of women and sheds light on the difficulty of the Christian experience for women.

Ulanov wrote *Religion and the Unconscious* (1975) with her husband. They begin by describing the intrapsychic relationship between consciousness and the unconscious, and how both depth psychology and religion mediate and illuminate numinous and primordial experiences of the psyche. They predict an assimilation of Jungian "active imagination" into religious institutions in the form of spiritual exercises. Like Ulanov's first book, the style of *Religion and the Unconscious* is lucid, smoothly written, methodical. But because it breaks new ground through a synthesis of two fields, the second book is more difficult to understand. *Religion and the Unconscious* is nevertheless exciting, hopeful, brilliant, and profound. It is ecumenical in the deepest sense in showing the universal psychic need for the processes that religion has codified into sacraments. The book is quiet in tone and written for a well-educated reader but will undoubtedly become a classic in its new field.

In *The Functioning Transcendent: A Study in Analytical Psychology* (1996), Ulanov tackles the manner in which the transcendent—or "God, the unknown, or the holy"—operates in our lives by demonstrating how it has operated in her clinical practice. Drawing on her observations, she discusses the spiritual aspects of analysis as they are manifested in cases involving issues such as weight problems in women, suicidal ideation, and masochism.

Ulanov and her husband, Barry, collaborated on *Cinderella and Her Sisters: The Envied and the Envying* (1998), a study of the emotion of envy. Using the fairytale's story as a basis, the Ulanovs consider the psychological aspects of envy and discuss the male and female aspects of the individual as well as relationships between persons of the same and/or opposite sexes.

In *The Female Ancestors of Christ* (1999), Ulanov attempts to resurrect the "female voice" in the Christian religion. The Gospel according to Matthew includes four women in Christ's genealogy—Ruth, Tamar, Rahab, and Bathsheba. Ulanov argues that these women merge issues of sexuality and spirituality and represent Jesus' feminine side. Critics have remarked that although the premise showed promise, Ulanov's obscure narrative style requires acceptance of her analyses on faith rather than as supported by logic.

Ulanov has a compassionate, perceptive viewpoint on both women and universal religious needs. She never waxes angry, and one feels trust in her always balanced, fair discussion of all issues. Her books will outlive contemporary controversies because she always takes the long view.

OTHER WORKS: *Primary Speech: A Psychology of Prayer* (1988). *The Witch and the Clown: Two Archetypes of Human Sexuality* (1990). *Men and Women: Sexual Ethics in Turbulent Times* (1991). *Transforming Sexuality: The Archetypal World of Anima and Animus* (1994). *The Wisdom of the Psyche* (1994). *The Wizard's Gate: Picturing Consciousness* (1994). *Receiving Woman: Studies in the Psychology and Theology of the Feminine* (1995).

BIBLIOGRAPHY: *American Journal of Psychiatry* (Aug. 1974). *Anglican Theological Review* (Oct. 1976). *Christian Century* (2 Mar. 1977). *Crosscurrents* (Summer-Fall 1972). *Religion in Life* (Winter 1976).

Other references: Barnes & Noble web site: http://www.barnesandnoble.com.

—STEPHANIE DEMETRAKOPOULOS,
UPDATED BY REBECCA C. CONDIT

UNDERWOOD, Sophie Kerr

Born 23 August 1880, Denton, Maryland; **died** 6 February 1965, New York, New York
Also wrote under: Sophie Kerr
Daughter of Jonathan W. and Amanda Sisk Kerr; **married** John Underwood, 1904 (divorced)

A well-educated woman, Sophie Kerr Underwood had diverse interests: cooking, writing, and a love of plants and flowers imparted to her by her father, a nurseryman. She held a B.A. from Hood College, an M.A. from the University of Vermont, and several honorary degrees. Underwood's marriage ended in divorce after four years.

A prolific writer, Underwood contributed to the *Saturday Evening Post*, the *Ladies' Home Journal, Collier's*, and *Harper's*. She edited the woman's page of the *Chronicle Telegraph* and the woman's Sunday supplement of the Pittsburgh *Gazette Times* and was managing editor of the *Woman's Home Companion*. She published more than two dozen works of fiction and drama.

Characteristic of Underwood's fiction is the novel, *The See-Saw: A Story of Today*, (1919). Marcia Grossey, the heroine, is beautiful, warm, gentle, and understanding of her husband, Harleth, who is a handsome, temperamental, restless, and very rich man. Although Harleth loves Marcia, he falls prey to a femme fatale, Leila. When Marcia divorces Harleth, he marries Leila for honor's sake. Several years later Leila divorces Harleth, who returns to the woman he always loved. *See Saw* is "woman's fiction"—furs, perfume, and jewels are given more attention than the characters, who are flat and predictable: good wife, erring husband, wicked adventuress. The plot line is obviously manipulated, built on the premise that all's well that ends well.

Typical of Underwood's short stories are those in the collection *Confetti* (1927), a work divided into four groups, each with a general theme. The section, "Greedy," has stories about food and jealousy; "Women" concerns envy, love, and discipline; "In America," the weakest section, details the efforts of three young men to marry; and the best section, "Country," insists that country life is not only healthier than city life but also more pleasurable. The stories are absolutely representative of the kind of fiction appearing in women's magazines for many years. Sentimentality rules: all the endings are happy, true love always wins, old virtues stand fast, as do the old aphorisms. Plots appear to have evolved from maxims, and characters who are indistinguishable from each other speak in dated and hackneyed language. In the short stories, as in the novels, Underwood's effectiveness is greatest in descriptions of country life, food, and scenery. She does not provide information or understanding of her era. She gave the readers of her day escape and entertainment, but the modern reader will not find either in Underwood's work.

OTHER WORKS: *Love at Large* (1916). *The Blue Envelope* (1917). *The Golden Block* (1918). *Painted Meadows* (1920). *One Thing Is Certain* (1922). *Mareea-Maria* (1929). *Tigers Is Only Cats* (1929). *In for a Penny* (1931). *Girl into Woman* (1932). *They're None of Them Perfect* (1933). *Big-Hearted Herbert* (with A. S. Richardson, 1934; film version, 1935). *Stay out of My Life* (1934). *Miss J. Looks On* (1935). *There's Only One* (1936). *Fine to Look At* (1937). *Adventure with Women* (1938). *Not a Cloud in the Sky* (1938). *Curtain Going Up* (1940). *The Beautiful Woman* (1940). *It Was a Lovely Meeting of the Flower Show Committee* (1940). *Michael's Girl* (1942). *Jenny Devlin* (1943). *Love Story Incidental* (1946). *Wife's Eye View* (1947). *The Sound of Petticoats* (1948). *As Tall As Pride* (1949). *The Man Who Knew the Date* (1951). *The Best I Ever Ate* (with J. Platt, 1953).

BIBLIOGRAPHY: *NYT* (8 Feb. 1965). *PW* (1 March 1965).

—HELEN S. GARSON

UNTERMEYER, Jean Starr

Born 13 May 1886, Zanesville, Ohio; **died** 27 July 1970, New York, New York
Daughter of Abram E. and Johanna Schonfeld Starr; **married** Louis Untermeyer, 1907 (divorced 1933, remarried, divorced again in 1951); **children:** Richard (died 1927)

An artistic child, Jean Starr Untermeyer was sent by her Midwestern family to Kohut's College Preparatory School in New York. She also attended special courses at Columbia University. In 1907 she married poet and editor Louis Untermeyer, a friend and associate of many leading literary figures. Several years later, Untermeyer began secretly writing poems, which her husband discovered and submitted to magazines. She felt she had absorbed poetry ''by osmosis'' from her husband and his coterie and that music was her ''major passion.'' A brief career as a lieder singer in Vienna and London in 1924 was interrupted by marital problems. The Untermeyers separated in 1926; but the suicide of their only child, Richard, in 1927, brought about a temporary reconciliation. They divorced in 1933, later remarried, and obtained a final divorce in 1951 after many years of separation. Untermeyer taught at Olivett College (1936-37, 1940) and at the New School for Social Research (1948-55).

Untermeyer's memoir, *Private Collection* (1965), describes her childhood, early married life, and acquaintances; but it is her poetry that reveals the more intimate, emotional aspects of her life. In an essay published in the *Bookman* (June 1923), Untermeyer defends the woman artist' right to use her own experience in her art. In addition—six years before Virginia Woolf published *A Room of One's Own*—Untermeyer discusses a woman's need for ''peace and privacy,'' for relief from domestic routine, and time in which to do creative work. Recognizing that ''the sexual instinct is. . .bound up with the artistic impulse,'' Untermeyer calls upon scientific research to discover something ''to liberate woman in her sex life.'' ''Love *minus* Art = Wife'' is a telling line in ''Love and Art,'' part of a dream sequence that concludes *Dreams Out of Darkness* (1921).

Untermeyer's most domestic work appears in her early poems. In ''Autumn'' (*Growing Pains*, 1918), she portrays in exquisite detail her mother, now ''so shaken and so powerless,'' when she was ''high priestess'' of her home, involved in the seasonal ritual of canning and preserving. ''Birth'' celebrates the ''exultation and. . .fertile pain'' of her sister's labor.

Numerous poems, published throughout Untermeyer's career, portray a woman whose lover has betrayed or abandoned her. She seeks solace in religion, music, or nature; or, she seeks to repress or renounce her self and, mystically, to achieve a state that provides, paradoxically, both security and freedom. Usually the woman counters faithlessness with faith and forgiveness. Although her suffering may leave her withdrawn, ''without elation,'' and ''disheveled,'' as in ''Overseen'' (*Love and Need*, 1940), she is strong and proud. Untermeyer also wrote light verse, occasional poetry, and many poems with war or nature as their subject.

Untermeyer translated Oscar Bie's *Schubert, the Man* (1928), the official Schubert centennial biography. Her highly praised translation of Hermann Broch's *The Death of Virgil* (1946) took her five years to complete. Her last book, *Re-creations* (1970), contains translations of French, German, and Hebrew poems.

Untermeyer's early poems were often highly imagistic, and many were in free verse, but she moved—counter to most of her contemporaries—to more traditional, rhymed forms. Critics praised her ear for sound and rhythm—qualities that reflect her love of music.

OTHER WORKS: *Steep Ascent* (1927). *Wingéd Child* (1936). *Later Poems* (1958). *Job's Daughter* (1967).

BIBLIOGRAPHY: Untermeyer, L., ed., *Modern American Poetry: A Critical Anthology* (1936).
Other references: *CSM* (5 Sept. 1942). *Poetry* (Aug. 1936, July 1941). *SR* (15 Feb. 1941).

—JEANNINE DOBBS

UPTON, Harriet Taylor

Born 17 December 1854, Ravenna, Ohio; died 5 November 1945, Pasadena, California
Daughter of Ezra B. and Harriet Frazer Taylor; married George W. Upton, 1884

Harriet Taylor Upton's family had a long history of pioneering and public service. Her father, a lawyer and later a judge, was a member of the U.S. Congress for 13 years. She and her husband, also a lawyer, lived in Warren, Ohio, and in Washington, D.C., when Congress was in session. Upton had ample opportunity to develop her interest in politics.

At first, she was antipathetic to the woman suffrage movement and worked actively against it; but in 1890, she changed her mind and joined the National American Woman Suffrage Association. She served as acting chairman of the congressional committee and through her efforts the national headquarters was for some time located in Warren. From 1902 to 1910, Upton edited the monthly *Progress*, which became the official organ of the association in 1907. When, in 1920, the vote of Tennessee was crucial in gaining acceptance of the 19th Amendment, Upton and Carrie Chapman Catt waged an active campaign there which was instrumental in winning approval.

Upton's political work was done primarily through the Republican party. During the Harding administration, she served as vice chairwoman of the Republican National Committee, probably the highest ranking position a woman had yet held in America. Later she did important social work in Ohio as liaison officer between Governor Myers Cooper and state institutions. She was also instrumental in opening the diplomatic corps to women, in placing women on the Advisory Committee of the Conference for the Limitation of Arms, and in the final reporting out and passage of the Child Labor Bill.

Upton wrote children's stories for *Wide Awake* and *St. Nicholas*. For a book for children, *Our Early Presidents and Their Wives and Children, from Washington to Jackson* (1890; also serialized in *St. Nicholas*), she did considerable research and wrote to the descendants of the presidents. The review in the *Nation* (22 Jan. 1891) acknowledges the minute detail in the description of home life, but the author is accused of ''an absolute affectation of intimacy'' in her style: ''This kind of baby talk is much to be regretted, for it weakens a book which otherwise appears to be thorough, authentic, and useful.'' Upton also wrote two several-volume works of local (Ohio) history.

The *New England Magazine* (March 1899) published an avant-garde love story by Upton, about a young Hollander, Rita, who is jilted by an American businessman. Rita still believes the U.S. is ''a woman's own land, and she can do what she wants to. She can study, work, go to college, and vote.'' Obviously, this was fantasy, as Upton recognized six years later. In 1905 she, Ida Husted Harper, and Susan B. Anthony visited President Theodore Roosevelt at the White House to call his attention to the action of Congress in forbidding the legislature of Hawaii to extend the suffrage to women, and ''to ask him to see that this outrage is not repeated in the Philippines.'' At this point he exclaimed with scorn, ''What! Give the franchise to those Oriental women!''

Upton contributed articles on women's rights to the *Ladies' Home Journal* and *Harper's Bazaar*. Characteristic is ''A Woman's View of Practical Politics,'' the lead article in the *Woman's Home Companion* (Aug. 1921). She urges a humanistic rather than a tough-minded approach to political problems. Politics, she feels, are only as good as the people themselves: ''Therefore, it is of the most tremendous importance that the women-people repudiate 'practical politics' as an excuse for dealing with government concerns in ways which they would never tolerate in their own personal affairs, and, instead, give to 'practical politics' its real meaning of straightforward, honest understanding of the science of government.'' She concludes by prophesying that men will not come to understand women's point of view in her generation: ''It is our granddaughters who will profit by men learning to understand women.''

In spite of her advanced ideas, Upton was a woman of her time, who still thought in terms of ''feminine'' traits and ''masculine'' traits and seemed unaware these might be the result of conditioning. The writer of this entry knew her personally and corresponded with her between 1920 and 1934. She was once told by Upton, ''You can do any job a man can do, but never forget that you are a woman. Always keep your shirtwaist and skirt pinned together so the safety pin doesn't show.''

OTHER WORKS: *A Twentieth-Century History of Trumbull County* (2 vols., 1909). *A History of the Western Reserve* (3 vols., 1910).

BIBLIOGRAPHY: Harper, I. H., *The Life and Work of Susan B. Anthony* (1908).

Other references: *Century* (Aug. 1923). *Ladies' Home Journal* 39 (Aug. 1922). *Literary Digest* 81 (May 1924). *Outlook* 136 (Jan. 1924). *Woman Citizen* (May 1924).

—FRANCELIA BUTLER

V

VALENTINE, Jean

Born 27 April 1934, Chicago, Illinois
Daughter of John and Jean Purcell Valentine; **married** James Chace, 1957 (divorced); Barrie Cooke, 1991; **children:** Sarah, Rebecca

Jean Valentine is a graduate of Radcliffe College (B.A. 1956). Her first book of poetry, *Dream Barker and Other Poems* (1965) was chosen by Dudley Fitts and published as the winner of the Yale Series of Younger Poets Award. She has taught at Yale, Barnard, Swarthmore, and Hunter Colleges, among others, and since 1974 has been on the faculty of Sarah Lawrence College.

Though over the years Valentine has not had the recognition accorded many of her contemporaries, she is considered by many to be among the finest American poets. Hayden Carruth has commented: "No other living poet gives me as keen a sense of intelligence, the mind at work there on the page, as [Valentine's].... Such poems are very, very rare." Valentine has received awards from many foundations and organizations including the National Endowment for the Arts (1972), New York Foundation for the Arts, New York State Council for the Arts, The Bunting Institute, and the Rockefeller Foundation. She was also the recipient of a Guggenheim fellowship in 1976, and was awarded the Maurice English Prize in 1991 and the Sara Teasdale Poetry Prize in 1992.

Her poetry makes of experience something spare and emblematic, dream-like. Her lines rely on image, and often time and objects become a haunting presence in her poems. She investigates what Richard Jackson calls the "hallowing of the everyday," using language to go places it seems most difficult or perhaps useless to go, to describe the moment things invisible become visible.

Valentine's early poems are more formal and explore language and images; she often alludes to classical and biblical narratives which give these poems a sense of depth and context, as seen in a few lines from "Waiting": You will not be forgiven if you ignore / The pillar of slow insistent snow / Framing the angel at the door / Who will not speak and will not go." Many of her poems range through the varied experiences of women's lives: first love, marriage, childbirth, family life. She often uses dialogue in a symbolic manner where voices in poems speak in associative rather than linear ways. And, as in "September 1963," people populate her poems much in the way they populate dreams, as figures floating between language: "With twenty other Gullivers / I hover at the door, / Watch you shy through this riddle of primary colors, / The howling razzle-dazzle of your peers."

In Valentine's subsequent volumes, her poems become more delineated and definite in the world they evoke. Wider political and social forces appear in tangible ways. And though Valentine's poems are perhaps less specifically concerned with her own private life, the experiences of others are still grounded in the physicality of life lived in bodies. This does not mean Valentine leaves the personal behind, she has just found a way to widen what is personal into ever overlapping circles which vibrate out from images in her poems: "Today we visited a field of graves— / slaves' or Indians' graves, you said—/ sunk, unmarked, green edges of hammered granite / sharp as a shoulder blade" ("Forces" *Home. Deep. Blue.*, 1989).

In her most recent book, *Growing Darkness, Growing Light* (1997), Valentine's poems are pared down and deal deeply with the presence of death and the spiritual. These are often evoked by the simplest of things as in "A Bit of Rice": "A bit of rice in a string bag: / the rice spills, / we have to sweep it up. . . / What will be left here when you die? / Not the rice / not the tea / left *somewhere* when the monk / knocked over the cup / not / not." As Alberta Turner comments, all of [Valentine's] poems, in one way or another, address "the threat of an empty universe." Valentine also returns to the world of women with a small series of poems (beginning with "Mother and Child, Body and Soul") which explore the often painful and deeply knotted relationships between mother and daughter.

Valentine's poems have appeared in *American Poetry Review, Atlantic Monthly, Field, Ironwood, New Yorker, Ploughshares, Poetry Ireland Review, Salt Hill Journal,* and many other journals and anthologies. Valentine currently lives in New York City, but spends part of her time in County Sligo, Ireland. Her newest book of poems *The Cradle of Real Life* is forthcoming in 2000.

OTHER WORKS: *Pilgrims* (1969). *Ordinary Things* (1974). *Turn* (chapbook, 1977). *The Messenger* (1979). *The River at Wolf* (1992).

BIBLIOGRAPHY: Jackson, R., *Acts of Mind: Conversations with Contemporary Poets* (1983). Kravis, J., *Teaching Literature: Writers and Teachers Talking* (1995). Upton, L., *The Muse of Abandonment: Origin, Identity, Mastery, in Five American Poets* (1998).

Reference works: *CANR* (1991). *CP* (1991).

Other references: *American Book Review* (May 1990). *APR* (Jan. 1980, July/Aug. 1991, interview). *Field* (Spring 1989). *Harper's* (Jan. 1980). *NYTBR* (7 Nov. 1965, 2 Aug. 1970, 21 Oct. 1979). *Ploughshares* (Fall 1993). *Poetry* (Oct. 1975, Dec. 1992). *Southern Review* (1997). *VLS* (23 May 1989).

—MICHAEL KLEIN AND GLYNIS BENBOW-NIEMIER

VALENTINE, Jo
See ARMSTRONG, Charlotte

VAN ALSTYNE, Frances (Jane) Crosby

Born 24 March 1820; Putnam County, New York; **died** 12 February 1915, Bridgeport, Connecticut
Wrote under: Fanny Crosby and some 200 others
Daughter of John and Mercy Crosby; **married** Alexander Van Alstyne, 1858 (died 1902)

At the age of six weeks, Frances Crosby Van Alstyne was permanently blinded as a result of an eye infection treated by hot poultices that destroyed the optic nerves. This trauma was compounded when her father died before she was one year old, but as an eight-year-old she wrote the lines: "O what a happy soul am I! / Although I cannot see, / I am resolved that in this world / Contented I will be!" Van Alstyne spent her childhood studying the Bible and developing the powers of her memory. In fact, she later told friends she had memorized the first five books of the Bible, the Psalms, and most of the New Testament.

At the age of fifteen, Van Alstyne enrolled in the New York Institution for the Blind, where she remained as a student for the next eight years. While there she developed her poetic talents by reciting topical poems for visitors, such as Jenny Lind and Henry Clay. She also recited on fundraising tours for the institution from 1842 to 1844. One of her favorites on such occasions began: "Contented, happy, though a sightless band, / Dear friends, this evening we before you stand." After graduating at the age of twenty-three, Van Alstyne stayed at the institution and taught a number of subjects for the next 15 years.

Van Alstyne's first volume of poetry, *The Blind Girl, and Other Poems* (1844), was published when she was twenty-four. Ironically, the preface states that "any pecuniary advantage" to the authoress will be appreciated since she is in "declining health." Van Alstyne died at the age of ninety-five. The volume concentrates on the extremely morbid subjects so popular at the time. Typical poems are "My Mother's Grave," "Ida, the Broken-Hearted," and "On the Death of a Child."

In her next volume of poetry, *Monterey, and Other Poems* (1851), Van Alstyne again appeals to her readers' sympathy: she states her health is "sadly impaired," while she hopes her "declining years" will be supported by the sale of this volume. The contents are even more maudlin, including "The Dying Daughter," "Let Me Die on the Prairie," "Weep Not for the Dead," "The Stranger's Grave," and "Reflections of a Murderer."

A Wreath of Columbia's Flowers (1858) is a collection of short fiction. Although Van Alstyne claims her writings are "natural and true to life," this volume contains the story "Annie Herbert," about a girl who hears flowers talking to her. Her final volume of poetry, *Bells at Evening, and Other Verse* (1897), includes a biographical sketch by Robert Lowry. Van Alstyne considered *Bells at Evening* her finest poetic effort. It contains such secular poems as "A Tribute to Cincinnati" and other patriotic fare. The final section includes some 65 of her most famous hymns.

Hymn writing was Van Alstyne's major claim to fame. She began writing popular songs with the composer George F. Root in 1851, and the two collaborated on about 50 songs, including "Rosalie, the Prairie Flower," which earned $3,000 in royalties. In 1864 Van Alstyne began writing hymns with William B. Bradbury, generally considered the father of Sunday school music in America. Over her long career, she wrote around 8,000 hymns. Not even she could remember the exact figure, since so many were published under her more than 200 pseudonyms. Her most successful hymns include "Rescue the Perishing" and "Safe in the Arms of Jesus," used by Dwight L. Moody and Ira D. Sankey in their missionary work and by Frances E. Willard in her temperance work.

Van Alstyne's final literary efforts were two versions of her autobiography, *Fannie Crosby's Life-Story* (1903) and the more detailed volume, *Memories of Eighty Years* (1906). In the latter volume she gives one paragraph to her marriage to another blind teacher at the institution. The two moved to Brooklyn, where Van Alstyne continued to write hymns and her husband worked as a music teacher until his death in 1902. One suspects, from Van Alstyne's autobiographical volumes, that beneath her saccharine surface she was a shrewd businesswoman who prospered by presenting to the public the popular sentiments they wanted to hear.

OTHER WORKS: *Ode to the Memory of Captain John Underhill* (1902).

BIBLIOGRAPHY: Van Alstyne, F. C., *Fanny Crosby's Life-Story* (1903). Van Alstyne, F. C., *Memories of Eighty Years* (1906). Reference works: *NAW* (1971).

—DIANE LONG HOEVELER

VAN DUYN, Mona

Born 9 May 1921, Waterloo, Iowa
Daughter of Earl G. and Lora Kramer Van Duyn; **married** Jarvis Thurston, 1943

The first woman named as poet laureate of the U.S. (1992), Mona Van Duyn was educated at the University of Northern Iowa (B.A. 1942) and the University of Iowa (M.A. 1943), where she was an instructor at the Writer's Workshop from 1943 to 1946. In 1946 she joined the faculty of the University of Louisville, leaving there in 1950 for a lectureship at Washington University in St. Louis. She later served as poetry consultant to the Olin Library Modern Literature Collection at Washington University, and was appointed Visiting Hurst Professor there in 1987. In 1973 she taught at the Salzburg (Austria) Seminar in American Studies; she also taught at the Breadloaf Writers Conferences. Van Duyn and her husband founded *Perspective: A Quarterly of Literature* and coedited the journal from 1947 to 1967.

Van Duyn has received an impressive array of awards, including the Pulitzer Prize in poetry in 1991, and the prestigious

Bollingen Prize (1971). She has been the recipient of fellowships from the National Endowment for the Arts (1966, 1985), the Academy of American Poets (1981), and the Guggenheim Foundation (1972). In addition to honorary degrees from Washington University and Cornell College, her honors also include the Shelley Memorial Prize (1987); National Book Award (1971); Harriet Monroe Memorial Prize, from *Poetry Magazine* (1968); Borestone Mountain Poetry Prize (1968); Hart Crane Memorial Award (1968); Helen Bullis Prize from *Poetry Northwest* (1964); and the Eunice Tietjens Memorial Prize (1956). In 1985 Van Duyn became a chancellor of the Academy of American Poets.

Van Duyn has been compared to such diverse poets as William Shakespeare, John Donne, Robert Browning, Wallace Stevens, Robert Lowell, and Elizabeth Bishop. Well received by critics, her work of almost four decades is frequently characterized as formalist. Examining the quotidian, her poetry is sometimes called ''domestic,'' a designation she decries for its sexism. She writes of married life and ordinary people, and speaks of love and its losses, often using ventriloquism to speak the stories of her family members. Sweet but painful, her poems provide glimpses into suburban life. Conventional in subject matter, they lack postmodern cynicism. Drawing from Greek mythology, the Bible, and employing colloquial language, her poetry combines the usual with the unusual.

Her seventh book, *Near Changes* (1990, Pulitzer Prize, 1991), asks, ''How can human love be unfearing?'' and asserts Van Duyn's belief in an essential goodness in human community. Even as she accuses the earth of ''uncaring'' in the ''The Accusation,'' she resolves that ''no lie can conceal the truth / that our kind was built to be caring.'' This world view permeates Van Duyn's work. Praised for its seemingly effortless crafting of formality, storytelling, and wit into a poetics of transformation, *Near Changes* marks her passage from middle age.

To See, To Take (1970, National Book Award, 1971) contextualizes the poet-speaker within a larger world, concentrating on observations of middle-class suburban life. *Merciful Disguises: Published and Unpublished Poems* (1973) acknowledges, in ''Open Letter, Personal,'' that ''We know the quickest way to hurt each other,'' but insists nevertheless, ''We love.'' Van Duyn reveals the disguises we use to distance ourselves from our deepest sorrows, to keep ourselves going despite the pain of living. In *Letters from a Father and Other Poems* (1983) Van Duyn projects an anecdotal, epistolary style as she explores relationships with aging parents. Autobiographical, the poems are without the high egocentricism of the confessional poets, and break through personal pain to celebrate joy and compassion.

Emphasis on the power of love and its healing properties remains a hallmark of Van Duyn's poetry. Preferring hope to despair, her work offers a vision where love peers through rage as it confronts the impossibility of satisfying human desire, quietly bringing gentleness to a world accustomed to hardness.

With *Firefall* (1993) Van Duyn takes up the familiar domestic topics with gentle cynicism, writing in ''We Are In Your Area'' about the ceaseless requests for old household goods which she is very reluctant to discard: ''old clothes that have learned our

old bodies, / old dear castiron skillets, the old chairs / we sit on, re- and re- covered since the fifties.'' In ''The Marriage Sculptor'' she imagines the broken halves of one wrecked marriage transformed into two happier marriages, not ignoring the pain of ''Time's tempests'' but seeing ''a larger work'' in the human lives ''stronger than Time.'' Van Duyn's favorite themes of love and loss converge in this volume at an emergency room, in a National Park (Yosemite, scene for the ''Falls'' of fire in her anchor poem), in the deathbed of a poet (several, in fact), in beginnings and endings (each has a separate poem here). These poems are comforting because they acknowledge pain as part of the process of living, not something to be escaped but something to be savored for what we can learn from it—from her.

Van Duyn has forged an equal place for women as poets in the 20th century not simply because of what she has done, but because of what she has not done. She has not insisted on special feelings or rights; she has not expected her readers to separate values from human experience or to divide those of one gender from the other. She has honored intimate family relationships and aging without shrinking from or exaggerating the difficulties of adjusting to either of these. Van Duyn encourages the reader to hope by showing the eternal present in the everyday, ''Firefall still blazing bright in memory.''

OTHER WORKS: *Valentines to the Wide World: Poems* (1958). *A Time of Bees* (1964). *Bedtime Stories* (1972). *If It Be Not I (Poems 1959-1982)* (1993).

BIBLIOGRAPHY: Reference works: *CA* (1974). *CANR* (1982, 1998). *CLC* (1975, 1977, 1991). *CP* (1991). *DLB* (1980). *FC* (1990). *Oxford Companion to Women's Writing in the United States* (1995).
   Other references: *APR* (Nov.-Dec. 1973). *Antioch Review* (Spring 1970). *Carleton Miscellany* (Spring/Summer 1974). *Nation* (4 May 1973). *NR* (6 Oct. 1973, 31 Dec. 1990). *NYT* (11 Jan. 1971, 21 June 1991). *NYTBR* (21 Nov. 1965, 2 Aug. 1970, 9 Dec. 1973, 18 Nov. 1990). *Parnassus* (1991). *Poetry* (Oct. 1990). *Sewanee Review* (Winter 1973). *Virginia Quarterly Review* (Spring 1965, Winter 1974). *WP* (10 April 1991, 15 June 1992). *WPBW* (6 Jan. 1974).

—LOLLY OCKERSTROM,
UPDATED BY KATHLEEN BONANN MARSHALL

VAN VORST, Bessie McGinnis

Born 1873, New York, New York; died 18 May 1928, Paris, France
Wrote under: Mrs. John Van Vorst
Daughter of John Jr. and Lydia Matteson McGinnis; married John Van Vorst, 1899 (died); Robert H. Le Roux, 1914

Bessie McGinnis Van Vorst was educated in New York City at private academies for women. She took up writing as a career after the death of her first husband. While living in France with her sister-in-law, Marie Van Vorst, she served as a correspondent for the New York *Evening Post* and a contributor to *Harper's, Century, Revue des Deux Mondes, Saturday Evening Post*, and *Ladies' Home Journal*. The close association with her sister-in-law was of crucial importance to the development of Van Vorst's career. Her first two book-length publications were written in collaboration with Marie. After Van Vorst ceased actively writing herself, she continued to consult frequently with her sister-in-law throughout Marie's more lengthy career.

Their first novel, *Bagby's Daughter* (1901) centers on the complications surrounding the rapid courtship and European honeymoon of a prominent American manufacturer's daughter. Although quite comical, perhaps unintentionally, the moderately successful novel was dismissed by contemporary reviewers as "a wild-goose chase, mental, moral, physical and literary, leaving the reader uncertain whether he has been at the vaudeville or the grand opera." Their second collaboration, *The Woman Who Toils* (1903), catapulted the two women into public prominence. To research material for this muckraking exposé of the working conditions, values, and aspirations of women wage earners, the two women from fashionable and well educated upper-middle-class families adopted pseudonyms and worked for several months in various mills and factories. In her section, Van Vorst—or Esther Kelley, as she called herself—relates her experiences in a Pittsburgh pickle factory, a western New York mill, and several Chicago clothing establishments.

Van Vorst is especially disturbed by what she considers the moral and spiritual bondage of the working woman: "vulgar and prosaic, there is nothing in the language they use that suggests an ideal or any conception of the abstract. . . . What could be the result upon the mind and health of this frantic mechanical activity devoid of thought?" Although sympathetic to the plight of her coworkers, Van Vorst is critical of the younger women, who, she believes, worked only to satisfy an egotistical desire for shoddy finery.

Van Vorst is in no way an advocate of equal pay for male and female workers. As a strident propagandist for the domestic orientation of women as the wives and mothers of the nation, Van Vorst sees the vast numbers of working women as potentially destructive to the family and feminine sensibilities. Believing effective reform would arise through altering working conditions and combatting the increasing tendency of American manufacturers toward shoddy mass production, Van Vorst espouses the theory most women wage earners should be taken out of the factories and put to work in the "industrial arts": lace-making, hand weaving, and embroidery.

In her novel, *The Issues of Life* (1904), Van Vorst is as critical of women of her own class for what she perceived to be a willful shirking of domestic responsibilities as she was of wage-earning women. In what is essentially a melodramatic arraignment of club women, Van Vorst describes those disasters that befall women who embrace eccentric, frivolous, or egotistical theories. Only the heroine, Madeline Dillion, who quits the club and returns to her husband, escapes the crimes of infanticide, suicide, divorce, and reckless driving to which her less maternal friends succumb.

Letters to Women in Love (1906) bears striking resemblance to today's self-help manuals. Here again, Van Vorst's focus is domestic as she counsels women on effective means of safeguarding an endangered hearth. "Fireside particulars" become the crux of all the social problems that besiege American society. The success of marriage, of the family as a viable, thriving unit and, ultimately, the future well-being of the nation depend on the ability of women to ameliorate, compromise, and cajole.

Too often didactic and uncompromising in their delineation of women's familial duties, Van Vorst's works are not likely to enjoy any significant renewal of popularity or influence. Only *The Woman Who Toils* receives any attention today. But her writing, perhaps because of its limitations, does provide interesting insight into one aspect of the ongoing debate about the proper sphere of influence and activity of the American woman.

OTHER WORKS: *A Popular History of France* (1906). *The Cry of the Children* (1908). *A Girl from China* (1926).

BIBLIOGRAPHY: Filler, L., *The Muckrakers* (1976). Hill, V. L., *Strategy and Breadth: The Socialist-Feminist in American Fiction* (dissertation, 1979). Maglin, N., *Rebel Women Writers, 1894-1925* (dissertation, 1975).
Other references: *Bookman* (April 1903). *Critic* (Jan. 1902, May 1904). *Independent* (26 May 1904, 10 Jan. 1907). *Literary World* (Feb. 1902, April 1904). *Nation* (19 Dec. 1901, 5 May 1904, 1 Nov. 1906). *Overland Monthly* (May 1903).

—VICKY LYNN HILL

VAN VORST, Marie

Born 23 November 1867, New York, New York; died 16 December 1936, Florence, Italy
Daughter of Hooper C. and Josephine Treat Van Vorst; married Count Gaetano Gaiati, 1916

Marie Van Vorst was the daughter of a financially prosperous and socially prominent family, and she was educated by private tutors; but most of her best-known writings are animated by a conscious dedication to social reform. She most likely inherited this commitment to reform from her father who, during his tenure on the New York City Superior Court, was involved in an investigation of urban corruption which contributed to the demise of the Tweed Ring.

Van Vorst began writing short stories, poems, and nonfiction essays for periodical publication during the late 1890s. Shortly after the death of her brother, John, she and her sister-in-law,

Bessie, moved to France where they both served as correspondents for American journals. With only occasional visits to the U.S., primarily to gather research material for her writing, Van Vorst lived in various European cities until her death in 1936. Although she wrote for many American, French, and British periodicals, her association with *Harper's* was the most sustained and significant. One of her most important assignments for *Harper's* was a cultural series, "Rivers of the World" (1906-09), which included information gathered at the Seine, Tiber, and Nile rivers.

Van Vorst began writing before her sister-in-law, but it was their collaboration on a novel and, particularly, on an exposé of women factory workers that initially brought the work of both women public attention. After the two ceased actively writing together, Bessie remained Van Vorst's most constant friend, critic, and consultant. Van Vorst and Bessie returned to the U.S., assumed aliases, and worked in factories to gather information for *The Woman Who Toils* (1903). As "Bell Ballard," Van Vorst worked in a shoe factory in Lynn, Massachusetts, and in cotton mills in South Carolina. Describing herself as a "mirror, expositor and mouthpiece" for working women, she was more sympathetic to her coworkers than Bessie. Although she never identified herself with these women, she was more understanding in her estimation of their values. Where Bessie criticized the women for their frivolity, Van Vorst saw in it an incipient rebellion against the deadening limitations of their lives. Similarly, she was more hopeful of reforms coming within the industrial workplace rather than by removing the women from the mills. Although sharply critical of "the abnormality, the abortion known as Anarchy, Socialism," she championed the cause of labor unions: "Organize labor, therefore, so well that the work-woman who obtains her task may be able to continue it and keep her health and self-respect."

Van Vorst's experiences in the cotton mills provided her with enough information to write a fictionalized account of the situation in one of her better novels, *Amanda of the Mill* (1905). She presents both the history of how the hill people came to work in the mills and the world they found there, primarily through two characters—the somewhat idealized, but none the less interesting heroine, Amanda Henchley, and the man she loves, Henry Euston, a drunkard whose reformation is effected through the dual inspirations of Amanda and reform-oriented labor organizing. The novel is memorable for its accurate and concerned reporting of industrial issues.

In *Amanda of the Mill*, Van Vorst leads her characters through a series of crises that could seemingly be resolved only through economic revolution. She avoids this conclusion through a propitious natural disaster, which clears the way for a new era without requiring confrontation with the problems the narrative so carefully raises. Although a tendency to equivocate also occurs in the later novels—in which dilemmas posed by marital incompatibility and illicit sexual passion predominate, and spouses conveniently die before virtue is endangered—these books are entertaining and occasionally of more lasting interest.

The most significant of the later novels is *Mary Moreland* (1915), the story of a stenographer in love with and loved by her employer, a married Wall Street financier. In *Mary Moreland*, Van Vorst writes her most sophisticated discussion of the moral issues surrounding marital dissatisfaction and infidelity and creates her most complex and admirable heroine. Mary, a self-supporting suffragist dedicated to her career while searching for a passionate love that is neither compromising nor limiting, is a memorable fictional portrait of a young American woman seeking her identity in a world of shifting social and sexual values.

First excerpted in *Colliers*, *War Letters of an American Woman* (1916) is a record of Van Vorst's experiences as a volunteer field hospital worker with the American Ambulance corps during the early months of World War I. Although primarily written to encourage American involvement in the war, it also provides interesting insight into Van Vorst's life and associations.

Although Van Vorst's fiction fails to fulfill the promise engendered by her vivid moral and economic observations, the novels, especially *Amanda of the Mills* and *Mary Moreland*, deserve some renewal of critical interest. Perhaps because of her continued inability to solve the problems she raises without resorting to catastrophe and coincidence, Van Vorst's writings provide a remarkable record of the turmoil of a society in transition. Although she never abandoned the traditional codes of behavior, she raised penetrating questions about their viability.

OTHER WORKS: *Bagsby's Daughter* (with B. Van Vorst, 1901). *Philip Longstreth* (1902). *Poems* (1903). *Miss Desmond* (1905). *The Sin of George Warrener* (1906). *The Sentimental Adventures of Jimmy Bulstrode* (1908). *In Ambush* (1909). *First Love* (1910). *The Girl from His Town* (1910). *The Broken Bell* (1912). *His Love Story* (1913). *Big Tremaine* (1914). *War Poems* (1916). *Fairfax and His Bride* (1920). *Tradition* (1921). *The Queen of Karmania* (1922). *Sunrise* (1924). *Goodnight Ladies!* (1931). *The Gardenia* (1933).

BIBLIOGRAPHY: Blake, F., *The Strike in the American Novel* (1972). Filler, L., *The Muckrakers* (1976). Hill, V. L., *Strategy and Breadth: The Socialist-Feminist in American Fiction* (dissertation, 1979). Maglin, N., *Rebel Women Writers, 1894-1925* (dissertation, 1975). Rose, L., "A Descriptive Catalogue of Economic and Politico-Economic Fiction in the United States, 1902-1909" (dissertation, 1936). Taylor, W., *The Economic Novel in America* (1942).

Reference works: *NAW* (1971).

Other references: *Athenaeum* (18 April 1908). *Bookman* (May 1902, April 1903, June 1905, Jan. 1910). *Critic* (Jan. 1902, Oct. 1903). *Dial* (1 Sept. 1906). *Overland* (May 1903). *SR* (18 August 1906).

—VICKI LYNN HILL

VANDEGRIFT, Margaret
See JANVIER, Margaret Thompson

VANDERBILT, Amy

Born 22 July 1908, New York, New York; **died** 27 December 1974, New York, New York
Daughter of Joseph M. and Mary Brooks Vanderbilt; **married** Hans Knopf, 1945

Amy Vanderbilt grew up on Staten Island with the rich cultural inheritance of the wealthy Vanderbilt family. She was educated at the Packer Collegiate Institute in Brooklyn, New York University, and the Heubi Institute in Switzerland, where she studied home economics. Vanderbilt began her career as an arbiter of manners with a stint as society reporter for the Staten Island *Advance*. She served as business manager for the *American Spectator*, worked as an account executive in an advertising firm, and served as vice president and later president of Publicity Associates, Inc., a public relations firm for a number of publishing houses.

Vanderbilt took up Doubleday's offer to write an etiquette book and spent four years in research and writing. With her often revised *Complete Book of Etiquette* (1952), she became the natural successor to Emily Post in the 20th-century field of common sense manners. She was an institution, combining the functions of adviser, consultant, editor, writer, and television and radio producer. Vanderbilt distinguishes between manners and custom: the first is largely an artificial and superimposed code, set by a small coterie of leaders, that people follow consciously and the second is the natural and unconscious response to social change and new contexts and relationships. With the dizzying rate of change in the political, economic, and social scenes, these two are rapidly merging into one. The comprehensive guidelines for the new contexts of post-World War I society provided in Emily Post's *Blue Book* (1922) are further developed, elaborated, and updated for the post-World War II generation.

Vanderbilt was hostess for a television program, *It's in Good Taste* (1954-60), and a radio program, *The Right Thing to Do* (1960-62). Her "Amy Vanderbilt's Etiquette" was a syndicated newspaper column, which ran from the early 1950s through 1974. She was also a regular contributor to *Ladies' Home Journal* and an etiquette consultant to the U.S. State Department.

As the new dean of American sociability, Vanderbilt held a prominent position in the increasingly female establishment of philosophers of public mores and manners—a guild of imaginative, adaptive, and inventive women writers, such as Emily Post, Jean Kerr, Peg Bracken, Abigail Van Buren, and Ann Landers. Like these others, Vanderbilt believed etiquette is at its heart a matter of fellow-feeling, of innovation, of a spirit of comfort and generosity, and of common sense, rather than the formal, prescribed ritual associated with the manuals of decorum of earlier eras. Vanderbilt's *Complete Book of Etiquette* (reprinted 1995) is "a guide to gracious living rather than a rule book." For the individual with a social conscience, it is a guide to discovering some common ground for behavior, which can be relied on even in the midst of a pluralistic society where other guidelines have been virtually abandoned.

OTHER WORKS: *Amy Vanderbilt's Everyday Etiquette* (1956, 1981). *Amy Vanderbilt's Complete Cook Book* (1961). *Amy Vanderbilt's Success Program for Women* (1964).

BIBLIOGRAPHY: *AB Bookman's Weekly* (20 Jan. 1975). *CB* (Feb. 1975). *Newsweek* (6 Jan. 1975). *NYT* (28 Dec. 1974, 29 Dec. 1974). *Time* (6 Jan. 1975).

—MARGARET J. KING

VENDLER, Helen Hennessy

Born 30 April 1933, Boston, Massachusetts
Daughter of George and Helen Conway Hennessy; **married**

Helen Vendler's sophisticated and demanding method and style have earned her a reputation as America's best "close reader" of poetry. She believes the close, passionate reading of a poem leads to the discovery of its human voice and emotion. Through her work as a scholar, critic, and teacher, Vendler offers readers the tools with which to understand and appreciate the artistry and power of poetry.

From 1950 to 1954, Vendler studied at Emmanuel College in Boston, where she took her B.A. in chemistry, summa cum laude. In the following years, she studied at the University of Louvain under a Fulbright Fellowship and at Boston University. She received her Ph.D. in English and American literature in 1960 from Harvard University, where she is now a professor.

Yeats's Vision and the Later Plays (1963) is Vendler's defense of *A Vision* against critics who find it incomprehensible or embarrassing as a statement of Yeats' belief in gnosticism and a supernatural reality. Vendler believes critics stress Yeats' philosophical and historical failure at the cost of the more successful aesthetic statement.

In *On Extended Wings: The Longer Poems of Wallace Stevens* (1969), which won the *Explicator* Prize, Vendler tries to approximate Stevens' actual experience in writing a line of poetry. She then scrutinizes the repetitions and variations of syntactical pattern, diction, and mood to elucidate what the poet is continually in the process of doing rather than what he is finally saying. She believes Stevens himself is unrelenting in demanding that poet and reader participate vigorously, line by line, in the metrical, metaphoric, grammatical, and intellectual action of the poem.

In *The Poetry of George Herbert* (1975), Vendler explains her dissatisfaction with Herbert's reputation as merely a beautiful phrasemaker whose expression of sentiments is wholly conventional. Like other critics, she finds beauty and originality in his language, but primarily she demonstrates his religious attitudes and use of religious conventions are also original.

With *The Odes of John Keats* (1983), Vendler proposes the odes are best understood when studied together, in sequence. When read this way, she argues, the odes raise and attempt to resolve a series of formal and philosophical questions about the nature of art. Vendler's original treatment of the odes as an artistic unity was welcomed by critics as a full and persuasive study of Keats' great poems.

Vendler studies Wallace Stevens' shorter poems in *Wallace Stevens: Words Chosen Out of Desire* (1984). She hopes to correct what she considers to be a popular misconception—that his work is remote and cerebral. Instead, she focuses on the "disappointment of desire" in Stevens' work, revealing the warmth and loneliness that permeate many of the poems.

In 1995 Vendler published *The Breaking of Style: Hopkins, Heaney, Graham* and *The Given and the Made: Strategies of Poetic Redefinition*, both of which are based on lecture series. In *The Breaking of Style*, she examines the nature and significance of the changes during the careers of Gerard Manley Hopkins, Seamus Heaney, and Jorie Graham. Vendler further explores the work of Irish poet Heaney in *Seamus Heaney* (1998). In *The Given and the Made*, Robert Lowell, John Berryman, Rita Dove, and Graham are the subjects of Vendler's discussion of how personal circumstances shape a poet's themes.

With *The Art of Shakespeare's Sonnets* (1997), Vendler ignores the historical detective work, which is so often associated with the sonnets, and instead focuses on how and why the poems work. Her commentaries on the 154 sonnets offer new perspectives on the imaginative, stylistic, and technical features in these poems. A compact disk of her reading 65 sonnets is bound with the book.

The Music of What Happens: Poems, Poets, and Critics (1988), a collection of previously published essays, includes discussions of contemporary poets, as well as articles on Wordsworth, Keats, and Whitman. In a particularly interesting introduction, Vendler explains her critical methods. Dismissing interpretation-centered and ideological criticism as "paraphrase and polemic," she argues that a work of literature, like any work of art, can best be understood only through a thorough consideration of the work's formal elements and their relationship to meaning. She calls her own method "aesthetic criticism" and claims that too often critics involved in both hermeneutic and ideological criticism overlook aesthetic achievement, thereby missing the essence of the artwork itself.

Because her method and style are so sophisticated and because of her belief that to enjoy poetry at all one must be conscious of the use of a wide range of technical devices, Vendler appeals most to other critics and scholars. In her reviews and essays for magazines, she becomes more accessible to the general reader. Some of these works have been collected in *Part of Nature, Part of Us: Modern American Poets* (1980), which won a National Book Critics' Circle award, and in *Soul Says: On Recent Poetry* (1995).

Vendler edited the *Harvard Book of Contemporary American Poetry* (1985), published in England as the *Faber Book of Contemporary American Poetry* (1986), and served as poetry editor of the *Harper Anthology of American Literature* (1987). In 1987 she edited and contributed to *Voices and Visions: American Poets*, a companion work to the Public Broadcasting System television series of the same name. Vendler also edited and introduced Wallace Stevens' *Poems* (1985), and W. B. Yeats' *Selected Poems* (1990). She has written regularly for the *New York Review of Books*, the *New Republic*, and the *New York Times Book Review*, and began as poetry critic for the *New Yorker* in 1978.

Vendler is the recipient of numerous professional awards including the National Book Critics Circle award for Criticism (1980) and a fellowship from the National Endowment for the Humanities (1986-87). She was a Fulbright lecturer at the University of Singapore in 1986 and at Trinity College, Dublin, in 1988. For many years she served as a judge for the Pulitzer prize in poetry and since 1990 has been a member of the board of that organization. She was the first woman to be awarded the A. Kingsley Porter University Professorship, the highest academic distinction Harvard awards faculty members.

BIBLIOGRAPHY: Donoghue, D., "The Supreme Fiction," in *NYRB* (28 Nov. 1996). Pettingell, P., "Vendler's Letter to the World," in *New Leader* (18 Dec. 1995). Weiss, T., "Reviewing the Reviewer," in *APR* (May-June 1996).

Reference Works: *CA* (1979). *CANR* (1989). *CB* (1986.) *MTCW* (1991).

Other references: *Journal of American Studies* (Aug. 1989). *Nation* (25 Dec. 1995, 29 Dec. 1997). *New Boston Review* (Mar. 1984). *NYT* (27 Nov. 1983). *TLS* (2 Mar. 1984, 24 May 1985, 8 July 1988). *Wilson Quarterly* (Winter 1984).

—PATRICIA LEE YONGUE AND MELISSA BURNS, UPDATED BY JANETTE GOFF DIXON

VICTOR, Frances Fuller

Born 23 May 1826, Rome, New York; **died** 14 November 1902, Portland, Oregon
Also wrote under: Frances Barritt, Dorothy D., Florence Fane, Frances Fuller
Daughter of Adonijah and Lucy A. Williams Fuller; **married** Jackson Barritt, 1853 (divorced 1862); Henry C. Victor, 1862 (died 1875)

Frances Fuller Victor was the eldest of five daughters, descended from an old colonial family. Victor and her sister Metta, with whom she wrote poetry, received their schooling at a young ladies seminary in Wooster, Ohio. At the age of nine she wrote verses on her slate and directed her fellow students in plays she had written. The publication of her verses in the Cleveland *Herald* in 1840 marked the beginning of a long writing career.

Victor's turbulent private life frequently interrupted her prolific writing career. When her father died in 1850, she stopped writing poetry and returned home to live with her family, who by then had moved to St. Clair, Michigan. Her first marriage broke up after a period of homesteading in Omaha, but Victor didn't obtain a divorce until March, 1862, two months before she married her sister's brother-in-law, Henry Clay Victor, a navy engineer. Victor and her husband moved to the West Coast, but his position in the navy often took him away for long periods of sea duty. Left alone, Victor embarked on a successful career as a historian, and continued it after her husband was drowned in 1875 in the wreck of the *Pacific*.

As teenagers, Victor and her sister Metta together wrote poetry and published it locally and eventually in the New York *Home Journal*. In 1848 they moved to New York, and in 1851 they published *Poems of Sentiment and Imagination*, a collection of descriptive and highly melodramatic poetry. The remainder of their poetry was written and published separately. After Victor moved west in 1862, she wrote numerous poems of a more descriptive quality for Western magazines.

In 1848 Victor published her first melodramatic romance, *Anizetta, the Guajira; or, The Creole of Cuba*. She abandoned this genre when she discovered she had more talent as a realistic dime novelist. For her brother-in-law's editions of Beadle's Dime Novels, Victor wrote *East and West; or, The Beauty of Willard's Mill* (1862) and *The Land Claim: A Tale of the Upper Missouri* (1862), both realistically treating Nebraska farm life, especially the hardships faced by women. Her short stories, published in the Western magazines, reflect this same concern for the hard lot of frontier women; the regional writing of Bret Harte was a major influence on these realistic short stories.

Victor's work as a satirist and crusader began when she moved to the West Coast in the 1860s. As Florence Fane, she took satiric pokes at all levels of society in regular contributions to the San Francisco *Bulletin* and the *Golden Era*. Her brief crusade as a temperance supporter resulted in one temperance tract, *The Women's War with Whiskey* (1874). She also served as a columnist for the *Call-Bulletin* under the name of Dorothy D.

The 30 years Victor spent as a historian and folklorist proved the most successful aspect of her writing career. She discovered history was her forte in 1864 when she began studying local Oregon history. She interviewed many Western pioneers and researched family papers and archives. *The River of the West* (1870), based on an interview with Joseph Meek, is his first person account of life as a Rocky Mountain trapper. Victor acknowledges in her introduction her debt to Washington Irving's *Astoria* (1836) and *Captain Bonneville* (1837), which reveal a romantic attachment to historical places.

Victor's second attempt at this new genre, *All Over Oregon and Washington* (1872) contains less folklore than *The River of the West*. The book covers the discovery, early history, natural features, resources, and business and social conditions of these two states. Victor's response to rapid social and economic change is nostalgic. She emphasizes her disappointment at the close of the frontier, but points with pride to the cultural developments of the Northwest Coast.

Victor's major historical endeavor was her contribution to Hubert Howe Bancroft's voluminous *History of the Pacific States* (1890); she contributed to all but two of the 28 volumes. Victor

joined the staff as a chief assistant and its only woman in 1878, three years after the death of her husband. By this time, she had accumulated a wealth of journalistic, literary, and historic experience. As a member of Bancroft's staff, she prepared all of the two-volume history of Oregon, Washington, Idaho, and Montana and was the major writer and researcher for the history of Utah. She also wrote over half of the two California volumes and researched *Northwest Coast* and *California Inter Pocula*. The series is written in textbook style, but Victor's volumes, like her other historical works, exhibit a sensitive response to the aesthetics of the land and a nostalgia for the past.

Victor's historical accounts reflect a keen understanding of the economic and social elements of a slowly diminishing frontier; these works also reveal a seemingly contradictory perception of the West as a land of hardships and cherished memories. Her main contribution to American letters rests with these history and travel books and their blend of fact and romance. Her realistic dime novels and short stories, her sentimental and descriptive poetry, and her satiric and crusading pieces, however, also earn a place for her in American letters.

OTHER WORKS: *The New Penelope, and Other Stories and Poems* (1877). *Eleven Years in the Rocky Mountains* (1879). *The Early Indian Wars of Oregon* (1894). *Poems* (1900). *Letters to Matthew P. Deady, F. G. Young, and Others, 1866-1902* (1902).

BIBLIOGRAPHY: Caughey, J. W., *Hubert Howe Bancroft: Historian of the West* (1946). Morris, W. A. "Historian of the Northwest: A Woman Who Loved Oregon," in *In Memoriam: Frances Fuller Victor; Born May 23, 1826; Died November 14, 1902* (1902). Morris, W. A., "The Origin and Authorship of the Bancroft Pacific States Publications," in *Oregon Historical Society Quarterly 5* (1903).

Reference works: *NAW* (1971).

—DONNA CASELLA KERN

VICTOR, Metta (Victoria) Fuller

Born 2 March 1831, Erie, Pennsylvania; **died** 26 June 1885, Hohokus, New Jersey

Wrote under: George E. Booram, Corinne Cushman, Eleanor Lee Edwards, Metta Fuller, Walter T. Gray, Rose Kennedy, Mrs. Mark Peabody, Seeley Regester, the Singing Sybil, Mrs. Henry J. Thomas, Metta Victor

Daughter of Adonijah (Adanigh?) and Lucy Williams Fuller; **married** Dr. Morse, circa 1850; Orville J. Victor, 1856; **children:** nine

Five years younger than her sister Frances, Metta Fuller Victor was eight years old when the family moved to Wooster Village, Ohio. Soon thereafter, she began her writing career. By the age of thirteen she was publishing in journals and papers. By fifteen, she had published *The Last Days of Tul: A Romance of the*

Lost Cities of Yucatan (1846). The same year, Victor began publishing as "The Singing Sybil" in Willis and Morris' *New York Home Journal*. Her poetry was much praised, but after producing one joint poetry volume with her sister, she turned her greatest energies to the writing of stories and novels.

Victor's early novels are often moralistic as well as melodramatic and focus on a particular social ill. One example, *The Senator's Son* (1853; sometimes called *Parke Madison*), is a temperance novel. It was also Victor's first bestseller, running to 10 editions in the U.S., and selling some 30,000 copies in pirated British editions.

There is some evidence that, by 1851, while living in Michigan, Victor was married to a Dr. Morse. Nothing is known about this marriage, which does not appear in records for St. Clair, Washtenaw, or Oakland County, Michigan. Her first marriage is even more mysterious than that of her sister to Jackson Barritt. It is known that in 1856 Victor married Orville J. Victor, a young journalist who would soon become one of the architects of the Beadle Dime Novel empire. Besides untold poems, stories, articles, manuals, and novels, Victor produced nine children. She was still an active writer when she died at age fifty-four of cancer.

Not surprisingly, Victor was one of Beadle's prime resources. She edited their journal, the *Home*, and was the author of manuals and cookbooks as well as fiction. She produced more than 20 books for Beadle. Dime Novel Number Four was Victor's *Alice Wilde* (1860). Her most popular Beadle novel was *Maum Guinea and Her Plantation Children*, first published in 1861. This impassioned story of slave life is said to have been praised by both President Lincoln and Henry Ward Beecher. It sold some 100,000 copies in the U.S. and was also reprinted widely in Britain.

Although Victor is perhaps best known for sensationalist sermons on issues like temperance and slavery, her most important contribution is probably her landmark work in the American detective novel. Under the pseudonym Seeley Regester, Victor produced *The Dead Letter*. First published by Beadle in 1866 (but believed to have been originally published two years earlier), *The Dead Letter* is one of the first detective novels. It antedates, by at least 12 years, Anna Katharine Green's *The Leavenworth Case*, which was long believed to be the first American detective novel.

Still a highly readable tale of treachery, true love, and murder, *The Dead Letter* features a professional gentleman sleuth named Mr. Burton. Besides the help of the young hero, Redfield, Burton also relies on the considerable talents of his young daughter, a psychic. Victor produced a second novel as Seeley Regester, *The Figure Eight; or, The Mystery of Meredith Place* (later called *A Woman's Hand*) in 1869. Other novels by Victor during this period, although not pure detective puzzles, feature violent crimes and their detection. One example, *Too True: A Story of Today* (1868), was published under Victor's real name and features a good deal of detection by a woman artist.

Victor deserves recognition as one of the earliest creators of the detective novel and as a writer with facility in any formula of popular fiction. She wrote romance, pioneer adventure, detective, sensation, and social issue novels. Late in her career she also

created a comic realm populated by bad boys, bashful men, and prosperous pork merchants. During the heyday of the American dime novel and serial Victor was in great demand. At one point in the 1870s, Victor received $25,000 for exclusive story rights from the *New York Weekly*.

Victor could easily be labeled a hack writer. But she was also a writer of undeniable skill whose inventiveness anticipated the needs of her reading public. Sensational thrillers like *The Dead Letter* opened new frontiers in popular fiction and have the power to entertain even a modern reader.

OTHER WORKS: *Poems of Sentiment and Imagination* (with F. F. Victor, 1851). *Fresh Leaves from Western Woods* (1852). *Fashionable Dissipation* (1854). *Mormon Wives* (1856). *The Arctic Queen* (1858). *Miss Slimmen's Window* (1859). *The Dime Cook Book* (1859). *The Dime Recipe Book* (1859). *The Backwood's Bride* (1860). *Myrtle: The Child of the Prairie* (1860). *Uncle Ezekiel and his Exploits on Two Continents* (1861). *The Emerald Necklace* (1861). *The Unionist's Daughter* (1862). *The Gold Hunters* (1863). *Jo Daviess' Client* (1863). *The Country Cousin* (1864). *The Two Hunters* (1865). *The Housewife's Manual* (1865). *Who Was He?* (1866). *Laughing Eyes* (1868). *The Betrayed Bride* (1869). *Black Eyes and Blue* (1876). *Passing the Portal* (1876). *Brave Barbara* (1877). *The Hunted Bride* (1877). *Guilty or Not Guilty* (1878). *The Locked Heart* (1879). *A Wild Girl* (1879). *A Bad Boy's Diary* (1880). *The Black Riddle* (1880). *Madcap: The Little Quakeress* (1880). *The Mysterious Guardian* (1880). *Pretty and Proud* (1880). *Pursued to the Altar* (1880). *The Blunders of a Bashful Man* (1881). *At His Mercy* (1881). *Miss Slimmen's Boarding House* (1882). *A Woman's Sorrow* (1882). *The Bad Boy Abroad* (1883). *Morley Beeches* (1883). *Naughty Girl's Diary* (1883). *Abijah Beanpole in New York* (1884). *Mrs. Rasher's Curtain Lectures* (1884). *The Bad Boy at Home* (1885). *A Good Boy's Diary* (1885). *The Brown Princess* (1888). *The Phantom Wife* (1888). *Born to Betray* (1890). *The Gay Captain* (1891). *Who Owned the Jewels?* (1891). *The Georgie Papers* (1897).

BIBLIOGRAPHY: Johannsen, A., *The House of Beadle and Adams*, Vol. 2 (1950).

Other references: *Cosmopolitan Art Journal* (March 1857).

—KATHLEEN L. MAIO

VINING, Elizabeth Gray

Born 6 October 1902, Germantown, Pennsylvania
Also writes under: Elizabeth Janet Gray
Daughter of John G. and Anne Izard Gray; **married** Morgan Vining, 1929 (died 1934)

Elizabeth Gray Vining, of Scottish descent, was born into a Quaker family and a Quaker environment. She attended Germantown schools and later received a B.A. from Bryn Mawr (1923) and a B.S. in library science from Drexel Institute in

Philadelphia in 1926 (now Drexel University). Her husband was a professor at the University of North Carolina. After his death in an automobile accident in 1934, Vining traveled widely, doing research for her historical novels. When World War II made travel impossible, Vining worked for the American Friends Service Committee as a writer of reports, articles, and appeals.

In 1946 Vining was selected by American officials, at the behest of Emperor Hirohito, to tutor Crown Prince Akihito of Japan. She was the first foreigner permitted inside the living quarters of the imperial palace. Vining was the tutor of Akihito's brother and three sisters as well, and became so close to the cloistered imperial family that she played cards with the emperor and empress. Vining published two accounts of her time in Japan, the bestselling *Windows for the Crown Prince* (1952) and *Return to Japan* (1960), the story of her return as a visitor to the country she had left 10 years earlier. Interest in Vining and these books was revived when Akihito ascended to the throne in 1988. Vining also authored other nonfiction works, which were imbued with her Quaker heritage. These include *Contributions of the Quakers* (1939), *Friend of Life: The Biography of Rufus M. Jones* (1958), and her autobiography, *Quiet Pilgrimmage* (1970).

Vining is a master of the art of recreating a historical period, with all its sights, sounds, and smells, and of creating realistic, believable characters to people her recreated worlds. Her greatest achievement in historical fiction for children, *Adam of the Road* (1942), won a Newbery award for excellence. It is the story of a 14th-century boy, son of a minstrel, who loses and then regains his father and his dog. Adam's journey through southeastern England is filled with fragments of English ballads and French lays and with fascinating details of life in inns, on farms, and in monastery schools.

Whether she is writing for children or for adults, whether her treatment is essentially biographical, as in *Flora: A Biography* (1966)—the story of Flora MacDonald, who is credited with saving the life of Charles II—or novelistic, as in *Take Heed of Loving Me* (1964)—based on the life of John Donne—Vining brings the same careful attention to finding and evaluating both primary and secondary sources. Moreover, her gift for creating characters allows her to make Flora, Donne, William Penn, and the young Walter Scott into real people rather than historical abstractions.

Vining has had similar success with the contemporary family story, exemplified by *The Fair Adventure* (1940) and *Sandy* (1945), winner of the *Herald Tribune* Spring Festival Award.

Although Vining has made important contributions as a chronicler of the lives of important Quakers and of the education of the Crown Prince of Japan, her greatest contribution to contemporary letters is to be found in her juvenile fiction, especially her historical novels. Vining lives in retirement in Kennett Square, Pennsylvania.

OTHER WORKS: *Meredith's Ann* (1929). *Tilly Tod* (1929). *Meggy MacIntosh* (1930). *Tangle Garden* (1932). *Jane Hope* (1933). *Young Walter Scott* (1935). *Beppy Marlowe of Charles Town*

(1936). *Penn* (1938). *Anthology with Comments* (1942). *The Virginia Exiles* (1955). *The Cheerful Heart* (1959). *I Will Adventure* (1962). *I, Roberta* (1969). *The Taken Girl* (1973). *Mr. Whittier* (1974). *Being Seventy: The Measure of a Year* (1978). *Harnessing Pegasus: Inspiration and Meditation* (1978). *John Woolman, Quaker Saint* (1981). *A Quest There Is* (1982).

BIBLIOGRAPHY: Reference works: *Junior Book of Authors* (1951). *Encyclopedia of Japan: Japanese History and Culture from Abacus to Zori* (1991).

Other references: *Books* (10 May 1942). *NYT* (30 Nov. 1930, 2 Oct. 1988). *SR* (9 Apr. 1966).

—KATHARYN F. CRABBE,
UPDATED BY ANGELA WOODWARD

VIRAMONTES, Helena María

Born 26 February 1954, Los Angeles, California
Daughter of Serafin and María LaBrada Viramontes; **married** Eloy Rodríguez, 1983; **children:** Pilar, Eloy

Helena María Viramontes is a short story writer, editor, and screenwriter, as well as faculty member at Cornell University. She was born in East Los Angeles and graduated from Garfield High School. Growing up in a working-class family with eight brothers and sisters, she learned about hard work at an early age. If working 20 hours a week while carrying a full load at Immaculate Heart College (B.A., 1975) were not enough, she had the added pressure of being one of only five Chicanas in her class. Her first collection of short fiction, *The Moths and Other Stories* was published 10 years after college, in 1985. Some of the stories, especially "Growing," have now been republished in several anthologies. This early fiction presents Chicana subjects who are a contradictory blend of strengths and weaknesses, struggling against lives of unfulfilled potential and restrictions forced upon them because they are women. While racial prejudice and the economic and social oppression of Chicanos form the backdrop, Viramontes focuses her narrative lens on the cultural values that shape women's lives and against which they struggle with varying degrees of success.

Most of her stories develop a conflict between a Chicana and the man who represents the maximum authority in her life, either father or husband, i.e., society mores dictated by the patriarch. To assume more independence and responsibility in their lives, these women must break with years of indoctrination by the church. In "Birthday," Alice's abortion radically redefines her relationship to her religion. In "The Long Reconciliation," Amanda's decision to abort because she cannot bear to "watch a child slowly rot" in poverty defies the values of her husband as well as the dictates of the priest: "It is so hard being female, Amanda, and you must understand that this is the way it was meant to be." The main character in "The Broken Web" reveals her disillusionment with "a distant God." "Her children in time would forgive her. But God? He would never understand. He was a man, too."

In most cases, Viramontes' characters pay dearly for breaking with traditional values, and the exploration of their sexuality outside the bounds of cultural norms often brings negative consequences. The two women who abort are either wracked with guilt or ostracized by their communities. By murdering her husband, the nameless woman of "The Broken Web" breaks a cycle of use and abuse but suffers both literal incarceration and the belief that she has condemned her soul to eternal punishment.

"Growing" and "The Moths" explores the relationship between the culture and female sexuality in that crucial phase in the life of a Chicana when she ceases to be a girl and must accept her role as "woman." In "Growing," Naomi rebels against the mandate that her life must change because her body has changed. When she asks for an explanation, her father responds in Spanish, "Tú eres mujer" (you are a woman, or a female), and her mother says nothing. She understands that she will always have other duties than her brother because she is a woman, and that she must be chaperoned, or watched carefully, also because she is a woman.

"The Moths" also depicts the coercive socialization of adolescent girls in femininity. The adolescent tomboy of the story is acutely aware that she is "different" from her "pretty" and "nice" older sisters. Estranged from her mother and sisters, she is close to her grandmother, whose body she bathes after her death in a cleansing ritual that is also a rite of passage. The words she whispers, "I heard you, abuelita. . .I heard you," suggest that she may have inherited from her grandmother the strength to alter her culture's definitions of "man" and "woman."

Two of Viramontes' strongest stories, for demonstrating in writing the ethnic and gender barriers to obtaining voice in the U.S. society, are "The Cariboo Cafe" from her book *The Moths* and "The Jumping Bean" published in 1995 in *Chicana (W)rites: On Word and Film*. In "Cariboo Cafe," a technique of unheard, parallel monologues provides for striking expression: a third-world feminist's meditation on the function of silence and the overtly sociopolitical commentary on the plight of those individuals displaced by either economic necessity or political horrors. The illiterate, the silent, the unintelligible, the senselessly violent, and those driven mad by life in extreme poverty all appear in quick strokes before the reader's eyes, as they come to the "zero zero cafe," a virtual no-man's-land. The police and strangers are to be feared at all times; these individuals' only safety lies in silence.

"The Jumping Bean," written several years later, represents an important moment in Viramontes' writing for the integration of the competing discourses of ethnicity, gender, and the aesthetic. A father brings home a bag of jumping beans, the result of an ethnic ridicule he suffers at his job, and gives them to his daughters to

play with. While a cruel joke was played on him, he turns the beans to a positive act by giving them to his children for playthings. His eldest daughter, however, wants to free the caterpillar in each bean, and diligently works at cracking the beans open, thus metaphorically freeing her ethnicity. When she is scolded, however, and told to account for one last bean, her younger sister swallows the bean rather than have it turned over, directly confronting her own fear and her father. The daughters, who express their pain when they are silenced by covering their mouths with their hands, have symbolically placed themselves in the dark interior of a jumping bean. The jumping beans represent speech and empowerment as well as the potential to overcome ethnic slurs and patriarchal silence. The father's behavior, however, is seen to be caused in part by harsh working conditions and the cruelty of coworkers.

Viramontes has said that her writing of this story helped her develop male characters more fully in her later work. In *The Moths*, her stories in effect screamed and shouted against the pain her female characters experienced, even as they were silenced. In later stories and especially in her novel *Under the Feet of Jesus* (1995), male characters are more "complicated." The principal male character in this novel, Perfecto, makes many sacrifices for his family, but is about to leave when he senses his common-law wife is pregnant again. Even so, he is seen as a human being who has been worn down by the conditions under which migrants must work. And he is a help to Estrella (the mother's oldest child) as she finds her own voice in this migrant family that keeps its civil papers (proving citizenship in this country) tucked into the feet of the plaster statue of Jesus disassembled and reassembled and mounted on an altar each time the family moves. Eventually, the statue is broken, and Estrella symbolically replaces the image as she stands tall atop the barn she has been forbidden to enter.

While accomplishing a superb work of fiction in *Under the Feet of Jesus*, Viramontes also continues to study and write critically. In 1987 she collaborated on a first book with fellow Los Angeleno, María Herrera-Sobek, editing *Chicana Creativity and Criticism: Charting New Frontiers in American Literature*, one of the first books of criticism on Hispanic writing by women. A provocative combination of original poetry, prose, criticism, and visual art, the book documented the continuing growth of literature by and about Chicanas. Through innovative use of language and images, the editors collected 1970s and 1980s discourse on economic and social injustice, gender roles, and female sexuality critical theory. Seven years later, Viramontes collaborated again with Herrera-Sobek on *Chicana (W)rites: On Word and Film*.

Viramontes has been awarded two consecutive first prize awards in fiction by the California State University at Los Angeles' *Statement* magazine, and a third prize award in fiction from the University of California at Irvine. In 1989 she received a National Endowment for the Arts Creative Writing Fellowship. Viramontes was selected from a national pool of nominees by Nobel Laureate Gabriel García Márquez to participate in a ten-day storytelling workshop sponsored by the Sundance Institute in

Utah. She completed an M.F.A. in creative writing at the University of California at Irvine in 1997, and is working on a novel titled *Their Dogs Came with Them* and her second collection of short stories, called *Paris Rats in East Los Angeles*. She lives in Ithaca, New York, and teaches at Cornell University.

BIBLIOGRAPHY: Corpi, L., ed., *Máscaras* (1997). McCracken, E., *New Latina Narrative: The Feminine Space of Postmodern Ethnicity* (1999). Rebolledo, T. D., *Women Singing in the Snow* (1995). *Talking Back: Toward a Latin American Feminist Literary Criticism* (1992).

Reference works: *CA* (1979). *CANR* (1989). *MTCW* (1991). *Oxford Companion to Women's Writing in the United States* (1995).

Other references: *Américas Review* (Fall-Winter 1987; Summer 1989). *Chasqui-Revista de Literatura Latinoamericana* (Nov. 1995). *Journal of American Studies* (Aug. 1989). *New Boston Review* (Mar. 1984). *NYT* (27 Nov. 1983). *TLS* (2 Mar. 1984, 24 May 1985, 8 July 1988). *Wilson Quarterly* (Winter 1984). *Women's Studies* (1989).

—YVONNE YARBRO-BEJARANO AND ELIZABETH COONROD
MARTINEZ

VOIGT, Cynthia

Born 25 February 1942, Boston, Massachusetts
Daughter of Frederick C. and Elise Keeney Irving; **married** Walter Voigt, 1974; **children:** Jessica, Peter

A graduate of Smith College (1963), Cynthia Voigt places independent, resilient, and intelligent young women at the center of all but two of her novels. She made her debut in the children's literature field in 1981 with *Homecoming*, the first of her Tillerman stories, which earned immediate critical applause.

The seven novels in the Tillerman family saga form the core of Voigt's substantial contributions to realistic young adult literature. Abandoned by their mother in a shopping mall parking lot, thirteen-year-old Dicey leads her siblings, intelligent James, reliable Sammie, and gifted Maybeth, on a long search for family. *Homecoming* documents their arduous journey from Massachusetts to their grandmother's house in Maryland. *Dicey's Song* (1982), winner of the Newbery Medal, explores their new family constellation. *Sons from Afar* (1987) depicts James and Sammie's attempts to find their father, while *Seventeen Against the Dealer* (1989) concludes the cycle with Dicey's encounter with her drifter father as she achieves a hard-earned focus on the future.

The three satellite novels, *A Solitary Blue* (1983), *The Runner* (1985), and *Come a Stranger* (1986), maintain the Chesapeake Bay setting integral to the Tillerman books while each tells the story of a relative or friend connected to the family. *The Runner* completes an intricate portrayal of their grandmother before the arrival of Dicey and her siblings. *A Solitary Blue* develops the character of Jeff Greene, Dicey's first friend in Crisfield, who becomes her steadfast boyfriend. *Come a Stranger* concentrates on Dicey's schoolmate, Mina Smiths, who feels the burn of racial prejudice when she is excluded from an all-white dance camp.

As she does with all of her characters, Voigt imbues each Tillerman with the fiber of individuality and the substance of family. Hard physical work, belief in positive change, and sheer will drive these determined characters. Love, generosity, and mutual respect temper them and deepen their emotional ties. Similar qualities within interdependent relationships characterize *The Vandemark Mummy* (1991) in which an intelligent, tenacious brother and sister team up to defeat a villain and solve a mystery in a small college town. *David and Jonathan* (1992) explores the ties of friendship as a Holocaust survivor disrupts a New England family.

Essential human bonds infuse not only Voigt's realistic novels but also those drawing on fantasy and myth. A tense gothic novel, *The Callender Papers* (1983), unearths dark family secrets as Jean Wainwright discovers her inner resources. *Building Blocks* (1984) transports Brann Connell from modern times to a recent past where he confronts his father as a boy. *Jackaroo* (1985) and *On Fortune's Wheel* (1990) share the same mythical setting of Kingdom but are separated in time by two generations. Voigt reshapes the well-known Robin Hood tale with vigor and freshness in *Jackaroo*, while the later book relates the escape and survival of spirited Birlie, Jackaroo's granddaughter, and her devoted companion, Orien, in a riveting adventure and love story. *Orfe* (1992) casts the Orpheus myth into a contemporary setting. *Tree by Leaf* (1988) also includes elements of the fantastic as it tells the very real story of a World War I soldier's agonizing return to his neglected family in Maine.

Since the early 1990s, Voigt has produced high caliber, unflinchingly honest young adult novels in both the realistic and fantasy genres. She has continued to garner high praise and a loyal readership. *The Wings of a Falcon* (1993) is her third book in the world of Kingdom. It is the story of two boys who together survive childhood on the island of a sadistic man called the Damall. The two very different heroes, one brave and self-assured, the other more reflective and likened in his resiliency to a strong bendable sapling, travel into brutal adventures together, undergoing the traditional rigors of the heroic quest. Yet Voigt's story is never stock. Rather, by dint of the author's fine prose and gift for storytelling, it is a gripping tale that becomes a reflection on the nature of heroism and identity, friendship, ethics, and love.

The action of *When She Hollers* (1994) takes place over the course of one day in the painfully realistic life of a seventeen-year-old girl who has been repeatedly molested by her stepfather. Voigt tells the tale unsparingly from Tish's point of view, true to her difficult and broken mental-emotional state.

Bad Girls (1996) and its sequel are funny, unrepentant stories of Mikey and Margalo, two likable bad girls with bravado and smarts. In the first book, they become friends—and allies in power—while in the fifth grade class of Mrs. Chemsky, which is where all the action takes place. It is a setting Voigt is familiar with from her years as a teacher, and this shows in the authenticity of her depiction of classroom cliques, factions, and power struggles.

Voigt writes adeptly beautiful fiction about interesting, well-realized characters in sometimes desperate situations. She writes without moralizing or shying away from the gritty and difficult realities of life. Her consistency alone would win her readers. She can be counted on to tell a "rattlin' good tale"—one enlivened by unexpected plot twists but satisfying in its honest, complete resolution. Her portrayals of trustworthy, capable adolescents can empower readers to effect meaningful change, and she shares with them her vision of a better world, strengthened by human connectedness.

OTHER WORKS: *Tell Me If the Lovers Are Losers* (1982). *Izzy Willy-Nilly* (1986). *Stories About Rosie* (1986). *Glass Mountain* (1991).

BIBLIOGRAPHY: Drew, B. A., *The 100 Most Popular Young Adult Authors* (1996). Felps, M. C., "Dicey's Story: A Contemporary Hero Following an Established Path" (thesis, 1992). Gillespie, J. T. and C. J. Naden, *The Newberry Companion* (1996). Henke, J. T., *Children's Literature in Education* (1985). Rahamut, J. C. "Family Relationships in Selected Young Adult Novels by Cynthia Voigt and Sue Ellen Bridgers" (thesis, 1995). Reid, S. W., *Presenting Cynthia Voigt* (1995). Sutherland, Z., *Newbery and Caldecott Medal Books: 1976-1985* (1986).

Reference works: *CA* (1982). *CLR* (1987). *CANR* (1986). *CLC* (1984). Helbig, A. K., and A. R. Perkins, *Dictionary of American Children's Fiction* (1986, 1993). *SATA* (1987). *TCCW* (1989).

Other references: *Children's Literature in Education* (Spring 1985). *CSM* (13 May 1983, 7 June 1985, 1 Nov. 1985). *Horn Book* (Aug. 1983). *Language Arts* (Dec. 1983, Dec. 1985). *PW* (July 1994). *SLJ* (Nov. 1983). *WPBW* (1 July 1985).

—CATHRYN M. MERCIER,
UPDATED BY JESSICA REISMAN

VOIGT, Ellen Bryant

Born 9 May 1943, Danville, Virginia
Daughter of Lloyd G. and Zue Yeatts Bryant; **married** Francis G. W. Voigt, 1965; **children:** Julia, William

"The fight is on between the will to live and the nature to die," wrote Ellen Glasgow in *Vein of Iron* (1935), set in the Piedmont area of Virginia. Ellen Bryant Voigt's poetry carries on this contest with passion and persistence.

Voigt grew up in a family of Southern Baptists rooted for generations in the foothills of the Blue Ridge, knowing rural life not as pastoral but as daily reality. Her mother was an elementary schoolteacher. Her own life growing up was mainly music, her most crucial teacher her music teacher; she worked her way through college and graduate school by playing the piano in various settings. She later wrote (in "The Chosen") that when a "clear melody / comes in to represent a grieving heart, / it will do so as a brook, rushing over stones, / approximates a flock of birds rising."

A graduate of Converse College (1964), Voigt earned an M.F.A. at the University of Iowa (1966), where she studied with Donald Justice. Settling in rural Vermont, she joined the core literature and writing faculty of the Adult Degree Program at Goddard College. There, in 1976, she founded the country's first low-residency M.F.A. program for writers, believing many writers, and particularly women, could benefit from a program that did not obligate them to be in residence throughout the term. In 1980 the faculty of the program transplanted itself as a body to Warren Wilson College in North Carolina, where Voigt continued to teach and beginning in 1984, to serve as chair of the academic board. She has held many other teaching positions and received many grants and awards, including fellowships from the Guggenheim Foundation and the National Endowment for the Arts.

In Voigt's first book of poems, *Claiming Kin* (1976), a strong physical compassionateness asserts itself in and against the wrenchings and separations of family life. The poet is gifted with lucid perception, musical speech, and a controlling sense of shapely form, "following the taut strands / that span flower and drain spout, / down the long loops, moving / through the spider's whole house" ("Dialogue: Poetics"). But her moral imagination is with the drowned, buried, and violated; it springs from something vital and inarticulate. Of the flailing body of a decapitated hen, she writes, "I knew it was this / that held life, gave life, / and not the head with its hard contemplative eye" ("The Hen").

The Forces of Plenty (1983, reprinted 1996) is alert to the delicate balances and subtle patterns that preserve love and trust in the world and sustain life in the face of danger. Often, as in the marriage poem "Liebesgedicht," where recurring masculine and feminine half-rhymes support a meditation of selfhood and otherness, she dwells on the fragility of connection. Momentarily suspended between love and loss, these poems are filled with poignant longing for a world where we "are buoyed past our individuating fear, / and. . .memory is not, as now, a footprint filling with water."

Voigt's third book, *The Lotus Flowers* (1987), leaves behind the stillness-in-motion of the lyric to embrace a more textured, inclusive, open world of narrative. It is a collection of elegies, but a newfound security of tone and richness of emotional, circumstantial, and symbolic reference enable the poems to reach beyond grief and loss toward a vision of community. The stars, which in an earlier poem for her father had failed to promise immortality, here are seen as constellations, even as the poet, learning to recognize her own mortality, gains new access to the world around her. "Staring down into her losses," she "fills her throat with air and sings," and even, in the last poem, dances with "all those who cannot speak / but only sing."

Two Trees: Poems (1992) refuses to rest in the achieved vision and art of *The Lotus Flowers.* Seeking truth, wary of the beautiful, these elliptic and difficult, often angry, bitter, or sardonic poems, refuse to mask the pain and cold-blooded savagery of the world. Art must get outside of itself, Voigt insists, must be "flung like a rope into the crater of hell" ("Song and Story"): only so can the knowledge of good and evil, in the myth of the title poem, lead us beyond our limits, toward a vision of the forever inaccessible tree of everlasting life.

OTHER WORKS: *Kyrie* (1995). *Poets Teaching Poets: Self and the World* (editor with G. Orrs, 1996). *The Flexible Lyric* (1999).

Poems in journals including: *American Poetry Review, Antioch Review, Atlantic, Ploughshares, Southern Review, Tri-Quarterly* and others.

BIBLIOGRAPHY: Pack, R. and J. Parini, eds., *Writers on Writing* (1991). Reference works: *CA* (1978). *CANR* (1984, 1990). *CLC* (1989). Other references: *Ellen Bryant Voigt Reading Her Poems with Comment in the Recording Laboratory* (audio, 1978). *Hudson Review* (Spring 1988). *John Peck and Ellen Bryant Voigt Reading Their Poems* (audio, 1980). *Nation* (6 Aug. 1977). *New Letters Review of Books* (Spring 1987). *NYTBR* (1 May 1977, 17 July 1983, 23 Aug. 1987). *Partisan Review* (Summer 1988, 1998). *Poetry* (Feb. 1984). *Southern Review* (April, 1993). *Tikkun* (July 1991). *Tri-Quarterly* (Winter 1988). *Yale Review* (Spring 1977).

—SARAH KAFATOU

VORSE, Mary Heaton

Born 9 October 1874, New York, New York; died 14 June 1966, Provincetown, Massachusetts

Daughter of Hiram and Ellen Blackman Heaton; married Albert W. Vorse, 1898 (died); Joe O'Brien, 1912; Robert Minor, 1920; children: three

Mary Heaton Vorse was born to an old New England family. As a child, she spent her summers in the college town of Amherst, Massachusetts, and her winters in New York City and Europe. Although seemingly cosmopolitan, Vorse wrote, in later life, about how the sheltered academic atmosphere of her youth

enabled her to acquire a dedication to intellectual speculation, but left her isolated from the industrial and economic changes characterizing late-19th-century America.

Vorse was married three times and had three children. After the death of her first husband, Vorse supported herself through her writing. Her earliest published writings were short sketches, which appeared in diverse periodicals including *Criterion, Critic, Woman's Home Companion,* and *Atlantic Monthly.* Both *The Very Little Person* (1911) and *The Prestons* (1918) include short fiction excerpted from these early publications. Vorse drew on the experiences of her first years of marriage to Albert Vorse in her first novel, *The Breaking-in of a Yachtsman's Wife* (1908). *The Autobiography of an Elderly Woman* (1911), an anecdotal and entertaining narrative, is told from the point of view of a woman her mother's age who resents the circumscriptions youth imposes on the aged.

In 1906 Vorse moved to Greenwich Village, where she and her husband founded the A Club, an experimental cooperative living arrangement frequented by Mark Twain, Theodore Dreiser, Mother Jones, Maxim Gorky, and others. Primarily a collection of liberal reformers who flirted with varieties of socialism, the participants in the A Club were devoted to a thoughtful and stimulating analysis of American society. Vorse wrote favorably about her experiences in the club. Still, she affectionately satirizes the Greenwich Village lifestyle in the novel *I've Come to Stay* (1915). The heroine, Camilla Deerfield, justifies the excesses and absurdities of the village residents as a necessary and long overdue response to their Calvinist heritage: "We are the flaming shadows cast by unfulfilled joys which died unborn in our parents' souls. We come of people who lived in the ordinary hypocrisies so long that some of us cast away even the decencies in our endeavor not to be hypocritical."

From 1906 through the mid-1940s, Vorse spent a portion of each year in Provincetown, Massachusetts, as did other members of the Greenwich Village radical intelligentsia. It was here that Vorse, prompted by a series of articles on infant education she had researched in Italy for *Woman's Home Companion,* organized a Montessori school. More importantly, it was here that Vorse was among the founding members of the experimental theater group, the Provincetown Players, the group that staged Eugene O'Neill's earliest plays.

In *A Footnote to Folly* (1935), an autobiographical account of the years 1912 to 1922, Vorse identified the 1912 Lawrence, Massachusetts, textile strike as the single most significant event in her political and literary development. She described how her experiences at Lawrence led both her and Joe O'Brien, the labor reporter who became her second husband, to active identification with the problems and struggles of the American working class. Henceforth, Vorse was to write the bulk of her work in explicitly politicized terms.

Vorse's dedication is reflected in the prolific writing of her major phase; for more than 30 years she was a tireless reporter of current events on labor and battle fronts throughout the U.S., Europe, and the Soviet Union. Most of this writing is ephemeral; it appeared in Hearst newspapers, *Harper's* the *Nation, New Republic, Advance, World Tomorrow, Outlook,* and the *Masses* (which she edited) and was never collected. As a war correspondent during World War I, Vorse covered the 1915 International Congress of Women in Amsterdam and the International Woman Suffrage Convention in Budapest. Her journalism was enhanced by personal involvement with the Red Cross, the American Relief Association, and the Committee for Public Information; her coverage of the war, like that of labor disputes, often focused on the ignored victims—women and children.

With the exception of *The Ninth Man* (1918), a novel set in 12th-century Italy, all of Vorse's book-length publications spring from her experiences as a radical journalist. They vary from compilations recording her coverage of actual events, such as *Men and Steel* (1920) and *Labor's New Millions* (1938), to fictionalized accounts of actual strikes, such as *Passaic* (1926) and *Strike* (1930), and novels springing from her impressions of a world in turmoil, such as *Second Cabin* (1928), based on an ocean voyage from inflation-ravaged postwar Germany to the U.S., after a visit to "optimistic" postrevolutionary Russia.

For the contemporary reader, unfamiliar with the events Vorse so passionately described throughout her lengthy career, the best introduction to her writing and sensibilities probably will be found in either *A Footnote to Folly*—in which she effectively describes the relationship between personal identity and political commitment and growth—and *Of Time and the Town* (1942). The latter deals with her years in Provincetown; the legends and

traditions of the fishing village provide a background for her history of the Provincetown Players and cultural attitudes during the first half of the 20th century. Both books reflect the perspective Vorse acknowledges in *A Footnote to Folly*: "Indeed, my book is the record of a woman who in early life got angry because many children lived miserably and died needlessly."

OTHER WORKS: *The Whole Family* (with others, 1908). *The Heart's Company* (1913). *Growing Up* (1920). *Fraycar's Fist* (1923). *Wreckage* (1924). *Here Are the People* (1943).

The Mary Heaton Vorse Collection is in the Archives of Labor History and Urban Affairs, Wayne State University, Detroit, Michigan.

BIBLIOGRAPHY: Aaron, D., *Writers on the Left* (1961). Blake, F., *The Strike in the American Novel* (1972). Hill, V. L., *Strategy and Breadth: The Socialist-Feminist in American Fiction* (dissertation, 1979). Overton, G., *The Women Who Make Our Novels* (1918). Rideout, W., *The Radical Novel in the United States, 1900-1954* (1956). Sochen, J., *The New Woman in Greenwich Village, 1910-1920* (1972). Sochen, J., *Movers and Shakers* (1973). "The Reminiscences of Mary Heaton Vorse" (transcript of interviews conducted for the Oral History Research Office of Columbia University, 1957).

Reference works: *American Women* (1939). *TCA*.

Other references: *Nation* (4 June 1908, 15 Jan. 1936). *NR.* (13 July 1942). *Time* (23 Dec. 1935).

—VICKI LYNN HILL

WAKOSKI, Diane

Born 3 August 1937, Whittier, California

Daughter of John J. and Marie Mengel Wakoski; **married** S. Shepherd Sherbell, 1965 (divorced); Michael Watterlond, 1973 (divorced); Robert J. Turney, 1982

Black Sparrow Press regularly prints a note at the end of Diane Wakoski's books saying her poems give all the important information about her life; but because she *invents* her autobiography as often as she records it, the information concerns her imaginative life more than her verifiable biography. Still, the poems indicate that she and one sister were born to poor Polish American parents and were deserted by their father in early childhood. Wakoski may have borne two children and given them up for adoption before 1971, and she has experienced at least two cycles of marriage and divorce.

Other published sources indicate Wakowski studied music and poetry at the University of California at Berkeley (B.A. in English, 1960) and moved to New York in 1960. In 1962 she published the first of more than 20 collections of poems. She worked in a bookstore until 1963 and then taught English at a junior high school until 1969. Since then, she has supported herself by her writing, poetry readings, and workshops and guest appointments at universities. Wakoski has written several long poems, such as the multivolume *Greed*, which she published in parts beginning in 1968, and was finally collected as *The Collected Greed* in 1984. She began putting out a sequence of autobiographical poems beginning with *Medea the Sorceress* in 1991, followed by *Jason the Sailor* (1993), *The Emerald City of Las Vegas* (1995), and *Argonaut Rose* in 1998. These four books, though concerned with the particulars of her personal life, such as the death of her ex-husband, all fall under the subtitle *The Archaeology of Movies and Books* and employ disparate allusive material, from L. Frank Baum's *The Wizard of Oz* through classical Greek myths, particularly the tale of Medea. Wakoski's essays have been collected in a book called *Toward a New Poetry* (1980). Although she has eschewed the politics of feminism, she has treated many of the most difficult issues faced by feminists.

Wakoski seeks to convert the imagination into something tangible and beautiful. Her poems can best be read as a record of her imaginative confrontations with the relationships between beauty and pain, love and rejection, identity and roles, power and submission, greed and generosity, sacrifice and reward, and loyalty and betrayal. Wakoski writes in an idiosyncratic form that allows her to be discursive or imagistic, factual or mythical, mundane or visionary, and to shift from one of these levels to another in the same poem without warning. The staples of her form are repetition and digression, used to hold the reader's

interest in the most ordinary aspects of experience, or to place a painful aspect in an unexpected perspective to reveal its potential beauty.

"Looking for the Bald Eagles in Wisconsin," from *The Man Who Shook Hands* (1978), begins with a story about Wakoski's ride with friends to the Mississippi on "black camels" and proceeds through several digressions on the natives' incredulity, the stubbornness of camels and men, America's history of destroying its mythical creatures, and her own ability to navigate on the back of her mythical beast to her direct experience of the bald eagles and her vision of the rising moon—whose landscape "is still not part of real/ life." Although the image of the camel ride holds the poem together, Wakoski's journey serves to affirm the different modes of transportation we can use on our own journeys. Relying for the most part on common language and ordinary rhythms of speech, Wakoski seeks to reveal the extraordinary dimensions of life, becoming alternatively an archaeologist, an astronomer, a magician, a goddess, a misfit, and an ordinary woman in the process.

Although Wakoski's experimental form and her attention to devalued (feminine, intellectual, and imaginative) aspects of human experience have provoked negative criticism, her talent, courage, seriousness, intelligence, and insight into human feelings seem likely to make this ambitious, coherent oeuvre one of the hallmarks of our time.

Wakoski's middle years have brought no extreme rupture with the poetics of her youth, but rather an organic process of refinement and development. As she says in "When Breakfast Is Brought by the Morning Star," from *Medea the Sorceress*, "New day doesn't mean new life;/ it means that you continue work out afresh/ each day/ the story, you were always destined/ to tell." She continues to work with loose forms, free imagination, coherent narrative, tangential digression, reiteration of images, and personal history and mythology to add to the poetic mosaic she is constructing of her life. This life work is a self-portrait of a woman across time—aging—and space: the West, the Midwest, and Europe orient Wakoski's work like a three-cornered compass rose. Because her project is essentially the weaving of an autobiography consisting of many individual poems, these poems are tightly interconnected. The full strength of the work can best be appreciated by taking it as a unified whole, a life in progress.

In 1988 Wakoski published *Emerald Ice*, a selection of her poems written between 1962 and 1987. This volume, like *The Collected Greed*, shows the development of the poet's technique and themes over the decades. *Medea the Sorceress* entwines poems with prose in the form of letters and excerpts from quantum physics texts. In this volume, her dark focus—on the humiliations of aging, human ugliness in its many forms, and what she perceives to be her own failures—lightens toward a calmer self-appreciation and acceptance.

Although Wakoski wholeheartedly engages many issues in contemporary women's lives, she avoids being labeled as political. ''I don't ever want a political point of view imputed to me,'' she said in a 1983 interview. Alliance with a political movement seems to run counter to her strong individualism: ''One of the reasons I have not been wanting to be called a feminist poet is that the label seems to lump all women writers together, as if we have a common message. I am not sure I have a message, but if I do, it is full of contradictions and paradoxes and perhaps even baffling'' (*Medea the Sorceress*).

Wakoski has received many awards and honors, including Guggenheim (1972), National Endowment for the Arts (1973), and Fulbright (1984) fellowships. She received a grant from the Michigan Arts Council in 1988 and the Michigan Arts Foundation award in 1989. Her selected poems, *Emerald Ice*, (1988) won the William Carlos Williams prize from the Poetry Society of America in 1989.

Wakoski has maintained a steady outpouring of publications, primarily poetry and occasionally essays. Her collections consistently show concern for the quality of books as physical objects and continue to be fine samples of the bookbinder's as well as the poet's art. She has long been an itinerant poet, supporting herself with numerous one-term teaching appointments at colleges across the country and by giving public readings. Nevertheless, she has been poet-in-residence at Michigan State University since 1975, where she was awarded a Distinguished Professorship in 1990. She continues to teach there, and to work on the series *The Archaeology of Movies and Books*.

OTHER WORKS: *Coins and Coffins* (1962). *Four Young Lady Poets* (1962). *Discrepancies and Apparitions* (1966). *The George Washington Poems* (1967). *Inside the Blood Factory* (1968). *The Magellanic Clouds* (1970). *The Motorcycle Betrayal Poems* (1971). *Smudging* (1972). *Dancing on the Grave of a Son of a Bitch* (1973). *Trilogy: Coins and Coffins, Discrepancies and Apparitions, The George Washington Poems* (1974). *Virtuoso Literature for Two and Four Hands* (1975). *Creating a Personal Mythology* (1975). *Waiting for the King of Spain* (1976). *Cap of Darkness* (1980). *Earth Light* (1981). *Saturn's Rings* (1982). *Divers* (1982). *The Lady Who Drove Me to the Airport* (1982). *Making a Sacher Torte* (1982). *The Magician's Feastletters* (1982). *Why My Mother Likes Liberace* (1985). *The Managed World* (1985). *The Rings of Saturn* (1986). *Roses* (1987).

The manuscript collection of Diane Wakowski is housed at the University of Arizona at Tuscon.

BIBLIOGRAPHY: Gerber, P., and R. Gemmett, eds., *A Terrible War: A Conversation with Diane Wakowski* (1970). *Women as Mythmakers: Poetry and Visual Art by Twentieth-Century Women* (1984).

Reference works: *CA* (1966). *CAAS* (1984). *CANR* (1983). *CLC* (1986). *CP* (1991). *FC* (1990). *Crowell's Handbook of Contemporary Poetry* (1973). *Contemporary Poets of the English Language* (1970). *Oxford Companion to Women's Writing in the United States* (1995).

Other references: *Boundary* (Spring 1982). *Gypsy Scholar* (Summer 1979). *Hudson Review* (Autumn 1985). *LATBR* (18 July 1982; 4 Nov. 1984). *Margins* (Jan-Mar. 1976).

—ESTELLA LAUTER,
UPDATED BY DONNA GLEE WILLIAMS AND ANGELA
WOODWARD

WALD, Lillian D.

Born 10 March 1867, Cincinnati, Ohio; **died** 1 September 1940, Westport, Connecticut
Daughter of Max D. and Minnie Schwarz Wald

The third of four children of a successful German-born dealer in optical goods, Lillian D. Wald grew up in an affectionate and cultured household within the Americanized German-Jewish community in Rochester, New York. Unsatisfied with the life of a well-to-do young woman, in 1889 Wald applied for admission to the New York Hospital training school for nurses, because she felt ''the need of serious, definite work'' and found nursing ''womanly [and] congenial.''

After graduating and working at the Juvenile Asylum in New York, Wald entered the Woman's Medical College of the New York Infirmary. While teaching home nursing on Manhattan's East Side, she was called to the bedside of a suffering woman in a filthy tenement. This ''baptism of fire'' inspired her to abandon medical school, move to the East Side with a friend from training school, and begin nursing her neighbors in their tenement homes. Aided from the first by wealthy Jews who felt a duty to their coreligionists crowding the slums, and later by other philanthropists, Wald founded the Henry Street Settlement and a visiting nurse service, which by 1915 served all of Manhattan and the Bronx and cared for more patients than three of New York's largest hospitals combined.

Wald did more than any other individual to invent and popularize the American version of public health nursing. She became a national figure in social reform and nursing circles, reaching her peak of influence in the decade before WWI when she spearheaded the successful drive for a federal children's bureau. Adept at conciliating people of differing views, Wald was a suffragist but not a militant.

Wald wrote for practical purposes and frequently had others, particularly Henry Street—resident Lavinia L. Dock, prepare her speeches and articles. Wald's briefer writings often described the methods of the Settlement and visiting-nurse service in business-like detail, leaving motives and goals vague. Her two books, *The House on Henry Street* (1915) and *Windows on Henry Street* (1933), show a similar disjunction between concrete fact and impalpable ideal. They juxtapose anecdotes of her experiences as a nurse, East Side resident, and participant in reform crusades with inspirational but fuzzy generalizations.

Wald did not formulate a consistent philosophy. But her writings show three fundamental loyalties which shaped her career: to the settlement movement; to women, children, and the family; and to the promotion of women's social mission. Her interest in settlements was based on her sense of kinship with all human beings and comradeship in social service and on her pragmatism. The powerful first chapter of *The House on Henry Street* recounts Wald's "awakening" to her ties to tenement dwellers and her immediate decision to live among them.

Wald's writings reveal her dedication to women and children, combined with a tendency to subsume their interests under those of the home and family. A skillful propagandist sharing many of the values of her readers, Wald plays on middle-class Americans' reverence for motherhood by presenting the immigrant and working-class women of her neighborhood as conscientious, perplexed mothers. She endorses statements of individual working women and the Women's Trade Union League that, as actual or potential mothers, women workers need unions, shorter hours, and legal protection from poor working conditions.

Wald's discussions of nursing best express her conception of women's social role. Nurses act on a traditional, womanly impulse to care for the young and sick. She sees public health nurses as part of a reform movement based on the new conviction that much disease could be prevented by teaching ordinary people what scientists had learned about hygienic living and by improving social conditions. In *Windows on Henry Street*, Wald claims that "intelligent medical men" recognize the "essential independence" of nursing. Despite similar origins, medicine and nursing have separate histories, because scientific advance sets the pace of medical development, while religious and humanitarian interests determine the growth of nursing.

The practicality, conciliatory charm, and unanalytical sincerity that made Wald a star fund raiser and effective witness before committees appear in her writings as a fondness for anecdotes and comforting generalities and an unwillingness to probe struggles in her own soul or in society. Other women in the settlement movement, including Jane Addams and Vida Scudder, used their autobiographies to explore how they came to pioneer new roles for women and launch a social movement. Wald wrote less personally and less critically. Although her books do not reveal her innermost life and do not explain the dynamics of American society, they have value as documents of women's leadership in the settlement and public health movements. Their concreteness, disjointedness, and optimism convey the élan of women confident of their special ability to make the world a kinder, more humane place, while finding freedom for themselves at the same time.

OTHER WORKS: The papers of Lillian D. Wald are at the New York Public Library and in the Butler Library, Columbia University, New York City.

BIBLIOGRAPHY: Daniels, D., *Lillian D. Wald: The Progressive Woman and Feminism* (dissertation, 1976). Duffus, R., *Lillian Wald: Neighbor and Crusader* (1938). Reznick, A., *Lillian D. Wald: The Years at Henry Street* (dissertation, 1973).
    Reference works: *DAB*, *NAW* (1971).
    Other references: *NR* (8 Jan. 1916, 27 June 1934). *NYT* (2 Sept. 1940, 2 Dec. 1940). *Survey Graphic* (Oct. 1940).

—SUSAN ARMENY

WALDMAN, Anne

Born 2 April 1945, Milville, New Jersey
Married to Reed E. Bye, 1980; **children:** one son

Anne Waldman has spent over 30 years writing and chanting poetry. She has published over 40 books, of which she has either written or edited. She ran the St. Mark's Poetry Project as assistant director from 1966 to 1968 and director from 1968 to 1978 at St. Mark's church in New York. The two *World* anthologies were derived from her work with other poets from the St. Mark's Poetry Project.

Waldman then went on to become the cofounding director of the Jack Kerouac School of Disembodied Poetics at the Naropa Institute in Boulder, Colorado, with Allen Ginsberg in 1974. The school revived the idea of poetry as a vocalization and a public art. Together with Ginsberg, Waldman taught poetry as a theatrical event. Her experience beginning at age six as a performer at the Greenwich Village Children's Theatre to her upbringing with a jazz culture to her Buddhist religion influenced her "expansive chant-like structures," which in turn gave her the basis for her teachings at the school. Ginsberg said of Waldman's performances: "Anne Waldman is a poet orator, her body is an instrument for vocalization, her voice a trembling flame rising out of a strong body, her texts the accurate energetic fine notations of words with spoken music latent in mindful arrangement on the page."

Waldman has won numerous awards, including the Dylan Thomas Award in 1967, the Cultural Artists grant in 1976, and a National Endowment for the Arts grant in 1980. Her poetic career in the 1960s was heavily influenced by the Beat Generation. She describes her post-Beat career as "a unique creative generation, a second generation Beat." It is from this Beat and post-Beat era that Waldman edited and contributed to *Women of the Beat Generation* (1996). The book is her attempt to give women the chance to express themselves artistically and poetically. This effort was due to her own struggles to become a writer in a male-dominated world. *Women of the Beat Generation* features prolific women writers in an attempt "to acknowledge. . .the suffering, difficulty, and dignity" of their lives. It includes an excerpt from several of Waldman's better known poems, including "Fast Speaking Woman," "Two Hearts," "A Phone Call From Frank O'Hara," and "I Am the Guard."

Fast Speaking Woman (1996), the 20th-anniversary expanded edition, is a collection of pieces published in the first two editions (1975 and 1978) and works from old files and notebooks never published before. The title poem, "Fast Speaking Woman," is almost 600 lines like the following:

"I'm the phenomena woman
the woman who studies
the woman who names
the woman who writes
I'm the cataloguing woman
water that cleans
waters that run
flowers that clean as I go"

The poem uses the word "woman" in nearly every line. The "water that cleans. . .as I go" break is a pause and shift in rhythm and cleanses the impulsiveness of the writing. This is a clear example of the rhythmic chant of Waldman's poetry.

"Fast Speaking Woman," is a tribute to Maria Sabina, the Mazatec Native American shamaness in Mexico who guided Waldman in a magic mushroom ceremony. Waldman began writing it during a trip to South America, intended for meditation. She continued writing it back in New York and then later in India. The poem is Waldman's intention to list-chant all the things women are to be, including her own personal intricacies (how she sees herself). Again, with this poem, Waldman concerns herself with women's roles and how Everywoman is both messenger and protector.

Iovis: All Is Full of Jove (1986) and *Iovis: Book II* (1993) are two of Waldman's masterpieces. The former book is a 336-page epic, where Waldman combs the masculine soul and the sources of its energy. She uses several distinct male voices including her grandfather, her son, and male deities from other cultures. She explores her own aggression and male energy in mostly English, but also in Greek, Spanish, French, Italian, German, Balinese, Indonesian, Mayan, Czech, Sanskrit, and Gaelic. It ends with "To blunt the knife," alluding to the continuation of the exploration of female energy, may it be compassion, overtaking male aggression.

Iovis: Book II is a continuation of *Iovis: All Is Full of Jove*. Its purpose of exploration, however, changes from male to female energy. It is in this second part that Waldman sets up themes about the confusion of women's roles in the 20th century. She explores the compassionate female energy and at the end exclaims the renewal of that feminine charge with "I rang him down."

Waldman is known for her chants, powerful performances, and quest for recognition for women writers. Her poems rhyme or don't; her books, such as *Journals & Dreams* (1976), include impulsive words from her travels, including poems and personal letters. She explores sexuality, cultures, and personality, and her words never lie flat on the pages—they chant to you as if she were performing them.

OTHER WORKS: *On the Wing* (1967). *Giant Night* (1968). *O My Life!* (1969). *The World Anthology: Poems from the St. Mark's Poetry Project, and Another World* (1969, 1971). *Baby Breakdown* (1970). *Giant Night: Selected Poems* (1970). *Goodies from Anne Waldman* (1971). *Holy City* (1971). *Icy Rose* (1971). *Memorial Day* (with T. Berrigan, 1971). *No Hassles* (1971). *Light and Shadow* (1972). *Spin Off* (1972). *The West Indies Poems* (1972). *Life Notes: Selected Poems* (1973). *Self Portrait* (with J. Brainard, 1973). *Fast Speaking Woman* (1975). *Shaman* (1977). *4 Travels* (with R. Bye, 1978). *Talking Poetics from Naropa Institute* (ed. with M. Webb, 2 vols., 1978-1979). *To a Young Poet* (1979). *Countries* (1980). *Cabin* (1982). *First Baby Poems* (1982). *Make-Up on Empty Space* (1984). *Invention* (1985). *Skin Meat Bones* (1985). *The Romance Thing* (1987). *Blue Mosque* (1988). *Helping the Dreamer: New and Selected Poems* (1989, 1992). *Not a Male Pseudonym* (1990). *Lokapala* (1991). *Nice to See You: Homage to Ted Berrigan* (edited, 1991). *Out of This World* (edited, 1991). *Disembodied Poetics, Annals of the Jack Kerouac School* (edited with A. Schelling, 1994). *Kill or Cure* (1994).

BIBLIOGRAPHY: Cloward, T. F., "The Shaman's Voice: Anne Waldman and Maria Sabina—Some Notes on Contemporary Performance Poetry" (thesis, 1992).
Reference works: *CP* (1996).
Other references: *Anne Waldman* (audiocassette, 1987). *Anne Waldman* (video, 1991). *Battle of the Bards* (video, 1990). *Cassady, Vega, Waldman: Three Women of (and Beyond) the Beat Generation* (video, 1998). *Fried Shoes, Cooked Diamonds* (video, 1978, 1989). *Inquiring Mind* (Spring, 1997).

—KIMBALLY A. MEDEIROS

WALDROP, Rosmarie

Born 24 August 1935, Kitzingen-am-Main, Germany
Daughter of Josef and Friederike Wolgemuth Sebald; **married** Bernard K. Waldrop

Poet and translator Rosmarie Waldrop's work has had a great impact on the world of contemporary American letters. The author of over 30 books of poetry and prose and the translator of more than 20 books of poetry, Waldrop's contribution to contemporary poetry and poetics has been both significant and influential. In addition to her writing and translating work, since 1968 Waldrop has been coeditor of Burning Deck Press, one of the most important publishers of experimental poetry and prose in the United States.

Waldrop was born in Nazi Germany in 1935, the youngest of three daughters. She learned English as a child, the result of living in what was to become, from 1945 on, an American occupation zone. The experience of having grown up (as a non-Jew) in Hitler's Germany is recounted in Waldrop's novel, *The Hanky of Pippin's Daughter* (1986), and issues relating to the themes of personal history and knowing are at the root of much of her work.

Waldrop began studying comparative literature at the University of Wurzberg in 1954. In that same year, she met Bernard Keith Waldrop, a recently discharged private from the United States Army, who was to become her husband. Waldrop finished her undergraduate studies at the University of Freiburg in 1958 and moved to the U.S. to undertake graduate work at the University of Michigan. She and Keith were married a month after she moved to the U.S.

Waldrop's German-language roots, and her life in an English-speaking country, have had a profound impact on her writing: "In crossing the Atlantic my phonemes settled somewhere between German and English. I speak either language with an accent. This has saved me the illusion of being the master of language. I enter it at a skewed angle, through the fissures, the slight difference." Finding it awkward and "artificial" to write in German after having settled in the U.S., where she was already "thinking in English, dreaming in English, living in English," Waldrop fastened on translating as a "natural substitute." While she began with translating American poets into German, she soon settled on translating poets such as Günter Grass and Gottfried Benn into English. Thus Waldrop's work with translation dates as far back as her poetic output; some of her most compelling and important thought stems from how these two projects are intertwined and in some sense overlapping. In 1963 Waldrop first had her work—both original poems and translations—published in journals. In 1964, with her dissertation not yet completed (she received her Ph.D. from the University of Michigan in 1966), Waldrop was hired to teach comparative and German literature at Wesleyan University. Since 1968 the Waldrops have lived in Providence, Rhode Island, where they're associated with the Creative Writing Department at Brown University.

Waldrop's first chapbook, *A Dark Octave*, appeared in 1967. Her first major collection, *The Aggressive Ways of the Casual Stranger*, appeared in 1972 from Random House. The period of time between these two events was both busy for Waldrop (in addition to a number of chapbooks, her doctoral dissertation was published, as was her translation of Peter Weiss' novel *Bodies and Shadows*), and formative. During a year spent in Paris in 1970-71, the Waldrops met and became friends and colleagues with Claude Royet-Journoud and Anne-Marie Albiach. Not only did these new friendships provide an important context for literary discourse, but it was through Royet-Journoud that Waldrop met Edmond Jabès. Waldrop, as of the late 1990s, has translated 10 volumes of Jabès' works and has become his major translator. The predominant themes of the poems in *Aggressive Ways* are gender, family, domestic life, and the body. Issues relating to gender identity continue to be in some way central to Waldrop's writing, yet her position vis-à-vis gender is complex and refreshingly nondogmatic. In a critical piece originally appearing in *Onward: Contemporary Poetry & Poetics* (edited by Peter Baker, 1996) and subsequently excerpted in *Moving Borders: Three Decades of Innovative Writing by Women*, Waldrop notes that "The fact [of being a woman] clearly shapes my writing; thematically, in attitude, in awareness of social conditioning, marginality—but does not determine it exclusively." In addition, she says, "I don't really see 'female language, female style or technique.' Because the writer, male or female, is only one partner in the process of writing. Language, in its full range, is the other. And it is not a language women have to 'steal back.'"

Also central to Waldrop's thought and practice as a poet is the handling of, the examination of, language itself, the structure of language, and notions of authorship. Again, from the piece in *Moving Borders*: "Language comes not only with an infinite potential for new combinations, but with a long history contained in it. The blank page is not blank. No text has one single author. Whether we are conscious of it or not, we always write on top of a palimpsest. . . . This is not a question of 'linear influence,' but of writing as dialog with a whole net of previous and concurrent texts, tradition, with the culture and language we breathe and move in, which conditions us even while we help to construct it."

OTHER WORKS: *Change of Address* (with K. Waldrop, 1968). *Camp Printing* (1970). *The Relaxed Abalone; or, What-You-May-Find* (1970). *Spring Is a Season and Nothing Else* (1970). *Body Image* (with N. Howe, 1970). *Until Volume One* (with K. Waldrop, 1973). *Words Worth Less* (with K. Waldrop, 1973). *Kind Regards* (1975). *Since Volume One* (with K. Waldrop, 1975). *Acquired Pores* (1976). *The Road Is Everywhere or Stop This Body* (1978). *The Ambition of Ghosts* (1979). *When They Have Senses* (1980). *Psyche & Eros* (1980). *Nothing Has Changed* (1981). *Differences for Four Hands* (1984). *Streets Enough to Welcome Snow* (1986). *Morning's Intelligence* (1986). *The Reproduction of Profiles* (1987). *Shorter American Memory* (1988). *A Form of Taking It All* (1990). *Peculiar Motions* (1990). *Light Travels* (with K. Waldrop, 1992). *Lawn of Excluded Middle* (1993). *Fan Poem for Deshika* (1993). *Concerned Stone, Split Infinites* (1994). *A Key into the Language of America* (1994). *Another Language: Selected Poems* (1997). *Blindsight* (1998). *In a Flash* (1998). *Well Well Reality* (with K. Waldrop 1998).

BIBLIOGRAPHY: Sloan, M. M., ed., *Moving Borders: Three Decades of Innovative Writing by Women* (1998).
    Reference works: *ANR* 39. *DLB* (1996).

—JESSICA GRIM

WALKER, Alice

Born 9 February 1944, Eatonton, Georgia
Daughter of Willie L. and Minnie Grant Walker; **married** Melvyn R. Leventhal, 1967 (divorced); **children:** Rebecca

Alice Walker is the eighth child of black sharecroppers. She attended Spelman College in Atlanta and Sarah Lawrence College (B.A., 1965). Deeply involved in the civil rights movement, she worked with voter registration in Georgia, welfare rights and Head Start in Mississippi, and the Welfare Department in New York City. She taught at Jackson State University (1968-69) and

Tougaloo College (1969-70), both in Mississippi. She has lived in Kenya, Uganda, and the Soviet Union, and now resides in Northern California where she is a fiction editor of *Ms.* magazine and continues to write poetry, fiction, and essays.

In *Once* (1968), Walker renders into verse her experiences in the civil rights demonstrations of the 1960s and her impressions of her African travels. Influenced primarily by Zen epigrams and Japanese haiku, Walker writes simple, brief, and mysterious poems about love, pain, struggle, and the joy of being alive and whole.

Revolutionary Petunia (1973) was written in honor of "incorrect" people like Sammy Lou, the heroine of the title poem, who "struggled against oppression and won." Much of the poetry is autobiographical, conjuring up a child's image of home—a small, rural southern Georgia town, a place where children and adults are aware of their roots and experience a sense of community.

Walker describes *The Third Life of Grange Copeland* (1970), her first novel, as a "grave book in which the characters see the world as almost entirely menacing." Spanning the years between 1900 and the 1960s, it is about three generations of black people, all descendants of Grange Copeland. He is the unifying force of the book and it is he who, after many painful years of white oppression, learns that black oppression can be even more deadly and dehumanizing—that there is never any excuse for the cruelty of blacks to each other. Walker's characters are painfully credible—painfully alive and painfully oppressed by others and by themselves.

In her one book of short stories, *In Love and Trouble* (1973), Walker explores—as do her two favorite writers, Zora Neale Hurston and Jean Toomer—"the oppressions, the insanities, the loyalties, and the triumphs of black women," the only people she respects "collectively and with no reservations." Although many of the women in the book suffer from everything from stifled creativity to stifled sexuality, they endure stoically. The subjects are often ghastly, but the book as a whole is not a sad one; it has its anguished grace.

In *Langston Hughes* (1974), a biography, Walker lovingly renders into language that young children can understand and appreciate the story of the poet laureate of Harlem. In 1977's *Meridian*, chronicles the coming of age of several civil rights workers, one of whom is white, during the 1960s in the South. The main character is Meridian, a mysterious, sensitive black woman dedicated to helping others and, more important, to living her life "against whatever obstacles, and not to give up any particle of it without a fight to the death, preferably *not* her own."

In the 20 years since publication of *The Third Life of Grange Copeland*, Walker became one of the best-known American writers. Among the numerous honors and awards she has won are the Pulitzer Prize and the American Book Award in 1983 for *The Color Purple*, the O. Henry Award in 1986 for the story "Kindred Spirits," and the Langston Hughes Award in 1988.

Set in the rural South in the early 20th century, Walker's epistolary novel *The Color Purple* (1982) describes the spiritual,

emotional, and practical growth of the protagonist Celie from a physically and emotionally repressed "slave" of black men and white men and women to a loving and loved, self-sufficient woman. This growth is largely a process of Celie's finding her own voice and learning to control it. In many respects, *The Color Purple* is a tribute to the work of Walker's "foremother," Zora Neale Hurston, particularly Hurston's novel *Their Eyes Were Watching God*.

The autobiographical essays of Walker's *In Search of Our Mothers' Gardens* (1983) range in subject from the civil rights movement to the writer Flannery O'Connor to discussions of beauty and childbearing. The book discovers and articulates a black feminist sentiment and tradition Walker calls "womanist." Walker recovers the work of African American women artists, locating art in the quilts and gardens of mothers and grandmothers, and reclaims writers, particularly black women writers, whose writing had been distorted or entirely ignored. It was in part due to this book that *Their Eyes Were Watching God* was elevated from a forgotten book to a near-canonical text.

A fourth collection of poems, *Horses Make a Landscape More Beautiful* (1984), attempts to come to grips with the complexities of what Walker elsewhere has called her "triple-blood," her inheritance from African American, European American, and Native American ancestors, within the political landscape of the contemporary U.S. The language of these spare poems often appears prosaically simple and almost artless, but is in fact tightly bonded by slant rhymes, alliteration, and repetition.

Living by the Word: Selected Writings 1973-1987 (1988) covers as wide a range of subjects as *In Search of Our Mothers' Gardens*. The overriding concern running through the diverse pieces of the later book is for a universal spirituality Walker hopes will redeem a world seemingly bent on destroying itself.

The novel *The Temple of My Familiar* (1989) represents 500,000 years of human history, investigating the cultural inheritance of black and white Americans through the medium of the oral tradition of storytelling. Instead of a linear narration, the novel consists of a series of stories, many told from the perspective of Miss Lissie, an elderly African American woman who can recall earlier lives and who switches back and forth in gender, race, nationality—even species. Miss Lissie is not the only storyteller in the novel; virtually all the characters tell stories in a variety of media: oral narratives, letters, diaries, songs. Some complete stories come from earlier books: the reader finds out more, for example, about the later history of Shug and Celie from *The Color Purple*.

In *Possessing the Secret of Joy* (1992), Walker again returns to characters from *The Color Purple*, using Tashi, the young African girl who marries Adam, as her heroine. Her story is about her struggle to reconcile her African heritage with the modern world. In order to show her solidarity with her Olinka people's fight against colonialism, Tashi embraces their traditions, including female circumcision, a practice that had proven fatal to her own sister. Political in intent, Walker's novel focuses on this controversial subject of clitoridectomy to call attention to a practice of submitting women to a patriarchal definition of sexuality that not only destroys their pleasure in sex but also endangers their health throughout their lives.

In the 1990s, Walker continued to produce work that is challenging, technically rich, and culturally acute. With fiction, wide-ranging essays, and journal works, Walker's writings reflect a deep and ever evolving passion for language and story, along with an integral commitment to activism and social change. In 1994 a controversy was sparked when two of Walker's stories were abruptly removed from a California 10th grade achievement test. The stories were removed because of complaints that they were, in the case of "Roselily" (1972), considered "antireligious," and, in the case of "Am I Blue?" (1986), labeled "anti-meat eating." Shortly thereafter, Walker was chosen to receive a California Governor's Award, which she politely declined. The stories are collected in a volume with an excerpt from *The Color Purple* (1982) and a detailing of the numerous attempts which have been made to censor these works, along with an introduction citing Walker's initial response and her eventual acceptance of the Governor's Award. The book, *Alice Walker: Banned* (1996) represents a unique entry in the literature of censorship.

A collection of essays on a myriad of topics, *Anything We Love Can Be Saved* (1997), roves from religion, daughters, and saving literary heritages to Fidel Castro and Jung's house in Zurich. The essays, beginning with "The Only Reason You Want to Go to Heaven Is That You Have Been Driven Out of Your Mind" (in which Walker writes of her quest for a spirituality beyond that of the Judeo-Christian tradition), are united loosely by Walker's activism and her "belief in the love of the world."

In the novel *By the Light of My Father's Smile* (1998), Walker unfolds the story of an anthropologist couple who take their two daughters to the Sierras in Mexico to study the Mundo, a mixed-race black and Indian tribe. When one daughter becomes intimate with a boy in the tribe, her father responds violently. The events that take place among the Mundo form the central knot of the novel. Through first person narrative, shifting gracefully from and between characters, time periods, life and afterlife, Walker ravels her reader into and out of the tangle. As is the case with much of Walker's work, the novel focuses on family relationships, social injustice, spirituality, and sexuality within a culturally diverse setting.

Walker's importance as a writer encompasses her skill as novelist, essayist, and poet as well as her role as a promoter and reclaimer of an African American women's cultural tradition. Her work has changed the shape of contemporary literature as her novels helped to put African American women fiction writers at the front of the American literary culture. Walker has also changed literary scholarship, reviving the work of nearly forgotten writers and articulating a black feminist criticism that has had a major impact on the increase in critical writings by African American women scholars.

Walker's writings evoke both criticism and delight while provoking both controversy and change. As she continues to write from her unique intellectual and spiritual perspective, her contribution to literature and social change grows ever more solid and abiding. Walker is dedicated to the continuation and preservation of the traditions that are hers as a black American. To her, to lose those traditions is not only to lose "our literary and cultural heritage but, more insidiously, to lose ourselves." Her works, though often painful, are refreshingly and lovingly real. As Grange Copeland says after the birth of his granddaughter, "Out of all kinds of shit comes something clean, soft and sweet smellin'."

OTHER WORKS: *Good Night Willie Lee, I'll See You in the Morning* (1979). *You Can't Keep a Good Woman Down* (1981). *Her Blue Body Everything We Know: Earthling Poems, 1965-1990* (1991). *Warrior Marks: Female Genital Mutilation and the Sexual Blinding of Women* (with P. Parmar, 1993). *The Complete Stories* (1994). *The Same River Twice: Honoring the Difficult* (1995). *Langston Hughes, American Poet* (1998).

BIBLIOGRAPHY: Bell, R. P., et al., *Sturdy Black Bridges* (1979). Benevol, D., *Alice Walker's The Color Purple* (1995). Bloom, H., ed., *Alice Walker* (1989, 1999). Butler-Evans, E., *Race, Gender, and Desire: Narrative Strategies in the Fiction of Toni Cade Bambara, Toni Morrison, and Alice Walker* (1989). Christian, B., *Black Women Novelists: The Development of a Tradition, 1892-1976* (1980). Dieke, I., ed., *Critical Essays on Alice Walker* (1999). Evans, M., ed., *Black Women Writers* (1950-1980). *A Critical Evaluation* (1984). Gates, H. L., Jr., *The Signifying Monkey* (1988). Gates, H. L., Jr., ed., *Reading Black, Reading Feminist* (1990). Gates, H. L., Jr., and K. A. Appiach, eds., *Alice Walker: Critical Perspectives Past and Present* (1993). Gentry, T., *Alice Walker* (1998). Howard, L. P., ed., *Alice Walker and Zora Neale Hurston: The Common Bond*, (1993). Humphries, J., ed., *Southern Literature and Literary Theory*, (1990). Jenkins, P. J., *The Wandering Soul: The Search for Identity in Chopin's The Awakening, Hurston's Their Eyes Were Watching God, and Walker's The Color Purple* (1995). Johnson, W. D., and T. L. Green, eds., *Perspectives on Afro-American Women* (1975). Lauret, M., *Alice Walker* (1999). Lazo, C. E., *Alice Walker* (1999). O'Brien, J., ed., *Interviews with Black Writers* (1973). Pendergast, T., and S. Pendergast, eds., *Gay and Lesbian Literature* 2 (1998). Simawe, S. A., *Music and the Politics of Culture in James Baldwin's and Alice Walker's Fiction* (1994). Tate, C., ed., *Black Women Writers at Work* (1983). Winchell, D. H., *Alice Walker* (1992). Witherspoon-Walthall, M. L., *The Evolution of the Black Heroine in the Novels of Jessie Fauset, Nella Larsen, Zora Neale Hurston, Toni Morrison, and Alice Walker* (1988).

Reference works: *African American Writers* (1991). *Black Literary Criticism* (1992). *CA* Online (1999). *CANR* (1989). *CLC* (1976, 1978, 1981, 1984, 1988, 1998). *DLB* (1980, 1984, 1994). *Oxford Companion to Women's Writing in the United States* (1995).

Other references: *American Scholar* (Winter 1970-71). *Black World* (Sept. 1973, Oct. 1974). *Callaloo* (Spring 1989). *CLA*

Journal (Sept. 1973, Dec. 1975, March 1981). *Essence* (July 1976). *Freedomways* (1971, 1974, 1976, 1979). *Ms.* (Feb. 1974). *NR* (14 Sept. 1974). *Newsweek* (24 Apr. 1989). *NY* (27 Feb. 1971). *NYRB* (29 Jan. 1987). *NYTBR* (5 June 1988, 30 Aug. 1989). *PMLA* (Oct. 1991). *Southern Literary Journal* (Fall 1998). *Third Woman* (1980). *Time* (1 May 1989). *Alice Walker and* The Color Purple (video, 1995). *Alice Walker: A Portrait in the First Person* (video, 1988). *Alice Walker: Possessing the Secret of Joy* (film, 1994). *Conversation with Alice Walker* (video, 1992). *Visions of the Spirit: A Portrait of Alice Walker* (film, 1989). *Walker, Alice, My Life as My Self* (recording, 1996). *Women's Rights: A Global Movement* (video,1995). *The World Is Made of Stories* (recording, 1995).

—LILLIE P. HOWARD,
UPDATED BY JAMES SMETHURST AND JESSICA REISMAN

WALKER, Margaret

Born 7 July 1915, Birmingham, Alabama; **died** 30 November 1998
Daughter of Sigismund and Marion Walker; **married** M. Alexander, 1943; **children:** four

Margaret Walker's middle-class parents were both university graduates; her father was a Methodist minister, and her mother a musicologist and third-generation educator. Walker graduated from Gilbert Academy (1930) and studied at Northwestern University (B.A. 1935) and the University of Iowa (M.A. 1940; Ph.D. 1965).

After working on the federal government's Writers Project in Chicago and as a newspaper and magazine editor, she began teaching. Beginning in 1949, Walker was a professor of English at Jackson State College, Mississippi. She also served as director of the Institute for the Study of History, Life, and Culture of Black People and organized black culture and writers' conferences, notably the Phillis Wheatley Poetry Festival (in November 1973), at which 20 black women poets read. Walker had four children.

Walker began writing poetry at the age of twelve. She was the first of her race to receive the Yale Younger Poets Award for her first volume of poetry, *For My People* (1942, reissued in 1989 and 1992), and other awards have followed. Her work is widely published in periodicals.

For My People is an early indication of Walker's poetic talent. She experiments with traditional and modern poetic forms. There are 10 occasional poems, written in unmistakably black poetic rhythms; 10 ballads with superimposed jazz rhythms or blues metrics; and six sonnets, the most traditional of her poetry in substance and structure. The volume begins at a dramatic, intense pitch, continues in a relaxed tone, and ends in contemplative

modulation. In *Prophets for a New Day* (1970), Walker limits her subject to the often fatal struggle to secure human rights—chiefly for blacks. Substance clearly dominates form, whether sonnet or ballad.

Walker dedicates *October Journey* (1973), a volume of 10 poems, to two of her greatest influences: her father and Langston Hughes, her "friend and mentor." Her verse is at its most melodramatic here. The first poem, "October Journey," establishes the volume's tone: "A music sings within my flesh / I feel the pulse within my throat." The final piece, "A Litany from the Dark People," is a skillful, rhythmic composition.

Jubilee (1966, 1999), Walker's gripping novel, spans several genres: Civil War epic, historical fiction, and the slave narrative. It is the story of Vyre, daughter of a slave and her master. She experiences simultaneously the rite of passage to womanhood and the change from slavery to freedom. Walker frees her epic from the traditional male-oriented sense of the heroic, structuring her novel around Vyre, her maternal great-grandmother. Vyre's first husband, a free and literate Negro, functions only in a supportive role to underscore Vyre's heroism. Walker's poetic style is evident in *Jubilee*'s rhythmic prose and biblical overtones.

Jubilee was conceived in part as an answer to Margaret Mitchell's *Gone with the Wind*. The former draws on both the modern form of historical fiction and the genre of the 19th-century slave narrative as well as oral African American traditions. Sometimes criticized for an overly conciliatory tone, the novel chronicles the survival and personal and spiritual growth of an African American woman, Vyre, in the face of slavery and incredible cruelty. Vyre not only withstands slavery but is able to transcend her hatred and forgive her former slave mistress, offering a vision of society without racism.

In *How I Wrote Jubilee and Other Essays on Life and Literature* (1972, 1990) Walker writes about her own artistic development, her experience as a woman teacher in traditionally black colleges, African American literature, and Southern literature. Walker's essays especially chronicle the difficulties of African American women who teach in colleges dominated by men.

Her biography *Richard Wright, Daemonic Genius* (1988) attempts to analyze the complex influences that molded Wright's particular literary vision. Walker brings to bear her skills as scholar and writer as well as her personal knowledge of Wright, with whom she had a close working relationship—Walker did much of the primary research for Wright's novel *Native Son*.

This Is My Century: New and Collected Poems (1989) is a collection of autobiographical poems, elegies, historical portraits, and meditations on the state of African American life in the 1980s. It contains a new group of poems, "This Is My Century," and another, "Farish Street," previously published only in periodical form. "Farish Street" describes and commemorates an African American community in Jackson, Mississippi, portrayed both as a specific place and as an archetype of African American life in the United States.

Walker's work, particularly her poetry, shares many formal and thematic concerns with other African American writers of her generation, notably in her use of the sonnet, epic free verse, and vernacular-based ballads. In her fiction, she shares with such women writers of her generation as Tillie Olsen and Meridel Le Sueur a feminist sensibility, portraying strong female protagonists and suggesting that a more humane society is possible in the U.S. through the maternal power of women.

OTHER WORKS: *A Poetic Equation: Conversations with Nikki Giovanni* (1974). *On Being Female, Black, and Free: Essays by Margaret Walker, 1932-1992* (1997).

BIBLIOGRAPHY: Carmichael, J. M., *Trumpeting a Fiery Sound: History and Folklore in Margaret Walker's Jubilee* (1998). Edwards, M. L., *The Rhetoric of Afro-American Poetry: A Rhetorical Analysis of Black Poetry and the Selected Poetry of Margaret Walker and Langston Hughes* (dissertation, 1980). Evans, M., ed., *Black Women Writers (1950-1980): A Critical Evaluation* (1984). Gwin, M. C., *Black and White Women of the Old South: The Peculiar Sisterhood in American Literature* (1985). McCray, J., *For My People: The Life and Writing of Margaret Walker* (video, 1998). Miller, R. B., ed., *Black Poets Between Worlds, 1940-1960* (1986). Pryse, M., and H. Spillers, eds., *Conjuring: Black Women, Fiction and Literary Tradition* (1985). Tate, C., ed., *Black Women Writers at Work* (1983).

Reference works: *African-American Writers* (1991). *CANR* (1989). *CB* (Nov. 1943). *CLC* (1973, 1976). *DLB* (1988). *Ebony Success Library* (1973). *Oxford Companion to Women's Writing in the United States* (1995). *Poetry Criticism* (1998).

Other references: *A Message from Margaret* (video, 1992). *African American Review* (1999). *Black World* (Dec. 1971). *Callaloo* (Winter 1999). *CSM* (22 Jan. 1990). *LATBR* (19 Feb. 1989). *Margaret Walker Interview with Kay Bonetti* (audiocassette, 1991). *Mississippi Quarterly* (1995). *Nation* (1999). *WRB* (July 1990). *Yale Review* (1943).

—ADRIANNE BAYTOP,
UPDATED BY JAMES SMETHURST

WALKER, Mary Spring

Born circa 1830s or 1840s; death date unknown
Married Reverend J. B. R. Walker

Mary Spring Walker's works are all temperance novels set in Connecticut. No biographical information, aside from her marriage to a minister, could be found to indicate the origins of her concern with the temperance movement. Her novels anticipate the great women's temperance crusade of 1873-74, and they precede Frances E. Willard's *Women and Temperance: or, The Work and Workers of the Women's Christian Temperance Union* (1883); nevertheless, reference to Walker's name or writing does not appear in connection with either of the two.

In *The Family Doctor; or, Mrs. Barry and Her Bourbon* (1868), Walker interweaves the stories of the Barry and Barton families. The narrator is Lizzie Barton whose father, a heavy drinker, squanders the family's income and drowns himself. From her vantage point as a lady's maid, Lizzie relates the tragedy of Mrs. Barry, a beautiful aristocrat, who becomes addicted to bourbon after her doctor prescribes it as a tonic. Lizzie reports the deterioration of the Barry household and, in graphic detail, the death of the eldest son, Philip, who also falls victim to alcohol. She attempts to help the Barry family, particularly the younger son and the father, salvage their lives.

Walker's primary theme is the irresponsible prescription of alcohol as medication. She blames the medical profession for ignoring the harmful consequences of alcoholism and portrays Dr. Sharpe, the offending family physician, as selfish and pompous. Sharpe becomes more villainous as the novel progresses; his careless prescription, while drunk, of a poisonous drug causes a death and serves as his own punishment for destroying many families.

Walker links a religious theme with temperance concerns in *The Rev. Dr. Willoughby and His Wine* (1869). In this novel, she launches an attack upon "ministers who do not minister." Scholarly Dr. Willoughby prefers conversation in his study to spiritual work among the needy. He and his fellow ministers enjoy port and cognac to lift their spirits after their Sabbath labors, which, ironically, are pious sermons on Christian charity.

Dr. Willoughby, the eldest and most influential minister in Hartford, undermines his position by his contradictory attitudes toward alcohol. Walker's long, complicated plot dramatizes the inability of many ministers and church members to recognize that even occasional intoxication leads invariably to incapacity and ruin. Because she establishes the church as an institution affecting all parts of society, Walker can involve numerous minor characters and subplots in extending her message to widely diverse socioeconomic groups. She is skillful in describing the impact of alcoholism on the family and home. Although her emphasis is on tragic effects, Walker redeems the ministry and congregations by also presenting a "teetotal parson" who leads an entire town in a successful war against rum sellers.

Walker's novels indict those in responsible positions for their social and moral complacency. She addresses a professional and middle class audience which does not realize that alcoholism affects not merely the poor and the laboring classes. Walker creates a large multilayered society which grows in awareness of mutual concerns through its connection with temperance issues. But she seldom penetrates her characters' exteriors or explores their reactions to problems other than lives ruined by drink. Her descriptions of a young wife's loyalty divided between her husband and her parents and of a poor mother's conflicting desires to keep her son or give him to wealthy foster parents show she had abilities beyond proselytizing that she rarely used.

OTHER WORKS: *Both Sides of the Street* (1870). *Down in a Saloon* (1871). *White Robes* (1872).

BIBLIOGRAPHY: Reference works: *Oxford Companion to Women's Writing in the United States* (1995).

—THADIOUS M. DAVIS

WALLACE, Michele

Born 4 January 1952, New York, New York
Daughter of Robert E. and Faith Ringgold Wallace

African American cultural critic and feminist theorist Michele Wallace received her B.A. (1974) and M.A. (1990) from the City College of New York, where she did graduate work in African American literature and feminist literary criticism. She has taught journalism at New York University, and creative writing and African American literature at the University of California at San Diego, the University of Oklahoma, and the University of Buffalo. Wallace joined the faculty of the City College of New York and the City University of New York Graduate Center in 1989, teaching literature and women's studies.

Wallace's articles, essays, short stories, and poetry have appeared in a number of anthologies, newspapers, and magazines. She is best known for her two books of cultural criticism, *Black Macho and the Myth of the Superwoman* (1979, reprinted with a new introduction by the author in 1990, and again in 1999) and *Invisibility Blues* (1990).

Black Macho and the Myth of the Superwoman, published when Wallace was twenty-six, generated an enormous amount of controversy; and the debates it provoked continue to resonate. Using autobiography, psychohistory, literary and political criticism, sociological study, and feminist theory, she examines the ways in which racism and sexism distort relationships between black men and women. She argues that black leaders and writers give credence to the stereotypes of the black stud and the super matriarch imposed on them by whites. These myths, she says, perpetuate hatred and self-hatred and leave black men and women at odds with one another and politically powerless. Wallace contends as well the black power movement failed because it equated manhood and masculinity with power and did not move beyond the sexual politics that play an important role in maintaining the oppression and marginalization of black women.

Some critics, like June Jordan, felt Wallace's youth invalidated her arguments, many of which were based on personal experience. Others criticized her for devaluing the civil rights and black power movements and for neglecting the additional factors leading to their demise, such as institutional racism, economic inequality, and political assassinations.

Many critics agreed with Wallace, however, seeing her as a harbinger for change and praising her for urging black women to assert their own identity. Even those who thought her vision was limited agreed that it provoked important and necessary discussion about the future of African Americans in general and of black women in particular.

In *Invisibility Blues* (1990), Wallace turns her attention to questions of representation, examining popular culture and its limited representations of black womanhood from a black feminist perspective. She discusses the ways in which black artists, ranging from her mother, artist Faith Ringgold, to pop superstar Michael Jackson, make a distinct contribution to American culture and at the same time challenge the status quo or disrupt the dominant discourse. Wallace repudiates the notion that black women are marginal to the production of culture or knowledge and explores the ways in which demands for their solidarity with black men often render women's contributions to the struggle for liberation invisible.

Invisibility Blues has been generally well received. Wallace's unique combination of popular journalism and rigorous scholarship makes an important contribution to the field of cultural studies and to the formidable and growing body of black feminist criticism.

OTHER WORKS: *Black Popular Culture* (with G. Dents, 1992, 1998). Contributor to many anthologies, periodicals and exhibition catalogues, including: *All the Women Are White, All the Blacks Are Men, But Some of Us Are Brave: Black Women's Studies* (1982). *Global Television* (1988). *Multi-Cultural Literacy* (1988). *Art in America* (Dec. 1990). *Out There: Marginalization and Contemporary Cultures* (1990). *Reading Black, Reading Feminist: A Critical Anthology* (1990). *Aperture* (Spring, 1992). *Our Town* (1992). *America Street: A Multicultural Anthology of Stories* (1993). *Aesthetics in Feminist Perspective* (1993). *Black American Cinema* (1993). *The Cultural Studies Reader* (1993). *Race, Identity, and Representation in Education* (1993). *Multiculturalism: A Critical Reader* (1994). *Constructing Masculinity* (1995). *Division of Labor: "Women's Work" in Contemporary Art* (1995). *Face Value: American Portraits* (1995). *Subjects and Citizens: Nation, Race, and Gender from Oroonoko to Anita Hill* (1995). *Ms.* (1995, 1996).

BIBLIOGRAPHY: Coleman, L. M., "Cultural Representations of Blackness: Discourse, Identity, and Voice in the Texts of bell hooks and Michele Wallace, 1979-1992 " (thesis, 1994). Exum, P. C., *Keeping the Faith* (1972).
  Reference works: *CA* (1983).
  Other references: *African American Review* (1995). *Black American Literary Forum* (Winter 1984). *Black Female Authors*

& Playwrights (video, 1989). *Black Women, Sexual Politics and the Revolution* (video, 1991, 1992). *College Literature* (Oct. 1993). *Essence* (Feb. 1979, Aug. 1979). *Journal of Communication* (Spring 1991, Autumn 1991). *Michele Wallace* (video, 1991). *Nation* (17 Feb. 1979, 15 July 1991). *New Directions for Women* (Jan. 1992). *New Statesman and Society* (30 Nov. 1990). *Newsweek* (5 Feb. 1979). *NYTBR* (18 Mar. 1979). *Signs* (Spring 1995). *Washington Monthly* (Feb. 1979). *Woman's Art Journal* (1999).

—MARJORIE BRYER,
UPDATED BY SYDONIE BENET

WALLER, Mary Ella

Born 1 March 1855, Boston, Massachusetts; **died** 14 June 1938, Wellesley, Massachusetts
Wrote under: M. E. Waller, Mary E. Waller
Daughter of David and Mary Hallet Waller

The early deaths of Mary Ella Waller's father and brother made it necessary for her to earn her own living—in a manner compatible with her genteel New England descent. Four years in Europe, acquiring languages, qualified her to teach at an exclusive Boston finishing school. She later held a similar post at the Brearly School in New York and then founded Miss Waller's School for Girls in Chicago.

Waller's first writings were children's stories and translations of German verse. Forced by poor health to give up her school, she turned to writing fiction and became a popular novelist. Her earliest books were most successful: *A Daughter of the Rich* (1903), *The Wood-Carver of 'Lympus* (1904), and *Sanna* (1905) ran through more than a dozen editions each. She also published magazine verse, *Our Benny* (1909, a Civil War narrative poem honoring Abraham Lincoln), and *From an Island Outpost* (1914), a semiphilosophical work in journal form.

Waller's work is similar to that of her contemporary Gene Stratton-Porter *The Wood-Carver of 'Lympus*, published the same year as *Freckles*, strikes the same vein: the crippled hero lies in bed at the center of the house carving exquisitely detailed wildflowers which are bought by wealthy New Yorkers. He also provides a home for a girl cousin whose illegitimacy creates a subplot. Customers bring science and culture into the rural retreat and are in turn restored by the woodcarver's wholesomeness. Thus sentimentality, goodwill, and a healthy dose of coincidence reconcile opposites: nature with art, the work ethic with aristocratic privilege, urban culture with rural simplicity, and physical helplessness with the ability to control one's life and influence the lives of others.

As her journal reveals, Waller sympathized with the downtrodden, and particularly with the Native American. At the same time, she was a social Darwinist; her belief in progress and manifest destiny made her see life as a competition in which the fittest succeed. She made sentimental use of the issues of the Progressive era. *Flamstead Quarries* (1910) is about an ex-convict's reform; both it and *The Little Citizen* (1902) deal with child labor, abandoned children, and the exploitation of children; *Out of the Silences* (1918) portrays Cree culture and religion; *A Cry in the Wilderness* (1912) deals with a working girl's loneliness and depression.

In a different vein, *A Year Out of Life* (1909), an epistolary novel about a German writer and his young American translator deals with the paradoxes of sexual politics. The heroine struggles not to fall in love for fear of losing her freedom; she aggressively declares her love because she knows forwardness will drive the man away and so save her from the decision of whether to marry him. The book, however, ends unsatisfactorily with an easy irony.

Waller was among the novelists considered safe for readers of all ages. Several elements in her usual story express a typically adolescent fantasy: the sense of being outcast, different, deficient, or unwanted and the belief that love can be earned by martyrdom. The lost-father plot solves the problems of the insecure adolescent or unhappy working woman by allowing a rich man to arrive and make all well. Waller has, however, given some deliberate thought to sex roles. Most of her heroines can catch and ride a horse; the nicest of her men can cook a meal or care for a baby without looking foolish. All of her admirable characters support themselves. Yet for both men and women the ideal is a life of cultured leisure. Though Waller pays lip service to hard work and the beauties of nature, express trains are continually rushing into her countryside laden with books, objects d'art, hothouse flowers, and out-of-season fruits.

Waller uses shifting viewpoints, with letters, diaries, and first-person narratives sandwiched in the midst of omniscient passages. She emphasizes the effect of events on people rather than the events themselves; only rarely does she write strong scenes. The sentimental tension works to sustain the early books; the lame newsboy's heroic ride to save the town from the bursting dam in *The Little Citizen* (1902) must touch responsive chords in the heart of anyone who has ever felt helpless and patronized. But because Waller deals primarily in melodramatic events of the sort usually found in plot-centered books and her emotional analysis is seldom profound, the novels are flat and anticlimactic. The vogue for Waller's sort of fiction ended with World War I, and, as her later novels failed to develop any new directions, they were dismissed by critics and public alike.

OTHER WORKS: *The Rose-bush of Hildesheim* (1889). *Giotto's Sheep* (1889). *Through the Gates of the Netherlands* (1907). *My Ragpicker* (1911). *Aunt Dorcas's Change of Heart* (1913). *Deep in the Hearts of Men* (1924). *The Windmill on the Dune* (1931).

BIBLIOGRAPHY: Overton, G., *The Women Who Make Our Novels* (1922).

Other references: *Nation* (19 May 1904). *NYT* (15 June 1938).

—SALLY MITCHELL

WALTER, Mildred Pitts

Born 9 December 1922, De Ridder, Louisiana
Daughter of Paul and Mary Ward Pitts; **married** Earl Lloyd Walter, 1947; **children:** Earl Jr., Craig

Mildred Pitts Walter began writing because she ''wanted to know why there were so few books for and about the children I taught who were black.'' She became an author ''out of the need to share with all children the experiences of a people who have a rich and unique way of living that has grown out of the ability to cope and to triumph over racial discrimination.''

Raised in Louisiana, Walter has spent her adult life in California and Colorado. After graduating from Louisiana's Southern University with a B.A. in English (1944), Walter accepted a position as a teacher and librarian in the Los Angeles Unified School System, where she taught for many years. She received an M.A. in education from Antioch Extension in Denver (1947) and later (1950-52) attended California State College in Los Angeles. With her husband, a city chairman of the Congress on Racial Equality, Walter worked with the American Civil Liberties Union and the National Association for the Advancement of Colored People toward desegregating the Los Angeles schools. She was also a consultant for the Western Interstate Commission of Higher Education and a consultant, teacher, and lecturer in Metro State College. In 1977 Walter served as a delegate to the second World Black and African Festival of the Arts and Culture in Lagos, Nigeria.

In her books, which range from picture format to young-adult novels, Walter sensitively incorporates issues of family, heritage, race relations, and change. She specifically builds her characters around ''the dynamics of choice, courage and change.'' Walter firmly believes that heritage is integral to identity: children must know their family and cultural heritage before they can know themselves.

Although she did not start her writing career until 1969, Walter has written more than a dozen children's books and received numerous awards and honors. In 1987 *Justin and the Best Biscuits in the World* (1986) won the Coretta Scott King Award, and *Because We Are* (1983) and *Trouble's Child* (1985) were Coretta Scott King Honor Books. The nonfiction *Mississippi Challenge* (1992) relates the history of the African American in Mississippi from slavery through the Civil War and Reconstruction, to the inception of the Mississippi Freedom Democratic Party.

Walter has also attempted to raise awareness of the African holiday Kwanzaa through her children's books *Have a Happy. . .* (1989) and *Kwanzaa: A Family Affair* (1995). The latter book is a guide to celebrating the occasion, including information on its origin, vocabulary, related family activities, and ideas for gift-giving. Another recent work is *Darkness* (1995), geared to the preschool level and addressing the fear of the dark. Despite the occasional awkward phrasing, Walter illustrates the beauty of darkness with symbolic and philosophical descriptions of good things taking place there.

Second Daughter: The Story of a Slave Girl (1996) is a novel based on the true story of Elizabeth ''Mum Bett'' Freeman, a slave who sued for her freedom in 1781, helping to end slavery in Massachusetts. The book has been praised for its extensive research, although the story gets heavy with historical details and the plot wanders at times. Walter's recent project, *The Suitcase* (1999), was just published.

Walter's strength in writing for children is her ability to bring life to everyday situations. Children's literature has been enriched through the warmth, sensitivity, love, gentleness, and caring that speak out in her work.

OTHER WORKS: *Contribution of Minorities to American Culture* (n.d.). *Lillie of Watts: A Birthday Discovery* (1969). *Lillie of Watts Takes a Giant Step* (1971). *The Liquid Tap* (1976). *Ty's One-Man Band* (1980). *The Girl on the Outside* (1982). *My Mamma Needs Me* (1983). *Brother to the Wind* (1985). *Mariah Loves Rock* (1988). *Little Sister, Big Trouble* (1990). *Mariah Keeps Cool* (1990). *Two and Too Much* (1990).

BIBLIOGRAPHY: Reference works: *Authors of Books for Young People* (1979). *Black Authors and Illustrators of Children's Books* (1988). *CLR* (1988). *SATA* (1986, 1992). *Sixth Book of Junior Authors and Illustrators* (1989). *TCCW* (1989).
Other references: *Booklist* (15 Nov. 1995, 15 Feb. 1996). *Horn Book* (Jan./Feb. 1991, 1996). *LJ* (Oct. 1995).

—SANDRA RAY,
UPDATED BY CARRIE SNYDER

WALTON, Evangeline

Born circa 1920s

Evangeline Walton's full name is Evangeline Walton Ensley and she has lived in Arizona. No other biographical information can be found.

Walton is one of several modern writers who have retold stories from the four branches (or first four stories) of the Mabinogion, a collection of ancient Welsh legends. Sex, magic, and heroism loom large in the Mabinogion, which encompasses in simple words a wide range of emotion, striking every note from the comic to the tragic.

In her first book, *The Virgin and the Swine* (1936), based on the fourth branch, Walton portrays magic as a demonstration of the powers of the mind. She lays great stress on the cleverness of the enchanter Gwydion, who is constantly overreaching himself in the tricks he plays on others and who emerges as a very human and fully rounded character.

Walton explains much that happens in the Mabinogion in terms of a shift from matrilineal descent and worship of the

Mother Goddess to patrilineal descent and neglect of the Mother Goddess, bringing about a deterioration in the relationships of men and women. She also attempts to recreate the religion of the Druids. Her characters believe in reincarnation, and Walton expresses this belief so wholeheartedly she appears to share it.

The Virgin and the Swine was not a success, and Walton went on to different subjects in her next books. *Witch House* (1945) tells of a battle between good and evil in a house that was built by a warlock in 17th-century New England. The struggle between the warlock's 20th-century descendants is intense and thrilling. In the end good triumphs.

The Cross and the Sword (1956, reissued 1960) is the story of a Viking who comes to England in Anglo-Saxon times and is converted to Christianity. There is tenderness, violence, cruelty, and a touch of magic in this story, which attempts to solve some historical puzzles.

Lin Carter, the editor of a popular fantasy series, reprinted Walton's first book under the title *The Island of the Mighty* (1970, reprinted several times, the most recent 1993) and asked Walton for any other stories she might have based on the Mabinogion. She brought out a 30-year old manuscript, based on the second branch. In *The Children of Llyr* (1971, 1992), Walton is particularly fascinated by the character of Evnissyen, an insanely spiteful young man who is finally induced by the goodness of his twin, Nissyen, to atone for his crimes. Walton suggests the good man is higher up the ladder of reincarnation than the bad man and must help him.

The Song of Rhiannon (1972, 1992) and *Prince of Annwn* (1974, 1992), based on the third and first branches, followed in rapid succession, completing the adventures of the characters in Walton's earlier retellings of the Mabinogion. These two suggest that this world and supernatural worlds beyond are connected in a gigantic chain of evolution.

Walton's chief claim to critical attention is the way in which she has fleshed out the spare narrative of the Mabinogion, giving a plausible explanation in human and historical terms for the strange and magical doings of its heroes and heroines. She is a mistress of fantasy and deserves her long-delayed success.

OTHER WORKS: *Son of Darkness* (1957). *Four Branches of the Mabinogion: In a Complete Boxed Set* (1974). *The Sword Is Forged* (1984).

BIBLIOGRAPHY: Carter, L., Introductions to *The Island of the Mighty* (1970), *The Children of Llyr* (1971), and *The Song of Rhiannon* (1972). Merla, P., Introduction to *Prince of Annwn* (1974). Zahorski, K. J., *Lloyd Alexander, Evangeline Walton Ensley, Kenneth Morris: A Primary and Secondary Bibliography* (1981).

Other references: *Children's Literature in Education* (Spring 1978).

—BARBARA J. BUCKNALL

WALWORTH, Jeannette (Ritchie) Hadermann

Born 22 February 1837, Philadelphia, Pennsylvania; **died** 4 February 1918, New Orleans, Louisiana
Wrote under: Ann Atom, Jeannette R. Hadermann, Mother Goose, Mrs. Jeannette H. Walworth
Daughter of Charles J. and Matilda Norman von Winsingen Hadermann; **married** Douglas Walworth, 1873

Jeannette Hadermann Walworth was one of seven children. Her father was a German political exile who came to this country in the 1820s, after supporting the attempted formation of a German republic. Not long after Walworth was born, her family moved to Washington, Mississippi, where her father became professor of modern languages at Jefferson College.

From the age of sixteen until the close of the Civil War, Walworth was a governess on Louisiana plantations. The desire for a writing career took her to New Orleans, where she wrote for the New Orleans *Times* under the name Ann Atom, earning little but attracting some interest. More lucrative endeavors soon followed, when two novels (written while she was serving as governess) were published. *Forgiven at Last* (1870) did not create more than polite interest, but *Dead Men's Shoes* (1872) outraged the residents of Tensas Parish, Louisiana, who believed the author had maligned a prominent family of the parish through her character portrayals.

After marriage to Major Walworth of Natchez, Mississippi, the couple lived for five years in Arkansas on the Walworth plantation, where she wrote *Against the World* (1873), *Heavy Yokes* (1876), and *Nobody's Business* (1878). For a short time the Walworths then lived in Memphis, Tennessee, where she wrote for the Memphis *Appeal* as "Mother Goose," before leaving the South for a 16-year stay in New York City.

In New York, Major Walworth established a law practice and Jeannette wrote for magazines and newspapers and also published many novels. The Walworths returned to Mississippi, where he was editor of the Natchez *Democrat* and she continued to write. She lived with relatives in New Orleans following the death of her husband in 1914.

A number of Walworth's novels reflect changes in the South following the war. These difficult times for both blacks and whites and the change from an agrarian life to one influenced by urban values are seen through her characters. *The New Man at Rossmere* (1886), *Baldy's Point* (1889), *On the Winning Side* (1893), and *Uncle Scipo* (1896) all have plantation settings. Perhaps because she was a journalist with more than casual knowledge of society beyond her own household, Walworth provides a kind of synthesis of the average postwar citizen's view of things. Her forte is the realistic novel, not light romance, and she is adept at giving substance to her characters and the places where they live. Many of the same character types (such as women who are noble, long-suffering, virtuous, and strong), reappear in her novels. They are not mere stereotypes, however, because she varies the patterns, and the major characters are often skillfully and at times powerfully developed.

Walworth attracted considerable attention from critics and readers for her condemnation, in *The Bar Sinister: A Social Study* (1885), of polygamy in Mormon Utah. It is somewhat different from her other novels in that she does not provide a happy ending for her protagonist, Anna Quinby, the legitimate wife of a Mormon convert.

Uncle Scipo: A Story of Uncertain Days in the South tells of a Yankee who goes South to check land titles for a firm that has bought 10 cotton plantations. Through a first-person account, the reader comes to know all the facets of life in the Delta country. There are good, insightful descriptions of the customs and folkways of the South, as well as a realistic portrayal of the postwar scene.

Walworth wrote nearly 30 novels, most set in the South. They are often melodramatic, in the accepted style of the period, and display strict religious moralizing. There are villains in plentiful supply, but usually they confess their wrongs and repent (and are compassionately forgiven by those who have been illused). Although the plots are somewhat obvious, Walworth uses a variety of characters from all levels of society, portraying them adequately and sometimes memorably.

OTHER WORKS: *Matsy and I* (1883). *Old Fulkerson's Clerk* (1886). *Scruples* (1886). *Without Blemish* (1886). *At Bay* (1887). *Southern Silhouettes* (1887). *The Silent Witness* (1888). *A Strange Pilgrimage* (1888). *That Girl from Texas* (1888). *True to Herself* (1888). *The Martlet Seal* (1889). *A Splendid Egotist* (1889). *An Old Fogy* (1895). *Ground-Swells* (1896). *Where Kitty Found Her Soul* (1896). *Three Brave Girls* (1897). *Fortune's Tangled Skein* (1898). *Green Withes* (1899). *A Little Radical* (1900). *His Celestial Marriage* (n.d.). *Stories of a Southern Country* (n.d.).

BIBLIOGRAPHY: Roberts, O. H., "A Criticism of Jeannette Ritchie Hadermann Walworth's Novels" (thesis, 1938).

Reference works: *A Bibliography of Fiction by Louisianians and on Louisiana Subjects* (1935). DAB. *Living Female Writers of the South* (1872).

—DOROTHY H. BROWN

WARD, Mary Jane

Born 27 August 1905, Fairmont, Indiana; died February 1981
Daughter of Claude A. and Marion Lockridge Ward; married
  Edward Quayle, 1928

Mary Jane Ward lived most of her life in Evanston, Illinois, where she attended Evanston High School and Northwestern University. She studied art and piano and won a year's scholarship at the Chicago Lyceum of Arts Conservatory. She began writing after her marriage to a statistician and published stories in such magazines as *Woman's Home Companion* and *Good Housekeeping*. *The Snake Pit* (1946), her best known book, is based on her experiences in a state mental institution, where she spent nine months after a nervous breakdown in 1941. Ward became an advocate for mental health, speaking and writing regularly on behalf of more progressive treatment of the mentally ill. In 1949, she was given the Women's National Press Club Achievement Award.

The Tree Has Roots (1937) deals with the lives of people without whom a university could not function: grounds crews, a night watchmen, a commons waitress, a stenographer. Ward is sympathetic to the everyday frustrations of lower class life during the Depression. In this first novel, she shows herself to be a fine craftsman, especially skillful with dialogue.

The Wax Apple (1938) treats the lives of two families living on the wrong side of Chicago during the Depression. Less touching than *The Tree Has Roots*, this is still a strong chronicle of the ultimate frustrations of life. *The Professor's Umbrella* (1948) is a slight work about the attempt of a Jewish college professor to find a new career after he is dismissed from his teaching position on a trumped-up charge of moral turpitude, which masks the college administration's anti-Semitism. Ward moves away from ordinary lives and takes up the politics of religion; in doing so, she unfortunately weakens the novel, creating flat types rather than characters. Less dogmatic and more diffuse is *It's Different for a Woman* (1952), Ward's closest approach to a feminist novel. Sally Cutter faces middle age, a roaming husband, a daughter's shaky romance, and the prospect of 40 uneventful and changeless years in an expensive suburb.

The Snake Pit is generally considered one of the most accurate and moving fictional accounts of insanity. The book follows the life in an asylum of Virginia Stuart Cunningham, writer and wife, who has had a nervous breakdown. One sign of her returning sanity is her increasing attention to the events of the asylum as "material for a story." Although Ward at the end applauds the ministrations of doctors, the story makes it clear that Virginia's recovery was born, shaped, and realized within her own mind.

Counterclockwise (1969) depicts a relapse that returns its heroine, the author of a bestselling novel about mental illness, to an expensive private hospital. The book effectively contrasts with *The Snake Pit*, for the heroine receives the kind of care that should have been available to Virginia Cunningham. Ward attempts to show that, properly treated, the mental patient can be fully cured and, above all, need not be feared nor rejected by society.

Neither as intense nor as focused as *The Snake Pit*, *The Other Caroline* (1970) is yet another treatment of a woman's return from insanity. In this novel, a woman is convinced her brain has been transplanted into the body of Caroline Kincaid, "the other Caroline" of the novel's title. As part of her therapy, she writes a fictionalized account of "the other Caroline's" life. By this structural device, Ward shows both the cause and the cure of the mental illness.

Ward presents in her early novels a world now unfashionable, but so concrete that her works could serve as social history. Although decidedly not a feminist, she possesses "sensitive and compassionate insight into feminine psychology." Her work, always meticulously crafted and skillfully organized, makes the subject of nervous breakdowns acceptable and even engaging; it thus creates a wide and receptive audience for her mental health crusades. Ward is an example of a single-subject writer who produces one great book and several minor gems.

OTHER WORKS: *A Little Night Music* (1951).

BIBLIOGRAPHY: Reference works: *American Novelists of Today* (1951). *CB* (June 1946). *TCA*.

Other references *NYTBR* (25 April 1937, 16 Jan. 1938, 7 April 1946, 14 April 1946, 11 Jan. 1948, 24 Feb. 1951, 9 Nov. 1952, 12 Oct. 1969, 23 Aug. 1970).

—LORALEE MACPIKE

WARFIELD, Catherine (Ann) Ware

Born 6 June 1816, Natchez, Mississippi; died 21 May 1877, Louisville, Kentucky

Daughter of Nathaniel A. and Sarah Ellis Ware; married Robert E. Warfield, 1833

Catherine Ann Ware Warfield was brought up by her father, a major during the War of 1812 and an amateur scientist, who had strict notions about home education and the benefits of travel. Her mother was institutionalized for insanity after the birth of her second daughter in 1820. Nathaniel Ware then sold his property in Mississippi and moved with his children to Philadelphia, where he obtained tutors for his daughters' social education, while he taught them academic subjects at home. Each year the family traveled for educational purposes in both the South and the North. After her marriage, Warfield settled at her husband's home in Lexington, Kentucky. In 1857 she and her family moved to Beechmoor, an estate near Louisville, where she lived in comparative retirement until her death.

Warfield and her sister, Eleanor Ware Lee, wrote poetry together and, with their father's encouragement, published *The Wife of Leon, and Other Poems* in 1843, followed by *The Indian Chamber, and Other Poems* in 1846. While none of the verse is attributed specifically to either of the sisters, clear hints of Warfield's later work pervade the poetry's tone, settings, subjects, and themes: the pieces are generally sentimental, while insisting on rigid principles of conduct and on moral absolutes. They are often stilted, with conventional rhythms, rhymes, and forms; yet the emphasis on character, first person voices, and narrative suggests the strengths of Warfield's fiction.

She ceased writing for a time after her sister's death in 1849. Her calm and secluded life at Beechmoor, however, evidently provided the proper atmosphere for a return to writing; Warfield wrote steadily after her first novel, *The Household of Bouverie* was published in 1860. This novel is not only one of her best, it is characteristic of her fiction. It is a lengthy, somewhat autobiographical study of a fascinating criminal scientist, Erastus Bouverie, who tortures his wife and, obsessed by monomaniacal jealousy and possessiveness, uses strange chemical processes to maim and murder those he resents. The first part of the narrative is written from the point of view of Bouverie's granddaughter, Lilian; the story is carried on by a detached narrator after Lilian's death; and the last third of the novel consists almost entirely of excerpts from the diary of Bouverie's wife. The plot depends heavily on mystery, suspense, and sensationalism, and is not always psychologically sound. The strengths of *The Household of Bouverie* lie in its experiments with point of view and its sometimes sharply drawn details; in its sustained, if windy, narrative; and in its emphasis on women's responses to bizarre exploitation.

In the story of the Bouveries, as throughout her writing, Warfield stresses primarily domestic tensions, but at times her social and political allegiances become explicit, as when she writes of the necessity of slavery, noting that "God intended the white man to govern the negro." The Civil War inspired Warfield to return to writing poetry, which she published in periodicals and anthologies. Her verse shows strong Confederate sympathies, as do her later novels.

Warfield deserves recognition in the history of American literature as one of the first female novelists of consequence in the South.

OTHER WORKS: *The Romance of the Green Seal* (1866). *The Romance of Beauseincourt: An Episode Extracted from the Retrospect of Miriam Monfort* (1867; also published as *Miriam's Memoirs*, 1876). *Miriam Monfort* (1873; parts 1 and 2 published separately as *Monfort Hall*, *Sea*, and *Shore*, 1876). *A Double Wedding; or, How She Was Won* (1875). *Hester Howard's Temptation* (1875). *Lady Ernestine; or, The Absent Lord of Rochester* (1876). *Ferne Fleming: A Novel* (1877). *The Cardinal's Daughter: A Sequel to "Ferne Fleming"* (1877).

BIBLIOGRAPHY: Brown, A., *The Cabells and Their Kin* (1895). Simpson, E. M., "The Meadows," in *Bluegrass Houses* (1932). Townsend, J. W., *Kentucky in American Letters* (Volume 1, 1913). Warfield, J. D., *The Warfields of Maryland* (1898).

Reference works: *LSL* (1910). *Southland Writers* (Volume 1, 1870). *Women of the South Distinguished in Literature* (1861).

—CAROLINE ZILBOORG

WARNER, Anna Bartlett

Born circa 1824, New York, New York; **died** 22 January 1915,
  West Point, New York
Wrote under: Amy Lothrop, Anna B. Warner
Daughter of Henry W. and Anna Bartlett Warner

Anna Bartlett Warner's mother died soon after she was born.
After the business depressions of mid-century, her father had to be
supported by Warner and her sister, Susan. For most of her long
life, Warner lived on Constitution Island, in the Hudson opposite
West Point. The Warners owned the entire island, making their
home in a Revolutionary War-era farmhouse. While the sisters did
not earn much money from their many books, they did manage to
spend most winters in New York City, where they had friends
among the literary set. Warner continued to live on the island with
two black servants for 30 years after the death of her sister. The
island is maintained by the Constitution Island Association, and
the Warner house is a historic landmark, open to the public during
the summer.

Both Warner and her sister published prolifically. Warner's
first book, *Dollars and Cents* (1852), published under the pseudonym Amy Lothrop, is not very good, but it enjoyed considerable
popularity. Based on her own experiences, it tells of the Howard
family's loss of fortune and retirement to country life. All ends
well, of course, with a marriage. She wrote a few other adult
novels with Susan, but most of her fiction is for children.

Warner's children's novels are all of a didactic nature intended for Sunday school readers. She did not have her sister's gift for
telling a story; somewhat unusual, however, is that not all of her
books have happy endings. The young readers are urged to
become Christians, give to missionaries, and obey their parents.
Poor children are described in most of her books, but not all of
them are rescued.

Warner is perhaps best known as the writer of the famous
children's hymn, "Jesus Loves Me," which appears in a scene in
Say and Seal (1860), sung by the hero as he walks the floor with a
dying child. Another of her hymns, "We Would See Jesus," from
the deathbed scene in *Dollars and Cents*, has achieved some
popularity. In addition to novels and hymns, Warner wrote some
nonfiction about the Bible and Christian life.

Her most distinctive work deals with gardening. *Pond Lily
Stories* (1857) is a collection of flower fables for children. Most
have a moral and teach something about plants, in the style of
mixed flower fantasy and botanical fact common at the time.
Three Little Spades (1868), a story that presents some of the
principles of gardening, and the sequel, *Blue Flag and Cloth of
Gold* (1879), are more instructional than *Pond Lily Stories*.

For adult readers, she wrote *Gardening by Myself* (1872),
encouraging women to do their own gardening, as she had done.
In a fictional companion volume, *Miss Tiller's Vegetable Garden
and the Money She Made by It* (1872), she tells how, with the help
of a wise boarder, a woman is able to support herself and her two
children with produce from her own backyard. For several years,

Warner had made her garden feed her family, selling produce on
the side.

A more active and outgoing person than her sister, Warner
was modest and self-effacing about her own accomplishments. In
her biography of Susan, she glorifies her sister's achievements,
perhaps at the expense of her own. While she was not gifted, she
was a hardworking and disciplined professional writer.

OTHER WORKS: (The following is a list of Anna Bartlett Warner's
more important works. A complete bibliography is included in
They Wrote for a Living, compiled by D. H. Sanderson, 1976). *My
Brother's Keeper* (1855). *Stories of Vinegar Hill* (1871). *Tired
Christians* (1881). *Tired Church Members* (1881). *Cross Corners*
(1887). *Yours and Mine* (1888). *Patience* (1890). *Up and Down
the House* (1892). *Fresh Air* (1899). *West Point Colors* (1903).
Susan Warner (1909).

BIBLIOGRAPHY: Hollingsworth, B., *Her Garden Was Her Delight*
(1962). Sanderson, D. H., *They Wrote for a Living* (1976). Stokes,
O. E., *Letters and Memoirs of Susan and Anna Bartlett Warner* (1925).

Other references: *Fourth Report and Yearbook of the
Martelaer's Rock Association* (1920-23). *N.Y. History* (April 1959).

—BEVERLY SEATON

WARNER, Susan Bogert

Born 11 July 1819, New York, New York; **died** 17 March 1885,
  Highland Falls, New York
Wrote under: Susan B. Warner, Elizabeth Wetherall
Daughter of Henry W. and Anna Bartlett Warner

Susan Bogert Warner's family was prosperous during her
childhood, but the depression of 1837 saw the collapse of their
fortunes. Thereafter, Warner and her sister Anna were responsible
for the support of themselves, their father (their mother had died
young), and a paternal aunt. Their father had purchased Constitution Island, in the Hudson River opposite West Point, as a summer
retreat, but the family was forced to make it their permanent home.
The sisters cooked, gardened, chopped wood, and fished.

At her aunt's suggestion, and because of a great need for
money, Warner wrote *The Wide, Wide World* (1850), which went
through many editions in many languages. She and her sister were
among the century's most prolific writers, but their earnings were
small, partly due to literary piracy.

A sensitive, rather morbid personality distinguished Warner
from her younger sister socially, but hers was the greater talent.

Although poverty and hard work narrowed her world, she managed to travel some, meeting Emerson and other New England literary figures in Boston. She spent almost every winter in New York, where she knew such writers as Alice and Phoebe Cary.

The Wide, Wide World, which had been rejected by several publishers, was a literary phenomenon. Its basic appeal is to girls and women. After her mother dies, Ellen Montgomery must live with other relatives—first an old maid aunt who runs her own farm and then a worldly Scottish family who claim her for a time. Ellen finds they try her Christian patience—and they disapprove of her priggish ways. No matter what the issue, Ellen expresses herself by bursting into tears. (Biographers say that Warner was apt to cry frequently herself.) However sentimental this novel appears today, Warner's ability to tell a story and to involve the reader in the lives of her characters is superior.

Warner's second novel, *Queechy* (1852), almost as popular as her first, tells how, after the death of her grandfather and the business failure of her uncle, young Fleda Ringgan helps support her family by selling flowers and garden produce. Throughout the novels of both sisters, young women in financial difficulties are commonplace; they are often furnished with a father, uncle, or guardian who cannot function once his money is gone. The autobiographical element is obvious. While the sisters preserved a pious respect for their father (who lived until 1875), their books reveal their annoyance with such helpless characters. In *Queechy* even the resourceful heroine feels faint if she must answer the door or eat with the hired girl, but the late novel *Nobody* (1882) shows a family of sisters who do their own work and thrive on it. Presumably, as the years passed, Warner became more accustomed to her status in life.

By herself and in collaboration with Anna, she wrote many children's books. Most of them are highly didactic and were popular in the Sunday school libraries of the time. Although both sisters were evangelical Presbyterians—they disapproved of the theater, but not of *all* novels—Warner's books are centered on accepting and serving Christ, with little interest in doctrinal or controversial themes.

Most of her adult novels are what she called "true stories" (she didn't like the word "novel"). The books usually have a good Christian heroine (or hero) who overcomes poverty and becomes successful. Meals of bread and molasses are to be found in these books, but generous meals are much more common.

In *Diana* (1877), Warner attributes her fascination with writing about food to her intimate knowledge of is preparation. "Sympathy and affection and tender ministry are wrought into the very pie crust, and glow in the brown loaves as they come out of the oven; and are specially seen in the shortcake for tea and the favorite dish at dinner and the unexpected dumpling." Warner had a gift for describing the material things of life; a reading of her novels will give the modern reader a close look into 19th-century American kitchen cupboards, desk drawers, and clothes closets.

Interest today in Warner's books is mainly historical. She is one of the best of the "damned mob of scribbling women" of her time, however, and deserves serious consideration from literary scholars.

OTHER WORKS: (The following is a list of Susan Bogert Warner's more important works. A complete bibliography is included in *They Wrote for a Living*, compiled by D. H. Sanderson, 1976). *The Law and the Testimony* (1853). *The Hills of the Shatemuc* (1856). *The Old Helmet* (1863). *Melbourne House* (1864). *Daisy* (1868). *Walks from Eden* (1870). *The House in Town* (1872). *A Story of Small Beginnings* (1872). *Willow Brook* (1874). Say and Do Series (1875). *Bread and Oranges* (1877). *Pine Needles* (1877). *The Broken Wall of Jerusalem and the Rebuilding of Them* (1878). *The Flag of Truce* (1878). *The Kingdom of Judak* (1878). *My Desire* (1879). *The End of the Coil* (1880). *The Letter of Credit* (1882). *Stephen, M.D.* (1883). *A Red Wallflower* (1884). *Daisy Plains* (1885).

BIBLIOGRAPHY: Baker, M., *Light in the Morning: Memories of Susan and Anna Warner* (1978). Sanderson, D. H., *They Wrote for a Living: A Bibliography of Susan Bogert Warner* (1976). Stokes, O. E., *Letters and Memoirs of Susan and Anna Bartlett Warner* (1925). Warner, A., *Susan Warner* (1909).

Reference works: *Oxford Companion to Women's Writing in the United States* (1995).

Other references: *American Quarterly* (Winter 1990). *N.Y. History* 40 (April 1959).

—BEVERLY SEATON

WARREN, Lella

Born 22 March 1899, Clayton, Alabama; **died** March 1982
Daughter of Benjamin S. and Lee Ella Underwood Warren; **married** John Spanogla, 1921; Buel W. Patch, 1941

Lella Warren's father's duties as a doctor with the U.S. Public Health Service took his family to many marine hospitals and quarantine stations before they settled in Washington, D.C., when she was twelve. Dr. Warren, however, returned his family to Clayton, Alabama, for frequent visits so they would retain ties with the state where Warren ancestors had been pioneers. Warren graduated from Western High School in Washington and attended Goucher College (1918-19) and George Washington University, where she received a B.A. (1921) and did graduate work. Warren and her first husband had one daughter.

Warren published short stories and features in Washington newspapers and national magazines. "Before the Flight," an in-depth feature on the preparations for Charles Lindbergh's transatlantic flight, with details checked by Lindbergh himself, appeared in *Collier's* (18 July 1931). She also worked in government, publicity, advertising, and education—meanwhile devoting years to extensive background research for her novels. In 1941, Warren was chosen one of the "women of the year" by the National Women's Press Club.

Warren describes her first novel, *A Touch of Earth*, (1926) as semiautobiographical. It follows Jick, the daughter of an Army doctor, from her childhood through her development as a woman and a writer. The novel's style becomes more mature and sensitive as Warren's heroine grows up.

Warren's father wanted a "true-to-life book about Southern planters," so she spent nearly 12 years researching *Foundation Stone* (1940) and a similar period on *Whetstone Walls* (1952). She used diaries, correspondence, court records, research at the Library of Congress, as well as interviews in Alabama with friends and relatives. *Foundation Stone* opens on a South Carolina plantation in the 1820s. Yarbrough Whetstone moves his family and possessions from the depleted South Carolina land to the Alabama wilderness, leaving behind luxury of the plantation life for the hardships of the frontier planter. Warren follows the family through the settlement years and the ravages of the Civil War. At the end of the book—the title, drawn from a passage in Stephen Vincent Benét's *John Brown's Body*, refers to Whetstone's wife, Gerda—the war is over and the remnants of the Whetstone family are collecting their resources to rebuild.

The sequel, *Whetstone Walls*, is a self-contained novel, set in the 1880s and 1890s. The focus is on the children and grandchildren of Gerda and Yarbrough.

The extent of Warren's research is reflected in her meticulous attention to details, such as pioneers' building methods, food preparation, and schooling, and her detailed attention to broader concerns, such as Indian affairs (Yarbrough attended the Alabama legislature to hear the farewell speech of Chief Yufala); difficulties of travel and the coming of the railroad; and the course and effects of the Civil War. The historical background, however, never overshadows the characters and plot. The events are important only as they touch the lives of the Whetstones and their friends.

Warren excels at characterization as she creates a range of characters comparable to that in Dickens's novels. The variety increases as the family grows in the third and fourth generations and the circle of friends widens. Warren believes "the *family* is a *way of life*. . . and will ultimately survive." However confused the casual reader may become by the multiplicity of characters, each individual is carefully delineated in relationship to the Whetstone family. Episodes that might be attacked as too coincidental are justified by the importance of family ties, even as members move to New Orleans and Washington. The family is the unifying force of the novels.

There are to be two more works in the Whetstone saga: an "interlude" novel about some minor characters, already in manuscript, and a novel in progress following Rob, one of the Whetstone grandchildren, through his medical career.

Even without future works, Warren fulfilled a prediction of William Rose Benét, who wrote one of her teachers about an early Warren short story: "The girl who wrote 'Red Brick' will inevitably be a writer."

BIBLIOGRAPHY: Atkins, L. R., *The Romantic Ideal: Alabama's Plantation Eden* (1978). Ross, J. C., *A Sense of Place: Fiction in the Agrarian Tradition* (1978).

Other references: *Alabama Librarian* (Jan. 1953). *NYTBR* (15 Sept. 1940, 8 Dec. 1940). *Perspectives: The Alabama Heritage* (ETV broadcast, 10 Jan. 1979).

—NANCY G. ANDERSON

WARREN, Mercy Otis

Born 25 September 1728, Barnstable, Massachusetts; **died** 19 October 1814, Plymouth, Massachusetts
Wrote under: A Columbian Patriot
Daughter of James and Mary Allyne Otis; **married** James Warren, 1754; **children:** five sons

Mercy Otis Warren was the third of 13 children. Her father, a staunch Whig, was a district judge whose life revolved around politics. Although women were customarily denied formal education, her father permitted Warren, his eldest daughter, to be tutored with her brothers by their paternal uncle, Rev. Jonathan Russell. Russell encouraged her to take lessons in all fields except Greek and Latin, so her elder brother James, an exceptionally brilliant young man, instructed her in these languages. Theirs was an unusually close relationship. He introduced her to Locke's *Essay on Government*, which became the foundation of the political theory they shared. Her writing shows the influence of Raleigh, Pope, Dryden, Milton, Shakespeare, and Molière, but she learned the art of writing from her study of her uncle's sermons.

Warren's husband, like her brother James, was a Harvard graduate. In this cultured and politically astute man she found a husband she loved and respected who returned her feelings, and they enjoyed a long and happy life together. She bore five sons to him between 1757 and 1766, all of whom survived to adulthood. Warren took much pride in his wife's intelligence and literary talents. He not only brought stimulating guests like John and Samuel Adams regularly into their home but he himself gave her companionship and stability.

During the early years of marriage, Warren served her literary apprenticeship, writing verse on every subject considered proper for poetry. She also wrote many letters. Perhaps her favorite correspondent was Abigail Adams, but she exchanged letters with many distinguished people on both sides of the Atlantic.

During the 1770s, Warren became active in politics, along with her husband, father, and brother. "Be it known unto Britain even American daughters are politicians and patriots," she wrote. She began writing political satires in the form of plays; none had much plot nor women characters. They were not stage-worthy pieces, but they were not intended to be. They accomplished their task, firing their readers' imaginations and urging them to turn the depicted events into reality and punish the easily recognized villains.

The Adulateur (1772), published anonymously in two installments in the *Massachusetts Spy*, presents "Rapatio, the Bashaw [ruler] of Servia whose principal mission in life is to crush the ardent love of liberty in Servia's freeborn sons," who clearly is the colony's Governor Thomas Hutchinson. The classical names of her characters do not obscure their identities: for example, Brutus is James Otis, Jr., champion of the patriots. The "play" was so well received that the names Warren had given the characters were widely and gleefully used in the community.

Her second play, *The Defeat* (1773), published by the Boston *Gazette*, continued Rapatio (Hutchinson) as arch villain. It pictures Rapatio planning to charge the improvements he has made on his house to the public taxes. Together with his self-incriminating letters then being circulated among the patriots, it brought about Hutchinson's disgrace and recall.

The Group (1775), the most popular of Warren's political satires, appeared in pamphlet form only two weeks before the clash of "Minutemen" and British soldiers at Lexington. John Adams himself arranged its printing and, years later, personally verified Warren was its author. Almost pure propaganda, the play has only villains, the Tory leaders who are the group of the play's title. Chief is Brigadier Hate-All, really the American-born Tory Timothy Ruggles, a longtime enemy of the Otis family. Other characters include Hum Humbug, Esq.; Crusty Crowbar, Esq.; Dupe; and Scrblerius Fribble.

After the collapse of the Confederation, Warren wrote *Observations on the New Constitution, and on the Federal Conventions* (1788), under the pen name "A Columbian Patriot," opposing the Constitution as it was originally proposed. She was an anti-Federalist who believed, as she said, in "a union of the states on the free principles of the late Confederation." The pen name caused some confusion, and the author's identity was in dispute until 1930.

Poems, Dramatic and Miscellaneous (1790) was dedicated to George Washington. The major works of the volume, "The Sack of Rome" and "The Ladies of Castille," had been published previously. Though much praised by her political friends, critics pointed out her poems have faulty versification, too much alliteration, and bad rhyme.

History of the Rise, Progress, and Termination of the American Revolution, Interspersed with Biographical and Moral Observations (1805) was published in three volumes nearly 17 years after Warren finished it. By this time, other histories of the Revolution had appeared. Hers, however, is the only contemporary history told from a Republican point of view. Much of its value lies in the fact that more than 10 percent of the work is devoted to character analyses of the people she knew. John Adams broke off their long friendship over her analysis of him, but a number of years later a mutual friend brought them together again. Her history did not enjoy the success she had expected or it deserved; yet it has endured, and her reputation survives principally upon its merits.

Warren was given a chance—rare for a woman—to use her talents, and she made the most of them. Although she was much respected in her own time, her reputation has dimmed somewhat—perhaps because so much of her writing was published in pamphlets and newspapers, so much of it was topical, and perhaps because so much of it reflects the classical pretensions of the time. Her history of the Revolution, however, is viewed by modern scholars as having enduring value as a strikingly realistic record of the struggle for independence.

BIBLIOGRAPHY: Anthony, K., *First Lady of the Revolution: The Life of Mercy Otis Warren* (1958). Brink, J. R., ed., *Female Scholars: A Tradition of Learned Women Before 1800* (1980). Brown, A., *Mercy Warren* (1896). Fritz, J., *Cast for a Revolution: Some Friends and Enemies 1728-1814* (1972). Schlueter, J., ed., *Modern American Drama: The Female Canon* (1990). Smith, W., *History as Argument: Three Patriot Historians of the American Revolution* (1966).

Reference works: *Benet's Reader's Encyclopedia* (1991). *Oxford Companion to Women's Writing in the United States* (1995).

Other references: *New England Magazine* (April 1903). *PMHS* (March 1931). *WMQ* (July 1953).

—BILLIE W. ETHERIDGE

WASSERSTEIN, Wendy

Born 18 October 1950, Brooklyn, New York.
Daughter of Morris W. and Lola Schleifer Wasserstein.

The plays that Wendy Wasserstein has written since the late 1970s capture with humor the hope and the despair, the joy and the anguish of her generation of well-educated, successful upper-middle-class women whose lives have defined, and been defined by, the progress of the women's movement in America during the last few decades of the 20th century. The women of Wasserstein's plays have ridden the exhilarating, yet sometimes disorienting, wave of the women's movement through college in the 1960s and 1970s, only to come crashing ashore in the 1980s to find the beckoning sands of professional success and personal fulfillment made rocky by the demands of relationships, family, and the "biological clock."

Wasserstein was raised in New York City, the youngest of four children of Jewish immigrant parents who prospered in the United States. She was educated at the Calhoun School (an exclusive Manhattan private school for girls), Mount Holyoke College (B.A., 1971), City College of New York (M.A., 1973), and the Yale School of Drama (M.E.A., 1976). For most of her life since Yale, she has lived in New York City in a world focused on the theater.

As a child, Wasserstein was introduced to dance and theater (she was especially fond of musicals) by her mother and wrote musical revues at the Calhoun School. While an undergraduate, she took a summer playwriting course at Smith College and performed in campus theatrical productions. After she graduated from Mount Holyoke, but before she enrolled at Yale, in 1973 her play *Any Woman Can't* was produced off-Broadway by Play-wrights Horizons.

While at Yale, Wasserstein collaborated on two musical works, *Montpelier Pa-zazz* and *When Dinah Shore Ruled the Earth*. She wrote a one-act version of *Uncommon Women and Others* as her master's thesis, and after completing her M.F.A., she expanded this play into two acts. The revised version was produced initially at the 1977 National Playwrights Conference at the O'Neill Theatre Center in Waterford, Connecticut, and then a few months later, by the Phoenix Theatre Company, at the Marymount Manhattan Theatre. *Uncommon Women and Others* (1978) was Wasserstein's first successful play; receiving an Obie award, among others. It was followed in 1981 by *Isn't It Romantic* (published 1984), also produced by the Phoenix at the Marymount Manhattan Theatre; a revised version opened off-Broadway late in 1983.

Wasserstein's most important work to date, *The Heidi Chronicles*, opened at Play-wrights Horizons in New York in 1988; after three months, it moved to Broadway. This play "chronicles" the life of Heidi Holland from her adolescence in the 1960s to her adulthood in the 1980s. Heidi voices disillusionment with the women's movement ("I thought the point was that we were all in this together"), yet in her commitment to rearing her adopted daughter (she remains unmarried), she makes an active statement of hope for the future.

The Heidi Chronicles received the Pulitzer Prize for drama and the Tony award as best new play of the year in 1989, as well as "best play" awards from the New York Drama Critics Circle, Outer Critics Circle, and Drama Desk; Wasserstein also received the Susan Smith Blackburn Prize and the 1988 Hull-Warriner Award from the Dramatists Guild. While her work has been criticized by some for lack of depth, it has been praised by many critics for its witty dialogue and honest insights into one particular contemporary social milieu.

Wasserstein has also written a one-act play, *Tender Offer*, produced in 1983, and collaborated on a musical, *Miami*, as yet

(1993) unproduced. She has written several scripts for television, including an adaptation of the John Cheever story "The Sorrows of Gin" for public television; she was also a regular contributor to the CBS series *Comedy Zone* in 1984-85. She coauthored with Christopher Durang the screenplay *The House of Husbands* and wrote *Maids in America* for Steven Spielberg (both still unproduces), and adapted Stephen McCauley's novel *The Object of My Affection* for Twentieth Century-Fox. She also adapted her own *Uncommon Women* for television (broadcast on PBS in 1978 and rebroadcast in 1991), and wrote a screenplay for *Isn't It Romantic* (unproduced).

In 1991 Wasserstein published *Bachelor Girls*, a collection of her personal essays on contemporary women's lives; many critics found these nonfictional prose writings less compelling than her dramatic work. Wasserstein has received several fellowships and grants, including a 1983 Guggenheim Fellowship and a 1984 NEA grant for playwriting.

Wasserstein's play *The Sisters Rosensweig* (1992), about the conflicts between Jewish ethnic/religious identity and cultural assimilation in the lives of three sisters, opened off-Broadway to favorable reviews. It moved to Broadway in early 1993 and won a Tony for Madeline Kahn.

In October 1995, *The Heidi Chronicles* was brought to television by the Turner network, starring Jamie Lee Curtis as the heroine. Some asked why make the award-winning play into a movie, and Wasserstein responded, "It would have killed me if Heidi never became a movie." She said she was going to bring it to public television, but there was no money until Curtis became interested and Turner picked it up. *The Heidi Chronicles*, Wasserstein explains, is "a play by a woman about women running on Broadway and commercially viable." Thus she opened the door for other women to do the same, to be funny, yet taken seriously. And she opened the door for other women playwrights to be brought to television.

The story, originally written as a reaction to Wasserstein's own disillusions, follows the flashbacks of a woman who is very successful yet feels stuck by the decisions she's made. Although when it was released on television there were fears that audiences would not relate to Heidi's character, women of today are relating to the recurring theme of "What if. . .?"

Wasserstein more recent play, *An American Daughter*, which she calls "a bitter and angry play" opened in Seattle in the spring of 1996 and in New York that fall.

OTHER WORKS: *The Heidi Chronicles and Other Plays* (1991). *Pamela's First Musical* (1996).

BIBLIOGRAPHY: Betsko, K., and R. Koenig, *Interviews with Contemporary Women Playwrights* (1987). Carlson, S. L., "Comic Textures and Female Communities 1937 and 1977: Clare Boothe and Wendy Wasserstein,'' in *Modern American Drama: The Female Canon* (1990). Keyssar, H., *Feminist Theatre* (1984). Raymond, M. G., ''Chronicling Our Selves: Hermeneutical Consciousness in Four Plays by Marsha Norman, Caryl Churchill, and Wendy Wasserstein'' (thesis, 1998).

Reference works: *CB* (July 1989). *CA* (1987, 1989, 1990). *CLC* (1990). *Contemporary Theatre, Film, and Television* (1986). *Feminist Companion to Literature in English* (1990). *Oxford Companion to Women's Writing in the Untied States* (1995). *National Playwrights Directory* (1981). *WWAW* (1984).

Other references: *Modern Drama* (Dec. 1984). *Women's Studies: An Interdisciplinary Journal* (1988, interview).

—STEVEN F. BLOOM,
UPDATED BY DEVRA M. SLADICS

WATANABE, Sylvia

Born circa 1950s or 1960s

Over the past 20 years, there has been a sort of renaissance of Hawaiian literature. Writers like Milton Murayama, Darrell Lum, Nora Okja Keller, Susanna Moore, and Lois Ann Yamanaka have written significant fiction with Hawaiian themes. Another writer to follow this theme in her work is Sylvia Watanabe. With the emergence of Watanabe and these other writers, Hawaii seems to be carving out its own place in contemporary American literature. Hawaii has for more than 100 years been seen as the land of the hula and smiling faces with greetings of ''Aloha.'' It is viewed as a land of tourist fare through TV shows and exotic travel brochures. However, the latest dawning of Hawaiian literature has redefined the state and locale, showing a more realistic view of life from the insider's point of view.

Watanabe, a Japanese American born and raised on Maui, has taken her place among today's literary voices with her first collection of stories, *Talking to the Dead* (1991, 1993, 1994). She evokes the everyday lives of Hawaiian villagers with a disarming blend of humor and pathos. Though for most Hawaii represents the dreamed-of vacation getaway, Watanabe adds some heart and soul, blended with some mysticism, to create a mood and picture that even the best vacation brochure could not provide.

Talking to the Dead is a collection of interrelated short stories revolving around a close-knit Asian community of Luhi in Hawaii. The stories depict Maui's Lahaina coast before it turned from fishing villages to tourist traps. The stories center on the community and family and often focus on interfamilial power struggles. Beneath the calm, normal exterior of the village, the reader will find some magic and dark family secrets.

The various stories are heartwarming and memorable. In ''Anchorage,'' the story that opens the collection, Little Grandma takes her granddaughter (the narrator) to her attic to show the granddaughter her life's work—a magnificent quilt: ''Though unfinished the quilt covered nearly the entire wall. From where I stood, perhaps 15 feet away, it seemed to contain every color in the entire world. As I moved closer, the colors began to cohere into squares, the squares into scenes—each scene depicting places and people in the life of the village.'' This story, like many others, celebrates Watanabe's relationship with her grandmother. This same celebration is relived in a collection edited by Mickey Pearlman, *Between Friends: Writing Women Celebrate Friendship* (1994). Watanabe's essay focuses on her mother and grandmother and on the heart-wrenching bedside vigil as her mother lies dying of pancreatic cancer.

''Anchorage'' and the other stories also evoke a fantastic portrait of this rural Hawaiian village. It is a way of life that is rapidly disappearing, being replaced by resorts and tourist destinations. Watanabe writes in an afterword, ''I wanted to tell how the Lahaina coast looked before it was covered with resorts. . . . I wanted to save my parents' and grandparents' stories.''

The title story of *Talking to the Dead*, winner of the O. Henry Award, explores the life of an elderly mystic, Auntie Talking to the Dead, who conducts funeral rites. She is joined by a young, local Japanese girl, who cannot be married off and who becomes her apprentice. The apprentice learns the medicinal uses of indigenous plants and Hawaiian healing chants. She learns the value of the gift of life passed on by the elderly woman and is able to use her knowledge after the woman's death to keep the traditions of the old culture alive.

Talking to the Dead was nominated for a National Book award in 1992. This first collection has allowed Watanabe to open the doors of opportunity before her even further. She has made an impressive start; her writing infuses her stories and characters with a timeless, boundless quality. Though the stories are rooted in the period of World War II and its effect on Japanese Americans, they intermingle the different generations and make the settings easily adjustable to the past, present, and future.

Watanabe has also edited two collections of Asian American works, *Home to Stay: Asian American Women's Fiction* and *Into the Fire: Asian American Prose* (1996), and her work has been included in additional volumes like the *1998 Pushcart Prize XXII: Best of the Small Presses,* edited by Bill Henderson. In addition, *Talking to the Dead* was nominated in 1993 for the PEN/Faulkner award for fiction.

OTHER WORKS: *O-bon: A Gathering of Joy* (1985).

BIBLIOGRAPHY: Bauermeister, E., *500 Great Books by Women.* Cheuse, A. and Marshall, C., eds., *Listening to Ourselves: More Stories From ''The Sound of Writing''* (1994). Frosch, M., *Coming of Age in America: A Multicultural Anthology* (1994).

Pearlman, M., ed., *A Place Called Home: Twenty Writing Women Remember* (1997). Penelope, J. and Valentine, S., eds., *International Feminist Fiction* (1992).

Other references: *American Book Review* (Nov. 1990). *Asian Week* (16 Oct. 1992). *International Examiner* (20 Apr. 1992). *NYT* (27 Sept. 1992). *PW* (6 July 1992). *San Francisco Chronicle* (6 Sept. 1992).

—DEVRA M. SLADICS

WATSON, Sukey Vickery

Born 12 June 1779, Leicester, Massachusetts; **died** 17 June 1821, Leicester, Massachusetts
Wrote under: "Fidelia," "A Young Lady of Worcester County"
Daughter of Benjamin and Susannah Barter Vickery; **married** Samuel Watson, 1804

Sukey Vickery Watson was educated at Leicester Academy and wrote poetry for the *Massachusetts Spy*, under the pseudonym "Fidelia" during 1801 and 1802. She also produced the first novel to be published in Worcester County, *Emily Hamilton* (1803). In 1804 she married Samuel Watson, a successful manufacturer and representative to the Massachusetts legislature.

Dr. Charles L. Nichols in his bibliography of Worcester attributed the novel *Emily Hamilton* to "Eliza Vicery," an error which was copied by other scholars and by the Library of Congress, by means of which the error has been perpetuated. Sukey Vickery Watson had a daughter Eliza, which may have been the reason for the confusion of names.

In the introduction to *Emily Hamilton*, Watson explains the function of a novel is to delight and to instruct the reader, but not to arouse false romantic expectations that could lead to "ruin." *Emily Hamilton* is an epistolary novel, consisting of some 70 letters spanning over four years. The principal plot concerns Emily, who is courted by one man, conceives a "guilty passion" for another, and becomes promised to a third. The first of these, Lambert, proves a villain and flees to Canada under sentence of death. The second, the miserably married Belmont, becomes a widower at a most opportune time. The third, Devas, is tragically lost at sea, thereby freeing Emily to marry Belmont.

Because events described in the letters have already taken place, the story lacks the immediacy of a present-tense narrative. Other handicaps are correspondents' lengthy reflections on the moral consequences of actions and Watson's overly elegant language: when Belmont attempts to convince Emily that they should be married quickly, "the pearly drop of sensibility gave additional lustre to his beamy eyes." Watson includes numerous poems in a variety of styles, almost all lengthy and undistinguished.

Emily Hamilton's chief virtue—and Watson's chief claim to fame—is as a sociological document rich in detail about upper-class life after the Revolution. Watson's "real life" novel shows

that American men and women of large landed estates and ritualistic courtesies still bore a striking resemblance to their English counterparts, from whom they had so violently severed themselves only 20 years before.

OTHER WORKS: The papers of Sukey Vickery Watson (poems, letters, and a fragment of her diary) are in the collection of the American Antiquarian Society in Worcester, Massachusetts.

BIBLIOGRAPHY: Bennett, J. B., *A Young Lady of Worcester County* (1942).

Other references: *Proceedings of the American Antiquarian Society* (1942).

—JEANETTE NYDA PASSTY

WATTS, Mary Stanbery

Born 4 November 1868, Delaware County, Ohio; **died** 21 May 1958, Cincinnati, Ohio
Daughter of John and Anna Stanbery; **married** Miles T. Watts, 1891

Mary Stanbery Watts wrote in 1918 that her childhood on an Ohio farm was the "greatest asset" in her writing career. Apparently, because of declining fortunes, the family lived at "The Lindens" in solitude enforced by their social superiority over their illiterate neighbors. She was educated at the Sacred Heart Convent in Cincinnati. She married a successful real estate agent and spent the rest of her life in Cincinnati.

Most of Watts' novels are set in Ohio, and she consciously chronicles Midwestern manners. One of the prevalent themes of the early novels is the once-prominent and wealthy family now down on its luck. Her first novel, *The Tenants* (1908), set in Columbus during the 1880s, concerns the fortunes of the Gwynne family and their management of the family mansion built by Governor Gwynne and now merely a burden to his heirs. As in two other early novels—*The Legacy* (1911) and *Van Cleve* (1913)—there is one sensible and responsible member to contrast with less reliable family members.

Watts' second novel centers not on a family on its way down but on a young man on his way up. *Nathan Burke* (1910), a historical novel with a wealth of interesting characterization, is set in the Scioto River country where Watts was born and in Columbus, where young Burke goes to seek his fortunes. He becomes a hero in the Mexican war and makes good as a lawyer. The novel was well received by reviewers in major critical papers.

With *The Rise of Jennie Cushing* (1914), Watts launched the dominant theme of all her later novels: the difficulties of marriages between classes. As a child, Jennie is taken from her home to become a ward of the state at the Girls' Home (a facility that actually existed near the Stanbery farm). A beautiful, hardworking, independent young woman, Jennie leaves the school at eighteen, works for a farm family, becomes a manicurist, then later works in private homes as a hairdresser. Donelson Meigs, a painter, falls in love with her and takes her to Paris. But when he finds out about Jennie's background, she, believing she'd only drag him down, goes back to America and runs a home for orphans in the country near the Girls Home. When Meigs comes after her, she refuses to marry him. Clearly, Watts believes this is the wise decision not only for Jennie but also for Meigs and his family.

The rest of Watts' novels all use romance and marriage to make the point, in the words of Mrs. McQuair of *The Noon-Mark* (1920), "the clay pots cannot float down stream with the brass pots; each to its own current." There are good and bad characters in both classes. In *Luther Nichols* (1923), a handsome, aggressive chauffeur's life ends tragically because of a flirtatious irresponsible society girl. In *The Noon-Mark*, two realistic young people break their engagement when they realize they are too widely separated in background. The lower-class heroine, a secretary, is rewarded by marriage to her employer. Watts does not gloss over these troubled relationships, and only in her last novel, *The Fabric of the Loom* (1924), about the terrible error made by Dick Meryon in marrying a middle-class "person" who does not share his family's tastes in pastimes or home decoration, does she become petty and absurd. Perhaps the best of these novels is *The Rudder* (1916), which contains varied characters in a humorous story about a young woman of good family who becomes a social worker. There are no deserving poor, according to the heroine, but "they've got to be taken care of whatever they are."

Watts herself said she modeled her work on the novels of such writers as Thackeray, Defoe, and Hardy; and she believed the depiction of ordinary life to be the highest goal of a writer. To a certain extent, she was successful, for her novels are rich in realistic characterization and incident. Perhaps her gift for describing the social milieu of a group of people and then relating them to people in other circumstances led to her preoccupation with class issues. Watts was a fairly competent writer whose novels are quite worth reading, although it is hard to imagine how a woman with such vision could have such narrow sympathies.

OTHER WORKS: *Three Short Plays* (1917). *The Boardman Family* (1918). *From Father to Son* (1919). *The House of Rimmon* (1922).

BIBLIOGRAPHY: Overton, G., *The Women Who Make Our Novels* (1922).
Other references: *Atlantic* (1910). *Bookman* (July 1910). *Dial* (1910). *Mentor* (15 Aug. 1919). *NYT* (21 May 1910, 25 Oct. 1914).

—BEVERLY SEATON

WEBER, Sarah Appleton
See APPLETON-WEBER, Sarah

WEBSTER, Jean

Born Alice Jane Chandler Webster, 24 July 1876, Fredonia, New York; **died** 11 June 1916, New York, New York
Daughter of Charles L. and Annie Moffett Webster; **married** Glenn F. McKinney, 1915; **children:** one daughter

Jean Webster was a grandniece of Mark Twain; her father was Twain's partner in his ill-fated publishing ventures. She attended the Lady Jane Grey School in Binghamton, New York, and graduated from Vassar College in 1901. She was a frequent contributor to college publications and literary editor of the yearbook. Webster's friend and roommate at Vassar, Adelaide Crapsey, was probably the inspiration for Patty in her books *When Patty Went to College* (1903) and *Just Patty* (1911). Webster became a freelance writer, lived in Greenwich Village, and traveled extensively touring the world in 1906-07. After her marriage in 1915 to a lawyer, she and her husband lived in New York City and the Berkshires. She died a day after the birth of her only child, a daughter.

When Patty Went to College collects sketches Webster began writing while still at Vassar. It depicts the escapades of Patty Wyatt and Priscilla Pond, seniors in a turn-of-the-century women's college where the students surreptitiously brew afternoon tea and evening cocoa on alcohol stoves in their rooms, receive gentleman callers in the parlor after a maid has carried up cards, dine in evening dress, evade obligatory chapel, and study Greek and ethics. A sequel, *Just Patty*, concerns the innocent adventures of Patty and Priscilla as seniors at a church boarding school.

The epistolary novel *Daddy-Long-Legs* (1912) presents a modern Cinderella, Jerusha Abbot ("Judy"), who leaves her lifelong home in a depressing orphanage to attend a women's college. She must report her progress to her nameless benefactor, whom she christens "Daddy-long-legs" and whom she marries four years later. Webster's dramatization became highly successful on Broadway, starring Ruth Chatterton, and appeared in several film versions, including a silent version with Mary Pickford. A 1915 reviewer criticized the drama on the ground that "the chief object of the play" was to provide "sentimentalism sentimentally interpreted, turnip smothered in sugar offered as an apple of life." The novel, however, largely avoids sentimentalism, and the brisk irreverence and piquancy of its humor have made it a perennial favorite with both adults and children.

Dear Enemy (1914), an epistolary sequel to *Daddy-Long-Legs*, follows Judy's college friend Sallie McBride as she arrives to reform the old-fashioned orphanage from which Judy had escaped and stays to fall in love with its dour Scotch doctor. Once again, a potentially sentimental story is saved from stickiness by the practical point of view and the lively prose of its narrator.

Both *Daddy-Long-Legs* and *Dear Enemy* remained in print for almost 70 years. Their strong stories and charming characters, together with Webster's real interest in reforms in the care of dependent children, will secure them an audience for many years to come.

OTHER WORKS: *The Wheat Princess* (1905). *Jerry, Junior* (1907). *The Four Pools Mystery* (1908). *Much Ado About Peter* (1909). *Asa* (1914).

The papers of Jean Webster are collected in the Lockwood Library of Vassar College.

BIBLIOGRAPHY: Simpson, A., *Jean Webster, Storyteller* (1984).
Reference works: *Junior Book of Authors* (1951). *NAW* (1971). *TCA.*
Other references: *NR* (13 March 1915). *NYT* (9 Nov. 1914, 13 Dec. 1914, 12 June 1916). *Vassar Quarterly* (Nov. 1916).

—SUSAN SUTTON SMITH

WEEKS, Helen C.
See CAMPBELL, Helen Stuart

WELBY, Amelia (Bell) Coppuck

Born 3 February 1819, Saint Michaels, Maryland; **died** 3 May 1852, Louisville, Kentucky
Daughter of William and Mary Shield Coppuck; **married** George H. Welby, 1838; **children:** one

Soon after Amelia Coppuck Welby's birth, her father, a mason, moved his family to Baltimore, where Welby received some formal education, and in 1834 the family moved to Louisville. By 1837 poems signed "Amelia" appeared in the Louisville *Daily Journal.* Welby's poems were quickly copied and circulated in other local papers, and by the 1840s she had gained national popularity. Five years later, her poems were collected in her only book, *Poems by Amelia* (1845); by 1860, it had appeared in 15 editions.

At the age of nineteen, Welby married an English businessman. While she continued to write verse after her marriage, it appears the work Welby had found important to her from girlhood no longer attracted her so powerfully toward the end of her life. She died two months after the birth of her only child.

Welby's poetic techniques and subjects are generally standard. She usually writes in slavishly exact and repetitive meter of nature, love, death, children, and religion; romanticized peasants, disappointed lovers, and sentimentalized brides abound. Equally conventional are the themes of her reflective lyrics and occasional dramatic narratives (such as "The Dying Girl" and "The Dying Mother"), in which she often juxtaposes innocence and sin. "The American Sword" and "My Own Native Land" reveal a passionate if sometimes brutal patriotism.

But Welby's sentimental conventionality does not obscure her real if unsustained strengths. Her poetry reveals a fanciful imagination and sensitive humor. She freely assumes the voice of the dew in "The Dew-Drop" and of the violet in "The Violet's Song to the Lost Fairy." Her humor appears less frequently in her earlier than in her later poems, in which she is able to smile even at love.

Welby shows understanding of character and skill in exploring first person speakers. For example, in appropriately childlike rhythms, she reveals her understanding of a small boy and his stepmother in "The Little Step-Son"; here, through the voice of the stepmother, Welby admires the cute but realistic child in stanzas punctuated by the refrain, "My sturdy little stepson, that's only five years old." With apparent ease, she assumes the male voice of a lover (as in "The Golden Ringlet" or in "Lines—to a Lady"), of a boy (as in "The Captive Sailor Boy") or of a soldier (as in "The American Sword"). She also uses her personae to explore her vague frustrations with her role as a woman; in "My Own Native Land," she writes: "Oh, had I the strength of my heart in my hand, / I'd fight for thy freedom, my own native land."

Whether expressed through her clearly fictional or suggestively autobiographical speakers, Welby's concern with various voices reveals an interest in self that never quite fully informs her poetry; still, her exploration of the first person rewards the careful reader as the poet writes as "I. . .a Minstrel Girl" in "The Stars" or as "I, the youngest, wildest one" in "The Sisters."

BIBLIOGRAPHY: Coggeshall, W. T., *The Poets and Poetry of the West* (1860). Poe, E. A., in the *Democratic Review* (Dec. 1844). Watts, E. S., *The Poetry of American Women from 1632 to 1945* (1977).
Reference works: *Daughters of America* (1882). *Female Poets of America* (1848). *Women of the South* (1860). *Women's Record* (1853).

—CAROLYN ZILBOORG

WELLS, Carolyn

Born 18 June 1869, Rahway, New Jersey; **died** 26 March 1942, New York, New York
Also wrote under: Rowland Wright
Daughter of William E. and Anna Wells; **married** Hadwin Houghton, 1918

A precocious child, Carolyn Wells hated formal schooling and refused to attend college. Scarlet fever, suffered at the age of six, caused her to become hard of hearing. Reared in New Jersey, she made her home in New York City after her marriage to Haldwin Houghton, of the Houghton Mifflin publishing clan. She loved puzzles, bridge, chess, charades, and detective stories (her discovery of a mystery by Anna Katharine Green was pivotal, inspiring her both to read voraciously and to write voluminously in that genre). Her literary career began almost by accident, with the contribution of jingles to humorous periodicals. She considered 1902 an important date in her career: by then she had written eight books and had begun composing juveniles; after this date she consistently published at least three or four books annually. From 1909 on she wrote mysteries, and she claimed in an autobiographical work (*The Rest of My Life*, 1937) to have written 170 books, including 70 detective stories—"so far."

Her other main literary activity was as an anthologist, but she was also an important collector and bibliographer of the works of Walt Whitman. Her parody of Sinclair Lewis' *Main Street* (*Ptomaine Street*, 1921), in which Carol Kennicott becomes Warble Petticoat, is funny and full of witty puns. Sometimes it misses its mark because both locale and social class are changed, but it wickedly refashions a number of episodes from the original.

Wells' juveniles are intended for young girls; different series are aimed at different age groups. Marjorie is in her early teens, for example, and is presented as a child, sometimes mischievous though generally a model little girl (in *Marjorie's Vacation*, 1907, and five other novels through 1912). Patty, on the other hand, is in her later teens, and the final books in her series lead to her marriage (in *Patty Fairfield*, 1901, and 16 other novels through 1919). In the middle are "two little women," who are fifteen when their series begins (see *Two Little Women*, 1915, and two other novels through 1917). All these novels are seriously dated by their intense concern for the social conventions of the early 20th century. For example, Patty's main problems and decisions grow from situations in which she has (either apparently or actually) been led to behave in an unconventional manner (such as going out without a chaperone).

Although also clearly limited by its time and place, Wells' detective fiction holds up somewhat better. She claimed the title of "Dean of American Mystery Writers" and was widely considered an authority. *The Technique of the Mystery Story* (1913; revised 1929), heavily larded with quotations of both primary and secondary materials, is a thorough survey of the field, written for aspiring authors. Unfortunately, Wells' own style is undistinguished; dialogue and dialect are often clumsily handled. Characterization is flat, characters often being hard to distinguish from each other. Her women are often irritatingly coy, shallowly coquettish ingenues—whom the reader is clearly expected to find charming—and she made it a rule that a woman could never be the murderer (though women were sometimes the victims in her stories). Although male figures are more varied, heroes and detectives are consistently well educated and wealthy. Plotting, however, is inventive, and Wells made interesting use of such conventional types as the "locked room" mystery.

Wells created a number of detectives, the best known and most frequently used (in 61 novels) being Fleming Stone, a professional detective who is a cultivated gentleman, moving easily in the elevated social circles in which Wells' mysteries occur. He was her first creation (*The Clue*, 1909), and she continued to use him until the end of her career (*Who Killed Caldwell?*, 1942). Similar to Stone in characterization and methods of detection is Kenneth Carlisle, but he is distinguished by

being a former screen star and matinee idol (in *Sleeping Dogs*, 1929, and two other novels). More interesting is the team of Pennington ("Penny") Wise and Zizi (in *The Man Who Fell Through the Earth*, 1919, and five other novels). His approach to detection is rational while hers is intuitive; both are fallible, although Zizi is more often right. She is presented as a mysterious young sprite of a girl who seems to have no background or past. Wells' other detectives are Lorimer Lane (in *More Lives Than One*, 1923, and another novel) and Alan Ford (in *Faulkner's Folly*, 1917, and two other novels). Wells' sleuths often work wonders of detection, but they occasionally err and thus illustrate her distaste, often expressed, for the "omniscient detective."

Once well known and highly respected, Wells's works now languish unread. She was too prolific, wrote too easily and rapidly, reflected her age too uncritically, and restricted herself too narrowly to popular genres and formulas. Her importance thus is largely historical, and is most clearly found in her practice of the detective novel.

OTHER WORKS: *The Jingle Book* (1899). *The Story of Betty* (1899). *Idle Idyls* (1900). *Folly in Fairyland* (1901). *The Merry-Go-Round* (1901). *Mother Goose's Menagerie* (1901). *Children of Our Town* (1902). *Abeniki Caldwell: A Burlesque Historical Novel* (1902). *Eight Girls and a Dog* (1902). *Folly in the Forest* (1902). *A Nonsense Anthology* (1902). *The Pete & Polly Stories* (1902). *A Phenomenal Fauna* (1902). *Trotty's Trip* (1902). *Folly for the Wise* (1904). *The Gordon Elopement: The Story of a Short Vacation* (with H. P. Taber, 1904). *In the Reign of Queen Dick* (1904). *A Parody Anthology* (1904). *Patty at Home* (1904). *The Staying Guest* (1904). *The Dorrance Domain* (1905). *The Matrimonial Bureau* (with H. P. Taber, 1905). *Patty in the City* (1905). *A Satire Anthology* (1905). *At the Sign of the Sphinx* (1906). *Dorrance Doings* (1906). *Patty's Summer Days* (1906). *Rubáiyát of a Motor Car* (1906). *A Whimsey Anthology* (1906). *The Emily Emmins Papers* (1907). *Fluffy Ruffles* (1907). *Patty in Paris* (1907). *Rainy Day Diversions* (1907). *A vers de société Anthology* (1907). *The Happychaps* (1908). *Marjorie's Busy Days* (1908). *Patty's Friends* (1908). *Year Book of Old Favorites and New Fancies for 1909* (1908). *Dick and Dolly* (1909). *Marjorie's New Friend* (1909). *Patty's Pleasure Trip* (1909). *Pleasant Day Diversions* (1909). *The Rubáiyát of Bridge* (1909). *The Seven Ages of Childhood* (1909). *Betty's Happy Year* (1910). *Dick and Dolly's Adventures* (1910). *Marjorie in Command* (1910). *Patty's Success* (1910). *The Gold Bag* (1911). *Marjorie's Maytime* (1911). *Patty's Motor Car* (1911). *A Chain of Evidence* (1912). *The Lover's Baedeker and Guide to Arcady* (1912). *Marjorie at Seacote* (1912). *Patty's Butterfly Days* (1912). *Christmas Carollin'* (1913). *The Eternal Feminine* (1913). *Girls and Gayety* (1913). *The Maxwell Mystery* (1913). *Patty's Social Season* (1913). *Pleasing Prose* (1913). *The Re-echo Club* (1913). *Anybody but Anne* (1914). *Jolly Plays for Holidays: A Collection of Christmas Entertainments* (1914). *Patty's Suitors* (1914). *Patty's Romance* (1915). *The Disappearance of Kimball Webb* (1915). *The White Alley* (1915). *The Bride of a Moment* (1916). *The Curved Blades*

(1916). *Patty's Fortune* (1916). *Two Little Women and Treasure House* (1916). *Baubles* (1917). *Doris of Dobbs Ferry* (1917). *The Mark of Cain* (1917). *Patty Blossom* (1917). *Two Little Women on a Holiday* (1917). *Patty—Bride* (1918). *Such Nonsense! An Anthology* (1918). *Vicky Van* (1918). *The Diamond Pin* (1919). *Patty and Azalea* (1919). *The Book of Humorous Verse* (1920; revised 1936). *In the Onyx Lobby* (1920). *Raspberry Jam* (1920). *The Room with the Tassels* (1920). *The Come Back* (1921). *The Luminous Face* (1921). *The Mystery of the Sycamore* (1921). *A Concise Bibliography of the Works of Walt Whitman, with a Supplement of Fifty Books about Whitman* (with A. F. Goldsmith, 1922). *The Meaning of Thanksgiving Day* (1922). *The Mystery Girl* (1922). *Queen Christmas: A Pageant Play* (1922). *The Sweet Girl Graduate: A Commencement Play* (1922). *The Vanishing of Betty Varian* (1922). *The Affair at Flower Acres* (1923). *Feathers Left Around* (1923). *An Outline of Humor: Being a True Chronicle from Prehistoric Ages to the Twentieth Century* (1923; revised edition, *World's Best Humor*, 1933). *Spooky Hollow* (1923). *Wheels Within Wheels* (1923). *Cross Word Puzzle Book* (1924). *The Fourteenth Key* (1924). *The Furthest Fury* (1924). *The Moss Mystery* (1924). *Prillilgirl* (1924). *Anything But the Truth* (1925). *Book of American Limericks* (1925). *The Daughter of the House* (1925). *Face Cards* (1925). *The Bronze Hand* (1926). *The Red-Haired Girl* (1926). *The Vanity Case* (1926). *All at Sea* (1927). *American Detective Stories* (1927). *American Mystery Stories* (1927). *Ask Me a Question: Over 2000 Questions and Answers on Interesting and Informative Subjects* (1927). *A Book of Charades* (1927). *The Sixth Commandment* (1927). *Where's Emily?* (1927). *The Crime in the Crypt* (1928). *Deep-Lake Mystery* (1928). *The Tannahill Tangle* (1928). *The Tapestry Room Murder* (1929). *Triple Murder* (1929). *The Doomed Five* (1930). *The Doorstep Murders* (1930). *The Ghosts' High Noon* (1930). *Horror House* (1931). *The Skeleton at the Feast* (1931). *The Umbrella Murder* (1931). *Fuller's Earth* (1932). *The Omnibus Fleming Stone* (1932). *The Roll-Top Desk Mystery* (1932). *All for Fun: Brain Teasers* (1933). *The Broken O* (1933). *The Clue of the Eyelash* (1933). *The Master Murderer* (1933). *Eyes in the Wall* (1934). *In the Tiger's Cage* (1934). *The Visiting Villain* (1934). *The Beautiful Derelict* (1935). *The Cat in Verse* (1935). *For Goodness' Sake* (1935). *The Wooden Indian* (1935). *The Huddle* (1936). *Money Musk* (1936). *Murder in the Bookshop* (1936). *The Mystery of the Tarn* (1937). *The Radio Studio Murder* (1937). *Gilt Edged Guilt* (1938). *The Killer* (1938). *The Missing Link* (1938). *Calling All Suspects* (1939). *Crime Tears On* (1939). *The Importance of Being Murdered* (1939). *Crime Incarnate* (1940). *Devil's Work* (1940). *Murder on Parade* (1940). *Murder Plus* (1940). *The Black Night Murders* (1941). *Murder at the Casino* (1941). *Murder Will In* (1942).

BIBLIOGRAPHY: Reference works: *Encyclopedia Mysteriosa* (1994). *Encyclopedia of Mystery and Detection* (1976). *NCAB*. *St. James Guide to Crime & Mystery Writers* (1996).

Other references: *NYT* (27 March 1942). *NYTBR* (4 Dec. 1937).

—MARY JEAN DEMARR

WELLS, Emmeline (Blanche) Woodward

Born 29 February 1828, Petersham, Massachusetts; **died** 25 April 1921, Salt Lake City, Utah
Wrote under: Amethyst, "Aunt Em," Blanche Beechwood, E.B.W., Emmeline B. Wells
Daughter of David and Deiadama Hare Woodward; **married** James H. Harris, 1843 (deserted); Newell K. Whitney, 1845 (died 1850); Daniel H. Wells, 1852; **children:** five daughters

Emmeline Woodward Wells converted to Mormonism when she was fourteen, married James Harris at fifteen, and moved the following year to Nauvoo, Illinois, then the Mormon headquarters. Deserted by Harris, Wells married Newell K. Whitney and joined the exodus of Mormons to Salt Lake City. After Whitney's death in 1850 she married Wells. Five daughters were born of Wells' last two marriages.

An ardent suffragist and women's rights advocate, Wells was a member of numerous national and state woman suffrage and other (especially literary) organizations. As president of the Utah Woman's Suffrage Association, she successfully lobbied for the inclusion of woman suffrage in Utah's constitution in 1895. In 1910, at age eighty-two, Wells was appointed general president of the Mormon woman's Relief Society, serving until three weeks before her death in 1921. The *Woman's Exponent*, a Mormon women's journal Wells edited from 1877 to 1914, gave her an influential voice in women's affairs. She used its editorial page to promote equal rights for women, and also to defend the Mormon practice of plural marriage.

Wells' only collection of poetry, *Musings and Memories*, (1896), is aptly named. The poems are reflective and personal, most of them a sentimental backward look at a past both pleasant and painful. "A Glance Backward" illustrates the portentous mood pervading much of her retrospective verse. The festive celebration in honor of two young lovers who "plighted their troth" is underscored by ominous intimations. Shadows of a fire creep "like spectres," trees stand "phantom-like," and laughter echoes "in a hollow sound." The lovers are doomed, yet choose to shun the "potent sway of dread" and exchange their vows in "fond expectancy." Wells subtly sustains the fateful mood, which she delicately balances on a thin narrative thread that gives the piece its unity.

"Memory of the Sea" evokes the same mood, heightened by the mournful cadence associated with Poe's "The Raven." Wells uses the sea as metaphor: it holds the answer to life's mysteries, but recklessly drives human hopes to and fro. Unyielding, it keeps its secrets "sleeping in its surging bosom," and frail humanity must find its answer elsewhere. One of the author's most effective poems, "Memory of the Sea" is persistently but restrainedly emotional.

As a poet, Wells fits comfortably under Hawthorne's rubric of "scribbling women." While much of her poetry has definite merit, it occasionally demonstrates the stilted manner and excessive sentiment typical of the period. Poetry, she said, was "a history of the heart." She wrote for a receptive local audience appreciative of her style; a second edition of her poems was published in 1915. Wells did not use poetry as a medium for polemics, reserving her feminist arguments for the editorial page. She left a collection of diaries spanning nearly half a century. A prominent figure in the Mormon female hierarchy, she wrote perceptively and intelligently, if not always disinterestedly, of events in Mormon history, especially during the critical period of 1876 to 1896. She is often frustratingly elusive in her references to personal affairs but remarkably informative in her observations of the effect on women of a changing Mormon society.

It is as a journalist that Wells is most noted. The majority of her editorials for the *Woman's Exponent* responded to the "woman question" of her century, her rhetoric often echoing the polemics of other feminists. In them she exercised both logic and analysis, sometimes interlacing her premises with poetic imagery. Other editorials dealt with local issues, particularly those centering on the religious and political tensions polarizing Utah and the rest of the nation. Writing initially as a contributor to the *Exponent* under the name of Blanche Beechwood, Wells dropped the pseudonym soon after becoming editor. She created another literary identity, however, "Aunt Em," who wrote 87 articles and stories incorporating traditional Victorian values and sentiments. Wells, the editor, and "Aunt Em," the contributor, symbolize the different views of woman battling for women's allegiance and formed the double dimension of Wells' literary personality.

Wells was a woman of her time, her literary products felicitously harmonizing with its concerns and values. While her poetry was addressed to another audience, her editorials are relevant to the contemporary woman's movement. One of the most influential of 19th-century Mormon women, Wells made a literary impact both substantial and effective.

OTHER WORKS: *Memorial of the Mormon Women of Utah to the President and Congress of the United States, April 6, 1886* (1886). *Charities and Philanthropies: Women's Work in Utah* (1893). *Songs and Flowers of the Wasatch* (edited by Wells, 1893).

BIBLIOGRAPHY: Anderson, R., "Emmeline B. Wells: Her Life and Thought" (thesis, 1975). Burgess-Olson, V., *Sister Saints* (1978). Crocheron, A. J., *Representative Women of Deseret* (1884). Gates, S. Y., *History of the Young Ladies Mutual Improvement Association, 1869-1910* (1911). Madsen, C. C., "'Remember the Women of Zion': A Study of the Editorial Content of the *Woman's Exponent*, A Mormon Woman's Journal" (thesis, 1977). Whitney, O.F., *History of Utah*, Vol. 4 (1904).

Reference works: *Latter-Day Saint Biographical Encyclopedia* (1914). *NAW* (1971).

Other references: *Improvement Era* (June 1921). *NYT* (27 April 1921). *Relief Society Magazine* (Feb. 1915, Feb. 1916). *Sunset* (May 1916). *Utah Historical Quarterly* (Fall 1974). *Young Woman's Journal* (April 1908).

—CAROL CORNWALL MADSEN

WELLS, John J.

See BRADLEY, Marion Zimmer

WELLS-BARNETT, Ida B.

Born 16 July 1862, Holly Springs, Mississippi; **died** 25 March 1931, Chicago, Illinois
Wrote under Ida B. Wells
Daughter of Jim and Lizzie Warrenton Wells; **married** Ferdinand Barnett, 1896; **children:** four

Ida B. Wells was born a slave, but her father was a skilled carpenter and she grew up in a house he had built and owned. Both of her parents emphasized the importance of education and were very active in civic and religious activities. The oldest of eight children, Wells attended Rust College in Holly Springs, Mississippi, a school for blacks that extended down to the primary grades. Her childhood ended in 1878 when an epidemic of yellow fever decimated Holly Springs, killing her parents and youngest brother. Wells was determined to keep the remaining children together, so she became a schoolteacher.

About five years later, Wells moved to Memphis, where she taught in a rural school while studying for the city's teacher's examinations. In May 1884 she was riding the train to work when the conductor told her to leave her seat and ride in the smoking car. Wells refused. When the conductor and baggage man tried to force her to move, she got off the train and sued the railroad. The law required separate but equal accommodations, and Wells did not consider the smoking car equal to the first-class car. The local court agreed and awarded her $500 in damages, but on appeal the Supreme Court of Tennessee supported the railroad's claim that the smoking car was acceptable for blacks. Wells was furious and dismayed to discover that the law was not on the side of justice.

In 1887 Wells wrote about this formative experience for a church paper. Readers and editors asked for more, and soon she was writing for a variety of church papers and secular black newspapers. She was then offered the editorship and part-ownership of a Memphis paper, the *Free Speech and Headlight*, which she shortened to *Free Speech*. In 1891 she wrote a series of articles criticizing the conditions in Memphis' segregated schools for blacks. Not surprisingly, the Memphis Board of Education responded by firing her from her teaching position. Wells was now a full-time journalist.

On 9 March 1892, three young black businessmen were lynched. They were owners of a Memphis grocery store, friends of Wells, and too independent and successful to be safe in a time of increasing racism. In response to their deaths, *Free Speech* called on Memphis blacks to stop spending money in white businesses, boycott the streetcars, and move west to a place where the laws would protect them. Hundreds of people—including two church congregations—left Memphis, and the superintendent and treasurer of the City Railway Company begged Wells to call off the boycott. Instead, she renewed her campaign against lynching.

After a fiery editorial appeared in *Free Speech*, a mob destroyed Wells' press in May 1892. She escaped only because she happened to be in Philadelphia reporting on a conference. Knowing that her life was in danger if she returned to the South, she began to write for the *New York Age* and tried to rally Northerners against lynching. Few were interested until Wells went abroad with her stories of American barbarism. In 1893 and again in 1894, Wells toured England, Scotland, and Wales, telling interested audiences about America's failure to live up to its promise of justice, liberty, and equality for all. She sent home articles that were published in the *Chicago Inter-Ocean* and other papers. In 1895 she published *A Red Record: Tabulated Statistics and Alleged Causes of Lynchings in the United States, 1892-1893-1894*. Wells' careful documentation and appeal to international opinion helped turn white popular opinion against lynchings and decrease the lynching rate.

Wells also remained concerned about the broader scope of American racism. She wrote *The Reason Why the Colored American is Not in the World's Columbian Exposition—The Afro-American's Contribution to Columbian Literature* (1893), denouncing the exclusion of all individual blacks and black groups from Chicago's great World's Fair. Wells had been very impressed with the English women's civic clubs that sponsored her lecture tours. After her return she helped found the first black women's clubs, which were devoted to community improvement and local and national activism.

In 1896 Wells married Ferdinand Barnett, an activist lawyer/journalist and a widower with two children. After the birth of their second child, she gave up newspaper work until her youngest child was eight and able to go to school by herself. She continued, however, to fight for racial justice. In 1901 the family moved into a white neighborhood. In 1910 Wells-Barnett founded the Negro Fellowship League, which was roughly modeled after Jane Addams' Hull House but located in the roughest part of Chicago. Whenever a race riot happened anywhere in the country, she would promptly go to the location, gather facts, and publish her reports in black newspapers. She remained active in black women's clubs, organized the first black women's suffrage club, and urged black men to use the power of the vote. As her children grew older, she returned to lecturing, and she always used her pen to document injustices. In 1928 she recorded the events of her life in *Crusade for Freedom: The Autobiography of Ida B. Wells* (published 1970). Despite increasing ill health, she kept active until a final illness of four days.

OTHER WORKS: *Lynch Law in Georgia* (1899). *To the Members of the Anti-Lynching Bureau* (1902). *On Lynchings* (1969). *Lynching and Rape* (1977). *Selected Works of Ida B. Wells* (1991). *The Memphis Diary of Ida B. Wells* (1995). *Southern Horrors and Other Writings* (1997).

BIBLIOGRAPHY: Bederman, G., *Manliness and Civilization: A Cultural History of Gender and Race in the United States, 1880-1917* (1995). Davidson, S., *Getting the Real Story* (1992). Lisandrelli, E., *Ida B. Wells-Barnett* (1998). McMurray, L., *To Keep the Waters Troubled* (1998). Miller, E. M., *The Other Construction: Where Violence and Womanhood Meet in the Writings of Ida B. Wells-Barnett, Angelina Gimké Weld, and Nella Larsen* (1999). Sterling, D., *Black Foremothers* (1988). Thompson, M., *Ida B. Wells-Barnett* (1990). Townes, E., *Womanist Justice, Womanist Hope* (1993).

Reference works: *African-American Orators: A Bio-Critical Sourcebook* (1996). *African-American Women: A Biographical Dictionary* (1993). *Black Women in America* (1993). *DLB 23*. *NAW*.

Other references: *Black Scholar* (1994). *Radical History Review* (1992). *Sage* (1991).

—LORI KENSCHAFT

WELTY, Eudora

Born 13 April 1909, Jackson, Mississippi
Daughter of Christian W. and Mary Andrews Welty

Although she is thoroughly Southern, Welty's family came from Ohio (her father's home) and West Virginia (her mother's home, which figures prominently in *The Optimist's Daughter*). Welty's childhood in Jackson was in a household of readers and in a town not yet industrialized, where schools and parks and grocery stores were all within walking distance of her home. Welty attended Mississippi State College for Women from 1925 to 1927, received her B.A. in 1929 from the University of Wisconsin, and spent 1930 to 1931 at Columbia University, studying advertising. With jobs scarce in Depression days and with her father's death in 1931, Welty returned to Jackson, where she has continued to live. Various jobs with local newspapers, Jackson radio station WJDX, and the Works Progress Authority (WPA) occupied her in the mid-1930s; but all the while she was writing, and her first story, "Death of a Traveling Salesman," appeared in *Manuscript* (May-June 1936).

Predictably, it was not easy to convince an editor to publish a collection of Welty's short stories before a novel appeared, but Doubleday, Doran did bring out *A Curtain of Green, and Other Stories* in 1941. The volume, distinguished in having an introduction by Katherine Anne Porter, brought Welty critical acclaim, and readers still find it contains many favorite stories—"Petrified Man," "Why I Live at the P.O.," "Keela, the Outcast Indian Maiden." These stories establish Welty's voice in portraying lower-middle class characters with convincing dialogue, in her lyrical descriptive power, and in her sense of place.

Reviewers were generally puzzled by *The Wide Net, and Other Stories* (1943), finding this second collection's stories (with the exception of "Livvie") radically different and less accessible than those in the first. Welty's third collection, *The Golden Apples* (1949), presents seven interrelated stories based on three generations of families in Morgana, Mississippi, whose lives intertwine publicly and privately. It is a work that draws heavily on myth to give added dimension to the lives and deeds of characters whose daily activities are of great interest.

Of the stories in Welty's fourth collection, not all are set in the South. The title story takes place in the boat train running from London to Cork, and ''Going to Naples'' aboard the *Pomona* en route to Palermo and Naples; ''Circe'' portrays the goddess on her enchanted island with Ulysses and his crew.

Welty's first novel, *The Robber Bridegroom* (1942), is a short work integrating stories of the Old Natchez Trace and remnants of Grimms' fairy tales and American frontier humor to relate the story of Clement Musgrove, his fair daughter Rosamond, and Jamie Lockhart, her ''robber bridegroom.'' As Welty has pointed out, this work is not a *historical* historical novel, and many critics see it as ''an examination of the theme of disenchantment in the pursuit of a pastoral, and fundamentally American, Eden.'' *Delta Wedding* (1946), Welty's first full-length novel, had its origin in a short story, ''The Delta Cousins.'' The novel is set in 1923, a year chosen for its relative calm so that domestic concerns in the Fairchild household might take precedence over outside involvements in a narrative presenting a Southern demiparadise on the verge of social change. Welty's comic masterpiece, *The Ponder Heart* (1954), has enjoyed success as a short novel and then as a Broadway play (adapted by Joseph Fields and Jerome Chodorov), in which the antics of Uncle Daniel and Bonnie Dee Peacock, Miss Teacake Magee, Mr. Truex Bodkin, the Peacock clan, and the populace of Clay, Mississippi, combine with the firm narrative voice of Edna Earle Ponder to form a work of boundless humor.

Two more novels appeared much later. After a virtual silence of 15 years, Welty published *Losing Battles* in 1970. A work of brilliant parts, *Losing Battles* is a long novel and has not pleased all readers; its diffusion and loose structure, however, are for many compensated by its comic richness—its eccentric characters, amusing situations, and details of places, names, and objects. Telescoped into a day-and-a-half, the novel presents the community of Banner, Mississippi, during the Depression, with kin and neighboring connections joined by choice or chance at the Beecham family reunion. It is an expression of Welty's persistent emphasis on the mystery surrounding human relationships and on the redeeming power of love.

For *The Optimist's Daughter* (1972) Welty won the Pulitzer Prize, an award many thought she should have received already. This novel presents both lower-middle class characters and the upper-middle-class citizens of Mount Salus, Mississippi. The second marriage of Judge Clinton McKelva to Wanda Fay Chisom evokes consternation in the town gossips, forces the Judge's daughter, Laurel McKelva Hand, to reassess her life, and in the end leaves her able to give up the ties of the past and to live in the present.

In addition to fiction, Welty has written introductions—for Jackson cookbooks, an anthology of suspense stories, and collections of others' stories—as well as occasional essays, reviews, and critical articles. *The Eye of the Story* (1978), containing 20 essays and 15 book reviews, attests to her skill as a critic. *One Time, One Place* (1971) marked the publication of photographs Welty had taken in the 1930s during her various assignments for the WPA in Mississippi. The photographs are of the Mississippi countryside,

its black farmers and teachers and workers, its churches, its crossroad stores, its houses and shacks. They reflect Welty's keen eye and her sensitive response to man and nature as surely as does her fiction.

A prominent theme in Welty's work, in the stories as well as the novels, is the mystery of human life and human relationships. For example, the nameless couple in ''No Place for You, My Love'' have come from unhappy relationships and meet by chance in a New Orleans restaurant. Their day together, however, does not result in a solution of the situations they left nor does it lead them into a love affair with each other. The force of mutability is another theme insistently at work as young characters discover love for the first time, as mothers and fathers watch their daughters grow up and marry and move away, as characters become aware of the approach of old age, as life is measured by the rituals of birthdays, reunions, weddings, and funerals. Some of these changes bring almost insufferable loneliness to characters: Miss Eckhart, in ''June Recital,'' loses all contact with pupils and society; Snowdie MacLain of ''Shower of Gold'' lives through the years of her husband's wandering; Virgie Rainey approaches middle age in ''The Wanderers,'' with her career as a pianist unrealized and her love life a series of second-rate affairs; in ''The Whole World Knows,'' Eugene MacLain, unhappy with his wife and living in San Francisco, far away from Morgana, the town of his youth, grieves for his dead daughter.

Equally important as a theme in Welty's fiction is the restorative power of love. Gloria and Jack Renfro (*Losing Battles*) may fail in their respective roles as intellectual and financial saviors, and their private world of marriage seems continually threatened by the imposing force and sheer numbers of the Beecham and Renfro families. The fact and power of their love, however, cannot be denied. Some characters experience an excess of love and joy, quite beyond their ability to communicate— Marjorie in ''Flowers for Marjorie,'' the American girl in ''The Bride of Innisfallen,'' the deaf boy in ''First Love,'' and Hazel in ''The Wide Net.'' If any writer has ever brought to life the dignity of the human spirit, Welty has certainly done so in the old, dying Solomon, husband to a young wife (''Livvie''); in the simple couple, Sonny and his woman (''Death of a Traveling Salesman''); and most assuredly in Phoenix Jackson in ''A Worn Path,'' whose persistent journey of selfless love and devotion indeed numbers her among the saints.

In Welty's first volume, Katherine Anne Porter praised her range of mood, place, tone, and material, and this wide range has been present in Welty's subsequent work. If place is usually the South, it is place particularized, made concrete, rendered visually and aurally. If, as some critics have charged, Welty has not often taken the South's social turmoil as subject matter, she has always been sensitive to the injustice of human beings to each other, has dealt with that injustice in her fiction, and has rightly maintained the necessity for a writer to be a writer, not a tractarian. (Her most explicit statement on this point is the essay ''Must the Novelist Crusade?'' in *The Eye of the Story*.) Welty's writing skill is particularly evident in the inevitably ''right'' dialogue, the tale-telling that reflects an individual's character. Welty has had success with scenes built on external confrontations as well as on internal meditation and reflection ("vortexes of quiet," they are called in "The Bride of Innisfallen"). She makes use of surrealism, of dream and fantasy and myth, of accurate details gleaned from careful observation and from a lifelong habit of insatiable reading.

A distinguishing feature of Welty's fiction is what she calls "that dateless quality"—detail. The varieties of roses in Ethel's garden in "Kin," the contents of the luncheon basket in "The Bride of Innisfallen," Granny's birthday gifts in *Losing Battles*, or the wedding activities in *Delta Wedding* are carefully and rightly chosen. Character names and place names emerge after thoughtful selection, as illustrated by Welty's explanation of the young husband's name change in "Death of a Traveling Salesman": "Rafe" in the 1936 version became "Sonny" when that story appeared in *A Curtain of Green* in 1941. The change was not only to a more indigenous name but to one that heightened an intended ambiguity.

The spirit of celebration, of lived life, is of singular importance in much of Welty's fiction. While there are always serious matters at the heart of her fiction, it is also true that the comic spirit is a significant force, not merely entertaining but also conveying thoughtful commentary. Standard comic devices are found: disingenuous characters (Leota in "Petrified Man"), eccentric characters (Aunt Cleo in *Losing Battles*), and homely figures of speech. In "Why I Live at the P.O.," Sister valiantly cooks away, trying "to stretch two chickens over five people and a completely unexpected child into the bargain without one moment's notice." Comedy of situation, comic one-liners, and ironic juxtapositions—used by Welty in a variety of stories—confirm the presence of the comic spirit at the base of Welty's fiction. She writes, in the essay "The Radiance of Jane Austen," that comedy "is social and positive, and exacting. Its methods, its boundaries, its *point*, all belong to the familiar." For Welty, the comic spirit is true and natural.

The publication of *The Collected Stories* (1980, winner of the American Book Award in 1981) gave critics the opportunity to reassess three decades of Welty's work. Reviewers were particularly impressed with the range of her work. Indeed, Walter Clemons found her "an experimental writer with access to the demonic. . . . She is bigger and stranger than we have supposed." If some of Welty's prose has occasionally been described as deformed, if she has sometimes been charged with presenting an imprecise landscape and using vague language, most of her fiction challenges our reading power, speaks to our hearts, and convinces us her world of fiction embodies the best and truest of human experience.

Her work spanning a period of more than 50 years, Welty ranks among the most extraordinary writers of the 20th century. Her lyrical passages, her transcendence of conventional narrative form, and her concern for the inner stirrings of her characters have invited comparisons to Virginia Woolf. Into commonplace events and surroundings Welty can infuse an illusory quality, invoking myths, and interweaving shades of memory. In this dreamlike light, she strikes what is true and concrete in human relationships. The unbridgeable gulfs that separate us, the experiences drawing us together—these, she writes, are her "true subjects."

In 1984 Welty published her autobiography *One Writer's Beginnings*. In this book, she celebrates the clarifying power of memory, capturing her past in a stream of individual moments and events. With all the humor and attention to detail Welty exhibits in her fiction, the author recreates the Jackson, Mississippi, of her childhood, once again painting a lasting portrait of the American South. Throughout *One Writer's Beginnings*, Welty focuses on her development as a writer. As a young girl, surrounded by books, reading constantly, Welty had begun to attune her ear to the rhythms and cadences of the written word. In addition, the gossip and anecdotes flying recklessly about her small hometown provided a fertile environment in which she learned the art of telling tales. Welty devotes the third and final chapter of *One Writer's Beginnings* to reflections on her career and on writing in general, offering a window on both the forces that move a master artist and the act of creation itself. The book achieved universal acclaim, and received an American Book award.

In 1989 Welty published *Photographs*, her second collection of what she likes to refer to as "snapshots." She also continued to contribute articles to such publications as *Atlantic*, the *New Yorker*, and the *New York Times Review of Books*.

Welty possesses the coveted honors America awards its writers: including the American Book Award, National Medal for Literature (1980), the American Academy of Arts and Letters Howells Medal, the National Institute of Arts and Letters Gold Medal for the Novel, the Presidential Medal of Freedom (1980), Commonwealth Award for distinguished service in literature from the Modern Language Association (1984), the Chevalier de l'Ordre des Arts et Lettres (1987), and the National Medal of Art (1987), the National Book Foundation Medal (1991), the Cleanth Brooks Medal in Southern Letters (1991), the PEN/Malamud Award for excellence in the short story (1993), induction into France's Legion of Honor (1996), and numerous honorary degrees.

Selecting Welty as the first living author for inclusion in the monumental Library of America series, the publisher cited Salman Rushdie's remark that her work is "impossible to overpraise." In honor of Welty's 90th birthday, 22 contributors describe her impact in *Eudora Welty: Writers' Reflections upon First Reading Welty* (1999). Barry Hannah marvels at her "soul-traveling magic" in creating such characters as a jazz virtuoso and a lonely salesman, and Doris Betts reflects that she "has influenced generations of writers while her lucid and luminous prose defies imitation."

At the end of the decade, osteoporosis made it difficult for Welty to leave her home in Jackson, and arthritis brought a stop to the writing career began in the 1930s. Her final book-length project was an anthology, the *Norton Book of Friendship* (1991), coedited with Ronald A. Sharp. A revised, silver anniversary edition of *One Time, One Place,* Welty's book of Depression-era photographs, appeared in 1996; "The Death of a Traveling Salesman" (1936) was reprinted in *The First Story* (1999), along with Welty's essay about the story's composition.

Although no comprehensive collection has been made of her letters, Michael Kreyling's *Author and Agent: Eudora Welty and Diarmuid Russell* (1991) is structured around more than 30 years of correspondence between Welty and the literary agent who offered her his assistance in 1940. Another important gathering is *A Writer's Eye: Collected Book Reviews* (1994), Pearl Amelia McHaney's edition of the 67 reviews Welty wrote between 1942 and 1984. According to McHaney, these pieces (most of them published in the *New York Times Book Review*) are "as sensory-laden, as thoughtful, and as well-crafted as her stories," whether she is discussing books about World War II or volumes of fairy tales.

Scholars have studied the full range of Welty's work, from the short stories that are considered her greatest achievement to her photographs, her bestselling 1984 memoir, and her longer fiction, most notably *Delta Wedding* (1946) and *Losing Battles* (1970). Emphasizing her "compassionate vision and memorable incantation," the novelist Reynolds Price predicts that American authors will continue to find Welty "a guide to both the threatening shades and the brilliant peaks of human life."

OTHER WORKS: *The Bride of Innisfallen* (1955). *The Shoe Bird* (1964). *One Time, One Place: Mississippi in the Depression. A Snapshot Album* (1971). *A Worn Path* (editor, with Ronald A. Sharp, 1991).

The manuscripts and papers of Eudora Welty are housed in the Department of Archives and History (Jackson, Mississippi) and at the Humanties Research Center of the University of Texas at Austin.

BIBLIOGRAPHY: Appel, A., Jr., *Eudora Welty* (1965). Binding, P., *The Still Moment: Eudora Welty, Portrait of a Writer* (1994). Bloom, H., *Eudora Welty* (1986). Brantley, W., *Feminine Sense in Southern Memoir: Smith, Glasgow, Welty, and Hurston* (1993). Bryant, J. A., Jr., *Eudora Welty* (1968). Carson, B. H., *Eudora Welty: Two Pictures at Once in Her Frame* (1992). Champion, L., ed., *The Critical Response to Eudora Welty's Fiction* (1994). *Civil War Women: The Civil War Seen Through Women's Eyes in Stories by Louisa May Alcott, Kate Chopin, Eudora Welty, and Other Great Women Writers* (reissue, 1990). Desmond, J. F., ed., *A Still Moment: Essays on the Art of Eudora Welty* (1978). Devlin, A., *Eudora Welty's Chronicle: A Story of Mississippi Life* (1983). Devlin, A., ed., *Eudora Welty: A Life in Literature* (1987). Dollarhide, L., and A. Abadie, eds., *Eudora Welty: A Form of Thanks* (1979). Gretlund, N. J., and K. Westarp, eds., *The Late Novels of Eudora Welty* (1998). Gygax, F., *Serious Daring from Within: Feminine Narrative Strategies in Eudora Welty's Novels* (1990). Harrison, S., *Eudora Welty and Virginia Woolf: Gender, Genre, and Influence* (1997). Howard, Z., *The Rhetoric of Eudora Welty's Short Stories* (1973). Isaacs, N., *Eudora Welty* (1968). Kreyling, M., *The Achievement of Eudora Welty* (1980). Kreyling, M., *Author and Agent: Eudora Welty and Diarmuid Russell* (1991). Johnston, C. A. *Eudora Welty: A Study of the Short Fiction* (1997). MacKethan, L. H., *Daughters of Time: Creating Woman's Voice in Southern Story* (1990). Manning, C., *With Opening like Morning Glories: Eudora Welty and the Love of Storytelling* (1985). Manz-Kunz, M., *Eudora Welty: Aspects of Reality in Her Short Fiction* (1971). Marsh, R., *The Dragon's Blood: Feminist Intertextuality in Eudora Welty's Golden Apples* (1994). McHaney, P. A., ed., *Eudora Welty: Writers' Reflections upon First Reading Eudora Welty* (1999). Mortimer, G., *Daughter of the Swan: Love and Knowledge in Eudora Welty's Fiction* (1994). Pingatore, D. R., *A Reader's Guide to the Short Stories of Eudora Welty* (1996). Polk, N., *Eudora Welty: A Bibliography of Her Work* (1994). Prenshaw, P., ed., *Eudora Welty: Critical Essays* (1979). Prenshaw, P., *Conversations with Eudora Welty* (1984). Prenshaw, P., ed., *More Conversations with Eudora Welty* (1996). Schmidt, P., *The Heart of the Story: Eudora Welty's Short Fiction* (1991). Senter, Lester (vocals), *The Memory Is a Living Thing: Songs Based on the Writings of Eudora Welty* (CD, 1996). Spacks, P., *Gossip* (1985). Trouard, D., ed., *Eudora Welty: Eye of the Storyteller* (1989). Turner, W., and L. Harding, eds., *Critical Essays on Eudora Welty* (1989). Vande Kieft, R., *Eudora Welty* (1962). Waldron, A., *Eudora: A Writer's Life* (1998) Westling, L., *Sacred Groves and Ravaged Gardens: The Fiction of Eudora Welty, Carson McCullers, and Flannery O'Connor* (1985). Weston, R., *Gothic Traditions and Narrative Techniques in the Fiction of Eudora Welty* (1994). Westling, L., *Sacred Groves and Ravaged Gardens: The Fiction of Eudora Welty, Carson McCullers, and Flannery O'Connor* (1985).

Reference works: *ANR* (1991). *CLC* (1998). *DLB* (1991; 1994). *FC* (1990). *Oxford Companion to Women's Writing in the United States* (1995).

Other references: *Atlantic* (Mar. 1984). *Boston Globe Magazine* (29 Nov. 1992). *Brightleaf: A Southern Review of Books* (Winter 1998). *Delta Review* (Nov. 1977). *Eudora Welty Newsletter. Mississippi Quarterly* (1973; 1986; 1997). *Newsweek* (20 Feb. 1984). *New Yorker* (20 Feb. 1984, 5 Oct. 1998). *NYTBR* (19 Feb. 1984, 22 Oct. 1989, 22 April 1990). *Oxford American* (Nov./Dec. 1998). *Shenandoah* (1969). *Southern Literary Journal* (Spring 1989). *Southern Quarterly* (Fall 1990, Fall 1993). *Southern Review* (Spring 1990, Autumn 1997). *TLS* (20 July 1984).

—ELIZABETH EVANS,
UPDATED BY JEROME CHOU AND JOAN WYLIE HALL

WEST, Dorothy

Born 2 June 1907, Boston, Massachusetts; **died** 16 August 1998, Oak Bluffs, Martha's Vineyard, Massachusetts
Daughter of Isaac Christopher and Rachel Pease Benson West

Novelist, short story writer, editor, and critic Dorothy West decided as a child that she never wanted to be the last leaf on the tree. Yet with her death at the age of ninety-one, the person Langston Hughes nicknamed "the Kid" of the Harlem Renaissance was indeed the last surviving member from a luminous group of writers, painters, musicians, poets, and other artists who created the most important cultural renaissance of the 20th century. With two novels, a collection of essays, and numerous short stories to her credit, West's talent and social awareness marked her as a writer of enduring significance.

West was the only surviving child of Rachel Pease Benson and Isaac Christopher West. She came of age in Boston, where her family joined the slim ranks of Boston's black upper middle class. Her father, born a slave, built a prosperous wholesale fruit and vegetable business in the shadow of Fanuiel Hall. This success allowed his family a fairly privileged life in predominantly white Brookline, Massachusetts. The Wests were among the first blacks to summer on Martha's Vineyard.

West began her formal education at age two under the tutelage of Bessie Trotter, sister of Monroe Nathan Trotter, then editor of the *Boston Guardian*. At age four, she entered Farragut School in Boston, where she proved herself capable of doing second-grade work. She completed her elementary education at Matin School in Boston's Mission District. A precocious writer, she began to write short stories at age seven. Her first story, ''Promise and Fulfillment,'' was published in the *Boston Globe*, and at age ten she won prizes from the *Boston Post*. After elementary school she went to the Girls' Latin School, graduating in 1923. She then took courses at Boston University and the Columbia University Graduate School of Journalism.

West's long association with Harlem began in 1926 when she and a cousin, Helene Johnson, both still teenagers, entered a national writing contest sponsored by *Opportunity* magazine. They were both invited to attend the annual awards dinner in New York City. They stayed at the Harlem Young Women's Christian Association (YWCA). When the two arrived at 125th Street in Harlem, West remembered, they were delighted to see ''all these colored people'' and, unable to imagine any other reason for such a gathering, asked, ''When is the parade?'' That night, West's entry, ''The Typewriter'' (1926), shared second place with Zora Neale Hurston, then 25 years of age. This story reflected West's fascination with people's hidden motivations. With this heady experience behind them, West and her cousin soon moved to the city.

During the 1930s she traveled to Russia to make a movie about the life of African Americans. Traveling with Langston Hughes and 20 other blacks, the film, *Black and White*, was a story of the oppression of American blacks. The project was dropped following accusations of association with communism.

When she returned from Russia, West felt guilty that at the age of twenty-five she had not written more. With her own $40, she published the first issue of *Challenge*. The periodical was only published quarterly for a few years, but it contained the best of black literature at the time. The work of Langston Hughes, Arna Bontemps, Zora Neale Hurston, and Claude McKay maintained the journal's high caliber of writing. With the failure of the periodical in 1937, a more ambitious version was launched. The renamed journal, *New Challenge*, listed West and Marian Minus as coeditors and Richard Wright as associate editor. Only one issue was published, but the magazine reflected West's increasing interest in class issues as well as the struggles of black people generally. When the second journal folded, West became a welfare investigator in Harlem, which inspired ''Mammy'' a story, published in *Opportunity* in 1940. She then joined the

Federal Writers Project of the Works Progress Administration (WPA) until its demise in the 1940s.

In the more than 60 short stories she wrote throughout her career, West showed that form to be her forte. Like Dostoyevsky, to whom critics have compared her narrative style, West probed deeply into the minds of her characters, who face ''moral, psychological, and social confinement,'' wrote Sally Ann H. Ferguson in the *Dictionary of Literary Biography*. And much like the Russian novelist, West also shared a belief in the innocent nature of children.

Although the short story was the mainstay of her career, West published two novels, *The Living Is Easy* (1948) and *The Wedding* (1995). In the first, she reveals the shadow side of the aspiring and proper black Bostonians. Adopting a tone of ironic humor, she satirized the pretensions of the Boston black elite, especially their desire to distinguish themselves from ''ordinary'' blacks. According to Mary Helen Washington, West wrote about the black middle class from the viewpoint of ''the marginalized insider, both a fierce critic of the bourgeois life and a loyal daughter upholding the values of family and class.'' The central figure of *The Living Is Easy* is Cleo Judson, a neurotic beauty who marries an older, financially secure man. She then invites her three sisters and their husbands to live with them, leading to the demise of all their marriages. The novel earned West high marks for its treatment of the class snobbery, insularity, and all-around shallowness of the New England black bourgeoisie, whom West termed the ''genteel poor.''

In the 1950s West began *The Wedding*. She was unable to find a publisher because its theme of interracial marriage may have been too controversial. West set the unfinished novel aside. She continued to write and contributed short pieces to the daily newspaper on Martha's Vineyard, where she made her permanent residence in 1943. She returned to *The Wedding* in the early 1990s and finished it. Published in 1995, the novel is set on Martha's Vineyard and tells the story of Shelby Cole, who, much to the consternation of her parents, Dr. Clark and Corinne Cole, is preparing to wed a white jazz musician. Lute McNeil, a compulsive womanizer, is determined to stop Shelby's wedding, confident that he can convince her to marry him. West tells Shelby's story while relaying the intertwined histories of her ancestors. The reader meets a fascinating cast of characters, from slaves to a college president, all the while being made privy to the striving for achievement, status, and light skin color that has marked the early decades of this family's history. One reviewer described the novel as ''an account of a journey down many roads, along with which the seeds planted so many generations ago have engendered a family tree of many colors.'' West draws the many strands of her story together in a genuinely cathartic ending.

A cross section of West's writing can be found in her collection *The Richer, The Poorer: Stories, Sketches, and Reminiscences* (1995). Her prize-winning piece ''The Typewriter,'' first published in 1926, is included, as is the widely anthologized ''Jack in the Pot'' from 1940. Numerous pieces from the *Vineyard Gazette* appear as well. West remained constant as a chronicler of several generations of black middle-class Bostonians. She was constant, too, in her devotion to the craft of writing.

BIBLIOGRAPHY: Reference Works: *African American Almanac* (1997). *African American Women* (1993). *Black Women in America II* (1993). *Black Writers* (1994). *Bloomsbury Guide to Women's Literature* (1992). *CA* 143 (1994). *Encyclopedia of African-American Culture and History* 5 (1996). *The Essential Black Literature Guide* (1996). *Harlem Renaissance and Beyond* (1990). *The Schomburg Center Guide to Black Literature* (1996). *Selected Black American Authors: An Illustrated Bio-Bibliography* (1977).

Other References: *NYT* (19 Aug. 1998). *NYT Magazine* (3 Jan. 1999).

—CELESTE DEROCHE

WEST, Jessamyn

Born 18 July 1902, near Butlerville, Indiana; **died** February 1984
Daughter of Eldo R. and Grace Milhous West; **married** Harry M. McPherson, 1923; **children:** one daughter

The eldest of four children, Jessamyn West was reared in Yorba Linda, California. She began writing—novels, short stories, essays, autobiography, articles, reviews—after a severe case of tuberculosis halted her formal education while she was in graduate school. West married Harry McPherson in 1923, and later adopted an Irish daughter.

The female maturation process is a frequent pattern in West's fiction, which treats girls' social, emotional, and familial joys and difficulties evenhandedly and well. A central problem for the young protagonists is often the mother-daughter relationship: mothers, uneasy with their own rigidly controlled sensuality, teach their daughters to fear sexuality; furthermore, they often insist the elder daughters help curb sexual impulses in their younger sisters.

In *The Witch Diggers* (1951) and *South of the Angels* (1960), the maturation stories are embedded in a cluster of subplots. Here, the healthy acceptance of sexuality is the symbol of genuine maturity and the ability to love. The locales, eras, and atmospheres of both books are beautifully wrought. Despite some problems with structure, these novels succeed through the power of the maturation device, and the portraits of the sisters Cate and Em Conboy in the first are splendid.

Leafy Rivers (1967) and *The Massacre at Fall Creek* (1975), both set on the Indiana frontier, provide variations of the female maturation pattern. In West's most traditional maturation novel, Leafy comes to terms with her flawed marriage by undergoing the usual *Bildungsroman* journey, presented in flashbacks. The story of the first whites to be executed for murdering Native Americans

is the subject of *The Massacre at Fall Creek*, told largely through the perceptions of Hannah Cape, who learns to accept her own limitations as well as those of her lover. Clearly, this novel compares Hannah's maturation with the coming of age of the frontier; the device is compelling and works well. These books present large casts of characters portrayed with West's usual sound insight.

One of West's most successful forms is the collection of a series of interrelated short stories into books having the impact of novels. *Cress Delahanty* (1953), set in the California of West's youth, is the sunniest of the female maturation pieces, the portrait of a gifted girl who learns to value herself and her abilities. *The Friendly Persuasion* (1945) and *Except for Me and Thee* (1969) draw upon the Quaker family background and Indiana locale of West's mother's memories, which provided West with "the look of the land, the temper of the people, the manner of speech." Probably the best known of her books, these "Quaker stories," depicting the deepening relationship and developing family of Jess and Eliza Birdwell, avoid sentimentality through an excellent use of humor. *The Friendly Persuasion* was made into a successful movie in 1956; *To See the Dream* (1957) is West's account of her work on the film.

Central to all West's work is her basic theme: genuine love is acceptance; the lover may not approve of all the traits and habits of the loved one, but to demand alteration as the price of love is unfair. This theme is stated most overtly in the autobiographical *The Woman Said Yes: Encounters with Life and Death—Memoirs* (1976, reprinted 1986), which celebrates Grace West's influence upon her daughters. The emphasis is on Grace's life-enhancing qualities, and West attributes both her own recovery from tuberculosis and her sister Carmen's capacity to defeat cancer (by choosing suicide) to strength learned from their mother.

A Matter of Time (1966), which is West's best novel, also deals with a mother's influence and love, but here redemptive understanding occurs late. As Tassie nurses Blix, her younger sister, through terminal illness, the middle-aged women discuss their mother's use of Tassie to control Blix's behavior. This exploitation has severely damaged the women and their relationship, but they now validate their sisterly love by acceptance of themselves and one another. The maturation story appears in flashbacks, its strength completely overshadowing any moral question arising from the fact Tassie helps Blix commit suicide. This decision is presented as a final affirmation of Blix's humanity and her will.

In *The Life I Really Lived* (1979), Orpha Chase, successful novelist, attempts to put her experiences into perspective. She recounts the central events of her Kentucky girlhood and of her later life in California and Hawaii. Each step of the real journey as well as the maturation journey is illuminated by Orpha's analysis of the people—parents, husbands, daughter, lover, friends—who influenced and formed her. As in *A Matter of Time*, the impact of a sibling is especially important. Serious and sometimes grim, *The Life I Really Lived* is less successful than *A Matter of Time* and sometimes recalls *The Massacre at Fall Creek*, for it reflects

West's clear grasp of the danger, difficulty, and complexity as well as the joys and triumphs of the life of her protagonist, who stands for the women whose lives bridged the gap between the frontier and "civilization."

Considered an able, serious craftsperson, West was noted for her detailed, accurate settings and the careful development of motivation which makes fine characterization a dominant quality in her sound work.

OTHER WORKS: *A Mirror for the Sky* (1948). *The Reading Public* (1952). *Love, Death, and the Ladies' Drill Team* (1955). *Love Is Not What You Think* (1959). *The Quaker Reader* (1962). *The Chilekings* (1967). *Crimson Ramblers of the World, Farewell* (1970). *Hide and Seek: A Continuing Journey* (1973, reprinted 1987). *The Secret Look* (1974). *Violence* (pamphlet, 1976). *Double Discovery: A Journey* (1980, reprinted 1981). *Collected Stories of Jessamyn West* (1986, 1987).

BIBLIOGRAPHY: Farmer, A. D., *Jessamyn West* (1982). Farmer, A. D., *Jessamyn West: A Descriptive and Annotated Bibliography* (1998). Sherwood, R. I., *A Special Kind of Double: Sisters in British and American Fiction* (1991). Shivers, A. S., *Jessamyn West* (1972). Shivers, A. S., *Jessamyn West: Revised Edition* (1992). Whistler, K. A. "Social Justice in the California Fiction of Jessamyn West" (thesis, 1996). Yalom, M. and M. B. Davis, eds., *Women Writers of the West Coast: Speaking of their Lives and Careers* (1983).

Reference works: *Oxford Companion to Women's Writing in the United States* (1995). *Twayne's Women Authors* (CD-ROM, 1995).

Other references: *EJ* (Sept. 1957). *Expl* (Dec. 1964). *Indiana Magazine of History* (Dec. 1971). *Nation* (30 March 1957). *NYTBR* (14 Jan. 1951). *SR* (24 Oct. 1970). *Writers Digest* (May 1967, Jan. 1976). *An Interview with Jessamyn West* (audiocassette, 1980). *Jessamyn West Talks About Her Career and About Other Writers, with Dick Cavett* (audio recording, 1980).

—JANE S. BAKERMAN

WEST, Lillie

Born 11 October 1860, West Burlington, Iowa; died 3 July 1938, Chicago, Illinois
Wrote under: Amy Leslie, Marie Stanley
Daughter of Albert W. and Kate Webb West; married Harry Brown, 1880 (divorced); Frank H. Buck, 1901 (divorced 1916)

Lillie West was the daughter of an Iowa newspaperman and banker. After graduating with honors from St. Mary's Academy in Notre Dame, Indiana, and receiving a gold medal from the Chicago Conservatory of Music, she joined the Grayson Comic Opera Company, one of the many troupes formed in the 1870s to tour the phenomenally popular Gilbert and Sullivan operetta *H.M.S. Pinafore*. West rapidly rose to prominence on the light-opera stage. She married singer Harry Brown, and they performed together on Broadway and toured with the famous Grau Opera Company. When her four-year-old son died of diphtheria, a grief-stricken West retired from the stage. She settled in Chicago, and she and Brown were later divorced.

Her second husband was a twenty-three-year-old bell captain at the Virginia Hotel, where West lived. In her forties at the time, West dyed her hair to win the man who was later to earn the nickname "Bring 'em Back Alive" as a big-game hunter and author. He divorced her in 1916, claiming she humiliated him in public, but they were good friends in her last years.

West began contributing brief sketches to the Chicago *Daily News* after the death of her son; she became the first woman racetrack reporter and finally worked as a drama critic. As such she served for over 40 years, using the pen name Amy Leslie. West's style might best be described, like her personality, as effervescent. In a 1906 feature story on Sarah Bernhardt's tent tour of Texas, for example, she writes: "If no cyclone blows Sarah clear over the Gulf of Mexico, and if the coyotes are protected by game laws and warned out of gunshot and the centipedes are still hibernating, Mme. Bernhardt will triumph prismatically and bring beauty of art, splendor of charm, amazement, and a superb example to the youth and femininity of Dallas by her courage, her repertoire, her inexhaustible ambition, her diet of applause through sixty years and her power of concentration on the American dollar unadulterated and beatified."

Through the years, West encouraged many beginning stage and screen performers whose careers brought justification to the early praise she had lavished on them. She was the personal friend of such outstanding actors and actresses as Edwin Booth, Helena Modjeska, Julia Marlowe, E. H. Sothern, and Lily Langtry, whose intimate portraits she sketched in *Some Players* (1899).

In 1930 West published her only novel, *Gulf Stream*, using the name Marie Stanley. In it a fair-skinned black heroine spends a lifetime trying to deny her ethnic heritage, but is finally chastened when her daughter grows up to affirm her blackness with pride.

West was a popular critic and personality. Among the many affectionate tributes to her is one written by Ben Hecht, upon the occasion of her retirement: "There is a high wind about Amy that blows your hat off. She is as hilarious as a feast day. Her conversation is as successful as a circus. And she looks like a Mardi Gras. . . .Her phrases still rise like Fourth-of-July balloon ascensions."

OTHER WORKS: *Amy Leslie at the Fair* (1893).
The New York Public Library has a collection of clippings and photographs relating to Lillie West (Amy Leslie).

BIBLIOGRAPHY: *Bookman* (Feb. 1901). Chicago *Daily News* (5 July 1939). Chicago *Herald Examiner* (4 July 1939). *Chicago*

Tribune (4 July 1939). *NYT* (30 Aug. 1930, 4 July 1939). *Show World* (17 Aug. 1907).

—FELICIA HARDISON LONDRÉ

WEST, Mae

Born 17 August 1893, Brooklyn, New York; **died** 22 November 1980, Los Angeles, California
Daughter of John and Mathilda Doegler West; **married** once (annulled)

Mae West's description of her childhood (in the early chapters of her autobiography, *Goodness Had Nothing to Do with It*, 1959) illustrates the qualities that were to become her caricature: she learned early that "two and two are four, and five will get you ten if you know how to work it." She began her performing career at age seven. When, as a young actress and singer, she was criticized for "wriggling" on stage during performances, she realized it was the "force of an extraordinary sex-personality that made quite harmless lines and mannerisms seem suggestive." Her one marriage was annulled; she had no children.

West was producer, author, and star of *SEX* (1927). At first, the title scared away both booking agents and theatergoers. Ultimately, however, the play was a success, firmly casting the stylistic idiom in which West, actress, author, and woman, would be known: the tough, street-smart, unashamedly sexual "dame"— no man's fool—whose unrelenting self-promotion is exceeded only by her vanity.

West believed *The Drag* (1928), in which she did not appear, was a serious approach to a modern social problem, but her sensitivity to the issue of homosexuality is relative to her time. She writes that the homosexual's "abnormal tendencies (have) brought disaster to his family, friends, and himself"—and her message is that "an understanding of the problems of all homosexuals by society could avert such social tragedies."

SEX and *The Drag* ran simultaneously—*SEX* in New York City (for 41 weeks, before, thanks to efforts by the Society for the Suppression of Vice, West was arrested and jailed for a short time) and *The Drag* in Paterson, New Jersey. The district attorney in New York had *The Drag* closed and the entire cast arrested after only two performances.

Diamond Lil (1932) was written specifically to attract the female audience her earlier plays had failed to draw. Later filmed (as *She Done Him Wrong*, 1933) and even turned into a novel (1932), it features perhaps the most famous West character in a "grand Bowery folk play." One critic wrote an appropriately picturesque summation: "It's worth swimming to Brooklyn to see her descend those dance hall stairs, to be present while she lolls in a golden bed reading the *Police Gazette*, murders her girlfriend, wrecks the Salvation Army, and sings as much of 'Frankie and Johnny' as the mean old law allows."

The novel follows the footsteps and idiom of Diamond Lil. The narrative is liberally dosed with slang and hickish diction; women are "skirts," policemen are "dicks," and are all vividly drawn. It is lively and reasonably well written, given the genre.

In *The Constant Sinner* (originally titled *Babe Gordon*, 1930), a novel, the siren Babe "starts low and ends up high"— reversing everything mothers tell their daughters about the fate of bad girls. Babe is celebrated by the author, in part, for knowing her own mind and keeping the control of her body up to no one but herself. Again, West deals with subjects (such as interracial sex) socially unmentionable in the U.S. of the 1930s; yet she does it all within the confines of her public's expectations of the West caricature.

Pleasure Man (1975), West's novelization of *The Drag*, is about a bisexual Broadway headliner, Rodney Terrill, "whose wild sex-affairs with women," West declares, "led to unexpected but well-deserved difficulties." Again, street talk prevails, but in the novel the prose is often laced with attempts at more eloquent diction—mixed usage with mixed results.

Beginning in 1932, West appeared in many films. She wrote (or cowrote—as with her plays and novels, her collaborative debts are often unclear) at least six of these. Films such as *She Done Him Wrong, I'm No Angel* (1933), and *My Little Chickadee* (1939)— the last of which was written with her costar, W. C. Fields—are considered comedy classics.

Her novel, stage, and film personae are one and the same, often a mirror of West herself: the woman who will not conform, in her words, to the "old-fashioned limits" men have "set on a woman's freedom of action." Unfortunately, West's sex-personality became legitimate for the American public only as she became more and more a caricature of herself. Her public self was laundered into a distant cousin, twice-removed, from West the woman, thereby making her frank yet refreshing sexuality laughable and comic, but legitimate.

An extension of American pulp literature, West's fiction receives little attention. She is well known, however, as the queen of the reverse sexist one-liners: Hatcheck Girl: "Goodness, what lovely diamonds!" West: "Goodness had nothing to do with it, dearie." Her contributions to American culture are immeasurable, yet—perhaps because her outrageous persona commands so much attention—her written work is virtually unrecognized. She was not only the performer but the author of plays and films in which she appeared, and she deserves to be acknowledged as a creative and successful comic playwright.

OTHER WORKS: *The Wit and Wisdom of Mae West* (edited by J. Weintraub, 1967). *Three Plays by Mae West* (1997).

BIBLIOGRAPHY: Baxt, G., *The Mae West Murder Case* (1993). Blubaugh, A., "Mae West and the Effects of the Camp Sensibility on the Sex Goddess" (thesis, 1997). Chipman, D., *Cool Women* (1998). Cole, W. and L. Phillips, eds., *Sex: Even More Fun You*

Can Have without Laughing (1990, published in Britain as *The Humour of Sex: From Aristotle to Mae West and Beyond*, 1990, 1995). Curry, R., *Power and Allure: The Mediation of Sexual Difference in the Star Image of Mae West* (1990). Curry, R., *Too Much of a Good Thing: Mae West as Cultural Icon* (1996). Hamilton, M., *When I'm Bad, I'm Better: Mae West, Sex, and American Entertainment* (1995). Ivanov, A. J., "Sexual Parody in American Comedic Film and Literature: 1925-1948" (dissertation, 1994). Janik, V. K., ed., *Fools and Jesters in Literature, Art, and History: A Bio-Bibliographical Sourcebook* (1998). Leider, E. W., *Becoming Mae West* (1997). Leonard, M., *Mae West: Empress of Sex* (1991). Malachosky, T., *Mae West* (collectors edition, 1993). Robertson, P., *Guilty Pleasures: Feminist Camp From Mae West to Madonna* (1996). Sochen, J., *Mae West: She Who Laughs, Lasts* (1992). Tuska, J., *The Complete Films of Mae West* (1992).

—DEBORAH H. HOLDSTEIN,
UPDATED BY SYDONIE BENET

WETHERALL, Elizabeth

See WARNER, Susan Bogert

WHARTON, Edith

Born 24 January 1862, New York, New York; **died** 11 August 1937, St. Brice-sous-Forêt, France
Also wrote under: Edith Jones
Daughter of George and Lucretia Rhinelander Jones; **married** Edward Wharton, 1885 (divorced)

The literary and social world of Edith Wharton's childhood was exclusive, old-fashioned, and wealthy: her parents were socially prominent and well-established in New York, with income derived from landholdings and tracing their family history back 300 years. Her childhood was spent wandering around Europe's most luxurious spas and cities with indolent and indulgent parents. When she was ten—already making up stories to amuse her parents and their friends—the family returned to New York City, where her adolescent years were spent in a brownstone on West 23rd Street and in a summer cottage at Newport.

Wharton was well educated in modern languages and good manners, but recognized an injustice immediately when she saw it. An early ambition to be the best-dressed woman in New York gave way to a stronger humanitarian instinct. When she organized an extensive refugee relief program during World War I the French government awarded her their Legion of Honor.

Her emotional life was vastly complicated: engaged to two other promising young men, she finally married the socially prominent Bostonian Edward Wharton. The early broken engagements—and the youthful death of one of her suitors—clearly

influenced the plots and themes of her fiction. Her marriage seems to have provided additional material since it was not only unhappy but sent both of the partners into profound depressions. Wharton coped with her own recurring bouts of illness by steadily writing, and trusting in close relationships with important literary and intellectual figures of her time including Henry James and Bernhard Berenson. Her husband turned to infidelity and embezzlement, which led to recriminations and finally to their divorce. Wharton was well aware of the intensity these dramas produced in her early writing, chiefly verse and short stories, and remarked in later years: "I regard them as the excesses of youth. They were all written at the top of my voice, and 'The Fullness of Life' is one long shriek. I may not write any better, but at least I hope that I write in a lower key."

Indeed Wharton's works of fiction with their keen social observation, rich detail, and penetrating satire have come to be regarded as masterful and important contributions to the literary tradition of the 20th century. In the course of her life and her writing Wharton rebelled against the rigid, traditional, stifling attitude toward women and toward the middle classes who had to work for a living. She began quietly with poems privately printed (by her mother) in 1878 and a quartet of short stories in *Scribner's Magazine*. Between those and her first full-length novel *The Valley of Decision* (1902) she produced many stories and three novellas: *Fast and Loose* (1867), *Bunner Sisters* (1892) and *The Touchstone* (1900). But this period of her life is most notable for *The Decoration of Houses* (1897), a study of interior arrangements and furniture in upper-class homes written with architect Ogden Codmen.

Her wildly successful novel, *The House of Mirth* (1905), with its contemporary theme and tragic heroine redeemed by an unexpected strength of character, brought instant fame to Wharton. It sold faster than any book ever published by Scribner's—and sold well over 140,000 copies in the first year. The novel's main character, Lily Bart, is a pathetic young woman trapped in the treacherous world of New York society and the murky depths of investment politics in turn-of-the-century America. Lily's determination to settle in a marriage of wealth and privilege leads her to compromise moral values, even to sacrifice love, in order to achieve her goal of a luxurious and idle life. This particular heroine and the times Wharton describes might have remained mysterious and unintelligible to modern readers without the happy coincidence that her stories are readily adaptable into screenplays. So her work has enjoyed a sort of revival in recent years. Several of Wharton's most famous novels including *The House of Mirth, Ethan Frome* (1911), and *The Age of Innocence* (1920) have appeared in respectable Hollywood versions, bringing her milieu—with its stiff tradition of innocent women, forced by circumstances or lack of moral judgement into social-climbing; and of ruggedly determined American men, grasping through necessity or design at wealth and its seductive power—to the sympathetic attention of the educated middle-class film buff.

Still it is a pleasure to pick up the *Library of America* two volume edition of her novels and stories. Here one finds her great novels of manners, *The Custom of the Country* (1913) and *The*

Age of Innocence. These two long studies of love affairs, entanglements, and marriages in the time between the "old New York" and the new era focus on the differences in depth and quality of feeling that protected the boundaries of established society from the errors of youthful exuberance. The indefatigable and magnificently lovely Undine Spragg dashes through *The Custom of the Country* at furious pace. She has several husbands from both the American and European aristocracy and trashes them with equal fervor and disregard.

Undine cares supremely for herself—the consequences to anyone else, of course, are unimportant—and demonstrates the tenacity and single-mindedness which made America a nation of great achievements: "If I were only sure of knowing what you expect!" her future father-in-law jokes with her at dinner; and she replies "Why, *everything!*" The perfect foil for Undine's vulgar scenes is the deep serenity of Countess Olenska (formerly Ellen Mingott) in *The Age of Innocence*. The Countess must tolerate the upstarts in New York society as she struggles to assert an identity against the pressures of her tyrant of a European husband and her unyieldingly stiff and unsympathetic American relatives. Ellen Olenska's gentleness and self-deprecating humor linger even as she slips away to Paris and obscurity while those less able but stronger dominate the rest of the novel: "When I turn back into myself now," she explains, " I am like a child going at night into a room where there's always a light."

Wharton died and was buried in her beloved French countryside, where she had lived contented for two decades; though she remained essentially American, the comforts of a European pace were irresistible to a writer.

OTHER WORKS: *Verses* (1878). *The Greater Inclination* (1897). *Crucial Instances* (1901). *The Joy of Living*, by H. Suderman (translated by Wharton 1902). *Sanctuary* (1903). *The Descent of Man, and Other Stories* (1904). *Italian Villas, and Their Gardens* (1904). *Italian Backgrounds* (1905). *Fruit of the Tree* (1907). *Madame de Treyms* (1907). *The Hermit and the Wild Woman, and Other Stories* (1908). *A Motor Flight through France* (1908). *Artemis to Actaeon, and other Verses* (1909). *Tales of Men and Ghosts* (1910). *The Reef* (1912). *Fighting France, from Dunkerque to Belfort* (1915). *The Book of the Homeless* (1916). *Xingu, and Other Stories* (1916). *Summer* (1917). *The Marne* (1918). *French Ways and Their Meaning* (1919). *In Morocco* (1920). *The Glimpses of the Moon* (1922). *A Son at the Front* (1923). *Old New York* (1924). *The Mother's Recompense* (1925). *The Writing of Fiction* (1925). *Here and Beyond* (1926). *Twelve Poems* (1926). *Twilight Sleep* (1927). *The Children* (1928). *Hudson River Bracketed* (1929). *Certain People* (1930). *The Gods Arrive* (1932). *Human Nature* (1933). *A Backward Glance* (1934). *The World Over* (1936). *Ghosts* (1937). *The Buccaneers* (1938). *Eternal Passion in English Poetry* (1939). *The Collected Short Stories of Edith Wharton* (2 vols., edited by R. W. B. Lewis, 1968).

BIBLIOGRAPHY: Ammons, E., *Edith Wharton's Argument with America* (1980). Ammons, E., *Conflicting Stories: American Women Writers at the Turn into the Twentieth Century* (1991). Auchincloss, L., *Edith Wharton* (1961). Bell, M., *Edith Wharton and Henry James: The Story of Their Friendship* (1965). Donovan, J., *After the Fall: The Demeter-Persphone Myth in Wharton, Cather, and Glasgow* (1989). Erlich, G., *The Sexual Education of Edith Wharton* (1992). Goodman, S., *Edith Wharton's Women: Friends and Rivals* (1990). Howe, I., ed., *Edith Wharton: A Collection of Critical Essays* (1962). Lawson, R. H., *Edith Wharton* (1977). Lewis, R. W. B., *Edith Wharton: A Biography* (1975). Lewis, R. W. B., and N. Lewis, eds., *The Letters of Edith Wharton* (1988). Lubbock, P., *Portrait of Edith Wharton* (1947). Lyde, M., *Edith Wharton: Convention and Morality in the Work of a Novelist* (1959). Maxwell, D. E. S., *American Fiction: The Intellectual Background* (1963). McDowell, M., *Edith Wharton* (1976). Nevius, B., *Edith Wharton: A Study of Her Fiction* (1953). Patterson, M. H., "Survival of the Best Fitted: The Trope of the New Woman in Margaret Murray Washington, Pauline Hopkins, Sui Sin Far, Edith Wharton and Mary Johnston, 1895-1913" (thesis, 1996). Springer, M., *Edith Wharton and Kate Chopin: A Reference Guide* (1976). Tuttleton, J., *The Novel of Manners in America* (1972). Waid, C., *Edith Wharton's Letters from the Underworld: Fictions of Women and Writing* (1991). Walton, G., *Edith Wharton: A Critical Interpretation* (1970). Wolff, C. G., *A Feast of Words: The Triumph of Edith Wharton* (1977).

Reference works: *Oxford Companion to Women's Writing in the United States* (1995).

Other references: *Critical Inquiry* (Mar. 1985). *Representations* (Winter 1985).

—KATHLEEN BONANN MARSHALL

WHEATLEY, Phillis

Born circa 1753, Senegal, Africa; **died** 5 December 1784, Boston, Massachusetts
Married John Peters, 1778; **children:** three, all of whom died young

Facts about Phillis (sometimes written as Phyllis) Wheatley's birth are unknown. The speculation of biographers that she was seven years old in 1760, when she was sold as a slave in Boston, is based on the condition of her teeth at the time. Susannah Wheatley, the wife of a prosperous Boston tailor, bought the frail, asthmatic child. It is inferred from her later recollection of a sunrise ritual and familiarity with Arabic script that her African background was that of a Senegalese Moslem.

Her nurturing with the Wheatley's two eighteen-year-old twins was remarkably pleasant and unique to the period. Struck by her sharp intellect, the Wheatleys, contrary to the law and the accepted morality of the times, immediately began to teach Phillis to read and write. In sixteen months, Wheatley was reading the Bible, and at the age of twelve, she began to learn Latin and read the classics of English literature.

Greatly influenced by Pope, Wheatley began poetry at thirteen. After she started publishing at seventeen, she received the attention of Boston society and was invited to social gatherings. Whether to advance their social status or to further Phillis's career, the Wheatleys greatly supported her success among the Boston elite. Her fame soon spread from Boston to New York, Philadelphia, and England. She became a freedwoman in 1772. In 1773, the Wheatleys financed her trip to England, where—on a visit cut short by Mrs. Wheatley's illness—Phillis Wheatley was presented to London society. In 1776 Wheatley was warmly received by General Washington, with whom she had corresponded and to whom she had addressed a 42-line poem, published in the *Pennsylvania Magazine*, edited by Thomas Paine (April 1776).

By 1778 the Wheatleys were either dead or had moved to England; Phillis fended for herself as a poet and seamstress. After marrying Peters, she moved to Wilmington, Massachusetts, and lived in poverty for the rest of her life. According to the Massachusetts Historical Society record, when Peters was jailed for debts, Wheatley experienced drudgery for the first time in her life, working in a boarding house for blacks in Boston. She bore three children, and two had died by 1783; the third died a few hours after her own death in 1784.

Wheatley's *Poems on Various Subjects, Religious and Moral* was first published in England in 1773; the first American edition did not follow until 1784. It includes 39 poems of varying merit, some published earlier in magazines. Most of the poems are occasional; some are elegies. "Niobe in Distress for Her Children Slain by Apollo" and "Goliath of Gath," both long poems, reveal the two all-encompassing passions in Wheatley's life, for the Bible and the classics. The first, along with short poems such as "An Hymn to Morning" and "An Hymn to Evening," exhibits her characteristic classical allusions and use of heroic couplets. A very few poems, such as her odes to Washington and Major General Charles Lee reflect her response to the war.

Wheatley has been criticized for not being concerned enough with her own background and the problems of her race. Only two poems, "On Being Brought from Africa" and "To S. M., a Young African Painter, on Seeing His Works," deal with African subjects. There are clear references to Africa in only another nine poems. Richard Wright suggests that Wheatley's lack of racial protest must be explained by her acceptance in Boston society. It may well be that what we consider weaknesses in the collection of her poetry are the results of the temper of contemporary New England and the literary tastes of Wheatley's time.

Wheatley was celebrated by her contemporaries as a child prodigy and poet and regarded as a skillful letter writer and entertaining literary conversationalist. Her poetry is impersonal, with a self-effacement that subordinates her racial and sexual identities to her identities as Christian and poet. She retains, however, the distinction of being the first famous black woman poet.

OTHER WORKS: *Letters of Phillis Wheatley, the Negro-Slave Poet of Boston* (edited by C. Deane 1864).

BIBLIOGRAPHY: Hughes, L., *Famous American Negroes* (1954). Mason, J., Introduction to *The Poems of Phyllis Wheatley* (1966, revised and expanded 1989). Odell, M. M., *Memoir and Poems of Phillis Wheatley* (1834). Richmond, M. A., *Bid the Vassal Soar: Interpretive Essays on the Life and Poetry of Phillis Wheatley and George Moses Horton* (1974). Robinson, W. H., *Phillis Wheatley in the Black American Beginnings* (1975). Robinson, W. H., *Phillis Wheatley: A Bio-Bibliography* (1981). Shields, J. C., *The Collected Works of Phillis Wheatley* (1988).

Reference works: *Benet's Reader's Encyclopedia* (1991). *Oxford Companion to Women's Writing in the United States* (1995).

—ADRIANNE BAYTOP

WHEATON, Campbell

See CAMPBELL, Helen Stuart

WHIPPLE, Maurine

Born 20 January 1903, St. George, Utah; **died** April 1992
Daughter of Charles and Anne McAllister Whipple

Maurine Whipple was born in an arid city in southern Utah settled by Mormons in 1861 as part of the "Dixie Mission." Her ancestors were religiously motivated pioneers who struggled against drought, floods, and pestilence to build a town that is now a tourist stop between Salt Lake City and Las Vegas. They, like many other 19th-century Mormons, were polygamists who struggled with domestic conflicts and psychological and sexual anguishes to support a social system abjured by the now respectable and conservative religion that spawned it. It is from these ancestors and this environment that Whipple drew subject and documentation for her writings.

Whipple spent her childhood and youth in the St. George area, attended the local Dixie College, and then graduated from the University of Utah (1926). She spent several years in Utah and California teaching in smalltown high schools, earning extra money by winning dance contests and playing bit parts in movies. In her spare time she wrote.

In 1937 a friend persuaded Whipple to submit a manuscript to a writers' conference in Boulder, Colorado. Members of the conference encouraged her to continue writing. She submitted an outline of a novel to Houghton Mifflin Company for which she was awarded their annual fiction scholarship of $1,000 in order to complete it. In 1941 Houghton Mifflin published *The Giant Joshua* (reprinted 1976), a novel about Whipple's ancestors and the environment from whence she came.

Whipple wrote a few magazine articles and *This is the Place: Utah* (1945), a delightful, if somewhat acerbic, tourist guide, accompanied by a series of photographs. *The Giant Joshua*, however, remained her only major work; its long awaited sequels were never completed. Whipple continued to live in St. George, having taught school there for many years.

The Giant Joshua revolves around the story of Clorinda Agatha ("Clory") a Mormon pioneer who settled Utah's Dixie and one of the women caught up in the polygamy system. She suffers physically for her commitment to build the "Kingdom" of the Mormons; she suffers mentally with the questions she has about the Mormons' curious beliefs; she suffers emotionally over vows which tie her to a husband three times her age and to sister wives torn with jealousies. With its poignant portrayals of the weaknesses inherent in such a system, the book was branded by the locals as scandalous, its author as heretical. Whipple has relished both appraisals through the years since its publication.

Although occasionally cloying and sentimental, the story remains firmly grounded in the historical milieu which it enlivens. Whipple owed much to documentary materials collected under the Work Projects Administration studies conducted in southern Utah in the 1930s. *The Giant Joshua* is an arresting book. It has a secure place in the literature of the West and of women, and stands as the single most significant fictional treatment of the 19th-century Mormon experience.

BIBLIOGRAPHY: Capener, B., *The Giant Joshua: Screenplay* (adapted Whipple's novel, 1986).

Reference works: *CB* (1941).

Other references: *Who* (November 1941). *NYTBR* (10 Jan. 1941). *SR* (4 Jan. 1941).

—KATHRYN L. MACKAY

WHITCHER, Frances (Miriam) Berry

Born 1 November circa 1813, Whitesboro, New York; **died** 4 January 1852, Whitesboro, New York
Wrote under: Aunt Maguire, Frank, Widow Bedott, Widow Spriggins
Daughter of Lewis Berry and Elizabeth Wells; **married** Benjamin Whitcher, 1847; **children:** Alice Miriam

The eleventh of 15 children, Frances Berry Whitcher was the daughter of a prominent Whitesboro innkeeper. Deemed a precocious child, she was educated both at home and at a local academy. In spite of close family ties, she recalled having a lonely childhood because of her keen sense of the ridiculous; the neighbors sternly disapproved of her caricatures of them. As a young woman, however, she participated in many community activities.

In her mid-thirties, Whitcher married an Episcopal minister and moved with him to his new pastorate in Elmira, New York. Although her marriage was happy, her life in Elmira apparently was not. In 1848 her husband resigned his pastorate and they returned to Whitesboro, where she gave birth to her only child, Alice Miriam. Whitcher died of tuberculosis at the age of thirty-nine.

Whitcher's first humorous sketches (published posthumously as *The Widow Spriggins*, 1867), written to entertain a literary society, are burlesques of a popular English sentimental novel, *Children of the Abbey* (1798), by Regina Maria Roche. The sketches ridicule both sentimental fiction and women who attempt to imitate literary heroines; Whitcher's persona, Permilly Ruggles Spriggins, is an uncouth sentimentalist who models her language and her every action on Roche's Amanda.

Whitcher's most famous series of sketches, written at the request of Joseph Neal of the *Saturday Gazette* (1846-47), are dramatic monologues presented entirely in the malapropian vernacular language of the Widow Bedott, who is a parody of a smalltown gossip. The sketches are laced with references to contemporary fads, such as phrenology lectures and literary society meetings.

Bedott devotes considerable energy to a search for a second husband. The first widower she shamelessly pursues seems about to propose, but instead asks for permission to court her daughter. Her second major effort succeeds when she encourages the rumor that she is a woman of means; she succeeds in marrying the Reverend Sniffles, who is as pompous as Bedott is conniving.

After Whitcher's move to Elmira, she began a third series of sketches for the widely popular *Godey's Lady's Book* (1847-49). Her new persona, Aunt Maguire, is more compassionate than her fictive sister Bedott and speaks a more colloquial language. Inspired by her own observations and experiences as a minister's wife, Whitcher satirizes the residents of small towns for their uncharitable conduct and genteel pretensions.

In one sketch, "The Donation Party," Whitcher satirizes the custom whereby parishioners augment their minister's meager salary by giving him "donations" of substantial commodities. In her story, the minister's guests bring only trifling gifts, break the wife's heirloom china, eat more food than they contribute, and exhibit crude and socially reprehensible behavior. At the end, the fictive minister resigns, declaring that one more donation party would ruin him financially.

Whitcher's most controversial Aunt Maguire sketches focus on a fictional sewing society ostensibly created for charitable purposes, but whose participants turn the meetings into malicious gossip sessions. The series ends when Aunt Maguire travels to a neighboring village where the inhabitants mistakenly believe it is their sewing society that served as the model for the story in *Godey's* and their minister's wife who is the offending author.

Although Whitcher's responsibility for the sketches had been a closely guarded secret, rumors persisted that the author lived in Elmira. So realistic and biting were the sketches that when Benjamin Whitcher confirmed his wife was indeed "Aunt Maguire," he was threatened with a lawsuit and ultimately forced to resign his Elmira pastorate. Not since Frances Trollope's *Domestic Manners of the Americans* (1832) had readers been so stung by a woman's social satire. Whitcher responded by abandoning humorous writing.

Following the tradition of writers such as Seba Smith (who created Jack Downing), Whitcher used first-person vernacular humor as a medium for social criticism. She was unique in humorously depicting smalltown life from a woman's perspective, and became one of America's first significant woman humorists. Her work was widely popular in the 19th-century, and modern readers will find much to admire and enjoy in her humor.

BIBLIOGRAPHY: Curry, J. A., "Woman as Subjects and Writers of Nineteenth-Century American Humor" (dissertation, 1975). Derby, J. C., *Fifty Years Among Authors, Books, and Publishers* (1884). Hart, J. D., *The Popular Book: A History of America's Literary Taste* (1961). Morris, Linda A. Finton, "Women Vernacular Humorists in Nineteenth-Century America: Ann Stephens, Frances Whitcher, and Marietta Holley" (dissertation, 1978). Neal, A., Introduction to *The Widow Bedott Papers* (1856). Whitcher, Mrs. M. L. Ward, Introduction to *The Widow Spriggins, Mary Elmer, and Other Sketches* (1867).

References works: *NAW* (1971).

Other references: *Godey's* (July 1853, Aug. 1853). *New York History* (1974).

—LINDA A. MORRIS

WHITE, Anna

Born 21 January 1831, Brooklyn, New York; **died** 16 December 1910, New Lebanon, New York
Daughter of Robert and Hannah Gibbs White

The fourth of five children who survived infancy, Anna White was a daughter of Quakers and a relative of prominent New Englanders. She attended a Quaker boarding school at Poughkeepsie, New York. At eighteen, she rejoined her family in New York City, learned tailoring, and was trained by her mother in "systematic benevolence to the poor." White's father, however, was the principal influence on her life. A successful businessman, he shocked his family by joining the Shakers. Despite family opposition and disinheritance by an uncle, she followed her father into Shakerism in 1849 at New Lebanon, New York.

In 1865 she was made second (or assistant) eldress, and at the death of Eldress Mary Antoinette Doolittle in 1887, she became eldress, a position she held until death. Described as "cheerful and vigorous," practical and intellectual, White was at the same time committed to mystical experiences, especially spiritualism and faith-healing. An ardent reformer, she served as vice president of the Alliance for Peace and the National Council of Women in the U.S. and met with President Theodore Roosevelt to discuss international arbitration. An active feminist as well, she belonged to the National American Woman Suffrage Association and spoke before the Equal Rights Club of Hartford, Connecticut, in 1903.

With Eldress Leila S. Taylor, White wrote *Shakerism: Its Meaning and Message* (1904), an authoritative history of Shakerism and the only published history by Shakers themselves. Written

when Shakerism was rapidly dying out, the book seeks proselytes and puts the case for Shakerism before the world. According to the preface, "Shakerism presents a system of faith and a mode of life, which, during the past century, has solved social and religious problems and successfully established practical brotherhoods of industry, besides freeing women from inequality and injustice."

Despite its polemics, *Shakerism: Its Meaning and Message* is a valuable account of the origins of Shakerism, its early leaders and first societies, its movement westward, and its numerical growth. It explains the principles of Shakerism, its theology, and its advocacy of pacifism, celibacy, and communism. Further, the history provides an insider's view of the practical lives of the Shakers, of their industries and inventions, and their instruction of children. *Shakerism: Its Meaning and Message* concludes with an exhortation to remaining Shakers to maintain their spiritual commitment. Prophesying Shakerism would rise again and flourish, the authors maintain that Shaker principles will continue to influence the world outside.

White also wrote songs and compiled two books of Shaker music. Her verse appeared in a book of poetry by members of the North family at New Lebanon. Although her talent as a poet was limited, her prose was forceful. In an essay on feminism, "Woman's Mission," written for the Shakers' official periodical, the *Manifesto* (Jan. 1891), White declares "Man has exercised his power over woman to a marked degree. She has either been worshiped by him as an idol, used as a plaything, or bandied about as a slave." White's formal education—an advantage many Shakers lacked—and her wide social concerns made her an intellectual leader and the most effective Shaker woman writer.

OTHER WORKS: *Original Shaker Music* (1884). *Affectionately Inscribed to the Memory of Eldress Antoinette Doolittle* (1887). *Voices from Mount Lebanon* (1899). *The Motherhood of God* (1903).

BIBLIOGRAPHY: Taylor, L., *A Memorial to Eldress Anna White and Elder Daniel Offord* (1912).
Reference works: *NAW* (1971).

—HELEN DEISS IRVIN

WHITE, Anne Terry

Born 19 February 1896, Ukraine, U.S.S.R.; **died** July 1980
Daughter of Aaron and Sarah Terry, **married** Harry D. White, 1918; **children:** two daughters

Anne Terry White's family came to the U.S. when she was eight years old. She grew up and attended school in New England, graduated from Brown University, and received an M.A. from Stanford University. She held positions as a teacher and social worker, but is best known as the author of nonfiction books for children.

White's wish to present great literature to her own two daughters in a way they would find entertaining and easy to understand resulted in her first book, *Heroes of the Five Books* (1937), about Old Testament figures. *Three Children and Shakespeare* (1938) grew out of questions her daughters asked when she read Shakespeare to them; it adapts and discusses four plays in a fictitious family setting.

White's books span a wide range of subjects. Many of them, such as *The First Men in the World* (1953) and *Rocks All Around Us* (1959), are aimed for third- to fifth-grade readers and are intended to serve as introductions to particular fields of study. Her "All About" books on natural science, geography, and geology are considered among the best of their kind for very young readers. Other books, such as *Lost Worlds* (1941) and *Men Before Adam* (1942), both on archeology, have great appeal to older youths and adults. *Lost Worlds*, a history of the discovery of Troy, the palace of Minos on Crete, the tomb of Tutankhamen, and other sites, was reprinted more than two dozen times by the 1980s and is regarded as one of her finest books.

White has translated a myriad of Russian stories, including works by Pushkin and old stories from oral tradition. All are highly readable. In addition, the subjects of her biographies range from scientist George Washington Carver to William Shakespeare, King David of ancient Israel, and socialist labor-leader Eugene Debs. All are greatly fictionalized. To known facts, White judiciously adds dialogue and details to produce entertaining as well as informative pictures of the people concerned.

White has skillfully adapted for young children many books by other authors. Some of these, such as *Treasure Island* (1956), *The Adventures of Tom Sawyer* (1956), and *Heidi* (1956) were originally intended for a young audience; while others were written for adults. Among the most notable of the latter are Rachel Carson's *The Sea Around Us* (1958) and the American Heritage books *Indians and the Old West* (1958) and *The American Indian* (1963). The last appears on lists of books regarded as essential for elementary and junior high school libraries. White has also successfully retold the stories of King Arthur and Odysseus, Aesop's fables, and European and Asian myths and legends.

Regardless of the literary form, White's books are distinguished by fluid and rhythmical prose and thorough research. Analogies drawn from everyday life clarify obscure points, and skillfully framed questions and anecdotes and an informal, conversational tone create a storylike atmosphere. Because of her remarkable ability to put difficult concepts into terms many (but not all) children can understand easily without finding her condescending, sentimental, or overly melodramatic, White is ranked among the foremost writers of nonfiction for young people.

OTHER WORKS: *Prehistoric America* (1951). *George Washington Carver: The Story of a Great American* (1953). *All About the Stars* (1954). *All About Our Changing Rocks* (1955; reissued as *All*

About Rocks and Minerals, 1963). *Will Shakespeare and the Globe Theater* (1955). *All About Great Rivers of the World* (1957). *The Golden Book of Animals* (1958). *All About Archaeology* (1959). *Natural Wonders* (1960). *The Solar System* (1960). *The St. Lawrence, Seaway of North America* (1961). *Birds of the World* (1962). *All About Mountains and Mountaineering* (1962). *Windows on the World* (with G. S. Lietz, 1965). *Secrets of the Heart and Blood* (with G. S. Lietz, 1965). *Built to Survive* (with G. S. Lietz, 1966). *When Hunger Calls* (with G. S. Lietz, 1966). *Man, the Thinker* (with G. S. Lietz, 1967). *The False Treaty* (1970). *Human Cargo: The Story of the Atlantic Slave Trade* (1972). *North to Liberty: The Story of the Underground Railroad* (1972). *Eugene Debs* (1974).

BIBLIOGRAPHY: Reference works: *Authors of Books for Young People* (1971). *CA* (1974). *More Junior Authors* (1963). *SAA* (1971).

—ALETHEA K. HELBIG

WHITE, Eliza Orne

Born 2 August 1856, Keene, New Hampshire; **died** 23 January 1947, Brookline, Massachusetts
Wrote under: Alex
Daughter of William O. and Margaret Harding White

Eliza Orne White grew up in an intellectual and artistic household; her father was a Unitarian minister in Keene, and her mother was the daughter of the self-taught portrait artist, Chester Harding. Lucretia Hale, author of *The Peterkin Papers*, was an old school friend of White's mother and visited the family each year. Though a happy and active child, White was apparently not a completely healthy one, for her education in the public schools of Keene was twice interrupted by illness: at fourteen she missed a year of school because of eye trouble and at sixteen suffered an attack of typhoid, which ended her public school education, although she later spent a year at Miss Hall's School for Girls in Roxbury, Massachusetts.

A prolific writer (she wrote 41 books, 29 of them for children), White began at age eighteen to publish children's stories under the pseudonym "Alex" in periodicals such as the *Christian Register*. Her first story for adults, "A Browning Courtship" (*Atlantic*, July 1888), is a witty social comedy based on the craze for Browning societies during the later years of the 19th century. Her first book for children was *When Molly Was Six* (1894), an episodic rendering of the life of a little girl, her older brother, her mother and father, and her young unmarried aunt. Each chapter is self-contained, and the book's unity is provided by the clearly defined and consistent characters.

The conception and execution of character, along with an eye and an ear for humor, are White's greatest strengths in both her books for children and those for adults. None of her stories are heavily plotted, but their virtues are clearly summarized by the reviewer of *Miss Brooks* (1890), who wrote, "The fortunes of a few interesting persons are followed. . . . As a study of social life, it shows capital observation and shrewd insight. . . ." Whether White's children's books are historical (as is *A Little Girl of Long Ago*, 1896, based on stories of her mother's life) or contemporary (as is *The Blue Aunt*, 1918, concerned with the home front manifestations, such as rationing, of World War I), whether they are grounded in autobiography (as is *A Borrowed Sister*, 1906) or are purely imaginative, White's books nearly always focus on New England families and realistic relationships between children and adults.

The families in White's children's books are clearly middle class. The fathers are doctors, businessmen, and artists; the children are aesthetically and morally sensitive, although they are liable to lapses in judgment out of which the episodes grow. In *Ednah and Her Brothers* (1900), for example, the children decide to make wine, so they pick the grapes their father had intended to sell, put them in tub, and stomp on them. The father is naturally displeased, but he quickly comes around to see the humor of the episode, and the children are forgiven.

The function of the adults in these books, then, is to protect the children from the dangers to which inexperience makes them subject. Beyond that, the adults are basically indulgent, charged with finding ways to let the child's natural goodness express itself. They invariably support children's activities, respect their humanity, and encourage their use of imagination. White's conception of the ideal relations between children and adults is perhaps most clearly expressed in her description of Lucretia Hale: "Aunt Lucretia. . .was the most perfect companion for any child. She never made you feel you were an inferior."

White had a long and productive life. Her last book, *When Esther Was a Little Girl* (1944), appeared 70 years after her first collection of short stories, and it is filled with interesting experiences and good, humorous characters, most drawn from White's childhood. Although by the end of her life she was very deaf and had been totally blind for nearly 30 years, she never lost her imaginative vision or her ability to write natural-sounding dialogues. She once wrote, "The good thing about imagination is that it defies time and bridges the gap between childhood and what to the uninitiated seems like age."

OTHER WORKS: *As It Should Be* (1873). *As She Would Have It* (1873). *Winterborough* (1892). *The Coming of Theodora* (1895). *A Browning Courtship, and Other Stories* (1897). *A Lover of Truth* (1898). *John Forsyth's Aunts* (1901). *Leslie Chilton* (1903). *An Only Child* (1905). *The Wares of Edgefield* (1909). *Brothers in Fur* (1910). *The Enchanted Mountain* (1911). *The First Step* (1914). *William Orne White: A Record of Ninety Years* (1917). *The Strange Year* (1920). *Peggy in Her Blue Frock* (1921). *Tony* (1924). *Joan Morse* (1926). *Diana's Rosebush* (1927). *The Adventures of Andrew* (1928). *Sally in Her Fur Coat* (1929). *The Green Door* (1930). *When Abigail Was Seven* (1931). *The Four Young Kendalls* (1932). *Where is Adelaide* (1933). *Lending Mary* (1934). *Ann Frances* (1935). *Nancy Alden* (1936). *The Farm*

Beyond the Town (1937). *Helen's Gift House* (1938). *Patty Makes a Visit* (1939). *The House Across the Way* (1940). *I: The Autobiography of a Cat* (1941). *Training of Sylvia* (1942).

BIBLIOGRAPHY: Moore, A. E., *Literature Old and New for Children* (1934).

Reference works: *Junior Book of Authors* (1934). *NAW* (1971). *NCAB* (1906).

Other references: *Horn Book* (Apr. 1955).

—KATHARYN F. CRABBE

WHITE, Elizabeth

Born circa 1637; **died** 1699
married 1657; **children:** one

Elizabeth White was born in New England, possibly in or near Boston, around 1637, and married in 1657; she had at least one child. There are apparently no extant records of her life, except for these sketchy details that she put into the one published work, her spiritual autobiography. *The Experience of God's Gracious Dealing with Mrs. Elizabeth White*, published as a short pamphlet in 1741, is a notable example of early American women's spiritual autobiography. It contains imaginative and personally revealing details about the psychic life of a Puritan woman in 17th-century New England. After White's death, this work was discovered in her "closet," a small room used for private meditation and writing. Although it was probably circulated among friends and relatives for many years (as was the practice), it was not published until four decades after White's death during a period of religious revival in New England; her confession would have evoked for its readers an earlier, much admired pious period.

The lack of polish and sophistication in White's autobiography is made up for by spontaneity and vividness as she reveals the internal landscape of the darkest recesses of her soul in an attempt to express her redemptive experience. Three experiences of deepest despair about her soul's destiny occurred concurrently with her marriage, the birth of her first child, and the weaning of this infant. A month before her marriage, she relates, her father desired her to take communion, but she suddenly had grave doubts about her preparedness for taking part in the sacrament. Similarly, she experienced a crisis three days after delivering her first child; she was tempted by the devil with a vision of the Trinity, but escaped Satan's clutches through the suckling of her infant and finally through sleep, in which she dreamt of her assured place in heaven, a place secured for her after death in childbirth. A third great trial coincided with weaning, and relates directly to White's stated feelings of guilt for the affection she lavished on her firstborn. Tempted to believe the Bible is not God's word, she was uplifted by Christ, and the darkness about her soul dispelled.

Although she felt renewed after this final experience, moments of doubt continued to plague her. But she felt secure enough in her salvation and regeneration to commit to writing her account of repentance and trust in Christ. In talking about the trials and religious doubt in the period of early womanhood, White reveals the deep-seated conflicts and uncertainties felt by a Puritan woman when facing the responsibilities and struggles of marriage and motherhood. As a Puritan, she views these external events only as markers by which she identifies moments of acute spiritual awareness. For the modern reader, the conjunction of White's internal and external experiences provides thought-provoking clues to the psychic life of Puritan women.

BIBLIOGRAPHY: Shea, D., *Spiritual Autobiography in Early America* (1968).

—JACQUELINE HORNSTEIN

WHITE, Ellen Gould (Harmon)

Born 26 November 1827, Gorham, Maine; **died** 16 July 1915, St. Helena, California

Daughter of Robert and Eunice Harmon; **married** James White, 1846 (died 1888); **children:** four

The daughter of a hatter, Ellen Gould White had only a third-grade education. Although baptized in the Methodist church, by the age of seventeen she was enthusiastically involved with the activities of William Miller—an itinerant preacher who believed the Second Coming of Christ and the end of the world would occur during the fall of 1844. In that year, White had the first of a series of over 2,000 visions, which revealed to her why Miller's prediction failed and what God intended her to accomplish.

White married a fellow "Millerite," and together they spread the message of the coming of Christ to the New England area. She had four children; the first died at sixteen and the last in infancy, but the other two boys became active in the church their mother helped found. The Whites moved to Battle Creek, Michigan, in 1855, and prompted by her visions White preached and wrote on the significance of the imminent (if unknown) coming of Christ, the validity of biblical prophecies, fundamental Christianity, and the divine desire for observing the Sabbath not on Sunday but on the seventh day of the week, Saturday. The Seventh Day Adventist church was eventually established on those principles in 1863. When her husband died in 1888, White increased her writing and speaking activities, campaigning for Adventist Christianity, health reform, and temperance. As many as 20,000 people gathered to hear her orations against alcohol. Her travels included two years touring Europe and 10 years as a missionary to Australia. In 1902 White moved the Adventist headquarters from Battle Creek to a suburb of Washington, D.C., and she settled in California. She died at the age of eighty-seven from complications following a hip fracture.

It has been estimated that White wrote over 105,000 pages of published and unpublished materials. She maintained that because of her poor health and lack of education, only God's visions enabled her to produce this literary corpus. Much of her writing was done late at night or in the early morning when domestic tasks were completed.

The foundation of the Seventh Day Adventist church rests on the belief that the Bible reveals the ultimate truth concerning the nature of God, the origin and purpose of human life, and the future of the world. Divine inspiration was not sufficient to convince most 19th-century Americans that Adventist doctrine was the ultimate truth; White wanted to show the continuity of biblical prophecy and the course of historical events. Five books, the Conflict of Ages series, are devoted to tracing the history of the battle between God and Satan as predicted in the Old and New Testaments. Four books tell the biblical story from Genesis to the Pauline epistles. *The Great Controversy* (1888), although actually written first, continues the story into the European and American historical settings. White used the history of Western civilization to underline certain central themes in Adventist belief: the reality of Satan, the evil of Roman Catholicism, and the redemptive quality of William Miller's proclamation.

Much of White's writings were composed during a period of general social reform in the United States. Women's rights, prison reform, the settlement-house movement, and prohibition were important issues at grassroots and national levels. Such late 19th-century reforms were a part of the "social gospel movement," which emphasized the role of Christianity as a force for social change, rather than as a promoter of the status quo. White fueled this movement with her tracts on health, education, temperance, and diet; and she encouraged her followers to adopt a lifestyle encompassing many of the contemporary reforms.

According to White, God intends humans to lead a simple life: pure air, deep breathing, regular sleeping and eating habits, and good sanitation promote moral as well as physical well being; tobacco, coffee, alcohol, meat, and sugar are all detrimental to the body, soul, and mind. Her views on dress reform echo some of the earlier sentiments of Amelia Bloomer and Elizabeth Cady Stanton. In *The Ministry of Healing* (1905), she condemns the restrictive and overly decorative style of contemporary dress: "Every article of dress should fit easily, obstructing neither the circulation of the blood nor a free, full, natural respiration. Everything should be so loose that when the arms are raised, the clothing will be correspondingly lifted."

Educational reform also figures prominently in White's writings. Education must include not only the biblical and historical basis of Adventism but also a foundation in physiology, diet, health, and medicine. Traditional secular education should be limited to basic English, arithmetic, and history ("from the Divine point of view"). She sought to purge from Adventist education "pagan" languages and literature, modern literature by immoral authors, frivolous fiction writers, non-Christian science, biblical criticism, spiritualism, and anarchy. Seventh Day Adventist education included girls as well as boys and even encouraged some fluidity in sex role education: "Boys as well as girls should gain a knowledge of household duties. . . . It is a training that need not make any boy less manly; it will make him happier and more useful."

White's writings on practical reforms have antecedents in the work of earlier reformers, but she was able to institutionalize them in the doctrine of the Seventh Day Adventist church. She remains a unique woman in the history of American religions, for her writings act as a foundation not only for a growing religious organization but for that religion's extensive system of schools, hospitals, and sanatoriums.

OTHER WORKS: *Sketches from the Life of Christ and the Experience of the Christian Church* (1882). *Christian Temperance* (1890). *Gospel Workers; Instructions for the Minister and the Missionary* (1892). *Steps to Christ* (1892). *The Story of Patriarchs and Prophets; the Conflict of the Ages Illustrated by the Lives of Holy Men of Old* (1890). *Christ Our Savior* (1895). *The Desire of Ages* (1898). *Christ's Object Lessons* (1900). *Testimonies for the Church* (1901). *Education* (1903). *The Acts of the Apostles in the Proclamation of the Gospel of Jesus Christ* (1911). *Counsel to Teachers, Parents and Students Regarding Christian Education* (1913). *Life Sketches of Ellen G. White, Being a Narrative of her Experience to 1881 as Written By Herself* (1915). *The Captivity and Restoration of Israel; the Conflict of Ages Illustrated in the Lives of Prophets and Kings* (1917). *Christian Experience and Teachings of Ellen G. White* (1922). *Counsels on Health and Instruction to Medical Missionary Workers* (1923). *Spiritual and Subject Index to the Writings of Mrs. Ellen G. White* (1926). *Principles of True Science* (1929). *Message to Young People* (1930). *Medical Ministry* (1932). *An Appeal for Self-Supporting Laborers* (1933). *A Call to Medical Evangelism* (1933). *Selections from the "Testimonies"* (1936). *The Sanctified Life* (1937). *Counsels on Sabbath School Work* (1938). *Counsels on Diet and Food* (1938). *Counsels to Editors* (1939). *Counsels on Stewardship* (1940).

BIBLIOGRAPHY: Noorbergen, R., *Ellen G. White: Prophet of Destiny* (1972). Numbers, R., *Prophetess of Health: A Study of Ellen G. White* (1976). Spalding, A. W., *There Shines a Light* (1976). White, A., *Ellen G. White: Messenger to the Remnant* (1969).

Reference works: *Comprehensive Index to the Writings of Ellen G. White* (1962-63). NAW (1971). *Oxford Companion to Women's Writing in the United States* (1995).

—M. COLLEEN MCDANNELL

WHITE, Helen Constance

Born 26 November 1896, New Haven, Connecticut; **died** 7 June 1967, Madison, Wisconsin
Daughter of John and Mary King White

In 1901 Helen Constance White's family moved to Boston, where she attended Girl's High School and Radcliffe College, receiving her M.A. in 1917. After teaching for two years at Smith, she moved west to the University of Wisconsin, where, except for study tours and research leaves, she remained until her death, living in the same apartment for over 40 years. She received her Ph.D. in English in 1924, and in 1936 was the first woman to become a full professor in Letters and Science at the university. She later served as chairman of the English department.

According to White, "Belonging to things is an occupational disease of the profession!" One year she was simultaneously president of the local University Club, president of the University of Wisconsin Teachers Union, and national president of the American Association of University Women. As the first woman national president of the American Association of University Professors, she took a firm stand for academic freedom. Twice she served as a U.S. delegate to UNESCO meetings.

White's scholarly works usually combine her competence in literature with her lifelong interest in religion. *The Mysticism of William Blake* (1927) and *The Metaphysical Poets* (1936) are critical studies of major literary figures. Other studies, such as *Tudor Books of Saints and Martyrs* (1963), analyze materials of greater religious and historical import than literary significance.

Such scholarly work served as impetus and background for the writing of novels centering on figures from Catholic history. Her fiction probed the minds and souls of sensitive men and women gallantly attempting to live out their ideals in a blemished church and world. In *Dust on the King's Highway* (1947), the competing goals of the pioneering Franciscan friars in California and the secular Spanish administration result in massacre and martyrdom. In *Not Built with Hands* (1935), the strong Countess Matilda, "Lord of Tuscany," loyally keeps her resources in the service of the vulnerable Pope Gregory VII. *To the End of the World* (1939) focuses on a young priest who, though he supports the ideas of the French Revolution, refuses to accept the Civil Constitution of the Clergy and goes underground. Each of the protagonists must in the end face partial defeat.

Critics suggested that editorial pruning would have improved the narrative line of White's fiction. In none of her novels is there a developed love story. Her readers often find her careful spiritual appraisals and rich descriptions slow and gentle in pace, but her concern for the spiritual is at once the strength and the weakness of her fiction. She confessed to a passion for history and steeped herself in the lore and traditions of monasticism and mysticism. She filled a broad canvas with lavish historical detail against which opposing forces of order and chaos, freedom and bondage, persuasion and violence, played themselves out. Her sympathetic delineation of the delicate conscience and missionary zeal is unsurpassed in spiritual insight.

OTHER WORKS: *Victorian Prose* (with F. Foster, 1930). *English Devotional Literature (Prose) 1600-1640* (1931). *A Watch in the Night* (1933). *Social Criticism in Popular Religious Literature of the Sixteenth Century* (1944). *Seventeenth-Century Verse and Prose* (with R. Wallerstein and R. Quintana, 1951). *The Tudor Books of Private Devotion* (1951). *The Four Rivers of Paradise*

(1955). *Bird of Fire* (1958). *Prayer and Poetry* (1960). *Changing Styles in Literary Studies* (1963).

BIBLIOGRAPHY: State Historical Society of Wisconsin Women's Auxiliary, *Famous Wisconsin Women* (1976).

Other references: *Catholic Library World* (Apr. 1940). *Catholic World* (May 1937). *Christian Century* (4 June 1947). *NYT* (2 June 1935). *RES* (Feb. 1965).

—ARLENE ANDERSON SWIDLER

WHITE, Nelia Gardner

Born 1 November 1894, Andrews Settlement, Pennsylvania; **died** 12 June 1957, New Hartford, Connecticut
Daughter of John A. and Anna Jones Gardner; **married** Ralph L. White, 1917; **children:** two

Nelia Gardner White, one of five children of a Methodist minister, lived in several small towns as she was growing up. Though the family had very little money, the atmosphere of the home was happy; life was filled with "books, friends, and fun." By taking many different sorts of jobs, White was able to attend Syracuse University for two years (1911-13) and the Emma Willard Kindergarten School (1913-15). After several years as a kindergarten teacher, she married a lawyer. The couple had two children.

During World War II, as a guest of the British Ministry of Information, White wrote articles about England. In 1948 she won the $8,000 prize in the Westminster Press Fiction Contest with her novel *No Trumpet Before Him*. White gives great credit for her start as a writer to Maude Stewart, a teacher in the kindergarten school who helped her toward an understanding of human character and of the various relationships between people. White contributed articles about child care to a kindergarten magazine. She began writing fiction with stories for kindergarten children and four novels for young people and then branched out to adult fiction. The rest of her life is a record of much industry and a great deal of success. Hundreds of her stories appeared in such popular magazines as the *American, Ladies' Home Journal, People's Home Journal, Midland, McCall's, Pictorial Review, Forum, and Good Housekeeping*. In addition, she wrote 25 novels.

Her fiction is notable for a clear and compassionate delineation of human characters and a smooth, almost poetic style. In her early writing, she frequently exhibits a facile sentimentality; later she was able to control this, so it could enhance rather than mar her narrative. Though all her life she used rural and smalltown settings and characters, near the very end she portrayed a few more sophisticated men and women against a city background. While certainly not "high brow," her fiction is not to be classed as "slick" or "light." According to one critic, her last novel, *The Gift and the Giver*, published the year of her death (1957), is "perhaps her most penetrating and at times disturbing book." Another critic wrote, "None of Mrs. White's prize winning novels has the brutal realism and the compassionate power of truth that *The Gift and the Giver* evokes."

Thus White's art grew and developed throughout the years, always illustrating her personal theory about writing. One must have discipline, she said, and "discipline comes through failure, through writing thousands of words and using only a hundred of them, through filling the mind with great literature, through stretching the imagination to the utmost, through forgetting markets and concentrating on the immediate work. A surface cleverness is not enough."

OTHER WORKS: *Mary* (1925). *Marge* (1926). *And Michael* (1927). *Jen Culliton* (1927). *David Strange* (1928). *Joanna Gray* (1928). *Kristin* (1929). *Tune in the Tree* (1929). *Toni of Grand Isle* (1930). *Hathaway House* (1931). *Mrs. Green's Daughter-In-Law* (1932). *This, My House* (1933). *Family Affairs* (1934). *The Fields of Gomorrah* (1935). *The Heaths and the Hubbells* (1937). *Daughter of Time* (1941). *Brook Willow* (1944). *The Pink House* (1950). *Woman At the Window* (1951). *The Merry Month of May* (1952). *The Spare Room* (1954). *The Thorn Tree* (1955). *A Little More Than Kin* (1956).

BIBLIOGRAPHY: *KR* (15 July 1957). *NYHTB* (19 Aug. 1956). *WLB* (Nov. 1950). *Writer* (Sept. 1955).

—ABIGAIL ANN HAMBLEN

WHITE, Rhoda E(lizabeth Waterman)

Born circa 1800s; **died** death date unknown
Also wrote under: Uncle Ben of Rouses Point, N.Y. Uncle Ben
Daughter of Thomas G. and (?) Whitney Waterman; **married** James W. White; **children:** six daughters, two sons

No biographical data on Rhoda E. White appears in the standard 19th-century sources; however, some general information about her background can be abstracted from *Memoir and Letters of Jenny C. White Del Bal* (1868), a book she wrote following her daughter's death. White was the oldest daughter of General Waterman, a New York state lawyer who married the eldest daughter of General Joshua Whitney, founder of Binghamton, New York. Her parents were socially prominent Episcopalians. She married a member of an exemplary Irish Catholic family. White converted to Catholicism in 1837, and the Catholic religion was one of the major influences in her life.

Her husband, a wealthy lawyer, became a judge of the Superior Court of New York City. She traveled in fashionable New York society, vacationed at Newport and Saratoga, and enjoyed the privileges of the rich, but her life was not idle. She studied throughout her marriage and received private lessons in all subjects from the best teachers. The mother of eight children, including six daughters, she tutored her family at their home, Castle Comfort.

The title page of *Jane Arlington; or, The Defrauded Heiress: A Tale of Lake Champlain* (1853) lists *The "Buccaneer" of Lake Champlain* as an earlier work of Uncle Ben. Any prior publications, however, have been lost. *Jane Arlington*, a short novel, is the story of a "young lady perfect and accomplished in every aspect" who, after she is orphaned, is deceived by her kindly stepfather's villainous brother into leaving home and finding employment in the frontierlike Lake Champlain region. The plot is predictable: Jane receives both charity and cruelty from employers and others she encounters, but her moral fortitude and personal goodness enable her to survive and regain her rightful inheritance. White does make use of the unprincipled scoundrel, but her premise is that villainy, or virtue, is frequently disguised and unanticipated. As a corollary, White exposes class pretensions and distinctions as inadequate measures of individual merit. In developing her theme of false class consciousness, she reveals a keen comic talent that emerges most fully in the caricatures of Mrs. Prim and her family.

White extends her humorous portrayal of human foibles in *Portraits of My Married Friends; or, A Peep into Hymen's Kingdom* (1858), a series of six sketches narrated by a wry old bachelor, Uncle Ben, who terms his married acquaintances "more fortunate" than he, but who mainly tells of the problems of marital discord and unhappy matches. Most of the portraits, whether comic or tragic, are slight, melodramatic treatments, but the most effective integrate character and theme with moral vision and social consciousness. One of these, "Jerome and Susan Daly," idealizes the love between a village couple and their children, while at the same time it contrasts child-rearing practices in the village with those in the city, depicts Scotch and Irish servant girls in the homes of the rich, and proposes "cultivated hearts" as a means of leveling class distinctions. Another effective portrait, "Kate Kearney," combines social realism—including graphic descriptions of tenement life and the plight of abused wives—with a strong story line.

White's main concern in *Mary Staunton; or, The Pupils of Marvel Hall* (1860), the most fully realized of her fiction, is the detrimental effects of poor training and environment on young girls, even if their natures are gentle, loving, and sensitive. The novel is an exposé of a fashionable boarding school in New York City, whose pupils acquire little meaningful education and only superficial training in social amenities. Mary is an unlikely heroine; mean, vengeful, and "coarse," she has been neglected by Mrs. Marvel, who is satirized for her false values. Deprived throughout her childhood of affection as well as of religious and moral instruction, she receives a chance for a different life when her long-absent father returns from India and attempts to repair the damage done to his motherless daughter. Although the novel is weakened by White's penchant for exaggerating virtues and faults, it is for the most part refreshingly frank and unsentimental.

Two ideas dominate White's fiction—Catholicism and education. Her recurrent theme is that children, regardless of their

socioeconomic status, develop best when they are instilled with faith and love. Her style is at times stilted and melodramatic, and she uses dialogue excessively in forwarding plots. Nevertheless, White captures voices accurately, particularly immigrant brogues and regional dialects, and she is skillful in rendering realistic scenes of both lower- and upper-class life. Her treatment of New York tenement dwellers and their living conditions, though neither extensive nor primary, is a forerunner of the work of Stephen Crane and Jacob Riis. All of White's writing stems from a sense of ethical and social responsibility, but her view of conventional situations is generally from an unexpected angle. Her humorous perspective raises even her most commonplace subjects from the level of cliché and stereotype.

—THADIOUS M. DAVIS

WHITING, Lillian

Born 3 October 1847, Olcott, New York; **died** 30 April 1942, Boston, Massachusetts
Daughter of Lorenzo D. and Lucretia Clement Whiting

Lillian Whiting was an only daughter and the eldest of three children. While she was still very young, her parents moved to a farm near Tiskilwa, Illinois, where both parents served as principals of the local school. Whiting, however, was educated privately and at home, where she became acquainted early with literary classics. With the assistance of her mother, her father became editor of the *Bureau County Republican*, published in Princeton, Illinois. A leader in the Grange movement and a fighter against the expansion of the railroads and for the expansion of waterways, he served as both representative and senator in the state legislature and assisted in framing the state constitution.

Whiting's writing career started when her articles were accepted by the local newspaper, of which she later became editor. In 1876 she went to St. Louis as a journalist and soon became associated with the idealist Philosophic Club. In 1879 she went to work for the *Cincinnati Commercial* after it published two papers she had written on Margaret Fuller. The following year, she moved to Boston to become the art editor—and later literary editor—of the *Boston Traveler*.

In 1890 she became editor-in-chief of the *Boston Budget*, to which she also contributed literary reviews (among them, favorable commentary on Emily Dickinson's poems) and a column, "Beau Monde," credited with helping to break down the artistic parochialism of contemporary Boston. In Boston, Whiting was a member of a circle that included James Russell Lowell, Lucy Stone, Mary Livermore, Frances Willard, Oliver Wendell Holmes, and many others active in the intellectual life of the time. She visited Bronson Alcott's School of Philosophy and attended Thomas Wentworth Higginson's Round Table. She went to Europe for the first time in 1895 (to do research for the first of several biographies, *A Study of Elizabeth Barrett Browning* (1899), and thereafter made 18 pilgrimages abroad. While there, she became the friend of artists such as Auguste Rodin, Harriet Hosmer, and Rosa Bonheur and the theosophist Annie Besant. Benjamin O. Flower, editor of the *Arena*, said of her that she "knew more men and women of letters than any other woman in America."

So widespread was Whiting's reputation as a writer and critic and as a spiritual influence that in 1897 a Lillian Whiting Club was formed in New Orleans with the aim of inspiring its members in matters relating to the arts and sciences. Whiting's spiritualist leanings had deep roots: her father was a descendent of Cotton Mather and her mother of a long line of New England Episcopalian ministers. She wrote 10 inspirational books and became one of the most popular of New Thought writers. (William James called New Thought the "religion of healthy-mindedness.") Liberal in her acceptance of a variety of religious sects—in *Life Transfigured* (1910), she discusses spiritualism, theosophy, Christian Science, the Vedantic philosophy, psychotherapy, and Bahai, all as means of salvation—her philosophy is optimistic. She believed in the primacy of the spiritual world and referred to death merely as "change"—she viewed the time she lived in as the "dawn of a new perfection." The death of the journalist Kate Field, a close friend, led Whiting to write *After Her Death: The Story of a Summer* (1897), which she considered her best work. It spells out her belief in communication between the living and the dead. The essays, such as "Success as a Fine Art," collected in the World Beautiful series (three volumes, 1894-96, which ran to 14 editions), are typical of Whiting's approach to living.

Boston Days: The City of Beautiful Ideals (1902) was the first of her eight books dealing with places she visited in North America, Europe, and Africa. The chatty tone of her accounts of popular landmarks and works of art as well as the liberal sprinkling of names of her famous acquaintances no doubt were the chief sources of the popularity of her travel writing. Whiting's third-person autobiography, *The Golden Road* (1918), is effusive rather than factual. She published one volume of poetry, *From Dreamland Sent* (1895). The poems are largely personal in subject and traditional in form and tone.

Whiting is of interest to those studying popular taste rather than excellence and originality in the literary arts. It is worth noting, however, that she achieved fame and success as a professional among professionals and moved freely in an international society of artists in a way few women of her time were privileged to do.

OTHER WORKS: *The World Beautiful* (1894-1896). *Kate Field: A Record* (1899). *The Spiritual Significance; Or, Death As An Event in Life* (1900). *The World Beautiful in Books* (1901). *The Life Radiant* (1903). *The Florence of Landor* (1905). *The Joy That No Man Taketh From You* (1905). *The Outlook Beautiful* (1905). *From Dream to Vision of Life* (1906). *Italy, the Magic Land* (1907). *Paris, the Beautiful* (1908). *The Land of Enchantment* (1909). *Louise Chandler Moulton: Poet and Friend* (1910). *The Brownings: Their Life and Art* (1911). *Athens, the Violet-Crowned*

(1913). *The Lure of London* (1914). *Women Who Have Ennobled Life* (1915). *The Adventure Beautiful* (1917). *Canada, the Spellbinder* (1917). *Katherine Tingley* (1919). *They Who Understand* (1919).

BIBLIOGRAPHY: Flower, B. O., *Progressive Men, Women, and Movements in the Past Twenty-Five Years* (1914). Gardner, W. E., *Memorial* (1942).

Reference works: *AW. NCAB.*

Other references: *Arena* (Apr. 1899). *Boston Globe* (1 May 1942). *Boston Herald* (1 May 1942). *NYT* (1 May 1942).

—VIRGINIA R. TERRIS

WHITMAN, Narcissa Prentiss

Born 14 March 1808, Prattsburg, New York; **died** 29 November 1847, Waiilatpu Mission, Oregon Territory
Daughter of Stephen and Clarissa Ward Prentiss; **married** Marcus Whitman, 1836; **children:** twelve

Narcissa Prentiss Whitman was the third of nine children. Her father, a prominent landowner, served for a time as associate justice of the Steuben County Court. In 1827 Whitman was among the first women admitted to Prattsburg's Franklin Academy and Collegiate Institute. After graduation, she taught at schools in New York state. Like her parents, Whitman was a Presbyterian. Attendance at a revival meeting in 1824 led to her decision to devote her life to missionary work, and in 1834 a minister convinced her of the need for Presbyterian missionaries in the Northwest. It is unlikely Narcissa knew Dr. Whitman, another prospective missionary, before his proposal of marriage. The match was a practical affair, because the American Board of Missionaries would not accept single men and women as missionaries. She and her husband set out immediately after their marriage in February 1836 for their mission in Oregon Territory and reached Fort Walla Walla in September. They established their mission station on the Walla Walla River, 25 miles from the fort, at a place called Waiilatpu, or "the Place of Rye Grass," among the Cayuse.

Whitman, with Eliza Hunt Spaulding, another missionary traveling with her husband and the Whitmans, was the first white woman to cross the continental divide. She and her husband have symbolized the pioneering spirit for countless American men and women. She learned the Cayuse language and established a mission school. She was also responsible for domestic economy. A daughter was born early in 1837, and over the years the Whitmans became foster parents of 11 children. Whitman's love of children, both Native American and white, aided the missionaries in their work among the Cayuse. The Native Americans, after an initial curiosity, became hesitant to receive the missionaries' religion. Language and cultural barriers began to seem insurmountable, and the idealism with which the Whitmans approached their mission faded in the face of reality. Despite Whitman's ill health and depression after the drowning death of her daughter in 1839 and despite criticism from other missionaries and the Board of Missionaries's threat to transfer them, the Whitmans were willing to work hard and overcome their difficulties. Whitman was in charge of the mission herself for the better part of a year, when her husband went east to convince the board to let them remain at Waiilatpu.

The Native Americans became increasingly skeptical of the missionaries' intentions because of the observed animosity between the Presbyterians and nearby Catholic missionaries and because of the pressure of growing white immigration. Late in 1847, a small band of Cayuse entered the Whitman mission and killed Whitman, her husband, and 11 others. Forty-seven people, mostly immigrants staying with the Whitmans, were captured. One result of the public sentiment raised by the Whitman massacre was that in 1848 Congress declared the region where the Whitmans had lived and died the Oregon Territory. With American control, immigration increased, and soon the area was heavily populated by white settlers who subdued or drove out the Native American population.

Whitman's experiences during the four-month trip on horseback and on foot from Missouri to her new home in the West are recorded in what started as a serial letter to her family and became a journal. Beginning with an entry written ''above the Platte River,'' and ending with a description of the Whitman's house at Waiilatpu, the journal is an invaluable account. Written by a well-educated woman, with an interest in botany and science, it is filled with details about the journey, the terrain the group covered, and Whitman's own responses to her new experiences. Unlike many later trail diaries written by women traveling west, Whitman was intensely aware that hers was a unique experience, and she was open to the beauties of the scenery around her.

Both the Whitmans were prolific letter writers. Whitman's letters to her parents and friends as well as her journal were meant for private eyes only. They are especially valuable and enjoyable reading for their candor. Because historians have been primarily concerned with the work of Marcus Whitman and the Oregon missions, comparatively little has been written about Narcissa, although her journal of their travels is often quoted. Certainly, more work should be done on the life and writing of this most remarkable American woman.

Whitman's journal was most recently published by the *Oregon Historical Quarterly* (1936-38). Her many letters remain largely unpublished and are located in various Oregon historical collections, as well as in private hands. The best catalogue of the Whitman letters is found in Appendix I of Clifford Drury's *Marcus and Narcissa Whitman and the Opening of Oregon* (1973).

BIBLIOGRAPHY: Brown, D., *The Gentle Tamers* (1958). Eaton, J., *Narcissa Whitman, Pioneer of Oregon* (1941). Nard, J., *The Great Command: The Story of Marcus and Narcissa Whitman and the Oregon Country Pioneers* (1959). Richardson, M., *The Whitman Mission* (1940).

—PAULA A. TRECKEL

WHITMAN, Ruth

Born 28 May 1922, New York, New York
Daughter of Meyer D. and Martha Sherman Basbein; **married** Cedric Whitman, 1941 (divorced); Firman Houghton, 1959 (divorced); Morton Sacks, 1966; **children:** Rachel, Leda, David

Poet, translator, editor, teacher, Ruth Whitman has won literary awards for 30 years, but she is best known for the imagined journals of two real women—Tamsen Donner and Hanna Senesh—in the last extraordinary months of their lives.

Born a New Yorker and a lawyer's daughter, Whitman in her adult life has been associated with academia and Cambridge, Massachusetts. She attended Radcliffe (B.A., 1944), graduating Phi Beta Kappa, magna cum laude, and three years later received her M.A. from Harvard University. She gained experience in publishing in the early 1940s with Houghton Mifflin, working first as an editorial assistant, then as educational editor. She served as a freelance editor for Harvard University Press from 1945 to 1960, from 1958 to 1963 as poetry editor for the Cambridge magazine *Audience*, and from 1980 as poetry editor of the *Radcliffe Quarterly*. Whitman has taught in Cambridge, giving poetry workshops at the Cambridge Center for Adult Education, 1965-68, and serving as a lecturer in poetry at Radcliffe and Harvard. During 1968-70, she was a fellow at the Bunting Institute at Radcliffe. Beginning in 1989 she was a visiting professor of poetry at the Massachusetts Institute of Technology.

Listing her religion as ''secular Jewish,'' Whitman often writes on Jewish themes. In *Blood and Milk* (1963), her first book of poems, Whitman celebrates her grandfather's life in ''The Lost Steps,'' ''The Old Man's Mistress,'' and ''Touro Synagogue.'' Her grandfather is also important in such personal poems as ''I Become My Grandfather'' in *The Marriage Wig* (1968), which begins with a prose paragraph on the custom of Jewish brides in Eastern Europe shaving their heads to wear the *sheytl*, or marriage wig, lest their beauty distract their husbands from proper study. Whitman has frequently translated Yiddish poetry: she edited and translated *An Anthology of Modern Yiddish Poetry* (1966) and translated Isaac Bashevis Singer in *Short Friday* (1966) and *The Seance* (1968). Her poem ''Translating,'' about King David and Abishag, and included in *The Passion of Lizzie Borden: New and Selected Poems* (1973), is dedicated to Jacob Glatstein, whom she edited and translated. In 1990 she published *The Fiddle Rose: Poems, 1970-1972* by Abraham Sutzkever. *Laughing Gas: Poems New and Selected, 1963-1990* (1991) contains a series of poems about being a present-day Jew as well as personal poems such as "Eighty-three," about her aged mother, and a beautiful elegiac sequence, "The Drowned Mountain."

Whitman in some of her later poetry turned away from celebrating her own life and experience to "bearing witness" to the experience of others. "I believe such poetry," she wrote in 1985, "teaches us how to live, how to cope with loss and disaster, how to survive." Four such works are: the title poem of *The Passion of Lizzie Borden*; *Tamsen Donner: A Woman's Journey* (1977), about a poet and teacher native to Newburyport, Massachusetts, who married the wagonmaster of the ill-fated Donner party; *The Testing of Hanna Senesh* (1986), about a young Hungarian poet who emigrated to Palestine in 1939, later to train with British intelligence, to parachute into Yugoslavia and be killed by the Nazis; and "Anna Pavlova," a short seven-part poem in *Laughing Gas* about the life and aging of the famous ballerina. All of these are meticulously researched. Whitman has also written a book-length poem, *To Dance Is to Live*, about the passionate life of Isadora Duncan, and *Hatshepsut, Speak to Me* (1992), a dialogue between the only woman pharaoh in ancient Egypt and the poet. *The Passion of Lizzie Borden*, as chamber opera, was performed in Santa Fe in 1986, and in 1988 in New York. Both *To Dance Is to Live* and *Tamsen Donner* have been performed as theater/dance by Julie Ince Thompson. To use Whitman's words, these works assert "the value of the individual in an apocalyptic world."

In her role as teacher, Whitman has frequently been poet in residence at universities in the U.S. and Israel. Books related to her teaching include *Poemmaking: Poets in Classrooms* (editor, with Harriet Feinberg, 1975) and *Becoming a Poet: Source, Process, and Practice* (1982). Whitman recorded her work for the Library of Congress in 1974 and 1981.

OTHER WORKS: *Sachuest Point* (television documentary, 1977). *Permanent Address: New Poems, 1973-1980* (1980). *Rhode Island Women on Women: A Poetry Chapbook* (1986).

The papers of Ruth Whitman are housed in the Schlesinger Library of Radcliffe College.

BIBLIOGRAPHY: Ferguson, M. A., ed., *Images of Women in Literature* (1991). Hartwell, D. and K. Cramer, eds., *Masterpieces of Fantasy and Wonder* (1993). Israel, B., *In Praise of Practically Nothing* (CD, 1999). Kates, J. and G. T. Reimer, eds., *Reading Ruth: Contemporary Women Reclaim a Sacred Story* (1994). Kaye-Kantrowitz, M. and I. Klepfisz, eds., *The Tribe of Dina: A Jewish Women's Anthology* (1989). McLennan, K. J., ed., *Nature's Ban: Women's Incest Literature* (1996). Macdonald, C., *Cynthia Macdonald and Ruth Whitman Reading Their Poems* (audiotape, 1981). Schwartz, H., and A. Rudolf, eds., *Voices Within the Ark: The Modern Jewish Poets* (1980).

Reference works: *CA* (1984, 1987). *CP* (1985, 1991). *Oxford Companion to Women's Writing in the United States* (1995). *WW in America* (1990-91).

Other references: *American Book Review* (June 1991, Feb. 1992). *Booklist* (1 May 1969, 15 July 1978). *Book World* (20 May 1973). *Choice* (Sept. 1978, June 1979). *Horn Book* (Dec. 1976). *International Journal of Aging & Human Development* (1991). *LJ* (1 Feb. 1969, July 1973). *Poetry* (May 1964, Mar. 1970). *Prairie Schooner* (Spring 1995). *SR* (15 Mar. 1969).

—JEAN TOBIN

WHITMAN, Sarah Helen (Power)

Born 19 January 1803, Providence, Rhode Island; **died** 27 June 1878, Providence, Rhode Island
Also wrote under: Helen
Daughter of Nicholas and Anna Marsh Power; **married** John W. Whitman, 1828 (died 1833)

Both of Sarah Helen Whitman's parents were from old Rhode Island families. Her father was absent from home for many years when, after being captured at sea by the British in 1813, he chose to continue his seafaring career until 1832. Whitman was educated, for brief periods, at private schools in Providence and at a Quaker school in Jamaica, Long Island, where she lived with an aunt. Although a taste for poetry and novels was thought pernicious, she preferred them to lessons and read the classics and French and German literature in the library of another aunt in Providence. She lived in Boston with her husband, an attorney, editor, and writer, but returned to Providence after his death in 1833. She traveled in Europe in 1857.

Whitman's first published poem was "Retrospection," signed "Helen" (*American Ladies Magazine*, 1829). The editor, Sarah Josepha Hale, encouraged further contributions. Whitman wrote scholarly essays on Goethe, Shelley, and Emerson and served as a correspondent for the *New York Tribune* and the *Providence Journal*.

Whitman was an advocate of educational reforms, divorce, the prevention of cruelty to animals, the liberal ethics of Fourier, women's rights, and universal suffrage. Opposing the materialism of the Protestant churches, she subscribed to the intellectual and spiritual idealism of the Transcendentalists. She was also noted for her belief in prenatal influences and occult and psychic phenomena.

A woman of unusual intelligence and charm, Whitman knew many prominent people, but today she is best known as a friend of Edgar Allan Poe. Following their first meeting on 2 September 1848, exchanges of poems, and a romantic correspondence, they were engaged to be married by the end of the year, but the engagement was broken at the time the banns were to be published. After Poe's death in 1849, Whitman cherished his memory and worked to exonerate the maligned author when, in many circles, it was not considered respectable to have been associated with him. She searched for and located materials and lent valuable items in her possession, and as the Poe controversy became international, she answered all inquiries about him.

Whitman's one volume of verse, *Hours of Life, and Other Poems* (1853), is more carefully composed than the work of most women who were her contemporaries, but it is too genteel and restrained to be of moment by comparison with rougher, more original writers. The subjects are typical for the period: dreams and memories of love, the reality of death, visions of paradise, and the comforts of serene religious faith. Her voice is subdued or languorous; her eyes are sensitive to light and color; her heart is tender. Sixteen poems are the record of her love for Poe; they constitute a structure of illusions for reconciling the "orient phantasies," the experience of mundane and rather ugly stresses, the shame and guilt, the grief, and what she calls the "silent eyes of destiny." The reconciliation freed her for the most radical writing of her career, *Edgar Poe and His Critics* (1860).

Having witnessed a decade of what she calls "remorseless violation" to the memory of Poe, Whitman wished her vindication of him to be impersonal and authoritative. She refrains from discussing her troubled romance with Poe but does take advantage of having known him, of long familiarity with what he wrote, and a scrupulous reading of all that had been written about him. She draws legitimately on the recollections of others who knew him and her own trenchant knowledge of literature and familiarity with the national scene.

Finally, taking into account Poe's mental desolation and periodic insanity, Whitman views his "unappeased and restless soul" in relation to an era when a prevailing skepticism and "divine dissatisfaction everywhere present" showed that the age was moving feverishly through processes of transition and development, "yet gave no idea of where they were leading us." Poe was, for Whitman, one of the men of "electric temperament and prophetic genius" who anticipate those latent ideas about to unfold themselves to humanity. Nothing would have been gained, she observes, had he been another Wordsworth or Longfellow. Whitman was a woman of courage, independent mind, tact, and dignity—and one of the most impressive of American literary critics of the 19th century.

BIBLIOGRAPHY: Harrison, I. A., ed., *The Last Letters of Edgar Allan Poe to Sarah Helen Whitman* (1909). Miller, J. C., *Building Poe Biography* (1977). Miller, J. C., *Poe's Helen Remembers* (1979). Osgood, F. S., *Poems* (1849). Ostrom, J. W., ed., *The Letters of Edgar Allan Poe* (1966). Robertson, J. W., *Edgar A. Poe: A Psychopathic Study* (1923). Ticknor, Caroline, *Poe's Helen* (1916).

Reference works: *American Female Poets* (1849). *NAW* (1971). *Oxford Companion to Women's Writing in the United States* (1995).

—ELIZABETH PHILIPS

WHITNEY, Adeline D(utton) T(rain)

Born 15 September 1824, Boston, Massachusetts; **died** 21 March 1906, Milton, Massachusetts
Wrote under: Mrs. A. D. T. Whitney
Daughter of John and Adeline Dutton Train; **married** Seth Whitney, 1843; **children:** four

Adeline Dutton Train Whitney was one of the second generation Boston Brahmins. She received a fine education and married a man 20 years her senior, a businessman like her father. She had four children—one of whom died in infancy—and did not begin her writing career until her children were grown. She tried her hand at all sorts of books, such as poetry collections, a cookbook, an attack on Christian Science, but her juvenile novels were the most popular.

In *Friendly Letters to Girl Friends* (1896), she calls novels "stories of human possibilities." Since most of her novels were written for girls, the "possibilities" she was concerned with were those of her young readers, and in novel after novel she counseled them to stay in woman's own sphere—the home. "Perfect homes must be the centres and starting-points of the perfect commonwealths," she writes in *Friendly Letters*.

This theme is evident in the four novels that make up the Real Folks series: *A Summer in Leslie Goldthwaite's Life* (1866), *We Girls* (1870), *Real Folks* (1871), and *The Other Girls* (1873). All the girls who meet one another in these lightly connected works find their happiness in home and family life, even if they have to go out as servants. One of Whitney's themes is that women should not want to work anywhere outside the home even if they have to earn money, so they should take jobs as servants in other women's homes above any other work. (Perhaps the most widely expressed grievance of Whitney's day among women of her class was the difficulty of finding good servants.) In all, Whitney's fiction defends the most traditional aspects of the lives of upper-class American women of her day. She perhaps tempers her support by some criticism of social snobbery and a respect for sincere religious profession.

Brought up in the Congregational and Unitarian churches, Whitney later became an Episcopalian. She was no evangelist, and her plots do not turn on the characters' conversions, but most of her novels touch on religion or Christian ethics. *Faith Gartney's Girlhood* (1863) was one of the standbys of Sunday school libraries for over 50 years. It was also her most popular and most interesting novel and has a rather common theme: Faith's family loses its money in a business depression; both parents are unable to cope with the change in their lives, but Faith offers a plan, in which they move to a country house they own and do some of their own work. Three women—her aunt, who runs her own home and maintains a rigid independence; her father's nurse, who though middle-aged and plain finds her life in service; and the servant girl taken in by the aunt, who is unlucky in love but is left the means to run a small orphan's home—serve as examples of paths women may tread without becoming unwomanly. Faith is one of the lucky ones; young and beautiful, she gets married and will have her own home, husband, and children.

It may not be intentional, but Whitney's novels set up a very woman-centered way of life and scheme of values, even as they promote the notion of woman's inferiority to man. Her wives are not seen much with their husbands, but with aunts, mothers, daughters, and girlfriends. Faith's father is a broken man when he loses his money: "I'm no more than a mere useless block of wood," he complains; his daughter answers, "We shall just have to set you up, and make an idol of you then!" Her girls are advised to seek a completely separate way of life from men. As she put it in *Friendly Letters*, "Puss, puss! run for the chimney-corner. And leave something outside for men to do, that there may still be chimney-corners."

Whitney was a writer familiar to several generations of American young women. While her prose style is murky and her diction high-flown, her depictions of ideal home life and successful girlhoods pleased her readers. Modern cultural historians find her novels of interest in the study of the segregation of the sexes in 19th-century America.

OTHER WORKS: *Boys at Chequasset* (1862). *The Gayworthys* (1865). *Patience Strong's Outings* (1868). *Hitherto* (1869). *Mother Goose for Grown Folk* (1870). *Pansies* (1872). *Sights and Insights* (1876). *Just How: A Key to Cook-Books* (1878). *Odd or Even?* (1880). *Homespun Yarns* (1886). *Bonnyborough* (1886). *Bird Talk* (1887). *Daffodils* (1887). *Ascutney Street* (1890). *A Golden Gossip* (1892). *White Memories* (1893). *The Open Mystery: A Reading of the Mosaic Story* (1897). *Square Pegs* (1899). *The Integrity of Christian Science* (1900). *Biddy's Episodes* (1904).

BIBLIOGRAPHY: Halsey, F. W., *Women Authors of Our Day in Their Homes* (1903).

Reference works: *Oxford Companion to Women's Writing in the United States* (1995).

Other references: *Horn Book* (June 1953). *NYT* (22 Mar. 1906).

—BEVERLY SEATON

WHITNEY, Phyllis A(yame)

Born 9 September 1903, Yokohama, Japan
Daughter of Charles J. and Lillian Mandeville Whitney; married George A. Garner, 1925 (divorced); Lovell F. Jahnke, 1950 (died); children: one daughter

Born of American parents, Phyllis A. Whitney first came to the U.S. at the age of fifteen, after living in Japan, China, and the

Philippines. She graduated from high school in Chicago. She married a businessman in 1950 and had one daughter, living in Staten Island, New York, and northern New Jersey. Whitney has written more than 50 novels, which she divides into three groups: novels for young people, mysteries for young people, and adult novels. Almost all of the last are gothic romances. During her long career, she has reviewed books for newspapers and has taught courses, lectured, and written widely on the business and craft of writing fiction. Two novels, *Mystery of the Haunted Pool* (1960) and *Mystery of the Hidden Hand* (1963), have received Edgars from the Mystery Writers of America, and she received the Grand Master award in 1988 for her lifetime achievement.

The novels for young people appeal to young girls rather than boys. Many of them carry girls' names in the title: *A Place for Ann* (1941), *A Star for Ginny* (1942), *A Window for Julie* (1943), *Linda's Homecoming* (1950), and *Nobody Likes Trina* (1972). A majority of these didactic novels have been favorably reviewed by educators and librarians, and Whitney's success in this field has made her an authority. She has also published how-to guidebooks, including *Writing Juvenile Fiction* (1947, revised 1960), *Writing Juvenile Stories and Novels: How to Write and Sell Fiction for Young People* (1976, 1985) and *Guide to Fiction Writing* (1984).

Her mysteries for young people can be easily recognized because, with the exception of *The Vanishing Scarecrow* (1971), each of them has a title beginning with "mystery" or "secret." These too are primarily written for girls, although the adventure aspect is strong. They are all characterized by vivid backgrounds. Whitney's early life abroad provided exotic background material for many of her novels. For many years, she made each of her many trips serve a double purpose: she used the background material gathered for one juvenile novel and one adult gothic romance. Thus a trip to the Virgin Islands produced both *Secret of the Spotted Shell* (1967) and *Columbella* (1966). She has set novels in Turkey, Norway, Japan, Greece, South Africa, and a wide variety of places in the United States.

Whitney's first adult novel was *Red Is for Murder* (1943), a straightforward mystery novel set in a department store. She did not return to adult fiction until sometime later; the next adult book, *The Quicksilver Pool* (1955), is a historical novel set on Staten Island during the Civil War draft riots. Although there is a domestic mystery, the most important aspect of the plot is a love story, a pattern she also uses in *The Trembling Hills* (1956), a novel about the San Francisco earthquake. After *Skye Cameron* (1957), a domestic novel of 19th-century New Orleans, Whitney turned to modern Japan for the background to *The Moonflower* (1958). The following three books—*Thunder Heights* (1960), a novel of the 19th-century Hudson River valley; *Blue Fire* (1961), a mystery of modern South Africa; and *Window on the Square* (1962), set on Washington Square in 19th-century New York— are similar to the novels preceding them. All deal with young women trying to make their way in the world and who marry their true loves after a series of dangerous adventures. The novels are competent romantic mysteries, but not nearly so well realized as the books to come.

After the successful contemporary romantic adventures *Seven Tears for Apollo* (1963) and *Black Amber* (1964), Whitney only once, in *Sea Jade* (1964), uses a historical setting for her novels. The mystery element becomes a more important part of the plot than it had been before. Whitney's preoccupation with women and their identities in these novels is often very sophisticated (she has written that she relies on Karen Horney for psychological insight about women). In novels such as *Columbella, Silverhill* (1967), *Lost Island* (1970), *Listen for the Whisperer* (1972), *The Turquoise Mask* (1974), and *The Golden Unicorn* (1976), she is increasingly concerned with relationships between mothers and daughters and with questions of feminine identity as they relate to the past—with the problems of women trying both to come to terms with and transcend their family background. In later years, most of her heroines sought their own identities through returning to their ancestral home or through a reconciliation with another woman in the family. The solution of the mystery provides both a conclusion for the plot and an answer to the significant questions asked by the heroine of her past.

Although each of these books ends with clear answers, the process of finding them is arduous and uncompromising. The mystery genre imposes limits on the ambiguity Whitney can allow in the resolution, but it does not keep her from an honest and rigorous development of the issues. Her women make mistakes: they marry the wrong man, they misjudge character, one of them has an illegitimate child; but they are allowed the opportunity to see what they have done and to change it and themselves. Many authors write gothic romances; very few write them with the continuing sophistication and wisdom of Whitney. Further testament to her enduring written powers are that most of her books are still in print, with three dozen or so titles reprinted in the 1990s alone.

OTHER WORKS: *The Silver Inkwell* (1945). *Willow Hill* (1947). *Ever After* (1948). *Mystery of the Gulls* (1949). *Island of the Dark Woods* (1951; alternate title, *Mystery of the Strange Traveler*). *Love Me, Love Me Not* (1952). *Step to the Music* (1953). *A Long Time Coming* (1954). *Mystery of the Black Diamonds* (1954). *Mystery of the Isle of Skye* (1955). *The Fire and the Gold* (1956). *The Highest Dream* (1956). *Mystery of the Green Cat* (1957). *Secret of the Samurai Sword* (1958). *Creole Holiday* (1959). *Secret of the Tiger's Eye* (1961). *Mystery of the Golden Horn* (1962). *Secret of the Emerald Star* (1964). *Mystery of the Angry Idol* (1965). *Hunter's Green* (1968). *Secret of Goblin Glen* (1968). *Mystery of the Crimson Ghost* (1969). *Secret of the Missing Footprints* (1969). *The Winter People* (1969). *Mystery of the Scowling Boy* (1973). *Snowfire* (1973). *Secret of the Haunted Mesa* (1975). *Spindrift* (1975). *Secret of the Stone Face* (1977). *The Stone Bull* (1977). *The Glass Flame* (1978). *Domino* (1979). *Poinciana* (1980). *Vermillion* (1981). *Emerald* (1983). *Rainsong* (1984). *Dream of Orchids* (1985). *The Flaming Tree* (1986). *Silversword* (1987). *Feather on the Moon* (1988). *Rainbow in the Mist* (1989). *The Singing Stones* (1990). *Woman Without a Past* (1991). *The Ebony Swan* (1992). *Star Flight* (1993). *Daughter of the Stars* (1994). *Phyllis A. Whitney Presents Malice Domestic 5: An Anthology of Original Traditional Mystery Stories* (1996).

A manuscript collection of Phyllis A. Whitney's work is housed in the Mugar Memorial Library of Boston University.

BIBLIOGRAPHY: Reference works: *CA* (1967). *Detecting Women* (1994). *Encyclopedia Mysteriosa* (1994). *St. James Guide to Crime & Mystery Writers* (1996).

Other references: *LJ* (June 1991). *NYTBR* (2 July 1967). *Time* (12 Apr. 1971). *Writer* (Feb. 1960, Feb. 1967).

—KAY MUSSELL,
UPDATED BY NELSON RHODES

WIGGIN, Kate Douglass

Born 28 September 1856, Philadelphia, Pennsylvania; **died** 24 August 1923, Harrow-on-Hill, England
Also wrote under: Mrs. Riggs
Daughter of Robert and Helen Dyer Smith; **married** Samuel Wiggin, 1881 (died 1889); George Riggs, 1895

Kate Douglass Wiggin was born to a prosperous Philadelphia lawyer and his wife, a native of Maine. Her childhood was spent in the village of Hollis, Maine, after the death of her father and her mother's remarriage. She was educated at home and then at various schools in New England. In the mid-1870s, she moved with her family to California, where they came on hard times.

Wiggin became interested in the new kindergarten movement and took a course under Emma Marwedel in Los Angeles, and then opened the Silver Street Kindergarten in a slum in San Francisco, the first free kindergarten in California. For a number of years, she was a national leader in the Kindergarten movement, and she began her own training school in San Francisco in 1880. To raise money for the free-kindergarten movement, Wiggin published privately two short sentimental novels, *The Story of Patsy* (1883) and *The Birds' Christmas Carol* (1887).

Her first husband, a lawyer, died in 1889. Wiggin had given up kindergarten work in 1884, and she began writing full time after the successful commercial publication of *The Birds' Christmas Carol* in 1889. She returned to the East Coast and lived in New York City and Hollis, giving readings from her works and traveling to Europe. Her second husband was a businessman. Among her New York circle were William Dean Howells, Mary E. Wilkins Freeman, and Carolyn Wells. Wiggin suffered periodically from nervous exhaustion; the opening chapters of *Rebecca of Sunnybrook Farm* (1903) were written in a sanatorium.

The Birds' Christmas Carol became a seasonal classic, published in multiple editions in various languages. In this edifying tale, Carol Bird, a wealthy but sick ten-year-old, gives a Christmas dinner for the children of a poor family in the neighborhood, the Ruggles. Although the heroine dies after the children leave on Christmas night, the book's popularity did not rest on sentiment alone; the portrayal of the Ruggles family is realistic and humorous.

Two children's novels set in California, *A Summer in a Canon* (1889) and *Polly Oliver's Problem* (1893), are not very good, and the same may be said of a series of travel novels, most of which have Penelope Hamilton as the heroine. Wiggin is best known for stories set in Maine, and these are undoubtedly her best work.

Timothy's Quest (1890) and some early short stories have Maine backgrounds, but Wiggin only began to concentrate on regional material after the success of *Rebecca of Sunnybrook Farm*. Today this is considered a children's book, but it was first a bestselling adult novel. Set in a village similar to Hollis, in the Saco River valley, the story is a classic orphan story without the orphan: Rebecca, the daughter of a poor widow, is sent to live with two maiden aunts in order to be "made." In traditional fashion, she wins their hearts, even that of the stern Aunt Miranda. A spirited child, Rebecca accomplishes many things in the course of the story, including the saving of her family fortunes. She graduates from boarding school in a cheesecloth dress, but her time at school has been a success—she is class president. Rebecca's character and the local color of her background are both appealing. This story did not end with a marriage, but with only the hint of an attachment. There was no sequel, only a volume of "missing chapters," or stories about Rebecca set in the time of the first novel, *The New Chronicles of Rebecca* (1907).

Mother Carey's Chickens (1911) is another of Wiggin's popular New England novels. A more saccharine story than *Rebecca of Sunnybrook Farm*, it tells how the Carey family, under the leadership of young Nancy, manages to survive economically after the death of their father. Other Maine stories with good regional description are another Christmas story, *The Old Peabody Pew* (1907), and *Susanna and Sue* (1909), which features a Shaker colony. *The Story of Waitstill Baxter* (1913) shows more mature character development than the average Wiggin novel. Set in the early-19th century, this novel of Saco valley life features a historical figure, the traveling evangelist Jacob Cochrane, and describes the disruption he brings to a family.

Wiggin's autobiography, *My Garden of Memory* (1923), is a charming and valuable document, revealing its author as a woman of spirit and sense. Several of her novels were filmed more than once. These movies mirror the popular modern conception of Wiggin as a silly sentimentalist, but her novels, slight as they are, belie that reputation. She was a chronicler of the romance of real life, not a romanticist. And while there is sentimentality in her earlier works, her major novels are free of it. Most of her heroines—Rebecca, Nancy Carey, Polly Oliver, Waitstill Baxter—are active, intelligent young women, unlike the Little Eva stereotype, Carol Bird. Wiggin argued for wholesomeness, not hypocrisy, in fiction, and her point of view was that of a sophisticated professional writer, not that of a sheltered matron. She was a popular writer who expressed what her contemporaries themselves thought of as "real life."

OTHER WORKS: *A Cathedral Courtship and Penelope's English Experiences* (1893). *The Village Watch-tower* (1895). *Marm Lisa* (1896). *Penelope's Progress* (1898). *Penelope's Irish Experiences* (1901). *Diary of a Goose Girl* (1902). *Rose o' the River* (1905). *Penelope's Postscripts* (1915). *The Romance of a Christmas Card* (1916). *Ladies in Waiting* (1919). *Creeping Jenny, and Other New England Stories* (1924).

Fifteen books, some collection of stories and some about kindergartens, written with her sister, Nora Archibald Smith.

BIBLIOGRAPHY: Benner, H., *Kate Douglass Wiggin's Country of Childhood* (1956). Smith, N., *Kate Douglass Wiggin as Her Sister Knew Her* (1925).

Reference works: *Oxford Companion to Women's Writing in the United States* (1995).

Other references: *Bookman* (1910, 1924). *Lamp* (1905). *London Bookman* (1910). *NEQ* (June 1968).

—BEVERLY SEATON

WIGGINS, Bernice Love

Born 4 March 1897, Austin, Texas; death date unknown
Daughter of J. Austin Love; **married** (Mr.) Wiggins

Bernice Wiggins may never have lived with her father, a college-educated black poet who worked as a laborer and later became state Sunday-school director for the Holiness church. When her mother died in 1902, Wiggins went to El Paso to live with an aunt. She grew up without a home library, but her first-grade teacher encouraged her in her habit of inventing and reciting rhythmical lines. In high school, Wiggins learned "something of the art of versification"—perhaps to her detriment, as her weakest poems are those that follow the conventions of white writing of her day. Folklorist J. Mason Brewer praises Wiggins as a dialect poet, calling her the best of her contemporaries and comparing her favorably with Paul Laurence Dunbar.

Wiggins' reputation was probably made chiefly through performances in her own community. One of her poems, "Miss Annie's Playing," is marked for piano accompaniment. "Church Folks," a satire in dialect, was immortalized by J. Mason Brewer, who not only published it but also recited it to open all his speeches during several decades. Wiggins also had poems published in the black press, including the *Houston Informer*, the *Chicago Defender*, and *Half-Century Magazine*. Much of her work deals with political issues: poverty, racism, women's rights, lynching, the black soldier's role in World War I. She even essays a work on the injustice of the laws against prostitution, in which she assumes the persona of a "vampire."

In 1925 Wiggins herself published a book of her poems called *Tuneful Tales*. This 174-page volume is the chief storehouse of her work, and its introduction by her former high school principal is almost the only published source of biographical data.

J. Mason Brewer mentions in 1936 that Wiggins had moved to Los Angeles. No further books by Wiggins have come to light.

The best poems in *Tuneful Tales* are characterized by excellent scansion, good narrative flow, and marvelous attention to detail. In ''A Race with a Corpse,'' a broadly humorous ballad, Wiggins carefully lays the groundwork by stating, ''dis t'ing yo' call 'Embalmin'/ Didn't hab dat in my day,'' and filling in details of a church funeral. Often her poems are tragicomic. In ''Who's to Blame,'' a man walks home in the snow and puts his only pair of shoes in the oven to dry. In the morning, his mother has built a fire and reduced the shoes to cinders. Wiggins' characteristically loving tone comes through as the character ponders, ''who's I gwine to blame fo' it,/ De party or de weather?'' He does not blame his mother or himself.

Wiggins often does fresh and original work in male personas. Her ''Sighs of a Soldier,'' for instance, picks up the voice of a black G.I., responding to ''dis sawed off Sarjunt'': ''He 'lows, 'Whose givin' orders here?' 'Alright,' I sez, 'I'se cumin'.'/ 'Why surtainly, I no yo' is, mak' 'ace, an' cum a runin'.'''

In ''Ethiopia,'' Wiggins observes that black patriots answered the call to arms only to face a resurgence of lynching at home. She suggests, through the persona of the race itself, the radical step of revoking loyalty to the nation: ''Take it back till they cease to burn them alive,/ Take it back till the white man shall cease to deprive/ My sons, yea, my black sons, of rights justly won.'' In the next stanza, the author comments: ''Mary forgave, 'twas her Savior son's will,/ Ethiopia forgives, but remembers still.''

In ''The Poetical Farmwife,'' Wiggins explains why it is difficult to write while doing housework. Yet many of her best works deal with relationships between parents and children and sacrifices lovingly made for family. More of her writing may be discovered among the papers of her friends or in the archives of churches or schools in one of her communities.

BIBLIOGRAPHY: Brewer, J.M., *Heralding Dawn* (1936).

—FRIEDA L. WERDEN

WIGGINS, Marianne

Born 8 November 1947, Lancaster, Pennsylvania

Daughter of John and Mary Klonis Wiggins; **married** Brian Porzak, 1965 (divorced 1970); Salman Rushdie, 1988 (divorced 1993); **children:** Lara

Novelist and short story writer Marianne Wiggins grew up in the Amish region of eastern Pennsylvania. Her father was a farmer and preacher and her mother was the daughter of Greek immigrants who had settled in Virginia. Wiggins' childhood was shaped both by the fundamentalist Christianity of her father and the ritual-filled Greek Orthodoxy of her mother as well as by the neighboring Amish community's endeavor to create an ideal religious society. These contentious influences permeate Wiggins' fictional themes in which she examines and dissects the tenacious yet mutable hold of religious mythology, romanticism, patriarchy, colonialism, and violence upon her characters' lives.

Married young and with a daughter who was born in Rome in 1968, Wiggins lived in Paris, Brussels, New York, and Massachusetts before settling in London, where she has resided since 1985. While a single mother, she supported herself with work in a stockbroker's office before the proceeds from her first novel, the semiautobiographical *Babe* (1975), enabled her to pursue a full-time career in writing. Her early work focuses in often comic fashion on the travails of young mothers attempting to make their way in the world despite loutish men and the conventions of traditional expectations for women.

Wiggins' third novel, *Separate Checks* (1984), features a matriarchal family full of eccentric overachievers and wild women characters as seen through the eyes of one of their daughters, Ellery McQueen. Ellery is composing her own version of the life histories of her female relatives, which serves as the framing device for the narrative. Through storytelling, Ellery is attempting to understand her own troubled inheritance of that ineffable mixture of emotions passed on from mothers to daughters. While the satirical language of the novel is uneven, shifting, as one reviewer noted, ''between the dazzling and the contrived,'' Wiggins largely succeeds in creating a portrait of the complicated, intimate, and not always welcome ties that bind this family of women.

In a collection of short stories, *Herself in Love* (1987), Wiggins turns an edgy eye upon the vagaries of romantic love and posits a nearly inevitable outcome of estrangement between women and men. Her characters suffer from odd disconnections, poignant regrets, and uneasy exile. There is an idiosyncratic range of content in these stories in which Wiggins demonstrates her ability to experiment with style and language, while still maintaining an attentive ear for the subtle nuances of dialect, locale, and period that so individuate her characters.

In her critically acclaimed novel *John Dollar* (1989), Wiggins successfully weaves together recurring themes from her earlier work into a caustic satire on the conceits of Christianity, imperialism, and the too easy descent of civilized society into barbarism. The book tells the story of Charlotte Lewes, a World War I widow, who accepts a position in Burma teaching the children of the smugly superior British colonialists living there at the height of the Raj. Once in Rangoon, Charlotte falls in love with sailor John Dollar and begins to shed the constraints of her English compatriots while adopting the customs of the Burmese. On an outing to name an island in honor of their king, the British colonialists are beset by catastrophes, perhaps brought on by their own brutality, leaving a paralyzed John Dollar and eight schoolgirls as the stranded survivors. In language alternately disturbing and lyrical, Wiggins depicts the relentless moral disintegration of the girls' social order. Forming a rigid hierarchy in a doomed attempt to survive, the girls instead devolve from petty bullying into ritualistic cannibalism, fated to recreate a nightmarish version of what they've seen modeled by their elders. With *John Dollar*, Wiggins is unsparing in her scathing critique of the myths of empire and of Christian sacrifice.

At the time of *John Dollar*'s publication, Wiggins was married to author Salman Rushdie. Their life together was severely disrupted by the death threat placed on Rushdie by Islamic zealots in response to the perceived blasphemy of his book *The Satanic Verses*. Wiggins and Rushdie were forced to live in hiding for a period of time and they subsequently separated and divorced. With respect to this episode, Wiggins has commented ironically on her obligation as a writer to point out the historical parallels with other eras in which religious doubters have been sentenced to death for voicing their skepticism.

In *Almost Heaven* (1998), Wiggins depicts a foreign correspondent, damaged by having witnessed too much violence in the Balkans, who returns to America, only to fall in love with a woman suffering from traumatic amnesia. The novel functions as an interrogation of the role of memory in human affairs and takes as its central metaphor the capricious nature of weather. However, *Almost Heaven* is less than satisfying due to its melodramatic prose and unwieldy plotting, which transpire at the expense of plausibility and depth of character development.

Throughout her novels and stories to date, Wiggins has established herself as an author willing to grapple with substantive ideas and with the darker cultural and political forces against which her characters enact their dreams and fears. At times her work is marred by overly clever wordplay, but more typically Wiggins infuses her writing with keen intelligence, a jaded vigilance toward hypocrisy, and the passionately acerbic sensibility of an expatriate. The recipient of a Whiting award, a National Education Association grant, and the Janet Heidinger Kafka fiction prize, Wiggins' next project is a novel about the American Revolution.

OTHER WORKS: *Went South* (1980) *Bet They'll Miss Us When We're Gone* (1991). *Eveless Eden* (1995).

BIBLIOGRAPHY: Reference works: *ANR* 60 (1998). *CA* 130 (1990). *CLC* 57 (1990).
    Other references: *Booklist* (1 Oct. 1995). *LATBR* (1 Apr. 1984). *MacClean's* (21 Aug. 1989). *NYT* (16 Feb. 1989, 4 Apr. 1990, 9 Apr. 1991). *NYTBR* (19 Feb. 1989, 15 Oct. 1995, 20 Sept. 1998). *PW* (17 Feb. 1989). *Salon* (17 Sept. 1998). *San Francisco Bay Guardian* (25 Nov. 1998). *WSJ* (19 July 1991). *WPBW* (6 Sept. 1998). *Writer's Digest* (Feb. 1991).

—CHERRI L. SHUR

WILCOX, Ella Wheeler

Born 5 November 1850, Johnstown Center, Wisconsin; **died** 30 October 1919, Short Beach, Connecticut
Wrote under: Ella Wheeler
Daughter of Marcus H. and Sarah Pratt Wheeler; **married** Robert M. Wilcox, 1884

Ella Wheeler Wilcox was the youngest of four children born to a music teacher turned farmer and a mother who had strong literary ambitions. She claimed that her mother's extensive reading of Shakespeare, Scott, and Byron was a prenatal influence that shaped her entire career. Her mother helped her to find time to read and write rather than work on the bleak Wisconsin farm.

Wilcox was influenced early by the romantic melodramas of Ouida, Mary J. Holmes, May Agnes Fleming, and Mrs. Southworth. At the age of ten, she wrote a "novel" in 10 chapters, printing it in her childish hand on scraps of paper and binding it in paper torn from the kitchen wall. The *New York Mercury* published an essay when she was fifteen. In 1867 she enrolled at the University of Wisconsin, where, however, she remained only a short time. She begged her family to be allowed to remain at home and write.

By the time she was eighteen, she was earning a substantial salary, which aided her impoverished family. People from Madison, Milwaukee, and Chicago began to seek out the little country girl with the "inspired pen," and she in turn was delighted to visit their city homes. By 1880 the "Milwaukee School of Poetry" was at its height with Wilcox as its shining light; the poets were all well known throughout the West, and some had even gained recognition in the East.

Maurine (1876), a narrative poem, introduces two types of women Wilcox often wrote about: Helen, a weak and passive person who bears a daughter and soon dies, and Maurine, an aggressive and highly intelligent artist who eventually marries an American poet-intellectual. Maurine travels to Europe, where her paintings are favorably received. Helen and Maurine reappear in more complex form as Mabel and Ruth, two of the characters in *Three Women* (1897).

When Wilcox attempted to publish *Poems of Passion* (1883), a collection of poems that had appeared previously in various periodicals, the book was rejected because of the "immorality" of several poems, and its author became the subject of unpleasant notoriety. When a Chicago publisher brought out the book, however, it was an immediate success, and Wilcox's reputation was made. In this work, she brought into her love poetry the element of sin. By 1888 she was a leader in what was called the Erotic School, a group of writers who rebelled against the stricter rules of conventionality. By 1900 a whole feminine school of rather daring verse on the subject of the emotions followed Wilcox's lead.

The symbolism of sexual passion is depicted throughout her poems as a tiger who is "a splendid creature," as in "Three and One" (*Poems of Pleasure*, 1888); sex for Wilcox is "all the tiger in my blood." In "At Eleusis," motherhood is praised and welcomed, a common theme of her poetry.

Wilcox wrote editorials and essays for the *New York Journal* and the *Chicago American* as well as contributing to *Cosmopolitan* and other magazines. In 1901 she was commissioned by the *New York American* to write a poem on the death of Queen Victoria and was sent to London, where she was presented at the court of St. James. During World War I, she toured the army camps in France, reciting her poems and counseling young soldiers on their problems.

Throughout her life, Wilcox enjoyed great popularity, and she took her work most seriously. In defending her poetry against critics, she maintained that "heart, not art," is most important in poetry and pointed out that her poems comforted millions of weary and unhappy people.

OTHER WORKS: *Drops of Water* (1872). *Shells* (1873). *The Birth of the Opal* (1886). *Mal Moulee: A Novel* (1886). *Perdita, and Other Stories* (1886). *The Adventures of Miss Volney* (1888). *A Double Life* (1891). *How Salvatore Won* (1891). *The Beautiful Land of Nod* (1892). *An Erring Woman's Love* (1892). *A Budget of Christmas Tales* (1895). *An Ambitious Man* (1896). *Custer and Other Poems* (1896). *Men, Women, and Emotions* (1896). *Poems of Power* (1901). *The Heart of the New Thought* (1902). *Kingdom of Love* (1902). *Sweet Danger* (1902). *Around the Year* (1904). *Poems of Love* (1905). *A Woman of the World* (1905). *Mizpah* (1906). *New Thought Pastels* (1906). *Poems of Sentiment* (1906). *New Thought Common Sense and What Life Means to Me* (1908). *Song of Liberty* (1908). *Poems of Progress* (1909). *Sailing Sunny Seas* (1909). *The New Hawaiian Girl* (1910). *Yesterdays* (1910). *The Englishman, and Other Poems* (1912). *Gems* (1912). *Picked Poems* (1912). *The Art of Being Alive* (1914). *Cameos* (1914). *Lest We Forget* (1914). *Poems of Problems* (1914). *World Voices* (1916). *The Worlds and I* (1918). *Poems* (1918). *Sonnets of Sorrow and Triumph* (1918). *Collected Poems* (1924).

BIBLIOGRAPHY: Ballou, J., *Period Piece: Ella Wheeler Wilcox and Her Time* (1940). Brown, N., *Critical Confessions* (1899). Town, C. H., *Adventures in Editing* (1926). Watts, E. S., *The Poetry of American Women, 1632-1945* (1977). Wheeler, M. P., *Evolution of Ella Wheeler Wilcox and Other Wheelers* (1921).

Reference works: *AA. NAW* (1971). *Oxford Companion to Women's Writing in the United States* (1995).

Other references: *American Mercury* (Aug. 1934). *Bookman* (Jan. 1920). *Cosmopolitan* (Nov. 1888). *Harper's* (Mar. 1952). *Literary Digest* (22 Nov. 1919).*London Times* (31 Oct. 1919). *NYT* (31 Oct. 1919). *Poetry and Drama* (Mar. 1913).

—ANNE R. GROBEN

WILDER, Laura Ingalls

Born 7 February 1867, Pepin County, Wisconsin; **died** 10 February 1957, Mansfield, Missouri

Daughter of Charles and Caroline Quiner Ingalls; **married** Almanzo Wilder, 1885; **children:** one son, one daughter

Born in a cabin in the Wisconsin woods, Laura Ingalls Wilder is perhaps America's best-known female pioneer. While her books do not follow the pattern of her early life exactly, they are very close. Her parents moved their family many times, searching for a better life for Wilder and her three sisters. After living in Missouri, Kansas, Iowa, and Minnesota, they settled in De Smet, South Dakota, where Wilder met and married her husband. After a difficult early married life, in which one daughter was born and a baby son died, the Wilders bought a farm near Mansfield, Missouri, where they lived the rest of their lives.

At Rocky Ridge Farm, Wilder raised chickens and made butter, helped her husband build their home, and began to write articles for various rural papers and a column, "As a Farm Woman Thinks," for the *Missouri Ruralist*. She stopped writing for the papers in 1924, but her daughter, Rose Wilder Lane, a writer herself, encouraged her to write about her early life. So, in 1930 at the age of sixty-three, Wilder began to write the Little House books.

The seven autobiographical volumes published during Wilder's lifetime cover the years from about age four to her marriage and reflect the changing point of view of the maturing heroine. *Little House in the Big Woods* (1932) describes life in a log cabin in the forest, as seen by a young child. This volume features stories about Pa's adventures in the woods, a jolly Christmas, and a maple sugaring dance. *Little House on the Prairie* (1935) takes the Ingalls family across the Mississippi into Indian lands, where they create a homestead but are forced by the government to leave. Minnesota is the scene of *On the Banks of Plum Creek* (1937), where Laura goes to school and first encounters Nellie Oleson, a tiresome brat who appears in later books as well. The Ingalls family's life in Minnesota is dominated by the plague of grasshoppers.

By the Shores of Silver Lake (1939) takes the family to South Dakota, where they live at a railroad camp, then spend the winter in the surveyor's house so they will be on hand when the town is established. *The Long Winter* (1940) describes the severe winter of 1881, which the family spends in a house in De Smet. The book ends with the arrival of the train (snowbound since fall) and the celebration of Christmas in May. *Little Town on the Prairie* (1941) gives scenes of Laura's life as a teenager in town. At the end of the book, she is given a certificate to teach school, although she is only fifteen. The final volume, *These Happy Golden Years* (1943), tells of her teaching and her courtship with Almanzo Wilder; they are married at the end of the volume. One other volume of the Little House books, *Farmer Boy* (1933), does not deal with her own life but with her husband's boyhood on a large farm near Malone, New York.

The other three books published under her name are all posthumous. *The First Four Years* (1971) covers the early, difficult years of her marriage, ending with the death of her baby boy and the burning of their home. *On the Way Home* (1962) is a journal she kept during their trip to Missouri and the beginning of their life at Rocky Ridge Farm. *West from Home* (1974) is a group of letters written to her husband from San Francisco when visiting Rose there in 1915.

The only major award won by Wilder was a special award given at the Newbery-Caldecott dinner in 1954, but her Little House books are among the most popular and beloved of children's classics, and have spawned many related series. The Children's Library Association set up the Laura Ingalls Wilder Award, of which she was the first recipient, to be given every five years. A popular television series was been based on her work, although the scripts departed a good deal from the themes and spirit of the original books, giving more emphasis to exciting and unusual events. Many of the places Wilder lived have memorials of some sort, and Rocky Ridge Farm is now a museum.

The Little House books' description of everyday life in pioneer times appeals to both children and adults. As children's fiction, their greatest achievement is the ease and grace with which Wilder speaks to children. She never patronizes, yet she retains a suitable perspective. Laura and her sisters are not glamorized; Laura is adventurous, but in contrast to children in other books about pioneer life, she performs no heroic deeds. Of course, these novels are cosmetic reality, for only a few of the harsher aspects of pioneer life are depicted, as a study of those parts of Wilder's life left out of the story reveals. No doubt the romance of pioneer life, aided by the appeal of a series, is no small part of the success of the Little House books, but the heart of Wilder's achievement is the literary artistry with which she uses a simple, declarative style and shapes her narrative around ordinary events.

BIBLIOGRAPHY: Alter, J., *Extraordinary Women of the American West* (1999). Anderson, W., *Laura Ingalls Wilder: A Biography* (1995). Anderson, W., *Pioneer Girl: The Story of Laura Ingalls Wilder* (1998). Bloom, H., ed., *Women Writers of Children's Literature* (1998). Erisman, F., *Laura Ingalls Wilder* (1994). Glasscock, S., *Laura Ingalls Wilder: An Author's Story* (1998). Hines, S. W., *I Remember Laura: Laura Ingalls Wilder* (1994). Miller, J. E., *Laura Ingalls Wilder's Little Town: Where History and Literature Meet* (1994). Miller, J. E., *Becoming Laura Ingalls Wilder: The Woman Behind the Legend* (1998). Neuman, J. M., "Cowgirl, Trailblazer, American: Laura Ingalls Wilder and the Ideology of New Traditionalism" (thesis, 1996). Perkins, C. N., *100 Authors Who Shaped World History* (1996). Romines, A., *Constructing the Little House: Gender, Culture, and Laura Ingalls Wilder* (1997). Ross, L. H., *To Sanctify the World: Skyscapes in the Fiction of Wilder, Guthrie, and Cather* (dissertation, 1991). Scherf, J. C., *The 'Wilder' Side of Laura Ingalls: The Role of Nature in the Little House Books* (1992). Spaeth, J., *Laura Ingalls Wilder* (1987). Subramanian, J. M., *Laura Ingalls Wilder: An Annotated Bibliography of Critical, Biographical, and Teaching Studies* (1997). Wadsworth, G., *Laura Ingalls Wilder: Storyteller of the Prairie* (1997). Wallner, A., *Laura Ingalls Wilder* (1999). Wheeler, J. C., *Laura Ingalls Wilder: A Tribute to the Young at Heart* (1992). White, D. L., *Laura's Friends Remember: Close Friends Recall Laura Ingalls Wilder* (1992). Zochert, D., *Laura* (1976).

Reference works: *Oxford Companion to Women's Writing in the United States* (1995).

Other references: *Atlantic* (Feb. 1975). *Children's Literature* (1975, 1978). *Commentary* (1998). *Horn Book* (Sept. 1943, Dec. 1953, Oct. 1965). *Legacy* (1998). *Lion and the Unicorn* (1979-80). *NYRB* (Dec. 1994). *NYTBR* (Aug. 1998). *PW* (Sept. 1992). *Signs* (Spring 1990). *Western Historical Quarterly* (1999).

—BEVERLY SEATON

WILDER, Louise Beebe

Born 30 January 1878, Baltimore, Maryland; **died** 20 April 1938, New York, New York
Daughter of Charles S. and Mary Harrison Beebe; **married** Walter R. Wilder, 1902; **children:** two

Louise Beebe Wilder was educated in private schools. With her husband, an architect, and her two children, she lived for many years in Pomona, New York, and moved in 1922 to Bronxville, then a fairly rural area. Very active in gardening club circles, she founded the Working Gardeners Club of Bronxville in 1925 and served as vice president of the Federated Garden Clubs of New York and editor of *New York Gardens*, its journal. She was also a director and member of the advisory council of the New York Botanical Garden. In 1937 the Garden Club of America awarded her a Gold Medal for Horticultural Achievement, a rare honor.

Between 1916 and 1937, Wilder wrote nine gardening books and many articles for magazines and newspapers. In her writing, she often mentions her own gardens, especially a large garden surrounding an old farmhouse in Pomona and her "suburban" garden in Bronxville.

Her first book, *My Garden* (1916), covers many topics and gives general advice. In the foreword, she points out the suitability of gardening and the manual labor involved in it as a pastime for women. *Colour in My Garden* (1918) discusses the use of color in garden design but again is fairly nonspecialized in its approach. These and other works by Wilder are distinguished from the usual general gardening books because she presents a good deal of original material.

Rock gardening was one of her special interests, dealt with not only in her general books but in *Pleasures and Problems of a Rock Garden* (1927). Wilder steers a course between the high cultists for whom rock gardening is an exotic and demanding pursuit and the average enthusiasts who plant their treasures in the backyard amidst clinkers and brick bits and are often criticized for a lack of skill in garden design. She points out that the enjoyment gardeners get from their gardens is what is most important.

The Fragrant Path (1932) is a thorough and charming book about the scents of a garden. Of the many books on this subject, this is the most comprehensive. There are chapters on such things as fragrant mushrooms as well as those on the more common herbs and roses. *Adventures with Hardy Bulbs* (1936) is a classic work on its subject. It is illustrated with photographs and line drawings by Wilder's son. She explains in the foreword her frequent use of the word "adventures" in her titles: "Adventure is of the mind—a mental attitude toward everyday events wherever experienced. One does not have to sit through the long night of an antarctic winter with an Admiral Byrd to know this, or to explore uncharted airways. Adventure may be met with any day, any hour, on one's own doorstep, just around the corner; it may lurk in the subway, on a bus stop, in the garden."

Wilder's gardening books are written with humor and grace. Behind her words lie a lifetime of real gardening experience and a lifetime of reading and research. Such gardening books may be out of print, but they can hardly be out of date.

OTHER WORKS: *Adventures in My Garden and Rock Garden* (1923). *Adventures in a Suburban Garden* (1931). *What Happens in My Garden* (1935). *The Garden in Colour* (1937).

BIBLIOGRAPHY: Andrews, L. L., *The Story of the Working Gardeners of Bronxville* (1976).

—BEVERLY SEATON

WILHELM, Kate

Born 8 June 1928, Toledo, Ohio

Daughter of Jesse T. and Ann McDowell Meredith; married Joseph Wilhelm, 1947; Damon Knight, 1963; children: three

Kate Wilhelm has two children from her first marriage and one from her second. She lives in Eugene, Oregon, with her second husband, a science fiction writer, critic, and editor. She was one of the directors of the Milford Science Fiction Writers Conference from 1963 to 1972. She lectured at the Clarion Fantasy Workshop from 1968 to 1970 and at Tulane University in 1971.

Wilhelm has long been recognized as an outstanding writer of science fiction. Yet this prolific author is proving more and more difficult to classify. She has successfully transplanted her economical prose and her imaginative ideas into a wide range of forms and genres; always she displays in her writing a sharp understanding of human psychology.

Wilhelm won the Nebula award from the Science Fiction Writers of America for the best short story of 1968 with "The Planners," from the collection *The Downstairs Room and Other Speculative Fiction*. The hero is a scientist who experiments with

monkeys, prison convicts, and developmentally challenged children. Rather than admit to his ethical doubts about these practices, he externalizes them in the form of an imaginary laboratory technician.

The Clewiston Test (1976) is also about a scientist who has ethical doubts. Anne has been testing a new painkilling drug on monkeys, who have become violent, shunning the friendly advances of the laboratory technicians, but the pharmaceutical company has ignored her report of these developments and markets the drug anyway. After Anne is seriously injured in a car accident and bedridden, she feels increasingly angry and isolated, and she avoids her husband, who wonders if Anne's rage is justified or unjustified (proof she has used the drug herself to ease the pain after the accident)?

Fault Lines (1977) follows the inner monologue of an elderly woman trapped in an isolated beach house following an earthquake. As she waits to die, she remembers her childhood, marriage, and love affairs and discovers the sources of guilt and blame in her life. She realizes the personal disasters she has tried to forget were simply predictable shifts, like earthquakes. *Fault Lines*, like many of Wilhelm's works, is about cycles: a preexisting weakness, a "fault line," shifts and reveals a stronger structure underneath.

Wilhelm is best known as a science fiction writer, and the science she fictionalizes is psychology. Sometimes it is physiological psychology (as in "The Planners" and *The Clewiston Test*), sometimes Jungian (as in *Margaret and I*, 1971, a novel based on Jung's theory of the unconscious), sometimes humanistic (as in *Fault Lines*). Her short stories range from the eloquent to the clever but superficial; her novels, however, are of more even quality. Her prose is economical and her psychological portraits engrossing.

Wilhelm second and third Nebula awards were earned for the novella "The Girl Who Fell into the Sky" (1988, from the collection *Children of the Wind*) and in 1989 for the short story "Forever Yours, Anna." The former contrasts sharply with Wilhelm's earlier short works, which are darker and more pessimistic. As in so much of her fiction, Wilhelm here explores "the inexplicable." Touched by the vast peace of the Midwestern prairie and by mysteries of the past, her characters find fulfillment beyond the colder pattern of the modern world.

This world and all its absurdities and threats is the focus of much of Wilhelm's work. Throughout her career, she has questioned whether or not we can accept the consequences of our scientific and technological advances. She writes with a strong sense of moral responsibility and social conscience. Her work—the majority of which has been categorized as social science fiction—raises questions about medical practices (*The Clewiston Test*), scientific research ("The Planners"), and environmental concerns (*Juniper Time*, 1979), and confronts a host of ethical issues.

Wilhelm has repeatedly demonstrated her literary versatility. Since 1980, she has ventured into the field of drama, collaborated in separate works with her husband, Damon Knight, and her son

Richard, and written mysteries, too. Against the varied, sometimes fantastic surroundings and situations of her fiction, her social commentary and her exploration of the human psyche remain constant.

In the collection *Listen, Listen* (1981), a novella entitled "With Thimbles, With Forks, and Hope" introduces two characters whose continuing stories act as something of a transitional vehicle for Wilhelm. The characters are psychologist Constance Leidl and her husband, Charlie Meiklejohn, a retired fire inspector and police detective. The transition takes place over the course of several stories pitting the investigative duo against mysteries with fantastic, science fictional elements. By the time the first Leidl-Meiklejohn novel appears, Constance, Charlie, and Wilhelm have taken up a more traditional place in the mystery genre. *The Hamlet Trap* (1987) has no elements of fantasy or science fiction, but is instead a thoroughly observed psychological mystery with satisfyingly believable characters.

Wilhelm, however, did not abandon the science fiction genre. Among the other Leidl-Meiklejohn novels is *The Dark Door* (1988), more of a tightly drawn thriller than a mystery featuring a supernatural foe; and *Crazy Time* (1988), also nominally science fiction, which achieves the same sort of hybrid status. It begins as generous farce and becomes a gripping comedy thriller that is also a rather profound metaphysical fantasy.

While some science fictional elements do appear in the following series of Leidl-Meiklejohn novels, the stories move solidly into reality-based investigations. Wilhelm also published a number of courtroom drama mysteries during this time. Chaos theory and superhuman powers are integral to the theme and plot of *Death Qualified: A Mystery of Chaos* (1991), but the novel is as much murder mystery and psychological study as it is science fiction. Following volumes with the same protagonist, criminal lawyer Barbara Holloway, *Malice Prepense* (1996) and *Defense for the Devil* (1999), are compelling works with Wilhelm's usual psychologically sophisticated character development and dexterous prose. *The Good Children* (1998), while it has the theme of haunting and the haunted house in common with several of Wilhelm's earlier works, is not a novel of the supernatural, but rather an exquisitely detailed account of the psychological problems affecting a boy when his older siblings cover up their mother's death. The resulting story is a believable and sensitive but unsentimental psychological portrait; it is also a taut gothic tale. Whatever the genre position, Wilhelm's fiction attains brilliance through her commitment to verity in the depiction of the human estate.

OTHER WORKS: *More Bitter Than Death* (1962). *The Mile-Long Spaceship* (1963, British edition as *Andover and the Android*, 1966). *The Clone* (with T. Thomas, 1965). *The Nevermore Affair* (1966). *The Killer Thing* (1967, British edition as *The Killing Thing*). *Let the Fire Fall* (1969). *The Year of the Cloud* (with T. Thomas, 1970). *Abyss: Two Novellas* (1971). *City of Cain* (1974). *The Infinity Box* (1975). *Where Late the Sweet Birds Sang* (1976). *Somerset Dreams and Other Fictions* (1978). *Axolotl* (play, 1979). *Better Than One* (with Damon Knight, 1980). *A Sense of Shadow* (1981). *Oh, Susannah!: A Novel* (1982). *Welcome, Chaos* (1983). *The Hindenberg Effect* (radio play, 1985). *The Hills Are Dancing* (with R.Wilhelm, 1986). *Huysman's Pets* (1986). *Smart House* (1989). *Cambio Bay* (1990). *Sweet, Sweet Poison* (1990). *State of Grace* (1991). *Naming the Flowers* (1992). *And the Angels Sing* (1992). *Seven Kinds of Death* (1992). *Justice for Some* (1993). *The Best Defense* (1994). *A Flush of Shadows: Five Short Novels Featuring Constance Leidl and Charlie Meiklejohn* (1995).

BIBLIOGRAPHY: Ash, B., ed., *Anatomy of Wonder: Science Fiction* (1976). Barr, M., *Lost in Space* (1993). Donald, M., *Patterns of the Fantastic* (1983). Marleen, S., *Future Females* (1985). Platt, C., *Dream Makers* (1980). Weedman, J., ed., *Women Worldwalkers* (1985).

Reference works: *DLB* (1981). *Science Fiction Writers* (1999). *St. James Guide to Science Fiction Writers* (1996).

Other references: *Anatomy of Wonder* (1987). *LATBR* (19 Dec. 1982, 3 Dec. 1989, 30 June 1991). *LJ* (Jan. 1999). *Newsweek* (9 Feb. 1976). *NYTBR* (10 Mar. 1974, 18 Jan. 1976, 22 Feb. 1976, 9 Mar. 1986, 1 Sept. 1991). *PW* (24 June 1968, Feb. 1990). *TLS* (3 Oct.1986). *Tribune Books* (17 Dec. 1989). *WPBW* (27 Apr. 1986, 29 Oct. 1989).

—KAREN FREIBERG,
UPDATED BY JEROME CHOU AND JESSICA REISMAN

WILLARD, Emma (Hart)

Born 23 February 1787, Berlin, Connecticut; **died** 15 April 1870, Troy, New York
Daughter of Samuel and Lydia Hinsdale Hart; **married** John Willard, 1809 (died 1825); Christopher Yates, 1838; **children:** one son

Emma Willard was the 16th of her father's 17 children, the ninth born to his second wife. Books were the center of life on the Hart family farm. Captain Hart had served in the Revolution, and in addition to Chaucer, Milton, and Shakespeare, the family savored stories of Washington and Lafayette.

Willard attended the Berlin Academy (where within two years she was teaching younger children), but she was extensively self-taught. She took advantage of the medical books of her husband—a fifty-year-old physician and politician who had four children from two previous marriages—and the books of his nephew—a student at Middlebury College who lived in their home in Vermont. Willard had been preceptress of a school in Middlebury before her marriage, and in 1814—to aid family finances—she opened the Middlebury Female Seminary, where she began to introduce "higher subjects," such as mathematics, history, and languages, in addition to the "ornamental" subjects usually deemed proper for women.

Willard realized that private means were too limited to provide suitable housing, adequate libraries, and the necessary

apparatus for quality education. She presented New York governor DeWitt Clinton with her *Plan for Improving Female Education* (1819), published at her own expense and sent to prominent
men throughout the country. It received enthusiastic response
from all quarters, but the legislature voted no funds. In 1821,
however, the Troy, New York, Common Council voted to raise
$4,000 for female education. Five years before the first public
high schools for girls opened in New York (and closed shortly
thereafter) and 16 years before Mary Lyon founded the Mount
Holyoke Female Seminary, Willard was offering women a serious
course of study equivalent to the best men's high schools and
sometimes superior to their college work.

She was supported in her work by her husband (until his
death in 1825), her sister, Almira Hart Lincoln Phelps, and later by
her one son and his wife. Her brief second marriage (to a man who
turned out to be a gambler and fortune hunter) was not successful,
but Willard had had the foresight to draw up an unusual prenuptial
financial agreement protecting her property, income, and school.

The work that established Willard's reputation is her *Plan for
Improving Female Education*. Incisive as any lawyer's brief, it
argues that the current system of privately financed education was
inadequate because most proprietors saw schools only as money-
making ventures and because many schools, particularly girls'
schools, had no entrance requirements, few regulations, and a
shallow curriculum. She declares that education "should seek to
bring its subjects to the perfection of their moral, intellectual, and
physical nature, in order that they may be of the greatest possible
use to themselves and others," and concludes by noting that since
women give society its moral tone, the country would benefit
from quality female education. In 1833 Willard expanded these
ideas in a series of lectures published as *The Advancement of
Female Education* to promote a female seminary in Greece.

Even while running the seminary herself, Willard found time
to write several textbooks, which made her financially independent. The first is *A System of Universal Geography* (1822), written
with William Channing Woodbridge. Older texts had been written
as if London were the center of the world and emphasized rote
learning. Willard encourages students to study and draw maps and
to use a globe. She describes the climate, customs, and history of
different countries.

Willard is best known for her history texts. *Republic of
America* (1828) begins with a chronological table dividing American history into 10 epochs and concludes with the "political
scriptures" she learned as a child. Lafayette endorsed her account
of the Revolution, and Daniel Webster wrote, "I keep it near me
as book of reference, accurate in facts and dates." It was popular
for both the student and the general reader.

Her Episcopal faith gave the books a popular moral tone. *A
System of Universal History in Perspective* (1837) details the
"virtues which exalt nations and the vices which destroy them."
In 1844 she published *Temple of Time*, the first in a series of books
in which she charted world history as a multistoried temple, in
which each floor is held up by groups of 10 pillars on which are
engraved the names of the principal sovereigns of each century.
Each floor contains various groupings of nations and the roof

displays the names of heroes. Although these books may appear
stilted and moralistic today, they were hailed as educationally
innovative, making history exciting in their time.

In 1820, at a time when the great popularity of millennial
speculation in the United States was just beginning, Willard
researched biblical prophecies to write *Universal Peace, to Be
Introduced by a Confederacy of Nations Meeting at Jerusalem*; 54
years later, she published an expanded version. Her commitment
to peace was such that during the Civil War she wrote two works
about how slavery might be modified in order to satisfy both sides.
She did not press the plan, however, after her nephew, a state
Supreme Court judge, told her the time for such suggestions was
long past.

Willard wrote many poems, but only "The Ocean Hymn; or,
Rocked in the Cradle of the Deep," written in 1831 on the return
voyage from a trip in Europe, became well known. Another of
Willard's interests was science. Although not as well known in the
field as was her sister Almira, she did argue in two works of the
1840s that there is a connection between respiration and the
circulation of the blood. Although she was made a member of the
Association for the Advancement of Science, she was somewhat
miffed when the idea was called the "American theory" rather
than the "Willardian."

Willard never participated in women's rights activities, but
she opposed Almira's Anti-Woman Suffrage Society. She wrote
to Celia Burr Burleigh in support of her career as a feminist
lecturer: "After all, you have only entered now upon a work that I
took up more than half a century ago—pleading the cause of my
sex. I did it in my way, you are doing it in yours, and as I have
reason to believe that God blessed me in my efforts, I pray that he
will bless you in yours."

OTHER WORKS: *Geography for Beginners; or, The Instructor's
Assistant* (1826). *Journal and Letters from France and Great
Britain* (1833). *Chronographer of Ancient History* (1846).
Chronographer of English History (1846). *Historic Guide to the
Temple of Time* (1846). *A Treatise on the Motive Powers which
Produce the Circulation of the Blood* (1846). *Respiration and Its
Effects, Particularly as Respects Asiatic Cholera* (1849). *Last
Leaves of American History* (1849 enlarged edition, *Late Ameri-
can History: Containing a Full Account of the Courage, Conduct,
and Success of John C. Fremont*, 1856). *Astronomy; or, Astro-
nomical Geography* (1853). *Morals for the Young; or, Good
Principles Instilling Wisdom* (1857). *Appeal to South Carolina*
(1860). *Via Media* (1862).

BIBLIOGRAPHY: Lord, J., *The Life of Emma Willard* (1873).
Lutz, A., *Emma Willard: Daughter of Democracy* (1929; rev. ed.,
Emma Willard: Pioneer Educator of American Women, 1964).
Woody, T., *A History of Women's Education in the U.S.* (1929).
Reference works: *NAW* (1971). *Oxford Companion to Wom-
en's Writing in the United States* (1995).

—NANCY A. HARDESTY

WILLARD, Frances (Elizabeth Caroline)

Born 28 September 1839, Churchville, New York; **died** 17 February 1898, New York, New York
Daughter of Josiah F. and Mary Hill Willard

In 1840 Frances Willard's family moved from New York to Oberlin, Ohio, where both parents attended classes at the then-young college. In 1846 they moved further west, to a homestead on the Wisconsin frontier. Willard had very little formal education before she enrolled in the Wisconsin Female College. After one year she transferred to North Western Female College in Evanston, Illinois, an institution affiliated with her family's church, the Methodist. Her parents joined Willard and her sister in Evanston, which was to be her home for the rest of her life.

Willard graduated in 1859 and then taught in local schools and at female seminaries and colleges in Illinois, Pennsylvania, and New York. She spent two years (1868-70) traveling in Europe, Russia, and the Near East, studying languages and meeting expenses by writing weekly articles for Illinois papers. As Jane Addams was to do in the 1880s, she returned from Europe determined to find independence and a career of service, but Willard meant to serve among the young middle-class women for whom she had already developed a great affection in her years as a student and as a teacher.

She was president of Evanston College for Women from 1871 to 1873, when it was absorbed by Northwestern University. She then became dean of women and professor of English and art. Her career as an educator ended with her resignation in 1874, probably due to conflicts with the university's president, who happened to be Willard's ex-fiancé.

This same summer, Willard was asked to lead the Chicago Women's Christian Temperance Union (WCTU). In October, she became secretary of the state organization, and one month later, at the Cleveland convention that founded the national WCTU, she was chosen as corresponding secretary. She was elected national president in 1879 and remained in that position until her death in 1898, leading for over two decades the largest organization of American women in the 19th century.

From 1876 to 1879 she was head of the publications committee, and she used the WCTU journal, *Our Union*, to promote her own views on the necessity of linking the temperance cause with other political issues, particularly woman suffrage. She lectured widely across the country and became a nationally known figure.

The WCTU advocated not temperance but prohibition. Willard was herself responsible for their slogan, "For God, Home, and Native Land," and regularly rang that theme in pamphlets such as *Home Protection Manual* (1879). This was to some extent a means to retain the support of a basically middle-class and conservative movement for the aims of the more radical Willard, but it is also a reflection of the fact alcoholism was not only an individual problem, but a threat to women and children who, in the 19th century, had little protection against the financial and physical exploitation of drunken husbands. In the 1890s, she became interested in socialism and argued that poverty is the cause of intemperance. Long before this country's experiment with prohibition, she came to believe that education, not prohibition, is the solution of the problem of alcohol abuse. After her death, however, the WCTU limited its attention to prohibition and abstinence.

As a feminist, Willard was most interested in the development of women's abilities and interests through their active involvement in the WCTU and in the improvement in their status that she hoped the political power of a strong WCTU might accomplish. Describing the temperance movement that began late in 1873 with spontaneous demonstrations of women in several Midwestern states, she writes in *History of the Women's National Christian Temperance Union* (1876): "A phenomenon no less remarkable, though certainly much less remarked, succeeded the crusade—indeed, is aptly termed its 'sober second thought.' This was the phenomenon of *organization*. The women who went forth by impulse, sudden, irresistible, divine, to pray in the saloons, became convinced. . .that theirs would be no easy victory." The image of women as the spiritual saviors (in the home) of a crass society was common in 19th-century America; working with a conservative group, Willard used this image when she discussed the organization of women outside the home.

With Mary A. Livermore, Willard edited *A Woman of the Century* (1893), the most important 19th-century biographical reference work on American women. In their preface, the editors draw attention to the "vast array of woman's achievements here chronicled, in hundreds of new vocations and avocations." The articles are laudatory, but also concise and factual.

Nineteen Beautiful Years (1864), Willard's first book, is a brief account of the life of her sister, who died in 1861. It is certainly sentimental, but considerably less so than the flowery preface by John Greenleaf Whittier to the second edition (1885). Her sentimentality is particularly evident in *What Frances Willard Said* (1905), a collection of aphorisms and brief exhortations such as the following appeal for woman suffrage: "by the hours of patient watching over beds where helpless children lay, . . . I charge you, give mothers power to protect, along life's treacherous high-way, those whom they have so loved." In fact, Willard developed a clear and fairly simple style in which, as in her organizational work, appeals to the ideals of piety, domesticity, and patriotism—although still unpleasant to the modern reader—are connected with a usually well-reasoned argument about the needs of women.

In *Glimpses of Fifty Years* (1889), Willard's sentimental tendencies are used to good effect in the autobiography of a feminist who did not mean to undervalue the "household arts or household saints. . . . All that I plead for is freedom for girls as well as boys, in the exercise of their special gifts and preferences of brain and hand." For personal and political reasons, Willard did not choose to dissociate herself from the sentimental or the domestic modes in either her writing or her organizational work.

OTHER WORKS: *Hints and Helps in Our Temperance Work* (1875). *Woman and Temperance; or, The Work and Workers of the Women's Christian Temperance Union* (1883). *How to Win: A Book for Girls* (1886). *Woman in the Pulpit* (1888). *The Year's Bright Chain: Quotations for the Writings of Frances E. Willard* (1889). *A Classic Town: The Story of Evanston by "An Old Timer"* (1891). *A Great Mother: Sketches of Madam Willard*, with M. B. Norton (1894). *Do Everything: A Handbook for the World's White Ribboners* (circa 1895). *A Wheel within a Wheel: How I Learned to Ride the Bicycle, with Some Reflections by the Way* (1895, reprinted 1991). *Occupations for Women*, with H. M. Winslow and S. J. White (1897). *Writing Out My Heart: Selections from the Journal of Frances E. Willard, 1855-96* (1995).

BIBLIOGRAPHY: Bordin, R. B. A., *Frances Willard: A Biography* (1986). Dobschuetz, B. S. "A Historical Study of the Religious Factors in Frances Willard's Development Before 1874" (thesis, 1992). Earhart, M., *Frances Willard: From Prayers to Politics* (1944). Gifford, C., *"My Own Methodist Hive": The Nurturing Community of Frances Willard's Young Womanhood* (1997). Leeman, R. W., *"Do Everything" Reform: The Oratory of Frances E. Willard* (1992). Mitchell, N. T., *Frances E. Willard: "Yours for Home Protection"* (1987). Shelton, C. J., "Frances E. Willard's Southern Tours for Temperance: 1881-1883" (thesis 1986). Slagell, A. R., *A Good Woman Speaking Well: The Oratory of Frances E. Willard* (dissertation, 1993). Stine, E. C., "Translating the Passive Voice into the Active Voice: An Examination of the Rhetoric of Frances Willard's Evangelical Feminism" (thesis, 1986). Strachey, R., *Frances Willard: Her Life and Work* (1912).

Reference works: *DAB. NAW* (1971). *NCAB. Oxford Companion to Women's Writing in the United States* (1995).

Other references: *Church History* (1997). *Feminist Studies* (Spring 1993). *Humanities* (July 1995).

—LANGDON FAUST

WILLARD, Nancy

Born 26 June 1936, Ann Arbor, Michigan
Daughter of Hobart H. and Marge Sheppard Willard; **married** Eric Lindbloom, 1964; **children:** James

Nancy Willard describes herself as having been a creative child with boundless curiosity, influenced by the fantasy of George Macdonald, the Oz books, and *Alice in Wonderland*. Drawing, writing, and storytelling were, and remain, her favorite activities. The dream quality in Willard's works comes from an early childhood experience to which she attributes her "call" to become a writer. Even as a child Willard created and designed books as gifts for friends and relatives. Her first poem was published when she was seven.

Born and raised in Ann Arbor where her father, a renowned chemist, taught at the University of Michigan, Willard describes her childhood home as a lively place with all sorts of characters in it and her writing often reflects memories of life there. Willard followed her insatiable love of story into the study of literature. Graduating from the University of Michigan (B.A., 1958), she studied for an M.A. (1960) at Stanford University, where her thesis in medieval literature opened "doors to all kinds of legends, . . .stories and fantasies." Equally important to Willard was the poetry she memorized as an undergraduate. "All those passages I learned are part of me, too." In 1963 she received her Ph.D. in modern literature from the University of Michigan. For years, Willard has lectured in English at Vassar College and taught at the summer Bread Loaf Writers' Conferences.

Between 1974 and 1990, Willard wrote 22 children's books. She says about writing for children: "I've always thought that questions are more interesting than answers," and she believes the most important question a children's author can ask is "What if?" Willard often uses a storyteller's voice while weaving a tapestry of fantasy, myth, legend, dreams, folk and fairy tales with her words. To this she adds mystical and magical elements, augmenting her own rich imagination. Two adult works also reflect her ability to make the ordinary extraordinary: a novel, *Things Invisible to See* (1984), and a book of poetry, *Household Tales of Moon and Water* (1982).

The recipient of numerous awards, in 1982 Willard became the first author ever to receive the Newbery award for poetry, given for *A Visit to William Blake's Inn: Poems for Innocent and Experienced Travelers* (1981), a whimsical fantasy inspired by Blake's poetry to which she had been introduced at the age of seven. Willard was also the recipient of a grant from the National Endowment for the Arts (1976).

Although she has written fantasy novels, her forte in children's literature is picture books. In two particularly enchanting early books, *The Snow Rabbit* (1975) and *Shoes Without Leather* (1976), the child's imagination invites magic to happen. Examples of Willard's sharing her own optimism, joy, and sense of the absurd are evidenced in *A Visit to William Blake's Inn* and *The Voyage of the Ludgate Hill: Travel with Robert Louis Stevenson* (1987). Nothing is impossible or improbable in her stories. Because she wants children to experience story, she rewrote *East of the Sun and West of the Moon* (1989) as a play, placing the characters and action in the present, thereby adding unexpected touches of comedy. In a later picture book, *The High Rise Glorious Skittle Skat Roarious Sky Pie Angel Food Cake* (1990, reprinted 1996), Willard answers the age-old dilemma—what to get a mother for her birthday—with poignancy and magic. By adding "What if?" she stretches the solution to the limitless heights of heavenly intervention.

OTHER WORKS: *In His Country: Poems* (1966). *Skin of Grace* (1967). *A New Herball: Poems* (1968). *The Lively Anatomy of God: Stories* (1968). *Testimony of the Invisible Man: William Carlos Williams, Francis Ponge, Rainer Maria Rilke, Pablo Neruda* (1970). *Nineteen Masks for the Naked Poet: Poems* (1971). *Childhood of the Magician* (1973). *The Carpenter of the Sun: Poems* (1974). *The Merry History of a Christmas Pie: With a*

Delicious Description of a Christmas Soup (1974). *Sailing to Cythera and Other Anatole Stories* (1974). *All on a May Morning* (1975). *The Well-Mannered Balloon* (1976). *Stranger's Bread* (1977). *Simple Pictures Are Best* (1977). *The Highest Hit* (1978). *The Island of the Grass King: Further Adventures of Anatole* (1979). *Papa's Panda* (1979). *The Marzipan Moon* (1981). *Uncle Terrible: More Adventures of Anatole* (1982). *Angel in the Parlor: Five Stories and Eight Essays* (1983). *The Nightgown of the Sullen Moon* (1983). *Night Story* (1986). *The Mountains of Quilt* (1987, 1997). *Firebrat* (1988). *Water Walker* (1989). *The Ballad of Biddy Early* (1989). *Pish, Posh, Said Hieronymas Bosch* (1991). *Beauty and the Beast* (1992). *A Starlit Somersault Downhill* (1992). *Sister Water* (1993). *The Sorcerer's Apprentice* (1993). *Telling Time: Angels, Ancestors, and Stories* (1993). *Bell Ringers of Kalamazoo* (1993). *Sister Water* (1993). *Simple Pictures are Best* (1994). *An Alphabet of Angels* (1994). *Among Angels* (1995). *Gutenberg's Gift* (1995). *The Good-Night Blessing Book* (1996). *Guest* (1997). *Cracked Corn and Snow Ice Cream: A Family Almanac* (1997). *The Magic Cornfield* (1997). *The Tortilla Cat* (1998). *Raggedy Ann and the Christmas Thief* (1999). *Shadow Story* (1999). *Swimming Lessons* (1999). *The Tale I Told Sasha* (1999). *When There Was Trees: A Poem* (1999).

BIBLIOGRAPHY: Datlow, E. and Windling, T. eds., *This Year's Best Fantasy and Horror: Ninth Annual Collection* (1996). Pearlman, M., ed., *Between Friends* (1994).

Reference works: *CA* (1980). *CANR* (1983). *CLC* (1977, 1986). *CLR* (1983). *Dictionary of American Children's Fiction, 1960-1984* (1986). *DLB* (1986). *MTCW* (1991). *SATA* (1983, 1985). *Writer's Directory* (1984-86).

Other references: *Book World* (May 1993). *Horn Book* (Aug. 1982).

—SANDRA RAY

WILLIAMS, Catharine (Read) Arnold

Born 31 December 1787, Providence, Rhode Island; **died** 11 October 1872, Providence, Rhode Island
Daughter of Alfred and Amey Read Arnold; **married** Horatio N. Williams, 1824 (divorced); **children:** Amey

Catharine Arnold Williams' father was a sea captain. Because her mother died when she was a child, Williams was raised and educated by two religious aunts. She did not marry until her mid-thirties, after which she and her husband moved to western New York. Two years later, Williams returned to Providence with her infant daughter, Amey, and secured a divorce, although she continued to call herself "Mrs. Williams." Williams opened a school, but soon abandoned teaching for health reasons. It was then that she turned to writing.

Williams' first book, *Original Poems on Various Subjects* (1828), sold by subscription, contains some poems that had been published previously. Her next book, *Religion at Home* (1829), was quite successful and went through several editions. During the next two decades, Williams wrote histories, biographies, and fiction. About 1849 she moved to Brooklyn, New York, to care for an aged aunt. When her aunt died, she returned to Rhode Island, but never to writing.

In theme and choice of subject, Williams always expressed patriotic, republican sentiments. *Tales, National and Revolutionary* (2 vols., 1830-35) and *Biography of Revolutionary Heroes* (1839) reflect her belief in American democracy and her desire to encourage good citizenship. In Williams' opinion, both men and women need to know about and emulate the heroism of Americans in defense of liberty; both need to understand the political and judicial systems. She praises the virtues of patience, industry and self-control, not the display of wealth and aristocratic style, as the marks of a good citizen.

Religion is also a major theme in her works. According to Williams, dignified and sincere religious expression, not showy religious fervor, was appropriate in the new nation. In *Fall River* (1833), for example, Williams argues that the religious display at camp meetings and revivals threatens people's morality, health, and self-control; genuine religion, accordingly, is practiced at home and expressed in the heart. Good manners and useful accomplishments blossom from pure religious sentiment.

There are admirable characters of both sexes in Williams' works. In *Religion at Home, Aristocracy; or, The Holbey Family* (1832) and other works, "true women" and admirable men are intelligent, sincerely pious, and courageous; they have good natures and even tempers. The men are distinguished from the women principally by their responsibilities and occupations. Honor and admiration characterize men's relationships with their wives; therefore, husbands frequently ask for their wives' opinions on public matters. Williams is critical of aristocratic pretensions in both sexes, but evil doing is mostly a male trait. When a reader pointed out to Williams that her worst characters are male, she responded in the preface to the second volume of *Tales, National and Revolutionary* that she only told stories as they were told to her.

Williams insists on the truth and high moral purpose of all her works. To prove that her stories are based on fact, she inserts written "proof" into the text, alluding to her personal acquaintance with the characters, explains where her information was gathered, or gives a historical account of the events behind her story. Sometimes this documentation becomes pedantic, as in *The Neutral French* (1841), but the attention Williams gives to historical truth is still impressive. To emphasize the moral of a story, Williams sometimes embellishes the facts, as she admits in *Tales, National and Revolutionary*, but she insists she never distorts them. Through her historical fiction, Williams warns her readers against errors in personal habits and governmental practices.

Williams described her own life as quiet; she said she excluded herself from gaiety not only to have time to earn a living, but also out of a sense of propriety. Prefatory remarks in *Religion at Home, Aristocracy; or, The Holbey Family* and elsewhere indicate that Williams was somewhat self-conscious about being a *woman* writer on political, legal, and historical topics, yet she never hid the fact of her sex from her readers. In recognition of her talents in those areas, Williams was elected to several state historical societies.

For contemporary readers, it is not Williams' moralistic fiction but her histories that are most interesting. *Fall River* is a fascinating study of ministerial corruption, female textile workers, and legal abuses in the early republic. *The Neutral French* is a gold mine of carefully collected information on the Acadians. *Tales, National and Revolutionary* and *Biography of Revolutionary Heroes* contain much information about Americans in Revolutionary times. One can't help but regret that this intelligent woman stopped publishing books some 25 years before her death.

OTHER WORKS: *Annals of the Aristocracy, Being a Series of Anecdotes of Some of the Principal Families of Rhode Island* (1843-1845).

BIBLIOGRAPHY: Rider, S. S., *Biographical Memoirs of Three Rhode Island Authors* (1880).
Reference works: *DAB.*
Other references:*Providence Daily Journal* (14 Oct. 1872).

—SUSAN COULTRAP-MCQUIN

WILLIAMS, Fannie Barrier

Born 12 February 1855, Brockport, New York; **died** 4 March 1944, Brockport, New York
Daughter of Anthony J. and Harriet Prince Barrier; **married** S. Laing Williams, 1887

Born, raised, and educated in the small town of Brockport, near Rochester, New York, Fannie Barrier Williams first encountered racial prejudice when she began her teaching career among the freedmen "in one of the ex-slave States." After graduating from the academic department of the Normal School at Brockport, she later attended the New England Conservatory of Music in Boston and the School of Fine Arts in Washington. She moved to Chicago after her marriage to a lawyer and spent most of her married life there.

Williams was the only black woman allowed to give a major address before the World's Congress of Representative Women at the World's Columbian Exposition at Chicago in 1893. She was the first black member in the Chicago Women's Club and an impelling force in the black women's club movement. She was also instrumental in founding the interracial Provident Hospital in 1891 and the Frederick Douglass Center in 1905 and was the first woman—black or white—to be appointed to Chicago's Library Board in 1924.

For many years, Williams gave lectures throughout the country. A prolific essayist, she wrote primarily for the *Voice of*

the Negro, but her articles also appeared in several other periodicals. *Progress of a Race: or, The Remarkable Advancement of the American Negro* (edited by J. W. Gibson and W. H. Crogman, 1902) features her long historical essay "Club Movement among Negro Women."

A pervasive concern evident in Williams' speeches and essays is the vindication of the morals of black women, which had been attacked by some because of the high number of illegitimate black babies. In an article in *Voice of the Negro* (June 1905), she writes, "It is because of this tyranny of race prejudice that the colored girl is called upon to endure and overcome more difficulties than confront any other women in our country." She maintains, in the essay in *Progress of a Race*, that equality will never come "until the present social stigma is removed from the home and the women of the race."

Williams was criticized by some blacks for her assertion in the 1893 speech in Chicago (printed in *World's Congress of Representative Women*, edited by M. W. Sewall, 1893) that the "colored people are in no way responsible for the social equality movement." Much of her later writing espouses a doctrine of assimilation.

The tone of all her writing, while eloquent, is moderate rather than militant. While a large part of her writing is concerned with her advocacy of justice for blacks, particularly women, as a well-educated, genteel woman writing at the turn of the century, Williams also wrote articles reviewing books, discussing art, advocating travel, and exploring domestic matters.

BIBLIOGRAPHY: Davis, E. L., *Lifting as They Climb* (1933). Flexner, E., *Century of Struggle* (1959). Lerner, G., *Black Women in White America: A Documentary History* (1972). Lowenberg, B. J., and R. Bogin, eds., *Black Women in Nineteenth Century American Life* (1976). Martin, C. E., *The Story of Brockport, 1829-1929* (1929?). Mossell, Mrs. N. F., *The Work of the Afro American Woman* (1908). Spear, A., *Black Chicago: The Making of a Negro Ghetto, 1890-1920* (1967).
Reference works: *NAW* (1971). *Oxford Companion to Women's Writing in the United States* (1995). *Profiles of Negro Womanhood, 1619-1900* (1964).

—MARILYN LAMPING

WILLIAMS, Sherley Anne

Born 25 August 1944, Bakersfield, California; **died** 6 July 1999
Daughter of Jesse W. and Lelia Siler Williams; **children:** John

Born in California to a sharecropping family, Sherley Anne Williams grew up picking cotton and fruit in the fields of the San Joaquin Valley alongside her parents. Overcoming the poverty of her childhood and the burden of being a single mother, Williams emerged as a well-known poet, novelist, and critic. As Lillie

Howard notes, her skillful use of blues cadences "attests to her role as a tradition bearer and puts her firmly in that long line of artists that stretches all the way back to the beginnings of black folk culture." A prolific voice and presence in African American literature and culture, Williams published poetry, novels, a historical drama, a stage show, numerous television programs, a screenplay (from her novel *Dessa Rose*, 1986), and numerous critical articles.

In 1966 Williams received a B.A. in English from California State University at Fresno, having used her earnings from cotton and fruit picking to pay her way through college. She began writing short stories around 1966, "with the idea of being published, not just to slip away in a shoebox somewhere." Williams' first published story, "Tell Martha Not to Moan," appeared in *Massachusetts Review* in 1967. It is her tribute to the women who "helped each other and me thru some very difficult years." Williams continued her studies as a graduate student at Howard University. In 1972 she earned an M.A. degree from Brown University, where she was also teaching in the black studies program. Williams' first book, *Give Birth to Brightness: A Thematic Study in Neo-Black Literature*, a critical text, appeared in 1972. Offering a thematic study of modern black (male) writers, the text articulates "a black aesthetic which grows from a shared racial memory and common future."

Williams' first book of poetry, *The Peacock Poems* (1975) was nominated for a National Book Award and a Pulitzer in 1976. The central image for the book is expressed in "The Peacock Song": "They don't like to see you with/yo tail draggin low so I try to hold mines up high." The poems follow a blues motif, "fingering the jagged edges of a pain that is both hers and ours," as Lillie Howard comments. Williams anticipates this pattern in her own poetry in her early *Massachusetts Review* essay, "The Blues Roots of Contemporary Poetry" (1977), and further explores the blues motif in her second book of poetry, *Some One Sweet Angel Child* (1982). Williams' life in the projects and the years spent "following the crops" are charted in her "Iconography of Childhood" (the fourth section of the book), where she demonstrates her central belief that "our migrations are an archetype of those of the dispossessed." In her work she wants "somehow to tell the story of how the dispossessed become possessed of their own history without losing sight, without forgetting the means or the nature of their journey."

Williams most notably demonstrates her attention to cultural memory and African American history in her critically acclaimed novel, *Dessa Rose* (1986, reprinted 1999), which fictionalizes and unites two historical incidents: a pregnant slave leads an uprising in 1829 and is sentenced to hang after the birth of her baby, and in 1830 a white woman, living on an isolated North Carolina farm, is reported to have sheltered runaway slaves. Williams amalgamates these stories and thus "buys a summer in the 19th century." This text (which is a revision of an earlier story, "Meditations on History") received much attention and praise from literary critics interested in postmodern texts rewriting the narratives of slavery.

Williams has been a Fulbright lecturer at the University of Ghana (1984), and taught at Brown and at Fresno State College before becoming professor of Afro-American literature at the University of California at San Diego. In 1987, Williams was chosen Distinguished Professor of the Year by the UC San Diego Alumni Association. She has been significantly influenced by the poetry of Langston Hughes, whose "black vernacular diction" encouraged her to write the "way black people talk." She also notes her connection to other African American literary figures such as Alice Walker, Zora Neale Hurston, and Toni Morrison, who "make a conscious effort to carry on the past of their ancestors in their writing." Black feminist critic Michele Wallace, a close friend of Williams, writes that for Williams fiction is "a sieve through which the culture has passed in an interesting and idiosyncratic way." Williams' second novel, *Working Cotton* (1992) was a Caldecott winner and awarded the Coretta Scott King Book Award. Her play, *Letters from a New England Negro* was performed during the National Black Theatre Festival in 1991 and at the Chicago International Theatre Festival in 1992.

Williams died of cancer on 6 July 1999. She was only 54 and in the prime of her writing and academic career. She left two unfinished novels, including a sequel to *Dessa Rose*, which is in its fourth printing and has been translated into German, Dutch and French.

OTHER WORKS: Contributor of poetry, fiction and critical work to several collections and anthologies, including: *Reading Black, Reading Feminist: A Critical Anthology* (1990), *Black Popular Culture* (1992, 1998), *Every Shut Eye Ain't Asleep: An Anthology of Poetry by African Americans Since 1945* (1994), *Centers of the Self: Stories by Black American Women from the 19th Century to the Present* (1994), *Richard Wright: A Collection of Critical Essays* (1995).

BIBLIOGRAPHY: Andres, P. M., *Literacies of Resistance: Script and Voice in Five 20th Century Women's Novels* (dissertation, 1998). Beaulieu, E. A., *Black Women Writers and the American Neo-Slave Narrative: Femininity Unfettered* (1999). Butler, R., *Contemporary African American Fiction: The Open Journey* (1998). Davenport, D., *Four Contemporary Black Women Poets: Lucille Clifton, June Jordan, Audre Lorde, and Sherley Anne Williams* (dissertation, 1985). Henderson, C. E., *The Body of Evidence: Reading the Scar as Text—Williams, Morrison, Baldwin, and Petry* (dissertation, 1996). Jordan, S. M., ed., *Broken Silences: Interviews with Black and White Women Writers* (1993). McDowell, D., and A. Rampersand, eds., *Slavery and the Literary Imagination* (1989). Mitchell, A., *Signifyin(g) Women: Visions and Revisions of Slavery in Octavia Butler, Sherley Anne Williams, and Toni Morrison* (dissertation, 1995). Schiff, J. L., *Rebellion into the Past: Sherley Anne Williams and the Quest for an Historical Voice* (1993). Ward, K. L., *From a Position of Strength: Black Women Writing in the Eighties* (dissertation, 1996). Tate, C., ed., *Black Women Writers at Work* (1983). Wall, C., ed., *Changing Our Own Words: Essays on Criticism, Theory, and Writing by Black Women* (1989). (1999).
Reference works: *African American Short Story, 1970-1990: A Collection of Critical Essays* (1993). CANR (1988). DLB

(1985). *Oxford Companion to Women's Writing in the United States* (1995).

Other references: *Black American Literary Forum* (Winter 1989). *Callaloo* (Summer 1989, Fall 1991). *Feminist Studies* (Summer 1990). *Genders* (Winter 1992). *History and Memory in African-American Culture* (1994). *Massachusetts Review* (Autumn 1977). *PW*.

—LISA MARCUS,
UPDATED BY SYDONIE BENET

WILLIS, Connie

Born Constance Elaine Trimmer, 31 December 1945, Denver, Colorado
Married Courtney Willis, 1967; **children:** Cordelia

Connie Willis was born in Denver, Colorado. She earned a B.A. in English from the University of Northern Colorado and taught elementary school from 1967 to 1969, serving as a substitute teacher for some years thereafter. After temporary residence in other states, the Willises settled in Greeley, Colorado, in 1984.

Her first story sale was "The Secret of Santa Titicaca" (1971) to *Worlds of If*, and her first novel, *Water Witch*, a collaboration with Cynthia Felice, appeared in 1982. *Fire Watch* (1985), her first short story collection, reveals Willis' gift for narrating both tragedy and hilarious satire in a clear, intelligent voice. The story "Fire Watch" (1982), which won the two most prestigious awards in the field—the Hugo (given by the World Science Fiction Association) and the Nebula (bestowed by the Science Fiction and Fantasy Writers of America)—concerns a 21st-century history student sent back to London during the Blitz of World War II. Working with the volunteers who attempt to save St. Paul's Cathedral from the Luftwaffe, he learns that history is not a matter of statistics but of living people, of human frailties and courage. In the Nebula-winning "A Letter from the Clearys" (1982), a teenager chafes against her family's strict rules and obsession with agriculture. With her discovery of a lost letter from some old friends, her parents' reaction and her own naive garrulity gradually enlighten the reader to the horrific reality of their society.

Willis' first solo novel, *Lincoln's Dreams* (1987), won the John W. Campbell Memorial award for Best Science Fiction Novel. Jeff Johnston, a researcher for an author of historical novels, is steeped in Civil War minutiae when he meets Annie, a woman suffering terrible nightmares that, he realizes, are actually a tangle of Robert E. Lee's memories. Falling in love with her, Jeff seeks to exorcise Annie's dreams, but as they tour the Southern battlefields, Annie determines to "finish the dreams" and exorcise Lee's guilt so he may literally rest in peace. With powerfully drawn characters and vivid descriptions of the horrors of war, Willis achieves an unforgettable drama of love, loyalty, and duty.

Doomsday Book (1992), like the later *To Say Nothing of the Dog, or, How We Found the Bishop's Bird Stump at Last* (1997),

is set in the same universe as "Fire Watch." In 2054 history student Kivrin visits medieval Oxford for her practicum, but because the time technician falls ill with an unknown virus, he accidentally sends her to 1384, the year of the Black Death. The story alternates between the two timelines, the characters in each fighting panic and plague. Willis identifies her themes as the psychological response to the end of the world, portraying religious faith, helplessness, and incredible heroism, "people who come and people who don't come and promises that are made that can't be kept and promises people will kill themselves in order to keep." This popular novel, a *New York Times* Notable Book, earned both the Hugo and the Nebula awards.

Impossible Things (1993) was Willis' second collection. Beginning with another Hugo and Nebula winner, "The Last of the Winnebagos," a novella about guilt, grief, and expiation in a near future where most animals have died out, the tales encompass all areas of the emotional spectrum. The Nebula-winning "Even the Queen" (1992) offers a witty commentary on how society might change were women allowed to avoid menstruation; in "Ado" (1988) political correctness forces English professors to bowdlerize Shakespeare to the point of meaninglessness; and in the heart-wrenching "Chance" (1986), an unhappy housewife wonders how her life might be today had she made a different decision 20 years earlier.

The collection also showcases the screwball comedies "Spice Pogrom" (1986) and "At the Rialto" (1989), another Nebula winner. Despite the grim subject matter that infuses so much of her fiction, Willis is famous as a humorist. *Remake* (1994), like "Ado," presents a future in which classic films are edited to remove any politically incorrect scenes, while two star-crossed lovers long for the days when movies told real stories with real actors. *Uncharted Territory* (1994), parodying science fiction clichés, suggests that space exploration will actually be bedeviled by stifling regulations and fussily bureaucratic aliens. *Bellwether* (1996) offers a screwball romance between a woman who studies fads and a chaos theorist who arrive at a cynical revelation of how human bellwethers start trends. *To Say Nothing of the Dog*, which won the 1999 Hugo Award, documents a time-traveler's misadventures in a madcap tour of Victorian England. As Willis said in an interview, "The time is ripe for comedy. . .but no one has a sense of humor about anything. We really are Victorians now—it's so distressing." Elsewhere she added, "This [the 1990s] is a very serious and pretentious time. The battle cry of the special interest groups is 'That's not funny.'"

Besides her talent for plotting and peopling screwball romances, Willis' comedies reveal her anger against the ineffectual busybodies who attempt to run society. Reviewers praise her bit-part characters, annoyances all: scientists with all the answers, inept nurses, middle managers and conference organizers, control freaks, overbearing do-gooders, hypocrites and political-correctness zealots of all stripes. She takes comedy seriously, saying, "There are real things at stake, and real things that matter. . . .[F]or every Coventry Cathedral rebuilt, for every uplifting moment—at the center is the burning down of these things, and the loss of things." Willis calls herself an optimist, though her narrative voice is that of a cheerful pessimist. Her settings are usually domestic rather than galaxy-spanning; her narrators frequently middle-aged women wondering what happened to their happily-ever-afters and still seeking romance, or young people struggling to find love and preserve beauty while hampered by imbeciles. At the end of the 1990s, Connie Willis has won more Hugos and Nebulas for fiction than any other writer in the science fiction/ fantasy genre.

OTHER WORKS: *Daisy, in the Sun* (1991). *Futures Imperfect* (1996). With Cynthia Felice: *Light Raid* (1989). *Promised Land* (1997).

BIBLIOGRAPHY: Burchette, B., "Subversive Housewife: An Interview with Connie Willis," in *Forbidden Lines* 9 (1992). "Connie Willis: Talking Back to Shakespeare," in *Locus* 29 (July 1992). "Connie Willis: Serious Funny Business," in *Locus* 38 (Jan. 1997). Doyle, C., "Lincoln's Dreams," in *Magill's Guide to Science Fiction and Fantasy Literature* (1996). Harrington, M., "Prize Writer," in *Denver Post* (23 Jan. 1994). Kincaid, P., "Willis, Connie," in *St. James Guide to Fantasy Writers* (1995). Mulcahy, Kevin P., "Doomsday Book," in *Magill's Guide to Science Fiction and Fantasy Literature* (1996). Roberts, R., "Uncharted Territory," in *Magill's Guide to Science Fiction and Fantasy Literature* (1996). Schafer, W. K., "Willis, Connie," in *The Encyclopedia of Fantasy* (1997).
Reference works: *CA* 114 (1985). *The Encyclopedia of Science Fiction* (1993).

—FIONA KELLEGHAN

WILLIS, Lydia Fish

Born April 1709, Duxborough, Massachusetts; died 25 January 1767, Malden, Massachusetts
Daughter of Thomas Fish; married Eliakim Willis, circa 1738; children: three, all of whom died in infancy

Lydia Fish Willis was the only daughter among five children. She developed an "early taste for reading" which led her, according to the anonymous editor who collected some of her letters, to an acquaintance with "authors, polite as well as religious." An unnamed friend reported that "she excelled most of her sex in a relish for works of genius. . . ."

Unidentified family difficulties in 1734 led Willis to seek employment outside her home, despite recurring health problems. She confided to her brother in a letter dated 13 September 1734 that she could not tell him "how shocking it is to think of leaving home, to go I know not where!" It is not clear from her extant letters whether she actually found employment.

Willis' father died in 1736, her mother in 1737. She married a minister, perhaps the following year, and lived in Dartmouth, New Hampshire, and later in Malden, Massachusetts, where her husband was called to parishes. She bore three children, a daughter who died in infancy and twin sons who were stillborn.

At the request of Eliakim Willis, after his wife's death in 1767, 21 of Willis' letters were collected and published in a memorial volume, *Rachel's Sepulchre*. Materials about Ann Stockbridge and Sarah Page were added to the 1788 edition. This second edition was intended to provide a female audience with examples of women "who were an honour to their sex." The editor offers the letters that "the ladies in other countries, by these examples [may] be fir'd with a laudable ambition to excel."

The published letters are generally melancholic, recording grief, sickness, family deaths, and spiritual struggle. They are apparently only a limited selection from among the papers she left at her death. The editor's selection criteria are not specified, so the collection may reveal more about the editor than Willis.

Willis excuses her occasionally self-pitying tone by writing to her brother that "it is not in my power to assume a language foreign to my heart, or to dissemble. . .my griefs so handsomely, as I could wish, if thereby I might be entertaining." The letters portray an unhappy woman who struggled with depression, a woman who felt that her life was "made up with blots and blurts." The source of her melancholy was unclear, even to Willis: "Don't think it an act of the will, but attribute it to the weak government of my passions.—If I murmur, it is *at* I don't know what."

BIBLIOGRAPHY: Cowell, P., *Women Poets in Pre-Revolutionary America, 1650-1775* (1981).

—PATTIE COWELL

WILLOUGHBY, Florence Barrett

Born 1900; died 29 July 1959, Berkeley, California
Wrote under: Barrett Willoughby
Daughter of Martin Barrett; married Robert Prosser

Florence Barrett Willoughby, daughter of a riverboat captain, was, as she comments in *Gentlemen Unafraid* (1928), literally raised on Alaska's waters. Some of her earliest Alaskan experiences are recounted in her first novel, *Where the Sun Swings North* (1922). She grew to love Alaska, its land, history, and people—and all but one of her novels have an Alaska setting. Many of her male protagonists are, like her father, riverboat captains, and all of her female protagonists share her love of the state. In addition to her novels, she wrote short stories, travel books, and character sketches of significant Alaskan pioneers.

Where the Sun Swings North centers on two sisters, Jean and Ellen. After giving Ellen's husband false information about the presence of gold on a deserted island, the evil and lecherous "White Chief" of Katleen, Paul Kilbuck, abandons them there, not returning with the winter provisions he had promised. He gives Ellen, whom he wishes to seduce, a homing pigeon, which she is to release when she decides she wants him. Meanwhile, his drunken bookkeeper, Gregg Harlan, attempts to warn the family but becomes a castaway too. Thanks to foraging, they all survive the winter; Harlan "dries out" and falls in love with Jean; Jean discovers a rich vein of gold, and Kilbuck gets his just desserts.

As in this first novel, all her others feature romance and outdoor adventure. *Rocking Moon* (1925) is about the independent, strong-minded Sasha Larianoff—who, to keep her Russian Orthodox father out of debt, sets up a successful fox farm on the island of Rocking Moon—and the men who are interested in her. *The Trail Eater* (1929) is loosely based on the adventures of Scotty Allen, which Willoughby had already described the year before in *Gentlemen Unafraid*. It traces Kerry Wayne's eventful and successful bid to win the All-Alaska Sweepstakes, a 400-mile dogsled race from Nome to the Arctic Sea and back, and, incidentally, the heart of Barbee Neilan, spunky ex-fiancée of his major opponent.

The title of *Spawn of the North* (1932) refers to both salmon and first generation Alaskans. Dian Turlon is the daughter of a canning king and has returned to Alaska for a nostalgic vacation before her marriage to a "Southerner." After many adventures and not much of a vacation, she discovers the vigorous North is preferable to the materialistic South and that she has opportunities in Alaska for independence, adventure, and accomplishment that she could never have "Outside."

Sondra O'Moore (1939) alternates between the adventurous seafaring days of Sondra's grandfather, Dynamite Danny, and contemporary Alaska. One of Sondra's suitors, Jean, tries to warn her that the other is illicitly involved with Japanese imperialists. Sondra is kidnapped, Jean rescues her, and all the protagonists are reconciled.

Willoughby writes Alaska potboilers bubbling with romance (at least three potential lovers per novel) and fast-paced adventure (usually on the high seas). She also celebrates Alaska—the land, the lifestyle, the traditions—so much so that all of her Alaska-born protagonists are fiercely loyal to the land and all of her Outside protagonists succumb to Alaska's lure. Most interesting in Willoughby's work are her portraits of almost mythic Alaskan women. All of her heroines are physically dauntless; they sail boats, ride horses, and drive dogsleds superbly. They are intensely interested in the work of Alaska, whether it be fishing or mining, and occasionally run their own businesses (*Rocking Moon*) or take over their father's (*Spawn of the North*). And they always marry the man who possesses the same physical attributes and interests. Willoughby has created the ideal "Daughter of Alaska"—independent, self-sufficient, intelligent, and devoted to her homeland.

OTHER WORKS: *Sitka, Portal to Romance* (1930). *Sitka: To Know Alaska One Must First Know Sitka* (1930). *Alaskans All* (1933). *River House* (1936). *Alaska Holiday* (1940). *The Golden Totem* (1945). *Pioneer of Alaska Skies: The Story of Ben Eielson* (with E. W. Chandler, 1959).

BIBLIOGRAPHY: Boston *Transcript* (24 June 1925). *NYT* (7 July 1929, 1 May 1932, 29 March 1936, 11 March 1945, 31 July 1959).

—CYNTHIA L. WALKER

WILSON, Harriet E. Adams

Born circa 1828, Milford, New Hampshire; died circa 1865
Wrote under: "Our Nig" (novel copyrighted by Mrs. H. E. Wilson)
Daughter of Charles Adams (probably, though not proven); married Thomas Wilson, 1851; children: George M. Wilson

Harriet E. Adams Wilson was the first African American woman to publish a novel in the U.S. and one of the first two black women in the world to publish a novel, *Our Nig; or, Sketches from the Life of a Free Black, in a Two-Story White House, North, Showing That Slavery's Shadows Fall Even There*. The work appeared on 5 September 1859, printed for Wilson by George C. Rang & Avery, Boston. The novel chronicles the hard life of a young woman named Frado, an indentured servant in an antebellum Northern household.

Our Nig is characterized by generic tension. At once autobiographical and fictional, it builds on two literary forms prevalent in Wilson's day: the slave narrative (a black male genre) and the sentimental novel (a white female genre). Wilson thus innovated a new literary form. In the view of Henry Louis Gates, Jr., Wilson not only provided "a 'missing link'. . .between the sustained and well-developed tradition of black autobiography and the slow emergence of a distinctive black voice in fiction," she "*created the black woman's novel.*"

The details of Wilson's life remain sketchy. It is believed she was born in Milford, New Hampshire in 1827 or 1828, although some sources give a date of 1808. In 1850 she moved to Massachusetts where she worked as a "straw-sewer" and servant and met Thomas Wilson, whom she married in 1851. He deserted her soon thereafter, leaving her to bear and support their son alone. Perhaps she received an education like that of her at least semiautobiographical character Frado: nine months of elementary schooling over three years. Wilson fought illness and poverty all her life, and wrote *Our Nig* at least in part to remedy her precarious situation. Her preface explains: "Deserted by kindred, disabled by failing health, I am forced to some experiment which shall aid me in maintaining myself and child without extinguishing this feeble life." Wilson's son died six months after *Our Nig* was published. Details of Wilson's death are unknown.

Our Nig vanished from view for more than a century after its publication, perhaps because of its unflinching portrait of Northern racism and its rendering of a marriage between a white woman and a black man. Since its rediscovery by Henry Louis Gates, Jr., and its republication in 1983, the text has been of special interest to scholars of African American autobiography and literature by African American women. Their work has focused on Wilson's expansion of the representation of black women beyond the conventions of the slave narrative and the sentimental novel and her novel's revelation of the impact of race, class, and gender on black women and their self-representations.

BIBLIOGRAPHY: Andrews, W. L., *To Tell a Free Story: The First Century of Afro-American Autobiography, 1760-1865* (1988). Bell, B. W., *The Afro-American Novel and Its Tradition* (1987).

Gates, H. L. Jr., ed., *Reading Black, Reading Feminist* (1900). Jackson, B., *A History of Afro-American Literature* (1989). Jacobs, H. A., *Incidents in the Life of a Slave Girl, Written By Herself* (1987). Pryse, M. and H. J. Spillers, eds., *Conjuring: Black Women, Fiction, and Literary Tradition* (1985). *Figures in Black: Words, Signs, and the "Racial" Self* (1989). Wall, C. A., ed., *Changing Our Own Words* (1989).

Reference works: *DLB* (1986). *FC* (1990).

Other reference: *American Quarterly* (1991).

—ELLEN WOLFF

WINDLE, Mary Jane

Born 6 February 1825, Wilmington, Delaware; **died** death date unknown

Born into a "large family circle," Mary Jane Windle was left fatherless at an early age and was supported by her mother. "A martyr to ill health" most of her life, she never married but led an active social life and had a large circle of male and female friends. This social life was crucial to her career as a society reporter and gossip columnist. Her four major books are all collections of previously published stories and articles.

As a writer of historical fiction, Windle is irritating and boring. "Grace Bartlett, an American Tradition," in the *Life at White Sulphur Springs, or Pictures of a Pleasant Summer* (1857) collection, is the overwrought tale of a young boy, Frank Winthrop, who is kidnapped from his Puritan home by Native Americans, raised by a British general, and given the mission of inciting Native American attacks on American villages near the Canadian border. Sent by his adoptive father to spy on his own village, he falls in love with Grace, a childhood playmate, but remains true to his dastardly task and betrays the town to his stepfather's Native American henchmen. Grace is one of the few survivors. By the end of the book, Grace and Frank, who has renounced spying, are happily married and surrounded by children.

Since the tale is set in colonial days, it makes no sense whatsoever for a British general to be under orders to destroy his fellow subjects. Windle never clarifies this point, however. She also does not say how Grace brought herself to forgive Frank for aiding in the slaughter of all her kin and neighbors. Windle's tales are short on logic and historical accuracy and long on swoons, brain fevers, and elision of time. These devices make explanations unnecessary, by Windle's standards.

Unlike her fiction, Windle's social sketches are crisp, witty, and interesting. *Life at White Sulphur Springs* contains a sprightly collection of gossip columns dealing with the parties, fashions, and flirtations at a summer resort for Washington's elite. *Life in Washington and Life Here and There* (1859), too, deals largely with presidential levees, state dinners, and fancy-dress balls. Interspersed with these gossip columns, however, are some shrewd articles about congressional proceedings just before Lincoln's election. An admirer of Henry Clay, Windle supports the Missouri

Compromise, Stephen Douglas' candidacy, states' rights, and slavery. She attacks several Southern congressmen for their "disunion sentiments" but praises their attacks on abolitionism.

In Windle's sketches, Southern delegates, cabinet members, and judges are all uniformly handsome, learned, and eloquent; Northerners are all cold, haughty, and wrongheaded. Southern women, of course, are prettier, more elegant, and more sweet-tempered. A brief trip to New York convinces Windle that slaves fare better than Northern servants and love their masters more. She displays her biases with innocence, and her staunch faith in a way of life so soon to be destroyed is moving.

Contemporary critics praised Windle for her "fascinating descriptive powers" and her "refined and ladylike prose." By modern standards, her fictional style is overheated, gushing, and coy. Her journalism, however, stands the test of time well. Windle's sketches of Washington society and congressional activity in the two years preceding the Civil War are particularly fascinating to read.

OTHER WORKS: *Truth and Fancy* (1850). *Legend of the Waldenses, and Other Tales* (1852).

BIBLIOGRAPHY: Reference works: *Women of the South Distinguished in Literature* (1861). *Female Prose Writers of America* (1857). *Oxford Companion to Women's Writing in the United States* (1995).

—ZOHARA BOYD

WINNEMUCCA, Sarah

Born circa 1844, Humboldt Sink, Nevada; **died** 16 October 1891, Monida, Montana
Daughter of Old Chief Winnemucca II and Tuboitonie; **married** an unidentified Native American; Edward Bartlett, 1871; Joseph Satwaller, 1878; Lewis Hopkins, 1881

Known as the "Princess of the Paiutes" by whites and as "Mother" by the Paiutes, Sarah Winnemucca served as interpreter, chronicler, and liaison for the Paiutes during their last days of freedom and their first decades of reservation life. Winnemucca's Paiute name, Thocmetony, means Shell Flower and she later took the name of her fourth and last husband, Hopkins. She is usually known today as Sarah Winnemucca.

Her life and the lives of all Paiutes were shaped by the invasion of the white settlers, who, in her words, arrived "like a roaring lion." Before the settlers' arrival, Paiutes ranged over what is now the lands of northwestern Nevada, northern California and into Oregon; afterwards, they were kept chiefly on small reservations, including one surrounding Pyramid Lake, Nevada. Winnemucca, however, lived a life caught between whites and Paiutes. As a girl, she lived with and worked for several white families. From them, she learned to read and write. She further educated herself on her own.

In her own time, Winnemucca was nationally known as a spokesperson for the Paiutes. She spent her life in a quest for a peaceful resolution to the clash between Paiute residents of the land and encroaching whites. She served as an interpreter, scout, and mediator. She made many heroic efforts for her people, at one time staging a daring midnight rescue of Paiutes who were being held prisoner by enemy Bannock tribe.

Most of her efforts were through negotiations or appeals to the American public and its politicians. One of those first efforts was a stage production depicting Paiute life that she performed with her father and sister; they presented it in San Francisco with a dual hope. They hoped to raise money for the Paiutes, and also to educate the whites about the plight of the Paiute people. The performances sold out, but public response was mixed, some of it condescending. Only a few responded as Winnemucca had hoped, with concern for the Paiute people. But she didn't give up her appeals to the white population. Through the years, she lectured many times both in San Francisco and on the East Coast and is reputed to have been an effective and impassioned speaker.

Winnemucca believed she could enlist the help of white citizens by revealing what was being done to the Native Americans: encroaching on their land; stealing food, clothing, and supplies meant for Native Americans confined on reservations; murdering Paiute people. Throughout her life, she attempted to communicate these crimes and to win redress and restitution.

Winnemucca is best known today for her one published book, *Life Among the Piutes [sic]: Their Wrongs and Claims* (1883, reprinted 1994). It was edited by Mrs. Horace [Mary] Mann, who, along with her sister Elizabeth Palmer Peabody, became a patron to Winnemucca after hearing one of her lectures. A year earlier, Winnemucca had also published an article, "The Pah-Utes," about Paiute ethnography for a periodical called the *Californian.*

Controversy surrounded Winnemucca's life. Some accused her of self-aggrandizement; some were disapproving of her divorces. As a teen, she was married to a Paiute man, who was abusive; she quickly left him. Later she was unhappily married less than a year to Lieutenant Edward Bartlett, a heavy drinker. In 1878, she was married for a short time to a man named Joseph Satwaller. In December 1881, she married Lieutenant Lewis H. Hopkins who is described by biographer Gae Whitney Canfield as "a bit of a dandy" and a gambler. He died of tuberculosis in 1887. Her divorces and her life as a single woman were considered scandalous in her day.

Reports also surfaced of Winnemucca's involvement in the occasional street brawl or other "unladylike" behavior. She established a reputation as a woman quick with a knife for any threats to her person, making it known she was able and willing to defend herself. Undoubtedly, she lived a colorful, adventurous life—too rich to be acceptable in her era. Still, even many of her contemporaries were able to completely discount the "scandals," and see her as a dedicated leader and defender of her people.

In her last years, Winnemucca spent any money she raised, along with her time and her talents, to educating the Paiutes. She had come to believe that education was their only route out of absolute dependence on the government. She established schools for Paiute children, keeping them open as long as her money held out, which was about four years. Soon afterward, at approximately age 48, she died of tuberculosis.

BIBLIOGRAPHY: Canfield, G. W., *Sarah Winnemuca of the Northern Paiutes* (1983). Gehm, K., S. W., *Sarah Winnemuca: Most Extraordinary Woman of the Paiute Nation* (1975). Liberty, M., ed., *American Indian Intellectuals* (1978). Peabody, E., *Sarah Winnemucca's Practical Solution of the Indian Problem* (1886). Ruoff, A. L. B., *American Indian Literatures: An Introduction, Bibliographic Review, and Selected Bibliography* (1990). Turner, K. C., *Red Men Calling on the Great White Father* (1951).

Reference works: *NAW* (1971). *Oxford Companion to Women's Writing in the United States* (1995).

Other references: *American West* (Nov. 1975). *Nevada Historical Society Quarterly* (Winter 1971). *Oregon Historical Quarterly* (June 1952).

—JUDITH HARLAN

WINSLOW, Anna Green

Born 29 November 1759, Nova Scotia, Canada; died 19 July 1780, Hingham, Massachusetts
Daughter of Joshua and Anna Green Winslow

Anna Green Winslow's father was commissary-general of the British forces in Nova Scotia. In 1770 she was sent to a finishing school in Boston, where she lived with her aunt and uncle, Sarah and John Deming. During her separation from her family, she kept a diary sporadically from November 1771 to May 1773. Her aunt apparently encouraged the effort as a penmanship exercise, but its chief function was to provide a running letter to her parents.

Much of the diary is a minute description of Winslow's daily routine. She summarizes sermons, details current fashions, tells jokes, and keeps her parents posted on family affairs. She mentions her fun at "dansing; danceing I mean," and asks to be allowed to dress in Boston styles: "I hope aunt wont let me wear the black hatt with the red Dominie—for the people will ask me what I have got to sell as I go along street if I do, or, how the folk at New guinie do? Dear mamma, you don't know the fation here—I beg to look like other folk." Winslow even admits to an occasional "egregious fit of laughterre" that caused her aunt to label her "whimsical."

But Boston life was not all fashion and frivolity; Winslow's "laughterre" was balanced by repeated descriptions of her industry at sewing, spinning, reading, and writing. The entry for 22 February 1772 is typical: "I have spun 30 knots of linning yarn, and (partly) new footed a pair of stockings for Lucinda, read a part of the pilgrim's progress, coppied part of my text journal. . .play'd some, tuck'd a great deal. . .laugh'd enough.'' Although most of Winslow's diary is preoccupied by such matters of social and domestic routine, the politics of pre-Revolutionary Boston occasionally attracted her attention. She notes, for example, that ''Col[onel] Gridley. . .taught [her] the difference between [Whigs and Tories],'' and she added some months later that the militia trained on Boston Common with drills that were ''very prettly perform'd.''

In all these descriptions of the world around her, Winslow reveals herself as well. References to her homesickness remind us that Winslow was, in 1771, a girl of twelve who wished desperately to please her parents. As she candidly remarked on 17 November 1771, ''I think I have been writing my own Praises this morning.'' Her homesickness may have been exacerbated by her concern at her father's neglect. The entry for 30 December 1771, for example, shows Winslow attempting to make light of a letter from her father to the Demings: ''I am told my Papa has not mention'd me in this Letter. Out of sight, out of mind.''

Winslow was reunited with her family in 1773 when Joshua Winslow moved them to Marshfield, Massachusetts. In 1775 he was exiled as a Tory; his family, including Winslow, remained behind. Before the end of the Revolution, Winslow died of tuberculosis in Hingham, Massachusetts. Despite her early death, her childhood diary remains an appealing document in the social history of colonial Boston.

OTHER WORKS: *Diary of Anna Green Winslow, A Boston School Girl of 1771* (edited by A. M. Earle 1894).

BIBLIOGRAPHY: Cowell, P., *Women Poets in Pre-Revolutionary America, 1650-1775* (1981). Forbes, H., ed., *New England Diaries, 1602-1800* (1923).

—PATTIE COWELL

WINSLOW, Helen M(aria)

Born 13 April 1851, Westfield, Vermont; died 27 March 1938
Also wrote under: Aunt Philury
Daughter of Don A. and Mary Newton Winslow

Educated at the Westfield Vermont Academy, the Vermont Normal School, and the New England Conservatory of Music, Helen M. Winslow began her literary career writing pastoral poems and short fiction for such children's periodicals as *Youth's Companion, Wide Awake,* and *Cottage Hearth.* Although she continued to write poetry and children's fiction sporadically throughout her life, she is best remembered not for these ''Aunt Philury Papers'' but for her newspaper and club work

Early in Winslow's career as a journalist, after the death of her parents, she lived in the Boston area with her three sisters.

During the 1880s, she wrote for numerous Boston papers, including the *Beacon, Transcript, Advisor,* and the *Saturday Evening Gazette.* Her first novel, *A Bohemian Chapter* (1886), the story of a struggling woman artist, was serialized in the *Beacon.* Her journalistic experiences led her to help form the New England Woman's Press Association (which she served as first treasurer) and the Boston Author's Club (which she served as secretary); she was also vice president of the Women's Press League.

Winslow's most sustained activity resulted from her involvement with the General Federation of Woman's Clubs. In the early 1890s, she was assistant editor of the *Woman's Cycle,* the federation's first official journal, and editor and publisher of its second journal, the *Club Woman.* She also edited the *Delineator's* ''Woman's Club'' department for 13 years and was founder and editor of the ''Woman's Club'' column in the *Transcript.* From 1898 through 1930, Winslow annually published the official *Woman's Club Register.* In addition to her direct affiliation with the club movement and its many publications, Winslow wrote numerous articles celebrating club women and their work in journals such as the *Arena,* the *Critic,* and the *Atlantic Monthly.* The most significant of these articles was her extensive history of American woman's clubs, ''The Story of the Woman's Club Movement'' (*New England Magazine,* June and October 1908).

Among the more interesting of Winslow's generally forgotten novels is *Salome Shepard, Reformer* (1893), an indictment of industrial working conditions with suggestions for reform. Salome, a young society woman, awakens to a sense of social responsibility after discovering the unsafe working and intolerable living conditions in the mills she has inherited from her father. Almost single-handedly, Salome initiates a series of reforms, including a model dormitory for the women workers, a social hall for the families of workers, and profit sharing.

Winslow partly duplicates this plot in *The President of Quex* (1906). In this novel, written in response to Agnes Surbridge's strident denunciation of club women in ''The Evolution of a Club Woman—A Story of Ambition Realized'' (*Delineator,* 1904), Winslow's heroine, the president of a woman's club concerned with municipal reform, becomes aware of abusive child labor conditions in her factories. Again, the women, this time through their club work, initiate and effect the necessary reforms, with no sacrifice to their home lives.

A Woman for Mayor (1909) is Winslow's most effective dramatization of the political sensibilities and capabilities of middle-class women. Written in support of the ''municipal-housekeeping'' concept of social reform, moderate women's rights, and the Progressive-era concept of expanded social services in local government, the novel relates the story of a young woman who is elected mayor on a platform dedicated to the eradication of political graft and corruption. For Gertrude Van Deusen, Winslow's heroine, the demands of public and domestic life are not only complementary but mutually reinforcing. It is difficult to tell whether she will be a good wife because she was a good mayor or was a good mayor because she was well versed in the skills of domestic efficiency.

Despite both her own achievements and those of her many heroines, Winslow showed a lifelong ambivalence about the public role of women. In each of her novels, the heroine, after ably demonstrating her superiority, retires willingly to marriage and an essentially domestic orientation. In *Spinster Farm* (1908), for example, Winslow chronicles the experiences of two women who create a productive, independent life for themselves by renovating and living on an abandoned farm. Both women articulate their preference for self-sufficient spinsterhood throughout the novel, only to marry in the final pages. In each novel, the heroine claims that her marriage will not end her public activism, although her primary focus will necessarily be on her home life. In no novel, however, does Winslow present her heroine after marriage. It is unclear whether this seeming ambivalence results from Winslow's desire to defend club women and meet the demands of a literary public in search of the happy ending or from an uncertainty about her own lifestyle—as her article "Confessions of a Newspaperwoman" (*Atlantic*, February 1905) might suggest. Whatever the reason, Winslow's fiction provides useful material for any reader interested in the ongoing debate about the public and private roles of women.

OTHER WORKS: *Mexico Picturesque* (with M. R. Wright, 1897). *Occupations for Women* (with F. Willard, 1898). *Concerning Cats* (1900). *Concerning Polly* (1902). *Little Journeys in Literature* (1902). *Literary Boston of Today* (1903). *Confessions of a Club Woman* (1904). *The Woman of Tomorrow* (1905). *The Pleasuring of Susan Smith* (1908). *The Road to a Loving Heart* (1926). *Keeping Young Gracefully* (1928).

BIBLIOGRAPHY: Blair, K., *The Clubwoman as Feminist: The Woman's Culture Club Movement in the United States, 1868-1914* (Ph.D. dissertation, State University of New York at Buffalo, 1976). Blake, F., *The Strike in the American Novel* (1972). Hill, V. L., *Strategy and Breadth: The Socialist-Feminist in American Fiction* (dissertation, 1979). Taylor, W., *The Economic Novel in America* (1942).

Reference works: *AW* (1939). *NCAB* (1927).

Other references: *Atlantic* (Dec. 1894). *Godey's* (Nov. 1893). *Independent* (26 Nov. 1893). *Literary World* (17 June 1893). *Picayune* (7 May 1893).

—VICKI LYNN HAMBLEN

WINSLOW, Ola Elizabeth

Born 1885, Grant City, Missouri; **died** 27 September 1977, Damariscotta, Maine
Daughter of William D. and Hattie Colby Winslow

Ola Elizabeth Winslow could trace her ancestry back to the Mayflower. Although born in the Midwest, she grew up in California, where she attended Stanford University (B.A. 1906, M.A. 1914). In 1922 she received a Ph.D. from the University of Chicago. From 1909 to 1961 she taught English at several colleges, on both coasts. She was professor of English at Wellesley College (1944-50) and instructor at the Radcliffe Seminars (1950-61). Winslow was fond of New England, and after her retirement spent her winters in Boston, doing research in the Boston Atheneum Library. In the summers, she lived in Sheepscott, Maine, in an old farmhouse she had restored. Here she enjoyed gardening and observing wildlife and did much of her writing.

Her biography of Jonathan Edwards won the Pulitzer Prize in 1941, acclaimed a masterpiece by one critic after another. One wrote, "This is by far the most complete and scholarly account of Edwards's career that has been written." Winslow followed the Edwards biography with *Meetinghouse Hill, 1630-1783* (1952), a description of religious life in colonial New England. It is so readable and informative it has been hailed as a valuable addition to any collection of Americana.

Then came a succession of seven books, each one notable for its careful scholarship, its exquisite craftsmanship, and its flashes of demure humor. Each has drawn praise from thoughtful critics. For instance, of *Master Roger Williams* (1957) one exclaimed that it is "certainly one of the most inspiring biographies about an American by an American written in recent years." And her history of Portsmouth, New Hampshire, written in 1966 for young children, was described as delightful reading, "a graceful, well-integrated narrative bringing the past to life." Although primarily occupied with American subjects, she produced a highly successful life of John Bunyan, the English mystic (1961). One reviewer proclaimed it the best biography of Bunyan in print.

Her primary interest lay with religious subjects, but she also wrote a book about Samuel Sewall, the judge at the Salem witch trials, and one about the conquest of smallpox. As her writings testify, she developed over the years a serene tolerance for the follies and errors of mankind. It was the sort of tolerance that comes only after much study of history and much thoughtful observing of the contemporary world.

OTHER WORKS: *American Broadside Verse* (1930). *Jonathan Edwards, 1703-1758* (1940). *John Bunyan* (1961). *Samuel Sewall of Boston* (1964). *Portsmouth: The Life of a Town* (1966). *Jonathan Edwards: Basic Writings* (1966). *John Eliot, Apostle to the Indians* (1968). *A Destroying Angel* (1974).

BIBLIOGRAPHY: Reference works: *Oxford Companion to Women's Writing in the United States* (1995).

Other references: *Boston Globe* (2 Oct. 1977). *Chicago Sunday Tribune* (27 Oct. 1957). *Christian Century* (4 May 1940). *NYT* (20 Oct. 1957). *NYTBR* (8 May 1966). *Yale Review* (Autumn 1940, Winter 1953).

—ABIGAIL ANN HAMBLEN

WINSLOW, Thyra Samter

Born 15 March 1893, Fort Smith, Arkansas; **died** 3 December 1961, New York, New York
Daughter of Louis and Sara Harris Samter; **married** John S. Winslow, 1920; Nelson W. Hyde, 1927

After leaving her smalltown Arkansas home, Thyra Samter Winslow made some attempt at gaining a formal education. She spent two years at the University of Missouri School of Journalism and later studied at the Cincinnati Art Academy and Columbia University. Her real education, however, began when she first went on stage as a chorus girl. The theatrical phase of Winslow's career ended in 1915 when she was hired as a feature writer on the *Chicago Tribune*. By this time she was regularly selling short stories and articles.

Between 1914 and 1923, her rueful stories of small-town life appeared almost monthly in H. L. Mencken and George Jean Nathan's widely read magazine, the *Smart Set*. Later, in 1934, she contributed to the *New Yorker* a regular series of sketches, which was later published as a book, *My Own, My Native Land*, in 1935. She also wrote book and theater reviews and, from 1937 to 1940, screenplays for major Hollywood studios. Her hobby was cooking, and late in her career she produced three diet books, expounding her own highly unscientific method of weight control.

Winslow's writing style is marked by shrewd observation of the absurdities of social ritual. She was acutely aware of the snobbery of the small town and often focused with ironic understatement on the strategies of the social climber. Courtship was for her of particular interest, especially those cases in which an outwardly naive young girl lures an unwitting suitor into matrimony. She also wrote extensively about theater people and about the sophisticated denizens of New York.

Show Business (1926) is a tale of an ambitious Missouri girl who finds glamour and financial reward in the chorus line. It is marred by a somewhat tedious plot as well as a lackluster central character. The novel's chief strength lies in its realistic depiction of the backstage milieu, complete with gold-digging chorines adept at "grafting" a dinner or a diamond from an attentive male. Given this sordid but wholly credible environment, it seems especially unlikely that the heroine remains virginal until a nice young millionaire proposes marriage. This novel, her only one, reveals the difficulties Winslow met in moving beyond the limits of the short story; in fact, more than 200 short stories make up the bulk of her published work.

Her concern with the three-generation household is exemplified in her best and most widely anthologized story, "A Cycle of Manhattan." This long story, which first appeared in the *Smart Set* (1919) and was later published in the volume *Picture Frames* (1923), traces the rapid assimilation of a Jewish immigrant family into the American mainstream. As the Rosenheimers move from rags to riches, their lifestyle grows increasingly pretentious and their family name becomes progressively more Anglo-Saxon: "Abe Rosenheimer" of the story's opening pages finally emerges as "A. Lincoln Ross." Winslow's sharp eye for social detail reinforces the sardonic humor behind the family's ascent. She clearly sees what these people have sacrificed in terms of emotional well-being for the sake of a fashionable veneer.

The story is typical of her, however, in that it lacks sympathy for its characters. She remains so scrupulously detached from her creations that she appears rather heartless. She is a master of the ironic twist, and it is the cleverness of her plotting far more than the sensitivity of her characterizations that made her popular.

OTHER WORKS: *People Round the Corner* (1927). *Blueberry Pie, and Other Stories* (1932). *Think Yourself Thin* (1951). *Winslow Weight Watcher* (1953). *The Sex without Sentiment* (1954). *Be Slim—Stay Slim* (1955).

BIBLIOGRAPHY: *NR* (11 Apr. 1923, 14 Apr. 1926, 17 Aug. 1927). *Saturday Evening Post* (11 Dec. 1943). *SR* (25 June 1927, 10 Aug. 1935).

—BEVERLY GRAY BIENSTOCK

WINTER, Ella

Born 17 March 1898, Melbourne, Australia; **died** 5 August 1980, London, England
Daughter of Adolph and Frieda Lust Winter; **married** Lincoln Steffens, 1924 (divorced, died 1936); Donald Ogden Stewart, 1939; **children:** one son

Ella Winter spent her early years in suburban Melbourne, where her German Jewish parents had settled in 1894 as baptized but nonbelieving Protestants eager to make a fresh start in a new land. The family moved to London in 1910. Winter graduated from the London School of Economics, where she associated with the Fabian Socialists. In the early 1920s, she was active in the Labor Party, spent a year at Cambridge, and translated two German books for English publication. Her first husband, the American radical journalist Lincoln Steffens, was fifty-eight when Winter married him shortly before their son was born. Although principled objections to formal marriage led later to a nominal divorce, the relationship continued unchanged until Steffens's death in 1936.

Winter combined a career in journalism with active support of leftist causes. Her trips to the Soviet Union provided material for two of her three books and many articles; she also wrote about California labor struggles in the 1930s and worked actively against fascism. Winter was one of the editors of two volumes of Steffens' letters and a collection of his later writings. She published an autobiography in 1963. Winter and her second husband, film writer Donald Ogden Stewart, left America under pressure of the McCarthy-era blacklists in the early 1950s. She lived in London until her death in 1980.

Red Virtue: Human Relationships in the New Russia (1933), Winter's best received and most noteworthy book, examines the social transformations accompanying the political and economic upheavals that followed the Russian revolution. Winter is interested especially in the new ethics and sexual morality, the changing patterns of marriage and family life, and the new psychology employed by the communists in "designing a new man." Winter's enthusiastic portrayal of Soviet Russia in 1931 is as revealing of the psychology of the observer as of the observed—in the early 1930s, Winter and the rest of the American Left still thought that the Soviets were designing mankind's utopian future. The book stands today as a kind of period piece, interesting as both portrait and product of its times.

I Saw the Russian People (1945) is competently written human-interest journalism, combining social commentary with a travel account to give a disjointed but comprehensive picture of Russian life in 1944. While Winter notes changes in Soviet society and policy since the publication of *Red Virtue*, her main focus is on the suffering and bravery of the Russian people in turning back the Nazi invaders.

When Winter wrote *And Not to Yield: An Autobiography* (1963), she could look back on a rich life filled with stimulating work, extensive travel, and close association with an extraordinary number of famous people. Unfortunately, although Winter's autobiography provides a usefully comprehensive reminiscence, the book is awkwardly narrated and fails to bring to life most of the people it portrays. Winter achieved some stature in her time as a journalist, political activist, and interpreter of Soviet society, but her contributions are overshadowed by those of other leftist writers more gifted than she was. Although Winter sought a career and an identity independent of her well-known husbands, she is remembered more for her connection with Steffens and with the American radical left than for her own accomplishments.

BIBLIOGRAPHY: Kaplan, J., *Lincoln Steffens: A Biography* (1974). Steffens, L., *The Autobiography of Lincoln Steffens* (1931). Steffens, L., *The Letters of Lincoln Steffens* (1938).

Reference works: *CB* (1946, 1980).

Other references: *London Times* (11 Aug. 1980). *Nation* (2 Nov. 1963). *NYT* (5 Aug. 1980). *NYTBR* (3 Nov. 1963). *SR* (30 Nov. 1963).

—PEGGY STINSON

WINWAR, Frances

Born Francesca Vinciguerra, 3 May 1900, Taormina, Sicily; **died** July 1985

Daughter of Domenico and Giovanna Sciglio Vinciguerra; **married** Bernard D. N. Grebanier, 1925; Richard W. Webb, 1943; F. D. Lazenby, 1949; **children:** one son

Frances Winwar spent her early years playing in and around the Greek theater of her native Sicilian town, peering between symmetrical columns at Aetna and the Ionian Sea. Her fascination with other cultures and languages was inspired by the many

foreign tourists who regularly visited the site, considered one of the most scenic in the world. Brought to America at the age of eight, she mastered English and demonstrated a talent for writing; soon she could claim a reputation as a book reviewer, translator, novelist, and biographer. As a concession to the editor of her first book, she agreed to anglicize her lengthy Italian name. She married three times and was the mother of one son.

Four books, beginning with *Poor Splendid Wings* (1933), form a tetralogy covering some of the major figures and movements of 19th-c. English literature. The first gained Winwar wide recognition, winning the *Atlantic Monthly* prize for the best nonfiction book of the year. A biography of those young artists who, during Queen Victoria's reign, started the movement known in England as the Pre-Raphaelite Brotherhood, it is imbued with sympathy and compassion for desperate souls who, despite strong wills and the superiority of talent and refined sensibilities, are frequently caught in the tragedy of circumstances beyond their control. The center of interest is Dante Gabriel Rossetti and his frustrating courtship and marriage to the idol of the brotherhood, Elizabeth Siddal. Assimilating a mass of material, Winwar retells familiar tales; but she does so with originality, for she represents the personal interrelationships of her subjects as they existed in a colorful age.

The Romantic Rebels (1935) is a composite biography in which Winwar, taking liberties with the historical facts, depicts the temperamental natures of Shelley, Keats, and Byron. She concentrates her efforts more on relating the eccentricities of her subjects than their poetic achievements and describes relationships that never actually existed between the three poets. Nevertheless, the book is well documented, even offering some previously unpublished letters, discovered by Winwar herself in the Morgan Library.

Farewell the Banner (1938) is a biography of William Wordsworth, his sister Dorothy, and Samuel Taylor Coleridge. Exploring the close and curious relationship of the famous literary trio, Winwar analyzes their individual yet merging personalities, stopping short of Freudian interpretations. She demonstrates the self-destructive nature of Coleridge's worship of Wordsworth, Dorothy's attachment to both men, and the eventual rupture between Wordsworth and Coleridge.

Oscar Wilde and the Yellow Nineties (1940) is a treatment both of an era, the decadent "yellow nineties," and a notorious figure of the age, Oscar Wilde. Winwar gives a full account of Wilde by relating his work to the aesthetic movements of the time and viewing his personal degradation against the backdrop of Victorian morality. Handling her controversial subject with frankness and sufficient delicacy to avoid offence, Winwar presents a moving account of the tragedy of Wilde's life.

The Life of the Heart (1945), a biography of George Sand and her times, proved the most popular with the general reading public. In it, one of the most fascinating women writers in history is brought to life by a woman biographer who is able to convey the authenticity of the Sand's many roles: wife, mother, mistress, novelist, political revolutionist. Since George Sand encountered many famous men in art and politics, Winwar created excellent individual portraits, including Chopin, Sainte-Beuve, Musset, Flaubert, and Louis Napoleon. The book's outstanding feature is the accurate assessment of George Sand in relation to the social revolution of her age and ours.

The Haunted Palace (1959) presents a romantic and psychologically facile portrait of Edgar Allen Poe. Carefully basing her flights of fancy upon a large body of published and unpublished material, Winwar reconstructs Poe's life, especially his emotional involvements and his inability to face the realities of rejection, poverty, and physical and mental suffering.

Neither an historian nor a literary critic, Winwar demonstrates a masterly handling of material as she heightens fact with imagination to recreate the lives of legendary figures from exciting epochs.

OTHER WORKS: *The Ardent Flame* (1927). *The Golden Round* (1928). *Pagan Interval* (1929). *Gallows Hill* (1937). *Puritan City* (1938). *American Giant: Walt Whitman and His Times* (1941). *The Sentimentalist* (1943). *The Saint and the Devil* (1948). *Immortal Lovers* (1950). *The Land of the Italian People* (1951). *Napoleon and the Battle of Waterloo* (1953). *The Eagle and the Rock* (1953). *The Last Love of Camille* (1954). *Queen Elizabeth and the Spanish Armada* (1954). *Wingless Victory* (1956). *Jean-Jacques Rousseau: Conscience of an Era* (1961). *Up from Caesar* (1965).

The papers of Frances Winwar are at the Brooklyn College Library, New York, and the Rutgers University Library in New Brunswick, New Jersey.

BIBLIOGRAPHY: Peragallo, O., *Italian American Authors* (1949).
Other references: *Atlantic* (May 1940). *Booklist* (1 Mar. 1959). *KR* (15 Nov. 1958). *NY* (8 Oct. 1938, 23 Mar. 1940, 10 Nov. 1945). *NYTBR* (24 Sept. 1933, 17 Nov. 1935, 25 Sept. 1938, 24 Mar. 1940, 23 Dec. 1945, 18 Jan. 1959). *SR* (7 Oct. 1933). *Time* (25 Mar. 1940, 29 Oct. 1945, 26 Jan. 1959).

—ANGELA BELLI

WOLF, Naomi

Born 12 November 1962, San Francisco, California
Daughter of Leonard and Deborah W. Wolf; **married** David Shipley; **children**: one daughter

Often heralded as a voice of feminism's third wave, Naomi Wolf came to international attention with the publication of her first book, *The Beauty Myth: How Images of Beauty are Used Against Women* (1990), published first in England, then in the U.S. It explores the beauty standards imposed on women and argues that these standards serve to maintain the status quo by continuously undermining women's advances—making women answerable to beauty standards set by a male-centered culture.

The book grew out of Wolf's work as a Rhodes scholar at Oxford University. She was exploring ideas about beauty in the 19th and 20th centuries when she made the connection to her own generation—females growing up in the 1970s. Her generation, despite the changes wrought by the second wave of the women's movement (the 1960s and 1970s), faced daunting beauty requirements; in response, many were succumbing to anorexia and bulimia. She further explored the idea that beauty standards circumscribe women in every occupation, subjecting them to required makeup, hair, and fashion routines that amount to a "third shift" of work. Successful women who want to continue up the corporate ladder know that looking young and vital is excruciatingly more important to them than to the male with whom they compete for promotions.

The Beauty Myth was a bestseller and embraced by many in the women's movement, though some questioned its depth of scholarship. It brought Wolf immediate fame and placed her in the celebrity circle of media attention. Her next book, *Fire with Fire: The New Female Power and How to Use It* (1993), was more controversial. In part, it was a critique of second-wave feminism, accusing it of becoming too rigid in its views and calling on feminists to broaden their self-definition. Wolf presented the idea of "power feminism," arguing that the time had come for women to embrace their political power (political parties were then courting women's votes). She urged women, too, to eschew "victim feminism" and to acknowledge, celebrate, and build their own power in business and in all of life's realms. Unfortunately, the term "victim feminism," Wolf told *Publishers Weekly* in 1997, was picked up by antifeminists. It was used in ways that Wolf "couldn't control," she said. She had meant to "acknowledge that women are victimized." Instead, the term has come to mean the equivalent of whining and has been used against established feminists ever since.

Wolf, meanwhile, gained fame as a talk show guest and speaker, as well as author of numerous articles. Her third book, *Promiscuities: The Secret Struggle for Womanhood* (1997), again tackled views of women's power, this time focusing on the sexuality and coming-of-age stories of young women. In it Wolf shares reminiscences of her own and those of old friends about their sexuality during the confusing teen years, and attempts to generalize from them. Critics varied in their response. A *New York Times* reviewer called Wolf "a sloppy thinker and incompetent writer." But a *New York Times Book Review* writer called the book "a searing and thoroughly fascinating exploration of the complex wildlife of female sexuality and desire." Some reviewers panned the book's format. The *Los Angeles Times* reviewer called it "chaotic and frustrating," adding that it "reads like several projects pasted together: a memoir, a polemic, a random assortment of readings on female sexuality." Wolf has said her book is "not a polemic, but a set of confessions." And she is aware her format is a combination of personal and theoretical information. *Promiscuities'* conclusions were questioned by some reviewers. The *Library Journal* stated that "overgeneralization abounds as she [Wolf] attempts to apply the microcosmic events of this mostly white, middle-class, liberal milieu to a whole generation." It also acknowledged that the book would likely be popular, and advised librarians to "purchase accordingly." Good advice. *Promiscuities* became a *New York Times* bestseller. Wolf continues to be a popular speaker and writer. In the 1997 words of *New York Times Book Review*'s Courtney Weaver, "One of Ms. Wolf's great strengths" is "blasting away myths." In the year following Weaver's review, Wolf was taking on many myths and closely held beliefs in a monthly opinion column in *George* magazine, exploring topics from patriotism, to the Virgin Mary, to the need for America to apologize for slavery. On the personal side, Wolf leads a busy life. She is married to political speechwriter David Shipley and has a daughter, born in 1995.

BIBLIOGRAPHY: Reference works: *CA* (1994). *CBY* (1993). *Who's Who in America* (1996).

Other references: *Commonweal* (25 Feb 1994). *George* (1998 passim). *LJ* (15 June 1997). *Los Angeles Times* (27 July 1997). *Nation* (9 June 1997). *NYT* (10 June 1997). *NYTBR* (8 June 1997). *PW* (30 June 1997). *Time* (30 June 1997).

—JUDITH HARLAN

WONG, Jade Snow

Born 21 January 1922, San Francisco, California
Daughter of Hong and Hing Kwai Tong Wong; **married** Woodrow Ong, 1950; **children:** Ming Tao (Mark Stuart), Lai Yee (Tyi Elizabeth), Lai Wai (Ellora Louise), Ming Choy (Lance Orion)

Jade Snow Wong's best-known work is *Fifth Chinese Daughter*. First published in 1950 and still in print in the 1990s, this third-person autobiography was one of the first books published by a Chinese American woman in the United States.

Fifth Chinese Daughter traces Wong's life in San Francisco through the mid-1940s. Like later works by Chinese American women as Maxine Hong Kingston's *The Woman Warrior* and Amy Tan's *The Joy Luck Club*, Wong's book documents a young woman's search "for balance between the pull from two cultures." The book poignantly recounts Wong's search for a "middle way" between the conflicting demands of the traditional Chinese culture of her immigrant parents, with its values of obedience, respect, and order and its assumption of women's inferiority, and the more individualistic American culture. It at once poses and tries to answer the question, "Am I of my father's race or am I an American?"

Wong's search for a "middle way" is crystallized in her book's form. She writes an autobiography, consistent with the American valuation of the individual and the individual's right to speak her mind. But in keeping with Chinese custom, which deems extensive use of the first person immodest (and perhaps, for women, unthinkable), she writes in the third person.

Women of today—those of Asian American descent and those who are not—continue to identify with Wong's autobiographical work. They can relate to her straightforward and honest storytelling of growing up in one world and growing into another

world upon reaching maturity. Many can even identify with having to prove themselves in the eyes of a male-oriented culture. Though Wong grows up in a very sheltered Chinese family, she must face many of the same challenges women face every day, even in today's culture. *Fifth Chinese Daughter* also explores the intricacies of the Chinese culture Wong grows up in, including the emphasis on males in the family, Chinese cooking and traditions, and Chinese festivals. The story also paints a vivid picture of Chinatown in San Francisco during the World War II. Her experiences and choices move her further from the confines of Chinatown and expands her horizons into the rest of American society. Wong herself said *Fifth Chinese Daughter* is still in print and used by schools to create an understanding between the worlds of the Chinese and Americans.

Wong continues to use third-person narration through much of *No Chinese Stranger* (1975), her less well-received sequel to *Fifth Chinese Daughter*. She uses the first person only after having narrated the death of her father. In addition to these autobiographical writings, Wong has written a column in the *San Francisco Examiner* and contributed to periodicals including *Holiday* and *Horn Book*. Educated at San Francisco Junior College (A.A., 1940) and Mills College (B.A., 1942), Wong is also an accomplished potter.

Wong has received recognition for both her work as a writer and for her accomplishments as a potter. In 1947 she received an award for pottery from the California State Fair, and again in 1949 she received an award for enamel. She also received a Silver Medal for craftsmanship from *Mademoiselle* magazine. For her treasured work in *Fifth Chinese Daughter* she was honored with a Silver Medal for nonfiction from the Commonwealth Club of San Francisco in 1976. She also holds an honorary doctorate of humane letters from Mills College. In addition, she has continued to honor her Chinese background as a member of the advisory councils for the China Institute of New York and as a director of the Chinese Culture Center from 1978 to 1981.

BIBLIOGRAPHY: Demirturk, E. L., *The Female Identity in Cross-Cultural Perspective: Immigrant Women's Autobiographies* (unpublished Ph.D. dissertation, University of Iowa, 1986). Kim, E. H., *Asian American Literature: An Introduction to the Writings and Their Social Context* (1982). Ling, A., *Between Worlds: Women Writers of Chinese Ancestry* (1990). Meissenburg, K., *The Writing on the Wall: Socio-Historical Aspects of Chinese American Literature, 1900-1980* (1986).

Reference works: *CA* (1983). *CLC* (1981). *Oxford Companion to Women's Writing in the United States* (1995).

Other references: *Amerasia Journal* (1971). *DAI* (Jan. 1987). *Hawaii Review* (1988). *MELUS* (Fall 1979, Spring 1982).

—ELLEN WOLFF,
UPDATED BY DEVRA M. SLADICS

WOOD, Ann
See DOUGLAS, Ann

WOOD, S(ally) S(ayward) B(arrell) K(eating)

Born 1 October 1759, York, Maine; **died** 6 January 1855, Kennebunk, Maine
Wrote under: Madam Wood, Sally Keating
Daughter of Nathaniel and Sarah Sayward Barrell; **married** Richard Keating, 1778 (died 1783); Abiel Wood, 1804 (died 1811); **children:** two daughters, one son

The first of 11 children, S. S. B. K. Wood (commonly referred to as Madam Wood) was born into a colonial New England family while her father was serving with General James Wolfe, British leader of the attack on Quebec. Her mother was the daughter of Judge Jonathan Sayward, with whom Wood lived until she was eighteen. During the American Revolution, Judge Sayward was a Loyalist, and much of his conservatism is evident in Wood's work.

Her first husband was a clerk in her grandfather's office. Judge Sayward gave them a house as a wedding present, and they settled into the cultivated social life that had surrounded her childhood. Two daughters and a son were born before Keating died suddenly in 1783. Wood turned to writing, not from any pressing financial need, but because it "soothed many *melancholy*, and sweetened many *bitter* hours." Her work was well received, and she gained a considerable literary reputation. She stopped writing when she married General Abiel Wood in 1804. "Madam Wood," as she was then known, took up writing again, after his death in 1811.

Following in the path of such early American novelists as Sarah Wentworth Morton, Susannah H. Rowson, and Hannah Webster Foster, Wood occupies an important niche in the development of American fiction, although her work does not mark a radical break from the traditions imported from England. In accordance with her 18th-century upbringing, she was serious, moralistic, and sentimental. Her stories generally follow a Cinderella pattern centering on a virtuous young woman who either is, or is reputed to be, a poor orphan but who after severe trial is rewarded with a wealthy marriage. Virtue, for Wood, is more than chastity; it is linked to intelligence and education with a strong infusion of patience and submission. Her heroines redeem, reform, or blunt the evil of the world by the example of their behavior, and if they are passive in suffering vicissitudes, they are strong in the face of vice.

Like many other 18th-century novelists, Wood uses rambling narrative interspersed periodically with side stories giving the history and background of various minor characters. These digressions relate to the main line through some plot complication, but they also serve as moral examples; most are object lessons in the dangers of falling from virtue. They serve to build suspense, vary the texture, and add scope to the central story.

Julia and the Illuminated Baron (1800) is perhaps her best-known work. Certainly it is the most complex, and Julia's progress from nameless orphan to respectably pedigreed wife and mother involves a set of characters (all related by blood) in a series of gothic adventures. The baron of the title is a member of the Illuminati, a secret society that shocked Wood; she presents him as an atheist, anarchist, and mystic who announces proudly, "I am to myself a God, and to myself accountable. . . . If anyone stands in my way, I put him out of it, with as little concern as I would kick a dog." The setting is France, but the characters are clearly recognizable as Americans in their actions and values.

Amelia or, The Influence of Virtue (1802) states her most constant theme. The gentle heroine, married to a rake, prefers death to divorce and meekly bears the taunts of her husband's mistress and rears his illegitimate children without complaint. She is rewarded in the end with a repentant husband, adoring children, and a respectable position in society. As in all her works, Wood does not plumb psychological depths, and the solution is simplistic, but the action is rapid, and her gift for creating melodramatic moments holds the reader's attention.

Ferdinand and Elmira (1804) is an adventure tale, again with intertwined lives of a single family, in a Russian setting that gives an exotic flavor to a moral tale. As it opens, Elmira is a captive in a mysterious castle, and the explanation of this circumstance leads to another mystery. This pattern (of one mystery following the solution of another) is consistent throughout, and the resultant suspense is the primary means of moving the action forward. The ending resolves all, pairs the heroine and hero, rewards the good, and permits the villains an extravagant repentance. Wood's focus is on the morality of the simple life as opposed to the corruption of courts; and, despite her Loyalist grandfather, the tale is clearly antiroyalist in tone.

Wood is one of the first writers to embody distinctly American ideals. She does not admire aristocratic idleness; indeed, one of her heroes is praised for his ambition to go into trade, and her young lovers rarely end with titles of nobility. She reflects strongly the responsibilities of freedom so uppermost in the consciousness of the young nation. Typical of her time in sentimental morality and her view of woman's place in society, her work nevertheless reveals an inquiring and imaginative mind searching for new horizons.

OTHER WORKS: *Dorval; or, The Speculator* (1801). *Tales of the Night* (1827).

BIBLIOGRAPHY: Gould, W., in *Collections and Proceedings of the Maine Historical Society* (1890). Dunnack, H. E. *The Maine Book* (1920). Freibert, L. M. and B. A. White, eds., *Hidden Hands: An Anthology of American Women Writers, 1790-1870* (1985). Petter, H., *The Early American Novel* (1971). Sayward, C. A. *The Sayward Family* (1890). Spencer, W. D. *Maine Immortals* (1932). Sprague, R. S., ed., *A Handful of Spice: Essays in Maine* (1968).
Reference works: *Oxford Companion to Women's Writing in the United States* (1995).
Other references: *Studies in American Fiction* (Spring 1988).

—HELENE KOON

WOODHULL, Victoria (Claflin)

Born 23 September 1838, Homer, Ohio; **died** 10 June 1927, Bredon's Norton, Worcestershire, England
Daughter of Reuben B. and Roxanna Hummel Claflin; **married** Canning Woodhull,1853; James Blood, 1866; John B. Martin, 1883

Victoria Woodhull was the seventh child of an itinerant worker who married a tavernkeeper's daughter in Pennsylvania and moved with her to Ohio. Woodhull and Tennessee Celeste, a younger sister, both demonstrated psychic powers in early childhood. These were exploited as the family, leaving Ohio hurriedly after a suspicious fire in Claflin's grist mill, set up a traveling medicine show promising psychic cures for a variety of physical ailments. Although Woodhull had little schooling, she was clearly an ambitious, intelligent child with extraordinary physical beauty and a strong sense of destiny. Her first marriage was a failure, although she had two children.

In 1868 obeying Woodhull's vision that fame and fortune awaited her in a city crowded with ships, she and Tennessee moved to New York City. For almost a decade, Woodhull was a notorious figure in New York, famous for her brilliance as an orator; her vigorous espousal of free love, spiritualism, woman suffrage, and the rights of workers; her establishment of a brokerage business in male-dominated Wall Street; and her publishing venture, *Woodhull & Claflin's Weekly*. Cornelius Vanderbilt provided help in her financial venture, but it was Woodhull's intensity, courage, and beauty that won not only public support for her causes but also the interest of public men such as the editor Theodore Tilton, the philosopher Stephen Pearl Andrews, and Congressman Benjamin F. Butler, an advocate of woman suffrage.

Woodhull earned the enmity of Henry Ward Beecher when she accused him of secretly practicing the free love doctrines she openly espoused. After publishing details of an alleged liaison between Beecher and Tilton's wife in her weekly magazine, Woodhull was attacked by the moralist Anthony Comstock and imprisoned for sending obscene matter through the mails. The suit was dismissed, but Woodhull, who at the height of her fame had been named the Equal Rights Party's candidate for president (black leader Frederick Douglass was nominated for vice president), had lost money, prestige, and health in the struggle. Shortly after Vanderbilt's death, Woodhull and Tennessee left for England amid rumors that money for the trip had been provided by Vanderbilt's son and heir, who did not wish the sisters to testify in a lawsuit contesting his father's will.

In England, Woodhull gave lectures such as "The Human Body, the Temple of God" and attracted the interest of her third husband, a banker. The prosperous comfort of her last years in England was a surprising end to her sensational career as lecturer, propagandist, and free thinker. Yet she continued to write and to publicize herself, attempting to refute through the press and by legal action those whom she accused of persecuting her. Woodhull's new causes—eugenics, a single moral standard, and educational reform—were pursued as vociferously as her earlier ones.

Although *Woodhull & Claflin's Weekly*—which was the first U.S. magazine to publish Marx's *Communist Manifesto*—reflected Woodhull's ideas, as did her lectures, there is a question as to how much of what was published under her name she actually wrote. Colonel Blood, her second husband, was an experienced writer and propagandist, and the commonly held notion that he wrote much of what she signed may be correct. On the other hand, Woodhull herself wrote extensively after their divorce.

Despite her lack of formal education, Woodhull had undoubted originality and intelligence, and a driving force that helped her rise from a childhood of poverty and social ostracism to become an internationally known spokeswoman for human freedom.

OTHER WORKS: *Origins, Tendencies, and Principles of Government* (1871). *Speech on Labor and Capital before the Labor Reform League* (1871). *Speech on the Principles of Finance* (1871). *The Elixir of Life* (1873). *Tried by Fire* (1874). *Breaking the Seals* (1875). *A Fragmentary Record of Public Work* (1887). *Stirpiculture; or, The Scientific Propagation of the Human Race* (1888). *The Garden of Eden* (1890). *The Human Body, the Temple of God* (1890). *The Rapid Multiplication of the Unfit* (1891). *Humanitarian Money* (1892).

BIBLIOGRAPHY: Anker, C., and I. Rosenberg, *Onward Victoria: A Musical* (1979). Johnston, J., *Mrs. Satan: The Incredible Saga of Victoria C. Woodhull* (1967). Marberry, M., *Vicky: A Biography of Victoria C. Woodhull* (1967). Sachs, E., ''The Terrible Siren'': *Victoria Woodhull, 1838-1927* (1928).

Reference works: *AA. NAW* (1971). *Oxford Companion to Women's Writing in the United States* (1995).

Other references: *London Times* (11 June 1927). *NYT* (11 June 1927).

—ANN PRINGLE ELIASBERG

WOODS, Caroline H.

Born circa 1840s; **died** death date unknown
Wrote under: Belle Otis

Stimulated by a restless curiosity about human nature, Caroline H. Woods observed, analyzed, and wrote about the people around her. If her two books, *Diary of a Milliner* (1867) and *Woman in Prison* (1869), can be accepted as autobiographical (which they claim to be), she opened a millinery shop after her husband died. A few years later her interest in reform led her to take the job of prison matron, which she kept until exhausted by overwork and lack of sleep.

In both books the author seeks to reveal the principles of human nature behind the personalities she meets; everyday encounters are material for generalizations and philosophical musings about her fellow women and men. But to a modern reader, her abstract cogitations are perhaps less interesting than her clear portrayal of her surroundings.

Diary of a Milliner humorously records the manners, eccentricities, and financial rituals of her predominantly middle- and upper-class clients. Her customers include the fussily pretentious woman who tries on every hat in the store without buying one, the "highway shopper" who custom orders a bonnet and then decides it is not what she wanted after all, the wealthy socialite who needs reassurance that she has purchased the most expensive hat in town, and the bold woman who just wants to "borrow" a mourning bonnet for a funeral. Woods has a quick-witted answer and apt sales psychology for dealing with every kind of client.

Woman in Prison, however, adopts a more serious tone, concentrating less on exposing the foibles of human nature than the shameful conditions in the women's section of the state penitentiary. Without condescension, her plain, unpretentious prose captures the personalities, feelings, slang, and behavior of the prisoners. Through the eyes of the new matron, we come to like and respect the inmates more than those in charge of them.

Woods' revelations about prison conditions support her assertion that if such institutions were open for public inspection, reform would inevitably follow. The small "stone dens" where prisoners live resemble the "low, narrow. . .cages of wild animals," where bedbugs, rats and mice, and colonies of insects freely gather. Because the prison master keeps the inmates busy doing contract work (mostly sewing) in the "shop," (which brings revenue to the prison's board of directors), he will not assign anyone to clean the cells. Prisoners also must sew and keep house for the master's family, while his wife receives a full-time salary as "Head Matron," without doing any work.

Other abusive conditions include long hours and minimal food—barely enough to keep the prisoners working. Punishment is arbitrary (inmates are not allowed to talk while working in the shop) and unrelated to the offense. Given the conditions Woods describes in *Woman in Prison*, one can easily see why she asserts that the prisoners leave the penitentiary more degraded and hardened in crime than when they entered the institution.

While the literary value of Woods' writings is slight, her clear rendering of two very different sides of American society will be useful to students of social history and psychology.

BIBLIOGRAPHY: *A Critical Dictionary of English Literature and British and American Authors Living and Deceased* (1900).

—MELANIE M. S. YOUNG

WOODS, Katharine Pearson

Born 28 January 1853, Wheeling, Virginia (now West Virginia); died 19 February 1923, Baltimore, Maryland
Daughter of Alexander and Josephine McCabe Woods

The oldest of three daughters of a tobacco merchant, Katharine Pearson Woods grew up in Baltimore. Her father was descended from an early Huguenot emigrant to Virginia, and her mother's family of Irish Protestants had been eminent in colonial Pennsylvania before an ancestor moved to Virginia at the time of the Revolution. In Virginia, the McCabes were prominent in literature and education, two important influences in the work of Woods.

In 1874 she became a postulant with the All Saints Sisters of the Poor, and although she withdrew because of poor health, the religious experience led to her work in charity and the religious and moral tone of her writing. For 10 years (1876-86), she taught in girls' schools and worked with the poor. The bulk of her writing was done in the 12 years from 1889 to 1901. After that period, she lived mostly in Baltimore, serving the community in charitable functions, social concerns, and feminist activities. From 1903 to 1912, she worked as a missionary and taught kindergarten. Of particular interest is a paper she read that "awakened" Charleston to the problem of woman suffrage (*Woman's Journal*, May 1891). In 1893-94, she received a fellowship from the College Settlements Association to study factory working conditions. Results of her investigation were published in the *American Journal of Statistics* (December 1895).

Woods' first novel, *Metzerott, Shoemaker* (1889), secretly written and anonymously published, reflects her experience among the German working people of Wheeling. In this and her two other social novels (*A Web of Gold*, 1890, and *From Dusk to Dawn*, 1892), Woods advocates a just relationship, based on Christian cooperation, between capital and labor.

John: A Tale of King Messiah (1896), Woods' first religious novel, is based closely on the biblical narrative of the lives and relationships of Christ and John the Baptist, beginning with Christ's rescue of a little girl, Ingar, from a burning village and continuing through the crucifixion and resurrection. There are occasional passages of beauty in her descriptions of the Holy Land, and the drama of the narrative itself is sustained by the biblical source. The flow, however, of the narrative is frequently interrupted by prolonged moralistic and didactic passages directed to the reader.

The Son of Ingar (1897) departs further from biblical sources and takes up the story of the girl, Ingar, and of her son, Theophilus, in the difficult years of the formation of the early Christian church. The first scene of the novel is well constructed and offers promising subtle undertones of an interesting study, but Woods almost immediately retreats into her more usual moral tone and digresses from her tale. The narrative as a whole is not well sustained, and Woods tends to lose some of the strands she has been weaving, leading to a final contrived unraveling.

In *The True Story of Captain John Smith* (1901), Woods makes a determined effort to redeem the somewhat tarnished reputation of Smith, the founder of Virginia. Family ties to Virginia no doubt influenced her choice of subject. As she explains in the preface, she attempts to "substantiate Smith's account of himself. . .by. . .enclosing, so to speak, his autobiography in a framework of the manners and customs of the times." The text includes documentary maps and photographs which are of interest to the student of colonial history. The text itself is readable, but useful only to the history student.

Woods' greatest strength in her fiction is evident in her description of natural settings, reflecting a deep love of nature; that love and appreciation is also evident in her poems, several of which were published in *Harper's* in the first years of the century. However, characterization in the novels lacks depth, and her narratives are strained. As a whole, her work is limited in literary quality by these formal problems as well as by the didactic moral tone.

OTHER WORKS: *Mark of the Beast* (n.d.).

BIBLIOGRAPHY: Reference works: *Handbook of Settlements* (1911). *LSL* (1907). *NAW* (1971).
   Other references: *Lippincott's* (Sept. 1890). *Nation* (Jan. 1923).

—BETTY J. ALLDREDGE

WOOLSEY, Sarah Chauncey

Born 29 January 1835, Cleveland, Ohio; **died** 9 April 1905, Newport, Rhode Island
Wrote under: Susan Coolidge
Daughter of John M. and Jane Woolsey

Sarah Chauncey Woolsey spent her formative years in a lively household, amusing her three younger sisters, brother, and cousin with games and stories. She was first educated in Cleveland private schools, then sent to a boarding school in Hanover, New Hampshire, nicknamed "The Nunnery." From 1855 to 1870, Woolsey lived with her parents in New Haven, Connecticut, where her uncle, Theodore Dwight Woolsey, was president of Yale University. During the Civil War, she spent one summer working with her friend Helen Hunt Jackson in the New Haven Government Hospital and 10 months serving as an assistant superintendent at the Lowell General Hospital in Portsmouth Grove, Rhode Island.

After her father's death in 1870, Woolsey moved to Newport, Rhode Island, a residence interrupted only by journeys to Europe, California, and Colorado and, in her later years, by summers in the Catskills. In 1871 her career as children's author began with the publication of *The New Year's Bargain*. The Katy series (1872-91) brought her fame. She also wrote poetry and magazine articles, served for a time as children's book reviewer for the *Literary World*, and worked as reader and editor for her publishers, Roberts Brothers.

Although *The New Year's Bargain* employs fantasy reminiscent of Hans Christian Andersen in a story of two German children who trick the months into telling them stories, *What Katy Did* (1872) establishes Woolsey as a writer of realistic juvenile fiction, similar to Louisa May Alcott in her gift of depicting real American girls in an appealing family setting. Katy Carr, an impulsive, boisterous, and ever well-intentioned girl who leads her younger sisters and brothers into scrapes, finally matures through suffering and the acceptance of responsibility. Her adventures continue in *What Katy Did at School* (1873) when Katy and her sister, Clover, become students at a New England boarding school and meet the irrepressible Rose Red, beloved by more than one generation of schoolgirl readers in America and England.

Katy travels to Europe and finds romance in *What Katy Did Next* (1886), where Woolsey uses the travelogue, a popular formula in children's literature of the period, to carry a rather pedestrian plot. The Katy series concludes with *Clover* (1888) and *In the High Valley* (1891), as the six Carrs grow up and marry. The charm of the final books lies less in the portraits of the young people than in the Colorado setting, which Woolsey remembered so vividly from her trips to visit Helen Hunt Jackson.

Woolsey's other juvenile novels also feature plucky girls in realistic settings, but none of the heroines has Katy's imagination and vitality. Motherless Isabella of *Eyebright* (1879) moves from a sheltered home to an island off the Maine coast where she risks her life to help a stranger. Although Lilly of *A Guernsey Lily* (1881) heals a feud, she is really a device to unify descriptions of the scenery, people, history, and legends of the Channel Islands. Because orphaned Candace of *A Little Country Girl* (1885) shows moral courage, she wins a place in her aunt's family, thereby continuing to enjoy the civilized pleasures of Newport.

Among the notable collections of Woolsey's short stories are *Mischief's Thanksgiving* (1874), *Nine Little Goslings* (1875), *Cross Patch* (1881), *A Round Dozen* (1883), and *Just Sixteen* (1889). These volumes illustrate her capacity for invention and her range—stories for children and for adolescents, tales of realism and of fantasy. *Nine Little Goslings* and *Cross Patch* cleverly translate Mother Goose stories into tales peopled with real children in contemporary settings.

Although Woolsey hoped to achieve distinction as a poet, her three volumes of verse for adults, *Verses* (1880), *A Few More Verses* (1889), and *Last Verses* (1906), reveal little more than careful workmanship, a sober acceptance of suffering and death, and a certain flair for the narrative poem.

A talented and versatile writer of children's fiction, Woolsey was once almost as popular as Louisa May Alcott in both England and America. Today she is still remembered for her stories of the incomparable Katy Carr.

OTHER WORKS: *For Summer Afternoons* (1876). *A Short History of the City of Philadelphia from Its Foundation to the Present*

Time (1887). *The Day's Message* (1890). *Rhymes and Ballads for Boys and Girls* (1892). *The Barberry Bush* (1893). *Not Quite Eighteen* (1894). *An Old Convent School in Paris, and Other Papers* (1895). *Curly Locks* (1899). *A Little Knight of Labor* (1899). *Little Tommy Tucker* (1900). *Two Girls* (1900). *Little Bo-Peep* (1901). *Uncle and Aunt* (1901). *The Rule of Three* (1904). *A Sheaf of Stories* (1906).

BIBLIOGRAPHY: Banning, E., *Helen Hunt Jackson* (1973). Darling, R. L., *The Rise of Children's Book Reviewing in America, 1865-1881* (1968). Kilgour, R. L., *Messrs. Roberts Brothers, Publishers* (1952). Meigs, C., *A Critical History of Children's Literature* (1969).

Reference works: *NAW* (1971).

Other references: *Horn Book* (1959).

—PHYLLIS MOE

WOOLSON, Constance Fenimore

Born 5 March 1840, Claremont, New Hampshire; **died** 24 January 1894, Venice, Italy
Wrote under: Anne March
Daughter of Charles J. and Hannah Pomeroy Woolson

Constance Fenimore Woolson was the sixth of nine children and the grandniece of James Fenimore Cooper. After the death of three older sisters from scarlet fever, Woolson moved at a very early age with her family to Cleveland. She attended school there until enrolling in Madame Chegary's school in New York City, from which she graduated in 1858. Her childhood summers were spent at the family cottage at Mackinac Island, later to become the setting for a number of her short stories. After her father's death in 1869, she traveled extensively in the South with her mother. Upon her mother's death in 1879, Woolson and her sister, Clare Benedict, traveled in Europe, where Woolson spent the remainder of her life. She died in Venice after falling or leaping from her bedroom window. Whether her death was the result of delirium from influenza or of depression has never been determined. At the time of her death, she had achieved a moderate degree of recognition as a writer; today her works are virtually unknown.

Woolson's writings reflect her experiences in the northern lake country, the South, and Europe. Much of her fiction appeared initially in magazines and was later in books. She also published several novels, the quality of which is usually inferior to that of her stories. Woolson's first book, *The Old Stone House*, a book for children, was published in 1872 under the pseudonym of Anne March. Of more importance, however, is the collection *Castle Nowhere: Lake-Country Sketches* (1875), which contains nine stories fashioned from her observations of Mackinac Island. *Castle Nowhere* has been compared favorably with Sarah Orne Jewett's *Deephaven* (1877) and Mary Noailles Murfree's *In the Tennessee Mountains* (1884).

Of even better quality is her second volume of short stories, *Rodman the Keeper: Southern Sketches* (1880), which sympathetically treats the Reconstruction period. One of the most skillfully written pieces in this collection, "Old Gardiston," depicts the downfall of an ancient Southern family, and concludes with the burning of their mansion before it can be possessed by a Northern businessman and his wife.

Anne (1882) was published as a novel shortly after its serialization in *Harper's*. Set in various places, including Mackinac Island, Pennsylvania, and West Virginia, the novel tells the story of Anne Douglas in a somewhat melodramatic plot including a love affair and a murder trial. In the 1880s, *Anne* was a popular novel; today it is a forgotten work deserving renewed attention.

For the Major (1883), set in Far Edgerly, a mountain village in western North Carolina, is a tale of Sara Carroll's return home from a long journey and her discovery her father, Major Carroll, has become senile and her stepmother is laboring to shield both the Major and the townspeople from this knowledge. Woolson's story provides an excellent blend of comic treatment of the inhabitants of Far Edgerly and a noble portrait of the declining Major and his compassionate wife. It is considered one of Woolson's finest works.

East Angels (1886), set in Florida, was also a popular work at the time of its publication. Woolson brings together a group of wealthy Northerners and impoverished Southern aristocrats in this postwar novel of reconciliation. In her novel *Jupiter Lights* (1889), Woolson incorporates Georgia, the Lake Country, and Italy as settings. Although the plot is contrived and the action melodramatic, the work has been noted for its advances in the psychological complexity of the characters, especially the heroine, Eve Bruce.

Woolson's final novel, *Horace Chase* (1894), set in Asheville, North Carolina, after the war, chronicles the marriage of Horace Chase, self-made millionaire, and Ruth Franklin, his headstrong young wife. Ruth becomes infatuated with a young man of her own age, but is forgiven by her husband, who says at the close of the novel, "I don't know that I have been so perfect myself, that I have any right to judge you." In a letter to Henry Mills Alden, Woolson notes that the essence of the novel lies in that last sentence and concludes, "Do you think it is impossible? I do not."

Two volumes of Italian stories, *The Front Yard, and Other Italian Stories* (1895) and *Dorothy, and Other Italian Stories* (1896), as well as a volume of travel sketches, *Mentone, Cairo, and Corfu* (1896), were published after Woolson's death. The Italian stories include some of her best work, such as "The Front Yard," the story of Prudence Wilkin, a New England woman who accompanies her wealthy cousin to Italy. Prudence marries an Italian waiter, who dies after their first year of marriage, leaving her a house inhabited by eight children and other assorted relatives whom Prudence supports until her death 16 years later.

A minor writer who produced a number of fine stories, Woolson is to be noted as a pioneer both in local color writing and in her depiction of a number of female characters—such as Ruth Franklin of *Horace Chase* or Margaret Harold of *East Angels*—which anticipates female characterization of 20th-century literature.

OTHER WORKS: A significant number of Constance Fenimore Woolson's papers are housed at the Western Reserve Historical Society in Cleveland, Ohio.

BIBLIOGRAPHY: Benedict, C., ed., *Five Generations (1785-1923)* (1929-30). James, H., *Partial Portraits* (1888). Kern, J. D., *Constance Fenimore Woolson: Literary Pioneer* (1934). Moore, R., *Constance F. Woolson* (1963). Tornsey, C. B., *Constance Fenimore Woolson: The Grief and the Artistry* (1989). Tornsey, C. B., ed., *Critical Essays on Constance Fenimore Woolson* (1992). Weimer, J. M., ed., *Women Artists, Women Exiles: "Miss Grief" and Other Stories* (1988).
Reference works: *Oxford Companion to Women's Writing in the United States* (1995).
Other references: *SAQ* (Apr. 1938, June 1940). *Mississippi Quarterly* (Fall 1976).

—ANNE ROWE

WORMELEY, Katharine Prescott

Born 14 January 1830, Ipswich, England; died 4 August 1908, Jackson, New Hampshire
Daughter of Ralph and Caroline Wormeley

Katharine Prescott Wormeley was descended, on her mother's side of the family, from Boston merchants and, on her father's, from a long line of Virginians. The family lived in England for many years, settling in the U.S. after her father's death in 1852.

At the beginning of the Civil War, Wormeley threw herself into volunteer work. She formed the local chapter of the Woman's Union in Newport, Rhode Island, and headed it until 1862. She also obtained a contract from the federal government to manufacture clothing for the troops, thus giving employment to otherwise destitute soldiers' wives. In April 1862, Wormeley began working for the U.S. Sanitary Commission, a private volunteer organization, as a matron on a hospital ship. Later that year, she became "lady superintendent" of Lowell General Hospital in Portsmouth Grove, Rhode Island. Her health, however, gave out after a year, and she returned home to Newport. After the war, Wormeley continued her charitable work. She helped found the Newport Charity Organization Society in 1874 and served it in various capacities for the next 15 years. She also established an industrial school for girls that offered classes in cooking, sewing, and domestic management.

Besides charity work, Wormeley's passion was for literature. Fluent in French, she translated many of the works of Balzac, Molière, Daudet, and Saint-Simon. In 1892 she published *A Memoir of Honoré de Balzac*. In *The Other Side of War* (1889),

Wormeley describes her function on the hospital ship *Daniel Webster*: "Our duty is to be very much that of a housekeeper. We attend to the beds, the linen, the clothing of the patients; we have a pantry and store-room, and are required to do all the cooking for the sick, and see that it is properly distributed according to the surgeons' orders; we are also to have a general superintendence over the condition of the wards and over the nurses, who are all men." Wormeley and her companions were on duty almost constantly; when they could relax, space and privacy were limited.

When Wormeley was loaned temporarily to the medical department of the Army, she discovered conditions that were, incredibly, worse than what she had already seen. Accustomed to abundant supplies of food, bandages, and medications, she found the Army lacked adequate stores of all three. Because of this many men died whom, Wormeley believes, the Sanitary Commission might have saved. The commission's example finally shamed the government into reorganizing its medical department in July 1862. Then, Wormeley claims with pride, the commission could resume its original functions, "inspecting the condition of the camps and regiments, and continuing on a large scale its supply business."

The Other Side of War is an appropriate title for Wormeley's work. As she notes, it is far too easy, both for her contemporaries and modern historians, to get caught up in the romance and glory of war without fully acknowledging the human suffering that invariably accompanies it. She and the countless other women who worked in the hospitals of the Civil War, in both the North and South, remind us of its true horror.

OTHER WORKS: *The United States Sanitary Commission: A Sketch of Its Purpose and Work* (1863).

BIBLIOGRAPHY: Brockett, L. P., and M. C. Vaughn, *Woman's Work in the Civil War* (1867). Massey, M. E., *Bonnet Brigades* (1966). Maxwell, W. O., *Lincoln's Fifth Wheel* (1956).

—JANET KAUFMAN

WRIGHT, Frances (Fanny)

Born September 1795, Dundee, Scotland; died 13 December 1852, Cincinnati, Ohio
Also wrote under: Madam D'Arusmont, Frances Wright
Daughter of James and Camilla Campbell Wright; married William P. D'Arusmont, 1831; children: one daughter

Frances (Fanny) Wright was a 19th century anomaly: in the age of the passive True Woman, she created a utopian community dedicated to abolishing slavery in America, edited a liberal journal, and lectured passionately on women's rights.

In 1818 Wright and her younger sister Camilla enthusiastically sailed to America for the first time. Encouraged by the great human progress allowed in a democracy, Wright kept an epistolary record of her American experiences which she published upon her return to England in 1820 (*Views of Society and Manners in America*, 1821). Her optimistic portrait of America and her implied criticism of Europe angered many of her non-American contemporaries.

In 1824 Wright returned to the U.S. with her sister, and this time, turned her attention to what she considered America's most significant problem—slavery. Wright believed slaves could be prepared for freedom if they worked for their emancipation. To this end, she founded Nashoba, an experimental community in southwestern Tennessee.

Purchasing slaves who would "work out" their freedom, and gathering together concerned individuals, Wright devoted much of her energy in 1826-1827 to her community. Nashoba attempted a radical implementation of sexual as well as racial equality. Wright declared that at Nashoba "no woman can forfeit her individual rights or independent existence." Because of her outspoken attitudes about sexual equality and because the white overseer at Nashoba and a black woman began "living together," Nashoba soon gained a notorious reputation, and was labeled "Fanny Wright's Free Love Colony." Wright herself became known as a "female monster," who wished to destroy marriage and the family. Though Nashoba suffered from a lack of fresh food, comfortable living arrangements, and economic stability, Wright did accomplish one goal—she took the Nashoba slaves to Haiti and settled them there.

In 1828 Wright became the editor of the *New Harmony Gazette* (soon to be renamed the *Free Enquirer*). Wright became disillusioned with a community that could not support itself and was constantly the subject of controversy. During the ensuing two years, she and her coeditor Robert Dale Owen (founder of the utopian community in New Harmony, Indiana) energetically urged women to break the fetters of false conventions and prejudices. Wright, purporting to be the "first woman speaker on the American platform," lectured widely, advocating increased rights for women and for workingmen. Wright was horrified a marrying woman "swore away her person and her property"— she impelled her audiences, in her Enlightenment-like style, to listen to reason. Always she lambasted cultural pressures which compelled women to be meek and obedient.

In 1830 Wright's vacation to Europe was indefinitely extended by her sister's sudden death in 1831 and her own hasty marriage to William Phiquepal D'Arusmont, a former Pestalozzian teacher at New Harmony. From 1930 on, Wright traveled extensively between the U.S. and Paris where her child and husband resided. She wrote little during this period and she spent the final years of her life battling her husband in court for her property and for custody of her daughter. She obtained neither, and died crippled and alone—a fitting end, many believed, for America's first woman-rights' advocate.

OTHER WORKS: *Altorf, a Tragedy* (1819). *A Few Days in Athens* (1822). *Course of Popular Lectures* (1829). *Fables* (1830). *England the Civilizer: Her History Developed in Its Principles*

(1848). *Biography, Notes, and Political Letters of Frances Wright D'Arusmont* (1849, reissued on microfilm, 1980). *Life, Letters and Lectures* (enlarged ed. of 1849 publication, 1972).

BIBLIOGRAPHY: Bartlett, E. A., *Liberty, Equality, Sorority: The Origins and Interpretation of American Feminist Thought: Frances Wright, Sarah Grimke, and Margaret Fuller* (1994). Follis, J. T., *Frances Wright: Feminism and Literature in Ante-Bellum America* (dissertation, 1983). Gilbert, A., *Memoir of Fanny Wright* (1855). Hartley, D., "The Embrace of Nature: Representations of Self and Other by Women Travel Writers of the Romantic Period" (dissertation, 1992). Kissel, S. S., *In Common Cause: The "Conservative" Frances Trollope and the "Radical" Frances Wright* (1993). Kuntz, K., "Toward a Religion of Humanity: Frances Wright's Crusade for Republican Values" (thesis, 1998). Lane, M., *Fanny Wright and the Great Experiment* (1972). Morris, C., *Fanny Wright: Rebel in America* (1984, 1992). Mullen, R., *Birds of Passage: Five Englishwomen in Search of America* (1994). O'Donnell, M. M., *Reflections on a Free Enquirer: An Analysis of the Ideas of Frances Wright* (dissertation, 1979). Perkins, A. J. G., and T. Wolfson, *Fanny Wright: Free Enquirer* (1939, 1996). Rutherford, V., "A Study of the Speaking Career of Fanny Wright in America" (dissertation, 1960). Waterman, W., *Fanny Wright* (1924). Sandlund, V. F., "To Arouse and Awaken the American People"—The Ideas and Strategies of the Gradual Emancipationists, 1800-1850 (dissertation, 1996).

Reference works: *Oxford Companion to Women's Writing in the United States* (1995).

Other references: *American History Illustrated* (April 1980). *Indiana's Guerrillas of the Philippines: Fanny Wright* (audiocassette, 1987). Lerner, G. *Frances Wright* (audiotape, 1962). *THQ* (Jan. 1932, Dec. 1947).

—CAROL A. KOLMERTEN

WRIGHT, Julia McNair

Born 1 May 1840, Oswego, New York; **died** 3 September 1903, Fulton, Missouri
Daughter of John McNair; **married** William J. Wright, 1859; **children:** two

Julia McNair Wright was born to an upper-middle class family who saw to her sound academic—and private—education. She was married at nineteen to a clergyman who, after serving churches for several years at a time in Ohio, West Virginia, Pennsylvania, Vermont, and New Jersey, became a professor of mathematics and then vice president at Westminster College in Fulton, Missouri. She had two children. Except for occasional one-to-two-year periods of silence—perhaps caused by the efforts of resettling her family or by travel in Europe, Wright published almost continuously. Her work ranged widely, including short stories and novels, histories, poems, religious tracts, moral lessons on temperance, cookbooks, and scientific works on botany. Many books were published by the Presbyterian Board of Publication or the National Temperance Society.

The idealism and morality pervading her writing are that of conventional middle-class Protestantism: some of her work displays anti-Catholic themes; and in some of her fiction she explicitly denies the importance of votes for women. Nevertheless, if she was inactive in the feminist movement and unsympathetic to some of its demands, her fiction and poetry rely heavily on the delineation of women's struggles, hopes, fears, and successes. Her heroines strike the modern reader as well conceived both aesthetically and psychologically.

Adam's Daughters (1892) has a provocative subject: three genteel and well-educated young women and their mother are left suddenly on their own with neither money nor means of support. As Wright explains in the preface: "'What shall we do for a living?' is a problem proposed to many women, maids, wives, and widows." She suggests in *Adam's Daughters* and in many of her short stories that women should be prepared to work in positions other than teaching or the home. They must, she insists, follow their interests and abilities. Van, one of her heroines who appears in a number of stories, struggles in unsuitable jobs until she recognizes that her real calling lies with the land. She reminds one of Willa Cather's later heroine Alexandra in *O Pioneers!*; each learns to run a successful farm against difficult odds.

Wright's fiction is characterized by the melodrama and sentimentality of the time, but it also conveys messages that go beyond rigidly conventional bounds. Fallen women survive, widows become independent, spoiled melancholic young women are treated with psychological sensitivity and perception. Medical care, especially in asylums for the poor, is realistically scrutinized in books such as *Under the Yoke, and Other Tales* (1897), *The Awakening of Kohath Sloan* (1897), and *Duncan's Errand* (1899).

Wright's botanical works contain descriptions of nature similar to those in most popular 19th-century poetry—roots, for instance, are called "treasures of darkness." But the books contain also a substantial amount of scientific information about plants and the care of seeds. She made a thorough reading of Thomas Huxley, especially of his analysis of arbitrary distinctions between plant and animal life. Her approach insists that nature always has its purposes, but she supports her philosophical ideas with close observation and extensive knowledge of her subject—a synthesis of love and understanding. The most important of these works, the Nature Reader series (1888-1901), was translated into several languages and into braille.

Wright's primary interest, in whatever she wrote, lay in her concern for the human soul. This concern took her from the nativism and prejudices of her *Secrets of the Convent and Confessional* (1872) to the Darwinian struggle to survive in society as a man or a woman, to the tragedy of intemperance, and to the lack of natural joy in the education of children. The latter themes appear in *The Temperance First Reader: Writing, Spelling, and Reading Lessons for Young Children* (1889).

Like an increasing number of popular and successful American women writers in the 19th century, Wright produced books with remarkable speed on a variety of subjects—books devoured by a growing audience always impatient for more. But she even outdid most of her peers in volume, and the popularity of her work suggests its influence on her times.

OTHER WORKS: *The Golden Life* (1867). *The Shoe Binders of New York; or, The Fields White to the Harvest* (1867). *Almost a Nun* (1868). *The New York Needle-Woman; or, Elsie's Stars* (1868). *John and the Demijohn: A Temperance Tale* (1869). *The New York Bible-Woman* (1869). *Our Chatham Street Uncle; or, The Three Golden Balls* (1869). *Almost a Priest* (1870). *How Could He Escape?* (1870). *Jug-or-Not* (1870). *Moth and Rust* (1870). *Priest and Nun* (1870). *Westward: A Tale of American Emigrant Life* (1870). *Saints and Sinners of the Bible* (1872). *Nothing to Drink* (1873). *The Life-Cruise of Captain Bess Adams* (1874). *The Early Church in Britain: Its Faith and Works* (1875). *Lights And Shadows of Sacred Story* (1875). *Patriot and Tory: One Hundred Years Ago* (1876). *A Strange Sea-Story: A Temperance Tale* (1876). *Circled by Fire* (1879). *The Complete Home: An Encyclopedia of Domestic Life and Affairs* (1879). *The Curse and the Cup* (1879). *Firebrands* (1879). *On London Bridge* (1879). *Twelve Noble Men* (1879). *A Day with a Demon* (1880). *Step by Step* (1880). *The Oath-Keeper of Forano* (1881). *Practical Life; or, Ways and Means for Developing Character and Resources* (1881). *No Cards, No Cake: Marriage Extraordinary* (1882). *Among the Alaskans* (1883). *Bricks from Babel: A Brief View of the Myths, Traditions, and Religious Belief of Races, with Concise Studies in Ethnography* (1883). *Hannah: One of the Strong Women* (1883). *Mr. Standfast's Journey; or, The Path of the Just* (1884). *A Wife Hard Won* (1884). *The Dragon and the Tea-Kettle: An Experience, and the Dopplegänger* (1885). *Roland's Daughter: A Nineteenth-Century Maiden* (1885). *Graham's Laddie: A Story of God's Providence* (1886). *Million Too Much: A Temperance Tale* (1886). *Rasmus; or, The Making of a Man* (1886). *The Heir of Athole* (1887). *In Black and Gold: A Story of Twin Dragons* (1887). *A Made Man: A Sequel to "Rasmus; or, The Making of a Man"* (1887). *Mother Goose for Temperance Nurseries* (1887). *ABC for Temperance Nurseries* (1888). *Nature Readers: Seaside and Wayside* (1888). *Rag Fair and May Fair* (1889). *Sara Jane: A Girl of One Talent* (1889). *A Plain Woman's Story* (1890). *Fraü Dagmar's Son* (1891). *The Temperance Second Reader* (1891). *A Modern Prodigal* (1892). *The House on the Beach* (1893). *Mr. Grosvenor's Daughter* (1893). *On a Snow-Bound Train* (1893). *The Temperance Third Reader* (1893). *Ragweed: A West-World Story* (1894). *Her Ready-Made Family* (1895). *A New Samaritan* (1895). *Cynthia's Sons* (1896). *The House on the Bluff* (1896). *Ladies' Home Cook Book: A Complete Cook Book and Manual of Household Duties* (1896). *The People's Millions: The Story of a Card House* (1896). *The Cardiff Estate* (1897). *Astronomy: The Sun and His Family* (1898). *Botany: The Story of Plant Life* (1898). *Toward the Glory Gate* (1898). *A Bonnie Boy* (1899). *Three Colonial Maids* (1900). *Studies in Hearts* (1902). *The Gospel in the Riviera: A Story of Italy* (n.d.). *My Five Wards; or,*

Aunt Huldah's Homilies (n.d.). *The True Story Library* (n.d.). *Two Boys* (n.d.).

The papers of Julia McNair Wright are housed in the Fulton Public Library (Missouri) and the Westminster College Library, also in Fulton.

BIBLIOGRAPHY: Dowland, W. A., *The Sum of Feminine Achievement* (1917). Neven, A., ed., *Encyclopaedia of the Presbyterian Church in the United States of America* (1884). Rice, J. J., ed., *History of Westminster College, 1851-1903* (1903).

Other references: *Collegian* (Apr. 1898). *Fulton (Missouri) Weekly Gazette* (4 Sept. 1903). *NYT* (4 Sept. 1903). Records of the Women's Christian Temperance Union.

—LOIS FOWLER

WRIGHT, Mabel Osgood

Born 26 January 1859, New York, New York; **died** 16 July 1934, Fairfield, Connecticut
Wrote under: Barbara
Daughter of Samuel and Ellen Murdock Osgood; **married** James O. Wright, 1884

Mabel Osgood Wright's father was a Unitarian minister who late in life became an Episcopalian; the Osgood family lived in a large house in lower Manhattan when there were still cows pastured nearby. Educated at home and at a private school, Wright was a keen amateur naturalist from her youth, enjoying long summer vacations at the family summer home. With her husband, a dealer in rare books and art (whom she referred to as "Evan" in her Barbara books), she lived in Fairfield, Connecticut. She apparently had no children.

Wright was the first president of the Audubon Society of Connecticut and a member of the American Ornithologists' Union and the Connecticut Society of Colonial Dames—a much more exclusive organization than the Daughters of the American Revolution, which she ridiculed in *A Woman Errant* (1904).

Wright's first published books were about nature. Three— *The Friendship of Nature* (1894), *Birdcraft* (1895), and *Flowers and Ferns in Their Haunts* (1901)—were written for adults, but most are for children. As was common in 19th-century children's nature books, Wright taught about nature in story form, creating fictional children to lead the little readers through their lessons. *Tommy-Anne and the Three Hearts* (1896) and its sequel, *Wabeno the Magician* (1899), tell of a young tomboy who discovers the "Magic Spectacles" that combine truth with imagination. Wearing her spectacles, she can converse with the grass, flowers, insects, squirrels, and even her dog, Waddles.

Among Wright's most popular works are the semiautobiographical Barbara books, particularly the first, *The Garden of a Commuter's Wife* (1901), which introduces her alter ego, Barbara, who lives in the country with her husband and shares her life with many eccentric friends. Wright calls this book and *The Garden, You, and I* (1906) "pages from Barbara's Garden Book." Three other Barbara books bear designations intended to reveal other aspects of Barbara's life. *People of the Whirlpool* (1903) is "from the Experience Book," *Princess Flower-Hat* (1910) is "from the Perplexity Book," and *A Woman Errant* is "from the Wonder Book." Wright blends fanciful fiction with social comment, showing that she was an interested observer of the changes taking place in New York society— particularly among her own class of people. Servants provide comic relief.

A Woman Errant is the most serious book of the series. It is a melodramatic statement of Wright's belief that woman lives for and through man. According to Wright, women who leave their proper sphere for a career become bisexual. She shows a woman doctor who causes her own son's death because of her lack of the right kind of ability. Wright's attack on career women is not atypical of popular writers, even the professional women writers.

Wright's novels, set in the same area as her Barbara stories, are all romances, and in most of them she focuses on marriage as the most important part of life. In her last, *Eudora's Men* (1931), she underlines the importance of men to women by tracing a family from the beginning of the Civil War down to the present, when one of the youngest generation, a woman doctor, almost ruins the life of her husband by her "unnatural" concept of marriage.

In her autobiography, *My New York* (1926), she writes of her life up to the death of her beloved father and her engagement, focusing entirely on the city. It is a beautifully written picture of life in lower Manhattan in the 1860s and 1870s, giving her gift for observation and social comment its best exercise; it memorializes old New York, which had all but vanished when she wrote the book. While Wright is historically an important figure in popular nature writing, she did not make a successful transition to fiction as did Gene Stratton-Porter. But her autobiography is a charming, nostalgic book written without the bitterness she showed in other books when writing of the changes in society.

OTHER WORKS: *Citizen Bird* (1897). *Four-footed Americans and Their Kin* (1898). *The Dream Fox Story Book* (1900). *Dogtown* (1902). *Aunt Jimmy's Will* (1903). *At the Sign of the Fox* (1905). *Gray Lady and the Birds* (1907). *The Open Window* (1908). *Poppea of the Post-office* (1909). *The Love that Lives* (1911). *The Stranger at the Gate* (1913). *Captains of the Watch of Life and Death* (1927).

BIBLIOGRAPHY: *NAW* (1971). *NYT* (18 July 1934).

—BEVERLY SEATON

WRIGHT, Mary Clabaugh

Born 25 September 1917, Tuscaloosa, Alabama; **died** 18 June
    1970, Guilford, Connecticut
Daughter of Samuel F. and Mary Duncan Clabaugh; **married**
    Arthur Wright, 1940; **children:** two

Mary Clabaugh Wright grew up in Alabama. She studied
European history at Vassar College (she graduated *summa cum
laude*) and then at Radcliffe, but early in her graduate career she
turned to the study of Chinese history. Her husband was also
involved in Chinese studies. Together they spent most of World
War II in an internment camp in Shantung. After their release in
1945, they decided to stay in Peking for a while. Wright assisted
the Hoover Institute on War, Revolution, and Peace as a researcher. She was resourceful in searching book markets and government agencies throughout the country; it is through her efforts that
the Hoover Institute became the center of documents and research
material on the Chinese revolution. She became the curator of the
institute's Chinese collection in Palo Alto when she returned to
the U S. in 1947.

During the next 10 years she received her Ph.D. at Radcliffe,
became the mother of two boys, and was recognized as a major
historian. In the 1950s, she defended victims of the McCarthy
hysteria, particularly China scholar Owen Lattimore. In 1959, she
became the first tenured woman faculty member at Yale University.

Wright's classic work, *The Last Stand of Chinese Conservatism: The Tung-chih Restoration, 1862-1874* (1957, reprinted
1967) analyzes the late Ch'ing dynasty. It describes the imperial
effort to rebuild China's social, cultural, and economic base,
which were being threatened by internal rebellion as well as by
foreign ideas and values. The book points out in what areas the
restoration of the Confucian order was a partial success; more
importantly, it analyzes the reasons why the movement ultimately
was doomed to fail. The reformers are portrayed as extraordinarily great men who fought a hopeless battle against changing times.

Believing that "there is no way in which an effective modern
state can be grafted onto a Confucian society," Wright shows the
policies of Chiang Kai-shek in more modern times in a new light.
She explains in the final chapter how the attitudes and policies of
Chiang Kai-shek and the Kuomintang after 1927 were influenced
by the conservative restorationists of the Tung Chih period. In
adopting the Restoration as a model for his own government,
Chiang Kai-shek fatefully affected the outcome of the Nationalist-
Communist struggle. The Kuomintang did not meet the needs and
share the values of the new age, and, like the Restoration, was
doomed to fail.

The Last Stand of Chinese Conservatism has often been
acclaimed as a work of prime historical scholarship. The author is
applauded for having studied a period in Chinese history often
been neglected because of the lack of sources in Western languages. Wright was able to use Chinese sources and to relate the ideas
and events of this era through the eyes of the Chinese.

In 1965, Wright organized a research conference on the
Chinese Revolution of 1911, with 22 participants from six countries. She edited the collection of their papers, *China in Revolution: The First Phase, 1900-1913* (1968, 1973), which has been
recognized as one of the best works on 20th-century China.
Martin Wilburn of Columbia University described her 60-page
introduction as a "masterful historical synthesis." She discusses
the unprecedented intellectual ferment and rapid social and institutional changes occurring in China during the first decade of the
20th century. She vividly portrays the anti-Imperialist nationalism
arising in a determined effort to save China from foreign domination, and she points out that the quest for rapid modernization and
the belligerent assertions of sovereignty displayed by the People's
Republic of China in the 1950s had close parallels 40 years earlier.

BIBLIOGRAPHY: *A Memorial Service for Mary Clabaugh Wright
(1917-1970)* (1970). Fairbank, J. K., *China Perceived* (1974).
Feuerwerker, A., *Approaches to Modern Chinese History* (1967).

Other references: *Annals of the American Academy of Political and Social Science* (Nov. 1969). *Choice* (Sept. 1969). *Journal
of American Studies* (Nov. 1970). *NYTBR* (23 Nov. 1969). *SR* (15
March 1969). *TLS* (5 June 1969). *VQR* (Spring 1969).

—PATRICIA LANGHALS NEILS

WYATT, Edith Franklin

Born 14 September 1873, Tomah, Wisconsin; **died** October 1958,
    Chicago, Illinois
Daughter of Franklin and Marian La Grange Wyatt

A self-designated "middle-class American," Edith Franklin
Wyatt spent her earliest years in Midwestern towns where her
father was a railroad and mining engineer. Settled in a modest,
neighborly Chicago home in the 1880s, she and her two younger
sisters shared wide-ranging interests with their mother, who was
later a privately published poet. Wyatt attended Bryn Mawr from
1892 to 1894 and taught at a local girls' school for five years.
Wyatt's first publication, "Three Stories of Contemporary Chicago" (1900), caught the attention of William Dean Howells, who
publicly praised her early fiction and remained an admiring
friend. While teaching at Hull House and participating in the Little
Room, Chicago's preeminent salon, she produced most of her
fiction during this decade.

After her *McClure's* report on the 1909 Cherry Mine fire,
Wyatt was in great demand during the 1910s as a social commen-
tator and Progressive activist, promoting the causes of working-class women, child laborers, victims of the Eastland pleas-
ure-boat disaster, and suffragists. A founding board member of
Poetry, her concurrent literary work included a report on working
women's budgets, a documentary play, poems, and literary criticism. Socially conscientious but temperamentally retiring, Wyatt
lived with her mother and maintained a few close friendships with
people who shared her commitments. Her creative talent seems to

have exhausted itself in 1923, when she published her second novel after a year as assistant editor for *McClure's*. Her remaining work was mostly retrospective; she memorialized deceased colleagues and Chicago's past and also collected her earlier short stories.

The stories first published in *Every One His Own Way* (1901) demonstrate Wyatt's attention to the everyday strengths and distinctive mannerisms of urban ethnic types as well as her exposure of genteel intolerance. Recurring characters and neighborhood settings link together stories ranging from tragedy to satire. "A Matter of Taste" is representative: it recounts a literary critic's disdain for the participative, popular musical tastes of a German American couple, while embodying Wyatt's own characteristic perspective in the clear-sighted observations of the critic's sister.

A similar dichotomy between conventionality and wholesomeness informs Wyatt's first novel, *True Love* (1903). Snobbish Norman Hubbard—whose "sepulchral" Chicago home traps visitors in vacuous conversation—engages himself to an equally convention-bound woman, until they can no longer stand each other's narrowness. A second romance between unpretentious Chicagoan Emily Marsh, whose simple family home welcomes friends to billiards and cards, and an equally ordinary country man, leads to marriage.

Wyatt believed heterogeneous Americans share primarily the experience of migration: "Movement through a variety of country" is, she declares, the unifying theme of the poems in *The Wind in the Corn* (1917). "To a River God" exemplifies her poetry's dynamic attention to geography, unity-in-diversity theme, and ritualistic, chanting rhythms, which occasionally disintegrate into sing-song. Most admired were Wyatt's urban poems: "November in the City" and "City Equinoctial" epitomize her unconventional portrayal of natural cycles in city as well as country scenes.

Original observation and social perspective mark Wyatt's literary criticism and social commentary. A well-chosen selection in *Great Companions* (1917) demonstrates her concerns with national literary culture, writers' attitudes toward women, and autobiographies of working people. "The Dislike of Human Interest" clarifies the political basis for her objections to standardized literary stereotypes.

Invisible Gods (1923) tries to combine Wyatt's fictional talents with her political commitments in a sociological novel about three generations of a Chicago family. But an uncharacteristically loose, episodic structure and wordy prose undercut her uncompromising vision and talent for characterization. Wyatt combined a pluralistic appreciation of common people and regional integrity with original observation and satiric humor in her fiction, poetry, literary criticism, and social commentaries. Her early fiction and essays represent her best work, as fine as that of Howells and undeservedly ignored by literary historians and critics.

OTHER WORKS: *The Whole Family* (with W. D. Howells, et al., 1907). *Making Both Ends Meet* (with S. A. Clark, 1911). *Art and the Worth While* (with R. M. Lovett, et al., 1929). *The Satyr's*

Children (1939). *Two Fairy Tales: The Pursuit of Happiness and The Air Castle* (n.d.).

The manuscripts of Edith Franklin Wyatt are housed in the Newberry Library in Chicago, and include both correspondence and three boxes of published and unpublished works.

BIBLIOGRAPHY: *Boston Transcript* (22 Dec. 1917). *Harper's* (Oct. 1901). *New York Tribune* (11 Mar. 1923). *North American Review* (May 1903, Mar. 1917). *Poetry* (Jan. 1918).

—SIDNEY H. BREMER

WYLIE, Elinor Hoyt

Born 7 September 1885, Somerville, New Jersey; died 16 December 1928, New York, New York

Daughter of Henry M. and Anne McMichael Hoyt; married Philip Hichborn, 1905; Horace Wylie, 1916 (divorced); William Rose Benét, 1923

Elinor Hoyt Wylie, the eldest of five children born into a socially and politically prominent family, grew up and attended private schools in Philadelphia and Washington, D.C. Her elopement in 1910 with a married Washington lawyer, Horace Wylie, and abandonment of her husband and son became a highly publicized scandal. To escape the notoriety, the couple lived for a few years in England as Mr. and Mrs. Horace Waring. There she published—privately and anonymously—her first book of poetry, *Incidental Numbers* (1912). The pair returned to the U.S. before World War I, living first in Boston, then in Augusta, Georgia, and Washington, D.C.

In Washington, Wylie became friendly with the writers William Rose Benét, Edmund Wilson, and John Dos Passos, who encouraged her to take her writing seriously. After separating from Wylie in 1921, she moved to New York and captivated the literary world with her beauty, elegance, conversation, and acid wit. She married Benét in 1923.

During the eight years from 1921 until her death, Wylie served as a contributing editor of the *New Republic* and wrote short stories, literary criticism, four volumes of poetry, and four novels. Two of the latter derive from her great interest in the Romantic movement, especially in the poet Shelley. *The Orphan Angel* (1926) is a fantasy of Shelley searching across the expanding American West for a mysterious and beautiful woman. *Mr. Hodge and Mr. Hazard* (1928) recounts the decline of romanticism in the tale of "the last Romantic poet" confronting the bourgeois world of the Victorians. Much careful scholarship went into the backgrounds of these novels.

Wylie's talent is notable, but problematic. A tension between opposing impulses often led her to miss her mark; but when these tensions were confronted and developed, her work achieved its full potential in powerful poems of heightened irony. Wylie's technical facility and taste for elegance produced in her novels and some of her verse a polished surface with little sustaining depth.

No doubt aware of this, she called her first full-length novel, *Jennifer Lorn* (1923), "a sedate extravaganza." One critic described it as "a dish of curds and cream flavored with saffron." The book's heroine is such a delicacy herself—elaborately confected, a visual delight, but entirely unsubstantial. One focus of the novel's rather mild satire is society's vision of women as decorative objects.

The Venetian Glass Nephew (1925, reprinted 1984) concerns itself with the conflicting claims of art and nature, but thematic development is submerged to elegant sensual richness. Rosalba Berni undergoes the painful transformation into glass in order to become a suitable bride for the manufactured Virginio. One of the characters notes, "The result, although miraculous, is somewhat inhuman. I have known fathers who submitted their daughters to the ordeal, husbands who forced it upon their wives."

In her best poetry, Wylie dealt more pointedly with the conflicts that claimed her attention: the problem of the feeling self smoldering beneath its decorative surface. Statements of this theme appear in "Sleeping Beauty," "Sanctuary," "Where, O Where?," "The Lie," and "Full Moon." In the last poem, the speaker, dressed elegantly in "silk and miniver," cries, "There I walked, and there I raged; / The spiritual savage caged...." Images of falsehood—masks, disguises, and costumes—convey the tension between beautiful exterior and turbulent interior, between felt passion and enforced restraint.

Carl Van Vechten called *Jennifer Lorn* "the only successfully sustained satire in English with which I am acquainted." Praise for her other works was equally adulatory. Recent criticism has been scanty and less favorable. The inclusion of Wylie in recently published anthologies of women poets indicates a reawakening of appreciation; it is time for her to receive a full-scale literary reappraisal.

OTHER WORKS: *Nets to Catch the Wind* (1921). *Black Armour* (1923). *Angels and Earthly Creatures* (1928). *Trivial Breath* (1928). *Collected Poems of Elinor Wylie* (1932). *Collected Prose of Elinor Wylie* (1933). *Last Poems of Elinor Wylie* (1943, 1982).

The Beineke Rare Book and Manuscript Collection at Yale University holds papers of Elinor Wylie and William Rose Benét; in addition, Wylie's correspondence is also housed with that of the Hoyt family in the Berg Collection of the New York Public Library.

BIBLIOGRAPHY: Auchincloss, L., *The Man Behind the Book: Literary Profiles* (1996). Blanck, J., *Bibliography of American Literature* (1991). Colum, M., *Life and the Dream* (1947). Farr, J. *The Life and Art of Elinor Wylie* (1983). Gaggke, C. T. et al, eds., *Poetry Criticism: Excerpts from Criticism of the Works of the Most Significant and Widely Studied Poets of World Literature, Volume 23* (1999). Gray, T. A., *Elinor Wylie* (1969). Gregory, H., and M. Zaturenska, *A History of American Poetry, 1900-1940* (1942). Howe, F., ed., *No More Masks! An Anthology of Twentieth-Century American Women Poets, Newly Revised and Expanded* (1993). Hoyt, N., *Elinor Wylie: The Portrait of an Unknown Lady* (1935). Kazin, A., *On Native Grounds* (1942). Olson, S., *Elinor Wylie: A Life Apart* (1979). Philip, N., ed., *Singing America* (1995). Ruihley, G. R., *An Anthology of Great U.S. Women Poets, 1850-1990: Temples and Palaces* (1997). Van Doren, C., *Three Worlds* (1936). Walker, C., *Masks Outrageous and Austere: Culture, Psyche, and Persona in Modern Women Poets* (1991). West, R., *Ending in Earnest* (1931). Wilson, E., *The Shores of Light* (1952). Woodard, D., *This More Fragile Boundary: The Female Subject and the Romance Plot in the Texts of Millay, Wylie, Teasdale, Bogan* (dissertation, 1993).

Reference works: *Oxford Companion to Women's Writing in the United States* (1995).

Other references: *Dial* (June 1923). *ES* (Dec. 1938). *NR* (5 Dec. 1923, 6 Feb. 1929, 7 Sept. 1932). *PMLA* (1941). *VQR* (July 1930).

—KAREN F. STEIN

Y

YAMADA, Mitsuye

Born 5 July 1923, Fukuoka, Japan
Daughter of Jack K. and Hide Shirake Yasutake; **married** Yoshikazu Yamada, 1950; **children:** Jeni, Stephen, Douglas, Hedi

Mitsuye Yamada was born in Japan of naturalized Japanese American parents and lived in Seattle, Washington, until the outbreak of World War II, when her family was relocated to the concentration camp at Minidoka, Iowa. Yamada left the camp to attend school at the University of Cincinnati and New York University (B.A., 1947). She earned an M.A. from the University of Chicago in 1953 and did further graduate study at the University of California at Irvine. A professor of English, Yamada taught in California at Fullerton College (1966-69) and at Cypress College from 1969 until her retirement in 1989. She has received several awards, including the Vesta award for writing from the Woman's Building of Los Angeles (1982) and the Women of Achievement award from the Rancho Santiago Foundation (1991).

Yamada's poetry, essays, and short fiction have appeared in numerous anthologies and periodicals, and she has published two books: *Camp Notes and Other Poems* (1976, 1992, 1998) and *Desert Run: Poems and Stories* (1988, reissued 1992). Her work is driven by her experience as a Japanese American woman growing up in 20th-century American society; in "Invisibility is an Unnatural Disaster," she claims membership in "the most stereotyped minority of them all, the Asian American woman." Her poetry and stories are charged with her sense of a double or divided identity, while her essays confront issues of race, gender, and justice that profoundly affect Asian American lives.

Some of Yamada's earliest poems, written during her internment, are included in *Camp Notes*. The short lines, simple stanzas, and matter-of-fact tone initially belie the poems' complexity, but the cumulative documentation of the daily indignities of camp life exposes the fundamental absurdity of the camps' existence. In the title poem of her later book, *Desert Run*, Yamada returns to the desert "with new eyes" for a reconsideration of the camp experience, and she discovers that "as an older Asian American woman [she has] come to identify with the desert." The poems and stories in this volume also explore the writer's connections to Japan and portray the cultural, generational, and sexual miscommunications between issei and nisei (first- and second-generation Japanese Americans) and between women and men.

Yamada maintains that Japanese Americans must acknowledge their often painful history in order to claim their identify. Because she believes that "art is a powerful force in effecting personal as well as social and political change," Yamada views her own writing as a means to exorcize racism and sexism and to create a more truly multicultural society. She actively supports other ethnic writers and artists; she has been an officer of MELUS (the Society for the Study of the Multi-Ethnic Literature of the United States), the founder of the Multi-Cultural Women Writers of Orange County, and the editor of two collections of ethnic literature. Yamada has also served on the national board of directors for the human rights organization, Amnesty International.

OTHER WORKS: *The Webs We Weave: Orange County Poetry Anthology* (with J. Brander, eds., 1986). *Sowing Ti Leaves: Writings by Multicultural Women* (with S. S. Hylkema, eds., 1991).

BIBLIOGRAPHY: Rountree, C., *On Women Turning 70: Honoring the Voices of Wisdom* (1999). Yamamoto, T., *Masking Selves, Making Subjects: Japanese American Women, Identity, and the Body* (1999).
   Reference works: *CA* (1979). *FC* (1990). *Oxford Companion to Women's Writing in the United States* (1995).
   Other references: *Amerasia Journal* (1991). *Contact Two* (1986). *MELUS* (Spring 1988). *Tozai Times* (Mar. 1989). "Mitsuye and Nellie [Wong]: Asian American Poets," Light-Saraf Films, Public Broadcasting System (1981). *Mitsuye and Nellie: Asian-American Poets* (video, 1981). *Mitsuye Yamada* (audiocassette, 1992). "A Woman is Talking to Death," an interview by Stan Yogi (audiotape, with Judy Grahn, KPFA, 1991).

—SUSAN B. RICHARDSON

YAMAMOTO, Hisaye

Born 23 August 1921, Redondo Beach, California
Wrote under: Napoleon
Daughter of Kanzo and Sae Tamura Yamamoto; **married** Anthony DeSoto, 1955; **children:** Paul, Kibo, Elizabeth, Anthony, Claude

Hisaye Yamamoto has been described as "not just one of the best Nisei [second-generation Japanese American] writers, not just one of the best Asian American writers, but. . .among the best short story writers today." Although she has written short stories over a span of more than 50 years, her work long remained relatively unknown. Most of it, which also includes some essays and poems, has appeared in West Coast Japanese American newspapers, literary magazines, and World War II camp publications. It was only with the publication of *Seventeen Syllables and Other Stories* (1994, reprinted 1998)—a collection of 15 stories dating from 1948 to 1987—that Yamamoto's work became generally accessible to American readers.

Yamamoto has tended to minimize her identity as a writer; in interviews she underscores the importance of her family life and describes herself as a housewife. Yet Yamamoto was among the first Japanese American writers to reach a national audience after World War II and one of the early few to receive national acclaim. During the late 1940s and 1950s, when anti-Japanese sentiment inhibited the publication of work by Japanese Americans, her stories appeared in such major journals as *Partisan Review, Harper's Bazaar, Furioso,* and the *Kenyon Review.* Four stories from this period were included on Martha Foley's annual list of "Distinctive Short Stories," and "Yoneko's Earthquake" (1951) was selected for Foley's 1952 collection of the *Best American Short Stories.* Yamamoto was awarded a John Hay Whitney Opportunity Fellowship in 1949 to support her writing. In 1952 she declined a Stanford (University) Writing Fellowship in order to join the *Catholic Worker* in New York. She received the 1986 American Book Award for lifetime achievement from the Before Columbus Foundation. When pressed, Yamamoto will admit to having her "little madness" for writing, and she concedes "if somebody told me I couldn't write, it would probably grieve me very much."

Born to immigrant parents, Yamamoto grew up on her father's strawberry farms among the Japanese American agricultural community of Southern California. She began publishing stories when she was still in her teens under the pen name "Napoleon." Before World War II, she earned an associate of arts degree at Compton Junior College, and she was writing columns for a Japanese American newspaper when the evacuation order relocated her family to the internment camp at Poston, Arizona. During her almost three years in Poston (1942-44), Yamamoto continued writing stories and columns for the camp paper, the *Poston Chronicle.* After the war, she worked three years for an African American newspaper, the *Los Angeles Tribune,* and spent several years writing full time before moving to New York in 1952 to join Dorothy Day and the *Catholic Worker* community on their Staten Island farm. Returning to Southern California in 1954, she married and subsequently combined writing with rearing five children. Her work has appeared regularly in West Coast publications, and she has continued a tradition established in the 1950s of contributing to the annual holiday literary issue of *Rafu Shimpo.* Yamamoto gives readings from her work throughout the country. *Hot Summer Winds,* a 1991 film shown on PBS' *American Playhouse,* was based on two of Yamamoto's stories.

Yamamoto's carefully crafted stories—delicate yet dense, small in scale but multilayered, spare of language yet laced with irony—portray the Japanese American experience. They are told by Japanese American narrators, most of them second-generation (nisei) women like Yamamoto herself; the narrator's age and the time and place of events tend to parallel the author's own life. Although not overtly political, the stories touch on issues of racism and the distribution of power in American society.

OTHER WORKS: Contributor to numerous anthologies and collections, including: *Aiiieeeee! An Anthology of Asian-American Writers* (1983, 1999); *Images of Women in Literature* (1991); *Imagining America: Stories from the Promised Land* (1991); *Short Stories by Japanese American Writers* (1991); *Charlie*

Chan is Dead: An Anthology of Contemporary Asian American Fiction (1993); *Growing Up Asian American: An Anthology* (1993); *Where Coyotes Howl and Wind Blows Free: Growing Up in the West* (1995); *Into the Fire: Asian American Prose* (1996).

BIBLIOGRAPHY: Bloom, H., ed., *Asian American Women Writers* (1997). Bloom, H., ed., *Asian-American Writers* (1999). Cheung, K., *Articulate Silences: Hisaye Yamamoto, Maxine Hong Kingston, Joy Kogawa* (1993). Cheung, K., and S. Yogi, eds., *Asian American Literature: An Annotated Bibliography* (1988). Hong, K. W., "Interethnic and Interracial Relations in the Short Stories of Hisaye Yamamoto" (thesis, 1995). Ignacio-Zimardi, J. T., "Self-Discovery and Subversive Expressions in Four Asian American Narratives" (thesis, 1993). Lim, S. and A. Ling, eds., *Reading the Literatures of Asian America* (1992). Pollack, H., ed., *Having Our Way: Women Rewriting Tradition in Twentieth-Century America* (1995). Schweik, S. *A Gulf So Deeply Cut: American Women Poets and the Second World War* (1991). Truchlar, L., ed., *Opening up Literary Criticism: Essays on American Prose and Poetry* (1986). Yogi, S. S., "Legacies Revealed: Uncovering Buried Plots in the Stories of Hisaye Yamamoto and Wakako Yamauchi" (thesis, 1988).

Reference works: *Asian American Literature: An Introduction to the Writings and Their Social Context* (1982). *Asian American Literature: Reviews and Criticism of Works by American Writers of Asian Descent* (1999). *Oxford Companion to Women's Writing in the United States* (1995).

Other references: *Amerasia Journal* (1990). *American Literature* (1999). *Calyx* (Summer 1992). *Chicago Review* (1993). *Comparative Literature Studies* (1996). *East-West Film Journal* (July 1993). *International Examiner Literary Supplement* (19 July 1989). *MELUS* (Fall 1980, Spring 1987). *Modern Language Notes* (1995). *Studies in American Fiction* (Autumn 1989). *Sunbury* (1981). *Tozai Times* (March 1989).

—SUSAN B. RICHARDSON

YAMANAKA, Lois-Ann

Born 7 September 1961, Ho'olchua, Molokai, Hawaii
Daughter of Harry and Jean Yamanaka; married John Inferrera; children: John

Lois-Ann Yamanaka was raised in the sugar plantation town of Pahala, Hawaii, by Japanese American parents. Yamanaka, the eldest of four daughters, grew up speaking pidgin, the dialect of working-class Hawaiians, as her first language. Formally known as Hawaii Creole English, pidgin originated with the influx of immigrant laborers from Japan, China, and the Philippines during the 19th century. Despite the fact that her mother was a teacher and her father a school administrator turned taxidermist, Yamanaka felt inferior to middle-class Japanese Americans who did not speak pidgin.

Yamanaka received a B.A. in education from the University of Hawaii at Manoa in 1983 and a masters in education from the same university in 1987. She credits poet Morgan Blair, one of her instructors, with helping her to overcome her fear of writing in pidgin. Blair introduced her to African American writers like Ntozake Shange and Thulani Davis who successfully wrote in dialect. Yamanaka was also encouraged by the members of Bamboo Ridge, a literary publishing collective formed in 1978 to encourage works by local-born authors of all ethnicities. Yamanaka's first book, *Saturday Night at the Pahala Theatre* (1993) is a collection of four verse novellas whose narrators are working-class Hawaiian teenagers. This debut work explores many of the issues Yamanaka is know for throughout her writing—ethnic identity, sexual development, peer pressure, self-hatred, and drug use. Yamanaka received critical praise for her first book and won several awards, including the Asian American Studies National Book Award, a Carnegie Foundation grant, and a National Endowment for the Arts creative writing fellowship, enabling her to take a sabbatical from her teaching position in order to write full time. She received a Pushcart Prize the same year for her novella *Yarn Wig*. Yet many Hawaiian educators criticized *Saturday Night at the Pahala Theatre* for its use of pidgin and its profanity. Of particular concern to educators was a passage in which a young girl repeats local stereotypes about Filipino men. Yamanaka was uninvited from several speaking engagements and her book was banned at many Hawaiian schools.

Yamanaka's next work, *Wild Meat and the Bully Burgers* (1996), is told in the pidgin dialect of narrator Lovey Nariyoshi, a Japanese American teenager in Hilo, Hawaii, during the 1970s. The story, which consists of a series of loosely collected anecdotes, revolves around Lovey's desire to be thin and Caucasian like the teen idols in her fan magazines. Yamanaka's other works also reveal the extent to which American culture has pervaded Hawaiian youth and replaced adherence to the traditions and customs of many ethnic groups with an affection for pop music, fast food, and Hollywood movies. Like *Saturday Night at the Pahala Theatre*, *Wild Meat and the Bully Burgers* also explores issues of class and ethnicity. Racism among different ethnic groups is a theme throughout the book as Lovey picks on a young Filipino girl in order to feel better about herself. Although *Wild Meat and the Bully Burgers* was nominated for an Asian American Studies National Book Award, criticism of the book within the association was so fierce no award was granted in 1996.

Yamanaka's third book, *Blu's Hanging* (1997), centers on its thirteen-year-old narrator, Ivah Ogata, her eight-year-old brother Blu, and her five-year-old sister, Maisie. The plot focuses on their attempts to come to terms with both their mother's death and their poverty-stricken lives. Ivah, who narrates in pidgin, watches helplessly as her father turns to drugs, Blu is sexually abused and develops an eating disorder, and Maisie quits speaking. The book's criminal and morally bankrupt characters are both Filipino and Japanese, which made Yamanaka's critics furious. She was awarded the 1998 Asian American Studies National Book Award for *Blu's Hanging* against her detractors' wishes, but the award was rescinded almost immediately.

Heads by Harry (1999) is another of Yamanaka's coming-of-age in Hawaii tales and has the most richly drawn characters of her books to date. The title takes its name from the Yagyuu family's taxidermy shop in Hilo. Sixteen-year-old underachiever Toni Yagyuu is from an offbeat but primarily stable family. The book, which is narrated in pidgin, revolves around Toni's relationship with her homosexual older brother, Sheldon, and beautiful younger sister, Bunny, who dreams of marrying a haole (Caucasian). The siblings grow older and share an apartment at college. Toni deals with a host of unexpected problems, including addiction, pregnancy, and poor grades. Like many of Yamanaka's characters, Toni has a wry sense of humor that sustains her throughout her troubles.

Yamanaka's recent work, *Name Me Nobody* (1999), is aimed at a younger audience than her previous works. The protagonist is thirteen-year-old Emi-Lou, who is overweight and whose only friends are her grandmother and her friend, Von. Emi-Lou struggles to overcome the nickname "Lumpy," given at school. She also tries to maintain her friendship with Von as the two grow older and it appears Von might be gay.

Yamanaka asserts that her work represents a more realistic picture of Hawaii than the "exotification" the islands receive in the mainstream media. Yamanaka's writing serves as an effective and just condemnation of the poverty and despair of Hawaii's immigrant minorities. She sees her books as helping to reclaim Hawaii's identity from the haole culture that has dominated the islands for the last several centuries. She also views her writing as a bridge linking pidgin-speaking students with literature to which they can relate. Yamanaka is a fierce defender of pidgin and a critic of what she sees as government attempts to eradicate the language. "Linguistic identity and cultural identity are skin and flesh. When you sever one from the other, you make it not okay to be who you are" (quoted in the *Knight-Ridder/Tribune News Service*). Yamanaka's unique voice makes it very clear she knows exactly who she is and that she is proud of it.

BIBLIOGRAPHY: Reference works: *CA* (1998).

Other references: *Atlantic Monthly* (Feb. 1999). *Harper's Bazaar* (Apr. 1997). *Knight-Ridder/Tribune News Service* (28 Feb. 1996). *Nation* (1 Mar. 1999). *Newsweek* (17 Aug. 1998). *People* (26 May 1997).

—LEAH J. SPARKS

YATES, Elizabeth

Born 6 December 1905, Buffalo, New York
Daughter of Harry and Mary Duffy Yates; married William McGreal, 1929 (died 1963)

Long summers on her father's farm south of Buffalo were the most memorable days of Elizabeth Yates' childhood and youth. After graduation from high school, she worked in New York City for three years, writing as much as possible. In 1929 she moved with her husband to London, where she continued her apprentice work, writing articles, book reviews, and short stories. Her first book was published in England in 1938. Because of her husband's failing eyesight, the couple returned to the U.S. in 1939, bought a small farm in New Hampshire, restored a century-old farmhouse, and created a new life focused around her writing, his work for the blind, and the fields and woodlands they both enjoyed. Yates' *The Lighted Heart* (1960) tells of this part of her life. Although her husband died in 1963, she has continued to live in New Hampshire, the setting of many of her works. She has been a staff member at writers' conferences and has received several honorary degrees as well as the Sarah Josepha Hale Award (1970) for a "distinguished author whose work and life reflect the literary tradition of New England." In *Patterns on the Wall* (1943), which received the *New York Herald Tribune* Spring Festival Award, a kind-hearted itinerant painter who decorates rooms with stenciled designs is held responsible for the severe weather of 1816 and tried for witchcraft. In *Hue and Cry* (1953, reprinted 1991), the same painter-farmer risks position and property 20 years later to befriend a disillusioned immigrant youth who has stolen a valuable horse.

Mountain Born (1943), a Newbery honor book, and *A Place for Peter* (1952, latest reissue 1994), a Boys' Clubs of America gold medal winner, depict the quiet, pastoral life on a sheep farm. The earlier book presents a detailed picture of the shepherd's life; the latter shows other farm activities, such as clearing brush and making maple syrup, and explores a growing boy's relationship with his father.

Amos Fortune, Free Man (1950, reissue 1989), the fictionalized biography of an obscure man of great strength and dignity, won the Newbery Medal in 1951 and the William Allen White Award in 1953. Born the son of a king in Africa, Fortune lived as a slave in Massachusetts until he was able to buy his freedom at the age of sixty. After purchasing the freedom of other slaves, including his wife and her daughter, he moved to New Hampshire, where he operated a tannery for 20 years and became a respected member of the community.

Carolina's Courage (1964, 1989) records the adventures of a small girl during the long trip by covered wagon from New Hampshire to Nebraska Territory. After she gives her doll, her only personal possession, to a Native American girl, the settlers receive a friendly welcome to the territory. *Sarah Whitcher's Story* (1971) is based on a published account of a little girl, lost in the woods, who was befriended by a black bear. *Rainbow Round the World* (1954), an interpretation of the work of UNICEF, won the Jane Addams Award for promotion of peace and world community. In *Someday You'll Write* (1962), Yates advises young people about practicing the writer's craft.

In her adult fiction, Yates writes about social and racial prejudice, emotional illness, and attempted suicide, but the books are suffused with an atmosphere of serenity, hope, and idealism rare in contemporary literature. Problems are resolved through the help of an understanding friend, through inspiration drawn from secular or religious literature, or through communion with nature.

Yates has also written biographies of the writer Dorothy Canfield Fisher, Howard Thurman, and Prudence Crandall, a courageous young woman who, in 1833, established a school for black girls in Canterbury, Connecticut. The latter was written for children.

Yates' writings are characterized by a faith in the nobility of people, love of nature and all creatures, family affection, religious belief, and detailed descriptions of crafts and occupations. Although she has written fiction and nonfiction for both children and adults, she is best known for her award-winning juvenile books. Though in her nineties, Yates has continued to write throughout the last decade of the century. Her recent book, *Open the Door: A Gathering of Poems and Prose Pieces* was published in 1999. Additionally, Yates was honored with an "Ageless Heroes" plaque from Blue Cross/Blue Shield of New Hampshire in March 1999 for her continuing creativity and "vitality." A proponent of community involvement, Yates has served on the Board of New Hampshire Association for the Blind for 25 years, and as a trustee of the Peterborough Town Library for 22 years. She still makes appearances in schools, and has donated 40 acres of land and her home in Peterborough for the creation of the Shieling Forest Learning Center.

OTHER WORKS: *Gathered Grace* (1938). *High Holiday* (1938). *Climbing Higher* (1939). *Hans and Frieda* (1939). *Haven for the Brave* (1941). *Around the Year in Iceland* (1942). *Under the Little Fir* (1942). *Wind of Spring* (1945). *Nearby* (1947). *Once in the Year* (1947). *Beloved Bondage* (1948). *The Young Traveller in the U.S.A.* (1948). *Children of the Bible* (1950). *Guardian Heart* (1950). *Brave Interval* (1952). *David Livingstone* (1953). *Prudence Crandall, Woman of Courage* (1955, 1996). *The Carey Girl* (1956). *Pebble in a Pool: The Widening Circles of Dorothy Canfield Fisher's Life* (1958; reissued as *The Lady from Vermont*, 1971). *The Next Fine Day* (1962, 1994). *Sam's Secret Journal* (1964). *Howard Thurman: Portrait of a Practical Dreamer* (1964). *Up the Golden Stair: An Approach to a Deeper Understanding of Life Through Personal Sorrow* (1966, 1990). *Is There a Doctor in the Barn? A Day in the Life of Forrest F. Tenney, D.V.M.* (1966, 1994). *An Easter Story* (1967). *With Paddle, Pipe, and Song: A Story of the French-Canadian Voyageurs* (1968, 1998). *New Hampshire* (1969). *On that Night* (1969). *The Road Through Sandwich Notch* (1973). *Skeezer, Dog with a Mission* (1973). *We, the People* (1974). *A Book of Hours* (1976, 1989). *Call It Zest* (1977). *My Diary—My World* (1981). *My Widening World* (1983). *One Writer's Way* (1984). *The Journeyman* (1990). *Sound Friendships: The Story of Willa and Her Hearing Ear Dog* (1992). *A Place for Peter* (1996). *Spanning Time: A Diary Keeper Becomes a Writer* (1996). *Swiss Holiday* (1996). *Iceland Adventure* (1997).

BIBLIOGRAPHY: Arbuthnot, M. H., and Z. Sutherland, *Children and Books* (1972). Greenberg, M. H. and Waugh, C., eds., *A Newbery Christmas: Fourteen Stories of Christmas by Newbery Award-Winning Authors* (1998). Hoffman, M., and E. Samuels, eds., *Authors and Illustrators of Children's Books* (1972). MacCann, D., and G. Woodward, *The Black American in Books for Children* (1972). Vaughn, R., *Elizabeth Yates' On That Night: Stageplay* (1978).

Reference works: *Junior Book of Authors* (1951). *Newbery Medal Books: 1922-1955* (1955). *SATA* (1973).

Other references: *Meet the Newbery Author: Elizabeth Yates McGreal* (filmstrip, Miller-Brody Productions, 1976).

—ALICE BELL SALO

YEZIERSKA, Anzia

Born circa 1880, Plinsk, Russian Poland; **died** 21 November 1970, Ontario, California

Daughter of Baruch and Pearl Yezierska; **married** Jacob Gordon, 1910; Arnold Levitas, 1911; **children:** one daughter

Anzia Yezierska was born into the poverty and orthodoxy of an East European shtetl. When her large family came to the Lower East Side of New York in the 1890s, her father clung to his life of full-time Talmudic study and the wife and children supported the family. Yezierska had little opportunity for formal education; she worked in sweatshops and laundries and learned what she could from night school English classes and borrowed books. A scholarship enabled her to attend a training program for domestic science teachers, and from 1905 to 1913 she taught cooking in an elementary school. Her determination to rise from the dirt and drudgery of poverty to "make from herself a person" led to an early break with her family, the failure of two brief marriages, and the surrender of her daughter to the father's care.

A meeting with John Dewey, then dean at Columbia Teachers College, led to a romantic involvement that Yezierska wrote about repeatedly, in disguised form, in her later fiction. Dewey wrote a number of poems to Yezierska during the years 1917 and 1918; two of these unearthed poems appear in Yezierska's books of 1932 and 1950, attributed only to the Dewey-figures "Henry Scott" and "John Morrow."

Yezierska published her first short story in 1915; in the next decade her stories appeared in respected magazines. Edward J. O'Brien praised "The Fat of the Land" as the best short story of 1919. When Hollywood bought the film rights to the short story collection *Hungry Hearts and Other Stories* (1920, reissued 1985) and also hired Yezierska as a salaried writer, the impoverished immigrant became overnight a wealthy celebrity.

But Yezierska could not write in materialistic Hollywood. She wrote productively in New York for a few more years, but by the time she lost her money in the Depression, she had also lost her creative inspiration. She joined the Work Projects Administration (WPA) Writers Project in the 1930s; published an autobiography in 1950 and then a few stories about old age; and was poor and forgotten long before her death in 1970.

In *Hungry Hearts*, 10 stories of Lower East Side life, Yezierska's immigrant characters struggle with the disillusioning

America of poverty and exploitation while they search for the "real" America of their ideals. The stories, like all of her fiction, are realistic, passionate, occasionally autobiographical, sometimes formless and overwrought; their effusive language suggests the style and intonation of an immigrant speaker. Women are the chief protagonists—women whose bodies are tied to sweatshop or household drudgery but whose spirits hunger for love, beauty, and some measure of independence, self-expression, and dignity.

In *Salomé of the Tenements* (1922), her first novel, she exhibits more passion than craftsmanship. It explores the attraction between two of Yezierska's stock character types: the "Russian Jewess," idealistic and emotional, and the rational, aloof, "born American" male. Sonya Vrunsky, poor girl of the ghetto, marries wealthy John Manning. But Sonya is not happy; she renounces her marriage and seeks to build an independent life based on her own talents.

Yezierska prefaces the short story collection *Children of Loneliness* (1923) with a revealing essay, "Mostly about Myself," in which she discusses her tortured efforts to write. The nine stories themselves are similar in style and substance to those of *Hungry Hearts*. They deal with conflicts between old- and new-world values, the insensitivity and ineptness of social service agencies, the corrupting influence of materialism, and the spiritual hunger of the poor.

Bread Givers (1925, reprinted 1975) is an autobiographical novel about a dominating, unbending Talmudic scholar and his daughter's struggle to break free of subservient roles and to forge for herself an independent, fulfilling life. It is worth rediscovering.

Arrogant Beggar (1927, reprinted 1996) mixes social criticism with sentimentality for an effect that is at once trite and moving. Adele Lindner is from a poor neighborhood on New York's East Side; her gratitude to the Hellman Home for Working Girls turns to disgust with the patronizing attitudes and policies of her rich benefactors. She denounces the home and finds true charity and a satisfying life among her own people. *All I Could Never Be* (1932), Yezierska's last and not very successful novel, is at least a useful companion piece to her autobiography. Its heroine is the intense and idealistic Fanya Ivanowna; in her unsuccessful but obsessive romance with an older professor, her writing career which first blossoms and then fades, and her lonely search for a meaningful life and for satisfying human contact, she lives a fictionalized version of Yezierska's own experiences.

Since Yezierska's fiction is frequently autobiographical, it is perhaps not surprising that her autobiography, *Red Ribbon on a White Horse* (1950, reprinted in 1981 and 1987), is semifictional. Autobiographical data is selectively presented and unreliable, but the book is interesting for its discussion of the bureaucratic absurdities of the WPA and for its account of Yezierska's painful attempts to come to terms with herself, her values, and her immigrant Jewish heritage, and to find some real happiness and peace.

Yezierska was not a master of style, plot development, or characterization, but the intensity of feeling and aspiration evident in her narratives often transcends the stylistic imperfections. Her work deserves consideration as one of the few chronicles of the immigrant experience from a woman's viewpoint and as an early attempt in American fiction to present the struggles of women against family, religious injunctions, and social and economic obstacles to create for themselves an independent identity.

OTHER WORKS: *The Open Cage: An Anzia Yezierska Collection* (1979). *How I Found America: Collected Stories of Anzia Yezierska* (1991). Contributor to several anthologies including: *Women of Valor: The Struggle Against the Great Depression As Told in Their Own Life Stories* (1990), *Imagining America: Stories From the Promised Land* (1991), *Women's Friendships: A Collection of Short Stories* (1991), *Growing Up Female: Stories by Women Writers From the American Mosaic* (1993), *Oxford Book of Jewish Stories* (1998), *The Urban Muse: Stories on the American City* (1998), and others.

BIBLIOGRAPHY: Batker, C. J., *Ethnic Women's Literature and Politics: The Cultural Construction of Gender in Early 20th-Century America* (dissertation, 1993). Baum, C., et al., *The Jewish Woman in America* (1975). Bloom, H., ed., *Jewish Women Fiction Writers* (1998). Burstein, J., *Writing Mothers, Writing Daughters: Tracing the Maternal in Stories by American Jewish Women* (1996). Hendriksen, L. L., *Anzia Yezierska: A Writer's Life* (1991). Hendriksen, L. L., *How I Found America: The Collected Stories of Anzia Yezierska* (1991). Jackson, P. *Beyond Gender: Constructing Women's Middle-Class Subjectivity in the Fiction of Wharton, Austin, Yezierska, and Hurston* (dissertation, 1997). Konzett, D. C., *Diasporic Modernisms: Displacement and Ethnicity in Anzia Yezierska, Zora Neale Hurston and Jean Rhys* (dissertation, 1997). Sigerman, H. M., *Daughters of the Book: A Study of Gender and Ethnicity in the Lives of Three American Jewish Women* (dissertation, 1993). Sullivan, R. M., *Anzia Yezierska: An American Writer* (dissertation, 1975).

Reference works: *Oxford Companion to Women's Writing in the United States* (1995). *TCA, TCAS.* Other references: *Bookman* (Nov. 1923). *Judaism* (Fall 1993). *MELUS* (1980). *NYT* (23 Nov. 1970, 6 Apr. 1978, 27 Apr. 1978, 24 Feb. 1980). *Social Education* (Jan. 1995). *Studies in American Jewish Literature* (Winter 1975, 1997, 1998).

—PEGGY STINSON

YGLESIAS, Helen

Born 29 March 1915, New York, New York
Daughter of Solomon B. and Kate Goldstein Bassine; married Bernard Cole, 1937 (divorced); Jose Yglesias, 1950 (divorced); children: Tamara, Lewis, Rafael

In her autobiographical sketch in *Starting Early, Anew, Over, and Late* (1978), Yglesias describes herself as the youngest in a

family of seven children (four sisters and two brothers) growing up in a crowded New York apartment overflowing with relatives. Her father, a Jewish immigrant, was hard-pressed to provide for his family on the earnings from his neighborhood grocery. By the time she was sixteen both of Yglesias' parents were invalids and America was in the midst of the Great Depression. She began to write a novel hoping to save the family financially; her older brother told her nobody would be interested in what she was writing, and Yglesias destroyed the manuscript. She recalled that her mother, watching her, grieved, "What are you doing to yourself: you're killing yourself. Stop killing yourself."

It was almost 40 years before Yglesias was able to recapture the career she destroyed with her first unfinished novel. During those years she worked in a print shop, became a member of the Young Communist League, married a union official who became a photographer, and became a wife and mother. Divorced and remarried at thirty-four, Yglesias remained at home, caring for children and doing political work until she was well into her forties. Then, after a few unrewarding jobs, she became the assistant to the literary editor of the *Nation*. When he died, Yglesias took over the job and worked there for five years (1965-70) before leaving New York and moving to Maine to begin her writing career.

Her career was heralded by the publication of *How She Died* (1972), which won the Houghton Mifflin Literary Fellowship. The novel chronicles the last days of Mary Moody Schwartz, a young radical activist who is dying of cancer. The book focuses not simply on the death of a single individual, but on the possibility of the death of a group—political death. More important, perhaps, than the dying Mary is her best friend, Jean, who becomes entangled in a love affair with Mary's husband. Jean watches while her friend becomes schizophrenic and is briefly incarcerated in an asylum. The object of her own children's neurotic needs, Jean tries, with the best will but with little effect, to make Mary's dying meaningful. Skillfully interwoven with the story of Mary's death is the story of the radicals who had tried to free Mary's mother from prison and who, during Mary's deathwatch, try to free themselves from their own failures. Yglesias's first book, the one she said she had waited decades to write, is a densely packed novel with sharp attention to the minute, often-hidden, details of her characters' lives, a clear sense of place and politics, and the sympathy of one who has lived long for one who is dying young.

Her second novel, *Family Feeling* (1976), while disclaiming the representation of any real persons, has a distinctly autobiographical flavor. Anne Goddard, the youngest daughter of Jewish immigrants, lives her childhood beneath the Myrtle Avenue El and listens to her mother's stories. She is torn between trying to escape her immigrant past and trying to come to terms with the love her mother gave her so unstintingly. Family conflicts, especially with one son, Barry, who is determined to make it big in America, threaten to unravel the Goddards' lives, and the murder of Anne's husband, Guy Rossiter, sends her home to Fort Greene in search of the past she has tried to forget. The novel's climax, in Barry's penthouse office overlooking the lights of New York

City, is Anne's attempt at reconciliation while still maintaining what she has won for herself.

Yglesias' third novel, *Sweetsir* (1981), uses a series of journalistic flashbacks to reveal the character of Morgan Beauchamp Sweetsir, a brutal, abusive husband who was fatally stabbed by his wife, Sally Stark Sweetsir, who is on trial for his murder. More important than just the story are the issues women face in their relationships with men. The questions of wife beating, the need many women have to stay with abusive husbands, and the roles women make for themselves in marriage are all painted with the deft hand of one who knows how to tell a story.

With *The Saviors* (1987), Yglesias returns once again to the questions of her own political past and to the issues of culture and ethnicity that filled her first two novels. The central question of the novel asks why people whose political goals are admirable are often less than admirable in their daily lives. Lionized by the political left for their life's work, Maddy Brewster Phillips and her husband, Dwight, are on their last political march. Maddy remembers her life with the Society of the Universal Brotherhood and with her lover, Vidhya, who has turned the principles of the society to his own ends. In one last effort to understand her life, Maddy says to her husband, "We're old, two old people. Death is right ahead of us, a step away. If we don't accept reality now, then when?" It is with this plea for reality that Maddy realizes only "love and faith and truth" matter to her, not the lies of her past or the myths the young make up about her.

Yglesias' nonfiction work, *Starting Early, Anew, Over, and Late*, not only reveals her own struggle to become a writer, but also chronicles the struggles of others who found their way at different stages in their lives. The first section, "Starting Early," features her son, Rafael Yglesias, a published novelist at age seventeen. "Starting Anew" and "Starting Over" focus on female and male ways of beginning again. "Starting Late" tells Yglesias' story and that of Helen and Scott Nearing, whose lives harmonized two central movements of the 20th century, socialism and ecology. *Isabel Bishop* (1988) is a vivid appreciation of the life and work of one of America's outstanding women artists whose compelling portraits of working women Yglesias had long admired.

In 1996 Yglesias published *Semblant*, followed by *The Girls* in 1999. Though starting late at the career she knew from her youth she was well suited for, this experience has given her an eye to see beyond the surface of people's lives into the essential truths of what it means to be human in the late 20th century. Now in her mid-eighties, she shows few signs of slowing down.

BIBLIOGRAPHY: Blumberg, B. L., "A Voice of Their Own—An Inquiry into the Theme of the Discovery of the True Self in the Writings of Helen Yglesias, Muriel Rukeyser, and Tillie Olsen" (thesis, 1982).

Reference works: *CA* 37-40 (1979). *CANR* (1985). *CLC* (1977, 1982). *FC* (1990).

—MARY A. McCAY

YOUMANS, Eliza Ann

Born 17 December 1826, Greenfield, Saratoga County, New York; **died** death date unknown
Daughter of Vincent and Catherine Scofield Youmans

Eliza Ann Youmans' father was a farmer and mechanic. As a young girl, she enabled her brother, Edward Livingston, to pursue his scientific studies despite his near blindness by reading to him and assisting in his experimentation; he founded and edited *Popular Science Monthly*, and a younger brother became a noted physician. Like her brothers, Youmans worked to disseminate scientific knowledge through writing and education. She hoped to establish botany as a fourth fundamental branch of education (with reading, writing, and arithmetic) to correct the "almost total lack of any systematic cultivation of the observing powers." Botany seemed the most suitable discipline to advance independent analysis and reasoned judgement because of its abundant and ever varying materials and precise vocabulary.

The First Book of Botany (1870) develops a new method of study founded on systematic observation and independent thought. It is copiously illustrated and written with the assumption that field samples are in hand. There were six editions of the book and a sequel for more advanced study, *The Second Book of Botany* (1873). This more close and thorough study introduces scientific notation; methods of gathering, pressing, and mounting specimens; and an explanation of plant processes. In the introduction, Youmans explains her wish to remedy the common faults of "carelessness in observation, looseness in the application of words, hasty inferences from partial data, and lack of method in the contents of the mind." The appendix, "On the Educational Claims of Botany," describes the natural laws of mental growth and their affinity to the study of botany.

To supplement the study of botany, Youmans adapted *Henslow's Botanical Charts* (1873) for American use by substituting native plants for English species not found in the U.S. and enlarging the diagram for classroom use. After the favorable reception of her translations in *Popular Science Monthly* of the lectures of Armand de Quatrefages de Breau on the newly established field of anthropology, the series was collected in *The Natural History of Man: A Course of Elementary Lectures* (1875). Again, her concern is for a basic discussion of important scientific disciplines. The unity of the human species, the antiquity and origin of man (in which the theory of evolution was refuted), and human races and cultures are covered. Youmans includes an essay explaining evolution to present a balanced treatment of a controversial issue. Youmans' interest in practical self-instruction and the systemization of basic skills led her to adapt the English handbook, *Lessons on Cookery* (1879); she includes an appendix on diet.

In Appleton's series of science textbooks, she combined her earlier works on botany in *Descriptive Botany* (1885) and abridged the series' sequel to her book *Bently's Physiological Botany* (1886). Youmans' commitment to the application of scientific knowledge to everyday life encompassed kitchen and classroom. She realized the potential value of systematic scientific study at an early age and of a general understanding of basic scientific principles, and her insights into the educational process are incorporated into teaching methods today.

BIBLIOGRAPHY: Reference works: *AA. Appleton's Cyclopaedia of American Biography* (1889). *CAL. A Critical Dictionary of English Literature and British and American Authors* (1871). *A Dictionary of American Authors* (1905). *A Dictionary of North American Authors Deceased Before 1950* (1951). *NCAB. A Supplement to Allibone's Critical Dictionary* (1891).

—ELIZABETH ROBERTS

YOUNG, Ann Eliza (Webb)

Born 13 September 1844, Nauvoo, Illinois; **died** after 1908
Daughter of Chauncey and Eliza Churchill Webb; **married** James L. Dee, 1863 (divorced 1865); Brigham Young, 1869 (divorced 1873); Moses R. Denning, 1883 (divorced 1893); **children:** two sons

Ann Eliza Young was the fifth child born to Mormon parents shortly after their prophet, Joseph Smith, was murdered by an angry mob in the Mormon community at Nauvoo. When she was only four, her family joined the Mormon exodus from Illinois, following Brigham Young to Salt Lake City. In compliance with Smith's doctrine of polygamy, her father married four more women in Utah; his second wife bore him 11 children. An especially strong bond developed between Young and her mother, strengthened by their mutual dislike of polygamy.

As Young reached maturity, her beauty attracted the attention of Brigham Young, who persuaded her to become an actress with the Salt Lake City Theatre and live with his many wives and daughters in his home. She was moderately successful in her stage career, and it was while acting that she met her first husband, James Leech Dee, a plasterer and amateur actor who was a Mormon convert. She was awarded a civil divorce in 1865 when Dee became interested in taking a second wife.

Young and her two sons lived with her parents until 1869, when she married Brigham Young because, she later claimed, he had threatened to excommunicate her parents and bankrupt her brother unless she did so. More likely, Young's hostility to plural marriage was overwhelmed by a proposal from the most powerful man in the Mormon church and community. In 1873 she filed for divorce from Young, and she immediately became a celebrity.

Young traveled the country with a highly profitable lecture tour. She developed three themes in her lectures: "My Life in Bondage" discussed her childhood and her tenure as a member of the Young household; "Polygamy as It Is" was a discussion of the institution of plural marriage from the viewpoint of women and children; and "The Mormon Religion" was a lecture devoted to denunciation of the horrors of the Mormon faith. To increase her appeal on the lecture circuit, she published the very successful *Wife No. 19; or The Story of a Life in Bondage* in 1876.

Attractive and ladylike, Young was a popular lecturer, discussing Mormon sexuality under the guise of lectures on the evils of polygamy. She spoke before members of Congress and President and Mrs. Ulysses Grant, and continued to lecture until passage of the Edmund Bill in 1882 which outlawed polygamy in the U.S and all its territories. She then lived with her third husband, Moses R. Denning, a wealthy lumber and coal dealer, in Michigan, where she devoted her time to the Christian Science church and the woman suffrage movement. She divorced Denning in 1893, charging him with adultery.

In 1907, due to financial problems and a fear that the U.S. Congress would seat as Utah's senator the polygamist Reed Smoot, Young revised *Wife No. 19*. Shortly after the publication of her second book, which was never the success its predecessor had been, she disappeared, and no record of her movements after 1908 can be found. The most notorious of all Brigham Young's many wives, popular author and lecturer, and at one time the most newsworthy woman in the U.S.—she died in anonymity.

Although authorship of *Wife No. 19* has been disputed, it is likely Young wrote the original draft from the notes of her lectures and then had it polished for publication by a professional writer. It was a very popular book in its time, although it was sold only by subscription. It was considered respectable by rigidly moral middle-class men and women shocked by polygamy at the same time that it appealed to their sexual curiosity. Overemotional, melodramatic, biased in content, and repetitive, it is filled with the tragic life stories of plural wives and diatribes against Mormon leaders and the institution of polygamy. At the same time, however, it gives the historian of Mormon family life an invaluable inside look at the household of Brigham Young and the effects of polygamy on family life.

BIBLIOGRAPHY: Wallace, I., *The Twenty-Seventh Wife* (1961). Woodward, H. B., *The Bold Women* (1953).
Reference works: *NAW* (1971).

—PAULA A. TRECKEL

YOUNG, Ella

Born 26 December 1867, Fenagh, County Antrim, Ireland; **died** 25 July 1956, Oceana, California

When she was three years old, Ella Young's family moved from northeastern Ireland to Limerick in the southwest, where she developed the love of the country so marked in her poems and stories. She was deeply religious even as a child, but tales of banshees, sprites, giants, and various other creatures of Irish folk lore nourished her imagination. She studied political economics, history, and law at the Royal University. Some years after graduation, she moved to Dublin, where she became involved with the Celtic Renaissance and the Irish National movements. She learned Gaelic and traveled around the countryside gathering myths and tales from the peasants. After the deaths of many of her friends in the conflicts with England, she emigrated to the U.S. in 1925. She taught Celtic mythology at the University of California at Berkeley for many years and lectured at other American colleges.

Young's earliest books were published in Ireland, but the first book published in America, *The Wonder-Smith and His Son* (1927), is also the first in which her style is truly distinctive. She retells stories gathered in Ireland; some are reproduced almost exactly as she heard them; all are true to the spirit of Irish folklore. The tales present a short biography of the Wonder-Smith, the Gubbaun Saor, maker of the universe and the gods. These are uncomplicated, fast-moving and highly entertaining tales, filled with humor and some terror.

Young wrote two more children's books based on Irish folklore, *The Tangle-Coated Horse* (1929) and *The Unicorn with the Silver Shoes* (1932). The last is not as successful as the first two; it exudes "old Irish charm," but events are contrived and the tone is condescending. She also published several books of poetry, both in Ireland and the U.S. As in her prose works, much of the subject matter stems from Irish folklore and much of the imagery is drawn from nature. Mostly regular in rhyme and meter, Young's poems are particularly notable for their evocation of haunting worlds of fairyland and mystery.

Flowering Dusk (1945) is Young's memoirs. Written in poetic prose with sharp flashes of imagery and humor, it includes many lively anecdotes and some tales and poems. Some critics praised it, but others found it excessively "arty" and self-conscious. The book is valuable, however, for the picture it gives of the intellectuals and nationalists—such as William Butler Yeats, George Russell, Maud Gonne, Seamus O'Sullivan, and Standish O'Grady—with whom Young associated at a critical period in Irish history.

Although Young made important contributions both as a teacher and writer to the knowledge and appreciation of Celtic literature, her works have not endured, being too romantic for present-day tastes. She had, however, a storyteller's eye for homely and magical detail. She had also a keen ear for euphonious language and the ability to capture the cadence of Irish speech. She once said that she had talked with elves and understood the language of forest and sea. It is her deep feeling for the Ireland of myth and magic and her skill in investing with life that ancient realm that make her books unique and led Padraic Colum to call her a "reincarnated Druidess."

OTHER WORKS: *Poems* (1906). *The Coming of Lugh* (1909). *Celtic Wonder Tales* (1910). *The Rose of Heaven* (1920). *The Weird of Fionavar* (1922). *To the Little Princess* (1930). *Marzilian* (1938). *Seed of the Pomegranate* (1949). *Smoke Myrrh* (1950).

BIBLIOGRAPHY: Reference works: *Authors of Books for Young People* (1964). *Junior Book of Authors* (1951). *TCA.*
Other references: *Horn Book* (May 1939).

—ALETHEA K. HELBIG

YOUNG, Marguerite

Born 1909, Indianapolis, Indiana
Daughter of Chester E. and Fay Knight Young

Marguerite Young was raised from early childhood by her maternal grandmother. She attended Indiana and Butler Universities (B.A. in English and French, 1930) and the University of Chicago (M.A., 1936). Working her way through graduate school, she read the works of Shakespeare aloud to a prominent woman who was bedfast due to opium addiction. From this experience, Young gained an insight into life and an understanding of the psychology of opium and dreams. Later, while studying at the University of Iowa, she became interested in the philosophies of Locke, Berkeley, Hume, and William James. She has taught creative writing at many universities, and after 1943 lived in New York City.

Young has published well-received poetry, *Prismatic Ground* (1937) and *Moderate Fable* (1945), both concerned with the fabulous and the illusory. The first deals especially with the hidden recesses of the mind, as in "The Dark Wood." In "Slow Motion," from the second volume, she makes use of an image of timelessness as fixed motion: "The heart is that camera of a slow motion."

Even in her reviews (such as "Fictions Mystical and Epical," *Kenyon Review*, Winter 1945, about Katherine Anne Porter's *The Leaning Tower* and Virginia Woolf's *A Haunted House*), she is most concerned with apparitions, ghosts, and the evanescent. Her style reflects her interest in what is obscure, in the fantastic and supernatural, "the certitude of the permanent possibility of sensation, which is the one reality."

Young is obsessed with utopian quests. *Angel in the Forest: A Fairy Tale of Two Utopias* (1945) is a poetic and fairly successful history of the Rappist and Owenite societies of New Harmony, Indiana. *Miss MacIntosh, My Darling* (1963, reissued and recorded in 1983) is an epic novel of illusion and reality. The heroine, Vera Cartwheel, journeys in search of reality as personified by her old Scotch Presbyterian nursemaid, Miss MacIntosh. Other characters—such as her mother, an opium addict—represent illusion. The novel concludes with Vera accepting ambivalence as a reality of life and marrying a stone-deaf man. Replete with detail, endless digressions, mythical legends, and arcane symbols, *Miss MacIntosh, My Darling*, even more than Young's other works, calls for suspended judgement on the part of an uncommon reader. If Young's style is obscure, it is an obscurity well matched with her subject matter and based on her extensive knowledge of a long history of symbolism, particularly of Elizabethan and Jacobean symbols.

OTHER WORKS: *Below the City* (1975). *Pacific Transport* (1976). *Leaves, Leaves* (1989). *Marguerite Young: The Collected Poems* (1990). *Nothing But the Truth* (1993). *Inviting the Muses: Stories, Essays, Reviews* (1994). *Harp Song for a Radical: The Life and Times of Eugene Victor Debbs* (1999).

BIBLIOGRAPHY: Etlin, M. E., "'Bee Bak in a Whale': The Matriarchal Vision of Marguerite Young's *Miss MacIntosh, My Darling*" (thesis 1983). Fuchs, M., ed., *Marguerite Young, Our Darling: Tributes and Essays* (1994). Newquist, R., *Conversations* (1967). Ruas, C., *Conversations with American Writers* (1985). Staley, R. E., *No Landscape but the Soul's: A Critical Study of the Work of Marguerite Young* (dissertation 1993).

Reference works: *CA* (1975). *World Authors, 1950-1970* (1975).

Other references: *Book Forum* (1977). *Book World* (Aug. 1994). *Cimarron Review* (Jan. 1995). *Marguerite Young Interview With Kay Bonetti* (audiocassette, 1983). *Paris Review* (1977). *Review of Contemporary Fiction* (1989).

—LORENE POUNCEY

YOUNG, Rida Johnson

Born 28 February 1875, Baltimore, Maryland; died 8 May 1926, Southfield Point, Connecticut

Daughter of William A. and Emma Stuart Johnson; married James Young, 1904

Rida Johnson Young attended Wilson College in Chambersburg, Pennsylvania. Her poems and stories had frequently been published in Baltimore-area newspapers. When she finished writing her first play, she decided, over parental objections, to take it in person to New York. Her persistence won her an interview with theater manager Daniel Frohman, who turned down the lengthy, 100-character play about Omar Khayyam but gave her a walk-on part.

Two years later, convinced she would never be a good actress, Young turned to songwriting for a music publisher. This experience was training for her later success as lyricist for her musical comedies. She collaborated with such composers as Victor Herbert, Jerome Kern, Sigmund Romberg, and Rudolf Friml. Her best-known songs were "Mother Machree" (*Barry of Ballymore*, 1911), "When Love is Young in Springtime" (*Brown of Harvard*, 1906), "I'm Falling in Love with Someone" (*Naughty Marietta*, 1910), and "Sweethearts" (*Maytime*, 1917).

In 1906 *Brown of Harvard* began the long string of her plays produced on Broadway. Until 1921 there were one or two of Young's works on Broadway every year. The longest running were *Naughty Marietta* (1910, revived 1929, 1931, 1936, 1964), *Maytime* (1917), *Sometime*, with Mae West and Ed Wynn (1918), and *Little Old New York* (1920). Young claimed that all but one of her plays had been successful in production. That one, *The Girl and the Pennant* (1913), was written in hopes of breaking a theatrical jinx: no play dealing with baseball had ever triumphed on Broadway. Young's manager sent her south with the Giants one winter to learn about baseball and write a play in consultation with pitcher Christy Mathewson, but the result only confirmed tradition. The considerable royalties from her plays went into a summer home at Bellhaven, New York, and an estate at Stamford, Connecticut.

The Lottery Man (1909), directed by Edith Ellis, was one of Young's most popular early plays. Its bumptious young hero hits upon a scheme to pay off his debts and to provide for his charming mother. He advertises a lottery at a dollar per ticket with his hand in marriage as the prize, and then—too late to cancel the lottery—he meets the girl he would like to marry. He, his mother, and the girl's aunt begin buying tickets in her name. The girl is properly scandalized at the whole idea of the lottery, but love finds a way in the end. As in most of Young's plays, the plot and its resolution are trite, but there is freshness and sparkle in the dialogue and comic business. In this play, she pokes fun at a current fad by having the wealthy aunt test various diet schemes (pills, massage, medicine balls) on her emaciated paid companion before trying them herself. A minor character is an Irish girl who affects a Swedish name and accent to promote her business as a masseuse. Young often used national types in her plays, most frequently Irish and Scotch Americans.

Asked for the secret of her success, Young said, "I know that a play cannot succeed if it does not please women.... I am supposed to write musical comedies which will please the 'tired business man.' But if they do not please the lady whom the tired business man brings with him, the show will not last long." Her plays usually feature a self-possessed, bright young woman with modern wit and old-fashioned values. The heroines of her novels *Out of the Night* (1925) and *Red Owl* (1927) both achieve financial success in a man's world before accepting the traditional fulfillment sought by heroines of popular romances—a husband, home, and family.

Author of over 25 plays and musical comedies, three novels, and approximately 500 songs, Young was—among such playwrights as Anna Caldwell, Catherine Chisholm Cushing, Edith

Ellis, Harriet Ford, Margaret Mayo, and Martha Morton—one of the most prolific and successful women dramatists of the 1910s and 1920s.

OTHER WORKS: *The Boys of Company B* (1907). *The Lancers* (1907). *Glorious Betsy* (1908). *Next* (1911). *The Red Petticoat* (1912). *The Isle o' Dreams* (1913). *Lady Luxury* (1914). *Shameen Dhu* (1914). *Captain Kidd, Jr.* (1916). *Her Soldier Boy* (1916). *The Little Widows* (1917). *Little Simplicity* (1918). *Macushla* (1920). *The Front Seat* (1921). *The Dream Girl* (1924). *The Rabbit's Foot* (1924). *Cock o' the Roost* (1924).

BIBLIOGRAPHY: *American Magazine* (Dec. 1920). *Good Housekeeping* (Nov. 1911). *NYT* (Sept. 1920, 19 Sept. 1920). *Theatre* (Nov. 1913, April 1917).

—FELICIA HARDISON LONDRÉ

Z

ZATURENSKA, Marya

Born 12 September 1902, Kiev, Russia
Married Horace Gregory, 1925

Marya Zaturenska emigrated to the U.S. with her parents and a younger brother in 1909; the family settled in New York City. At fourteen, she began working in a factory by day and attending high school at night. She also worked briefly as a newspaper reporter. Her education, at Valparaiso University and the University of Wisconsin, where she spent her last year (1925) in the library school, was financed by scholarships. Her husband was a poet and critic.

Zaturenska's poems are traditional in form and meter. Because of the delicate, abstract quality of much of her work, they have little emotional impact unless a number of poems are read together, allowing for an accumulation of insight and feeling. An extensive reading also reveals how she uses stock images, usually drawn from nature—suns, moons, water, gardens—to form pastoral and dreamlike landscapes. Characters from myth, literature, art, and history people Zaturenska's poems; she has written only a few "personal" poems, in which the persona and the poet seem to be one. These poems, such as "The Invaders," about children growing up and away from their parents, and "Another Snowstorm," in which the poet's faith reconciles her to approaching death (both from *The Hidden Waterfall*, 1974), seem timeless. However, the ones that lean heavily on tradition too often seem mere exercises, and those that remain abstract seem hollow or cryptic.

Frequently, Zaturenska's poems are about a romantic and mysterious character who, renouncing passion, has become a recluse or whose lover is lost or dead. This interest in romantic figures lies behind the choice of subjects for her prose studies as well: she has written on Christina Rossetti, Elizabeth Siddal, and Algernon Charles Swinburne.

A sense of loss pervades much of Zaturenska's poetry—not only the loss of love but the loss of homeland, innocence, youth, and joy. She has a gift for capturing a sense of the duality of human experience. The girl in "Girl and Scarecrow" (*Cold Morning Sky*, 1937) exults in the joy of beauty and youth while the "face of a scarecrow sorrow-worn and sick" lurks behind her mirror. In "Rare Joy" (*Cold Morning Sky*), she shows that the price of peace is a loss of passion. Such a loss may not be great, since passion can be disturbing, but it is accompanied by nostalgia or yearning.

For over 40 years, Zaturenska has polished her craft. She has received a number of awards, the most prestigious being the Pulitzer Prize, which she received in 1938 for *Cold Morning Sky*. While highly dependent on the past, she is, as she herself puts it, "an independent"—true to her own interests, her own voice, and her own vision.

OTHER WORKS: *Threshold and Hearth* (1934, 1983). *The Listening Landscape* (1941). *The Golden Mirror* (1944). *A History of American Poetry, 1910-1940*, with H. Gregory (1946). *Christina Rossetti: A Portrait with Background* (1949). *Selected Poems* (1954, 1983). *Terraces of Light* (1960). *The Crystal Cabinet: An Invitation to Poetry*, with H. Gregory (1962) *Collected Poems* (1965).

BIBLIOGRAPHY: Axelrod, L. S., *Moonsongs: Seven Poems For Soprano and Piano* (musical score, 1986).
Reference works: *Contemporary Poets* (1975).
Other references: *NYT* (3 May 1938). *Poetry* (Feb. 1935, Sept. 1941, May 1975).

—JEANNINE DOBBS

ZOLOTOW, Charlotte

Born 26 June 1915, Norfolk, Virginia
Daughter of Louis J. and Ella Bernstein Shapiro; **married** Maurice Zolotow, 1938 (divorced); **children:** two

When she was young, Charlotte Zolotow moved with her parents to New York City, where she attended public schools. As a shy fourth grader, she discovered that writing was her way to reach out to the world through a persona when she wrote a first-person essay "as told by a Boston bull terrier," and says she has been writing for "the child within" ever since. She studied writing at the University of Wisconsin and then returned to work in New York, eventually becoming a senior editor in the children's division at Harper & Row. She worked under Ursula Nordstrom, whom Zolotow credits not only with building the department from its original staff of three to a complement of nearly 50, but also with being, as the editor of imaginatively illustrated books dealing with contemporary subjects and problems, a truly seminal force in the development of modern children's literature.

Zolotow began writing children's books after leaving her editorial job in 1944 to stay home with the first of her two children. She returned to Harper & Row in 1962 and resigned as vice president and associate publisher of Harper Junior Books in 1981, when she was given her own imprint, Charlotte Zolotow Books. She still remains an editorial consultant for Harper Junior Books, unable to give up a job she loved so much. Many believe her success as an editor is attributed to her talent for matching the right illustrator with the right author. The same is true for her own works. She was divorced from her husband, also a writer, in 1970.

Many of her best books, considering both their quality and popularity with children, have been those that deal honestly with situations and problems that prior to the "new wave of realism" were not considered suitable subjects for this genre. Three examples would be *The Quarreling Book* (1963), *The Hating Book* (1967), and *The Unfriendly Book* (1975), all of which recognize that children, like adults, can harbor unpleasant emotions, be negatively affected by gloomy weather and gloomy behavior, and be downright antisocial at least some of the time. Earlier literature eschewed discussion of sibling rivalry and the displacement of an older child with the coming of a new baby, but Zolotow deals frankly with this topic in both *If It Weren't for You* (1966) and *Big Sister and Little Sister* (1966).

Several of her books humorously set forth a child's point of view about adult rules for the behavior of children, as in *When I Have a Little Girl* (1965) and *When I Have a Son* (1967). She addresses the once taboo subject of one-parent families in *The Night When Mother Went Away* (1961; reissued as *The Summer Night*, 1974), which shows a father dealing with the situation, and in *A Father like That* (1968), which shows a young boy telling his mother what his father would be like if he had one. In the latter, the subject is handled very subtly; we are never told if it has been death or divorce or an unmarried mother that has caused the father's absence, and Zolotow resolves the problem posed by having the child's mother agree with his dreams of an ideal father and reassure him that when he grows up, he can be such a parent.

A special favorite with feminists is *William's Doll* (1972). Its main character is a little boy who wants a real "baby doll," despite all the negative reactions from his big brother and the boy next door. His father brings home a basketball, which William enjoys, and electric trains, for which William builds model towns. Only his grandmother understands that he wants to "practice being a father." The point is clearly made, although Zolotow claims like all her other work, it was not written to "get a point across," but rather to let children see other children have shared the same emotions, frustrations, and joys.

Zolotow's work is lyrical, but not overstated. One of the finest examples is *Mr. Rabbit and the Lovely Present* (1962), in which Mr. Rabbit helps a child find the perfect gift for her mother, who is especially fond of red, yellow, green, and blue. Paul Williams identified it as an all-time favorite: "It is a perfect presentation of something rich and rare and untouchable, the time that exists between friends."

In *Someone New* (1978), she presents a boy puzzled by a difference in his life, which he is unable to pinpoint. He packs away his babyish toys and stuffed animals, realizing that he has a new interest in his shell collection, and finally comes to know that it is *he* who has changed. Zolotow closes with "Someone is gone. Someone is missing and I know who. It is I. I am someone new."

In a genre sometimes accorded less importance than it deserves, Zolotow's contribution has been tremendous. For many decades, she has provided leadership by example with books that are successful both artistically and commercially; she has reached children by communicating with them through the child within

herself and has evoked a response in adults as well. In every respect, Zolotow must be considered a major voice in the area of juvenile literature today.

Zolotow's career has also been punctuated with different honors, including the Harper Gold Medal for editorial excellence awarded in 1974, the 1974 Christopher Award for her writing, and Honor Book citations from the distinguished Caldecott and Newbery selection committees. She also is a teacher of the editorial and writing crafts she practices, lecturing widely to audiences around the country. Zolotow has participated in both the University of Colorado Writer's Conference of Children's Books and the University of Indiana Writer's Conference. And astoundingly enough, while being dedicated to her editorial responsibilities, she has published more than 60 of her own books for children since the writing of her first book, *The Park Book*, in 1944.

OTHER WORKS: *The Park Book* (1944). *But Not Billy* (1947). *The City Boy and the Country Horse* (1952). *Indian, Indian* (1952). *The Magic Word* (1952). *The Storm Book* (1952). *The Quiet Mother and the Noisy Little Boy* (1953). *One Step Two* (1955). *Not a Little Monkey* (1957). *Over and Over* (1957). *Do You Know What I'll Do?* (1958). *The Bunny Who Found Easter* (1959). *Aren't You Glad?* (1960). *Big Brother* (1960). *In My Garden* (1960). *The Little Black Puppy* (1960). *The Three Funny Friends* (1961). *The Man with the Purple Eyes* (1961). *When the Wind Stops* (1962; revised 1975). *The Sky Was Blue* (1963). *Thomas the Tiger* (1963). *The White Marble* (1963). *I Have a Horse of My Own* (1964). *The Poodle Who Barked at the Wind* (1964). *A Rose, A Bridge, and a Wild Black Horse* (1964). *Someday* (1965). *All that Sunlight* (1967). *I Want to Be Little* (1967). *Summer Is* (1967). *My Friend John* (1968). *The New Friend* (1968). *A Day in the Life of Yani* (1969). *The Old Dog* (1969). *A Day in the Life of Latef* (1970). *Flocks of Birds* (1970). *River Winding* (1970; rev. ed., 1978). *Where I Begin* (1970). *Wake Up and Goodnight* (1971). *You and Me* (1971). *The Beautiful Christmas Tree* (1972). *Hold My Hand* (1972). *Janey* (1973). *My Grandson Lew* (1974). *It's Not Fair* (1976). *May I Visit?* (1976). *If You Listen* (1980). *Say It!* (1980). *The Song* (1982). *I Know a Lady* (1984). *Everything Glistens and Everything Sings: New and Selected Poems* (1987). *I Like to Be Little* (1987). *Something is Going to Happen* (1988). *The Seashore Book* (1992). *Smippets* (1992). *This Quiet Lady* (1992). *The Moon Was Best* (1993). *The Old Dog* (1995). *When the Wind Stops* (1995). *Who is Ben?* (1997).

BIBLIOGRAPHY: Hopkins, L. B., *Books Are by People* (1969). Wintle, J., and E. Fisher, *The Pied Pipers: Interviews with the Influential Creators of Children's Literature* (1974)

Reference works: *Children's Literature Review* (1976). *SATA* (1971).

Other references: *Houston Post* (10 Apr. 1976). *Mademoiselle* (Jan. 1973). *New Orleans Times-Picayune* (30 Apr. 1974). *New York Daily News* (18 May 1971). *Palo Alto Times* (20 Sept. 1976). *Prism* (Dec. 1974). *PW* (10 June 1976).

—EDYTHE M. MCGOVERN,
UPDATED BY DEVRA M. SLADICS

ZUGSMITH, Leane

Born January 1903, Louisville, Kentucky; **died** 1969
Wrote under: Mrs. Carl Randau
Daughter of Albert and Gertrude Zugsmith; **married** Carl Randau, 1940

Leane Zugsmith spent most of her childhood in Atlantic City, New Jersey. Her formal education consisted of a year each at Goucher College, the University of Pennsylvania, and Columbia University. She lived in New York until her death, except for a year in Europe and some months in Hollywood, where she worked as a screenwriter for the Goldwyn studio. She has also worked as a copy editor for pulp magazines like *Detective Stories* and *Western Story Magazine* and written advertising copy. In the early 1940s, after marrying a newspaperman, she was a special feature writer on the staff of the New York newspaper *P.M.*

Her first novel, *All Victories Are Alike* (1929), is the story of a newspaper columnist's loss of ideals. *Goodbye and Tomorrow* (1931), which Zugsmith said is "shamelessly derivative of Virginia Woolf," is about a romantic spinster who becomes a patron of artists. *Never Enough* (1932) is a panorama of American life during the 1920s. *The Reckoning* (1934) tells the story of a New York slum boy.

A Time to Remember (1936) is concerned with labor troubles and unionization in a New York department store. Its heroine, Aline Weinman, a Dreiseresque, middle-class, Jewish employee of the store, goes out on strike. She pays the price of painful separation from her family for her political ideals because her father, who has lost his job, would disapprove if he knew Aline's politics.

The Summer Soldier (1938) is about a small group of men and workmen, mostly Northerners, who travel by train to a Southern county to hold a hearing on the abuse of black workers. Their mission, however, is not successful. The novel is a slick character sketch of different political types.

Home Is Where You Hang Your Childhood (1937) is a collection of short stories. "Room in the World" describes the desperation unemployment causes in a young family. The title story, about a very young high school girl's movement from childish innocence to experience, uses one of Zugsmith's favorite themes. *Hard Times with Easy Payments* (1941) is another collection of short stories, all from *P.M.*

With her husband, Zugsmith wrote *The Setting Sun of Japan* (1942) about their flying trip through the Far East for *P.M.*; a mystery story, *Visitor* (1944); and *Year of Wrath*, a novel serialized in *Collier's* in 1942. Stories by Zugsmith appeared infrequently until 1949 in *Good Housekeeping*, the *New Yorker*, and *Collier's*.

In the early 1940s, Zugsmith was considered one of the most promising young left-wing novelists. She said her greatest influences were Albert Maltz and Irwin Shaw in the short story and Josephine Herbst in the novel. All of her six novels are political, and her political themes gained considerable sophistication and some cynicism during the decade of her productivity (1929-38). Her sympathetic treatment of Jewish characters is of interest to the history of Jewish American writers because her Jewish characters solve the problem of assimilation by becoming socialists. Zugsmith belongs with those Jewish writers of the 1930s who attempted to transform ethnic background into meaningful politics. Her work became dated and of historical interest after World War II and the anti-Soviet backlash of the 1950s.

BIBLIOGRAPHY: Madden, D., ed., *Proletarian Writers of the Thirties* (1968). Ravitz, A. C., *Leane Zugsmith: Thunder on the Left* (1992).

Reference works: *CAA* (1944). *TCA. Universal Jewish Encyclopedia* (1943-48).

Other references: *Science & Society* (Spring 1994).

—CAROLE ZONIS YEE

GENERAL INDEX

Brown, Sandra, I, 144
Browne, Martha Griffith, I, 145
Brownmiller, Susan, I, 145
Brownson, Sarah N., I, 146
Bryan, Mary Edwards, I, 147
Bryant, Anita, I, 148
Buchanan, Edna, I, 149
Buck, Pearl S., I, 150
Buckmaster, Henrietta, I, 152
Burke, Fielding *See* Dargan, Olive
    Tilford
Burnett, Frances Hodgson, I, 153
Burnham, Clara L. Root, I, 154
Burr, Esther Edwards, I, 154
Burton, Katherine Kurz, I, 155
Burton, Virginia Lee, I, 156
Butler, Octavia E., I, 157

Cabeza de Baca, Fabiola, I, 159
Cade, Toni *See* Bambara, Toni Cade
Caldwell, Taylor, I, 160
Calhoun, Lucy *See* Monroe, Lucy
Calisher, Hortense, I, 160
Campbell, Helen Stuart, I, 162
Campbell, Jane C., I, 163
Campbell, Juliet Lewis, I, 163
Caperton, Helena Lefroy, I, 164
Carlson, Natalie Savage, I, 164
Carmichael, Sarah E., I, 165
Carrighar, Sally, I, 166
Carrington, Elaine Sterne, I, 166
Carroll, Gladys Hasty, I, 167
Carson, Rachel, I, 168
Cartoonists
    see Hollander, II, 221
Carver, Ada Jack, I, 170
Cary, Alice, I, 171
Cary, Phoebe, I, 172
Caspary, Vera, I, 173
Castillo, Ana, I, 174
Cather, Willa Sibert, I, 175
Catherwood, Mary Hartwell, I, 178
Catholic fiction
    see Banning, I, 59; Brownson, I,
        146; Dorsey, I, 304; Frankau, II,
        69; Fremantle, II, 73; Gordon, II,
        125; Howard, II, 233; Keyes, II,
        307; O'Connor, III, 215; Tiernan,
        IV, 138; Tincker, IV, 140; White,
        IV, 229
Catt, Carrie Chapman, I, 179
Caulkins, Frances Manwaring, I, 180
Cazneau, Jane McManus, I, 181
Cervantes, Lorna Dee, I, 181
Cha, Theresa Hak Kyung, I, 182
Chandler, Elizabeth Margaret, I, 183
Chapelle, Georgette Meyer, I, 184

Chapin, Katherine Garrison, I, 185
Chaplin, Jane Dunbar, I, 185
Chapman, Lee *See* Bradley, Marion
    Zimmer
Chapman, Maria Weston, I, 186
Charnas, Suzy McKee, I, 187
Chase, Ilka, I, 188
Chase, Mary Coyle, I, 189
Chase, Mary Ellen, I, 189
Chehia *See* Shaw, Anna Moore
Cheney, Ednah Littlehale, I, 190
Chernin, Kim, I, 191
Cherry, Kelly, I, 192
Chesebrough, Caroline, I, 193
Chesler, Phyllis, I, 194
Chesnut, Mary Miller, I, 195
Chidester, Ann, I, 196
Child, Julia, I, 197
Child, Lydia Maria, I, 198
Children's drama
    see Bates, I, 69; Chase, I, 189; Field,
        II, 41; Gerstenberg, II, 98; Gra-
        ham, II, 136; Latham, III, 11;
        Lawrence, III, 18; L'Engle, III,
        30; Merington, III, 130; Smith,
        IV, 63; White, IV, 224
Children's fiction
    see Allee, I, 20; Benét, I, 77; Brink,
        I, 129; Carlson, I, 164; Cheney, I,
        190; Chute, I, 204; Cleary, I, 213;
        Diaz, I, 283; Foote, II, 57; Fox,
        II, 67; Hale, II, 162; Haven, II,
        191; Hunt, II, 243; Hunt, II, 244;
        Hurst, II, 249; Janvier, II, 271;
        Jones, II, 285; Judson, II, 292;
        Konigsburg, II, 326; Lenski, III,
        31; Leslie, III, 36; Lindbergh, III,
        45; Maynard, III, 98; Meigs, III,
        128; Miller, III, 142; Neville, III,
        192; Newman, III, 195; Nor-
        ton, III, 208; Parton, III, 255;
        Petersham, III, 269; Petry, III,
        270; Polacco, III, 283; Pratt, III,
        293; Ramsay, III, 305; Rich, III,
        323; Sachs, IV, 1; Seawell, IV,
        29; Seredy, IV, 36; Shindler, IV,
        48; Skinner, IV, 57; Snyder, IV,
        73; Stein, IV, 92; Tepper, IV,
        128; Waller, IV, 195; White, IV,
        229; Yates, IV, 275
Children's poetry
    see Bailey, I, 52; Bates, I, 69; Benét,
        I, 77; Chute, I, 205; Field, II, 41;
        Follen, II, 56; Freeman, II, 72;
        Gould, II, 130; Janvier, II, 271;
        Kroeber, II, 327; L'Engle, III, 30;
        Livingston, III, 52; Marks, III, 84;

Norris, III, 207; Rawlings, III,
310; Schaeffer, IV, 19; Scott, IV,
24; Suckow, IV, 111; Turnbull,
IV, 155; Tyler, IV, 159; Uhnak,
IV, 164; Warren, IV, 201; Welty,
IV, 212; Wyatt, IV, 270
Fantasy
    see Brackett, I, 117; Bradley, I, 118;
        Castillo, I, 174; Fritz, II, 80;
        Gould, II, 130; Howe, II, 238; Le
        Guin, III, 21; McIntyre, III, 118;
        Moore, III, 162; O'Neill, III, 220;
        Ozick, III, 242; Pollack, III, 284;
        Rice, III, 319; Rusch, III, 351;
        Salmonson, IV, 4; Scarborough,
        IV, 18; Tepper, IV, 128; Walton,
        IV, 196; Willard, IV, 246; Willis,
        IV, 250
Farley, Harriet, II, 32
Farmer, Fannie Merritt, II, 33
Farnham, Eliza Woodson, II, 34
Farnham, Mateel Howe, II, 35
Farquharson, Martha See Finley, Martha
Farrar, Eliza Rotch, II, 35
Faugeres, Margaretta V., II, 36
Fauset, Jessie Redmon, II, 37
Felton, Rebecca Latimer, II, 38
Feminist critic
    see DuPlessis, I, 314
Feminist fiction
    see Barnes, I, 63; Blake, I, 93;
        Breuer, I, 126; Broner, I, 131;
        Brown, I, 141; Chopin, I, 202;
        Dargan, I, 259; Didion, I, 287;
        Ferber, II, 39; Gardener, II, 89;
        Gestefeld, II, 99; Gould, II, 130;
        Green, II, 140; Harris, II, 184;
        Heilbrun, II, 194; Holley, II, 222;
        Irwin, II, 255; Johnson, II, 275;
        Johnston, II, 281; Jong, II, 287;
        Lane, III, 5; Lathen, III, 12; Le
        Sueur, III, 23; Lerman, III, 33;
        Morrison, III, 172; Piercy, III,
        277; Reno, III, 317; Russ, III,
        353; Smedley, IV, 61; Tyler, IV,
        161; Ward, IV, 198
Feminist literature
    see Addams, I, 11; Anneke, I, 33;
        Anthony, I, 34; Ayer, I, 47;
        Blackwell, I, 90; Bloomer, I, 97;
        Brown, I, 141; Carmichael, I,
        165; Chesler, I, 194; Child, I,
        198; Daly, I, 255; Davis, I, 265;
        Davis, I, 268; Doolittle, I, 300;
        Dorr, I, 303; Duniway, I, 316;
        Eastman, II, 4; Eddy, II, 10;
        Farnham, II, 34; Flanner, II, 50;

Friedan, II, 78; Fuller, II, 81;
Gardener, II, 89; Gilmer, II, 108;
Goodsell, II, 122; Hacker, II,
159; Hasbrouck, II, 189; Heilbrun,
II, 194; Herschberger, II, 205;
Howe, II, 234; Howe, II, 235;
Howland, II, 240; Janeway, II,
270; Johnston, II, 281; Jong, II,
287; Malkiel, III, 81; Martin, III,
89; Millett, III, 144; Moers, III,
154; Moore, III, 162; Murray, III,
185; Orvis, III, 231; Ozick, III,
242; Papashvily, III, 249; Phelps,
III, 272; Sanger, IV, 8; Shaw, IV,
44; Sontag, IV, 75; Walker, IV,
189; Wells, IV, 210; White, IV,
224; Wright, IV, 266
Feminist poetry
    see Broumas, I, 136; Flanner, II,
        50; Gilman, II, 106; Giovanni,
        II, 109; Grahn, II, 137; Grif-
        fin, II, 146; Hacker, II, 159;
        Herschberger, II, 205; Jong, II,
        287; Laing, III, 1; Le Sueur, III,
        23; Menken, III, 129; Millay, III,
        138; Piercy, III, 277; Rich, III,
        320; Smith, IV, 63; Treadwell,
        IV, 146
Feminist writers
    see Broumas, I, 136; Brownmiller,
        I, 145; Charnas, I, 187; Cliff,
        I, 216; Cooey, I, 223; Daly,
        I, 255; Davis, I, 263; Deming,
        I, 277; Derricotte, I, 280;
        DeVeaux, I, 282; Drexler, I, 311;
        Dworkin, I, 319; Ehrenreich, II,
        11; Emshwiller, II, 23; French, II,
        76; Gearhart, II, 94; Gornick, II,
        128; Griffin, II, 146; Grumbach,
        II, 152; Harding, II, 178; Hite, II,
        214; Hollander, II, 221; hooks, II,
        226; Howard, II, 233; Howe, II,
        234; Howe, II, 238; Hunter-
        Lattany, II, 246; Jackson, II, 261;
        Jacobs, II, 265; Jones, II, 283;
        Kizer, II, 321; Le Guin, III, 21;
        Le Sueur, III, 23; MacKinnon, III,
        76; Mairs, III, 81; Millett, III,
        144; Miner, III, 146; Moraga, III,
        167; Morgan, III, 169; Nussbaum,
        III, 210; Owens, III, 238; Ow-
        ens, III, 239; Paglia, III, 246;
        Paretsky, III, 250; Piercy, III,
        277; Rich, III, 320; Sanchez, IV,
        5; Schaeffer, IV, 19; Scott- Max-
        well, IV, 26; Showalter, IV, 48;
        Shulman, IV, 50; Steinem, IV, 95;

French, Lucy Smith, II, 76
French, Marilyn, II, 76
Friedan, Betty, II, 78
Frings, Ketti, II, 79
Fritz, Jean, II, 80
Fulbright grants
    see Huxtable, II, 252; Le Guin, III,
        21; Plath, III, 281; Porter, III,
        286; Vendler, IV, 174
Fuller, Margaret, II, 81

Gage, Frances Dana, II, 85
Gale, Zona, II, 86
Gallagher, Tess, II, 86
Garber, Marjorie, II, 87
Gardner, Helen Hamilton, II, 89
Gardner, Isabella, II, 90
Gardner, Mariam See Bradley, Marion
    Zimmer
Gardner, Mary Sewall, II, 91
Garrigue, Jean, II, 92
Gates, Eleanor, II, 93
Gates, Susa Young, II, 93
Gearhart, Sally Miller, II, 94
Gellhorn, Martha, II, 95
Genêt See Flanner, Janet
Geographer
    see Semple, IV, 36
George, Jean Craighead, II, 96
Gerould, Katharine Fullerton, II, 98
Gerstenberg, Alice, II, 98
Gestefeld, Ursula N., II, 99
Gibbons, Kaye, II, 100
Gilbert, Fabiola Cabeza de Baca See
    Cabeza de Baca, Fabiola
Gilbert, Sandra M., II, 101
Gilchrist, Annie Somers, II, 103
Gilchrist, Ellen, II, 103
Gill, Sarah Prince, II, 105
Gilman, Caroline Howard, II, 105
Gilman, Charlotte Perkins, II, 106
Gilmer, Elizabeth Meriwether, II, 108
Giovanni, Nikki, II, 109
Glasgow, Ellen, II, 110
Glaspell, Susan, II, 113
Glück, Louise, II, 114
Godchaux, Elma, II, 116
Godwin, Gail, II, 116
Golden, Marita, II, 118
Goldman, Emma, II, 119
Goodman, Allegra, II, 120
Goodman, Ellen, II, 121
Goodsell, Willystine, II, 122
Goodwin, Doris Kearns, II, 123
Goodwin, Maud Wilder, II, 124
Gordon, Caroline, II, 125

Gordon, Mary Catherine, II, 126
Gordon, Ruth, II, 127
Gornick, Vivian, II, 128
Gothic and grotesque
    see Andrews, I, 30; Bradley, I, 118;
        Church, I, 203; Daniels, I, 258;
        Farnham, II, 35; Harris, II, 186;
        Henley, II, 200; Holding, II, 220;
        Kennedy, II, 303; Lurie, III, 68;
        Martin, III, 91; Oates, III, 220;
        O'Connor, III, 215; O'Donnell,
        III, 217; Read, III, 312; Scarbo-
        rough, IV, 17; Schoolcraft, IV,
        21; Voigt, IV, 180; Whitney, IV,
        235; Wood, IV, 261
Gottschalk, Laura Riding See Jackson,
    Laura
Gould, Hannah Flagg, II, 130
Gould, Lois, II, 130
Grafton, Sue, II, 132
Graham, Isabella Marshall, II, 133
Graham, Jorie, II, 134
Graham, Katharine, II, 135
Graham, Shirley, II, 136
Grahn, Judy, II, 137
Grant, Margaret See Franken, Rose
Graphologists
    see Roman, III, 339
Grau, Shirley Ann, II, 138
Graves, Valerie See Bradley, Marion
    Zimmer
Gray, Angela See Daniels, Dorothy
Greek tragedies
    see Norman, III, 206
Green, Anna Katharine, II, 140
Green, Anne, II, 141
Green, Olive See Reed, Myrtle
Greenberg, Joanne, II, 142
Greene, Sarah McLean, II, 144
Greenfield, Eloise, II, 144
Greenwood, Grace See Lippincott, Sara
    Jane
Griffin, Susan, II, 146
Griffith, Mary, II, 147
Grimes, Martha, II, 148
Grimké, Angelina, II, 149
Grimké, Sarah Moore, II, 150
Gruenberg, Sidonie Matzner, II, 151
Grumbach, Doris, II, 152
Guernsey, Clara F., II, 154
Guernsey, Lucy Ellen, II, 154
Guggenheim fellowship
    see Adams, I, 9; Betts, I, 85; Bishop,
        I, 88; Boyle, I, 114; Brooks, I,
        133; Carson, I, 168; Clark, I, 211;
        Colum, I, 219; Fox, II, 67;
        Gordon, II, 125; Hardwick, II,

III, 15; Laut, III, 16; Lew-
is, III, 41; Linington, III, 46;
Lothrop, III, 60; MacInnes, III,
75; Martin, III, 90; McDowell,
III, 114; McKenney, III, 119;
Meaney, III, 126; Meigs, III, 128;
Miller, III, 140; Morrow, III,
174; Morton, III, 176; Murfree,
III, 183; Niles, III, 202; Nor-
ton, III, 208; Oemler, III, 224;
Pinckney, III, 279; Porter, III,
286; Putnam, III, 300; Roberts,
III, 333; Sachs, IV, 1; St. Johns,
IV, 2; Schmitt, IV, 21; Scott, IV,
24; Seawell, IV, 29; Sedgwick,
IV, 31; Seredy, IV, 36; Seton, IV,
37; Stephens, IV, 97; Thane, IV,
132; Turnbull, IV, 155; Walk-
er, IV, 192; Walton, IV, 196;
Wharton, IV, 220; White, IV,
228; Whitney, IV, 235; Williams,
IV, 247; Windle, IV, 253; Woods,
IV, 263; Woolson, IV, 265
Historical poetry
    see Gould, II, 130; Morton, III, 176
Historical romance
    see Plain, III, 280
Hite, Shere, II, 214
Hobart, Alice Tisdale, II, 215
Hobson, Laura Z., II, 216
Hoffman, Alice, II, 217
Hoffman, Malvina, II, 218
Hogan, Linda, II, 219
Holding, Elisabeth Sanxay, II, 220
Hollander, Nicole, II, 221
Holley, Marietta, II, 222
Hollingworth, Leta Stetter, II, 223
Holm, Saxe See Jackson, Helen Hunt
Holmes, Mary Jane Hawes, II, 224
Holmes, Sarah Stone, II, 225
Hooks, bell, II, 226
Hooper, Lucy, II, 227
Hooper, Lucy Jones, II, 228
Hope, Laura Lee See Adams, Harriet
    Stratemeyer
Hopkins, Pauline, II, 228
Hopper, Hedda, II, 229
Horlak, E. E. See Tepper, Sheri S.
Horney, Karen, II, 230
Horror
    see Rusch, III, 351
Horticulturists
    see Fox, II, 67
Houston, Jean, II, 231
Howard, Maureen, II, 233
Howe, Florence, II, 234
Howe, Julia Ward, II, 235

Howe, Susan, II, 237
Howe, Tina, II, 238
Howes, Barbara, II, 239
Howland, Marie, II, 240
Hugo award
    see Butler, I, 157; Le Guin, III, 21;
        McIntyre, III, 118; Russ, III,
        353; Wilhelm, IV, 242; Willis,
        IV, 250
Hull, Helen, II, 241
Hulme, Kathryn Cavarly, II, 242
Hume, Sophia, II, 242
Humishuma See Mourning Dove
Humor
    see Alther, I, 24; Bombeck, I,
        103; Brown, I, 141; Cleary, I,
        213; French, II, 75; Hollander,
        II, 221; Hunter-Lattany, II, 246;
        Lathen, III, 12; Le Guin, III, 21;
        Lowry, III, 64; McCarthy, III,
        104; Mitford, III, 152; Phelps, III,
        272; Powell, III, 292; Rinehart,
        III, 328; Shulman, IV, 50; Skin-
        ner, IV, 58; Smith, IV, 67;
        Stephens, IV, 97; Welty, IV, 212;
        Whitcher, IV, 223
Hunt, Irene, II, 243
Hunt, Mabel Leigh, II, 244
Hunter, Rodello, II, 245
Hunter-Lattany, Kristin, II, 246
Huntington, Susan, II, 247
Hurd-Mead, Kate C., II, 248
Hurst, Fannie, II, 249
Hurston, Zora Neale, II, 250
Hutchins, Maude McVeigh, II, 251
Huxtable, Ada Louise, II, 252
Hyde, Shelley See Reed, Kit
Hymn writers
    see Chapman, I, 186; Moise, III,
        155; Oberholtzer, III, 223; Smith,
        IV, 64; Van Alstyne, IV, 170;
        Warner, IV, 200

Illustrators
    see Alexander, I, 19; Comstock, I,
        221; Foote, II, 57; Keith, II, 294;
        Mansfield, III, 84; O'Neill, III,
        220; Polacco, III, 283; Seredy,
        IV, 36
Imagism
    see Graham, II, 134; Niedecker,
        III, 199
Imperialism
    see Griffin, II, 146; Owens, III, 239
Indian-American literature
    see Divakaruni, I, 294

Kirkland, Caroline M. Stansbury, II, 320
Kizer, Carolyn, II, 321
Knapp, Bettina Liebowitz, II, 322
Knight, Sarah Kemble, II, 323
Knox, Adeline Trafton, II, 324
Koch, Adrienne, II, 325
Kohut, Rebekah Bettelheim, II, 325
Konigsburg, E. L., II, 326
Kroeber, Theodora, II, 327
Kübler-Ross, Elisabeth, II, 328
Kumin, Maxine W., II, 329

Labor and social problems
    see Perkins, III, 266; Scott, IV, 25
Laing, Dilys Bennett, III, 1
Lamb, Martha Nash, III, 1
Lamott, Anne, III, 2
Landers, Ann, III, 3
Landon, Margaret, III, 4
Lane, Gertrude Battles, III, 5
Lane, Rose Wilder, III, 5
Langdon, Mary See Pike, Mary Green
Langer, Susanne K., III, 6
Larcom, Lucy, III, 8
Larsen, Nella, III, 9
Lasswell, Mary, III, 11
Latham, Jean Lee, III, 11
Lathen, Emma, III, 12
Lathrop, Rose Hawthorne, III, 14
Latimer, Elizabeth W., III, 15
Latin American literature
    see Benítez, I, 78
Latsis, Mary Jane See Lathen, Emma
Laut, Agnes C., III, 16
Lauterbach, Ann, III, 17
Lawrence, Elizabeth L., III, 17
Lawrence, Josephine, III, 18
Lawrence, Margaret Woods, III, 19
Lawyers
    see Bres, I, 126; Murray, III, 185;
        Ricker, III, 326; Todd, IV, 142
Lazarus, Emma, III, 20
Le Guin, Ursula K., III, 21
Le Sueur, Meridel, III, 23
Le Vert, Octavia Walton, III, 24
Lea, Fannie Heaslip, III, 25
Lee, Eliza Buckminster, III, 26
Lee, Hannah Sawyer, III, 26
Lee, Harper, III, 27
Lee, Marion See Comstock, Anna
    Botsford
Lee, Mary Elizabeth, III, 28
LeGallienne, Eva, III, 29
L'Engle, Madeleine, III, 30
Lenski, Lois, III, 31
Lerman, Rhoda, III, 33

Lerner, Gerda, III, 34
Lesbian feminist writers
    see Anzaldúa, I, 37; Cliff, I, 216;
        Deming, I, 277; DeVeaux, I, 282;
        Gearhart, II, 94; Grumbach, II,
        152; Moraga, III, 167
Lesbian fiction
    see Forrest, II, 64
Lesbian writers
    see Allen, I, 21; Anzaldúa, I, 37;
        Bradley, I, 118; Broumas, I,
        136; Brown, I, 141; Cliff, I,
        216; Deming, I, 277; French,
        II, 76; Gearhart, II, 94; Gil-
        bert, II, 101; Grahn, II, 137;
        Grumbach, II, 152; Hacker, II,
        159; Herbst, II, 204; Johnston, II,
        281; Moraga, III, 167; Morgan,
        III, 169; Newman, III, 195; Rich,
        III, 320; Routsong, III, 344; Russ,
        III, 353; Sarton, IV, 12
Lesbianism
    see Brown, I, 141; Myles, III, 186;
        Stein, IV, 92
Leslie, Annie Brown, III, 35
Leslie, Eliza, III, 36
Leslie, Miriam Follin, III, 37
Letters
    see Adams, I, 5; Anthony, I, 35;
        Clappe, I, 210; Dickinson, I, 284;
        Graham, II, 133; Grimké, II, 149;
        Grimké, II, 150; Hale, II, 166;
        Lindbergh, III, 43; Lippincott, III,
        48; Madison, III, 80; Mead, III,
        124; O'Connor, III, 215; Orvis,
        III, 231; Ramsay, III, 305; Rob-
        ins, III, 335; Schoolcraft, IV, 21;
        Secor, IV, 29; Shindler, IV, 48;
        Smith, IV, 70; Stewart, IV, 99;
        Thaxter, IV, 133; Toklas, IV, 143;
        Towne, IV, 145
Levertov, Denise, III, 38
Lewis, Elizabeth Foreman, III, 39
Lewis, Estelle Robinson, III, 40
Lewis, Janet, III, 41
Libbey, Laura Jean, III, 42
Librarians
    see Bishop, I, 87; Estes, II, 26;
        Hunt, II, 244; Mojtabai, III, 156;
        Newman, III, 194; Norton, III,
        208; Ruddy, III, 346; Sachs, IV,
        1; Shannon, IV, 43
Lincoln, Victoria, III, 43
Lindbergh, Anne Morrow, III, 43
Lindbergh, Reeve, III, 45
Linguistics
    see Elgin, II, 15; Le Vert, III, 24

Martin, Del, III, 89

Martin, George Madden, III, 90

Martin, Helen Reimensnyder, III, 91

Martin, Valerie, III, 91

Martínez, Demetria, III, 92

Martyn, Sarah Smith, III, 94

Marxism

    see Davis, I, 263

Maso, Carole, III, 94

Mason, Bobbie Ann, III, 95

Materialism

    see Naylor, III, 189

Mathews, Frances Aymar, III, 97

Matthews, Adelaide, III, 97

May, Sophie *See* Clarke, Rebecca

    Sophia

Maynard, Joyce, III, 98

Mayo, Katherine, III, 99

Mayo, Margaret, III, 100

Mayo, Sarah Edgarton, III, 100

McBride, Mary Margaret, III, 101

McCaffrey, Anne, III, 102

McCarthy, Mary, III, 104

McCloy, Helen, III, 106

McCord, Louisa Cheves, III, 107

McCormick, Anne O'Hare, III, 108

McCrackin, Josephine Clifford, III, 109

McCrumb, Sharon, III, 109

McCullers, Carson, III, 110

McDermott, Alice, III, 113

McDowell, Katherine Bonner, III, 114

McGinley, Phyllis, III, 114

McGrory, Mary, III, 115

McGuire, Judith Brockenbrough,

    III, 116

McIntosh, Maria Jane, III, 117

McIntyre, Vonda N., III, 118

McKenney, Ruth, III, 119

McLean, Kathryn Anderson, III, 120

McMillan, Terry, III, 121

McPherson, Aimee Semple, III, 122

McPherson, Sandra, III, 123

Mead, Kate C. *See* Hurd-Mead, Kate C.

Mead, Margaret, III, 124

Meaney, Mary L., III, 126

Means, Florence Crannell, III, 127

Medical/medicine

    see Fisher, II, 45; Gibbons, II, 100;

        Johnson, II, 275; Johnson- Mas-

        ters, II, 279; Mitford, III, 152;

        Wilhelm, IV, 242

Meigs, Cornelia, III, 128

Melodrama

    see Barnes, I, 61; Luce, III, 66;

        Mortimer, III, 175; Parker, III,

        251; Ritchie, III, 330

Meloney, Franken *See* Franken, Rose

Memoir

    see Bergman, I, 81; Buchanan, I,

        149; Calisher, I, 160; Cleary, I,

        213; Clifton, I, 217; de Mille,

        I, 274; Graham, II, 135; Grif-

        fin, II, 146; Grumbach, II, 152;

        Highsmith, II, 210; Howard, II,

        233; Lamott, III, 2; Le Sueur, III,

        23; Lurie, III, 68; Mairs, III, 81;

        Maynard, III, 98; McCarthy, III,

        104; Munro, III, 182; Santiago,

        IV, 11; Schwartz, IV, 22; Simon,

        IV, 54; Uchida, IV, 163

Menken, Adah Isaacs, III, 129

Merington, Marguerite, III, 130

Meriwether, Elizabeth Avery, III, 131

Merriam, Eve, III, 132

Merril, Judith, III, 133

Meyer, Annie Nathan, III, 134

Meyer, June *See* Jordan, June M.

Miles, Josephine, III, 136

Millar, Margaret, III, 137

Millay, Edna St. Vincent, III, 138

Miller, Alice Duer, III, 139

Miller, Caroline Pafford, III, 140

Miller, Emily Huntington, III, 141

Miller, Harriet M., III, 142

Miller, Isabel *See* Routsong, Alma

Miller, Mary Britton, III, 143

Miller, Vassar, III, 144

Millett, Kate, III, 144

Milward, Maria G., III, 146

Miner, Valerie, III, 146

Minimalism

    see Howe, II, 238; Ozick, III, 242

Ministers

    see Blackwell, I, 91; Bowers, I, 111;

        Fahs, II, 31; Hanaford, II, 174;

        Hume, II, 242; McPherson, III,

        122; Shaw, IV, 44; Smith, IV, 62;

        Smith, IV, 65; White, IV, 227

Minot, Susan, III, 148

Mirikitani, Janice, III, 148

Missionaries

    see Elliot, II, 18; Lewis, III, 39;

        Nicholson, III, 197; Smith, IV,

        62; White, IV, 225; Whitman,

        IV, 231

Mitchell, Agnes Woods, III, 150

Mitchell, Margaret, III, 150

Mitchell, Maria, III, 151

Mitford, Jessica, III, 152

Mixer, Elizabeth, III, 153

Modernism

    see de Burgos, I, 272; Sontag, IV, 75

Moers, Ellen, III, 154

Mohr, Nicholasa, III, 154

III, 210; Oates, III, 220; Owens, III, 239; Sanchez, IV, 5; Scott-Maxwell, IV, 26; Seid, IV, 33; Shange, IV, 42; Sontag, IV, 75; Terry, IV, 131; Wasserstein, IV, 203; Willard, IV, 246; Williams, IV, 248

Poetry

see Allison, I, 23; Bergman, I, 81; Bishop, I, 88; Brooks, I, 133; Cha, I, 182; Cherry, I, 192; Chin, I, 201; Crapsey, I, 238; Deutsch, I, 282; Dickinson, I, 284; Dinnies, I, 291; DuPlessis, I, 314; Gallagher, II, 86; Hadas, II, 160; Harper, II, 181; Hejinian, II, 196; Hirshfield, II, 213; Howe, II, 237; Jackson, II, 260; Johnson, II, 276; Johnson, II, 277; Kenyon, II, 304; Lauterbach, III, 17; Lee, III, 28; Levertov, III, 38; Lowell, III, 63; Martínez, III, 92; Miles, III, 136; Mitchell, III, 150; Monroe, III, 158; Moore, III, 165; Myles, III, 186; Notley, III, 210; Obejas, III, 222; Reese, III, 315; Rukeyser, III, 349; Sarton, IV, 12; Sewell, IV, 39; Sigourney, IV, 51; Smith, IV, 65; Stein, IV, 92; Swenson, IV, 113; Tepper, IV, 128; Troubetzkoy, IV, 148; Vendler, IV, 174; Wakoski, IV, 185; Waldman, IV, 187; Waldrop, IV, 188; Welby, IV, 208; Wilcox, IV, 239; Woolsey, IV, 264

Poets

see Ai, I, 13; Allen, I, 21; Álvarez, I, 25; Angelou, I, 31; Brooks, I, 133; Broumas, I, 136; Brown, I, 142; Cervantes, I, 181; Chernin, I, 191; Clampitt, I, 208; Clifton, I, 217; Cooper, I, 230; de Burgos, I, 272; Derricotte, I, 280; Dove, I, 309; Erdrich, II, 25; Evans, II, 28; Forché, II, 59; Giovanni, II, 109; Glück, II, 114; Golden, II, 118; Graham, II, 134; Grahn, II, 137; Hacker, II, 159; Harjo, II, 180; Hogan, II, 219; Jones, II, 283; Jong, II, 287; Jordan, II, 290; Kizer, II, 321; Kumin, II, 329; Lerner, III, 34; Levertov, III, 38; McPherson, III, 123; Merriam, III, 132; Miles, III, 136; Mirikitani, III, 148; Morley, III, 170; Niedecker, III, 199; Nye, III, 212; Oates, III, 220; Olds, III,

226; Oliver, III, 227; Olsen, III, 228; Osbey, III, 231; Ostriker, III, 234; Owens, III, 239; Ozick, III, 242; Paley, III, 247; Pastan, III, 257; Piercy, III, 277; Rich, III, 320; Rodgers, III, 337; Sanchez, IV, 5; Shange, IV, 42; Song, IV, 74; Stone, IV, 103; Swenson, IV, 113; Valentine, IV, 169; Van Duyn, IV, 170; Voigt, IV, 181; Wakoski, IV, 185; Walker, IV, 189; Walker, IV, 192; Whitman, IV, 232; Wilhelm, IV, 242; Willard, IV, 246; Williams, IV, 248; Yamada, IV, 273

Poets laureate

see Dove, I, 309; Van Duyn, IV, 170

Polacco, Patricia, III, 283

Political activists

see Angelou, I, 31; Chernin, I, 191; Davis, I, 263; Deming, I, 277; Guy, II, 157; Herbst, II, 204; hooks, II, 226; Kingsolver, II, 314; Levertov, III, 38; MacKinnon, III, 76; Millett, III, 144; Mirikitani, III, 148; Olsen, III, 228; Paley, III, 247; Randall, III, 307; Sontag, IV, 75; Steinem, IV, 95; Walker, IV, 192

Political literature

see Acker, I, 3; Arendt, I, 39; Boyle, I, 114; Chernin, I, 191; Clapp, I, 209; Cleghorn, I, 215; Coit, I, 219; Dargan, I, 259; Davis, I, 263; Dawidowicz, I, 269; de Burgos, I, 272; Deming, I, 277; DeVeaux, I, 282; Didion, I, 287; Drew, I, 309; Drexler, I, 311; Evans, II, 28; Fairbank, II, 32; FitzGerald, II, 47; Glasgow, II, 110; Hahn, II, 161; Herbst, II, 204; hooks, II, 226; Howland, II, 240; Irwin, II, 255; Ivins, II, 257; Jordan, II, 290; Kingsolver, II, 314; Koch, II, 325; Lane, III, 5; Le Sueur, III, 23; Levertov, III, 38; Millay, III, 138; Millett, III, 144; Miner, III, 146; Paley, III, 247; Piercy, III, 277; Porter, III, 289; Ridge, III, 327; Ruether, III, 347; Smedley, IV, 61; Smith, IV, 63; Smith, IV, 70; Steinem, IV, 95; Strong, IV, 107; Taggard, IV, 118; Thompson, IV, 137; Tuchman, IV, 153; Ty-Casper, IV, 158; Warren, IV, 202; Zugsmith, IV, 287

Schofield, Sandy *See* Rusch, Kristine
  Kathryn
Scholars
  see Appleton-Weber, I, 38; Brée, I,
    124; Daly, I, 255; Heilbrun, II,
    194; Howe, II, 234; Jacobs, II,
    265; Lerner, III, 34; Nye, III, 211;
    Oates, III, 220; Ruether, III, 347;
    Russ, III, 353; Sanchez, IV, 5;
    Silko, IV, 52; Sontag, IV, 75;
    Walker, IV, 189; Wallace, IV,
    194; Wilson, IV, 252; Wolf,
    IV, 259
Schoolcraft, Mary Howard, IV, 21
Schwartz, Lynne Sharon, IV, 22
Science and technology
  see Alther, I, 24; Butler, I, 157;
    Gearhart, II, 94; Mojtabai, III,
    156; Swenson, IV, 113; Wilhelm,
    IV, 242
Science fiction
  see Brackett, I, 117; Bradley, I,
    118; Butler, I, 157; Calisher,
    I, 160; Carroll, I, 167; Charnas,
    I, 187; Elgin, II, 15; Emshwiller,
    II, 23; Forrest, II, 64; Ham-
    ilton, II, 173; Le Guin, III,
    21; McCaffrey, III, 102;
    McIntyre, III, 118; Merril, III,
    133; Moore, III, 162; Piercy, III,
    277; Pollack, III, 284; Reed, III,
    313; Rusch, III, 351; Russ, III,
    353; Salmonson, IV, 4; Sargent,
    IV, 11; Wilhelm, IV, 242; Willis,
    IV, 250
Science historian
  see Haraway, II, 176
Science journalism
  see Angier, I, 32
Scott, Anne Firor, IV, 24
Scott, Evelyn, IV, 24
Scott, Joan Wallach, IV, 25
Scott, Julia *See* Owen, Mary Alicia
Scott-Maxwell, Florida, IV, 26
Screenwriters
  see Brackett, I, 117; Caspary, I, 173;
    Ephron, II, 24; Frings, II, 79;
    Gordon, II, 127; Grafton, II, 132;
    Loos, III, 56; Mead, III, 124;
    Millett, III, 144; Minot, III, 148;
    Moore, III, 162; Rand, III, 306;
    St. Johns, IV, 2; Slesinger, IV,
    59; Spewak, IV, 84; Sture-Vasa,
    IV, 110; Turney, IV, 156; West,
    IV, 219; Winslow, IV, 257
Scudder, Vida Dutton, IV, 27
Sculptors

  see Hoffman, II, 218; Millett,
    III, 144
Seaman, Elizabeth Cochrane, IV, 28
Seawell, Molly Elliot, IV, 29
Secor, Lella, IV, 29
Sedges, John *See* Buck, Pearl S.
Sedgwick, Anne Douglas, IV, 30
Sedgwick, Catharine Maria, IV, 31
Sedgwick, Susan Ridley, IV, 32
Seeley, Mabel, IV, 33
Seid, Ruth, IV, 33
Seifert, Elizabeth, IV, 35
Semple, Ellen Churchill, IV, 36
Sentimental fiction
  see Jacobs, II, 265; Wilson, IV, 252
Sentimental novels
  see Blake, I, 93; Elder, II, 15; Evans,
    II, 29; Gates, II, 93; Harper, II,
    181; Hazlett, II, 193; Hooper, II,
    227; Jackson, II, 259; Jamison, II,
    270; Moore, III, 163; Morton, III,
    176; Oemler, III, 224; Pike, III,
    279; Prouty, III, 297; Rankin, III,
    309; Thompson, IV, 136; Under-
    wood, IV, 166
Seredy, Kate, IV, 36
Serialized fiction
  see Corbett, I, 231; Franken, II, 70;
    French, II, 75; Gale, II, 86;
    McLean, III, 120; Richmond, III,
    325; Scarberry, IV, 16; Wright,
    IV, 269
Seton, Anya, IV, 37
Settle, Mary Lee, IV, 38
Sewall, Harriet Winslow, IV, 39
Sewell, Elizabeth, IV, 39
Sexton, Anne, IV, 40
Sexuality
  see Dove, I, 309; French, II, 76;
    Hite, II, 214; Johnson-Masters, II,
    279; Mairs, III, 81; Martin, III,
    91; Naylor, III, 189; Olds, III,
    226; Phillips, III, 275; Swenson,
    IV, 113; Walker, IV, 192; Wolf,
    IV, 259
Shange, Ntozake, IV, 42
Shannon, Dell *See* Linington, Elizabeth
Shannon, Monica, IV, 43
Sharon, Rose *See* Merril, Judith
Sharp, Isabella Oliver, IV, 44
Shaw, Anna H., IV, 44
Shaw, Anna Moore, IV, 45
Sheehy, Gail, IV, 46
Sheldon, Ann *See* Adams, Harriet
  Stratemeyer
Sherwood, Mary Wilson, IV, 47
Shindler, Mary Dana, IV, 48

Short story
    see Boyd, I, 113; Cherry, I, 192;
        Davis, I, 265; Emshwiller, II, 23;
        French, II, 74; Gallagher, II, 86;
        Goodman, II, 120; McCrumb, III,
        109; Minot, III, 148; Moody, III,
        161; Moore, III, 164; Mukherjee,
        III, 181; Neely, III, 191; Obejas,
        III, 222; Prose, III, 296; Scott-
        Maxwell, IV, 26; Watanabe, IV,
        205; Wiggins, IV, 238
Showalter, Elaine, IV, 48
Shreve, Anita, IV, 49
Shulman, Alix Kates, IV, 50
Sidlosky, Carolyn *See* Forché, Carolyn
Sigourney, Lydia Huntley, IV, 51
Silko, Leslie Marmon, IV, 52
Simon, Kate, IV, 54
Sinclair, Bertha Muzzy, IV, 55
Sinclair, Jo *See* Seid, Ruth
Singer, June K., IV, 56
Singers
    see Anderson, I, 27; Bond, I, 105;
        West, IV, 218
Singleton, Anne *See* Benedict, Ruth
Singmaster, Elsie, IV, 56
Skinner, Constance Lindsay, IV, 57
Skinner, Cornelia Otis, IV, 58
Slade, Caroline, IV, 59
Slave narratives
    see Jacobs, II, 265; Prince, III, 296;
        Stowe, IV, 104; Walker, IV,
        192; Williams, IV, 248; Wilson,
        IV, 252
Slave owners
    see Andrews, I, 27; Browne, I, 145;
        Dorsey, I, 305; McCord, III, 107
Slaves
    see Gage, II, 85
Slesinger, Tess, IV, 59
Slosson, Annie Trumbull, IV, 60
Smedley, Agnes, IV, 61
Smith, Amanda, IV, 62
Smith, Anna Young, IV, 63
Smith, Betty, IV, 63
Smith, Eliza Snow, IV, 64
Smith, Elizabeth Oakes, IV, 65
Smith, Eunice, IV, 66
Smith, Hannah Whittal, IV, 67
Smith, Lee, IV, 67
Smith, Lillian, IV, 69
Smith, Lula Carson *See* McCullers,
    Carson
Smith, Margaret Bayard, IV, 70
Smith, Rosamond *See* Oates, Joyce
    Carol
Smith, Sarah Pogson, IV, 70

Smith, Susy, IV, 71
Snedeker, Caroline Dale, IV, 72
Snyder, Zilpha Keatley, IV, 73
Soap opera
    see Carrington, I, 166; Nixon, III,
        205; Phillips, III, 274
Social activists
    see DeVeaux, I, 282; Ehrenreich, II,
        11; Levertov, III, 38; Randall, III,
        307; Sanchez, IV, 5; Steinem,
        IV, 95
Social criticism
    see Goldman, II, 119; Mannes, III,
        82; Mitford, III, 152; Monroe, III,
        159; Older, III, 225; Sontag, IV,
        75; Stein, IV, 92; Strong, IV, 107
Social history
    see Andrews, I, 27; Arnow, I, 42;
        Banning, I, 59; Beard, I, 72;
        Breckinridge, I, 122; Chesnut, I,
        195; Farrar, II, 35; Gruenberg, II,
        151; Harper, II, 182; Lamb, III, 1;
        Laut, III, 16; O'Keeffe, III, 219;
        Ripley, III, 329; Robinson, III,
        335; Rourke, III, 343; Royall, III,
        345; Stewart, IV, 99; Watson, IV,
        206; Windle, IV, 253; Wright, IV,
        269; Yezierska, IV, 277
Social realism
    see Beattie, I, 73
Social reformers
    see Abbott, I, 1; Addams, I, 11;
        Blackwell, I, 90; Blackwell, I, 91;
        Blackwell, I, 92; Breckinridge, I,
        122; Campbell, I, 162; Goldman,
        II, 119; Mott, III, 177; Phelps, III,
        272; Strong, IV, 107; Todd, IV,
        142; Wald, IV, 186; Ward, IV,
        198; White, IV, 224; Woodhull,
        IV, 262; Wyatt, IV, 270
Social satire
    see Ritchie, III, 330; Victor, IV, 175;
        Whitcher, IV, 223
Social workers
    see Abbott, I, 1; Addams, I, 11;
        Balch, I, 56; Blackwell, I, 91;
        Breckinridge, I, 122; Henry, II,
        201; McPherson, III, 122; Slade,
        IV, 59; Smith, IV, 65; Stern, IV,
        98; Strong, IV, 107
Socialism
    see Avery, I, 47; Blackwell, I, 90;
        Blatch, I, 96; Cleghorn, I, 215;
        Day, I, 270; Earle, II, 1; Eastman,
        II, 4; Flynn, II, 55; Grumbach, II,
        152; Howland, II, 240; Kelley, II,
        297; Lane, III, 5; Lumpkin, III,